Palgrave Studies in the History of Economic Thought

Series Editors
Avi J. Cohen
Department of Economics
York University & University of Toronto
Toronto, ON, Canada

G. C. Harcourt
School of Economics
University of New South Wales
Sydney, NSW, Australia

Peter Kriesler
School of Economics
University of New South Wales
Sydney, NSW, Australia

Jan Toporowski
Economics Department,
SOAS University of London
London, UK

Palgrave Studies in the History of Economic Thought publishes contributions by leading scholars, illuminating key events, theories and individuals that have had a lasting impact on the development of modern-day economics. The topics covered include the development of economies, institutions and theories.

The series aims to highlight the academic importance of the history of economic thought, linking it with wider discussions within economics and society more generally. It contains a broad range of titles that illustrate the breath of discussions – from influential economists and schools of thought, through to historical and modern social trends and challenges – within the discipline.

All books in the series undergo a single-blind peer review at both the proposal and manuscript submission stages.

For further information on the series and to submit a proposal for consideration, please contact the Wyndham Hacket Pain (Economics Editor) wyndham.hacketpain@palgrave.com.

Ashwani Saith

Cambridge Economics in the Post-Keynesian Era

The Eclipse of Heterodox Traditions

Volume II

Ashwani Saith
International Institute of Social Studies
Erasmus University Rotterdam (EUR)
The Hague, The Netherlands

ISSN 2662-6578　　　　　ISSN 2662-6586　(electronic)
Palgrave Studies in the History of Economic Thought
ISBN 978-3-030-93018-9　　　ISBN 978-3-030-93019-6　(eBook)
https://doi.org/10.1007/978-3-030-93019-6

© The Editor(s) (if applicable) and The Author(s), under exclusive licence to Springer Nature Switzerland AG 2022
This work is subject to copyright. All rights are solely and exclusively licensed by the Publisher, whether the whole or part of the material is concerned, specifically the rights of translation, reprinting, reuse of illustrations, recitation, broadcasting, reproduction on microfilms or in any other physical way, and transmission or information storage and retrieval, electronic adaptation, computer software, or by similar or dissimilar methodology now known or hereafter developed.
The use of general descriptive names, registered names, trademarks, service marks, etc. in this publication does not imply, even in the absence of a specific statement, that such names are exempt from the relevant protective laws and regulations and therefore free for general use.
The publisher, the authors and the editors are safe to assume that the advice and information in this book are believed to be true and accurate at the date of publication. Neither the publisher nor the authors or the editors give a warranty, expressed or implied, with respect to the material contained herein or for any errors or omissions that may have been made. The publisher remains neutral with regard to jurisdictional claims in published maps and institutional affiliations.

This Palgrave Macmillan imprint is published by the registered company Springer Nature Switzerland AG.
The registered company address is: Gewerbestrasse 11, 6330 Cham, Switzerland

Preface

A Subaltern Window

One thing leads to another, and hindsight often makes one wish it hadn't. The project of this book emerged organically from the earlier intellectual biography of Ajit Singh (Saith 2019), in particular from the short narrative there on 'Faculty Wars' in which Ajit was a key figure. That chapter provided an introductory, highly compressed version of the untold story, and the folded leaves of that concertina are opened to full stretch in this book, relying on a much wider range of archival and other inputs.

An effort has been made, as far as reasonably possible, to keep the persona of the author out of the narrative, even though I spent much of the 1970s in Cambridge, the time when the battle lines were being drawn for the purges to come. I had arrived as a doctoral researcher in 1972, the momentous year when Frank Hahn returned triumphantly to a professorship in Cambridge, and so was part of the melee—initially as an observer and then for a couple of years as an occasional protagonist when I joined the Faculty in a lowly academic position reserved for slaves serving the professoriate. As such I had the questionable benefit of being both a marginal participant and a non-participant, observer viewing events unfold through the personal window of my cubby hole in the DAE wing on the top floor of the Faculty building. Life as a PhD scholar was seriously underprivileged but wildly exciting; the temptations and enticements in the ever-changing window displays at Bowes and Bowes—said to have been the oldest bookshop in Britain, now sadly gone—guaranteeing a quick slide into what Amit Bhaduri termed perpetual indebtedness; it was a tough choice: the delights of The Copper Kettle (as was, not as is) on King's Parade, or the odd pint or two at the Hat & Feathers on Barton Road, or treats from the kindly old ladies of Fitzbillies (again, as was, not as is) versus the tactile pleasure of leafing through one's own copies of Mario Nuti's pair of edited volumes of essays of Michal Kalecki, then hot off the press; Kalecki easily won that one, but there were fresh challenges; the following week saw the bespectacled young Gramsci looking one in the eye over the title of *Selections from the*

Prison Notebooks of Antonio Gramsci. Natural empathy and political solidarity with the cause of the striking coal miners was intensified by personal experience, as the OPEC price hikes worked their cost-plus way through to one's shopping basket, quickly halving the real value of the meagre Commonwealth scholarship stipend of GBP 78 per month—much of it earmarked for the Trinity landlady on Grange Road who might well have been charging a locational quasi-rent on account of being next door to the Robinsons—making a luxury even of the weekly 3-pound, 3-minute trunk calls to 'back home' from the red 'Dr Who time-machine' phonebooths. Half-way through, Rekha, my wife, registered for a PhD in Sociology, widening the interface with local intellectual life. The decade of the 1970s saw the arrival of a large cohort of PhD scholars from South Asia, with enough bench strength to kick off its own dedicated seminar and, needless to say, its own cricket team which took the field against a Faculty XI, replete with dodgy umpiring and dubious scorekeeping, usually with a return revenge game. Survival, or at least getting to the jam part of Micawber's equation, depended on the acquisition of college assignments for supervising undergraduate groups, and earnings were generally around GBP 2–3 per session per group of 2–3 students—the tiny payment slips were eagerly awaited and cheque withdrawal amounts at Lloyds on Trinity Street seldom exceeded the luxurious amount of GBP 5/-. As with mountain climbing or village field-work in the Indian summer, these 'character-forming' experiences all seem rather more exciting from the safety of a distant future; on the ground in real time, it was more an episode, with reruns, of hard times. Things eased when I was offered the post of Faculty Assistant in Research (FAR), a position I held for two years, bringing with it the thrill of close continuous contact with DAE and Faculty members otherwise only spotted distantly at Sidgwick Site as they disappeared into their respective sides of the building or encountered in the IBM Computer Room, access to which was through a bizarre route: males and females had to walk through their respective convenience facilities on the lower ground floor under the Marshall Library to re-emerge and be reunited in a dark corridor (stacked with boxes of supplies) in the dungeon on the other side, where there was a research students' workroom with a couple of discarded typewriters waiting their time to enter antique auctions, but also a couple of gleaming devices that were worth getting up early for: a Hermes manual typewriter—IBM golf-ball typewriters were still a long way into the future—and an electronic calculator with a huge footprint and a lurid red display of about a dozen digits, of which any 2 or 3 would have to be guessed as some horizontal or vertical section was always on the blink. Passage through the doors at the far end got you into the small engine room: there were the card punching and reading machines and the IBM computer, and here you waited anxiously for the beast to spit out your results, putting you instantly in a buoyant or foul mood.

As the FAR slave, I was assigned to work with William Brian Reddaway (WBR) and Ajit Singh, mostly to produce the weekly class statistical handouts that Brian was cunningly devising to bamboozle, harangue and then enlighten undergrads in his upcoming lecture.[1] This was a daunting, but hugely rewarding learning exercise; WBR took no hostages, was very demanding, quite brusque though never unfriendly or impolite; and on rare occasions he even managed a smile and a compliment, well measured, lest it might lead to any smidge of complacency. A regular stream of Reddaway-type tasks: This, or that, can't be random; can you do some scatters and check? Why do you have the same number of decimal spaces for all the columns of the table? Somehow, this number (in a publication) doesn't seem right, please go back to the original source and check it is a misprint there; and so on. In between, there were exchanges about real applied economics, what the tables were all about, possible explanations and qualifications, as he would sometimes try out some part in his upcoming lecture using me as a proxy for the class. He was genuinely delighted at my independently acquired facility with the double-quick, rough-and-ready Reddaway-method of deseasonalising time series. The Faculty tearoom was usually to be avoided, not least because there was an existential uncertainty about the nature of the experience lying in wait, ranging from being in the crowds enjoying an entertaining biff-baff between some seniors, to suddenly being biffed and baffed yourself over some stray remark. The Buttery provided the more predictably congenial company of PhD co-workers—a time for frivolity and seriousness in equal measure before everyone disappeared again with furrowed brows to plough their data sets or equations. The market for information, aka gossip, was far from being missing—if anything, there was a high velocity of circulation and a tale heard today was reheard from another source a day or two later enlivened by additional spicing. And of course, there was enough to grin or grumble about, given the fractions and frictions within the deeply divided Faculty; each week brought a fresh tournament of jousting white knights and blackguards. At my personal humble level, this extended sojourn in the 1970s served as a great observation post for keeping track of the daily skirmishes and battles across the divide. In the narrative that follows, I have assiduously attempted to avoid undue reliance on personal experience though inevitably this will have influenced, perhaps subliminally, the gathering and interpretation of 'evidence' and 'facts'.

The *Rashomon* Syndrome

The narrative stretches more than might be usual across time and space, locations and events, and so occupies a panoramic canvas. Assorted materials are used: archival sources for the investigation of some of the key episodes; published personal recollections of various actors and commentators, some long

[1] A cherished acquisition then was an acknowledgement in the first footnote on the first page of the first article, 'What has become of Employment Policy?' by Joan Robinson and Frank Wilkinson, in the first issue of the first volume of *Cambridge Journal of Economics*, a lot of self-proclaimed firsts' there, utterly trivial to the wider world, but for a few days I did not need the lift or staircase, I could just float up on a cloud to my top-floor cubicle in the Faculty building—what little it took to lift the spirits of slaves.

lost; and inputs from interviews or communications with several surviving members of the cast, many of whom had direct personal experience of the events. It cannot be said that the characters and actors are all fictional and bear no resemblance to any real person living or dead. That caveat does not apply; as far as possible, the players are named and made to speak for themselves in their own words drawn from archival and secondary sources, often via interviews available in the public domain. It needs to be emphasised that the purpose of the book is to investigate the reorientation of the trajectory of economics as a discipline in Cambridge; while the views and actions of specific individuals or groups are scrutinised and interrogated, this is not to be interpreted as, or conflated in any way, with impugning in any form the character or integrity of the persons concerned; the interpretations and commentaries are strictly intended to be kept at the intellectual level within this extended case study of the sociology of 'knowledge' production and control.

A declaration of interest as an author: no disingenuous pretence is made of being 'neutral', and the story telling is not 'impartial', or 'balanced', say a là BBC *News*, where an artificial superficial equality is notionally projected by granting each side equal media time for making their respective 'party political broadcasts'. It follows, rather, the BBC *Panorama* 'expose' template; it is explicitly an uncompromising narrative from one side of the battle lines and, as with the reporting of a war correspondent, the narrative consciously and admittedly tells one 'truth' as revealed by available evidence while explicitly acknowledging its relativity and mindfully highlighting its perceived contingencies and qualifications. There are very many more tomes by victors on how they won their wars than by losers on how these were lost; the triumphalist history according to the orthodox victors has been told and retold; it has become part of the Cambridge ether; in contrast, stories and memories from the other side have generally tended to lapse into a distressed post-trauma silence—but there are still voices from the scattered periphery or beyond the grave that need to be recorded and archived so that they are not obliterated altogether.

Lawrence Klein (1991: 108) set out his personal retrospective view of the 1944–1947 years at the Cowles Commission, induced by his dissatisfaction at the available 'insider' and 'outsider' accounts of that dynamic formative period. The econometrician suddenly turns anthropological in method: "some of the published accounts are from scholars who were not on hand for the whole period of interest to me, and some are based purely on historical research. Without having been on the scene, historians cannot capture voice inflections, gestures, body language, purely oral commentary (often informal discussion) and other pieces of unrecorded information. There were daily discussions and frequent reliance on oral traditions at the Cowles Commission, then, and the 'outside' accounts sometimes miss relevant points that related to this reliance on oral tradition. Lapses of memory can also affect 'insider' views." In the present case of the Cambridge purges, the acknowledged issues of the methodology of memory recall are compounded by the traumatic nature of the experience that the memory is meant to hold. Often, as a survival mechanism, memories of periods of acute episodic distress are shut down and not easily revived and reached, and this applies both to short-term post-trauma memory loss and to time-distant experiences, indicative perhaps of some form of a generic syndrome-labelled dissociative amnesia. Said one, when asked: "That whole period around 1984–1985 is a bit hazy for me, maybe the sheer unpleasantness of what happened during the period is something that I have expunged from my memory"; said another apologetically: "Sorry my memory is a bit confused. It was a very trying time for many of us and for many years I have done my best to put it behind me"; and said a third: "I feel a bit depressed whenever I think about Cambridge and so I put things off (I am usually a rather cheery person)"; [the respondent referred to the narrative of this book as] "rather depressing even upsetting"; and there were other similar reactions as well. Fortunately, or rather unfortunately, a sufficient number of persons had been cleansed through the purges to enable the construction and validation of what could be appropriately regarded as a collective syncretic memory through rounds of iteration and triangulation, including testing against documentary or archival evidence where available.

The admittedly idiosyncratic writing style takes its inspiration from manner, and manners, of the protagonists in their debates and duels; draining away all that passion in favour of a dismal, dour narration normally associated with the discipline of economics would be disrespectful of the fiery no-holds-barred Cambridge tradition of face-to-face intellectual exchanges in those times, and the reader might encounter a scattering of passages that carry a polemical, pamphleteering or on occasion even a prosecutorial air, and it can only be hoped that this might lighten and brighten the reader's lengthy journey.

While this rendition cannot really escape being partial, in both senses of the word, there is a fair attempt at being fair, though not at the expense of not calling a spade what it really is. I have had the benefit of close consultations with several of those intimately involved in the narratives and they are all wholly absolved of the responsibility for any errors of fact or interpretation that I might have accidentally made. Indeed, following the proverbial pejorative, these 'n' economists might well hold 'n+1' opinions about some of the stories told. As emphasised in the intellectual biography of Ajit Singh, the lead political commissar and Chief Whip of the radical heterodox tribes in these battles, the narrative resonates with Ryunosuke Akutagawa's *Rashomon*, immortalised by Akira Kurosawa, or Lawrence Durrell's *The Alexandria Quartet*—the door remains ajar for readers to enter the open space of oral history with their versions of what happened, whodunnit and howdunnit, and to express their preferences and choices about how it all transpired. At a minimum, what I have attempted is to insert one rendition of the story as seen from the perspectives of the vanquished, firmly into this choice set.

Cigars, Smoke, Mirrors

In stories of cigars, smoke and mirrors, with corpses and smell of cordite but no swaggering gunslingers, an occasional element of speculation is unavoidable in joining the dots, in making judgements from forensic as well as circumstantial evidence. In pursuing the whodunnit mystery, associations, affinities, opportunities, motivations, animosities and grudges, visceral vendettas and poisoned polarities and so on all come into play in constructing plausible scenarios that explain specific events or outcomes. That said, these somewhat amorphous aspects find their credence only in combination with a core of citable archival and personal recollections; in this sense, the speculative dimension, unavoidable as it sometimes is, is held within reasonable limits.

At various turns, the stories offer revelations about the unexpected roles, actions or inactions, of several key players whose linkages to the various purges have generally remained in occluded grey zones of silence, seldom going beyond puzzlement or whispers—reminiscent of the other Cambridge pastime of hunting for the fourth or the fifth man in that infamous spy ring. If nothing else, this adds a flavour of zest and spice to a bubbling brew. What emerges is a spectrum of involvement or culpability: from a direct hands-on hostile action; to strategic and tactical support for one of more purges at specific points in decision-making processes; to oppositions which unwittingly or unintentionally feed the purge campaigns; to wilful, or ostensibly accidental, inaction or passivity and lack of support for the various heterodox groups under threat, despite being regarded as members, friends or fellow travellers; or to careless, wanton actions unmindful of their potentially negative consequences for the heterodox side. It is possible to raise queries of one form or another about several names, some of whom perhaps had a direct, if quiet, hand in the proceedings, while others seemed to be onlookers not raising a hand to help the heterodox cause at critical points along the way. What becomes obvious is that while the central battle lines were clearly between the neoclassical orthodox group against the heterodox tribes, the campaigns of the purges were assisted by the opportunistic, active or passive, support of an intermediate group which, while not answering to the neoclassical label, practised forms of heterodoxy, or had political leanings, or held personalised grudges, that placed them in opposition to the main heterodox groups at specific conjunctures; and similar behaviour of some others was suggestive possibly of the pursuit of individual career agendas over professed political loyalties.

Some cautions are necessary. The closed version of the story, telling as it is, requires that the explanation avoids the risk of seeking a total answer within; the open version demands that in the search for greater completeness, the narrative does not slide into reductionism or determinism, into scripting a short history of the world outside, of everything. Then, there is the usual red herring, the easy allegation of flirting with 'conspiracy theorising'. The explanatory power of coincidence is perhaps oversold, a naïve euphemism for ignorance, or a wilful one for obscuring a cover-up—what enthrals audiences Bollywood audiences might not work equally well in historiography. The forensic art of chasing clues and converting coincidence into explanation often attracts the pejorative of 'conspiracy theorizing', this predictably, from the conspiratorial corner itself. Taking 'conspiracy' out of explanation would often yield a pathetically low R-squared value. Julius Caesar did not accidentally trip and lurch 23 times from dagger to naked dagger, all of which just happened to have bypassed security, held firmly, each pointing in his direction just at that time on that particular day in the Senate. And behind a 'conspiracy' usually lies some uncloaked constellation of hostile interests. That said, not all plots are well planned, not all 'conspiracies' succeed and, of course, not everything answers to the description of a plot; history is not a summation of plots, but that does not rule out their existence or salience of the exercise of coordinated collective agency at specific turning points.

"What If … ?"

And then, the discerning reader might find the narrative replete with rich opportunities for indulging in that useless game of 'what if …' counterfactuals—opening up arrays of intriguing simulations for happy-go-lucky modellers. On the one side, these highlight the role of coincidental conjunctures and contexts, accidents, individual idiosyncrasies, follies or percipience; on the other, these turning points beg the question whether, if the 'what if' factor had not occurred, some other constellation of factors might have emerged as a substitute from the deeper material configurations of the time. Even so, the what-if game does raise some teasing and tantalising scenarios. Consider a handful that distracted the author's eye during the labour process.

Take first the interventions of the grim reaper. Bob Rowthorn lamented the early death of Nicky Kaldor; in his view, "the fact that he died relatively young was a great loss; Cambridge economics would have been very different if he had lived another ten years" (Rowthorn 2008). Would it have? By the time of Kaldor's demise in 1986, much of the strategic damage was already done, and further, some of it was attributable to decisions in which Kaldor was himself a culpable party, if not, if accidentally or innocently, a moving spirit. The more, most, obvious 'what-if' surely would be the even more premature death of Keynes in 1946 at the cusp of a critical period for the subject globally and in Cambridge, and in the real world. Or, at a group level, what if the longevity of the neoclassical, neoliberal cohort, with an average age at death around 93 years, was matched by that of the Cambridge heterodox seniors whose average age fell, roughly reckoned over small cohorts, well more than 10 years short of that. Another crucial what-if: Lionel Robbins was struck by the influenza bug very many times in his life and happily survived well; but the unfortunate Allyn Young was struck just once and died within a few days, opening the space for Robbins to take over LSE economics and reorient it towards the Austrian and Chicago camps. Given Young's affinity with Cambridge economics (cf. Sraffa's 1926, and Young's 1928 *EJ* papers, and Keynes's letter of condolence to Allyn

Young's wife), LSE and British economics could have taken a distinctly different trajectory, potentially of significance given the sustained antagonistic stance adopted by LSE under the Robbins-Hayek regime. Then, there was an earlier what-if, in the form of the desire of Sidney Webb to appoint Keynes as the Director of LSE in 1919, instead of Beveridge, which again would surely have precluded, or diluted, the entry of Austrian and Walrasian traditions into LSE and the UK. And what if Frank Hahn had not been twice invited to Cambridge, once via Kaldor who might much later have had second thoughts and regrets and then by the likes of Kahn and Reddaway following Kaldor's managed appointment of Robert Neild (over Hahn) to the vacant Joan Robinson chair? And what if Richard Goodwin or Luigi Pasinetti or Geoff Harcourt had been appointed instead; or if, at a potentially game-changing turn, say, Pasinetti, and not Robin Matthews, had been appointed as the new Professor of Political Economy when Brian Reddaway retired in 1980; or perchance, later in the 1980s, the two professorships had gone, again, to someone from that list, or to others from the rising cohort of Francis Cripps or Hashem Pesaran or Ajit Singh? Kaldor had seen Luigi as the lead practitioner of the Cambridge post-Keynesian tradition of 'grand theorizing'; Francis was widely regarded as a potential natural inheritor of the Wynne Godley mantle; and Ajit was a highly accomplished applied economist straddling diverse research specialisations. In such alternative what-if scenarios, could the then ongoing and subsequent purges of heterodoxy have happened or continued with the same gusto and outcomes? Then, David Hendry (2004) recalled that after studies in Aberdeen, "I applied to work with Dick Stone in Cambridge. Unfortunately he declined, so I did an M.Sc in econometrics at LSE with Denis Sargan", becoming one of the stars of the young cohort of 'nephews' in the Hahn-Gorman years there; hindsight induces the speculation whether the tribulations and trajectories of the DAE macroeconomic teams might have gone differently if Stone had said 'yes' and Hendry had settled down instead to a fine career with Stone at the DAE in Cambridge? Then, the professorial vacancy to which Dasgupta was appointed emerged when Robert Neild retired hurt prematurely, six years short of the Cambridge retirement age of 67; what if Robert, with his mild-mannered and persuasive personality, had withstood the heat in the Faculty kitchen till then and fought the decent fight for applied and heterodox economics within the professoriate—later on he came out with trenchant critiques calling mainstream economics "a disgrace in need of a reformation"? So many hypothetical questions, so few firm answers.

Moving to the national stage, what about the committed Labour MP and family doctor, Sir Alfred Broughton, who had insisted even on his death bed to be driven to London to cast his vote in the No-Confidence motion introduced by Margaret Thatcher in 1979; his honourable wish was declined by Callaghan on ethical grounds, and Labour lost the motion 311–310; as Roy Hattersley (2009) recalled later, Labour was in trouble, but getting a few more months—a long time in politics—in government for Labour could well have changed the immediate political climate and discourse, and kept Thatcher out, at least at that time. In turn, this could have kept the umbrella of political protection over the Cambridge left-Keynesian groups for another term and pre-empted the political pressures brought to bear on the SSRC and Michael Posner at the time of the rejection of SSRC funding for the DAE's macroeconomic modelling teams. Or what if Tony Benn, with the Alternative Economic Strategy of the left, had not lost the crucial election to the deputy leadership of the Labour Party, by less than one per cent of the vote, through the combined midnight machinations of the Callaghan, Healey and Kinnock groups which then became a turning point for left labour? All such illicit game-playing in counterfactuals, imagining 'paths not taken' at direction-changing crossroads, is as intriguing as it is futile. Indeed, what if the enraged nationalist 18-year-old student, Gavrilo Princip, had not used his deadly pistol in Sarajevo on 28 June 1914? Or what if .... Oh, the pleasures and pitfalls of idle rumination.

COVID Caveat

Completing large manuscripts is a fraught business anyway, but the overlay of the pandemic made it rather more so. Multiple rounds of unexpected and extended lockdowns in India brought distress, dislocation and delay; travel restrictions to, and in, Europe added to the disruption. More significantly, this affected the possibility of personal access to libraries, of conducting some more personal interviews and made it impossible to consult additional archival materials in London and Cambridge. A year was lost, but then, unlike so very many unfortunate others, one lived to tell the tale; I confess the virus might merely have provided an alibi for an existential reluctance to bid farewell to the manuscript much earlier and consign it irretrievably to the publisher; and, even if disingenuously, one can cite the extended vacant stretches enforced by the pandemic as an alibi for the unusual length of the book.

The Hague, The Netherlands   Ashwani Saith

Cover

St Michael's victory over the devil.
Jacob Epstein, Coventry Cathedral

On 14–15 November 1940, "a bright moonlit cloudless night made navigation simple" for the Luftwaffe operation—fatefully code-named *Moonlight Sonata*—of the blanket bombing of Coventry in which "almost a third of the city was flattened" with its medieval cathedral reduced to rubble. (GCHQ 2021). Wynne Godley was married to Kitty Garman, daughter of Kathleen Garman and the famous sculptor Jacob Epstein, one of whose creations lives on the wall of the cathedral in Coventry evoking the unbroken spirit of the city, with Benjamin Britten composing his *War Requiem* for the consecration of the reconstructed cathedral in 1962. It depicts St Michael—representing the good—slaying the devil. Epstein used a model of his "impossibly handsome" son-in-law, Wynne, to sculpt the head of St Michael. Though Wynne and his research team, along with other celebrated heterodox lineages, lost out proverbially to "the devil" in the Cambridge war of economics, there has subsequently been a defiant phoenix-like revival of the reputation and work of the famous Godley-Cripps Cambridge Economic Policy Group of the 1970s, as well as of other renowned radical traditions nurtured since the 1920s in Cambridge, the crucible of heterodox economics. The allegorical symbolism of Sir Jacob Epstein's sculpture resonates with the leitmotif of the book.

Acknowledgements

Much appreciation is due to very many for varied and valuable inputs at different stages of the writing process: from supplying the simple ingredient of encouragement that sustains, facilitating access to sources and materials or to spotting banana skins before I did. The episodes narrated in this book are of a shared lived experience, often traumatic and locked away, of a dynamic cohort of accomplished, radical, socially motivated economists of various heterodox persuasions, of their expulsion or exile from their vibrant intellectual habitat in Cambridge, enforced to different degrees and in variable forms by a sustained onslaught by orthodox economics and its practitioners. This book could not have been written if they had not, to the last woman/man standing, been willing to relive and recount details of those episodes, however personally distressing might have been such exercises of reclaiming and piecing together a lost collective memory of a game-changing turning point in the history of Cambridge economics. In a real sense, I have merely been a scribe, the weaver of this fabric of suppressed untold stories, working the warp and weft to expose patterns formed by knotting together the many individual strings and threads. For generous and unfailing support in reading through, clarifying, correcting and validating various texts, for face-to-face interviews in real or later in virtual space, I am indebted to: Amiya Bagchi, Terry Barker, Bob Blackburn, Vani Borooah, Heinrich Bortis, Jo Bradley, Brendan Burchell, Ha-Joon Chang, Andy Cosh, Ken Coutts, Francis Cripps, Michael Ellman, Valpy FitzGerald, Matthew Frost, Geoff Harcourt, Wendy Harcourt, Alan Hughes, Jane Humphries, Alex Izurieta, Sandeep Kapur, Michael Landesmann, Marc Lavoie, Tony Lawson, Maria Cristina Marcuzzo, Peter Nolan, Jose Gabriel Palma, Prabhat Patnaik, Jill Rubery, Sunanda Sen, Ron Smith, Servaas Storm, John Toye, Brian Van Arkadie, Terry Ward, Frank Wilkinson and Ann Zammit. I hope the final outcome justifies their generosity. They are all hereby absolved of any errors of commission, omission or interpretation that remain.

The editors of the Palgrave series *History of Economic Thought* readily took on this project in its original incarnation and then did not blink as it stretched to three times its initially planned scale; I would like to thank them for their expressed confidence, in particular to Geoff Harcourt—sadly till a week ago, joint senior guru with Luigi Pasinetti, of Cambridge heterodox economics and economists. Geoff encouraged and supported the book from its inception as a chapter in my intellectual biography of Ajit Singh, almost all the way to completion, and it will remain a gnawing sadness that he was taken before he could write a foreword or examine the first copy off the press blocks. Other stalwarts from the times of the tales told here will also be much missed, especially Ajit Singh, John Toye, Mario Nuti and Frank Wilkinson.

I am much in debt to Paula Bownas for her precise and timely editorial preparation of a challenging manuscript for the publishers, though I messed it up again after her work was done; and then to successive teams at Palgrave Macmillan: Rachel Sangster and Joseph Johnson in the commissioning phase, and after that to Wyndham Hacket Pain, to Srishti Gupta, to the production team especially to Dhanalakshmi Muralidharan, Hemalatha Arumugam and Sujatha Mani, and to Palgrave's legal experts, for efficiently and calmly guiding the manuscript through the rest of its sometimes complex journey to publication; and to Srishti and Frido Steinen-Broo for the expeditious processing of my suggestions for the cover design. I would like to express my appreciation to the several anonymous readers of various draft versions for their very valuable feedback during the multiple rounds of reviews. As always, thanks are due to several librarians in Cambridge: to Simon Frost for the efficient and pleasant accommodation at short notice of my requests at the Marshall Library Archives; to Katrina Dean, Jill Whitelock and Michelle Barnes for kindly facilitating quick access to archival materials at the University Library; and to Patricia McGuire, Peter Monteith and Thomas Davies at the King's College Archives.

A collective salaam for the comradely support received from my scattered gang of friends, many of whom also shared the Cambridge journey; and loving familial appreciation for Sanjeev Saith and for the Wazir clan for keeping me in good cheer and high spirits, often literally. The unending, indeed forever extending, canvas of the manuscript exacted its toll of time and life, crowding out both this as well as that—the invisible price paid by someone else for an author's self-indulgence. And so, from the first page to the last, for caring and forbearance beyond calls of anything and everything, an open-arm acknowledgement and salutation for Rekha—gratitude begins at home.

Praise for *Cambridge Economics in the Post-Keynesian Era*

"This book is awesome in both its depth and range. It is avowedly a story of how the Economic Faculty of Cambridge University where not just Keynesian economics but macroeconomics was born and became home not just to Keynesians such as Joan and Austin Robinson, Nicholas Kaldor and Brian Reddaway but also Marxists such as Maurice Dobb, was converted into a fortress of not just neoclassical but neoliberal economics from the 1980s. Saith traces the change in the political atmosphere with the rise to power of Margaret Thatcher and Ronald Reagan. But he also shows how there was a planned attack on heterodox economics and economists by Matthews, Hahn and Dasgupta, who saw to it that only people of their choice were appointed to the Faculty and to all prestigious committees and editorial boards of journals, not only in Cambridge but everywhere else in Britain. They found allies in the LSE and in Chicago and Cambridge, Mass. overseas. The attackers took advantage of dissensions among the leaders of Keynesian economics in Cambridge. Saith also brings in sociology, development and economic history in his intense focus. This book should be required reading for everybody interested in the survival of people-friendly heterodox social sciences, including economics. Readers would realize that very similar tactics have been used by neoliberal economists wherever they have been able to obtain a foothold. That acquisition has been made easier with the omnipresence of the IMF and the World Bank. Saith's book is a notable addition to the history of economic thought and to the history of our times."
—Amiya Bagchi, Emeritus Professor and Emeritus Director, *Institute of Development Studies, Kolkata*; Adjunct Professor, *Monash University, Australia*

"This book explains how Cambridge (and indeed British) preeminence in post-Keynesian economics was undermined in the 1970s. With outstanding forensic scholarship, Saith reveals the institutional and personal networking that replaced a distinctive and empirical tradition in political economy by neoclassical orthodoxy. The book is destined to become the definitive account in the history of economic thought of how neoclassical economists reinforced their hegemony over the academic discipline in the 20th Century."
—Terry Barker, Former Director, *Cambridge Growth Project, Department of Applied Economics, University of Cambridge*; Coordinating Lead Author, *IPCC 1996–2006*; Director, *Cambridge Econometrics Ltd.*

"The Economics Faculty at the University of Cambridge is, arguably, one of the most famous in the world, suffused with the history of great ideas and the remarkable achievements of distinguished men and women. As a history of this Faculty, with particular emphasis on the past 75 years, Ashwani Saith's book is a tour de force. This is a compelling account of the jousts between the heterodox defenders of the Cambridge castle, who eschewed quantitative methods in economics, and their foreign invaders in the form of neoclassical economists who were devoted to the American tradition of using

mathematics and statistics. Saith tells a fascinating story of how the seemingly impregnable citadel fell to a combination of enemies within the faculty, aided by the university administration, and with the active assistance of the government of the day in the UK. Was this a Pyrrhic victory, which reduced a once great and independent faculty to an imitation of US economics departments, or was such an overthrow long overdue? And who were the winners and losers? and what became of them? These are all issues addressed by the author in this fascinating analysis of the fall of economics at Cambridge from its glory days."
—Vani Borooah, *Emeritus Professor and Chair of Applied Economics, University of Ulster;* Past President, *Irish Economic Association, and Secretary, Royal Irish Academy*

"The Keynesian-Sraffian double revolution of the *Years of High Theory (1926–1939–1960)* laid the basis for the Keynesian triumph from, broadly, 1945 to 1975—*We are all Keynesians now!*—became a current saying. In his immensely important book Ashwani Saith now pictures in great detail the tragedy linked to the systematic destruction of the Keynesian tradition at Cambridge through the neoclassicals from 1975 onwards. His book represents a substantive contribution to the recent history of economics."
—Heinrich Bortis, *Emeritus Professor of Political Economy, History of Economic Theory and Economic History, Department of Economics, University of Fribourg, Switzerland*

"I came to Cambridge in 1985 to work in the Department of Applied Economics as part of an interdisciplinary project involving Economics, Sociology and Social Psychology, progressing onto a lectureship in Social and Political Sciences (SPS) and finally a Chair and sometime Head of Department in Sociology. This book makes it clear why such a career path is no longer an option and does a lot to make sense to me of the period from the mid 1985s until now. It also explains, in a large part, why the Faculty of Economics has, for a long time now, been seen as an outlier amongst Cambridge institutions, cut off from the other social sciences. Reading this manuscript forced me to reflect deeply on just how things worked out like they did. Perhaps for now the music has stopped, but when (as it invariably will) the music starts playing again, I hope that someone with Ashwani Saith's eye for details and the bigger picture will be around to write the sequel!"
—Brendan Burchell, *Professor in the Social Sciences;* Chair, *Archaeology, Anthropology and Sociology Degree Committee;* President of Magdalene College, *University of Cambridge*

"This book opens up the shadowy world where academic orthodoxy aligns with neo-conservative politics and corporate power to block applied research in the Keynesian tradition making the search for solutions to long-standing global problems very, very hard if not impossible. Ashwani Saith digs deep to uncover not only the procedures through which protagonists of the neo-classical paradigm purged researchers whose evidence stood in their way but also the doubts and hesitations of the galaxy of world-famous economists who contributed to the rise and subsequent demise of Keynesian economics at its birthplace in Cambridge. The author describes the step-by-step process of demolition of the Cambridge Department of Applied Economics and purge of heterodox teaching of economics, sociology, development and economic history at a Faculty that had been the birthplace of the twentieth century Keynesian revolution,

attracting graduate students from around the world. People who share concerns about governance in the twenty-first century should read this book and think hard about how damage done in the last quarter of the twentieth century can be repaired and how open and plural research environments demanded by contemporary students can be restored."
—Francis Cripps, Director, *Alphametrics Co., Ltd, Bangkok, Thailand*

"The strange death of Cambridge heterodox economics is a significant development in intellectual history and is well worth the detailed attention it gets in this book. It has an excellent source basis: relevant archival documents, a wide range of publications, and interviews or email exchanges with many of those directly involved. The book covers a wide range of Cambridge issues, from Hahn's self-image as John the Baptist to the critiques of economics by Polly Hill and Michael Postan. However, the book is not confined to internal Cambridge matters but pays attention to national and international developments outside Cambridge that influenced or determined the outcome. These range from the decisions by the SSRC & ESRC to stop funding the major research programmes at the DAE (Department of Applied Economics), to the creation and activities of the Mont Pelerin Society and the vicissitudes of Keynesianism in the USA. This remarkable and well-written book is a mine of information. It is well worth reading and recommending to colleagues and libraries."
—Michael Ellman, Emeritus Professor, *University of Amsterdam, Awarded 1998 Kondratieff Gold Medal*; Co-editor, *Cambridge Journal of Economics*

"I had the great pleasure to read early versions of this meticulously researched history of the rise and demise of Cambridge heterodox economics in the post-Keynesian era. I warmly congratulate Ashwani for his tour de force."
—Geoffrey Harcourt, (27 June 1931–7 December 2021), *Emeritus Professor of Economics, University of Adelaide, Australia; Emeritus Reader in History of Economic Theory, University of Cambridge*

"Ashwani Saith has written a carefully researched and compelling account of the means by which the Cambridge Faculty of Economics and Politics was purged of heterodox applied economic analysis in the last quarter of the twentieth century. It draws on memoirs and interviews with participants in the contest for control, and a detailed archival analysis to reveal the methods by which this was achieved. These methods extended beyond the Faculty into the operations of major research funders. It should be read by anyone with an interest in the ways in which power can be exercised to control the nature of academic discourse and for the implications this may have for the future and relevance of the economics discipline."
—Alan Hughes, *Emeritus Margaret Thatcher Professor of Enterprise Studies and Director*, Emeritus, *Centre for Business Research, Judge Business School, University of Cambridge*; Life Fellow, *Jesus College, Cambridge*

"History is usually written by the victors, but Ashwani Saith speaks for and from the other side of the battlelines of how Cambridge Economics came to expunge its vibrant heterodox traditions, closed its hitherto distinguished applied department, narrowed its methodological approach and rejected

scholarly dissent. It is a voice that should be heard, and a book that must be read, certainly by anyone interested in making economics socially meaningful and fit again for the pursuit of public purpose."
  —Jane Humphries, Centennial Professor, *London School of Economics*; *Emeritus Professor of Economic History, University of Oxford*; *Fellow of All Souls College, Oxford*

"When I joined the University of Cambridge in early 2002 and was invited to tutor students of the Faculty of Economics, I was shocked to see that none of those I met ever read Kaldor or Robinson, and the only thing about Keynes they came across was the IS-LM caricature portrayed by Mankiw. Frequent conversations with Ken Coutts, Francis Cripps, John Eatwell, Wynne Godley, Geoff Harcourt, Ajit Singh and others helped uncover important pieces of the puzzle. But this comprehensive and rigorous book offers a full picture. Ashwani's opus excels. Through the painstaking account of events at Cambridge there grows an unmistakable appreciation of the imperative for the economics profession worldwide to become meaningful again."
  —Alex Izurieta, Senior Economist, *UNCTAD, Geneva*; Former Senior Researcher, *Judge Business School, University of Cambridge*

"Ashwani Saith's book is monumental, enthralling, beautifully written with its occasional satirical tone, but as we are being warned, depressing. It explains how the Faculty of Economics of the University of Cambridge—the world centre of post-Keynesian economics—was gradually and entirely taken over by neoclassical economics and why the Department of Applied Economics, also at the heart of heterodox economics, eventually came to be dismantled. This was so far an untold story, except for a chapter on 'Faculty wars' in Saith's previous book, the intellectual biography of Ajit Singh. The current book provides 14 chapters of a meticulous detective story, relying mostly on Cambridge archives, but also on testimonies, interviews, emails, and previous articles of participants to these events. The book makes clear that, besides possible strategical mistakes by the incumbent heterodox economists, there were inexorable and ineluctable outside forces that led to this dismal state of affairs, through the Americanization of the economics profession and through the changing political winds that blew out heterodox and left-wing economics nearly everywhere in the world. The last chapter shows that all is not lost, both in Cambridge and elsewhere in the world."
  —Marc Lavoie, Professor Emeritus, *University of Ottawa, Canada*; Professor Emeritus, *Université Sorbonne Paris Nord, France*

"This is an important book, and one that makes compelling reading for anyone interested in the developments in economics over the last few decades. It is a fascinating investigation into how ideas are shaped and in turn shape power relations within the academic world, and a passionate defence of the side which was defeated in Cambridge in the feud between heterodox and mainstream

economics. Ashwani Saith witnessed the events and, while standing firmly on the side of those who lost the battle, manages to remain fair, balanced and scholarly. Highly recommended."
—Maria Cristina Marcuzzo, Professor, *Accademia dei Lincei, Università di Roma 'La Sapienza'*

"Henry Kissinger once said that "The reason that university politics is so vicious is because stakes are so small". This is often true, but not in the case of the Faculty of Economics at Cambridge in the 1980s. The elections of Thatcher and Reagan and the rise of neo-liberalism made the conflict at Cambridge the exception: the stakes were high because this was part of a much larger conflict. When I started my academic career, Cambridge was the place where to be; but when I got an appointment in 1981, little did I know of what was coming! When I joined, the intellectual life of the Faculty consisted mostly of its own internal controversies between two powerful intellectual groups; those controversies kept everyone on their intellectual toes. But political changes in the outside world gave one group the opportunity to ally themselves with powerful external political interests and with internal bureaucracies always all-too eager to acquiesce to external demands. What this group could not win by the power of ideas they achieved through brute force. Little by little, as it's made clear by the meticulous research in Saith's brilliant book, they squeezed heterodox economics out of the Faculty. When I retired in 2014, a member of the other group told me jokingly: there goes the last of the Mohicans! As a great psychoanalyst discusses in his work, there seems to be an inverse relationship between the expectation of understanding the real, and the tolerance of dissent. As soon as the 1980s began to show the limitation of neo-liberalism as an ideology and neo-classical economics as an economic theory, the dread of having misunderstood the real led to a desperate need for the annihilation of disagreement—as soon as the DAE rightly predicted that Thatcherism will lead to unemployment jumping to 3 million the writing was on the wall. In other words, when expectation of understanding the real is high, difference of opinion is tolerable, but when there is little or no expectation of understanding, the need for agreement is absolute. This brings the destructive instinct into play, turning a belief system into an absolutist one, and this into an engine of ideological genocide. From this perspective Ashwani Saith's book is not just a great contribution to the history of economic thought, but also to the understanding of the intellectual obscurantism of our times."
—Jose Gabriel Palma, Senior Lecturer Emeritus, *Faculty of Economics, University of Cambridge*; Professor of Economics, *University of Santiago, Chile*; Joint Editor, *Cambridge Journal of Economics*

"The Keynesian Revolution was not just about the vacuity of Say's Law or the correct understanding of the determinants of the interest rate. It revolutionized economics as a whole, by completely opening up the subject, liberating it from the straitjacket of a belief in the desirability of perfect markets, and

bringing in bold, new thinking in many spheres. In development theory for instance it created room for the entry of structuralism; and in development policy it encouraged novel forms of state intervention within the *dirigiste regimes* that came up in the post-decolonization era. The Sraffa Revolution, though of a somewhat esoteric nature, had a similar liberating effect. As both revolutions began in Cambridge, it became a magnet for economists from all over the world. The capture of Cambridge by economic orthodoxy therefore was a major episode in the counter-revolution against the liberation of economics. It occurred not because of the superiority of orthodox ideas, but above all through the use of political and economic power. Ashwani Saith's book is a meticulous and comprehensive discussion of this capture. It is a *tour de force* that throws valuable light on the sociology behind the dominance of ideas. Given the profound significance of this capture, which prepared the intellectual ground for the subsequent ascendancy of neo-liberal thinking, it should be of interest to every economist, not just those who were directly involved; and it is written with remarkable scrupulousness and lucidity. An essential read."
—Prabhat Patnaik, *Emeritus Professor of Economics, Centre for Economic Studies and Planning, Jawaharlal Nehru University, New Delhi*

"This book chronicles the sustained undermining of heterodox economics and the severing of the links between economics and other social sciences in the Cambridge economics faculty from the 1970s onwards. This mattered as Cambridge was the renowned centre for Keynesian and heterodox economics and the suppression of this legacy was important in securing the domination of the neoclassical mainstream. This process was spreading across the world but as Ashwani Saith makes clear, through the most amazingly detailed evidence-based account, it was the specific strategies and practices deployed in Cambridge over decades by a small coterie of powerful academics that led to the evisceration of heterodoxy and cognate disciplines from the Economics Tripos. Painful as it was to relive through this outstanding book the years of intrigue, disrespect and intense job insecurity that I had to experience in a key period of my academic life, for me the saddest consequence is that young people now are denied the inspiring, theoretically diverse and interdisciplinary education that I enjoyed in Cambridge in the early 1970s. After the financial crisis economics students across the world started to ask why the economics curriculum no longer had power to explain or resolve real world problems. Many of the answers are to be found here."
—Jill Rubery, *Emeritus Professor of Comparative Employment Systems, University of Manchester*, Former Director, *Work and Equalities Institute at Alliance Manchester Business School*

"Ashwani Saith has produced a fascinating social anthropology of the warring tribes of Econ at one of their earliest settlements. Drawing on a wealth of original documents and the accounts of a host of participant-observers, he carefully documents the battles for the control of the priesthood, the seminar rituals and

the sacred journals, in the liminal time before the old gods of Cambridge Economics were finally displaced. It is both a revealing account of internecine academic warfare and an entertaining read."
—Ron Smith, *Professor of Applied Economics, Department of Economics, Mathematics and Statistics, Birkbeck, University of London*

"The history of Cambridge Economics in the Post-Keynesian Era is a story that needed to be told—and Ashwani Saith's book does it extremely well. In what reads as a detective story-cum-period-novel-cum-family-drama, Saith offers a persuasive, richly documented and fascinating account of how productive, relevant and innovative heterodox economic traditions were purged from the Faculty of Economics of Cambridge University, for reasons of 'ideology' and in order to align the divided department with an increasingly irrelevant mainstream economics. Saith brilliantly manages to contextualise the local happenings in Cambridge within the global rise of the 'neoliberal thought-collective', highlighting the crucial roles of individual knowledge brokers, networks, thinktanks, politicians and donors. Fundamental theoretical, ideological and methodological disagreements between the major actors in this drama are discussed with impressive clarity and purpose, and with a keen eye for biographical detail and historical setting. In the end, it is the sad story of the better road not taken. Saith's book brings us back to the fork in the road—and forces us to consider and reconsider our earlier decision. Cambridge Economics in the Post-Keynesian Era is an extraordinary piece of research, lovingly told and immensely worthwhile for the new light it sheds on the epoch-making purge of Keynesian thinking right in its original stronghold."
—Servaas Storm, Senior Lecturer, *Faculty of Technology, Policy and Management, Delft University of Technology, The Netherlands*, Joint Editor, *Development and Change*

"This book should be read by anyone with an interest in the freedom of academic study. Ashwani Saith accurately describes the events surrounding the creation of the Cambridge Department of Applied Economic and its development into a successful and prestigious centre for research into economic and social policy, attracting researchers from around the world, and its subsequent dismantling and eventual closure. It is the story of how those who did not subscribe to the dogmas of neoclassical economics, who believed that to start from unrealistic abstract assumptions was not the best way to build models of reality or of understanding behaviour, were driven out of the University, in a number of cases to pursue their research in the private sector. In many cases, they were highly successful in doing so, but to the detriment of economics in Cambridge and to the students who came to study there, attracted by the legacy of Keynes and a desire to understand how economies work and the factors underlying economic and social development. The book is a testament to the investigative skills of the author and his painstaking pursuit of how a shameful episode in Cambridge University history unfolded by uncovering and crawling through countless documents in various archives and interviewing a great many of those that were directly involved. Although it brings back painful personal memories, it is a story that is important to tell, to show how those who have gained academic power can dictate what can be taught, what research questions it is legitimate to try to answer and what methods can be used to do so."

—Terry Ward, Research Director, *Applica srl. Brussels*;
Managing Director, *Alphametrics Ltd. U.K.*

Contents of Volume II

10 Sociology: The Departure of 'Stray Colleagues in a Vaguely Cognate Discipline'   691
    10.1   *Early Years: Hostility, Neglect, Subordination*   692
    10.2   *Sociology: Growing Up Amongst Economists*   716
    10.3   *Hostile Public Spaces: SSRC, Rothschild-1982 and Sociology*   726
        10.3.1   *Entrenched Resistance to the Emergence of SSRC*   726
        10.3.2   *In the Court of Public Opinion: Open Season on Sociology*   728
        10.3.3   *The Joseph–Rothschild Assault*   730
    10.4   *Back in Cambridge, 1984–1986: To Remain Or to Exit, That Was the Question*   734
        10.4.1   *Sociology in the DAE Review: Crossfire and Crossroads*   734
        10.4.2   *Cometh the Hour, Cometh ... Tony Giddens*   736
    10.5   *Archival Insights: Harboured Preferences Revealed*   744
        10.5.1   *Do Please Stay, Pleaded the Heterodox*   744
        10.5.2   *Clear Out Now, Growled the Orthodox*   746
        10.5.3   *Do What Is Best for You, Whispered the Faculty Board*   747
        10.5.4   *Time to Choose: The Sociologists Speak*   748
    10.6   *Leaving Home, a Space of Its Own*   755
    References   758

11 Development on the Periphery: Exit and Exile   765
    11.1   *Cambridge Development Studies: The Heterodox Inheritance*   767
        11.1.1   *The Capitalist Economy and Its Cambridge Critics*   767
        11.1.2   *Bridges to Development*   769

11.2		*Evolution of the Teaching Project: Multiple Identities*	777
	11.2.1	*Timelines*	777
	11.2.2	*In University Space: The Professionalisation of 'Development Studies'*	779
		The Early Years: Fine-tuning Imperial Instruction, 1926–1969	779
		Turbulence and Transformation: Revising the Mandate, 1969–1982	787
	11.2.3	*In Faculty Space: The Disciplining of 'Development Economics'*	800
	11.2.4	*Against the Mainstream: Subaltern Perspectives*	808
11.3		*Development Research: Ebbs and Flows*	810
	11.3.1	*Cambridge–India Highway: Cambridge in India*	810
	11.3.2	*Cambridge–India Highway: India in Cambridge*	818
	11.3.3	*Not Just India*	821
	11.3.4	*Bi-modal Distribution of Development Interest*	826
11.4		*1996: Divorce and Eviction*	828
11.5		*A Credible Counterfactual*	832
		Appendix 11.1: Arguments in Support of Continuation of Development Studies Course in Cambridge	836
		References	839

12 From Riches to Rags? Economic History Becomes History at the Faculty of Economics 845

12.1		*Introduction: Economics and Economic History*	846
12.2		*The Pre-War Period: 1939, Marshallian*	847
	12.2.1	*At the Faculty of History*	847
		Cunningham to Clapham via Marshall	847
		Clapham to Postan via Power	849
	12.2.2	*At the Faculty of Economics and Politics*	852
		Maurice Dobb, 1900–1976	852
12.3		*Post-War Period-I, 1945–1980s: Post-Keynesian*	860
	12.3.1	*At the Faculty of Economics and Politics*	860
		On the DAE Side	861
		On the Faculty Side	875
	12.3.2	*At the Faculty of History*	881
		'Munia' Postan	881
		The Turn to Business Studies-I, David Joslin 1965–1970	892
		The Turn to Business Studies-II, Donald Coleman 1971–1981	895
12.4		*Post-War Period-II, 1980s: Unravelling and Divergence*	898
	12.4.1	*At the Faculty of History*	898

		The Turn to Business Studies-III, Barry Supple 1981–1993	898
		Modern Times: Martin Daunton 1997–2015	899
	12.4.2	At the Faculty of Economics: Turbulence, Transitions and Affinities	902
		Cluster 1: Humphries—Horrell	903
		Cluster 2: Kitson—Solomou—Weale	914
		Cluster 3: Ogilvie—Edwards	918
		Cluster 4: Toke Aidt	924
12.5	c.2020, Here, to Where?		926
	12.5.1	Economic History at the Faculty of Economics: Full Stop?	926
	12.5.2	At the Faculty of History: New Turnings	931
Appendix 12.1: Economic History and Accounting at the DAE			934
Appendix 12.2: Locating Phyllis Deane in National Accounting and Feminist Discourse: A Supplementary Note			938
References			953

13 Research Assessment Exercises: Exorcising Heterodox Apostasy from 'Economics' — 965

13.1	The Agenda	966
13.2	The Teaching Body: Unification, Hierarchy, Control	968
13.3	1986: Swinnerton-Dyer and the Genesis of the RAE	973
13.4	1986–1989: Frank Hahn and the Orthodox Capture of the RES	976
13.5	Through the RES: Controlling Panel Selection	983
13.6	Outcomes	989
13.7	Consequences and Critiques	991
	13.7.1 Gaming	992
	13.7.2 Competition and Conflict: Managerialism	993
	13.7.3 Individual Stress	995
	13.7.4 Medium Over Message: Diamonds for Ever	997
	13.7.5 Unethical Research Practices and Shaky Quality Proxies	998
	13.7.6 The Atrophy of Collective Research Traditions and Environments	1000
	13.7.7 The Loss of Intrinsic Values	1001
	13.7.8 Undervaluation of Undergraduate Teaching	1002
13.8	The Suppression of Heterodox Economics and Economists	1003
13.9	Follow Big Brother: Elimination of Heterodoxy in USA	1007
13.10	1662, Deja Vu	1012
References		1014

14 Reincarnations — 1019
- 14.1 In a Nutshell, à la Joan — 1020
- 14.2 Purges and Purification — 1021
- 14.3 Triumphalism — 1023
- 14.4 A Royal Mess: The Queen's Question — 1028
- 14.5 Students Speak Up — 1031
  - 14.5.1 In Cambridge — 1031
  - 14.5.2 Elsewhere — 1032
- 14.6 Faculty Performance: A Summary Report Card — 1033
  - 14.6.1 Global Ranks — 1034
  - 14.6.2 RAEs, REFs — 1034
- 14.7 Exiles and Reincarnations — 1036
  - 14.7.1 The DAE Flagships: CGP and CEPG — 1037
  - 14.7.2 DAE Industrial Economics: Alan Hughes and the CBR — 1038
  - 14.7.3 Judge Business School — 1038
  - 14.7.4 The Economic Historians — 1042
  - 14.7.5 Sociology: That 'Vaguely Cognate Discipline' — 1043
  - 14.7.6 Development — 1043
- 14.8 Reluctant Regrets — 1045
  - 14.8.1 Robin Matthews — 1045
  - 14.8.2 Frank Hahn — 1046
  - 14.8.3 David Newbery — 1047
  - 14.8.4 Tony Atkinson — 1048
  - 14.8.5 Francois Bourguignon — 1052
  - 14.8.6 Alan Blinder — 1053
  - 14.8.7 Peter Diamond — 1054
  - 14.8.8 Partha Dasgupta via Robert Neild — 1054
  - 14.8.9 Another Snowflake Moment? — 1056
- 14.9 Donors: Leveraging a Reboot? — 1057
- 14.10 The Great Banyan — 1068
- Appendix 14.1: Letter of Protest by Graduate Students, 2001 — 1073
- References — 1075

References — 1079

Name Index — 1147

Subject Index — 1175

Contents of Volume I

1. **Cambridge, That Was: The Crucible of Heterodox Economics** — 1
   - 1.1 *The Narrative* — 1
   - 1.2 *Evolutions and Revolutions* — 4
     - 1.2.1 The Great Banyan of Heterodox Traditions — 4
     - 1.2.2 Cohorts — 6
     - 1.2.3 The Cambridge Habitat — 9
     - 1.2.4 Which Cambridge? — 11
   - 1.3 *Regime Change* — 14
     - 1.3.1 The World of Cambridge: Stories Within — 20
     - 1.3.2 Worlds Beyond Cambridge: Neoliberalism at the Gates — 22
   - 1.4 *The Dialectic of Competing Paradigms* — 26
     - 1.4.1 Laissez-Faire: "Receding at last into the distance" — 27
     - 1.4.2 The Force of Ideas — 29
     - 1.4.3 Opposition Brewing — 32
     - 1.4.4 Evolutions and Hegemonic Incorporation — 33
     - 1.4.5 Ideological: Not the Techniques but the Purposes of Economics — 36
     - 1.4.6 Sociological: Mathematical Whiz-Kids and Ageing Dinosaurs — 38
     - 1.4.7 Beyond Kuhnian Reductionism — 39
     - 1.4.8 Mankiw's Pendulum — 40
     - 1.4.9 Solow's À La Carte Approach — 42
     - 1.4.10 Silos and Trenches — 43
     - 1.4.11 Joan Versus Hahn—History Versus Equilibrium — 46
   - 1.5 *Semantics and Pedantics* — 56
   - *References* — 63

2 The Warring Tribes — 69
- 2.1 *A Sanctuary of Sages* — 70
  - 2.1.1 Class to Community: *The Cement of War* — 70
  - 2.1.2 Community to Conflict: *Cement to Sand* — 76
  - 2.1.3 *A Pride of Savage Prima Donnas* — 78
- 2.2 *Faculty Wars* — 95
  - 2.2.1 *Paradise Lost* — 102
  - 2.2.2 *Fault Lines Within* — 103
    - Wynne Godley: No Legacy No Synthesis, No Textbooks—The Samuelson Factor — 103
    - Shifting Student Preferences? — 104
    - "Irrelevance" and Irreverence: Joan and K-Theory — 106
    - Inbred Insularity, Complacency — 108
    - Simultaneities in the Demographic Lifecycle — 111
    - Lack of Internal Group Coherence — 115
    - The Heterodox Camp: No Chairs—Sorry, Standing Room Only — 127
    - A Break in Intergenerational Transmission, in the Reproduction of Traditions — 128
- 2.3 *Godfathers, Uncles and Nephews: The Gathering Foe* — 129
  - 2.3.1 *The Trojan Horse: By the Pricking of My Thumbs* — 129
  - 2.3.2 *Forming the Academy* — 132
    - Meanwhile, at the Orthodox Party—A Merry Game of Musical Chairs — 136
  - 2.3.3 *The Chess Master* — 138
- 2.4 *The Campaign: How the War Was Lost and Won* — 150
  - 2.4.1 *The Orthodox Gambit: Capture the External Commanding Heights* — 150
  - 2.4.2 *Carrots and Commanders* — 153
  - 2.4.3 Modus Operandi: *Masters, Mandarins and Interlocking Committees* — 169
- References — 172

3 Worlds Beyond Cambridge: The Global Web of the 'Neoliberal Thought Collective' — 179
- 3.1 *Conjunctures* — 181
  - 3.1.1 *1930s, The Prelude* — 181
    - LSE Versus Cambridge — 181
    - Émigré Economists: The Benefactions of Lenin and Hitler — 185
  - 3.1.2 *1940s, The Cascade* — 191
  - 3.1.3 *Keynesianism: Divergent Receptions* — 192
    - Post-war Affinity in the UK — 193
    - Post-New Deal Hostility in the USA — 193

3.2		Spreading the Word: Messiahs, Messages, Methods	195
	3.2.1	Ideas and Ideologies: Manufacturers and Retailers	195
	3.2.2	USA: Early Ideological Entrepreneurs of Libertarianism	202
		Harold Luhnow: The Volker Fund and its Dollars	202
		Foundation for Economic Education (FEE) and its Facilitators	210
	3.2.3	Europe: Friedrich Hayek and the Mont Pelerin Society	212
		Antecedents	212
		Pilgrims Atop a Mountain, Mont Pelerin, Switzerland, April 1947	218
		Financial Sponsors	219
		The First Meeting of Minds	222
		Sarcastic Schumpeter, Sceptical Solow, Scathing Samuelson	227
	3.2.4	UK: Antony Fisher, Global Venture Capitalist of Think Tanks	229
3.3		Branding the Message: The 'Nobel' Prize	234
	3.3.1	The Stockholm Connection: Ideological Entrepreneurs	235
	3.3.2	Some Early Awards: Setting the Direction	240
		Jan Tinbergen—Ragnar Frisch 1969	240
		Samuelson 1970	241
		Gunnar Myrdal—Friedrich von Hayek 1974	242
		Milton Friedman 1976	246
	3.3.3	Mont Pelerin Society and the 'Nobel'—A Golden Embrace	249
	3.3.4	Cambridge Heterodoxy?	250
	3.3.5	'An Ideological Coup'	251
3.4		Reaching Politics: Weaponising the Message	253
	3.4.1	Santiago de Chile: Pinochet the Pioneer	253
		Chicago and its Cowboys	253
		Thatcher: Romancing Pinochet's Chile	257
	3.4.2	The White House: Reagan, a Disciple	262
	3.4.3	10 Downing Street: Thatcher, a Devotee	264
		More than its Weight in Gold—The Market Price of Symbolic Capital	269
	3.4.4	Pulling Together	269
3.5		Besieging Cambridge: The Chicago–MIT–LSE Trinity	271
	3.5.1	A Cross-Atlantic Triangle	271
	3.5.2	Diversity of Practice	271
	3.5.3	Unity of Purpose	275
References			285

4	Camp Skirmishes Over Interstitial Spaces: Journals, Seminars, Textbooks		295
	4.1 The Battle of Teruel—The Day before		296
	4.2 Journals		297
		4.2.1 EJ Leaves 'Home'—The Loss of a Flagship	297
		4.2.2 CJE Arrives—A Forum of One's Own	305
		4.2.3 Cambridge Economic Policy Review: One Crowded Hour of Glorious Life	319
	4.3 Seminars		322
		4.3.1 Cambridge Economic Club—A Marshallian Precursor: 1884–1890, 1896–?	329
		4.3.2 Political Economy Club: From Keynes to Robertson to Kahn—Dazzling to Dour	330
		4.3.3 The Marshall Society: A Socialisation into Economics and Its Purposes	334
		4.3.4 Piero Sraffa's Research Students Seminar: A Precocious Nursery	339
		4.3.5 In Retrospect, Austin Robinson on the Cambridge Circus: The Engine Room of The General Theory	344
		4.3.6 Cambridge–LSE Joint Seminar: Jousting Juniors	345
		4.3.7 Kahn's 'Secret' Seminar at King's: Fires in the Kitchen	347
		4.3.8 The Richard Stone Common Room: Typhoo and Typhoons	353
		4.3.9 Ajit Singh's Political Economy Seminar at Queens': Young Turks	356
		4.3.10 Arestis and Kitson Political Economy Seminar at St. Catherine's College	360
		4.3.11 Hahn's Churchill Seminar: Only Maths and Neoclassicals, Others Beware	361
		4.3.12 Cambridge Growth Project Seminar at DAE	362
		4.3.13 Hahn's 'Quaker' Risk Seminar: The Rising Tide	363
		4.3.14 Matthews's CLARE Group: The Master's Lodge of Moderate Practitioners	364
		4.3.15 Lawson—Realism and Social Ontology: Ways of Seeing and Framing	367
	4.4 Textbooks		369
		4.4.1 Distant Thunder: Keynes and McCarthy, Tarshis and Samuelson	371
		4.4.2 Lawrence Klein and the Paradox of The Keynesian Revolution	377
		Puzzle	378
		Ph.D.—At Samuelson's Feet	378
		Cowles Commission—The New Dealers	379

		The Keynesian Revolution: *The Extra Chapter—*	
		Klein, Then a Closet Marxist?	380
		Beyond Keynes	385
		UMich and McCarthyism	386
		Policy to Forecasting	391
		Resolution	393
	4.4.3	'Death of a Revolutionary Textbook': Robinson and Eatwell	394
	4.4.4	An 'Applied Economics' Textbook That Wasn't: Joan and Young Friends	399
4.5	The Battle of Teruel—The Day After		403

Appendix 4.1: First off the Blocks: Mabel Timlin's Keynesian
Economics, *1942*   403
References   406

5 The DAE Trilogy   415
  5.1 Origins and Evolution   415
    5.1.1 Origins   415
    5.1.2 Evolution: Substance and Styles   417
    5.1.3 Foundations of Stone   420
    5.1.4 Reddaway's Method: Eclectic Development   423
    5.1.5 Godley: Turbulent Times   426
  5.2 End of the Golden Age: The Decade of Discontent   430
  5.3 The Trilogy: Discrete Episodes or a Serial Campaign?   433
Appendix 5.1: DAE—Finding a Good Home   436
References   437

6 Cambridge Economic Policy Group: Beheading a Turbulent Priest   439
  6.1 Charged Conjuncture   442
    6.1.1 Imbroglios of 1974: Old Versus New Cambridge Versus the Establishment   442
    6.1.2 The Enigma of Kahn   444
    6.1.3 Kaldor: On Radical Policy Implications of New Cambridge, 1976   453
    6.1.4 Cambridge Squabbles: Spillover into Whitehall?   456
    6.1.5 Triggering Crisis: The Pivot of the OPEC Price Hikes   460
    6.1.6 1979: Enter Margaret Thatcher, Right-Wing, Upfront   464
    6.1.7 The Case of the Odd Consensus: The Letter by 364 Economists, 1981   466
    6.1.8 Thatcher in the Garage of the Federal Reserve   470

		6.1.9	1981: Brixton Riots, Toxteth Fires: "A Concentration of Hopelessness"	472
		6.1.10	The CEPG: A Thorn in the Thatcher Hide	474
		6.1.11	The Bogey of Import Controls and the Spectre of Bennism	477
	6.2	SSRC and CEPG: Dispensing Instant Injustice		484
		6.2.1	Posner's Parlour	484
		6.2.2	Posner's Process	489
	6.3	Epilogue		493
		6.3.1	Vengeance	493
		6.3.2	The Team Scattered	494
		6.3.3	The Model Reincarnated	496
		6.3.4	The Rehabilitation of Wynne	500
		6.3.5	Wynne Godley: 'My Credo' ...	502
		6.3.6	The Pacification of the CEPG	505
	Appendix 6.1: Old Cambridge, New Cambridge, 1974: and All the King's Men			509
		1. Letter WG to RFK 23 May 1974. JVR/vii/228/3/3		509
		2. Letter NK to RFK 20 May 1974. JVR/vii/228/3/14-16		509
		3. Letter from RFK and MP to NK 24 May 1974. JVR/vii/228/3/17-20		509
		4. Letter from RFK and MP to NK 28 May 1974. JVR/vii/228/3/24		510
		5. Letter from FC to RFK 29 May 1974. JVR/7/228/3/25		510
		6. Reply from RFK to FC 6 June 1974. JVR/7/228/3/24		510
		7. In the interim, NK replied to RFK and MP. JVR/7/228/3/26		510
		8. Letter from NK to RFK. RFK/12/2/132/3		511
	References			511
7	'Unintended' Collateral Damage? The Cambridge Economic Policy Group and the Joseph-Rothschild-Posner SSRC Enquiry, 1982			517
	7.1	Joseph—Rothschild—Posner—Godley		518
	7.2	The Posner-the-Saviour Narrative		520
	7.3	Setting Up the Enquiry		533
	7.4	Who Proposed Rothschild?		534
	7.5	Rothschild Report Writing Process		537
	7.6	The Judgement of Rothschild		539
	7.7	Between Draft and Release and Response: Handshakes and Cigars		540

	7.8	Did Posner Get Away with Just a Change of Name?	543
	7.9	CEPG—Collateral Damage? Or, Traded Down the River?	548
	7.10	The Rothschild Report: Gleanings on Macroeconomic Modelling	550
	7.11	Lord Kaldor—Off the Record, Off the Cuff, Off the Mark?	551
	7.12	Lord Harris' Vitriol	555
	7.13	Catholicity and Independence	556
	7.14	Rothschild's Last Word	559
	7.15	Joseph's Last Laugh	560
	References		560

8 Cambridge Growth Project: Running the Gauntlet   563

	8.1	Background and Conjuncture	564
		8.1.1 The Decision	566
	8.2	Substantive Issues	569
		8.2.1 No Innovation?	569
		8.2.2 Catholicity, Turnover and the Value of Disaggregation	569
		8.2.3 Use of Input-Output Tables	572
		8.2.4 CGP Presence in Policy Debates	573
		8.2.5 Insularity	574
		8.2.6 On Exploiting the Cheap Labour of Graduate Students	574
	8.3	Issues of Procedural Probity	576
		8.3.1 Shifting Goalposts Across Evaluations	576
		8.3.2 Unequal Application of Criterion of Commercial Funding	577
		8.3.3 Public Good or Private Resource?	577
		8.3.4 ESRC Ignored CGP Model Performance: Why?	579
		8.3.5 Compromised 'Independent' Evidence	580
	8.4	Other Concerns	582
		8.4.1 'Reds'?	582
		8.4.2 Crowding Out Competitors?	582
		8.4.3 Deadweight Loss of Built-up Intellectual Capital	582
		8.4.4 Gratuitously Offensive: Up Close and Out of Order	584
		8.4.5 The Consortium: 'Revived Talk of Conspiracy Theory'	585
		8.4.6 In Defence, a Lone Voice, Overruled	586
	8.5	Epilogue: CGP—Life After Death?	587
	Appendix 8.1: CGP Staff Members, Timeline 1960–1987		594
	Appendix 8.2: Publications of CGP Staff		595
	References		596

9 The DAE Review 1984–1987: A Four-Year Inquisition — 597
- 9.1 *The Campaign of Attrition* — 598
  - 9.1.1 *Occluded Origins* — 599
  - 9.1.2 *Two Stages, Two Committees* — 604
- 9.2 *The Orthodox Gambit* — 607
  - 9.2.1 *The Agenda Revealed* — 608
  - 9.2.2 *The Game Plan: Four Options* — 617
    - Closure — 617
    - Separation — 618
    - Absorption — 620
    - Capture — 623
  - 9.2.3 *External Critiques: Collusion as Consultation?* — 625
- 9.3 *The Heterodox Defence* — 631
  - 9.3.1 *Solidarity, Testimonies, Rebuttals* — 633
  - 9.3.2 *Chinks in the DAE Armour?* — 643
- 9.4 *On the Rack: Bleeding the DAE* — 648
  - 9.4.1 *The Secretary General,* The Prince *and the Chess Master* — 654
  - 9.4.2 *The Capture* — 657
  - 9.4.3 *How it Transpired, Perhaps Not Just by Chance* — 660
  - 9.4.4 *Checkmate: A Constitutional Coup* — 670
- 9.5 *Epilogue* — 675
- *Appendix 9.1: DAE Review Committees: Composition and Terms of Reference* — 680
  - *First Advisory Committee. Constituted: Easter Term 1984; Reported: May 1985* — 680
  - *Second Advisory Committee: Constituted: Easter Term 1985; Reported April 1987* — 680
- *Appendix 9.2: Labour Studies Group: Dispersed, Not Defeated* — 681
- *References* — 687

LIST OF TABLES

Table 2.1	Faculty of Economics and Politics—professorships, 1828–2000	80
Table 2.2	Early retirements in the Faculty of Economics, 1981–1985	114
Table 2.3	The CLARE Group of like-minded economists, 1977–2003	147
Table 2.4	Career tracks and the glittering prizes	156
Table 2.5	Cambridge-Oxford-LSE—Musical chairs	160
Table 2.6	Management positions in the Faculty of Economics and DAE	164
Table 2.7	Past Editors of *The Economc Journal*	165
Table 2.8	Past Presidents of Royal Economic Society	166
Table 3.1	Some honours awarded in the tenure of Margaret Thatcher, 1979–1990	266
Table 4.1	Cambridge economics seminars, 1890s–	323
Table 7.1	Timelines of actions and decisions leading up to the closure of the Cambridge Economic Policy Group, DAE Cambridge	521
Table 9.1	Research staff who have left the DAE since July 1984 or who will be leaving by the end of 1986–1987 academic year	651
Table 10.1	Three Decades of Empirical Sociology at the DAE	693
Table 11.1	A century of development teaching—A Cambridge timeline	780
Table 12.1	Economic historians at the Faculty of Economics and Politics, 1924–2021	853
Table 13.1	Presidents and council members of the Royal Economic Society, 1975–2019	980
Table 13.2	RAE panels 1989, 1992, 1996	985
Table 13.3	Journal publications of members of RAE Economics Panels 1989–1996	986
Table 13.4	References in publications of members of Economics Panels, 1989, 1992, 1996	987
Table 13.5	Standing of Cambridge economics in successive RAEs and REFs	990
Table 13.6	Elimination of heterodox economists and economics from 'economics': RAEs 1992, 2001, 2008	1005
Table 14.1	QS global ranks of selected Cambridge units, 2013–2019	1035

CHAPTER 10

Sociology: The Departure of 'Stray Colleagues in a Vaguely Cognate Discipline'

Abstract This chapter comes with a health warning: it tells a story of the evolution of sociology in Cambridge, as pieced together by an economist, the act of presumption partially justified by the fact that Cambridge sociology was fostered since its birth, well or poorly, in the twin Faculty and DAE homes of Cambridge economics where it resided till well into adulthood, when the hostility of the orthodox economists' campaign against the heterodox groups intensified the attraction, and opened up a realistic prospect, for 'leaving home' and seeking an independent existence in the institutional melee of the social sciences in Cambridge, hoping at the end to establish a department of its own. The turning point was the university review of the DAE of 1984–1987 in which the Hahn-Matthews camp lobbied vehemently for sociology and sociologists to be shown the door, and so it transpired, despite the almost universal and strongly expressed support for sociology and sociologists by their economist colleagues of various heterodox persuasions, both from within the DAE and the Faculty. This departure further strengthened the numerical hold of the orthodox Hahn-Matthews group over decision making in the Faculty of Economics, the prime, if covert motivation for its ostensibly academic 'purification' campaign. This episode is explored, using archival materials, within a wider discussion of the evolution to maturity of sociology as a taught discipline in the face of hostile academic and institutional environments in the UK, dominated by vocal economists and scientists. The heterodox economists of Cambridge, in the DAE and in the Faculty, with their realization of the worth

---

The phrase alludes to the term used by David Newbery is his comments to the General Board in the course of the DAE Review; for the context in which the term is originally used, see Chap. 9, p. 13.

of multidisciplinary research, stand out as exceptions in this regard. The narrative here offers some novel insights into the period of the life of Cambridge sociology spent in the home of Cambridge economics.

10.1 Early Years: Hostility, Neglect, Subordination

In 2015, the Cambridge Faculty of Archaeology and Anthropology celebrated its centenary. Writing at the time about the evolution of social anthropology in Cambridge, Alan Macfarlane remarks that "the Department [of Social Anthropology] has had long and complex relations with its two sister departments in the faculty, Archaeology and Biological Anthropology (known until the 1980s as 'Physical anthropology'). The three departments had been undivided in one faculty until the later 1960s and I have heard that this led to a good deal of tension". Presumably, physical and social anthropology hadn't really worked out the yin and yang of their co-habiting relationship; there seemed to be little chemistry in it: one lot was more interested in digging up and measuring bones of the dead, the other more in observing goings-on of the living. "When they separated, the situation eased. …. Other issues continued to create tension for another 20 years, but as they grew further apart and demarcations became established, this has declined" (Macfarlane, 2015, pp. 23–24). Seemingly, distance did make the heart grow fonder.

In comparison, sociology in Britain is a relatively young discipline. But while its history is much shorter, its life has been perhaps even more turbulent and tempestuous. The first department of sociology, at the London School of Economics, was formed in 1904, and remained for long the singular exception. In contrast, in Cambridge, though funding had been obtained for a Professorship in Sociology in 1944, the chair remained unfilled till 1969; and even then, it was a chair without a department or a Tripos to go with it: the Professorship of Sociology was located in the Faculty of Economics and Politics, and "sociology was only taught in combination with other subjects, first as part of the economics Tripos in 1961, and then, from 1969, within the Part II course in Social and Political Studies" (Halsey, 2004, pp. 101–102).

Table 10.1 Three Decades of Empirical Sociology[a] at the DAE

Year	Projects	Researchers
1957	Economic Circumstances of Old People	J.E.G. Utting; D.E. Cole; S. Meadows.
1958–1964	Economic Circumstances of Old People; Survey of Graduate Employment; Adaptation of Engineering Graduates to Industry; White-collar redundancy; Effects of Redundancy in Railway Workshops Attitudes to Work in relation to Production Systems and Community Structure: The New Working Class[b]; The Causes of Small Strikes; Demarcation Rules and related projects; Conditions of Employment of Manual and non-Manual Workers; Political Socialisation[c]	Dorothy Cole Wedderburn; J.E.G. Utting; J.C.Craig; F. Bechhofer; Peter Jenner; J.H. Goldthorpe; D. Lockwood; H.A. Turner; Garfield Clack; John Bescoby; G. Roberts; Philip Abrams.
1965–1966	Adaptation of Engineering Graduates to Industry; White-collar redundancy; Attitudes to Work in relation to Production Systems and Community Structure: The New Working Class; The Causes of Small Strikes; Demarcation Rules and related projects; Conditions of Employment of Manual and non-Manual Workers; Political Socialisation; Labour Relations in Mining; Job Evaluation; Social Mobility and Patterns of Anxiety[d]; British Elections[e]	Dorothy Cole Wedderburn; J.E.G. Utting; J.C.Craig; F. Bechhofer; Peter Jenner; J.H. Goldthorpe; D. Lockwood; H.A. Turner; Garfield Clack; John Bescoby; G. Roberts; Philip Abrams; L.J. Handy; R. Crompton; Jennifer Platt; E.I. Hopper; K.H. Boehm; B.R. Mitchell; F.G. Pyatt
1966–1967	Attitudes to Work in relation to Production Systems and Community Structure: The New Working Class; The Causes of Small Strikes; Demarcation Rules and related projects; Conditions of Employment of Manual and non-Manual Workers; Political Socialisation; Labour Relations in Mining; Job Evaluation; Relationship between Technology and Attitudes to Employment; The Affluent Worker: Political Attitudes and Behaviour; Comparative Study of Factory Organisations	Dorothy Cole Wedderburn; J.E.G. Utting; J.C.Craig; F. Bechhofer; Peter Jenner; J.H. Goldthorpe; D. Lockwood; H.A. Turner; Garfield Clack; John Bescoby; G. Roberts; Philip Abrams; L.J. Handy; R. Crompton; Jennifer Platt; Michael Fores; J.M. Mann; R.M. Blackburn
1967–1968	Attitudes to Work in relation to Production Systems and Community Structure: The New Working Class; The Causes of Small Strikes; Demarcation Rules and related projects; Conditions of Employment of Manual and non-Manual Workers; Political Socialisation; Labour Relations in Mining; Job Evaluation; Relationship between Technology and Attitudes to Employment; The Affluent Worker: Political Attitudes and Behaviour; Comparative Study of Factory Organisations; Variations in Trade Union Organisation Among White-Collar Workers; Management Organisation and Industrial Relations	Dorothy Cole Wedderburn; J.E.G. Utting; J.C.Craig; F. Bechhofer; Peter Jenner; J.H. Goldthorpe; D. Lockwood; H.A. Turner; Garfield Clack; John Bescoby; G. Roberts; Philip Abrams; L.J. Handy; R. Crompton; Jennifer Platt; Michael Fores; J.M. Mann; R.M. Blackburn; K. Prandy; A. Stewart

(continued)

Table 10.1 (continued)

Year	Projects	Researchers
1968–1969	Conditions of Employment of Manual and non-Manual Workers; Labour Relations in Mining; Job Evaluation; Management Organisation and Industrial Relations; Variations in Trade Union Organisation among White-collar Worker; Social and Industrial Determinants of Workers' Attitudes	Dorothy Cole Wedderburn; J.C.Craig; H.A. Turner; Garfield Clack; G. Roberts; L.J. Handy; J.M. Mann; R.M. Blackburn; K. Prandy, A. Stewart; D.J. Roberts
1969–1970	Conditions of Employment of Manual and non-Manual Workers; Labour Relations in Mining; Job Evaluation; Management Organisation and Industrial Relations; Variations in Trade Union Organisation among White-collar Workers; Social and Industrial Determinants of Workers' Attitudes; Cost-Benefit Returns of manpower Recruitment System in the Steel Industry; Economic and Social Effects of Migration to and from Great Britain; Social Status in Great Britain	Dorothy Cole Wedderburn; J.C. Craig; H.A. Turner; Garfield Clack; G. Roberts; L.J. Handy; J.M. Mann; R.M. Blackburn; K. Prandy, A. Stewart; D.J. Roberts; F. Wilkinson; B. M. Deakin
1970–1971	Labour Relations in Mining; Job Evaluation; Management Organisation and Industrial Relations; Social and Industrial Determinants of Workers' Attitudes; Cost-Benefit Returns of manpower Recruitment System in the Steel Industry; Economic and Social Effects of Migration to and from Great Britain; Social Status in Great Britain; Labour Problems in Underdeveloped Countries; Wage Determination and Wage Drift in the Construction Industry; Price and Incomes Policy; Life-time Earning Patterns	H.A. Turner; D.J. Roberts; D.A.S. Jackson; L.J. Handy; S.F. Wilkinson; A.H.M. Fells; J.C. Craig; R.M. Blackburn; K. Prandy; A. Stewart; J.A. Banks; K. Dixon; M. Green; J.M. Mann.
1971–1972	Management Organisation and Industrial Relations; Social Status in Great Britain*; Labour Problems in Underdeveloped Countries; Wage Determination and Wage Drift in the Construction Industry; Price and Incomes Policy; Lifetime Earning Patterns; Variations in Trade Union Patterns among White Collar Workers*; Social and Industrial Determinants of Workers' Attitudes*; Elites in the British Class Structure*[f]	H.A. Turner; D.J. Roberts; L.J. Handy; S.F. Wilkinson; D.A.S. Jackson; J.C. Craig; Aubrey Jones; R.M. Blackburn; K. Prandy; A. Stewart; J.M. Mann; J.A. Banks; K. Dixon; M. Green; D. Donald; Anthony Giddens; Geoffrey Ingham; Philip Stanworth; Lucy Slater.

(continued)

Table 10.1 (continued)

Year	Projects	Researchers
1972–1973	Management Organisation and Industrial Relations; Social Status in Great Britain;[g] Labour Problems in Underdeveloped Countries; Wage Determination and Wage Drift in the Construction Industry; Price and Incomes Policy; Life-time Earning Patterns; Variations in Trade Union Patterns among White Collar Workers; Social and Industrial Determinants of Workers' Attitudes; Elites in the British Class Structure; Labour Restrictive Practices; National Job Evaluation; Human Prospects of the Tropical Mining Areas; Deprivation, Work Experience, and the Legitimation of Authority	H.A. Turner; D.J. Roberts; L.J. Handy; Patricia Fosh; S.F. Wilkinson; D.A.S. Jackson; J.C. Craig; Aubrey Jones; R.M. Blackburn; K. Prandy; A. Stewart; J.M. Mann; J.A. Banks; K. Dixon; M. Green; D. Donald; Anthony Giddens; Geoffrey Ingham; Philip Stanworth; Lucy Slater; D. Webb; J. Scott; G. Rendle; P.H. Stanworth.
1973–1974	Some Economic and Social Implications of Immigration to Britain; Differentiation and Structural Change in Peasant Agriculture in Kenya; Management Organisation and Industrial Relations; Wages in the Coal Mining Industry; Labour Problems in Developing Countries; Incomes Policies; Unfair Dismissal; Labour Restrictive Practices; National Job Evaluation; Conditions of Manual and Non-Manual Workers; Human Prospects of Tropical Mining Areas; Development, Income Distribution and Social change in Egypt 1952–1970; Variations in Trade Union Organisation Among White-Collar Workers; Deprivation, Work Experience, and the Legitimation of Authority; Social and Industrial Determinants of Workers' Attitudes; Social Status in Great Britain; Elites in British Class Structure.	B.M. Deakin; K. Prandy; A.N.E. Jolley; D.M.G. Newbery; M. Cowen; H.A. Turner; D.J. Roberts; L.J. Handy; K.J. Coutts; D.A.S. Jackson; P. Fosh; G. Macpherson; T.S. Papola; G. Roberts; J.C. Craig; M. Fores; D. Wedderburn; P. Daniel; M. Abdel-Fadil; C.H. Feinstein; R.M. Blackburn; A. Stewart; J.M. Mann; D. Webb; K. Dixon; D. Donald; M. Green; J. Scott; A. Giddens; P.H. Stanworth; M. Hughes.
1974–1975	Some Economic and Social Implications of Immigration to Britain; Development, Income Distribution and Social Change in Egypt, 1952–70; Differentiation and Structural Change in Peasant Agriculture in Kenya; Labour Problems in Development Countries; Incomes Policies; Unfair Dismissal; National Job Evaluation; Human Prospects of Tropical Mining Areas; Deprivation, Work Experience and Legitimation of Authority; social and Industrial Determinants of Workers' Attitudes; Social Inequality	B.M. Deakin; K. Prandy; A.N.E. Jolley; D.M.G. Newbery; M. Cowen; M. Abdel-Fadil; C.H. Feinstein; H.A. Turner; D.A.S. Jackson; G. Macpherson; J.C. Craig; P. Daniel; K. Prandy; R.M. Blackburn; J.M. Mann; A. Stewart.

(*continued*)

Table 10.1 (continued)

Year	Projects	Researchers
1975–1976	Some Economic and Social Implications of Immigration to Britain; Human Prospects of Tropical Mining Areas; Social and Industrial Determinants of Worker' Attitudes; Variations in Trade Union Organisation among White-Collar Workers; Social Inequality; Career Structures; Childhood Skin Diseases	B.M. Deakin; K. Prandy; P. Daniel; H.A. Turner; R.M. Blackburn; J.M. Mann; A. Stewart; I. Birnbaum;
1976–1977	Labour Markets in Declining Inner-City Areas[h]; The Effect of the Abolition of Wages Councils; The Economics of Institutionalised Wage Determination; Social and Industrial Determinants of Workers' Attitudes; Variations in Trade Union Organisation Among White-Collar Workers; Social Inequality; Career Structures; Childhood Skin Diseases	B. Moore; J. Rhodes; F. Wilkinson; R. Tarling; J.C. Craig; J. Rubery; R.M. Blackburn; J.M. Mann; K. Prandy; A. Stewart; R.G. Jobling
1977–1978	Labour Markets in Declining Inner-City Areas; The Effect of the Abolition of Wages Councils; The Economics of Institutionalised Wage Determination; Social and Industrial Determinants of Workers' Attitudes; Variations in Trade Union Organisation Among White-Collar Workers; Social Inequality; Career Structures; Reproduction of Social Inequality[i]; Childhood Skin Diseases	B. Moore; J. Rhodes; F. Wilkinson; R. Tarling; J.C. Craig; J. Rubery; R.M. Blackburn; J.M. Mann; K. Prandy; A. Stewart; R.G. Jobling
1978–1979	Labour Markets in Declining Inner-City Areas; The Effect of the Abolition of Wages Councils; The Economics of Institutionalised Wage Determination; Social and Industrial Determinants of Workers' Attitudes; Variations in Trade Union Organisation Among White-Collar Workers; Reproduction of Social Inequality; Childhood Skin Diseases	B. Moore; J. Rhodes; F. Wilkinson; R. Tarling; J.C. Craig; J. Rubery; R.M. Blackburn; J.M. Mann; K. Prandy; A. Stewart; R.G. Jobling; D. Donald; R. Volpato; J. Holmwood; M.A. Hutton.
1979–1980	The Effects of the Abolition of Wages Councils; Home-working in ex-Wage Council Industries; The Determinants of Informal Payment Structures[j]; Labour Markets in Declining Inner-City Areas; Social and Industrial Determinants of Workers' Attitudes; Reproduction of Social Inequality; Childhood Skin Diseases	J.C. Craig, J. Rubery, R. Tarling, F. Wilkinson; B. Moore; J. Rhodes; R.M. Blackburn; J.M. Mann; K. Prandy; A. Stewart; R. Volpato; R. Jobling
1980–1981	The Effects of the Abolition of Wages Councils; The Determinants of Informal Payment Structures; Labour Markets in Declining Inner-City Areas; Economic Development and Social Differentiation in the Andean Peasant Economy; Reproduction of Social Inequality	J.C. Craig; J. Rubery; E. Garnsey; R. Tarling; F. Wilkinson; B. Moore; J. Rhodes; R.M. Blackburn; J.M. Mann; K. Prandy; A. Stewart; L. Miller-Bernal; D. Lehmann; M. Murmis

(continued)

Table 10.1 (continued)

Year	Projects	Researchers
1981–1982	The Determinants of Informal Payment Structures; Labour Markets in Declining Inner-City Areas; Economic Development and Social Differentiation in the Andean Peasant Economy; Reproduction of Social Inequality; Inequality in China	J.C. Craig; J. Rubery; E. Garnsey; R. Tarling; F. Wilkinson; B. Moore; J. Rhodes; R.M. Blackburn; J.M. Mann; K. Prandy; A. Stewart; L. Miller-Bernal; D. Lehmann; M. Murmis; P. Nolan; D.G. White
1982–1983	The Determinants of Informal Payment Structures; Inequality in China; Reproduction of Social Inequality; Understanding and Evaluation of Income Differentials in the Context of Social Stratification; the Importance of Social Stratification	J.C. Craig; J. Rubery; E. Garnsey; R. Tarling; F. Wilkinson; R.M. Blackburn; J.M. Mann; K. Prandy; L. Miller-Bernal; P. Nolan; D.G. White;
1983–1984	Agricultural Reform in China; Reproduction of Social Inequality; the Importance of Social Stratification	P. Nolan; R.M. Blackburn; K. Prandy; A. Stewart; L. Miller-Bernal
1984–1985	Social Change and Economic Life: The Northampton Labour Market[k]; Reproduction of Social Inequality; The Importance of Social Stratification; Social Identity and the Understanding of Economic Change in a Geographical Context	F. Wilkinson; R. Tarling; J. Rubery; B. Burchell; R. Jobling; C. Fraser; C. Marsh; R.M. Blackburn, K. Prandy; A. Stewart; L. Miller-Bernal; D. Lovatt
1985–1986	Social Change and Economic Life: The Northampton Labour Market; Reproduction of Social Inequality; The Importance of Social Stratification; Social Identity and the Understanding of Economic Change in a Geographical Context; An Occupational Classification and Coding Scheme for Social Research; Social Change and Economic Life	F. Wilkinson; R. Tarling; J. Rubery; B. Burchell; R. Jobling; C. Fraser; C. Marsh; R.M. Blackburn, K. Prandy; A. Stewart; L. Miller-Bernal; D. Lovatt; R. Volpato; G. Lowe
1986–1987	Social Change and Economic Life: The Northampton Labour Market; Reproduction of Social Inequality; The Importance of Social Stratification; An Occupational Classification and Coding Scheme for Social Research	F. Wilkinson; R. Tarling; J. Rubery; B. Burchell; R. Jobling; C. Fraser; C. Marsh; R.M. Blackburn, K. Prandy; A. Stewart; L. Miller-Bernal

[a]This table is assembled from information contained in the Annual Reports of the Department of Applied Economics. The projects listed include those of the "sociology group", but also several of the "labour studies group" when these are judged to have a significant social, or sociological, slant in objectives and methodology. For the earlier period, the latter was referred to as the "industrial relations and labour" group. Apart from these categories, there were also research projects in the "economic history" rubric, but these dwindled and disappeared, as the main researchers, for instance Charles Feinstein, left Cambridge, or others, such as Phyllis Deane, retired; and there was no fresh recruitment in the Faculty in these areas. Further, there was significant research done in the field of development, though this was not formally organized in the form of, and listed under, DAE projects, and therefore was not visible in the Annual Reports, except indirectly sometimes in the lists of academic visitors, and of course in the list of publications, mostly in Occasional Paper series of the DAE. A list of (a dozen) such publications on development-related themes is provided in Chap.; such publications emerged from projects undertaken variously by visiting scholars, or DAE staff, or members of Faculty

Table 10.1 (continued)

[b]"The main aim of the project is to test the proposition that the 'affluent' manual worker in Britain is becoming 'middle-class'" (DAE Report 1958–1964, p. 21). The main researchers involved were Goldthorpe and Lockwood; the team included Bechhofer and Platt

[c]"A Study of the political attitudes of young people in the fifteen to thirty age group", conducted by Philip Abrams. (DAE Report 1958–1964, p. 22)

[d]"This project is concerned with the problem of specifying some of the structural conditions in which upward social mobility is likely to be associated with various patterns of anxiety, especially with feelings of relative deprivations" (DAE Report 1965–1966, p. 14)

[e]"This project was conceived ... with the aim of collecting data on post-war electoral history and analyzing it in more sophisticated terms than the usual 'swing' concept" (DAE Report 1965–1966, p. 14); the researchers involved were Boehm, Mitchell and Pyatt

[f]The asterisked multi-year projects together constitute a significant and innovative intervention in the empirical sociological analysis of dimension of the evolving British class structure, using extensive data collection and biographical information processed through computer analysis using specially devised programmes

[g]The scale of the research projects in empirical sociology is impressive. In the research project on "Social Status in Great Britain" involving Blackburn and Stewart at the DAE examined "the stability of structural inequality" making use of scales of social stratification devised in the research; "a programme of 200 interviews as a pilot to the main study was completed in early summer 1973. The data have been extensively analysed and an internal working paper with approximately 175 tables and graphs is to be circulated. The main body of 6000 interviews in four centres York, Glasgow, Leicester and Cambridge, is now under way". And in the project studying "Elites in the British Class Structure", directed by Tony Giddens, the focus was on "the computation of data on those who have held elite positions in Britain between 1900 and 1970" (DAE Annual Report 1972–1973, p. 12)

[h]"The aim of the research is to find out quantitatively what has been happening to population and employment in all the major inner-city areas of the UK, to assess the speed at which economic decline has taken place, to disentangle so far as possible the causes of this decline, whether arising from government policies, local authority policies or market forces, and to discuss the kinds of policy change which may be helpful in alleviating the problem. One feature of the methodology is the setting up of 'control groups', such as outer city areas, smaller free-standing cities and new towns, so that relative changes taking place in each inner-city area can be properly assessed" (DAE Annual Report, 1975–1976, p. 12)

[i]This project commenced in May 1978, and "is concerned with the general area of social inequality and social change, seeking to move towards a more dynamic model of social stratification which takes account of processes of reproduction of societies" (DAE Annual Report 1977–1978, p. 23)

[j]"The aim is to explore the relationship between workforce characteristics, the structural constraints within which firms operate, and the development of payment structures. The emphasis is on the employment of women in small firms which tend not to have formalized payment systems" (DAE, Annual Report, 1979–1980, p. 12)

[k]In March 1985 a Cambridge team was selected to participate in the ESRC's interdisciplinary Social Change and Economic Life initiative which involved the study of six local labour market areas in England and Scotland, each under the responsibility of a separate team, with the Cambridge team researching Northampton. The aim of the initiative is to study social change and economic life in the Northampton labour market from an interdisciplinary perspective and through a range of different methods: from the perspective of employers, individuals and households, involving research by economists, sociologists, social psychologists and statisticians; and the research would have both an historical and a contemporary dimension, apart from cross-regional comparative analysis. The project involved several rounds of heavy data generation on the basis of a range of surveys. The team assembled at DAE included Frank Wilkinson, Roger Tarling, Jill Rubery, Ray Jobling, Colin Fraser, Cathie Marsh, Robert Blackburn, Ken Prandy and Brendan Burchell; in addition, their research publications included contributions from Joan Robinson, Jane Humphries and John Devereux and Sara Horrell—the last two being research students linked to the project

Not surprisingly, then, the story of the advent of sociology in Cambridge usually begins with the established disciplines of economics, anthropology and history being roundly castigated for their obstructive attitude in preventing a formal acknowledgement of sociology as a sufficiently mature academic field, and hence an endowment with space in the curricula or a position in the professoriate. Such annoyance is evident in the accounts of Noel Annan, who argued the case for sociology with little success in the early decades, Halsey, Barnes and Runciman.

Defending sociology under attack from right-wing peers in the House of Lords, Lord Annan argued that "there was a good deal of crude academic politics in this. No post in sociology was established at Cambridge until the 1960s, and even later at Oxford. At the London School of Economics and Bedford departments of sociology flourished, but they were small in terms of the numbers of students who came through the departments. That was the reason why, when in the 'sixties there was an overpowering desire at last to expand this subject and to recognise that it was a subject of importance, as had been recognised for years in France and Germany—and in all major American universities—no cadres of young academics existed to fill the new posts" (Annan, in House of Lords, (1983)).

Two decades later, W.G. Runciman,[1] the Cambridge sociologist, amplified Annan's remarks.

> At Cambridge, it was widely believed that Talcott Parsons had been invited for a year as a deliberate tactic to forestall the recognition of sociology for which Noel Annan, in particular, had been campaigning. Whether or not that is true, Parsons did the cause of sociology in Cambridge no good, and the well-entrenched dominance of economics and anthropology virtually guaranteed that if it was admitted at all, it would be as an adjunct to one or other of them. ... Sociology was finally admitted under the wing of the economists and David Lockwood and Michael Young appointed as lecturers. But the university still declined to create a chair, and by the time, in due course, that it would have been handed to Lockwood on a plate he had, understandably, no inclination to leave the University of Essex.[2] It

---

[1] In this 1982 debate, Annan puts in a jestful word for Runciman at Cambridge: "But let no one doubt that there are excellent men and women in this subject. If I may cite one who is the son of a Member of your Lordships' House, there is Mr. Runciman, who combines being the managing director of his family shipping business and writing illuminating books on sociology as a Title B Fellow of Trinity which, as a Cambridge man whose affection for Oxford is unassailable, I would describe as being at least equal in distinction to that of a Fellow of All Souls."

[2] Michael Young, later Lord Young of Dartmouth, and the first Chairman of the newly created Social Science Research Council in 1965, was at Cambridge, as a fellow of Churchill College and lecturer in sociology; the younger David Lockwood was in Cambridge during 1958–1968 also as lecturer, and left for a professorship at the University of Essex in 1968 after being passed over for the new chair in sociology which went to John Barnes. Lockwood was part of group of highly distinguished graduate students at LSE, including Ralf Dahrendorf, and Halsey regarded him as the most impressive of the group (Rose, 2014). Lockwood later played a significant role in the life of Cambridge sociology: when the General Board of the University conducted a questionably motivated Review of the Department of Applied Economics, he was included as the expert external sociologist to advise especially on the particular item in the terms of reference which asked whether sociology should remain in the DAE or leave to Social and Political Science; this was a game-changing point for sociology; the Review Committee, presumably led on this point by Lockwood, advised an exit.

was symptomatic, too, that Cambridge's first Professor Sociology was an anthropologist. Not that John Barnes's achievements or qualifications were in doubt—far from it. But his appointment sent an ambiguous message about the university's attitude to sociology to the wider world. And to this day [2004], sociology in Cambridge remains yoked in an uncomfortable multi-disciplinary troika in a way that no other university I can think of would contemplate. (Runciman, quoted in Halsey, 2004, p. 220)

Then, in 1963, came the momentous Robbins Report on Higher Education (Robbins, 1963), and, on its heels, Crosland's binary higher education policy, which changed the shape of British tertiary education almost instantaneously through its recommendations for a rapid increase in university places through both expansion and restructuring. The impact on sociology, as on other social sciences especially economics, was dramatic: the number of sociology departments increased fivefold from 7 in 1961 (when Lionel Robbins took up the assignment) to 35 by 1974,[3] and the number of academic staff in sociology departments rose from 40 in 1960 to 613 by 1975 (Grimley, 2019). Sociology had arrived as a pursuit in university academic life both as a degree option for students and a career track for would-be academics, and the case of the Cambridge sociologist, Geoffrey Hawthorn provides an apposite exemplar.[4] However, Downes (1992, p. xiii) adds a sobering note in pointing out that "In the process, false, as great, expectations were generated about what might flow from such expansion". And sure enough, sociology soon came under sustained criticism from academics in other social science disciplines, especially economics, on grounds of substance and quality, and from the political right for its inherent tendency to ask awkward questions.

Noel Annan, who had campaigned from the start for the institution of a Chair of Sociology in Cambridge, put up a robust rebuttal of charges against the discipline in the House of Lords debate in 1982 on the Rothschild Report on the SSRC, where sociology came under a withering assault.[5] Adopting attack as the best form of defence, he laid the blame at the feet of Oxbridge academics. "On sociology, I would say this. There are undoubtedly a number

---

[3] Downes provides a differing profile of growth: "the general expansion of higher education following the Robbins Report of 1964 (sic) and the announcement of Crosland's binary policy in 1965 fueled a heady rate of growth of sociology departments: from one only in the immediate post-war period—at the LSE—to 50 or more by 1970" (Downes, 1992, p. xiii). Possibly, Grimley's numbers refer to university departments, while Downes's figures might include polytechnics.

[4] "I had wanted to go to the LSE as I had heard about the social sciences in a vague way and read some prospectuses"; he eventually got there ... "started doing a PhD; I had a sociology plan because the new universities had been announced and they were going to set their face against the traditional subjects; they were to start in 1964–65 and I thought that if I did graduate work I could then teach as I wanted to be an academic". "After three weeks, Alan Little [his supervisor] suggested I applied for a job in sociology at the new Essex University; I applied for an assistant lectureship and got it, and went to teach at Essex at twenty-three with no qualifications whatsoever for the job" (Hawthorn, 2009). There is one answer to Lord Rothschild's open query whether the expansion of the universities in the 1960s outpaced the production of qualified sociologists!

[5] Lord Annan: Debate on SSRC Rothschild Report, House of Lords, 30 May 1982; Hansard 432.

of weak departments of sociology and of social studies in British universities today, and the report says so. Why is this? It is not the fault of the subject: it is the fault of dons of Oxford and Cambridge, and to some extent of London; in the 40 years between 1920 and 1960, the bitter enmity by historians and economists to a subject which already had major figures at the turn of the century in Weber and Durkheim, had a disastrous effect".

Indeed, there was hostility expressed from the outset by Cambridge economists against any prospect of the acknowledgement, let alone the establishment, of sociology as a 'proper' discipline in Cambridge, and this is evident in the attitude of Henry Sidgwick as much as Alfred Marshall.

Martin Bulmer (1985, p. 23) writes: "Victorian Cambridge had been guided in its attitude to sociology by Henry Sidgwick. In 1885, he told the British Association that sociology was 'in a very rudimentary condition' and that the task of establishing a genuinely scientific evolutionary sociology must take place at some other university". Thirty years later, Alfred Marshall, in his *Principles* says that "the present movement towards Sociology in America, England and other countries recognizes the need for the intensive study of economics and other branches of social science. But perhaps the use of the term Sociology is premature. For it seems to claim that a unification of social sciences is already in sight: and though some excellent intensive studies have been published under the name of Sociology, it is doubtful whether those efforts at unification which have been made so far have achieved any great success beyond that of preparing the way and erecting danger posts at its pitfalls for the guidance of later generations" (Marshall, 1916, 771n1, quoted by Arena, 2006). This kind of negativity prompted John Barnes, appointed the first Professor of Sociology in Cambridge in 1969, to open his Inaugural Lecture in 1970 with a response to Sidgwick, even if 85 years later: "somewhat unfairly I took the Cambridge philosopher and reformer Henry Sidgwick as my anti-hero", mainly to emphasise how much time had elapsed before sociology was admitted as a valid subject in Cambridge. Barnes, incidentally, "tried to emphasise that sociology is inherently an iconoclastic social science, and that its students must be expected to be iconoclasts" (Barnes, 1970, 2011, p. 45), an assessment perhaps born of, and immediately proven by the student protest movements from the late 1960s in which sociology students were most often in leading roles; such an assessment would no doubt have reinforced the opposition from academic truth seekers such as Sidgwick and Marshall, though not from the Faculty radical economists who were Barnes's contemporaries and were in full support, along with the Faculty Board, of the students in the famous Sit-in at The Old Schools in February 1972.[6]

---

[6] John Barnes was one of the few staff members who sat through the student meetings in Lady Mitchell Hall that immediately preceded the Sit-in, and later gave evidence in support of the position of the Faculty Board—which in turn was supportive of the students' demands for curriculum and exam reforms—to Lord Devlin who conducted the subsequent formal enquiry into the episode. For an account of this, including the roles of Faculty radicals such as Ajit Singh and Bob Rowthorn, and strong support also from Robert Neild, see Saith (2019, pp. 70–77).

Marshall's objections to sociology seem to have been strongly perceived. In a letter to Ludwig Brentano in August 1903, Marshall writes:

> I declined to join the English Sociological Association, partly because I thought the people who were getting it up were not quite the right men for doing it if it had to be done; and partly because I have never ceased to be ashamed of being a member of the so-called 'Institut International de Sociologie'. Its publications seem to me to have no adequate *raison d'etre*. Sociology is a magnificent aspiration: but the greater part of sociologists seem to me to divide their time impartially between prehistoric institutions, without much knowledge of early history; and the last new fashion in philanthropy without a knowledge of economics. Perhaps the gas may be squeezed out of it in the coming time, but I am too old to meddle with it".[7]

Marshall had also written to John Neville Keynes about Rene Worms, the founder of the Institut, having "seduced me with sweet phrases; and he has never done me any harm. But he has not yet made it clear to me why the Institut exists".[8]

In another letter, to *The Daily Chronicle* in 1904 in generous appreciation of Herbert Spencer, Marshall observes: "his attempt to lay down the outlines of a unified sociology was, in my opinion, premature by at least 100 years".[9] And, as cited above, his views are no different ten years later in the *Principles*. On the other side, Patrik Aspers (2006) makes Marshall's ideas more conciliatory and argues that "Marshall's approach[10] encourages a closer connection between sociologists interested in economic phenomena and economists", and points to a "resemblance of Marshall's analysis to those offered by Max Weber and Thorstein Veblen".

Perhaps a couple of points of mitigation could be cited that to an extent soften these perceptions of Marshall's antagonism towards sociology as a legitimate academic discipline. The first arises from his statement that "the use of the term Sociology is premature. For it seems to claim that a *unification of social sciences* is already in sight" (emphasis added); this could suggest that he might have been targeting the grander claim equating "sociology" with an integrated holistic social science, rather than to sociology as a rising separate discipline within the general domain of social sciences. Marshall, while not at all being enamoured of Walrasian abstractions and the general equilibrium template, nevertheless believed in such a separation of the disciplines, each with its own core concerns and methods, economics for instance having to be concerned with

---

[7] Alfred Marshall to Ludwig Joseph Brentano, 18 August 1903, Letter 768 (Whitaker, 1996, p. 53).

[8] Whitaker (1996, p. 54, Editor's fn 5).

[9] November 1904, Letter 811 (Whitaker, 1996, p. 97).

[10] Aspers (2006) cites three of Marshall's concerns: "how preferences are generated, the theory of action, and finally the introduction of a fourth factor of production, organization".

everything, in daily life, that came under the measure of money. But he equally saw the profound significance of organisations, institutions and other behavioural norms in setting the framework within which 'economic' questions could/ should be analysed. So to a considerable extent, the Marshallian approach was accommodative of interdisciplinarity, though based on the interaction between separately defined and developed disciplines and therefore some of his strictures against "sociology" can be read as denying, at the time, the maturity of any synthetic social science discipline that could replace both economics and sociology.

Second, Marshall's opposition to sociology within the university could also be read at the level of institutional competition, where the emergence of sociology was regarded as a potentially hostile or damaging development from the perspective of the established disciplines such as social anthropology, history or economics. The stronger statements attributed to Marshall are made in the early years of the 1900s, when Marshall was deep into the setting up of the Economics Tripos, which started in Cambridge in 1903.[11] Part of these efforts were directed at rescuing economics from economic history and the moral sciences, with which the discipline had been traditionally imbricated. As such, the emergence of another potential disputant, in sociology, in shared or contiguous instructional and institutional space might not have been particularly welcome. Matthews and Supple (1991) make such an argument in explaining Marshall's parallel, unaccommodating, if not hostile, stance in relation to economic history in relation to economics. Be it as it may, history, when viewed from the vantage point of the vanquished sociologists, with fair justification remained unequivocal in its perception of the hostility of economists, the victors in this jostling.

A decade later still, in 1925, there was the strong prospect of Cambridge being endowed with a Professorship in Sociology by the Laura Spelman Rockefeller Memorial, but this was allowed through indifference to slip by,[12]

---

[11] On Marshall and the setting up of the Economics Tripos, see Groenewegen (1988).

[12] The case of the offer of financial support for a chair in sociology at Cambridge University sparked a lively and acrimonious exchange about the hegemonic role of American philanthropic foundations in influencing the framing and orientation of the social sciences, in this case, sociology as a new entrant into the field; with Donald Fisher challenging the role of the foundations, and Bulmer putting up an indirect defence (Bulmer, 1982, 1984; Fisher, 1980, 1983, 1984). Fisher (1984, p. 580) complains against being treated shabbily by Martin Bulmer; the former's argument, based on his extensive research, was broadly that such foundations did systematically attempt to exert such influence, while Bulmer rejects any such interpretation, citing this case of Cambridge rejecting the LSRM funding offer as evidence for his position. Fisher tries "to partially set the record straight". "I am charged with exaggeration, misrepresentation, distortion, presenting a caricature of events, utilizing inadequate theory, being tendentious, and, with subscription to a conspiracy theory of history" (ibid.); leaving nothing to chance, Bulmer, according to Fisher feels that he (and a co-researcher) "are characterized as radical critics who espouse the crude determinism of Marxist theory". Fisher puts up a firm and comprehensive defence, in the process turning the tables on Bulmer, while reasserting his basic position concerning the agenda-setting strategies of philanthropic donor organisations such as Rockefeller. Fisher gives prime importance to the analysis of the institutional policy process; using Gramsci and Bourdieu in his work, he emphasizes that "the question of who controlled this process is central"; yet, Fisher argues that Bulmer "virtually ignores the policy making process …". Further, "When referring to the establishment of a Chair in Sociology at Cambridge

though the accompanying offer of a Chair in Political Science was accepted; Bulmer concludes that "institutionally sociology remained an unacceptable subject" ... "and the power of the antipathy to sociology is shown by the fact that it was nearly half a century after the Memorial's offer before a chair in the subject was established" (Bulmer, 1985, p. 25). There was another failed attempt at expanding the teaching of sociology in the 1930s, and following the Clapham Report of 1946, Cambridge University received funds for social science, including resources for a Chair in Sociology, "but either the university failed to find a suitable person, or it could not agree upon the type of person it wanted, for no appointment was made. According to one account T.H. Marshall was informally offered the chair and declined it. Another version has it that his election to the chair was blocked by the economists as part of faculty politics" (Bulmer, 1985, p. 25, also citing Johnson, 1978, pp. 154–155). According to W. G. Runciman, "a move to create a professorship which [T.H.] Marshall would be invited to occupy was—lamentably—defeated" (Runciman, quoted in Halsey, 2004, p. 220).[13] This money was utilised instead to finance a scheme for visiting professors in social theory, with Talcott Parsons being the first

---

University, Martin Bulmer presents negative evidence concerning the control exercised by Rockefeller philanthropy on recipient institutions. He notes that Cambridge 'rebuffed' the offer by the Laura Spelman Rockefeller Memorial to endow the new chair. While we disagree about the details of the story ... it is the case the Cambridge did not take up the offer. The significance here is that from my preliminary analysis of the relations between Rockefeller philanthropy and recipient institutions in Britain, the USA and Canada, this piece of negative evidence stands out as an exception. The material evidence on more than 100 recipient institutions and on the thousands of negotiations that were conducted between these bodies and Rockefeller philanthropy leads me to conclude that offers were hardly ever rejected. One has to question the sort of scientific methodology that Martin Bulmer is employing" (ibid., pp. 580–581). Stepping away from this, it also happens that Rockefeller Foundation provided generous grants that were crucial in the setting up of the Department of Applied Economics immediately after the war; a tentative understanding had emerged, leading to a visit to the USA by Keynes and Austin Robinson to finalise matters. Certainly, in this case, there was no scope for the donor to influence the agenda of the grantee.

[13] Much later, Marshall was to return from UNESCO in Paris (where he had been the Director of the Department of Social Sciences (1956–1960)) to Cambridge after he retired from UNESCO in 1960, and was in close contact with two eminent sociologists of the next generation—David Lockwood, his student at LSE who had been appointed to a lectureship in sociology in the Faculty of Economics in 1960; and John Goldthorpe, who had been elected to a fellowship in sociology at King's College in 1960. Prior to the return, in an exchange with Austin Robinson, Marshall had tested the waters in Cambridge.

"Thank you very much for your letter about the situation in Cambridge as regards sociology. It would seem that the prospects of establishing a place for sociology are now very good, but that there are still doubts as to the timetable. The proposals for the economics tripos are now clear and practical and should lead to very interesting results. Naturally I would like to know whether there is any chance that my services, in a modest way, might be of use next year. Although paper 12 in Part II deals very definitely with a part of the subject on which I lectured for many years at LSE, I am a little out of touch with recent developments and should need time to bring myself up to date. As I have explained before, my only interest is in being associated in some small way with this new development and in time regaining a status in the academic world at Cambridge when I return to live there." T.H. Marshall to E.A.G. Robinson, Letter dated 7 March 1960; signed "Tom"; T.H. Marshall, Director, Department of Social Sciences, UNESCO, Paris.

invitee in 1953–54—a move roundly criticized by W.G. Runciman, as reported by Halsey (2004), and by David Lockwood, as reported by David Rose (1996, 394n3): "It is related (and it may have been David Lockwood who told me this) that Parsons put back progress towards sociology's recognition at Cambridge for well over a decade when he told the economists that they were dealing with a mere sub-system of society, thereby leaving them with the impression that sociology still sought to be the queen of the social sciences."[14]

In the late 1950s, arguments abounded about an appropriate home and mode of delivery of sociology teaching with a range of opinion, with claims by history, economics (by Robin Marris) or anthropology, though "Jack Goody pointed out that … the most satisfactory solution might be to allow sociology to be taught in its own right, administered by a committee to organize lectures on the model provided by other 'new' subjects" (Bulmer, 1985, p. 26). And so began sociology teaching from 1960 with two papers on sociology in Part II of the Economics Tripos.[15] Michael Young, David Lockwood and Philip Abrams held university positions for periods in the 1960s, with W.G. Runciman holding a fellowship at Trinity, and John Goldthorpe at King's. This was still an unsatisfactory interim arrangement, and "the proponents of sociology, however, aspired to see the subject established in its own right", a prospect furthered by the Boys-Smith Committee on the Organisation of the Social Sciences which recommended in 1968 that while sociology should remain connected with economists, historians and philosophers, a separate Part II Tripos should be established in Social and Political Sciences, leading to a formal proposal to the University, giving sociology a prominent role in this venture. After much public argumentation, this move led in due course to the setting up in 1968 of the Social and Political Sciences (SPS) Committee located within the Faculty of Economics and Politics which brought together sociology, politics and social psychology into a single administrative unit (Bulmer, 1985). Alongside, also in 1968, the University established the first Chair in Sociology, also within the Faculty of Economics and Politics, with John Barnes, the social anthropologist, appointed to the Chair in 1969, a position he held till his premature retirement in 1982.

Barnes ended up in Anthropology but had started with intentions to spend the first two years for doing the Part 2 of the Maths Tripos before switching to take Part 2 of the Economics Tripos in his third year and graduating with a

---

[14] Professor Brendan Burchell anecdotally recalls that during the 2000–2010 period, there was an initiative, mooted by some sociologists to construct a Social Sciences Tripos, including economics and several other disciplines; economics, it seems, would have nothing to do it, and also opposed the idea, as without economics, the queen of the social sciences, there couldn't really be a 'social sciences' tripos (personal communication).

[15] In his special interviews with Maria Cristina Marcuzzo, Richard Kahn, reflecting in the mid-late 1980s on earlier times, observed: "as an economist in the post-War period I was heavily involved in the work of the Faculty of Economics and Politics, on which I served as Chairman for two years. I took part in a radical reform of our examination system and the introduction of Sociology into the University" (Kahn & Marcuzzo, 2020, p. 26).

B.A. in 1939. "He joked about his choice of anthropology as an option: it was advertised as explaining the meaning of civilization and the origins of culture: he thought he would like to find out about that, 'but I never did'" (Young, M.Y., 2011, p. 5, quoting Hiatt (1986)). As he wrote in his autobiography, *Humping My Drum*: "in the light of my subsequent disciplinary affiliations it may be surprising that I thought that all the world's troubles could be solved by the right economic decisions, but that was what I thought at the time" (Barnes, 2007, p. 45). But "it did not take long for me to discover that economics, at least at Part One level, was a very dull subject I never understood why, if the government was short of money, it couldn't just print more bank notes". Even in his innocence, he had put his finger on a central issue of contention in the subject; had he by mischance hit upon an exceptionally boring set of teachers? Be that as it may, "I gradually forgot about switching to economics in my third year and settled down to studying mathematics" (ibid., pp. 46–47). John "enjoyed the austere logical structure of mathematics, especially pure mathematics" (ibid., p. 46), and Michael Young in his obituary refers to John's "appreciation of what he called 'the aseptic logical imperturbability of mathematics'" (Young, M. Y., 2011, p. 9).

The economists were generally in poor standing with the sociologists and carried the stain of their opposition to the new subject from Marshall's times, though it is questionable if this negative depiction carried validity into the post-War era, especially from the decade of the 1960s—when Barnes picked the sociologists' bone with the economists in his Inaugural Lecture,[16] for illustration he had to hark back to the persona of Henry Sidgwick. Of course, a new neo-classical breed of opponents was maturing under the eye of Frank Hahn in the Faculty of Economics, though they would spring into local action a little later

But, there were apparently other antagonists lurking in the wings. In writing his appreciation of Meyer Fortes, Adam Kuper recalls: "When Fortes mounted his campaign against sociology, more specifically against the introduction of sociology in Cambridge, his basic argument was that anthropology dealt with primitive society, and so was quite different from sociology. After all, he noted, introducing his Presidential address to the Royal Anthropological Institute in 1966, totem and taboo—the subjects of his talk—were typical of the sorts of things that preoccupied social anthropologies and did not interest sociologists

---

[16] Barnes delivered his Inaugural Lecture in Cambridge in the politically charged environment of student protests, including several associated with the Faculty of Economics & Politics where his own chair was located. It is notable that later, in 1972, during the red-hot meeting of the protesting students held in Lady Mitchell Hall at Sidgwick Site—from where the students moved en bloc to stage the Sit-in at The Old Schools—John Barnes was one of two professors of the Faculty (the other being the newly appointed Robert Neild) who attentively sat through the meetings, and later gave evidence, supportive of the stand of the students, to Lord Devlin's Enquiry. Barnard reports that "one reviewer [of his Inaugural Lecture] did comment that 'it will hardly set the Cam on fire', but Barnes answered with characteristic reason couple with humour that this had not been his intention. Rather, he 'had merely hope to explain to the university why its sociology students [who were in the vanguard of the protests and Sit-in in Cambridge] might try to burn its building'" (Barnard, 2011, p. 38). For an account of the Sit-in, see Saith (2019, pp. 71–73).

at all. More pragmatically, Fortes feared that a sociology tripos would draw undergraduates away from anthropology. He fought off calls to establish a chair of sociology at Cambridge, but when the university at last decided to move, Fortes use his political skills to ensure that the first professor of sociology, appointed in 1969, was an anthropologist—none other than his friendly critic John Barnes" (Kuper, 2016, p. 136), whom Kuper refers to also as "his more than sympathetic commentator" (ibid., p. 134).

Alan Barnard in his appreciation of John Barnes for the British Academy suggests that Barnes might not have been unaware of such undercurrents, when he, as a social anthropologist, was appointed to the first chair of sociology while several other admired and aspiring sociologists looked on. "Barnes's unexpected decision to return to Cambridge in 1969, his choice of a newer college over an older one, and above all his decision to abandon an anthropology chair for a sociology one, all caused bemusement in some circles. He later revealed that the decision to change jobs and countries had had to do with the fact that he feared doing so later in life would have been impossible, although his documented disagreements with his colleague Derek Freeman at ANU perhaps also played a part. Barnes was a peace-loving man, and he shied away from academic politics when he could. For Barnes, the unexpected thing was that he should have been chosen for the Cambridge post at all. He was concerned that some might say that Meyer Fortes, who was William Wyse Professor of Social Anthropology there at the time and a member of the appointment committee, had acquired a second chair of anthropology through the back door. This led him to resist, at first, the invitation to teach an anthropology course at Cambridge, although later he did so" (Barnard, 2011, pp. 34–35).

Barnard writes that "Barnes was perhaps most at home in the eclectic style of social science that spanned conventional sociology and social anthropology and gave prominence to a history which embraced both social change and continuity, to relations between structure and individual action, and to the nature of virtually all contemporary societies" (Barnard, 2011, pp. 27–28). "To many of us today, social anthropology and sociology are very different disciplines. To John Barnes, they never were, and perhaps for this reason some social anthropologists came to regard him as more of a sociologist, while sociologists often saw more the anthropologist in him. Although he made great contributions to both subjects, he found such disciplinary boundaries distasteful, and the rigid separation of sociology and anthropology in the minds of others perhaps marginalised his work more than it might have. He may have resented this, although, it seems, he never explicitly said so" (Barnard, 2011, pp. 35–36). "In some incarnations", Paul Henley (2011, p. 13) writes in his appreciation of John Barnes "he was a sociologist, in others an ethicist whilst he was also on the leading academic experts on lying". "That is, ON lying, I hasten to add, not AT lying—for John as an academic was as straight and honest as the day is long." It is difficult to see how his appointment could have actively harmed the progress of Cambridge sociology, in the manner that Runciman said Talcott Parsons's Cambridge sojourns had done. As Runciman, even while complaining that the appointment of social anthropologist to the sociology chair broadcast the wrong signals, he was clear in clarifying: "Not that John Barnes's achievements or qualifications were in doubt—far from it" (Runciman, quoted in Halsey, 2004, p. 220).

David Lockwood (1929–2014) was thought of at the time as the rising star who transformed British sociology through his early work—some of it achieved jointly at the DAE in his years at the Faculty of Economics & Politics—on the study of class, analysing class consciousness, class structure and status, embourgeoisement. *The Blackcoated Worker* (1958) on clerical staff, as distinct from manual workers, and *The Affluent Worker in the Class Structure* (1969), co-authored with his Cambridge/DAE colleagues John Goldthorpe, Frank Bechhofer and Jennifer Platt, were game changers and set new agendas for their discipline. David Lockwood was born in 1929 in a working-class family in Holmfirth, what was then a mill town in West Yorkshire later (after he had left for university) put on the tourist map by the BBC's serial (1973–2010) *Last of the Summer Wine*; Lockwood studied sociology at LSE, graduated in 1952, and was appointed lecturer in 1953—according to Halsey, the leading light of an eminent cohort of sociology graduates, including Ralf Dahrendorf. "In 1958 he left the LSE on his appointment to a fellowship at St John's College, Cambridge and a University Lectureship in the Economics Faculty. Why economics, you may ask? The simple reason was that Cambridge did not then offer degrees in sociology, but only the odd optional sociology course within the economics degree. It was to be another ten years before Cambridge University decided, after a fierce and acrimonious debate, that sociology was a fit and proper degree subject for its students to pursue. There can be little doubt that the argument in sociology's favour was swayed by the importance, quality and undoubted scholarship of the work of David Lockwood and his colleagues at Cambridge. This culminated with one of the best-known studies ever undertaken by British sociologists, *The Affluent Worker*. As its name implies, this study examined the lives and aspirations of the new working class of post-war Britain. *The Affluent Worker* was published in 1968, the year David came to Essex as Professor of Sociology", and in the inaugural issue of *Sociology*, Goldthorpe et al. (1967) provide an entrée to the extensive research to appear imminently in their three volumes (Goldthorpe et al., 1968a, 1968b, 1969).[17]

---

[17] *The Affluent Worker* research was based on "a sample of 229 manual workers drawn from the hourly-paid employees of three progressive manufacturing firms sited in Luton. All these firms had advanced personnel and welfare policies and were noted for their good industrial relations records. Our sample was limited to men who were (1) between the ages of 21 and 46; (2) married; (3) earning regularly *at least* GBP 17 per week (October 1962); and (4) resident in the town of Luton itself or adjacent housing areas. The sample was also constructed so as to enable comparisons to be made between workers at different skill levels and involved in different types of production system. For further comparative purposes, we also took a sample of 54 lower-level white-collar workers based on two of the firms. The manual workers were interviewed twice; once at their place of work and then again, together with their wives, in their own homes. The white-collar workers were interviewed at home only" (Goldthorpe et al., 1967, pp. 14–15).

The overall conclusion of the grand project is previewed thus by the team: "the point emerging ... is the following: that the dynamics of working-class politics cannot be regarded as forming part of any

David Rose writes that "beyond his contribution as a scholar, he has played a vital role in the establishment of sociology both in the country as a whole and (perhaps more of a challenge) in the University of Cambridge" (Rose, 1996, p. 385); "the struggle to have sociology formally recognized and accepted by the University as a proper academic subject with its own Faculty Board and Tripos was one in which Lockwood was actively involved" (ibid., p. 388). In Rose's assessment in the mid-career appreciation assembled by disciplinary colleagues, "David Lockwood is not merely outstanding sociologists, but is ranked among the world's foremost sociologists" (Rose, 1996, p. 386); "where Tom Marshall pioneered, David Lockwood subsequently colonized and expanded" (Rose, 1996, p. 386). Marshall had been his teacher at the LSE, and in later years, Marshall, after his retirement from UNESCO in 1960, and Lockwood, after he joined Cambridge as a lecturer in sociology that year, overlapped there till 1968 when Lockwood left for Essex, a few years prior to the arrival in Cambridge of his famous LSE student, Tony Giddens.

Commenting in retrospect on the selection of the first professor of sociology, Bob Blackburn, the head of the sociology unit in the DAE, observes that "David Lockwood and John Goldthorpe[18] were both candidates and regarded

---

inexorable process of social change deriving from continually rising standards of living. Certainly, the sequence, assumed in much previous discussion, of affluence—*embourgeoisement*-Conservative voting is generally unsupported by our findings." The null hypothesis of embourgeoisement thus stands rejected. They elaborate: "The acquisition by manual workers and their families of relatively high incomes and living standard does not, on our evidence lead to widespread changes in their social values and life-styles in the direction of 'middle-classness' is not, after all, simply a matter of money; and politics has never been reducible to a mere epiphenomenon of economic conditions. The position of a group within a system of social stratification is not decisively determined by the income or possessions of its members, but rather by their characteristic life-chances and experiences and by the nature of their relationships with other groups. And it is in this context that their politics must be understood—a context which changes much more slowly than their relative levels of wages and salaries or patterns of consumption. Our affluent workers remain, in spite of their affluence, men who live by selling their labour power to their employers in return for wages; and, in all probability, they will still be so at the end of their working days. Again, although they and their families enjoy a standard of living comparable to that of many while-collar families, their social worlds are still to a large extent separate from those of the latter, except where bridges of kinship, or to a lesser degree of neighbourhood, can span the social distance between them. Nor is there much indication that affluence has encouraged the desire to *seek* acceptance in new social milieux at higher status levels" (ibid., pp. 27–28).

Thus, workers' wages could be flexible and mobile, but working-class identities would be sticky and sluggish to respond—a river, to a glacier. Embourgeoisement wasn't happening, and wouldn't happen in a hurry. However, the upheavals from the 1970s were to throw up fresh challenges to this general assessment.

[18] John Goldthorpe was born (in 1935) in a Yorkshire mining village; his father was a colliery clerk and mother a dressmaker. He took a 1st class with honours in history at UCL, then graduated in sociology from LSE, followed by a junior research fellowship, and then an Assistant Lectureship in the Department of Sociology, Leicester from 1957–1960 in the era of Ilya Neustadt and Norbert Elias; in 1960, he was elected to a Prize Fellowship in Sociology at King's College Cambridge, the first such position to be established in sociology at the University. He taught, with Lockwood, in sociology courses in Part II of the Economics Tripos. Again, like Lockwood, he had a close relationship with T.H. Marshall during the Cambridge years, 1960–1969, after which he was elected to an Official Fellowship at Nuffield College, Oxford, and retired there in 2002. Geoff Ingham, sociologist in the Faculty of Economics, was one of his students. Goldthorpe developed a 'core'

as strong candidates. The sociologists were united in supporting Lockwood (though well-disposed to Goldthorpe) and expected him to be appointed. However, the appointing committee was made of anthropologists, economists, etc., and chose an anthropologist. The Sociologists were VERY (emphasis in original) annoyed and there was considerable upset. Luckily John Barnes[19] proved to be a good man."[20]

David Lockwood, John Goldthorpe, Michael Young[21] and Philip Abrams,[22] meanwhile, all went their own ways. The departure of this group arguably marks a major turning point for sociology in Cambridge; it was a game changer. It broke with the impressive and widely respected body of research on the analysis of social classes that the group had been accumulating, especially through their projects at the DAE. Substantive and institutional control over the further development of the discipline was placed in the hands of a social anthropologist whose work stood at a discrete distance from that of this group; and the prospect of greater autonomy from the power brokers of social anthropology was diminished; all this, regardless of the positive personal or intellectual qualities of John Barnes.

Recently, Mike Savage (2016, p. 57) has argued forcefully that "the past fifteen years has seen a dramatic revival of interest in social class in the UK. Class—often in intersection with other inequalities such as gender, race and ethnicity—is indeed, the main topic within contemporary British

---

model of intergenerational class mobility, along with Robert Erikson and Walter Muller; also, the Erikson-Goldthorpe-Portocarero (EGP) class schema was used after 2002 in British official statistics, which encountered controversy because his schema of social class analysis was based on the family, focussing entirely on men taken definitionally as the head of household, as in the male-breadwinner household model.

[19] Prior to his appointment as the first professor of sociology in Cambridge in 1968, Barnes had been Professor of Anthropology at the University of Sydney (1956–1958), and Professor of Anthropology at the Australian National University (ANU) (1958–1969) and, amongst many other positions, had also served as President of the Sociological Association of Australia and New Zealand.

[20] Personal communication, email dated 30 March 2020.

[21] Michael Young (1915–2002), who had not slept in a bed of his own till he was 19 (Dartington. org) studied economics at LSE, and then law to become a barrister; had a university lectureship between 1961 and 1963, kept his Churchill fellowship till 1966, and then left to pursue his remarkable multiple-track career as a "one-man thinktank": as a socially oriented institutional entrepreneur, including, amongst many other initiatives, his role in the launch of The Open University (having set up a prototype on Anglia TV), a name attributed to him; he initiated the move to establish the SSRC of which, when it was eventually founded, he became its first Chairman; founder of the Consumers' Association, and *Which*; also served as President of Birkbeck College; introduced the concept of "meritocracy"; was a utopian socialist; had been Secretary of the Labour Party Research Department and involved in drafting the 1945 Manifesto, though he drifted towards the SDP later; had six children from three marriages; and the Wiki entry against his name informs that "although an egalitarian, Young accepted a life peerage on 20 March 1978, taking the title Baron Young of Dartington; his many projects required frequent travel to London and the peerage offered free rail travel and attendance allowance at a time when he had run out of money"; this, and very much more, all in one lifetime.

[22] Philip Abram, who chaired the SPS Committee for its first three years, 1968–1971, then went to Durham University (Bulmer, 1985, p. 26).

sociology. This is a remarkable recovery. Having been criticised as a tired and redundant concept in the 1990s, criticised by many of the key sociologists in the UK, [amongst others] by Zygmunt Bauman, Ulrich Beck, ... and Anthony Giddens, the concept has returned with a vengeance. How? Why?"

He demarcates three periods: "the 'golden age' of British class analysis from 1950 to the mid-1970s was characterised by the heady fusion of British social science around a particular focus on the working class as harbinger of progressive social change"; followed by "the decline of class analysis from the mid-1970s to the late 1990s", this, partly due to the erosion of working-class culture, but also because the expression and methods of academic discourse "undermined the popular interest in class itself"; followed then by the present revival of the concept of class after 2000, driven, in material terms, by the rise of extreme inequalities, and inspired in disciplinary and intellectual terms, in Savage's view, "by Bourdieu's capacity to open up the cultural aspects of class in telling ways ... it now operates as a term of dialogue and argument across boundaries" (Savage, 2016, p. 58), shifting and widening the contours towards the production and reproduction of privilege in the middle classes and upper class elites.

Savage (2016, p. 59) argues that the key benchmark works[23] which had established the distinctive intellectual profile of British sociology in its post-War phase of explosive expansion, especially after the Robbins Report, had a focus entirely devoted to class, and more particularly to the "working class". Savage cites "the spirit of the initial heroic generation of class analysis" (ibid., p. 58) and endorses "the paradigmatic significance of this remarkable generation of British sociologists" (ibid., p. 60). "This heroic generation was fixated on the prospects for the working class to bring about social change, and more particularly by the ambivalent position of the working class within British society, at the one moment being a central figure in bringing about the first industrial society in the world, but at another moment remaining outside the "gentlemanly", cosy world of the British establishment" (Savage, 2016, p. 60).

Pride of place is given to the cohort of sociologists which prominently includes those that kick-started its teaching in Cambridge, and whose works, written during their tenures there in the 1960s, are given landmark status in making the working class the centre of sociological study. In different capacities, various sociologists with a Cambridge connection are named as members of this 'heroic generation': there is Tom Marshall, who set down early goalposts, who on various accounts would, and should, have got a chair in sociology in Cambridge had opposing disciplinary lobbies not

---

[23] The works that Savage cites as beacons are: "T. H. Marshall's *Citizenship and social class*, (1951) through the ethnography of a mining village in the brilliant *Coal is our life* (Dennis et al., 1956), to Willmott and Young's *Family and kinship in East London (1958)*, David Lockwood's *The black coated worker* (1958), to John Goldthorpe and David Lockwood's *The affluent worker* (1968/69), Paul Willis's *Learning to labour* (1975), and John Goldthorpe's *Class structure and social mobility in modern Britain* (1980). Many of the generation of sociologists who were also to become prominent from the 1970s also wrote extensively about social class—with Anthony Giddens being an especially prominent example" (Savage, 2016, pp. 59–60).

intervened in the 1940s; Savage places huge emphasis, rightly, on the individual and collective work of David Lockwood and John Goldthorpe (and Michael Young), all sociology teachers in Cambridge in the 1960s, in placing the working-class centre-stage in the concerns of UK sociology and certainly the work of the applied sociologists of the DAE led by Bob Blackburn in their ... Goldthorpe—objective technical measurement, stats replace voices, different epistemological approach to social class analysis—but early breakthrough work nevertheless. Also to an extent Goldthorpe in post-Cambridge research. Then, the shift away from class analysis is also propelled from Cambridge, this through Tony Giddens, whose role is also explicitly underscored by Savage.

The intervention of this heroic generation also carried immediate relevance in that "this sociology was implicitly or explicitly highly political, and all of the key figures made no bones about the political significance of their work. ... This is nowhere more apparent than for Michael Young, who had written the Labour Party manifesto in 1945 and was a major figure in social democratic thinking. But it was also true in somewhat different ways for T. H. Marshall, who clearly articulated the Fabian LSE tradition to elaborate a conception of citizenship which sought to include the working classes. In short, there were direct political stakes in debates about class, with academic and political arguments cross fertilising each other" (Savage, 2016, p. 60).

There was also a break in the epistemological approach and associated methodologies and tools of investigation. "These interventions also elaborated a raft of methodological repertoires which became canonical for sociology itself, as well as the social sciences more broadly. These methods were championed explicitly as devices which allowed those who had previously been outside the purview of social research to gain some kind of voice. The qualitative in-depth interview and the representative survey were central here. Both of these proved means of eliciting accounts and views of a wider range of people outside the educated middle classes, and hence providing a more balanced understanding of social divisions as a whole" (Savage, 2016, p. 60). The legacy of this pioneering epistemological initiative is housed in the archives of the University of Essex, David Lockwood's academic home after his years in Cambridge.[24] "This

---

[24] The archive was created in 1961–1962 at the University of Essex, where David Lockwood was a professor after he left Cambridge, and the following entry on the records was compiled by John Southall of Qualidata, UK Data Archive, University of Essex. "The study covers the period 1950–1962. The papers—semi-structured interview transcripts—are stored in twenty archival boxes. Part One (The Luton area study) is held in Boxes One to Fourteen and Part Two (The Cambridge area study) in Boxes Fifteen to Twenty. Box One and Two contain 100 interviews with Vauxhall car workers; Boxes Three to Five contain 113 interviews with Skefco workers; Box Six contains 34 interviews with Laporte workers; Boxes Seven to Fourteen contain 551 interviews with workers in their home; Box Fifteen to Twenty contain 316 Cambridge area interviews. The Affluent Worker project was undertaken during 1961–1962 to test empirically the, then widely accepted, thesis of working class embourgeoisement. Married male workers from three Luton factories were firstly interviewed at work and then, again, with their wives at home. A number of white-collar workers from the same companies were also interviewed in their home,

heroic generation was therefore truly formative, not only in establishing a powerful form of scholarship, but also in forging a set of research tools which came to have much wider provenance within the social sciences as a whole. These tools allowed a new kind of social group—the working class—whose voices and identities had been obscured by the dominant genteel inflection of British culture, to be heard. These methods were part of a radical current during the 1960s which swept into British public life and which "made the working class visible" (Savage, 2016, p. 61).

However, Savage argues, "this heroic generation of sociology was also an elegiac and romantic one: it finally brought the white male working class fully into visibility at the very same time that the social foundations of this formation were beginning to be radically undermined. It was ultimately unsustainable" (Savage, 2016, p. 62). "The working class was very largely seen as 'white': the 1960s was the last decade when it was the white working class, rather than ethnic minorities, who were the prime 'outsiders knocking to come in'. It was also focused on men. Although the situation was already changing dramatically as a result of feminist politics and changing labour market and personal relationships, the 1960s was the last decade when women could largely be left out of the picture or—as with Willmott and Young—be predominantly identified as mothers. Thirdly, the world of the working class was being deconstructed at the very moment that it finally was to have its place in British culture—with the radical programme of public housing renewal and the final phases of slum clearance, as well as the continue decline of manufacturing industry" (Savage, 2016, p. 62). Therefore, "the great tradition of class analysis established in Britain in the immediate post war decades was unsustainable. It was premised on a model of the white male worker which could only be seen as nostalgic in the context of late twentieth century Britain. It is therefore completely explicable why growing interests in gender inequality and changing position of women, and concerns with racism and the position of ethnic minorities could only appear to undermine the project of class analysis as a whole" (Savage, 2016, p. 62).

"The solidaristic and cohesive worlds of the working class, defined by common relationships to production and the workplace, were the template here for understanding why and how class mattered. This approach had an appeal when there was evidence of solidaristic class politics, whether through trade unions,

creating an additional sample group. This material formed the basis for the influential Affluent Worker publications of the 1960s. In addition to the research material gathered in Luton, this collection also includes the earlier, Cambridge Area Study. Primarily a pilot, this is a substantial set of interviews (300+) made with teachers, grocers, bank employees and factory electricians, in the Cambridge area, and examined the same broad areas of middle and working class borders." The interviews are listed to cover these subjects: "aspiration; class consciousness; class differentiation; education; employment; factory workers; family life; industrial sociology; social mobility; social stratification; social structure".

Goldthorpe, J. H., Lockwood, D. Bechhofer, F. & Platt, J. (1961–1962). *The Affluent Worker Collection*. University of Essex Special Collections, GB 301 Q045; 20 archival boxes, 6.60 metres. https://archiveshub.jisc.ac.uk/search/archives/3e385b64-60d5-3914-939d-8ae03d38c5ba.

community mobilisation, or whatever, but this was unable to deal with the fragmentation of social relations embedded in the 'neo-liberal' shift towards a marketised economy from the 1970s. And so it was inevitable that the dramatic de-industrialisation of Britain from the 1970s alongside the deregulation of economic regulation and marketization of public services, could only be interpreted as undermining class—as it had been historically understood in the heroic age" (Savage, 2016, p. 63). Of great relevance here is the work of Guy Standing (2011) with his analysis of how contemporary processes of capitalism have led to a structural metamorphosis in the conditions of labour, employment and work, from an organically integrated working class towards the emergence of "a precariat, the new dangerous class". The material and political conditions underlying this transformation also explain the weakening of the idea and reality of 'the working class' as in the genre of 'the heroic generation' of sociologists.

When set against this context elaborated by Mike Savage, the rejection of David Lockwood for the professorship in Cambridge in 1968, and his, and John Goldthorpe's, consequent exit could indeed be regarded as a game changer. W. G. Runciman thought that the professorship should have been handed to Lockwood 'on a plate'; the sociologists in Cambridge wanted him appointed, but a committee without any sociologist made a different choice, presumably because they saw things differently.

Thus, sociology had its first professor, and SPS its new leader. Hawthorn (2009) explains: "The idea was that SPS as a Tripos would largely consist of bits drawn from elsewhere—political thought from history, some of the more comparative sociological things from anthropology, bits of social psychology from management and engineering; there were things that were not available in the University so in addition, three lectureships were established in 1969 in SPS to provide those inputs, where the appointees were Malcolm Ruel for comparative sociology, Martin Richards for development psychology, and Geoff Hawthorn for teaching methods for sociology".[25]

In his interview with Alan Macfarlane (Hawthorn, 2009), Geoff provides a valuable discursive sketch of life in early SPS: "In the early years of SPS we had external chairmen who could be very powerful, like Moses Finley, and a lot of the leg work was then done by the junior staff who were the academic secretaries as the chairman only appeared every other Tuesday afternoon". Things changed with John Barnes. John Barnes was "a very good anthropologist, …

---

[25] Hawthorn (2009) recalls being interviewed for his job—a university lectureship in sociology (statistics) to teach methods—at Cambridge in candle-light as suddenly there was a power cut [this was the pre-OPEC 1st price-hike era marked by regular strikes]: "I remember … Leach gave the impression of being asleep then asked how I thought men were different from animals"; "John Barnes very politely asked if I knew anything about statistics, which I said I didn't; … in the darkness they must have made a mistake but anyway I got the job". Geoffrey Hawthorn stayed the full course in Cambridge, a keen observer and participant in the evolution of the field, eventually switching from sociology to retire as Professor of International Politics when that new department was established in 2009.

[but] there were two difficulties: he was more of an anthropologist than a sociologist; he was not very interested in modernity but sociology is largely about that; there was a paper [in the Economics Tripos] on the sociology of economic life where people talked largely about industry, labour and management; John gave a lecture on peasants which perhaps symbolized the nearest he could come ...; secondly, he did not really want to take much responsibility and didn't like administration"; "John Barnes was, however, a true liberal, a very decent man .... The ideology of SPS was much more left-wing; nevertheless, being a liberal, he suited SPS very well as it would have been very difficult if we had had someone who imposed a particular vision of the social sciences. My wider view of SPS is that it was a notionally radical entity created in the most deeply conservative of circumstances; it was a set of compromises where everybody from genetics to theology wanted to have a say, as a result of which no one intellectual voice was primary; I think that in many ways that was a good thing; my experience of the social sciences is that when they start institutionally trying to define themselves, excluding other things, then a rigid theoreticism and methodological obsession takes hold; I think the environment of Cambridge and John's character kept SPS plural; quite inadvertently it sustained its conservative inspiration".[26][27]

Alan Macfarlane, in his "preliminary" jottings on Cambridge Anthropology, writes that in the early 1970s, "there was a complex political relation" and much-shared teaching between Anthropology and the undivided Social and Political Sciences group, and "there was a good deal of talk of a merger between Archaeology and Anthropology, or at least Social Anthropology, and SPS into a Faculty of Social Science. After the anthropologist John Barnes was succeeded by Anthony Giddens as Chairman of SPS, in the early 1980s, the two teaching courses were severed and the relations became less close" (Macfarlane, 2015, p. 24).

---

[26] John Barnes was also interviewed in the Alan Macfarlane series, and notably by Jack Goody but this was in 1983, the year after his retirement, the starting point of the subsequent turbulent institutional and organisational evolution from the time of SPS to the new institutional mapping of the various disciplines. Barnes and Goody do not stray at all into earlier SPS institutional matters. All we learn is that John Barnes started off in the 1930s doing a mathematics Tripos, but "I wasn't really interested in mathematics", so he switched to an arrangement where he could take Part II of the Economics Tripos while doing his maths, and read on the Part I of Economics in his spare time, "but it didn't take me very long to discover that economics was the dullest subject imaginable"; and so he switched to the Archaeology and Anthropology (A&A) Tripos which, according to his handbook, "would enable me to answer questions like the origin of civilization, what's the meaning of culture, and so on, and I thought I'd like to know the answers to those questions, so I switched to A&A, but I still haven't found the answers to the questions" (Barnes, 1983). As it happens, on SPS and related themes, the interview with Jack Goody conducted in 1991 by Eric Hobsbawm is also a complete blank (Goody, 1991), as is the one of Garry Runciman (2014), interviewed by Alan Macfarlane in 2014.

[27] There is much underlying resonance here to the character and course of teaching in the field of Development in Cambridge in those times, under the influence of Austin Robinson, and then the anthropologist Paul Howell.

It could be pertinent here to insert a brief reflection on the contiguous domain of Anthropology, as then practised in Cambridge under the sway of its greats, especially Jack Goody, who was heading the department at the time. Geoffrey Hawthorn was "a tremendous admirer ... I love the range and intellectual openness, his almost matter-of-fact originality, that he will take cooking or flowers to be self-evidently as serious a subject as kinship; he is so prolific ... [his] creation of a welcoming environment seemed to me terrific; ... Ernest Gellner was much more deeply reflective, Leach in his own tortured way, much more brilliant, Marilyn Strathern is very intense, but Jack has a set of qualities which none of them had—just his presence seems to me to have been crucial to the subject of anthropology in the 1970s and 80s, ... the subject has a genius for reinventing itself, unlike sociology which has drifted into some sort of sterile backwater, at least for the moment [spoken in 2011]; it [this sense of anthropology] was particularly vivid in Cambridge because Jack was so good at energizing the subject; John Barnes had the same liberality but not the same energy" (Hawthorn, 2009). What perhaps needs adding to this personalised account is that some of the leitmotifs of Jack Goody's work created rich contours of potential interfaces with sociology and political economy, in particular through his propositions concerning the central role of economic surplus in societal change, in the role of communication technologies, urbanisation, bureaucratic and State authority displacing traditional forms; there are obvious conversations here with the sociology of industrialisation and modernity on the one side, and, as an illustration, to the genre of work à la Maurice Dobb's *Studies in the Rise of Capitalism*, and differently, on the role of economic surplus in planned industrialisation in developing economies. The arena and the times were imbued with possibilities, many or most of which lapsed with the passage of their human carriers and protagonists.[28]

10.2 Sociology: Growing Up Amongst Economists

In Cambridge, sociology was fostered in the extended family of economists and, in some respects, its story of early development is the familiar one: a young discipline having to survive and fend for itself in a subordinate position on the fringes of the established territory of its older, albeit accommodating and supportive, social science sibling. That said, life wasn't too bad for it and things could have been worse.

1960 was an especially noteworthy year in the timeline of the Department of Applied Economics (DAE) with three significant developments. First, the iconic Cambridge Growth Project (CGP) was launched under the leadership of Alan Brown and Richard Stone; second, sociology entered the Faculty through the teaching of a paper in the Tripos, and the appointment of two sociologists within the Faculty; and third, as with sociology, teaching on economic

---

[28] A view that needs noting is that Jack Goody had a reputation for adopting a very tough stance on the issue of granting tenure to junior staff.

development was recognized in the Faculty through a paper on Economic Development in the Economics Tripos. Following this augmentation of the remit of the Faculty of Economics and Politics, both development and sociology, like economics, moved on parallel tracks: teaching in the Faculty, and research in the DAE. For sociology, this dual arrangement marked the period 1960 till 1987; on both sides of the disciplinary and organisational lines, there was evidence of interaction and cooperation in this evolution through till 1968, in the form of joint research projects in the DAE, and the creation of interdisciplinary courses in Tripos teaching.[29]

Indeed, sociological themes had entered the research portfolio of the DAE even prior to 1960.[30] What is perhaps striking is the alacrity with which DAE takes up the cue and widens its remit, indicating that it welcomed, rather than resisted, the formal entry of sociology and sociologists into its enterprise. Indeed, DAE, on its own volition, had sprinted off the blocks even earlier: the DAE Report for the years 1954–1957 includes a description of the research project on "The Economic Circumstances of Old People" (paragraphs 35 & 36) and describes pilot surveys ongoing in 1957 in Greenwich and in Bedford: "The main purpose of this inquiry is to provide a detailed picture of the economic circumstances of people over retirement age in Britain at the present time". In addition, "a number of socio-economic factors are also being investigated; ... the material collected will also provide data for a further investigation of the life cycle of income and expenditure" (ibid., p. 9). If the experience of the pilot was positive, the intention was to launch a nationally scaled-up project. This was a theme with a life cycle of its own, and was picking up from Brian Reddaway's immediately pre-war study of *The Economics of a Declining Population* (Reddaway, 1939), a prescient treatment of a phenomenon that is now widely manifest in mature economies inducing serious policy concern. This first project also illustrates the synergetic potentialities for research between the disciplines and their practitioners. The project involved J.E.G. Utting and Mrs D.E. Cole; the latter takes over the running of the project and is cited in the following, fifth DAE Report, as Mrs Dorothy Cole Wedderburn—she had been married to W. A. Max Cole, but after that

---

[29] The first reference to sociological research in the DAE is to be found in the records for 1960, when the Minutes of the Committee of Management registers the desire to encourage such work in the DAE. The DAE Report for the years 1958–1964 lists seven "principal developments" during this period, and the first one on this list refers to sociology: "First, an increase in scale and scope of the Department's research activities, notably in the field of sociological research (after the scope of the Faculty had been enlarged to cover sociology) and in the provision for research into the economic problems of developing countries (which now constitutes a paper in the Tripos" (Department of Applied Economics 1965, 'Fifth Report: Activities in the Years 1958–64', DAE, Cambridge, April).

[30] Martin Bulmer notes that in the late 1950s, "sociological perspectives were also opened up by the teaching of industrial sociology by a group in the Engineering Department and by the existence of the Institute of Criminology" (Bulmer, 1985) founded in Cambridge in 1959 through the initiative of Rab Butler. In all probability, Bulmer is referring to Dorothy Wedderburn's sociological research at the DAE, shifted later to the engineering department of Imperial College, London.

marriage broke up in 1960, she was married for 1962–1968 to the leftist lawyer Bill Wedderburn (later Baron Wedderburn of Charlton). This is perhaps how sociological research began in the DAE, and it is striking that the first main investigator, Dorothy Wedderburn, was an economist (who worked at the DAE for 15 years) engaging in sociological research; she was later to emerge as one of the leading industrial sociologists of the country.

Somewhat surprisingly, in his otherwise densely informative review of the advent and early years of the institutional life of sociology as a discipline in Cambridge, Martin Bulmer does not make any mention of the presence of the team of sociology researchers within the DAE. This is a significant gap that needs bridging. The dismissive antagonisms of Sidgwick and Marshall to sociology had long lapsed, and later Cambridge economists were far from united in their ascribed hostility towards sociology as a new academic entrant. Attitudes had changed within post-war economics, and this was reflected in full measure in the DAE, especially after 1955 when Reddaway took over as Director from Richard Stone. Sociology was readily accepted, and encouraged, as a sister discipline next to applied economics. Ajit Singh (2008, p. 13) in his appreciation of Brian Reddaway, writes thus:

> Reddaway did so with great energy and total conviction. He changed the direction of the department's research towards applied economics and economic policy. Under his leadership in the 1960s the DAE was a vibrant and exciting place, which was generally regarded as one of the world's leading institutions for applied economic research. Reddaway, as many observers have noted, was in his element as the Director. He was a liberal academic in the best sense of the term and let a hundred flowers bloom. The DAE hosted projects on a wide range of subjects, including notably economic history, corporate finance, labour markets, regional economies and economic sociology, to each of which he himself made significant contributions.

The DAE provided a generous, appreciative and respectful home for the small team of sociologists within its midst. The inclusive conceptualisation of the overall DAE project at inception evolved over time. The DAE vision, while framed in terms of economics, was wide and holistic, reflecting the eclectic, heterodox view it had of the subject. A wide range of curiosities was found worth of investigation. Predictably, the central focus was on the core projects of national income, capital formation, consumer behaviour, industrial and corporate economics. But there were also projects on underdeveloped countries especially on agriculture, and on constructing their national income accounts. The UK research agenda included projects on 'the causes of small strikes', 'status of manual workers', 'income, expenditure and savings of old people' (suggesting an interface with socially disaggregated treatments of aggregate economic variables with strong sociological and demographic implications, themes pursued by Richard Stone, and later by Brian Reddaway, both Directors of the DAE); and several others on labour and employment, all of which offered fertile interdisciplinary space. And then there were projects, in the early 1960s, on the 'study of political ideology', and another, suggested intriguingly by Graham Pyatt, on 'psephological research', both of which received sympathetic support from the Committee of Management; and if there is still residual doubt about the open approach of the DAE to the empirical study of economy and society, there was a project on 'the economics of car parking'. Back in 1960, the year that Richard Stone and Alan Brown set up the CGP, there was an explicit assertion in the DAE's Committee of Management of the desire of the DAE to promote sociological research; and serious consideration was being given to the setting up of a Survey Research Centre at the DAE. The regional and local dimensions had always been strong within the DAE; there was a project on the Social Accounts of Cambridgeshire more or less from the start; a very early clue to the breakthrough, much later, associated with Pyatt and Stone on Social Accounting Matrices.

Thus, after 1960 within the DAE, the portfolio of sociological research projects developed steadily and came to occupy a significant space in the overall research output of the DAE, with demonstrable synergy between the sociologists and the applied economists on overlapping themes of mutual concern. The DAE's impressive research productivity was the product of a highly fertile intellectual ecology of applied research, often hybrid, rooted in different disciplines but on similar themes. Apart from the two large-scale modelling projects, viz., the CGP and the Cambridge Economic Policy Group (CEPG), there was the highly regarded labour studies group, the well-established team working on industrial economics, a group working on regional economic issues, the eminent group of economic historians, and the sociologists who were thought, by their peers both within and outside Cambridge, to be producing excellent research. In 1985–1986, at the point of separation, the research portfolio of the sociology group included a set of four separate projects funded by the Economic and Social Research Council (ESRC), all dealing with the salience and empirical dynamics of social stratification, inequality and social identity in a geographical context, and a project on an occupational classification and coding scheme for social research—collectively suggestive of the wide potential interface between the applied economists and empirical sociologists. It is not for nothing then that Tony Giddens, on becoming Professor of Sociology, wished to prioritise the development of a Centre for Social Research emulating the success of the DAE. And definitely not to be overlooked is the landmark research and writing on theoretical sociology by Tony Giddens on the Faculty side of the line: while there was impressive sociological work carried out in the DAE (from Lockwood, Goldthorpe, Abrams) on the sociology of class formation and political attitudes, including the studies on 'the affluent worker', Giddens, from the Faculty side, produced a series of theoretical texts, *Capitalism and Modern Social Theory* (1971), *The Class Structure of the Advanced Societies* (1973), *New Rules of Sociological Method* (1976), *Central Problems in Social Theory* (1979), *The Constitution of Society* (1984), amongst other contributions. It would, therefore, be difficult, indeed incorrect, to argue that sociology and sociologists, both on the DAE and the Faculty sides of the internal demarcation, were not highly productive during the period leading up to 1986/87, the time when the door was opened for them to leave the DAE and Faculty of Economics and Politics.

Over the years, the (not invariably) friendly cooperation notwithstanding, there was a progressive churning and polarisation as sociology evolved as a discipline within Cambridge and outside. There were new visions and ambitions within the groups of sociologists on the one side, and the emergence of divisions amongst the economists on the other, the latter reflecting the intrinsic value attached to the intellectual project of interdisciplinarity—which was 'very little' for the mainstream orthodox camp, and 'very considerable' for the diverse heterodox lineages within the Faculty. The US-led mathematical revolution in economics had invaded and begun to take hold in UK universities, and its supportive neoliberal political infrastructure was fully operational on a global basis; at Cambridge, the neoclassicals were launching their drive to stage a coup and take charge of the Faculty of Economics, and devising strategies to do so. Bearing in mind the hostility of the orthodox economists clearly rising into power in the Faculty, it was both expeditious and wise for the sociologists to think of alternative accommodation. But that does not diminish the intellectual loss of the intrinsically valuable project of interdisciplinarity that had long been an evolving feature of Faculty teaching and DAE research.

In this regard, a reflection on the contrasting positions of a few leading economists of the orthodox as against the heterodox persuasion is pertinent. At a more philosophical level, some of the main economists of the era took a far more holistic view of economics and economic behaviour, irreducible to the neoclassical universal simplification of individuals separately maximizing something called utility, and firms maximizing profits. The methodological perspectives of Reddaway, of Stone, of Joan Robinson, were quite open to the role of sociological factors and influences at both theoretical and policy levels. Thus, the narrative of the sociologists on the advent and subsequent evolution of their discipline needs to fill this lacuna, or otherwise be deemed to be flawed. The very fact that sociology, and also other related social sciences, including the study of economic development, came to be housed in SPS which was located institutionally within economics bears testimony to the openness of the larger majority of economists to welcoming the 'new' disciplines into their curricula, on to their Faculty Board, and into their staff common room.

Richard Stone could be misread with one eye as being a theoretical and applied econometrician interested in developing techniques and tests; of course, he was vastly more than that. Underlying even the most technical of works is a social framework constructed from carefully selected social categories; and there are economic, social and policy concerns that set the questions that the techniques are meant to answer; all this while handling with the greatest care the collection and processing of the statistical data to be employed in the exercises. This broad interface underlies the national income project and is even more immediately visible in Stone's pioneering work towards developing a system of social and demographic statistics (see UNSO, 1975).[31] The archives of his papers hold a handwritten manuscript, c.1974, running to 57 pages on Social Indicators, dealing inter alia with issues to do with epistemological questions, objective vs subjective approaches; changes in social norms and attitudes; participation and democracy; infrastructure and investment; data and empirics; modelling. This paper far precedes the later, simplistic and problematic, human development index and was written the same year that Jan Drewnowski published his much-overlooked study *On Measuring and Planning the Quality of Life*, where he acknowledges (Drewnowski, 1974, p. 6, fn) the pioneering work of Stone in the setting up of the system of social and demographic statistics. The Social Accounting Matrix embodies the full spectrum of questions and methods, tools and techniques for useful social ends. This is but one example, but any young social scientist with an interest in conversing with empirics would have found Stone a remarkable resource.

Reddaway, who was the Director of the DAE during the dynamic and expansionary 1955–1970 period, was a supremely accomplished, pragmatic, eclectic applied economist, with a masterly command over the utility (and futility) of different genres of research methods. Yet he generally looked askance at econometric modelling, arguing that real-life systems were far too complex and had too many variables on the run to capture in the reductionist specifications necessary to start the econometric game; these models were inherently underdetermined but pretended not to be so. An analogous logic and critique can be transferred to disciplinary, that is, unavoidably reductionist, forms of economic enquiry, where posing an 'economics' question demands abstraction from changes and movements in a multitude of phenomena that in reality interact with economic ones. Thus, seeking a holistic understanding of real processes requires this acknowledgement in the investigative frame, which is thereby rendered multidisciplinary in one direction or another, depending on the

---

[31] Graham Pyatt (2005) explains the significance of Stone's innovative contribution in this multidisciplinary domain. "Come the 1970s, Stone refocused his energies yet again, this time on demographic accounting. His initial ideas on the subject were given their first airing in the 1970 series of Radcliffe Lectures at Warwick University. And they finally evolved into a new treatise *Systems of Social and Demographic Statistics* that was published by the United Nations in 1975 [endnote 9]. The central concern in *Systems* is to account for people. Stone sets the problem in a dynamic context in which individuals are born into, and then move (migrate) between a set of mutually exclusive and exhaustive states or categories before they eventually die. Age groups provide the obvious example of a set of states that can be used to classify the population within this framework. But there are many other potentially interesting taxonomies relative to which Stone's framework of forward and backward stochastic differential equations can be deployed, such as in tracing the movement of a population through an education or health system, or the spatial location of a moving population. And here we should note that Stone's framework for sociodemographic data is analogous to his work on the SNA in so far as the framework serves not only as an interesting way of presenting the facts: it is also a powerful framework for collating the facts and reconciling inconsistent and fragmentary data; and the architecture of the system is at least suggestive of the way in which the facts might be modelled. All of which may explain why *Systems* is yet another of Stone's contributions over the years that relevant authorities consider to be seminal."

substance of the research enquiry. As such, there is not just the potential, but also the imperative, to analyse societal processes not as purely economic ones, or in purely sociological terms, but within a holistic approach which allows the interdependencies to be made explicit. If that meant that received 'neat' theory and packaged tailored methodologies had to be rethought, well, so be it. Reddaway's angst over econometrics resonates with, perhaps draws from that of his teacher, Keynes who expressed himself quite forcefully in his critique of Tinbergen's econometric approach. All this is a far cry from the approach of orthodox schools of mainstream neoclassical economics and associated econometrics practitioners.

Unusually, it is R.C.O. Matthews who approvingly points to Joan Robinson's appreciation of the need for economics to learn from cognate disciplines. "One characteristic of the book [*Accumulation of Capital*, 1956] is the sharply different roles and motivations attributed to different types of economic agents (wage earners, entrepreneurs, rentiers). Joan was hostile to the now more fashionable notion of an undifferentiated utility maximizing economic agent. She held that economic conduct was culturally conditioned. .... This was a fruitful area for exploration, though, as Joan admitted, her own treatment was rudimentary. 'Economic analysis requires to be supplemented by a kind of comparative historical anthropology which is still in its infancy as a scientific study' (Joan in *Accumulation of Capital*, p. 56)" (Matthews, 1989). Joan, of course, was far from being an applied economist, but the breadth of her disciplinary perspective is reflected in these comments on the appropriate conceptualisation of social categories in terms of which economic theory was to be constructed.[32]

Compare this with the assessment of Paul Samuelson's contributions to economics by Assar Lindbeck, the man behind the throne of the Nobel Economics Prize; the occasion was the 1970 award.

> One basic theme in Samuelson's work, perhaps in his *Foundations* in particular, is his demonstration of the unity of methodology and theoretical structure in various fields of economic theory. He showed the basic formal similarity between such diverse areas as production economics, consumer behaviour, international grade, public finance and macro analysis. In most of these fields, maximization

---

[32] In her "Equilibrium versus History" paper in 1974, she argued: "Before we can discuss accumulation, we must go back to the beginning and deal with the questions which Walras and Pigou left unanswered. In what kind of economy is accumulation taking place? Is it Frank Ramsey's classless cooperative, a collection of peasant and artisans, or a modern capitalist nation? Is a property-owning democracy in which the rate of saving depends on the decisions of household? If so, by what means is saving converted into additions to the stock of inputs? Or if investment depends on the decision of industrial firms, how do they get command of finance and what expectations of profits are guiding their plans? Is there a mechanism in the system to ensure growth with continuous full employment? And if an increasing value of capital per man leads to a prospective fall in the rate of profit, do the firms go meekly crawling down a pre-existing production function or do they introduce new techniques that raise output per unit of investment as well as output per man?" (Robinson, J., 1974, p. 10).

(minimization) under constraints and the exploitation of second-order conditions for reaching unambiguous conclusions, were proven fundamentally to play the same analytical role. As in the natural sciences, the logic of *maximization* was proved to be a useful method of analysis, even if there are no obvious behaviour units engaged in conscious maximizing behaviour. … His analysis … may also be regarded as a basis for the later formulations of the theory of economic policy. (Lindbeck, 1970, pp. 343–344)

The position of the orthodox camp is perhaps well captured anecdotally by pulling out a revealing extract in a frank navel-gazing conversation between two reflective members of that lineage: Nick Stern interviewing his close friend Tony Atkinson in 2017 shortly before the latter sadly passed away. Stern confesses: "the testimony of theories of search behaviour and of institutions, which have no content in a perfectly competitive perfectly functioning world, have increasing centrality to understanding how badly we got it wrong before". Atkinson joins in: "Yes. I can remember the lecture given by Jacques Dreze, called 'the firm in general equilibrium theory'. He said, 'How do you get the firm into general equilibrium theory? Well, you blow up a paper bag, and then you puncture it'. And so you let all the air out. The firm has no real existence" (Atkinson & Stern, 2017, p. 14). And you could say the same for the Schultzian farmer assumed to be endowed with perfect foresight, just carrying on being 'poor but efficient', or for that matter for the entrepreneur. By its inherent nature, the basic neoclassical paradigm drives out all space for agents and agency; everyone and everything is on autopilot, driverless, moving inexorably (or rather hopefully) towards the ultimate nirvana of general equilibrium. So, not much existential room there for sociology, or sociologists then practising their humble trade; as Hahn said of papers written in prose—all blah blah.

A candid generic statement of the disdain in which orthodox neoclassical economists hold the other social sciences is provided by American economist, Alan Blinder (1988, p. 118). "We economists proudly distinguish ourselves from the lower social sciences by pointing to our illustrious theoretical heritage. In the economist's world, rational and self-interested people optimize subject to constraints. The resulting decision rules equating 'marginal this' to 'marginal that' lead to supplies and demands, which interact in markets to determine prices. These prices, in turn, guide the allocation of resources and the distribution of income. If not interfered with, markets tend to be highly competitive and have a strong tendency to clear by price. … These are the canons of our faith. They are what gives economics the unity and cohesion that, say, sociology lacks. Rightly or wrongly, they also imbue economists with an imperialistic attitude toward the other social sciences—rather like Kipling's attitude toward India. We have a tight theory; they don't. We should treat the heathen kindly, if condescendingly, while we firmly propagate the faith."

Hahn, of course, accepted the applicability of the 'neoclassical' label to himself (though Joan would have put him in the neo-neoclassical box). "There are three elements in my thinking which may justify it: (1) I am a reductionist in that I attempt to locate explanations in the actions of individual agents; (2) In theorizing about the agent I look for some axioms of rationality; (3) I hold that some notion of equilibrium is required and that the study of equilibrium states is useful" (Hahn, 1984, pp. 1–2). The application of these, and other related postulates, become the basis for Hahn's mission: the "reconstruction ... based on a dynamic theory of general equilibrium that would integrate time, money and growth" (Beaud & Dostaler, 1995, p. 251), as prophesied by him in his "I come as John the Baptist" speech to the Association of University Teachers of Economics (AUTE) congregation in the early 1970s. His was an abstract vision where the inconvenience of historical time and process was eliminated by assumption.

This provides an appropriate backdrop for the reassertion of historical/evolutionary and institutional/sociological dimensions into the frames of analyses arising from broader societal and intellectual vantage points. In sharp contrast to Hahn's three-point reductionist distillation of the world according to neo-classicism, his contemporary Robert Neild offers (much later) his preferred three-point condensation as expounded by the Cambridge sociologist Garry Runciman's (1989) in his evolutionary theory of societal change. "[Runciman] argues that:

1. Society is shaped by the pursuit of power, defined as the ability to influence or dictate the behaviour of other people in one's favour.
2. Power comes in three forms: economic power (which Marx dogmatically said was predominant); persuasive power (from the pulpit to modern media); and coercive power (the threat or use of force).
3. As technology and human ideas evolve, these three types of power change in a manner analogous to the genetic evolution of species: new machines, new weapons, new means of communication and new means of organising society keep changing the way each type of power may be exercised and its strength.

What it implies is that you cannot predict how society is going to evolve because new technological ideas and social ideas evolve as unpredictably as new mutations and recombinations of genes in nature. Just as a biologist may be able to explain after the event, but not before, why a new species found a niche and prospered, so we may be able to say after the event why a new species of power was successful in changing a society" (Neild, 2013, pp. 12–13).

Neild, the eclectic, institutional, practical, short-term Keynesian and long-term Schumpeterian, endorses the approach of Runciman the sociologist: "This theory does not mean that there are no exceptional people who are not driven by a greedy pursuit of power. Nor does it mean that there is no free will or anything like that. Moreover it may be possible to make intelligent short-run predictions when you see that a new species of power is emerging. ... I find this a wonderfully rational, unmoralistic and coherent approach to understanding society."[33] Joan and Nicky might not have yielded as much ground to the ascribed explanatory power of unpredictable evolutionary processes but, with their historically rooted Schumpeterian or Marxian or related approaches, might well have pitched their tents somewhere in this quadrant. Robert Neild (2013) wrote passionately about "Economics in Disgrace", referring to the takeover of the subject by the neoclassical mathematical general equilibrium school à la Hahn, and the consequent huge costs imposed on the world by its adoption in right-wing policy frames in governments and the Bretton Woods institutions. The point to elicit really is that apart from these hard-core neo-neoclassicals, the other groups of Cambridge economists worked within social imaginations and theoretical frameworks which were potentially open to multidisciplinary analysis. Regrettably, and at great cost, that openness was shut down by the cloistered, mono-focal orthodox vision that came to dominate the subject in Cambridge, and beyond. The 'vaguely cognate disciplines' of sociology, history and development studies were systematically exiled or expelled from the reading and staff lists.[34]

Lord Rothschild had sought feedback from a wide range of expertise in the course of his enquiry into the Social Science Research Council (SSRC) in 1982; one of his earliest correspondents was Lord Kaldor. While his three-page missive deals primarily with SSRC and research on economic issues, he does unambiguously convey his disdain for sociological research funded by SSRC. Was money being wisely spent by SSRC? Not so, says Kaldor (1982) citing thoughtless empirical research involving "endless fact-gathering with no clear purpose", mostly by sociologists worrying about "the number of times a week people take a bath or go to the cinema etc."; Tony Giddens had complained that "sociology was sneered at by quite a few of the established people at that time"; some senior scholars expressed "academic scorn for a relatively new subject at Cambridge" (quoted in Grove, 2017); Nicky Kaldor seemed to be providing a caution not to simply conflate heterodoxy with multidisciplinarity.

On the side of the Faculty, there was a basic schism, with most of the heterodox economists being in strong support of the 'new' subject and its practitioners, and most of the hard-nosed neoclassical general equilibrium *wallahs*, led prominently by Frank Hahn, being against this intrusion into their rarefied abstract theoretical space. On the other side of the Austin Robinson building, the DAE economists, perhaps with the exception of just one or two Hahn followers, were both intellectually and institutionally in unambiguous support of the sociologist colleagues and their research projects which in general displayed an active synergy with the applied research of various teams of DAE economists. In fact, these divisions ranged from the DAE staff and the sociology supporters amongst Faculty economists in opposition to the remaining orthodox Faculty economists who tended to be hostile to sociology. Not that all sociologists were iconoclasts, as described by John Barnes in his 1970

---

[33] See also, Neild (2017) where he develops his case for adopting an evolutionary approach.
[34] The three preceding paragraphs are drawn from the opening chapter of the book.

inaugural lecture, but it was obvious that on virtually all institutional issues and struggles between the radical, heterodox groups of economists and the orthodox group led by Hahn, the large majority of the sociologists would stand behind the radical group—and especially in the crucial democratic exercise of electing the members of the all-powerful Faculty Board. In due course, in 1987, this division was to create the conditions for the expulsion of sociology and sociologists from the DAE as one outcome of the University Review of the DAE.

While being heterodox did not automatically imply multidisciplinarity, sociology and sociologists within the economists' family on the whole had lived and worked in a relatively sheltered environment with good measures of respect, resources and representation. But conditions were changing, and not for the better, with rising polarisation and faculty battles between the mainstream orthodox and the heterodox clans in economics, and it became increasingly apparent that there could be serious fallout for sociology and sociologists, depending on which side came out on top; as such, sociology needed a strategy of insurance against future existential risk and institutional uncertainty. On the other side of the coin, Cambridge, as often, presented a sharp contrast to the hostility vis-à-vis sociology in the public spaces of the academic and institutional worlds outside.

10.3 Hostile Public Spaces: SSRC, Rothschild-1982 and Sociology

Three short exposés illustrate the hostility the rising and aspiring discipline of sociology encountered in structured or open public space.

10.3.1 *Entrenched Resistance to the Emergence of SSRC*

After two destructive world wars which together had left virtually no British household and family unscathed by death, disability, deprivation or distress, the 1940s was an era of collective optimism generated by the solidarity of the war efforts ending in 'victory'. Michael Young, the first Chairman of the Social Science Research Council (when it was eventually formed in 1965), reflected: "there were high hopes, even among some normally cautious administrators, about what social sciences should do to illuminate public policy" (ESRC, n.d., p. 4). But the setting up of the SSRC had been an uphill task, pushing against the deadweight of opposition born of preconceived and ill-informed prejudice and hostility, not least from the natural sciences. An early proposal for setting up a social sciences council "was swiftly killed off by one of the ... existing institutions, the Medical Research Council: 'we should have some difficulty in accepting the view that sociology had arrived at such a stage of scientific development that an Advisory Council for Sociological Research could be justified as an official Government body'" (ibid.). Looking back, Lord Moser, a founding member of the SSRC Council, felt that "time and again, rational arguments for establishing a Council encountered a mixture of prejudice coupled with ignorance of what the social sciences were really about" (ibid., p. 5). In 1944, Clement Attlee asked the Cambridge economic historian Sir John Clapham to chair another committee; after two years it reported that social science research was in a poor state and needed more resources, but warned against setting up a separate council for the social sciences citing "a danger of a premature crystallization of spurious orthodoxies"[35] (ibid.). The Lord President of the Council, Herbert Morrison, asked, "What is social science?" (ibid.). Further lobbying met with robust resistance from Lord Hailsham, the succeeding Lord President of the Council in the 1950s who wanted to prioritise funds for the natural sciences, regarding the diversion of resources to the social sciences as wasteful, encouraging a "happy hunting ground for the bogus and the meretricious" (ibid.). Sustained pressure eventually succeeded, with the granting of the Royal Charter to SSRC in October 1965. Twenty years, a generation, of research had been waylaid, if not lost. Robin Matthews chaired the SSRC during 1971–1975; those years, he observed later, "were the last of the SSRC's honeymoon period" (ibid., p. 12). Three research programmes of special note were the History of Population and Social Structure at Cambridge University; the Industrial Relations Research Unit at Warwick University; and the research programme for the study of Transmitted Deprivation which had been initiated after the controversial speech by the Secretary of State for Social Services, Keith Joseph, on intergeneration transmission of deprivation, from deprived parents to their children, and on again; the latter two programmes were to acquire special significance, though in political rather than academic terms, round the corner in 1982, when Joseph launched the Rothschild Enquiry into the Social Science Research Council with what was widely perceived to be an agenda for the closure of the SSRC altogether. In the event, the SSRC was wounded but survived the wide-ranging criticisms levied by Lord Rothschild, even as he recommended its continued existence.

The ESRC retrospective continues (ibid., p. 18):

Howard Newby, Chairman of the Council between 1988 and 1994, argued, however, that not all the results of the Joseph/Rothschild interregnum were

---

[35] L. C. Robbins, R. H. Tawney as members, and T. H. Marshall, Raymond Firth, Chichele Professor of Economic History, Hancock, as those whose views were sought, all supported the idea of the formation of an SSRC. Strikingly, J. R. N. Stone did not: Nicol (2001, p. 12) reports that "Professor J. R. N. Stone, director of the Department of Applied Economics at Cambridge University, mentioned four different approaches, one of which was an agency which would bring together workers outside government and provide funds. It would also direct university research workers to problems. He did not want an SSRC. He argued in favour of something that arose spontaneously from the desires of workers in the field. Funds, he thought, should come from the UGC".

negative. 'Sir Keith Joseph was probably the individual who had the most significant influence on the overall direction of the Council,' he now reflects. 'As a result of the Rothschild Report, the 1980s saw a major shift towards a more empirical orientation which had to be seen as a positive development'. Newby has since pointed to a trend in the 1970s in which British sociology 'moved away from its strengths (and)…indulged in an orgy of theorising, which became ever more speculative and distanced from the real world'. In retrospect, recalls Newby now, the measures arising from the Rothschild Report were probably necessary to sharpen up the Council and, in the long term, make the social sciences more robust.

"Sir Keith Joseph was probably the individual who had the most significant influence on the overall direction of the Council…." One might need to add, for good or for ill.

10.3.2 In the Court of Public Opinion: Open Season on Sociology

Academics, even in Oxbridge, do not live in ivory-tower seclusion; they tend to step into the bustling world of public opinion, media and entertainment—and the 'scholarly' opposition to sociology behind closed doors of committee rooms was often interlaced with the visceral, and mirthful, hostility in the public domain, where brickbats were illiberally thrown from all sides, especially from hecklers in the right-wing galleries.[36]

Julius Gould (1977), then a Sociology Professor at Nottingham University, had come up with a florid 'exposé' of Marxist and radical penetration of higher education in Britain; his earlier career had been at LSE, where, in a comprehensive treatment of LSE Sociology, Husbands (2019, p. 119) states that "his principal later reputation was as a virulent right-wing critic opposing the alleged left-wind penetration of higher education". Gould soon set up a right-wing think tank, Social Affairs Unit, supported by Arthur Seldon who, with Ralph Harris, had been the pioneer of the Institute of Economic Affairs—both with connections with the Mont Pelerin Society; Seldon was also on the Academic Advisory Council of the Bruges Group, a predominantly Conservative Party, avowedly anti-EU super right-wing think tank—with extensive links to the IEA and overlaps with the Mont Pelerin Society—which has the mission, euphemistically speaking, "to promote discussion on the European Union and to advance the education of the public on European affairs" (Wikipedia: Bruges Group [United Kingdom]; see also Platt, 2003, pp. 119–120).

Halsey refers to the Gould Report of 1977 as "a low point", and describes it as

> a scholarly but denunciatory analysis on behalf of the Institute for the Study of Social Conflict (ISC) criticizing Marxist infiltration of sociology as a threat to

---

[36] See, for instance, Sklair (1981); Husbands (1981).

established customs of research and teaching.[37] The BSA [British Sociological Association] responded angrily, and Gould refused to appear before what he doubtless thought was a kangaroo court of Comrades. … the significant underlying fact was that sociology, an increasingly powerful force in both university and society, was simultaneously derided and attacked by both academic and political interests. The 1980s dealt severe blows to the subject. Posts were abolished, postgraduate scholarships were reduced, research resources were impoverished, departments were closed, and the SSRC was wounded and banished to Swindon under a new name. Yet, later, in that decade the demand for student places revived, there was some institutional recovery, some reinvigoration of funded research, and then, in 1992, ironically from a Conservative government, there came the admission of polytechnics and colleges of higher education into the university system, doubling the number of sociology students and staff. It was almost as if adversity had never struck. By the end of the twentieth century, a huge expansion of the British university system had taken place with the additions of the 1990s dwarfing all previous extension and converting the university from the restrictive experience of a highly privileged minority into the normal expectation of a near majority. (Halsey, 2004, pp. 122–123)

John Eldridge, the sociologist, remembers those turbulent days: "what a busy lot we were and for the most part all unpaid labour". He uses the two contemporary novels of Malcolm Bradbury to draw out popular perspectives and prejudices of the times. In *The History Man*, "the anti-hero was a sociologist working in a new university, who was amoral, deceitful and exploitative, skilled in deploying a left-wing vocabulary to achieve his devious ends. The novel became a television series. I was told of a Vice-Chancellor who adjourned a committee meeting to go and watch the latest instalment. True or not, it catches the structure of feeling at the time about the subject and its standing, later amusingly to be portrayed by Maureen Lipman in an advert for BT, when she tells her grandson who has only passed sociology in his exams: 'well at least it's an "ology"'" (Eldridge, 2011).[38]

In 1975, with cruel mirth, had appeared Malcolm Bradbury's *The History Man* on the public stage. "This was after all the year of Margaret Thatcher's election"[39] … and soon "sociologists were to become recurrent characters in Thatcherite demonology. It was from the mid-1970s onwards that sociology

---

[37] The attacks on 'Marxist' sociology were choreographed and orchestrated from the libertarian quarter, involving various right-wing organisations and their leaders, including Brian Crozier at the ISC with links to the Mont Pelerin Society, Le Cercle, the Hoover Institution; David Marsland, a Brunel Professor of Epidemiological research, at the Social Affairs Unit; Digby Anderson, an ordained priest of the Church of England, and founder-director of the Social Affairs Unit, an offshoot of the Institute of Economic Affairs which stood at the core of the rapidly evolving revolutionary right institutional network.

[38] Eldridge (2011) also picks out some words from Bradbury's later satire, *Cuts*: "It was the summer of 1986, and everywhere there were cuts … 'cut' was the most common noun, 'cut' was the most regular verb… they were chopping at the schools, hewing away at the universities, scissoring at the health service, sculpting the hospitals, shutting down operating theatres …".

[39] As Leader of the Conservative Party.

suffered a precipitous fall from grace, particularly in British universities." Bradbury denied responsibility, but there is nothing as destructive of reputations as effective topical satire. "I don't believe novels make that kind of difference", he said, (Rosenthal, 2006) though he was clearly being too modest about his achievements in this regard. The 1970s and 1980s were open season for attacking sociology, with commentators, from vice chancellors to priests to medics to ministers vying for the top prize in wit and sarcasm. A few examples culled from Grimley's (2019) dark-humour account of the times: from a historian: "a detestable and deplorable subject that will destroy any historian who gets involved in it"; another historian: "the 'sociology' more often met with nowadays consists of seeking support for a preconceived notion, usually of a notably shallow type, from selected or invented material. It is the sociology of the paperback and the colour supplement"; Isaiah Berlin, according to Noel Annan, said sociology had produced no single thinker of any significance, "no, not even Weber"; sociology, sociologists and sociology students were all too quickly accused of being the provokers of protest; sociology was the home of Marxist bias that was dripping into the other disciplines; "too many people in charge of the morals of the young have been brainwashed by sociologists"; passing sentence on a group of student radicals in 1972, a judge pronounced, "undoubtedly a warped understanding of sociology has brought you to the state in which you are"; warnings by a senior conservative politician of "the dangerous and demeaning delusion, that man can properly be regarded as raw material for the sociologist to mould as he sees fit", as Grimley comments, "portraying the sociologist as a sort of demonic social engineer"; "Lynda Lee-Potter cited graffiti in the gents' toilets at Liverpool University, where someone had written 'sociology degree, take one' over the toilet paper dispenser"; a philosopher, denigrating modern sociology as "largely a vehicle for mindless statistics and political prejudice", a "sociological liturgy … simply the easy rigmarole of the 'second order' mind which substitutes ready-made concepts for critical understanding"; Terence Miller: "sociology is in about the condition chemistry was when they called it alchemy"; and someone equating degrees in social science to Florida University's degrees in waterskiing. It was the open season, if not decade, in Tony Giddens's words, for "sneering", or in John Eldridge's words, of "casual kicks" aimed at sociology and sociologists, the academic "barbarians".

10.3.3   *The Joseph–Rothschild Assault*

The SSRC drama was staged against two backdrops. First, following the Robbins Report (1963), there was a phenomenal expansion of university education in Britain. A prime beneficiary of this was the new discipline of sociology, where the number of university departments of sociology leapt from seven in 1961 to thirty-four[40] in 1974 (Halsey, 2004, p. 126). Second, shortly after this explosive expansion, there was another abrupt change of direction, as the newly elected Thatcher government launched its deep conservative revolution hallmarked by its programme of cuts in expenditure on welfare and the social sectors, including education and the SSRC.

The new regime was especially hostile to the social sciences, and sociology was particularly singled out for trashing and thrashing.[41] Paul Flather, who had an inside track with Rothschild, recalls: "Keith Joseph had decided that sociology, particularly, but maybe humanities more generally, was too left-wing; … anyway he was convinced it was all a big Marxist plot, and he set up this inquiry, ostensibly to abolish the Social Science Research Council, and he appointed Victor Rothschild to chair it" (Flather, 2019). Rothschild, an eminent natural scientist, had earlier chaired a similar enquiry into the natural sciences, and it was generally expected that he would carry that approach, with the usual anti-social science prejudices popularly ascribed to natural scientists, to his analysis, findings and recommendations. On the whole, Joseph was to be disappointed, since Rothschild came down unequivocally and volubly on the side of protecting the social sciences—but within this plot, he singled out sociology for a lashing.

King (1998, p. 415) argues, on the basis of archival research, that in both the USA and in Britain, "the political context played a key role in the development" of their public funding regimes for social science, the National Science Foundation and the Social Science Research Council, respectively: "the conception of social science institutionalized in these organizations was positivist, that is, it was assumed that social and political phenomena could be studied in a way broadly analogous to the scientific methods of natural science"; … "in each country the need politically to stress the neutrality of social research … produced a bias towards positivist scientific methodology, untempered by ideology".

Lord Rothschild seemed to have reserved much of his withering wit for the new subject and its practitioners. The ESRC review of its first forty years had spoken of "intellectual snobbery" and "hostility"; and Rothschild picked up that negative refrain from where earlier supercilious critics had left it (ESRC, n.d.). "Rothschild threw one-liners to the gallery on sociology and the SSRC's administrative costs and opened the way for the Tories to flog a hobbyhorse in

---

[40] Different commentators provide marginally differing statistics on the expansion of sociology in terms of numbers of departments and staff, but the variations are insignificant in relation to the substantive point about rapid growth.

[41] Of relevance here is Keith Joseph's bruising and dramatic brush with 'sociology' when earlier he was making his bid for the leadership of the Conservative Party, and thereby to be its prime ministerial candidate. He had made a name by focussing on the theme of the intergenerational transmission of deprivation and poverty and the need to break this cycle, a speech that had been well received, but then his bid had gone down in flames when later he translated all this into some kind of a fertility control message that suggested that mothers from such deprived backgrounds lacked the capability to raise families properly, as he saw it. SSRC had funded substantial research on these themes, and the outcome rankled; Joseph's old scars had not fully healed.

the shape of allegedly marxisant SSRC research on industrial relations" (Walker, 2016, p. 46).

A.H. Halsey, a leading and respected sociologist—who had critical views on the treatment of sociology and SSRC, and had unusually been taken off the SSRC Council after serving just one term—provided a reflection and rebuttal to the Rothschild Report. In contrast to other social science disciplines, including social anthropology, sociology got a separate chapter and, in it and elsewhere in the Report, a battering. Halsey (2004, pp. 139–140) questions Rothschild's treatment of his discipline: "the lay reader would gain the impression that sociology was a pretentious mistake now discredited and replaced by more sensible [and in Rothschild's words] 'less ambitious and better established disciplines which are the heirs to the grander claims of sociology—for example, human geography, social psychology and social anthropology'". Halsey rightly protests: "this was a highly tendentious and ill-informed judgement" (ibid., p. 140).

The SSRC "was subjected to a sharp reduction in the flow of cash. The real resources of the Council both for research projects and postgraduate studentships were cut step by step. In 1979 (at 1980 survey prices) the SSRC received just over GBP 20 million; by 1982 it was down by a quarter to GBP 15.2 million. In that year the number of postgraduate student awards for the main social science disciplines was less than one half of what it had been in the mid-1970s. During the 1980s, the SSRC (later ESRC) research budget was halved and the number of doctoral students supported by it fell by 75 per cent. The Council was also urged to direct its activities to problems of the national interest as understood in Whitehall and Westminster" (Halsey, 2004, p. 137).

Specifically, with respect to sociology, Rothschild makes some pointed observations and recommendations. First, he asks for the SSRC's Industrial Relations Research Unit (IRRU) at Warwick University and the Industrial Relations Panel to be formally subjected to an independent enquiry to investigate the allegation of political bias made against the unit by Max Beloff, the right-wing politics professor knighted in 1980 immediately after Thatcher took power, and elevated to Baron the following year. This recommendation was followed up; the charges were found untenable and the IRRU fully exonerated, but not before the two-year process had led to considerable collateral damage to the Unit's research prospects and its researchers' careers. Second, the SSRC was enjoined "not to help establish new departments or sub-departments of sociology, nor finance those which specialists consider to be sub-standard". This recommendation resonates with Rothschild's throwaway comment in his Epilogue to the Report: he asks, without giving an answer: "was the expansion of the Universities in the 1960s so great as to make it impossible to fill all the Departments of Sociology then created with academics of high enough calibre?" (Rothschild, 1982, p. 90).

The occasion of the tabling of the Report in the House of Lords provided further opportunity for mocking sarcasm directed at the worth and ways of sociological research (House of Lords, 1982). Noel Annan, with typical erudition and wit, Michael Young, and Bill Sefton with his hallmark vigour and passion, put up a strong defence of sociology and the SSRC.

Annan: "I think the SSRC was right to support a struggling subject—a subject which has made important contributions to knowledge. It is sociology and the study of society which has transformed historical research. Historical research is now unrecognisable from what it was before the days of Marc Bloch and the great French school which centred round the periodical Annales in the Sixième Section of the Collège de France".[42]

While philistine Thatcherites were predictably haranguing the SSRC for funding research on quaint topics concerning exotic lands and people, or anything that remotely appeared (from the project titles) as being politically radical, Lord Sefton of Garston, son of a Liverpudlian docks capstan driver, reminded the house "of some of the problems which concern the SSRC: crime, poverty, race riots, drug addiction, urban deprivations, unemployment and the state of the economy. If anyone wants a lesson in trying to gauge the necessary amount of resources to meet those problems, I recommend him to go and live in and try to manage a local authority such as Merseyside", said the son and flag-carrier of Merseyside. "We talk about dismembering the Social Science Research Council, or we talk about putting their responses out to the market forces, or carrying out research where somebody finds a need for research and is willing to pay for it. What happens to the young kid in Liverpool who is now glue sniffing? Who pays for the research into that social problem? That can be applied to every social problem that exists. There is no question of applying market forces to the examination of social problems for which the economy is responsible, and for which ultimately the Government are responsible." ... "It will be a crime against the Humanities, against the academic life of this nation, if the academic world in this nation cannot come up with a solution perhaps to reorganise the SSRC into another body, perhaps to rename it, perhaps to give it more resources. But to dismember it will be disloyal to the nation's academic profession and, worse still, disloyal to the nation itself."[43]

---

[42] These post facto esoteric references would have made little impact on Rothschild who, the course of his Enquiry, had sought the learned opinions of, amongst others: Ralf Dahrendorf, W.G. Runciman, R. Illsley, Jean Floud, D.G. Macrae, T.B. Bottomore, Robert Blackburn, Brian Abel-Smith, Raymond Firth, John Barnes, Jack Goody, A.H. Halsey, Edmund Leach, Teodor Shanin, Peter Townsend, Michael Young. Noticeably, Tony Giddens is missing from the list: it could be that his advice was conveyed privately (as in the case of Nicholas Kaldor), or it was sought without receiving a response, or it was not sought—Giddens, at the time, was a lecturer in the Faculty of Economics and Politics in Cambridge, soon to be professor and lead sociology out to an independent existence; noticeably, the list of respondents includes Bob Blackburn, then a research officer at the DAE. The list is biased heavily, perhaps unavoidably, in favour of London and Oxbridge; it remains striking that the extreme strictures that Rothschild places on sociology and departments of sociology should have survived feedback from this elite of the discipline.

[43] This extract overlaps partially with the quotation of Lord Sefton's speech reported in Chap. 7 and is reproduced here for convenience of reference.

These public castigations and humiliations aired in the House of Lords, even though not directly aimed at Cambridge sociology, formed the backdrop when the matter of the continuation of sociology within the DAE came up for consideration at the point when the General Board of the Faculties announced its Enquiry into the Department of Applied Economics in 1984. It would not have been lost on the leadership of the Sociology groups that the high-profile Cambridge Economic Policy Group had been brazenly shut down by SSRC and its associated networks—ominous portents for Cambridge heterodox economics. This would surely have served as an early warning that should Sociology continue to live in the extended family arrangement of Economics and SPS, it could become increasingly vulnerable as its traditional support base, the groups of heterodox economists, itself came under internal attack from the orthodox camp led by Hahn and Matthews (strengthened in 1985 by the arrival of their young recruit Partha Dasgupta), and suffered from external challenges—for funding from ESRC, or hostile treatment in the Research Assessment Exercise—often choreographed by the group.

10.4   Back in Cambridge, 1984–1986: To Remain Or to Exit, That Was the Question

10.4.1   Sociology in the DAE Review: Crossfire and Crossroads

The short five-year period of 1982–1987 arguably marks the second major turning point in the institutional trajectory of Cambridge sociology, and it comprises two interconnected episodes: first, the retirement of John Barnes in 1982 and the appointment of Tony Giddens to the (now permanent) chair in 1985; and second, the two-stage University Review of the DAE which led eventually to the separation of sociology from its long-standing location in the economics home. After floating along quietly for several decades, it entered the rapids, with fast changing circumstances, pushes and pulls from well-wishers and detractors, with the ideological and disciplinary power struggles in economics within a divided faculty impinging on the prospects for sociology, simultaneously posing threats and offering opportunities it could not have contemplated earlier.

In the 1980s, the contiguous domains of SPS—anthropology, archaeology, sociology—entered an unsettled zone of turbulence, both external and internal, with clashes of incompatible energies and emergent perspectives on if, where and how these fields, with their distinct imaginations and structures, could or should combine, or go their own ways. The muddling-through era of lightly managed mutual co-existence and accommodations, minding toes and elbows, of intellectual laissez-faire, had served its purpose, perhaps of ensuring productive survival; but all that had had its day, and kaleidoscopic change was afoot.[44] Cambridge sociology arrived at a crossroads, with the newly promoted

---

[44] Geoff Hawthorn recalls: "SPS in the middle years was not easy and there was a moment in the late eighties when I would have gone to Harvard"; he didn't, and stayed in SPS and Cambridge,

Tony Giddens in command of his band, including the eager and the reluctant, directing traffic, piloting a safe passage through the minefields of the warring tribes of economics.

What was the fight about? Amongst themselves, the economists were engaged in their perennial power struggle between the orthodox neoclassical and the multiple lineages of heterodox economics. The outcome of these battles had implications for the prospects for sociology and sociologists, as practised in the Faculty of Economics in terms of teaching, and in the DAE, in terms of research. The clash could justifiably be viewed as reflecting the divergent intrinsic value systems associated with the orthodox and heterodox schools, with the former dismissing sociology as irrelevant for economics, and the latter seeing intrinsic intellectual merit in the multidisciplinarity afforded by the presence of sociology and sociologists in the midst of economics and economists. Be it as it may, it was also possible to read the contestation in terms of the arithmetic of political control in the Faculty, through coming out on top in the elections to the Faculty Board. This provided an additional, perhaps dominant, dimension to the game; the positions taken by the rival groups of economists were perhaps driven more by their own tribal interests than by pure solidarity in helping the sociologist colleagues with their own agendas. The sociologists, though internally conflicted, generally wanted an alliance with heterodox economics, but such a course was not risk-free. They could see that the tide was turning in favour of the orthodox gang winning the Faculty wars, which would potentially make life for sociology and sociologists uncomfortable, if they chose to remain with economics. And, while acknowledging and appreciating all the support they had received within the Faculty and DAE from their heterodox colleagues, the sociologists nevertheless wanted to strike out for an independent space of their own; and in this venture, Giddens would not have wanted his plans for sociology to be corralled by Faculty decision-making, especially if the Board was controlled by the orthodox camp. It is revealing to see all these and other considerations become visible in the Review process: the testimonies and exhortations from the different groups and from individual staff make for intense reading and throw fresh light not just on how sociology as a subject, and the sociologists as scholars, were viewed and valued, but also on the playing out of hidden agendas and strategies to achieve the unstated ultimate objective of the orthodox camp, viz., to gain control of the Faculty Board by expelling the group of sociologists that usually and overwhelmingly supported the radical, heterodox side in Faculty decision-making.[45]

Matters came to a head with the sudden arrival of the Review of the DAE by the General Board in 1984. The terms of reference for the Review were not set

though for personal reasons, and "was very glad I did because things got better". He spent some time in the early 1970s in Harvard, soon after the Harvard Khanna demography-population-fertility study and the critique by Mamdani—something he taught on when there.

[45] The number of sociologists, scattered across institutional locations, could add up to around 10, and Brendan Burchell remembers the two-line whip and arm twisting to ensure they duly turned up at key Faculty Board votes—to side with the heterodox group.

after consultation with the DAE, or with the Faculty Board, though it was widely acknowledged that the two senior professors of the orthodox camp had been the key instigators of the Review and had critical inputs into the agenda of the Review. Thus, 'Item Seven' of the terms of reference was pointedly addressed to the question of the desirability of the continuation of sociology within the DAE. This opened wide the door for debate, and potentially for departure; the Review of 1984–1987 was therefore a fateful event in the life of Cambridge sociology. The three-person DAE Review Committee, appointed by the General Board of the Faculties of the University in 1984, declared itself to be unfit to adjudge on this aspect (and other substantive discipline-related issues concerning economics), and an enlarged committee, also including David Lockwood as the sociology expert, subsequently reported and recommended that the sociologist group of the DAE should be relocated, along with their financial allocations and claims, to join their other sociologist colleagues in the already existing SPS sub-Faculty which functioned autonomously under the institutional umbrella of the Faculty of Economics.

10.4.2 *Cometh the Hour, Cometh ... Tony Giddens*

Sociology and SPS had been under the charge of John Barnes, the sole professor for the field even in the absence of a conventional department. There were sociologists both in the Faculty and in the DAE where Robert Martin (Bob) Blackburn[46] was the head of sociological research. There was a change of guard after Barnes retired in 1982, and Tony Giddens took over the chair, in 1985,

---

[46] Bob Blackburn graduated in Maths and Philosophy at Cambridge, then spent two years doing National Service in Army as electronic engineer; followed by another two years at Cadbury with a Qualified Certificate of Industrial Administration (some social science but no sociology). He taught maths, stats and some philosophy in Liverpool in the Social Science Department. He says he "found Sociology interesting, and so learnt it—the only person to be taught sociology in the Mersey tunnel—my colleagues Joe and Olive Banks used to give me a lift home which took a long time in the traffic for the tunnel and I learn a lot by listening to them, then later joining in". Bob was later appointed to a lectureship; and then when the big expansion occurred after the Robbins Report, "John Goldthorpe sent me particulars of the DAE Directorship of sociology, for which I reluctantly applied. I was also offered a chair in one of the new Departments, which I might have been wise to accept, but I chose Cambridge. The post I applied for was Director of Sociological Research but at the interview I was told it was not yet approved by University and I was quite young, so I would be SRO for 2 years then be Director. It never happened.

While in DAE I published 5 books, introduced CAMSIS scale with colleagues Prandy and Stewart—the first measure to demonstrate the occupational hierarchy, and extensively used internationally—, proved that the Gini coefficient was simply Somers' D and so able to obtain vertical and horizontal components, proved that the Index of Dissimilarity (previously measured with a term for each occupation) was just a difference of proportions in a 2 by 2 table, proved that other popular measures of Segregation were differences in the same table distorted by inappropriate weightings, established that the Marginal Matching measure, which I had previously introduced for education, could be effectively used for other subjects. I list this selection just to show I had been active.

The DAE economists took up my case and suggested a professorship. The result was I was given the title Head of Sociological Research with no rise in salary. Senior Research Officer was the highest anyone could achieve in the DAE. Towards the end I was so fed up with treatment of DAE that

and its demanding responsibilities. The status of the professorship was also changed from a one-tenure appointment (as was done for Barnes) to the first permanent chair of sociology.

SPS was clearly a contested space between, and even within, diverse tribes; agreement could be elusive and impermanent. John Barnes passed away in 2010, and his close ally Geoff Hawthorn wrote a fine appreciation of the man and the academic in 2011, where he looks back on the early days, and the decades seemed not to have softened the cutting edge of the knife. Obviously, though not explicitly, alluding to Tony Giddens, he starts his memorial piece on John Barnes thus:

> "The man who succeeded John Barnes in the chair of sociology at Cambridge claimed that it was he who had established Social and Political Sciences in the University (Boynton, 1997). As Barnes himself had observed, conception and the reckoning of descent are often in question and genealogies of fatherhood more vulnerable than many to 'structural amnesia'. A truer history of Social and Political Sciences would reveal that it was conceived by many in the course of the 1960s and when it emerged in 1968, weak and imperfectly formed, was to be claimed and disclaimed by many. A genealogist might claim that Barnes marked the institutional fatherhood of sociology itself in the University. He was elected, in agnatic caution, for one tenure only—by a committee on which as he put it no 'card-carrying' sociologist served (Barnes, 2007, p. 377)". "Barnes himself remarked that there would never be an adequate history of social anthropology in Britain or Australia, where he had worked before, until libel laws were repealed.[47] So will it be for a history of sociology" (Hawthorn, 2011, p. 35).[48]

Born in 1938, Tony Giddens took a first degree at Hull, the first in his family to have gone to university; did a Masters at LSE with a dissertation supervised by David Lockwood, on Sport and Contemporary Society, stimulated perhaps by virtue of being a dedicated supporter of Tottenham Hotspur, his local club; moved to a lectureship at Leicester with Ilya Neustadt and Norbert

---

I became a tutor in Clare College. Anything I suggested at Clare was accepted positively, in contrast to the University attitude."

Later, after the relocation from Economics, Blackburn was in contention for heading the unit, but as he says, "the move to SPS became another battle after Giddens left, and I lost". (Personal communication, Emails dated 18 and 30 March 2020). See also 34n44 below for references to his book publications.

[47] "For an example of dry, donnish humour, subscribers to the *Australian Anthropological Newsletter* [Barnes, 1986] can read John's tongue-in-cheek, postprandial address to Churchill college fellow in 1984. 'Where lies the truth?' tells how he became a professor of sociology in Cambridge despite a lack of qualifications; it plays upon his ignorance of Latin, despite having taken the school certificate examination no fewer that five times without gaining a credit" (Young, M. Y., Young, 2011, p. 10). Barnes was an acknowledged expert on the study of lying, and authored the widely read book, "Who Should Know What".

[48] Incidentally, the 22 boxes containing the Faculty Board Papers for the 1968–2011 period, part of the Archives of the Faculty of Social and Political Sciences held at the Cambridge University Library, are closed to scholars for a period of 80 years from the date of creation; the unusual length of the period of embargo speaks for itself.

Elias as seniors; then to a lectureship in sociology in the Faculty of Economics and Politics at Cambridge University and a fellowship at King's College; and was promoted, after 14 years as a lecturer, to a readership in 1984,[49] but then almost immediately to Professor of Sociology in Cambridge in 1985,[50] following the retirement in 1982 of John Barnes, the first holder of the chair since 1969, when it had been created as a single-tenure position. Tony Giddens had been prolific in his publications and was visionary in his ambitions for his discipline. On assuming the leadership of Cambridge sociology in this tumultuous period, Giddens's perspectives for the discipline, within Cambridge and beyond, were extensively featured in *Network*, the newsletter of the British Sociological Association, and his blueprint is clear.

> He sees his main task at Cambridge to be the establishment of a Part I Tripos in Social and Political Sciences, so as to allow students to read for a full degree in sociology, but he is nevertheless enthusiastic about the interdisciplinary context of sociology teaching at Cambridge. He argues that this encourages students to develop a view of social theory in its broadest sense, and he hopes to build greater links with the Faculty of Archaeology and Anthropology, were Ernest Gellner has recently been appointed as Professor. He is especially keen to see further collaboration between economics and sociology, particularly through the key 'Sociology of Economic Life' lecture course. The primary advantage of gaining a Part I in SPS, however, is that it would give teachers of SPS a greater degree of control over entry to the degree, allowing them greater flexibility in the planning and continuity of courses. SPS currently recruits many students who 'discover' it after their arrival at Cambridge, and King's is one of the few colleges to actively recruit undergraduates wishing to specialise in sociology. [51]The other task which Giddens sees as priority is to 'establish a presence for empirical social research' at Cambridge, building on the success of the Department of Applied Economics, and he hopes to see the creation of a Research Centre for the study of industrial societies. Cambridge must, he argues, move firmly into the centre of developments in the discipline: 'Oxford and Cambridge must play a leading role in the further development of sociology', and should become the twin pillars of the sociological mainstream. Giddens believes strongly that it is necessary to 'enhance the visibility of Oxbridge sociology'. (Network, 1985a)

---

[49] Robert Boynton (1997) in interviewing Tony Giddens after his appointment as the Director of the LSE reports on a remark with a touch of dark humour by Ajit Singh, Chief Whip and political commissar of the radical younger cohort of Cambridge economists, and a close friend of Tony Giddens: "Tony and I had a contest for who could be passed over the greater number of times"; in the end, Ajit won the contest at a canter—Tony, was made a Reader on his tenth consideration over a 14-year period, 1970–1984, but Ajit remained a lecturer for 23 years, from 1968 to 1991; there was a price to pay for challenging orthodoxy.

[50] The same year, Sandy Stewart, a sociologist in the DAE, was appointed Professor and Head of Department at Edinburgh University; at DAE he had been working jointly with Bob Blackburn and Ken Prandy on research projects on social stratification (Network, 1985a).

[51] On Brendan Burchell's recollection, with the establishment of the full Tripos, numbers increased explosively from around 60 in Part II to a total of around 300, all to be handled initially with the same staff strength; the expansion could then be used strategically in institutional negotiations by Tony Giddens.

There is a clear indication that Giddens intended to combine the parallel tracks of the theoretically oriented sociologists (epitomised by Giddens himself) in the Faculty, with the strong and sustained research of the empirically oriented sociologists led by Bob Blackburn in the DAE. On the one side, Giddens explored developed critical analytical perspectives, with major theoretical departures, focussing on the current phase of modernity and its possibilities, risks and dangers both at a global and at the British level; on the other, Blackburn and his research collaborators were accumulating a substantial body of empirical sociological research on work, workers and the working class, on labour, employment, gender occupational segregation, trade unions, and social class analysis, viewed frequently through a gendered prism and using a diverse set of methodologies ranging from traditional interviewing on the factory floor, explorations of working class ideologies, to quantitative techniques using the DAE's skills in computing for the work on measuring class structures, and to the stability and reproduction of social and structural inequality.[52] There was clearly a strong interface with the team of DAE (and Faculty) researchers who focussed on similar themes within an applied political economy framework. Put together, these groups formed a formidable resource, with a significant creative potential for cross-discipline and cross-method exchanges (see Table 10). What is striking is that apart from the odd exceptional initiative, the body of research focussed almost exclusively on Britain. Worth noting also is the fact that the first four (of the six) volumes published in the book series *Cambridge Studies in Sociology* were all authored by the group of sociologists in the DAE.

The imperative to raise the visibility and profile of Oxbridge sociology led to another far-sighted initiative: unfazed by the contraction in the academic book market, Giddens, together with David Held and John Thompson, co-founded Polity Press, now a flourishing enterprise, and the outlet for many of his books.

> Polity Press was launched towards the end of 1984 as a self-proclaimed innovative venture in social science publishing. The company has already established a reputation for the quality of its output, and plans to publish 200 books by 1990. ... Although its policy is to concentrate on the higher education market, a number of books from a broad left perspective will appear in its lists ... a major target for Polity is the market for student textbooks—Tony Giddens sees this not simply as good financial sense, but also as a way of defending the social sciences and supporting social science teaching in schools and colleges. (Network, 1985b)[53]

---

[52] See, for instance: Stewart et al. (1973); Stewart and Blackburn (1975); Blackburn and Stewart (1977); Blackburn and Mann (1979); Stewart et al. (1980); Prandy et al. (1982); Prandy et al. (1983).

[53] "What makes the venture unique is its corporate structure as a joint venture between an established publisher and a group of social scientists. Tony Giddens, David Held, and John Thompson are the owners and directors of Polity Press, based in Cambridge, and are jointly responsible for the assessment and commissioning of books for publication. The technical and financial side of book production and marketing are handled by the old-established family firm of Basil Blackwell ... and the corporate structure ensures that all decisions on which books to publish are taken by the academics themselves. Initial publications by Polity include some books transferred from the Blackwell

This move by Giddens to proactively create a secure publishing space with intellectual affinity resonates with the formation of the *Cambridge Journal of Economics* in 1977 by a group of forward-looking radical economists, including his friend Ajit Singh. The initiative provided an intellectual and publishing space relatively free from the potentially thwarting prejudices of mainstream traditionalists who looked askance at rising sociological imagination, paralleling the motivation for the launching of the *CJE*.

In the space of just a few years, Tony Giddens had visibly emerged as a major force in sociology: he had risen from a lecturer in 1983 to the holder of the Cambridge sociology chair in 1985; shrewdly set up the forward-looking, vertically-integrating label of Polity Press, not least catering to the explosive expansion of sociology teaching in the universities in the previous 20 years; and in 1984 had published his *The Constitution of Society: Outline of the Theory of Structuration*, a major intellectual contribution that was likely to "be regarded as the most important piece of grand sociological theory in English of the past decade", according to Mark Poster, "taking its place alongside such major statements of sociological theory as those of Parsons and Habermas".

Alongside this, external events were shaking up the institutional lie of the field of sociology, in Cambridge and beyond. The Joseph-Thatcher hostility to the social sciences, often singling out leftist sociology and Keynesianism with a finger pointing in the Cambridge direction, had led to the Rothschild Enquiry into the SSRC in 1982, the Report of which had been especially critical of the state of sociological teaching and research in general in the UK. And after a period rife with unsettling rumours, the University of Cambridge had taken the unusual step of launching a review into the Department of Applied Economics, one of the long-standing homes of sociological research, within a multidisciplinary, applied environment in Cambridge. In 1981, the new government had also terminated its funding of the Development diploma; and in 1982, the SSRC had abruptly discontinued its regular grant to the high-profile Godley-Cripps CEPG team in DAE—moves that had further unsettled the institutional environment of the social sciences in Cambridge. The portents could be regarded as threatening, but the imminent and immanent crises also offered the proverbial opportunity to trigger change. Cometh the hour, cometh Tony Giddens, the man who guided Cambridge sociology through this crucial phase to forming an independent academic and institutional identity in the university.

Sociology came to be taught from the Faculty of Economics & Politics by a group led by Tony Giddens, later (at the time of separation from the Faculty)

---

list and others which were originally edited by Giddens. Its policy is to publish major works of social science for higher education, both new books and translations of foreign editions ... special series in Feminist Perspectives, Human Geography and Political Economy. Plans ... include an ... involvement in the humanities and history" (Network, 1985b).

including Geoff Ingham, Ray Jobling,[54] Gavin Mackenzie, John Thompson[55] and Cathie Marsh.[56] Under his leadership the sociologists of the Faculty formed

[54] Ray Jobling's research on the sociology of medicine is remarkable, in that it treats his own lifelong experience of the condition of psoriasis as the focus and field of his sociological analysis. His professional and human sense of his work is best conveyed in his own words. "My understanding, such as it is, rests on nearly 50 years of having and treating psoriasis and over 30 years of involvement in The Psoriasis Association. Psoriasis is characterised by extended chronicity. It affects around 2% of the population and decades of continuous daily treatment are a not uncommon experience. Psoriasis patients encounter *breakthrough* after *breakthrough*, with fanfare and loud promise ending ultimately in disappointment. It is a challenging and frustrating disease, with only rarely risk to life but an insidious potential for damage to self-esteem, nagging anticipated threat of social rejection and debilitating distracting impairment of well-being and quality of life. Psoriasis patients are frequently reminded that they are not 'ill'. Whatever the intended meaning, they can be nonetheless 'ill at ease'" (Jobling, 2005, p. 53). "Living with psoriasis is a lifetime experience. The lack of a cure combines with a peculiar public response of disinterest if not prejudice and stigmatization. Various factors account for changes in quality of life measures that seem independent from disease severity and effectiveness of treatment. Merging a qualitative and individual case analysis with assessment of quality of life would represent a direction for future studies" (Jobling & Naldi, 2006, p. 1438). Jobling, and with 25 others, has converted such perspectives into a policy framework for the EU for dealing with the systematic treatment of psoriasis vulgaris (Jobling et al., 2015).

[55] John Thompson was a student under Tony Giddens, and the influence of the teacher was evident in the presentations made by both at the celebratory symposium in 2018 marking the 50th Anniversary of the formal arrival of sociology in Cambridge. Starting with his early work, Thompson has focussed primarily on the sociology of mass communications and culture, introducing questions about ideology into the frame (Thompson, 1991); amongst other themes, he has also drawn attention to the "shifting boundaries of public and private life which have become a new battleground in modern societies, a contested terrain where individuals and organizations wage a new kind of information war, a terrain where established relations of power can be challenged and disrupted, lives damaged and reputations sometimes lost" (Thompson, 2011), and has carried this analysis into the public and political domains (Thompson, 1993, 2005). John Thompson became the head when the new Department of Sociology was created, and in this sense inherited the mantle of Giddens.

[56] The career of the gifted sociologist-statistician Cathie Marsh was cut short by a tragically early death in 1993 aged 42. Like Jill Rubery, she left Cambridge for Manchester, though primarily for family considerations. At the Faculty and the SPS, her interests and publication displayed an enormous spectrum, held together essentially by her interest and expertise statistics and quantitative methods applied to social-science questions. She laid down key markers for her future work in her early questioning of the SSRC in closing down its Survey Unit. "It may seem untimely to start worrying about the philosophical basis of survey research at a time when the main difficulty facing any of us is most probably getting cash to do the research at all. However, perhaps for that very reason, arguments, which are declaring that survey research is after all perhaps not on a very sound epistemological footing are gaining currency; I was forced to reflect hard on the process of decision-making in large-scale organisations when the S.S.R.C. suddenly discovered in 1975, when funds were beginning to dry up, that it had changed its mind on the importance of survey research and decided to close the S.S.R.C. Survey Unit. Many of those arguments and arguments since have made vague references to unease about survey research as a method applicable to producing sociological theory, and some of them I think touch chords in all of us when we consider what contributions to sociological theory have actually been made by survey research" (Marsh, 1979). In another epistemological turn, she explored "the effect of opinion polls on public opinion" (Marsh, 1985),

a cohesive group, perhaps not least because several of their numbers had the shared identity of having started their careers in Leicester under the watch of Ilya Neustadt and Norbert Elias. Giddens and Mackenzie put together a festschrift for the legendary teacher and mentor, with 13 contributions; notably, of this group, Giddens, Goldthorpe, Ingham and Mackenzie all later held appointments in the Sociology group in Cambridge, and to this could be added T. H. Marshall (Hon. D. Litt. Leicester 1970), and Mehboob Ali Rattansi who was supervised by Tony Giddens for his PhD. "The outstanding feature of what may be called the legacy of Leicester is undoubtedly the remarkably high proportion of teachers of sociology in British universities whose careers in sociology began in Neustadt's Department in Leicester. … It is a familiar part of the academic landscape, and it was achieved in just over 30 years, starting from scratch. The reputation of the department has been not only a British one, but an international one" (Giddens & Mackenzie, 1982, p. xv). Neustadt became the Head of Department in 1959, and Professor in 1962, thus predating the launch of the chair in Sociology at Cambridge by several years. In his warm homage to Neustadt, Giddens writes: "from his very first years at Leicester, Neustadt drew to him some of the ablest students in the university; many were to go on to distinguished careers in academic life and outside"—and this would surely apply to Giddens himself. "Sociology in his view is the core social science; its concepts and findings are relevant to all the others. Studying sociology is far more than just receiving an education in a particular vocational area, it is a quest for social understanding that at the same time demands self-interrogation; learning sociology means looking at one's own life with new eyes" (Giddens, 2011). The reflexivity inherent in the search for an overarching vision again is perhaps evocative of Giddens's own approach.[57]

At SPS as well, Giddens had (evolved) around him a like-minded group of staff. Brendan Burchell, who joined as a sociologist on the ESRC multidisciplinary project in the midst of the DAE Review when some of the significant

---

inspired perhaps by Keynes's pithy aside that "Americans are apt to be unduly interested in what average opinion believes average opinion to be". A joint piece with her colleague Brendan Burchell explores the serious, but generally side-tracked, methodological issue of "the effect of questionnaire length on survey response" (Burchell & Marsh, 1992); in other joint contributions, citing the example of European countries, a case is made for the release samples of anonymized records from the population census, and arguing that "the potential benefits from census microdata are large and that the risks in terms of disclosure are very small" (Marsh and 7 others, 1991; Skinner et al., 1994); with L. Giorgi (Giorgi & Marsh, 1990), she turned her attention on the data sets of the European Value Survey to test the central contention that a consensual Protestant work ethic, work values and understandings of the meaning of work, underlie modern industrial societies; and with Robin Blackburn, on a reassessment of the working of the 1944 Education Act. She wrote two influential books, *The Survey Method* (Marsh, 1982) and *Exploring Data* (Marsh, 1988, Marsh & Elliot 2nd. ed., 2008). She became an ad hominem professor in Manchester in 1992; the computing room in the HSPS Faculty was named after her, as also the Cathie Marsh Institute for Social Research at the University of Manchester.

[57] Goodwin and Hughes (2011) provide an insightful exploration of the Neustadt-Elias equation and the development of sociology at Leicester.

teams of DAE were beginning to wind down, recalls the absence of conviviality over tea in the staff room when SPS was located in the old Cavendish Laboratory—of Rutherford fame—and the contrast after it moved to its premises in Jesus Lane, where there were a strong coffee culture and lunch group meetings as had been the practice in the DAE. The SPS group numbered about ten, it was cohesive and informal; Tony Giddens was part of the group; Brendan says, "we all felt like round-table equals" (personal communication).

But outside these groups, not everyone seemed to be on board the ship with Giddens as skipper, and not everyone liked the fare served at its table, and some would have steered to other destinations if they had been at the wheel. Over the 14 years that he had (been) held (to) the rank of lecturer, Tony Giddens had been steadily accumulating an international reputation; the readership came in 1984, and the chair the following year. But not all were overjoyed. Robert Boynton (1997) put it thus: "Some of his colleagues disliked the interdisciplinary nature of his work and thought it thin and unduly broad, while others resented what they perceived to be his undeserved renown. ... he [had] edged out the presumed favorite candidate, Geoffrey Hawthorn, for the newly established permanent chair in sociology. Following Giddens's appointment, Hawthorn (1986) published an essay in the *London Review of Books* attacking his work as 'unusually disappointing ... simply a bland rehearsal of what others have been saying for twenty years.' Another prominent sociologist accused Giddens of 'purveying trendy waffle.' Many speculated that part of Giddens's motivation in establishing the S.P.S. Faculty, which he did that same year, was a desire to find a more congenial base for himself at Cambridge. He spent the next twelve years reconciling the ancient institution to the new discipline. The skill with which he did so helped improve his relations with some of his colleagues."

Nor did Hawthorn, or those for whom he spoke, accept the imaginary that Giddens had for the discipline. "We need a popular name for the kind of political theory that is emerging now. There was communism, socialism, capitalism, Thatcherism, and we have something else now. It boils down to 'a theory of social justice and individualism in the context of the global market society', but we need a shorter name. Perhaps an acronym? I'll have to think about that" (Giddens, in Boynton, 1997). That was the field Giddens had been seeding and growing all along from the 1980s.

But a bruised Geoff Hawthorn went public with a damning commentary implicitly, but not so indirectly, on the Cambridge decision "to take the conservative turn" in appointing Anthony Giddens as the new professor of sociology after John Barnes: "in refusing institutionally to reconsider the relation between the newer sorts of philosophical conversation and a social theory which might interest us; in insisting on the sharp separation of sociology from anthropology; and by implication insisting also on its super-ordinate relation to politics, it is set to re-invent misunderstanding and ensure sterility." Hawthorn doesn't stop there and moves from the institutional to the personal. "Social theorists are understandably perplexed. Are they still trying to represent social reality, or not? Some are. The failure of the old historical schemes has even prompted a few into an intellectually more orthodox reappraisal of the long run. Some are not. They just play. And some cannot make up their minds. Thus Giddens. He rejects 'objectivism' and 'naturalism' and all the other constraining old 'isms'. He will have nothing to do with laws or even with generalisations about people. Generalisations, he says—is this one exempt?—can always in principle be subverted by those they are generalisations about. He nevertheless dislikes disputes and avoids the more subversive of the Modernists' claims. He simply distils the common denominator; ... His equivocation is accordingly complete. ... In fact, Giddens is interesting merely because in trying at this desperate an unilluminating level of abstraction both to hold onto history and to deny it, both to talk of all the world and to talk of a world which is only talk, he reveals the dilemma into which general social theory has now precipitated itself. It is caught between a nostalgia for the old search for certainties across all time and space and the Modernists' cheerful rejection of that search; and as a result, it has come to haunt a nether world of nearly nothing" (Hawthorn, 1986).

Looking back on those charged episodes of the professorial appointment, Bob Blackburn, his friend Tony Giddens's counterpart heading the team of applied or empirical sociologists on the DAE side of the building, recollects: "Giddens and I thought we were the two main candidates and agreed to stay on and support the other if we lost. We saw Tony as the favourite but not a certain winner. In fact, Hawthorn, who firmly declared he was not a sociologist, applied. He had friends on the appointing committee and almost won. I think that would have been a disaster and a shock to people outside Cambridge. Happily, Tony won". But, evidently, there were mutineers on board his ship.

10.5 Archival Insights: Harboured Preferences Revealed

10.5.1 *Do Please Stay, Pleaded the Heterodox*

An independent external opinion from John Goldthorpe, writing from Nuffield College, Oxford, sees strong advantages in the continuation of empirical sociological research within DAE, and "were it to cease, I would foresee damaging consequences for the teaching of sociology at Cambridge, especially within SPS ... Already the content of this teaching tends to be insufficiently research-based, creating the impression that sociology is the product merely of writing books rather than of the conduct of some form of inquiry"; he goes on to emphasise the importance and the high potential of interdisciplinary academic collaboration: "research projects carried out in the department on ostensibly 'economic' issues would in many cases benefit if they were designed to have a sociological dimension, and if economists and sociologists could work on these projects alongside each other", and he singles out the labour market, industrial relations and employment groups as having high potential and rewards in this regard (John H. Goldthorpe to K.J.R. Edwards, Letter dated 3 October 1985; UA GB 859.426, p. 2).

Strong support, on intellectual grounds, comes from others, including Jobling, who cites the mutual value-addition through the collaboration of economists and sociologists, across the Faculty-DAE divide, in both teaching and research projects, including instances where such collaboration is explicitly mandated by the ESRC, all this leading him to speak of "a unity of perspectives across traditional disciplinary differences", creating the "distinctive Cambridge contribution and 'slant'"; he hastens to add that "none of this diminishes of course the contribution made by sociologists working in SPS, Engineering, Education" (Ray Jobling to K.J.R. Edwards, Letter dated 7 September 1985; UA GB DAE Review 983–985, p. 1).

Willy Brown, the newly appointed Montague Professor of Industrial Relations, whose work was centred on some of these themes, worries that should sociology move, 'it would make it considerably more difficult for me to develop my own subject there'. But the basis of his vehement support is not personal: "I should be very sorry if the DAE were to lose its distinguished sociological tradition. It would deny Cambridge economics one of its most distinctive and important features. Defensive demarcation lines between the social sciences are a major obstacle to originality in most other universities. For the DAE the tradition of eclecticism has been particularly valuable to the development of policy-oriented research, where a sensitivity to more than one discipline is almost always important. Multi-disciplinarity does not come from committee or external imposition but from the opportunity for specialists in different disciplines to meet informally, day-by-day, and to chew over their current pre-occupations. The opportunity to do this in the excellent and lively DAE common room is a thing to be treasured" (Willy Brown to K.J.R. Edwards, Letter dated 2 October 1985).

Firm confirmation comes from Frank Wilkinson about the multidisciplinary nature of the participation of the DAE labour team in the ESRC's Social Change and Economic Life initiative where "the collaboration between sociology, social psychology and economics is a feature of research at each level. It is worth saying the Cambridge team is by far the most integrated of any of the six teams participating in the Initiative. This I attribute in large measure to past co-operation fostered by the important part played by sociology in the teaching and research of the Faculty" (Frank Wilkinson to K.J.R. Edwards, Letter dated 24 March 1986; UA GB DAE Review).

A progressive heterodox economist's view comes from Tony Lawson who had direct experience in both the DAE as a researcher and in the Faculty as teaching staff: "I recommend most strongly to the committee that the 'sociological' research be maintained and encouraged in the DAE. Economics can only suffer if such interdisciplinary possibilities as exist are not maintained. Indeed, I wish they could be extended" (Tony Lawson to K.J.R. Edwards, Letter dated 14 October 1985; UA GB.858.119, p. 2).

In his response, when interviewed, Ajit Singh offers his support: "He [Ajit Singh] told us [the Review Committee] that the standing of the DAE in the outside world e.g. USA, is as high now as ever it was under Reddaway and that the sociological work in the Department also has a high reputation outside Cambridge" (Notes of Meeting of the General Board's Committee to Review the Department of Applied Economics, 29 November 1984; the Notes are dated 4 December 1984, and refer to the interviews with Frank Hahn, Robert Rowthorn and Ajit Singh).

In another strongly argued and worded letter, the representative of the Faculty of Economics on the SPS Committee, John Wells, first castigates the General Board: "I presume that raising this issue corresponds to the frequently heard wish amongst orthodox economists to 'get rid of the sociologists', in the hope that this might also have a favourable effect for them for the distribution of power". He goes on: "most orthodox economists feel that sociological issues are extraneous to the study of economic issues. This is clearly absurd. ... If economists and others had a better appreciation of the peculiar character of the British class structure and of the particular social and political institutions to which it gave rise, then Britain's post-war economic performance may well have been stronger". He argues for increasing the role of sociologists and sociology in the Faculty, "by getting economists to spell out the implications of most of their policy prescriptions for specific groups in society. Perhaps, in this way, we might avoid the present climate of confrontation in our country, which must surely be damaging to its long-run development" (J.W. Wells to K.J.R. Edwards, Letter dated 14 November 1985; UA GB DAE Review 983–985, p. 4).

10.5.2 *Clear Out Now, Growled the Orthodox*

Unsurprisingly, the orthodox neoclassical camp has a distinctly contrasting view: in the collective response of seven signatories to a letter to the General Board, they declare: "it seems to us anomalous for the D.A.E. to include a group of sociologists as it does at present, and in the long term the obvious solution is for this group to be transferred to S.P.S. to form the core of a research group there taking some of the University's current financial contribution to the D.A.E. with them" (Frank Hahn, Margaret Bray, J.S.S. Edwards, Partha Dasgupta, A.W. Peterson, David Newbery, Timothy Kehoe, Letter to the General Board; DAE Paper 28; UA DAE Review Box 983, p. 3).

In a similar vein, R.C.O. Matthews ends his nine-page submission to the General Board with his reflection on Item 7 on Sociology. "Sociology was first introduced into Cambridge within the Economics Faculty, as Professor Lockwood and Sir Kenneth Berrill [Matthews is directly addressing two key members of the Advisory Committee] will recall. It was natural, therefore, at that time that sociological research should take place in the DAE. The situation has now changed. Sociology now has another home, admittedly not an ideal one, in SPS. It would therefore be appropriate for DAE Sociology research to be transferred to SPS as well. I believe this would be in the interests of both economics and sociology. DAE sociology is always likely to have an unsatisfactory position and so command a low priority in competition for resources. This would not, of course, preclude the occasional appointment of sociologists as members of interdisciplinary groups within the DAE. It would be reasonable if such a shift to SPS of sociological research at present in the DAE were accompanied by a 'dowry', in the form of a transfer to SPS of a proportion of the annual allocations that would otherwise have come to the DAE and possibly also a transfer of a the DAE's accumulated resources" (R.C.O. Matthews to K.J.R. Edwards, DAE Review, September 1985, p. 9).

The imagery used by Matthews portrays him with the mantle of the patronising father, handing over the bride, and a bribe, in the form of a dowry. There is a subliminal glimpse of hierarchical superiority and subordination, a fleeting flash of the implicit gendering of disciplines: economics as alpha male, sociology following meekly a few steps behind; such hierarchies seem imprinted on the disciplinary DNA of mainstream economics and examples are easily on view elsewhere, whether at the Delhi School of Economics, or the London School of Economics. Multidisciplinarity was not invited, not welcome and to be escorted out if it did somehow gate-crash into the exclusive club of mainstream neoclassical economics.

And David Newbery, in words sounding somewhat supercilious, adds to the orthodox case for showing sociology the door: "It is also unclear why stray colleagues in vaguely cognate disciplines should be members of the electorate. There is a powerful case for excluding sociologists who are members of SPS, for reasons not dissimilar to that for excluding the DAE" (David Newbery, Note to K.J.R. Edwards, 1985, DAE Review).

10.5.3 *Do What Is Best for You, Whispered the Faculty Board*

Set against the force of such argument the submission of the Faculty of Economics seems anaemic, tentative and defensive. It rightly reaffirms the great value of interdisciplinarity and provides strong evidence of cross-border partnerships of high quality within the DAE and between DAE and Faculty sociologists—something of great value not just to cherish but also to sustain. But then, in what can only be interpreted as a friendly gesture towards the sociologists, it allowed them to negotiate their own position without interference or opposition from the Faculty Board where the heterodox group were obviously distinctly unhappy to see them go.

It would appear that the orthodox camp was pushing the sociologists against an open door. What mattered in the end were the collective views of the two groups of sociologists, that is, those in the DAE (led by Bob Blackburn) and those in the SPS group (led by Tony Giddens) within the Faculty of Economics. Also of relevance would be the position taken by the Faculty Board of Economics (which prominently included Ajit Singh and Bob Rowthorn): in the end, this Board left the matter open, saying that it should be considered separately from the other issues pertaining to the DAE per se. But this was hardly likely to happen, since Item Seven of the terms of reference of the DAE Review Committee explicitly sought an answer to this question, which in any case had been postponed from the first stage of the University's review to the second, when the advisory committee would be strengthened explicitly with expertise to deal with this issue. In taking such a position of ambivalence, if not silence, on this matter, the Faculty effectively ruled itself out of this conversation, thereby removing all opposition to the departure of the DAE sociologists and their relocation within SPS. The force of expediency made strange bedfellows of the conservatively oriented economists and the more radically inclined sociologists: the orthodox economists wanted the sociologists out of sight from Sidgwick Site, and so, for their own reasons, did the sociologists themselves—greener pastures beckoned, and they had a shepherd with the considerable skills and vision of Tony Giddens.

10.5.4 Time to Choose: The Sociologists Speak

The ball was finally in the court of the sociologists themselves, and they dutifully and beautifully fell into a collective line, led by their creative leader, Tony Giddens, the newly appointed Professor of Sociology. The writing was on the wall in large characters. The group of DAE sociologists write a joint letter expressing full support for the position taken by Giddens; and, in a joint letter of their own, so do the sociologists within the Faculty of Economics;[58] with alacrity, the SPS Committee underscores its agreement, and Tony Giddens sums it all up in his purposeful statement to the General Board.

More appropriate than the bridal imagery of Robin Matthews would be that of a young woman, if sociology is indeed gendered female, leaving after living (even if not entirely) alone in the parental home to find a room or field, a space, of her own, where she could exercise independent choice over her domestic arrangements, her preferences for alliances and partnerships—single or multiple, sequential or simultaneous, for life ahead; the bride called sociology wanted to control the body of her own discipline. Life had not been bad in the parental home; economics had been patriarchal but not overbearingly so, and economics and sociology did bridge their disciplinary divides and construct specific shared spaces. However, it would have become apparent that there was an existential threat forming from the emerging dominance of the neoclassical camp which had no time or space—even literally, as there was an acute shortage of rooms—for those they variously labelled as being 'vaguely cognate

---

[58] Joint Letter from five sociologists to K.J.R. Edwards, dated 11 April 1986; UA GB DAE Review, Paper 53. "We, the sociology lecturers in the Faculty of Economics, wish to indicate our support for the establishment of a social research unit as proposed by our colleagues in the DAE and Professor Giddens. We understand that the sociology section of the DAE would form the new unit attached to SPS, and that we would have the same access to the unit as we do at present to the DAE. In our view, a social research unit, provided it is adequately endowed will help to extend the University's achievements in the field of social research and further enhance its reputation."

disciplines', an 'anomalous' presence, 'an historical relic'. Differently, the separation could be viewed as a secession arising from the assertion of the right to self-determination; sociology became its own country, with its own new President, Tony Giddens, who assembled and guided the bands of sociologists and their fellow travellers, scattered, like Kurds, across various Faculty, Department and Committee boundaries, into one viable critical mass. Giddens needed no lessons in the value of multidisciplinarity, but he was also acutely aware that even though the past had been good, the future could become much worse within the Economics formation, and would be far better and more secure in an independent department outside it. That could also provide a more equal institutional platform for developing cross-disciplinary alliances and initiatives. Thus, while the heterodox economists were genuinely sorry to see the sociologists go, the orthodox camp was thoroughly pleased; and the sociologists themselves picked up their scattered baggage and left, even if willingly and voluntarily, some with heavy hearts.[59]

Tony Giddens pulls it all together, lays out a crystal-clear vision and strategic plan, sets the tone for the change, and eventually has the last word in his statement to the General Board of 27 March 1986. He pays unqualified tribute to the "extraordinarily high" quality of the research of the DAE sociologists who "have an established international reputation based on formidable research work"; "a move to SPS would not in any way inhibit either intellectual or practical connections with research in economics"; but that said, "the opportunities for fruitful interchange with colleagues in the social sciences [read SPS] would be considerably expanded within SPS, since the number of overlapping interests and competences is considerably greater"; so "the optimum solution for the DAE sociologists is to move across to SPS to form a social research unit"; "this would greatly strengthen the research side of SPS and contribute services to members of SPS staff"; "a social research unit would be much more 'visible' to outside fund-granting bodies than would the current set-up of the sociologists in the DAE" where "being a small group in a much larger entity … has hampered their chances of obtaining research funding". Giddens further asserts that in institutional terms, SPS is "already developed and autonomous"; and he places all this crucially within the frame of the "need to centralise both teaching and research in the social sciences in the University … which has the potential to become a major force in this area, but rationalisation of existing

---

[59] Bob Blackburn observes that the DAE sociologists had good relations with DAE Directors: "Stone was no longer Director, however he was friendly; Reddaway was his usual self, efficient and reasonably friendly; I don't think Godley was interested in sociology but not hostile and accepted us as part of the DAE; I forget the name who followed Godley, but had the impression he was hostile." There were many reasons for wanting to leave—questions of finance, of participation in decision-making, recognition and isolation; while acknowledging these, Bob adds: "relations with DAE economists were good and friendly, and I think that applies to all sociologists. While projects were run by project teams (sociology by sociologists etc) we talked regularly and could ask advice when it was relevant; … the DAE economists were good friends. I did not know they wrote supporting our staying (or do not remember) but I am not at all surprised. They were the only reason for not wanting to go" (Personal communication; email dated 18 February 2020).

resources is needed to achieve this". Financially, it was already virtually agreed, amongst other finer points, that DAE sociologists could carry across their pro rata share of the pot of resources given by the University, and Giddens even points to availability of rooms in the Free School Lane SPS site. And the new social research unit within SPS, absorbing the DAE sociologists, would be a vital step in this direction. He points out that "there are still anomalies to do with the institutional structure of SPS", implying that it does not have the status of an independent Department—which is clearly what Giddens has within his sights. And an independent Department of Sociology indeed came into existence down the line.

In his first response to the General Board in the course of the first phase of the DAE Review, Bob Blackburn, the head of the sociological unit within the DAE, noticeably avoids any comment on substantive academic issues and limits himself to the organisational, resource and decision-making implications of being a small group of sociologists in a large department of applied economists (R.M. Blackburn to D.E.C. Yale, Letter dated 4 December 1984; UA DAE Review, p. 3). However, this stance, aimed at negotiating better terms for the continuity of sociologists within the DAE, was soon to change. Within a year, when the matter is placed before the second phase of the DAE Review, there is distinct and dramatic shift in the position of the sociologists.

The Committee also sought advice from external experts. John Goldthorpe,[60] writing from Nuffield College, Oxford, points out that his association with the DAE ended in 1970, and his feedback to the Review Committee was based on "a fairly thorough knowledge" of the published work of the three main sociologists, Blackburn, Prandy and Stewart, and "some acquaintance" with that of the group of economists in the Labour Studies Group, viz., Rubery, Tarling and Wilkinson. The letter pays several backhanded compliments, and while offering qualified support providing ample ammunition to defend, or to question, DAE sociology and sociologists, depending on the proclivity of the recipient of the feedback. The academic work of the sociologists was of "a relatively high technical standard"—though with "some curious decisions about sampling"; "in the context of present-day British sociology ... to be reckoned as not inconsiderable merits"—"but my ultimate response to this work is a sense of opportunity missed". They "should have produced better monographs than they have"; he sees "the immediate source of this failure to realise the full potential of their research as lying in their preoccupation with establishing a distinctive 'theoretical' position of their own and with demonstrating faults in what they took to be the positions of almost everybody else. This has entailed much contorted ... and impenetrable argument ...; and this leads into the assessment that "these shortcomings might have been less had these researchers worked under more confident leadership, been more ready to engage in discussion with others' work in similar fields, especially within the international sociological community. But in fact, they have given the impression of being a

---

[60] Goldthorpe, J. Letter to K.J.R. Edwards, dated 3 October 1985.

rather introverted group, unduly anxious about the possibility of criticism". Goldthorpe "doubt[s] the wisdom of going on as now, with a small sociology programme that is more of less isolated from the mainstream of the Department's concerns"; "I suspect that some of the less attractive features of the work of the sociologists ... have arisen from their sense of insecurity, of at least of their marginality, with the Department and in turn within the University at large". But all said, Goldthorpe supports the idea of sociological research in the DAE, though "under stronger leadership and with some new blood". Responding explicitly to "Item vii"—about the desirability of the continuation of sociological research within the DAE—Goldthorpe points out that "there is no other centre in the University ... in which empirical sociological research has become established ... according to the standards of technical competence that generally prevail in the Department"; closure, then, would have "damaging consequences for the teaching of sociology at Cambridge, especially within the SPS". And then comes a sting in the tail: "already, in my view, the content of this teaching tends to be insufficiently research-based, creating the impression that sociology is the product merely of writing books rather that of the conduct of some form of inquiry". (Giddens, the prodigious book-writer, had incidentally been appointed professor of sociology in Cambridge in the same year.) He ends with a call for great interdisciplinary collaboration between sociologists and economists working jointly in teams, as successfully demonstrated by initiatives on the Continent. Qualified and finely balanced as these comments are, it is not difficult to read the subliminal messages between Goldthorpe's lines.

However, the fast-moving game was moving on apace. In a Note from SPS to the DAE Review dated 25 October 1985 (DAE Paper 19 [55 801]), it is clear from both the orientation and the content that the sociologists expect a relocation: it emphasises and lists the "extremely good" research work publications "which would rank amongst the best in British sociology", of the DAE sociologists (prominently including the work of Tony Giddens); it highlights the SPS teaching contributions and plans for a Tripos reform enabling "the teaching of sociology in the University as a whole"; it asks for the status of the DAE researcher sociologists to be protected in any move; and also significantly, draws attention, with examples, to "the clear connections between economics and sociology" within the DAE and asserts that "the Committee [SPS] is anxious that the continuation of the such interdisciplinary collaboration should not be inhibited by any changes in the existing form of the Department [DAE] which the Review Committee might make".

Bob Blackburn and the other DAE sociologists write in strong support for the formation of a social research unit within SPS, to which the DAE researchers would be transferred. "Professor Giddens, we know, shares essentially the same views, but will be writing to you separately". The letter is almost entirely devoted to detailing the institutional, financial and logistical arrangements necessary for such a transfer. But there is also a nuanced statement which hints at a significant change in orientation: the unit "would help to foster interdisciplinary cooperation between the disciplines of SPS; at the same time we would hope to keep close links with the DAE" (R.M. Blackburn, B. Burchell, D. Lovatt, K. Prandy, Letter to K.J.R. Edwards, dated 2 April 1986).

It is interesting to note that Blackburn's first letter to the Review Committee of Stage I was concerned entirely with matters of logistics and appropriate representation of the small sociologist group within the DAE as was; a second note from him to the Review Committee of Stage II simply asks the Review Committee to refer to his earlier note. Then comes this joint letter, which is cast in an entirely different frame, viz., one that is virtually predicated upon the acceptance of a breakaway from DAE. Part of the explanation lay perhaps in the appointment, in the interim, of Giddens to the sociology professorship in 1985; but according to Bob Blackburn, it was due primarily to the hostility faced by the DAE in general and DAE sociology in particular.

So, when, in 1984–1986, the time came and the key question of separation and divorce was posed, the sociologists with Tony Giddens as their leader, after a good deal of individual and collective rumination, came down clearly as a group in favour of an amicable divorce. One reason, entirely justifiable, was that the sociologists in DAE were structurally dominated by the economists, simply by virtue of the wide differential in the size of the two groups, whether in the DAE or in the Faculty of Economics. But another major pull factor was that sociology was plainly on the move in Cambridge, and so the disciplinary clan needed to mass together to achieve critical mass—size mattered in all kinds of dimensions that would influence the claim to become a separate academic unit altogether. Their economist colleagues of the DAE believed in dynamic economies of scale and scope in industrial production—and the argument held here in knowledge production as well. It is significant to read through the evidence in the archives: even as sociologists opt out, there is little recrimination or rancour against the DAE or its economists; it is just that they have outgrown the parental home, and need to move on and set up on their own homestead in Cambridge and the world beyond; and in Tony Giddens they had the catalysing visionary and ambitious leader who saw and wished it, and could make it happen. What lay ahead to be negotiated was a virtual spaghetti junction of established and embryonic disciplines: sociologists of the DAE, the SPS with anthropology, social anthropology, archaeology, development economics and development studies—all entered the zone of lane changes, made choices, with varying degrees of freedom or coercion, of directions, partners and co-habiting arrangements; and thus emerged, at the other end, a new configuration of social science disciplines lodged in various department and faculties, based on an amalgam of institutional expediency and academic affinity, all leavened with personal traits of the prime movers and committee decision makers. Sociologists of the DAE and of the SPS sub-Faculty within the Faculty of Economics assembled under their disciplinary standard, and under the skilful navigation of Tony Giddens, eventually attained their desired status as the new Department of

Sociology in 2004.[61] The spaghetti junction had released powerful latent centrifugal tendencies as well: the academic composition of the traditional social/anthropologists was framed by intrinsic curiosities over the stationary social grammars of tribes and castes and 'others' such, though slow incremental change was admissible; in contrast, the youthful sociological imaginary was dominated by the immediacy and imperatives of rapid kaleidoscopic change in modern industrial societies in the post-war era. Surely the two were not separable worlds, and the twain could certainly have met, in courses and committees, under more congenial circumstances. As it happened, they each went their own way—Sociology became an energetic Department in its own right; Anthropology and Archaeology kept its status; and Economics, to the delight of the orthodox camp and the dismay of those of heterodox persuasions, sanskritised and took a step towards its purification by expelling an alien genetic strain from its imagined pure DNA. Trampled underfoot on the spaghetti junction was the original, albeit hazy, vision of interdisciplinarity—that project of the past was now jostled into the future.

And then we have from Geoff Hawthorn, speaking freely in 2009, one insider's view of the dramatic changes in the course of sociology and related disciplines in the 1980s, a swirling period of 'all change'. The central player in this perhaps was Tony Giddens, and from a distance after the dust has long settled, Geoff provides a clear and frank reflection on the significance and impact of Tony Giddens.

> There was nobody else around who could have done what Tony Giddens did; tremendous confidence, managerial energy, will and determination to get something done; I was very nervous about doing what he did when he did it as I didn't think we had the resources; he took the view that he had to introduce a Part I and try to extend the number of students because that was the only way to get more money; meanwhile the load on the staff was terribly heavy; we disagreed about that; also thought that in contrast to Barnes and Goody, Tony wasn't a very liberal character; it still seems to me that Cambridge flourished because it tolerates intellectual heterogeneity; it hires clever people and lets them do what they want to do; for Tony the corollary of giving a faculty an institutional identity was disciplinary distinctiveness; what that meant was that a particular vision of sociology was given pre-eminence over politics and social psychology, and there was no connection with anthropology because he wasn't interested in it; I didn't think that it was right for this place, but at the same time I can see its practical point; it made the University sit up, made the Schools acknowledge its existence, but I think quite a high price was paid for it; what Tony did bringing it together in this way caused the later explosion that led into separating departments as there were too many of us who were not happy to be corralled in this way. (Hawthorn, 2009)

---

[61] Tony Giddens, meanwhile, had left Cambridge in 1997 to become the Director of the London School of Economics.

Underlying these institutional reconstitutions, there were deeper intellectual currents, and Hawthorn sounds rueful about the way sociology has gone, about the path not taken.[62] He confesses:

> I have had a problem with sociology all the time; when I came into sociology I was attracted by ethnographies of British society, ... seemed to be terrific that sociology was going to say what life was like in Britain. [But] sociology had two other sets of ambitions: one was to be a generalizing science, and Tony was something of that; the other was to agonize about a distinctive method, ... I had been employed to teach it and completely lost my faith in it. I think that the subject got distracted by these two dispositions—obsession with method and the desire to be a synthetic science—and lost its ethnographic impulse; where are the ethnographies of modern Britain? They exist in novels, and some work by anthropologists or social historians ... Cambridge is a very abstracted university and inclines people much more to theory ... where there is a temptation to very high levels of excessively generalizing abstraction, and this has been a bad environment for sociology; this is just one view and many people would say I never really was a sociologist anyway, and perhaps I wasn't; this great hope of the sixties, nowhere is it on the intellectual front line; psychology has moved into the study of neurology, philosophy has broadened out and has become interesting again, anthropology keeps finding a new life for itself, the study of history keeps renewing itself, English has broadened into cultural studies—these subjects are alive, where has sociology gone?—nowhere really. At Harvard [also], the professionals were moving in and wanted more methodologists and theorists, and the subject was being killed. (ibid.)

This is a powerful indictment of the modernising direction taken by sociology as the discipline of studying contemporary modernisation. Hawthorn would like to feel more the fresh breath of a breadth of vision, a deeper digging into things historical, of honest analytical narration, of a reflective experiential basis for theories, in lieu of grand sociological theorising; he would clearly prefer osmosis seeping and creeping through fuzzy permeable porous boundaries

---

[62] Borrowing a phrase from Emma Rothschild, the creative connector of the past, present and future. "I was sheltering from the rain in a shop doorway when Emma Rothschild also took shelter; she asked what I was doing and encouraged me to read Thucydides; I read him and it was a complete transformation, ... an extraordinary book, at last I was reading something that wrote about politics as they should be written about; then I thought it could be the basis of an undergraduate course ... so perhaps one should take the radical view of how to educate them in the second year, and so [I decided that] instead of doing a survey course in the Michaelmas term, they should all just read Thucydides; they were in a state of shock because firstly the whole reason they were doing the course was to understand what was happening in Iraq tomorrow, and secondly it was one whole, old book; it turned out to be an enormous pedagogical success and the course became very popular; they loved the book, thought about it, wrote well about it ... that is where I am at now; I taught it until I retired and I am now writing a book about Thucydides" (Hawthorn, 2009). Well done, Emma; and well done, Geoff, is what one might wish to say. 'Iraq' probably still dominates the students' imagination. What Hawthorn conveys is the value, indeed, the imperative, of visa-free travels and crossings, chasing curiosities across increasingly gated disciplinary boundaries. Hawthorn's *Thucydides on Politics* was published in 2014 (Hawthorn, 2014).

instead of the drive for hard borders artificially defining separate identities for what really were intrinsically co-habiting, contiguous subjects; he would wish for less disciplined disciplines. But all this would undermine any institutional ambition to have a separate department of sociology, or anthropology, or archaeology, or politics .... So, at the end, the key question re-emerges: should the old loose and fuzzy SPS type of construction have continued? Perhaps Giddens's thinking might have been that crossing boundaries would not be ruled out by the existence of boundaries, and that subterranean boundaries did exist even within the superficially open space of SPS. It remains true that specialisation is the new pathway, and this calls for definitive 'core courses' and 'methodologies and epistemologies' and 'evidential bases' that set the identity of each 'subject'; the secret perhaps lies more in the art of the practice of the profession than in descriptions in the curriculum. Be it as it may, over the course of growing up over a quarter-century in the foster home surrounded by economists, sociology and sociologists registered strong contributions both in terms of 'grand theorising' and 'honest empiricism'—both traditions well established and much appreciated within Cambridge heterodox economics; they carved out a viable and productive space for the discipline and its practitioners on both sides of the Austin Robinson Building, in terms of teaching in the Faculty, and in research within the DAE.

10.6 Leaving Home, a Space of Its Own

At the end of the day, the net outcome was that SPS and sociology walked out, pushed along the way by the group of orthodox economists, from both the Faculty of Economics and the Department of Applied Economics. Whatever commensality arrangements and co-habiting relations might have evolved in the New Cambridge departmental and faculty organograms of sociology, anthropology, archaeology, politics, international politics, land economy and development studies, it is clear that regular economics was not at the table; and the loss of a serious integrating component, if not a spinal scaffolding, of political economy could only have weakened their respective intellectual projects. On the other side, the loss of these co-habiting intellectual partners would make economics in its orthodox incarnation, even more reductionist, more blinkered, more useless. The original multidisciplinary vision of a combined home for an extended family—economics, politics, sociology and economic history—had run its course with a centrifugal breaking up and spinning off into nuclear 'disciplinary' organisational identities.

As the holder of the first permanent chair in sociology in Cambridge, Giddens "bulldozed his way through Cambridge's byzantine bureaucracy to establish the Social and Political Sciences Faculty and became its first Chairman" (Boynton, 1997)—terms that Giddens himself used in his allusion to his experience of the institutional establishment of sociology. In 1986 the SPS Committee became a fully-fledged Faculty of Social and Political Sciences with its own Tripos, offering a one-year Part I and a two-year Part II. As Brendan

Burchell recalled, student numbers jumped about fivefold; the SS Sociology had raised anchor. The subsequent evolution of sociology in Cambridge is a series of twists and turns, of separations and mergers, like an ambitious, conflicted, fostered youngster struggling to find independent space, a quest realised eventually in January 2004, when another vigorous spin of the centrifuge saw further breakdowns of the molecular structure of the complex physical compound into its constituent elements, and the SPS Faculty was formally divided into three separate Departments: archaeology (physical); social anthropology and sociology which now had a space of its own.

The three-some became a four-some with the addition, in 2009, of the new Department of Politics and International Studies (POLIS),[63] and the four (alongside several others) together constituted the new formation of the Faculty of Human, Social and Political Sciences. From 2011, POLIS included several Area Studies Centres, and in 2012, the Centre for Development Studies was formally established within POLIS. The swirling vortex had now deposited its payload on *terra firma*. Complex formations and magnetic polarities, with their frictions and fissions, had been sorted out and all reduced to constituent elements. Perhaps it was all too much to manage internally and called for the expert agency of an externally visible hand. 'Professor William Brown, the Montague Burton Professor of Industrial Relations at the University of Cambridge and Master of Darwin College was appointed the external Chair of our Faculty Board. The Faculty is delighted to note that Professor Brown was awarded a CBE in the Queens' Honours List. Professor Brown, a member of the ACAS Panel of Arbitrators, is well qualified to head the Faculty through a time of governance change and stringent budgets.'[64] There was now a Department of Sociology, on its own and no nonsense; a Department of Archaeology, including biological anthropology; a Department of Social Anthropology, on its own; a new Department of International Politics and International Studies; individual centres of international/regional studies were housed in POLIS space, including most prominently, the Centre of Development Studies from 2012.

---

[63] As in sociology, even before the department was formed, there was a chair in international politics, with Geoffrey Hawthorn as its occupant. Having started in the ranks as a lecturer in sociology in 1970, he was promoted to a personal chair in 1998: "the question was what do I call myself; John Dunn insisted that I shouldn't call myself professor of politics, but I was no longer a sociologist; so decided on 'international politics' but then realized that if I called myself Professor of International Politics I needed to know something about the subject; simultaneously with this, the educational structure of SPS was changing … I then went home and hurriedly read some textbooks; Cambridge is wonderfully indulgent; … I have been so lucky as every fancy that has taken me, Cambridge seems to have said yes to…" (Hawthorn, 2009). In his obituary for Geoffrey Hawthorn, Stefan Collini (2016) writes: "it is thanks to him more than to any other individual that Cambridge now boasts a flourishing Department of Politics and International Studies". POLIS, as it is known, is also now the institutional home of Cambridge Development Studies. (On some prehistory of sociology and political science at Cambridge in the 1920s, see Bulmer, 1981.)

[64] SPS Faculty Annual Report 2002–2003, p. 3.

The centrifugal process had started from 1986, and by 2014, one needed an organogram and a city map to navigate between the various units and sub-units of the new human, social and political sciences formation—which seems generously to include everything, barring the core discipline of political economy. Sociology left its economics home after living (not quite) alone for four decades; be it as it may, 'economics' had purified itself, and sociology had defined itself as a field of its own. There were advantages no doubt to such independence and specialisation; the collateral damage was the project of multidisciplinarity centred around political economy as a core discipline. Not all sociologists were pleased, and nor were all economists displeased; especially amongst the economists, there were sharp differences, and the orthodox neoclassical group was pushing its undeclared agenda to expel the intellectual impurity of sociology, and to expel the left-oriented sociologists from the college of voters in the Faculty Board, and thereby tilt the electoral balance and control over the Faculty decision-making process in its favour. How, and why, did Sociology come to leave its original home located in Cambridge economics in the 1980s? Was this a 'victim' being turfed out, or was it the exercise of 'agency', a unilateral declaration of independence?]

Disciplining 'purity' and purging 'impurity' are well entrenched in the grammar of some theoretical traditions in sociology, and the idea of mingling and rubbing shoulders at home and abroad with all and sundry from other disciplines might not have been a prospect that appealed to all sociologists, whether in the intellectual or institutional domain. Sociologists are arguably no more committed to the greater project of multidisciplinary research than any other social science. This existential ambivalence, or duality, is readable in its statement of identity on its web page: 'While Cambridge sociology has always existed within an interdisciplinary context, it has also maintained a distinctive profile as a centre of excellence for outstanding work in social theory and empirical sociological research'.[65]

Runciman complained bitterly about sociology being made to exist within a troika alongside anthropology and economics, and his stance is readily understandable from the vantage point of a discipline—deemed embryonic by its castigators but mature by its practitioners—that has not been allowed an independent identity. Subsequent evolution of the social sciences in Cambridge, however, confirm the atrophy of multidisciplinarity, with each discipline sanskritising and marking its intellectual and institutional boundaries through language and labels emphasising differences between one another, all dancing around the vacant central space of political economy—Hamlet without the prince, or social sciences without the queen. But at the end of the day, perhaps the biggest loss of potential value was for the Faculty of Economics, though that might not have been their own view. Through the expulsion of 'othered' strains and traditions of economics and social sciences, the brand of orthodox economics preached in the Faculty became increasingly monocultural,

---

[65] See: https://www.sociology.cam.ac.uk/about.

inward-looking and inbred, eliminating the interrogations and challenges that might have come from other constructions of society and economy, through shared courses, research projects, or common rooms. In this sense, paradoxically, it now became more easily possible to restore a sense of multidisciplinarity on the periphery to which the 'others' had been despatched, say within Development Studies (housed in POLIS) through the inclusion of political economy in the staff teaching and research profiles, coupled with regular academic transactions with sociology, anthropology, politics and international studies. Viewed from such a vantage point, the loser was mainstream economics; but this species of economists was of a shared conviction that through these expulsions, they had cleansed their heaven of impurities.

Thus, over the 1980s, at the epicentre that was the Faculty of Economics and Politics, the purges of 'others' and the orthodox purification rituals of sanskritisation proceeded apace: at the Department of Applied Economics, post-Keynesian macroeconomic quantitative analysis expunged with a return to the chosen orthodox microeconomic path; and then the DAE terminated in toto in 2003; sociology and sociologists were waved goodbye from the DAE and from the Faculty; heterodox economics and economists were squeezed out by an application of the RAE penal code—itself devised by the head priests of orthodoxy; development economics and development studies were roughed up and pulled out to the periphery, the natural habitat matching their intellectual concerns; economic history, once a feather in the DAE cap, was made history; the offending word 'politics', a reminder of the bad old days, was deleted from the name of the Faculty; and the banner of the republic of 1662 hoisted up again in a new promised land of disciplinary purity, of a single faith, of orthodox neoclassical economics. Over a century ago Marshall had pronounced that sociology was 'premature' by 100 years; now, his neoclassical descendants, from the Cambridge side of the parental line, seemed still be of the same retrogressive view, set on repeating history. Counterfactuals get no one anywhere, though it is tempting to speculate on possible future pathways for sociology, economics and the social sciences in the Faculty and the DAE had the heterodox clans been able to retain and assert their intellectual imaginations and institutional strategies.

References

Annan, N. (1983, February 3). How should a gent behave? *New York Review of Books.* https://www.nybooks.com/articles/1983/02/03/how-should-a-gent-behave/?pagination=false

Arena, R. (2006). *On the relation between economics and sociology: Marshall and Schumpeter.* https://www.lib.hit-u.ac.jp/service/tenji/amjas/Arena.pdf

Aspers, P. (2006). The economic sociology of Alfred Marshall: An overview. *American Journal of Economics and Sociology, 58*(4), 651–667.

Atkinson, A. B., & Stern, N. (2017). Tony Atkinson on poverty, inequality, and public policy: The work and life of a great economist. *Annual Review of Economics, 9,* 1–20. https://doi.org/10.1146/annurev-economics-110216-100949

Barnard, A. (2011). John Arundel Barnes, 1918–2010. *Proceedings of the British Academy, 172*, 27–45.
Barnes, J. (1970). *Sociology in Cambridge: An inaugural lecture*. Cambridge University Press.
Barnes, J. (1983). *Interview of John Barnes by Jack Goody, Cambridge 19 December 1983*. Filmed and edited by Alan Macfarlane and Sarah Harrison. http://www.alanmacfarlane.com/DO/filmshow/barnes1_fast.htm
Barnes, J. A. (1986). Where lies the truth? *Australian Anthropological Society Newsletter, 64*, 4–9.
Barnes, J. A. (2007). *Humping my drum: A memoir*.https://www.amazon.com/Humping-my-drum-J-Barnes/dp/1409204006
Barnes, J. A. (2011). Sociology in Cambridge: An inaugural lecture. *Cambridge Journal of Anthropology, 29*, Special Issue in Memory of John Barnes, 45–60.
Beaud, M., & Dostaler, G. (1995). *Economic thought since Keynes: A history and dictionary of major economists*. Routledge.
Blackburn, R. M., & Mann, M. (1979). *The working class in the labour market* (Cambridge studies in sociology) (Vol. 1). Palgrave Macmillan.
Blackburn, R. M., & Stewart, A. (1977, September). Women, work and the class structure. *New Society*.
Blinder, A. S. (1988). The fall and rise of Keynesian economics. *Economic Record, 64*(4, December), 278–294.
Boynton, R. (1997). *The two Tonys: A profile of LSE's Anthony Giddens*. https://www.robertboynton.com/articleDisplay.php?article_id=41
Bulmer, M. (1981). Sociology and political science at Cambridge in the 1920s: An opportunity missed and an opportunity taken. *The Cambridge Review, CII*(22623, April 29), 156–159.
Bulmer, M. (1982). Support for sociology in the 1920s: The Laura Spelman Rockefeller memorial and the beginnings of modern, large-scale, sociological research in the university. *The American Sociologist, 17*, 185–192.
Bulmer, M. (1984). Philanthropic foundations and the development of the social sciences in the early twentieth century: A reply to Donald Fisher. *Sociology, 18*(4), 572–579.
Bulmer, M. (1985). The development of sociology and of empirical social research in Britain. In M. Bulmer (Ed.), *Essays on the history of British sociological research* (pp. 3–36). Cambridge University Press.
Burchell, B., & Marsh, C. (1992). The effect of questionnaire length on survey response. *Quality and Quantity, 26*, 233–244.
Collini, S. (2016, January 17). Obituary: Geoffrey Hawthorn. *The Guardian*.
Dennis, N., Henriques, F., & Slaughter, C. (1956). *Coal is our life: An analysis of a Yorkshire mining community*. Eyre & Spottiswoode.
Downes, D. (Ed.). (1992). *Unravelling criminal justice: Eleven British studies*. Macmillan.
Drewnowski, J. (1974). *On measuring and planning the quality of life*. Institute of Social Studies and Mouton.
Eldridge, J. (2011). Half-remembrance of things past: Critics and cuts of old. *Sociological Research Online, 16*(3), 20. http://www.socresonline.org.uk/16/3/20.html
ESRC. (n.d.). *SSRC/ESRC: The first forty years*. ESRC. https://esrc.ukri.org/files/news-events-and-publications/publications/ssrc-and-esrc-the-first-forty-years/

Fisher, D. (1980). American philanthropy and the social sciences in Britain, 1919–1939: The reproduction of a conservative ideology. *The Sociological Review, 28*, 297–315.

Fisher, D. (1983). The role of philanthropic foundations in the reproduction and production of hegemony: Rockefeller Foundations and the social sciences. *Sociology, 17*(2), 206–233.

Fisher, D. (1984). Philanthropic foundations and the social sciences: A response to Martin Bulmer. *Sociology, 18*(4), 580–587.

Flather, P. (2019, January 9). *Paul Flather interviewed by Alan Macfarlane.* https://www.sms.cam.ac.uk/media/3058954

Giddens, A. (2011, October 22). Obituary: Professor Ilya Neustadt. *The Independent.* https://www.independent.co.uk/news/people/obituary-professor-ilya-neustadt-1473958.html

Giddens, A., & Mackenzie, G. (Eds.). (1982). *Social class and the division of labour: Essays in honour of Ilya Neustadt.* Cambridge University Press.

Giorgi, L., & Marsh, C. (1990). The protestant work ethic as a cultural phenomenon. *European Journal of Social Psychology, 20*(6), 499–517.

Goldthorpe, J., Lockwood, D., Bechhofer, F., & Platt, J. (1967). The affluent worker and the thesis of embourgeoisement: Some preliminary research findings. *Sociology, 1*(1), 11–31.

Goldthorpe, J., Lockwood, D., Bechhofer, F., & Platt, J. (1968a). *The affluent worker: Industrial attitudes and behaviour.* Cambridge University Press.

Goldthorpe, J., Lockwood, D., Bechhofer, F., & Platt, J. (1968b). *The affluent worker: Political attitudes and behaviour.* Cambridge University Press.

Goldthorpe, J., Lockwood, D., Bechhofer, F., & Platt, J. (1969). *The affluent worker in the class structure.* Cambridge University Press.

Goodwin, J., & Hughes, J. (2011). Ilya Neustadt, Norbert Elias, and the Leicester Department: Personal correspondence and the history of sociology in Britain. *British Journal of Sociology, 62*(4), 677–695.

Goody, J. (1991). *Jack Goody interviewed by Eric Hobsbawm.* Film interviews with leading thinkers, Alan Macfarlane archive, University of Cambridge. https://www.sms.cam.ac.uk/media/1117872

Gould, J. (1977). *The attack on higher education: Marxist and radical penetration. Report of a study group of the Institute for the Study of Conflict.* ISC.

Grimley, M. (2019). You got an ology? The backlash against sociology in Britain, 1945–90. In L. Goldman (Ed.), *Welfare and social policy in Britain since 1870: Essays in honour of Jose Harris* (pp. 178–196). Oxford University Press.

Groenewegen, P. D. (1988). Alfred Marshall and the establishment of the Cambridge Economics Tripos. *History of Political Economy, 20*(4), 627–667.

Grove, J. (2017, June 11). Lord Giddens: Accidental academic who reached the top. *The Times Higher Education Supplement.* www.timeshighereducation.com/news/lord-giddens-accidental-academic-who-reached-top

Hahn, F. H. (1984). *Equilibrium and macroeconomics.* Basil Blackwell.

Halsey, A. H. (2004). *A history of sociology in Britain: Science, literature and society.* Oxford University Press.

Hawthorn, G. (1986, November 6). Sociology in Cambridge. *London Review of Books, 8*(19). https://www.lrb.co.uk/the-paper/v08/n19/geoffrey-hawthorn/sociology-in-cambridge

Hawthorn, G. (2009). *An interview of Professor Geoffrey Hawthorn about his life and work*. Filmed by Alan Macfarlane on 23rd April 2009 and edited by Sarah Harrison. https://www.sms.cam.ac.uk/media/1120434

Hawthorn, G. (2011). Across the fields: John Barnes in Cambridge. Special issue: In memory of John Barnes. *The Cambridge Journal of Anthropology, 29*, 35–44.

Hawthorn, G. (2014). *Thucydides on politics*. Cambridge University Press.

Henley, P. (2011). John Barnes: An appreciation. *Cambridge Journal of Anthropology, 29*, 13–15.

Hiatt, L. (1986). An interview with John Barnes. *Australian Anthropological Society Newsletter, 63*, 4–15.

House of Lords. (1982, June 30). Debate on Social Science Research Council: Rothschild Report, 30 May 1982. *Hansard, 432*, 288–321.

Husbands, C. T. (1981). The anti-quantitative bias in postwar British sociology. In P. Abrams, R. Deem, J. Finch, & P. Rock (Eds.), *Practice and progress: British sociology 1950–1980*. Allen and Unwin.

Husbands, C. T. (2019). *Sound and fury: Sociology at the London School of Economics and Political Science, 1904–2015*. Palgrave Macmillan.

Jobling, R. (2005). Therapeutic research into psoriasis: Patients' perspectives, priorities and interests. In M. D. Rawlins & P. Littlejohns (Eds.), *Delivering quality in the NHS 2005* (pp. 53–56). Radcliffe Publishing.

Jobling, R., & Naldi, L. (2006). Assessing the impact of psoriasis and the relevance of qualitative research. *Journal of Investigative Dermatology, 126*(7), 1438–1440.

Jobling, R., et al. (2015). European S3-Guideline on the systemic treatment of psoriasis vulgaris. *Journal of the European Academy of Dermatology and Venereology, 29*, 2277–2794. http://publicatio.bibl.uszeged.hu/12736/1/3015633_Nast_et_al_2015_Journal_of_the_European_Academy_of_Dermatology_and_Venereology_u.pdf

Johnson, H. G. (1978). The shadow of Keynes. In E. S. Johnson & H. G. Johnson (Eds.), *The shadow of Keynes: Understanding Keynes, Cambridge and Keynesian economics*. Basil Blackwell.

Kahn, R., & Marcuzzo, M. C. (2020). Richard Kahn: A disciple of Keynes. *History of Economics Review*, 57p. https://doi.org/10.1080/10370196.2020.1767930

Kaldor, N. (1982). *Letter to Lord Rothschild concerning the Enquiry into the SSRC*. NK/3/98/2-4; 22 February. King's College Archives, University of Cambridge.

King, D. (1998). The politics of social research: Institutionalizing public funding regimes in the United States and Britain. *British Journal of Political Science, 28*(3), 415–444.

Kuper, A. (2016). Meyer Fortes: The person, the role, the theory. *Cambridge Journal of Anthropology, 34*(2), 127–139.

Lindbeck, A. (1970). Paul Anthony Samuelson's contribution to economics. *Swedish Journal of Economics, 72*(4), 342–354. https://www.nobelprize.org/prizes/economic-sciences/1970/ceremony-speech/

Macfarlane, A. (2015). *Cambridge anthropology: Preliminary notes*. Berghahn Books.

Marsh, C. (1979). Problems with surveys: Method or epistemology. *Sociology, 13*(2), 293–305. Reprinted as: Marsh, C. (1984). Problems with surveys: Method or epistemology? In M. Bulmer (Ed.), *Sociological research methods*. Palgrave. https://doi.org/10.1007/978-1-349-17619-9_5

Marsh, C. (1982). *The survey method: The contribution of surveys to sociological explanation*. Allen & Unwin.

Marsh, C. (1985). Back on the bandwagon: The effect of opinion polls on public opinion. *British Journal of Political Science, 15*(1), 51–74.
Marsh, C. (1988). *Exploring data: An introduction to data analysis for social scientists.* Polity Press.
Marsh, C., & Elliot, J. (2008). *Exploring data: An introduction to data analysis for social scientists* (2nd ed.). Polity Press.
Marsh, C., et al. (1991). The case for samples of anonymized records from the 1991 Census. *Journal of the Royal Statistical Society: Series A (Statistics in Society), 4*(2), 305–340.
Marshall, A. (1916 [1890]). *Principles of economics* (7th ed.). Macmillan.
Matthews, R. C. O. (1989). Joan Robinson and Cambridge – A theorist and her milieu: An interview. In G. R. Feiwel (Ed.), *Joan Robinson and modern economic theory* (pp. 911–915). Palgrave Macmillan.
Matthews, R. C. O., & Supple, B. (1991). The ordeal of economic freedom: Marshall on economic history. *Quaderni di Storia dell'Economia Politica, 9*(2–3), 189–213. Also available as a typescript in E.A.G. Robinson Papers, Marshall Library Archives, University of Cambridge, EAGR 6/4/16, 23p.
Neild, R. (2013). *Economics in disgrace: The need for a reformation.* GIDS Discussion Paper No. 01-13. Graduate Institute of Development Studies.
Neild, R. (2017). The future of economics: The case for an evolutionary approach. *Economic and Labour Relations Review, 28*(1), 1–9.
Network. (1985a). Glittering prizes. *Newsletter of the British Sociological Association, 32,* 1. https://www.britsoc.co.uk/files/NETWORK%20NO32%20MAY1985.pdf
Network. (1985b). New ventures in social science publishing. *Newsletter of the British Sociological Association, 32,* 2. https://www.britsoc.co.uk/files/NETWORK%20NO32%20MAY1985.pdf
Nicol, A. (2001). *The social sciences arrive: The Social Science Research Council is established.* Economic and Social Research Council.
Platt, J. (2003). *The British sociological association: A sociological history.* Routledge.
Prandy, K., Stewart, A., & Blackburn, R. M. (1982). *White collar work* (Cambridge studies in sociology) (Vol. 3). Palgrave Macmillan.
Prandy, K., Stewart, A., & Blackburn, R. M. (1983). *White collar unionism* (Cambridge studies in sociology) (Vol. 4). Palgrave Macmillan.
Pyatt, G. (2005). *Sir Richard Stone: An appreciation.* https://www.copsmodels.com/webhelp/viewhar/index.html?hc_stone2.htm
Reddaway, W. B. (1939). *The economics of a declining population.* George Allen and Unwin.
Robbins, L. (1963). *The Robbins Report. Higher education: Report of the Committee appointed by the Prime Minister under the Chairmanship of Lord Robbins 1961–1963.* Her Majesty's Stationery Office.
Robinson, J. (1974, Autumn). History versus equilibrium. *Thames Papers in Political Economy,* 11p. https://docs.gre.ac.uk/__data/assets/pdf_file/0025/122578/TP_PPE_74_3_compressed.pdf
Rose, D. (1996). For David Lockwood. *British Journal of Sociology, 47*(3), 385–396.
Rose, D. (2014, June 29). David Lockwood obituary. *The Guardian.* https://www.theguardian.com/education/2014/jun/29/david-lockwood
Rosenthal, T. (2006, February 5). How Malcolm Bradbury killed sociology. *The Independent.*

Rothschild, N. M. V. (1982). *An enquiry into the Social Science Research Council.* Her Majesty's Stationery Office.
Runciman, W. G. (1989). *A treatise on social theory: Volume II, Substantive social theory.* Cambridge: Cambridge University Press.
Runciman, W. G. (2014, June 3). *Garry Runciman interviewed by Alan Macfarlane.* Film interviews with leading thinkers. Alan Macfarlane archive, University of Cambridge. https://www.sms.cam.ac.uk/media/1729998
Saith, A. (2019). *Ajit Singh of Cambridge and Chandigarh: An intellectual biography of the radical Sikh economist.* Palgrave Macmillan.
Savage, M. (2016). The fall and rise of class analysis in British sociology, 1950–2016. *Tempo Social, 28*(2), 57–72. http://eprints.lse.ac.uk/68676/1/Savage_The_fall_and_rise_of_class_analysis_published_LSERO.pdf
Singh, A. (2008). *Better to be rough and relevant than to be precise and irrelevant: Reddaway's legacy to economics.* Working Paper No. 379. Cambridge University Centre for Business Research. www.cbr.cam.ac.uk/fileadmin/user_upload/centre-for-business-research/downloads/working-papers/wp379.pdf
Skinner, C., Marsh, C., Openshaw, S., & Wyner, C. (1994). Disclosure control for census microdata. *Journal of Official Statistics, 10*(1), 31–51.
Sklair, L. (1981). Sociologies and Marxisms: The odd couples. In P. Abrams, R. Deem, J. Finch, & P. Rock (Eds.), *Practice and progress: British sociology 1950–1980* (pp. 163–167). Allen and Unwin.
Standing, G. (2011). *The precariat: The new dangerous class.* Bloomsbury Publishing.
Stewart, A., & Blackburn, R. M. (1975). The stability of structural inequality. *The Sociological Review, 23*(3), 481–508.
Stewart, A., Prandy, K., & Blackburn, R. (1973). Measuring the class structure. *Nature, 245,* 415–417. https://doi.org/10.1038/245415a0
Stewart, A., Prandy, K., & Blackburn, R. M. (1980). *Social stratification and occupations* (Cambridge studies in sociology) (Vol. 2). Palgrave Macmillan.
Thompson, J. B. (1991). Mass communication and modern culture: Contribution to a critical theory of ideology. *Sociology, 22*(3), 359–383.
Thompson, J. B. (1993). The theory of the public sphere: A review article. *Theory, Culture and Society, 10*(3), 173–189.
Thompson, J. B. (2005). The new visibility. *Theory, Culture and Society, 6, 31–51.*
Thompson, J. B. (2011). Shifting boundaries of public and private life. *Theory, Culture and Society, 28*(4), 49–70.
UNSO. (1975). *Towards a system of social and demographic statistics.* United Nations. ST/ESA/STAT/SER.F/18.
Walker, D. (2016). *Exaggerated claims? The ESRC, 50 years on.* Sage Publications.
Whitaker, J. K. (Ed.). (1996). *The correspondence of Alfred Marshall, economist* (Towards the close, 1903–1924) (Vol. 3). Royal Economic Society Publication. Cambridge University Press.
Young, M. Y. (2011). John Arundel Barnes (1918–2010). *Cambridge Journal of Anthropology, 29,* 4–12.

CHAPTER 11

Development on the Periphery: Exit and Exile

Abstract In the period after the orthodox neoclassical group took control of the Faculty and the Department of Applied Economics, the teaching (and teachers) and research (and researchers) on radical development economics and development studies steadily moved out to other institutional locations in the university. By the mid-1990s, this process of exile to the periphery had been completed. This effectively undermined the existence of a branch of the subject that had been prominent in Cambridge at the university and later at faculty levels since its inception in the 1920s. The engagement with "development" over the past century can be roughly divided into three distinct, though overlapping historical eras: first, the Colonial-Imperial, 1920s–1940s; second, Decolonisation, Third World National Development, 1950s–1970s; and third, Neoliberal Globalisation, 1980s onwards. Each era had its distinctive features which reflect changing political and intellectual imaginations, programme objectives and substantive academic orientation, cultural ethos and institutional dimensions within which the demand and supply sides of development teaching were handled.

Having negotiated and survived the vicissitudes of the late period of empire and then of the confused imperial hangover, teaching on development made a recovery from the turbulence of the era of decolonisation, though there was a continual reassessment by the ODA of the utility of such training in the context of rapidly changing economic and political relations between the UK and the ex-colonies; and on the part of the university concerned about standards and profiling and the push towards academic professionalisation in place of the old style 'training' mission increasingly characterised as anachronistic. This led the university to accept the initiative of younger academic staff, of launching a new M.Phil in Development Studies in the mid-1970s, with funding not from the ODA but the SSRC, with the longstanding Diploma in Development Studies

© The Author(s), under exclusive license to Springer Nature Switzerland AG 2022
A. Saith, *Cambridge Economics in the Post-Keynesian Era*, Palgrave Studies in the History of Economic Thought,
https://doi.org/10.1007/978-3-030-93019-6_11

running in parallel. The period from the early 1970s till the mid-1980s witnessed a remarkable upswing in the demand for development teaching, in the diploma, the M.Phil and the PhD programmes in the Faculty—but then the climate first turned unfriendly and then hostile in the Faculty of Economics, and the phase ended with the closure, in 1995, of the M.Phil programme started in the Faculty in 1977; development studies was moved out and relocated in the Department of Land Economy till 2012, when, in view of the sustained strength of development teaching and research, the now flourishing Centre of Development Studies was established with its own M.Phil and PhD programmes. A bizarre paradox emerges from the narrative: the accumulated and accomplished heterodox and multidisciplinary teaching and research capacities in Development Studies/Economics are virtually eliminated from the Faculty by the orthodox group, and the time frame over which this expulsion takes place, roughly 1980–1995, is precisely the period where development issues dramatically come to occupy the foreground in global economic policy discourse, matched by a huge expansion in the demand for taught and research degrees in development, inducing a matching supply response in most major universities, including the London School of Economics and the School of Oriental and African Studies in London; in contrast, the Faculty of Economics in Cambridge decided to go the opposite way, thus highlighting the ideological basis of this expulsion.

The webpage entry for the Centre of Development Studies makes the history of the development project in Cambridge seem relatively simple.

> The tradition of research and teaching on development at Cambridge goes back at least to the 1930s, when some of those who were later to be the founding fathers in the field studied here as graduate students under John Maynard Keynes. In the eighty years since then research and teaching in the subject has taken place across many faculties and departments, especially Economics, Social and Political Sciences, Social Anthropology, Geography, Land Economy, the Judge Business School, and the Centres of African, South Asia, Latin American and International Studies. ... After many years operating as the Development Studies Committee, the Centre of Development Studies was formally established in January 2012 as an independent centre within the Department of Politics and International Studies, POLIS.[1]

But behind this hides a complex and convoluted story of many vicissitudes and zigzags in the evolution of 'development', both 'studies' and 'economics', as subjects of teaching and research at Cambridge, both within

---

[1] https://www.devstudies.cam.ac.uk/welcome.

inter-departmental university space and also within the domain of the Faculty of Economics and Politics. In unravelling these crosscutting pathways and timelines, it is useful to separate teaching and research in their multifarious forms and locations in Cambridge in the century over which they evolved.

11.1 CAMBRIDGE DEVELOPMENT STUDIES: THE HETERODOX INHERITANCE

11.1.1 The Capitalist Economy and Its Cambridge Critics

It is essential to recognise the unique intellectual and disciplinary heritage in which development studies is embedded and where it stands in the line of descent in the family tree of Cambridge heterodox traditions, and thus its potential status as another radical, oppositional project to uncontrolled free-market capitalist development.

Cambridge was the home, of course, of Alfred Marshall, the father of neo-classical economics; his words written and spoken were disciplinary authority personified. His *Principles of Economics*, for decades the bible of the subject, was first published in 1890 with an eighth edition in 1920, the year in which his student and successor Arthur Cecil Pigou published his *The Economics of Welfare*, the founding text of modern welfare economics, which introduced the concept of externalities that undermined some of the key neoclassical claims of the efficiency and superiority of the free market. Though Pigou was a thoroughbred neoclassical, this can arguably be regarded as the *first* internal element of critique of free-market capitalism, even though its author was himself a standard bearer of the Marshallian tradition; "it's all in Marshall", was an aphorism Pigou was wont to use.

Later in the same decade, in 1926, came the second challenge from within the Cambridge fold when the base of the high pedestal of Marshallian economics was vigorously shaken by two contrasting but highly significant interventions: first, in his powerful public polemic, John Maynard Keynes, much favoured by Marshall, proclaimed *The End of Laissez Faire*; and even more importantly, Piero Sraffa, who, escaping from fascism, had been brought over to Cambridge from Italy by Keynes after seeing his 1925 work, published his iconoclastic article in *Economic Journal*, that effectively demolished the key premises that formed the basis of Marshall's well-behaved neoclassical microeconomics theorising. Shortly thereafter, in 1933, came Joan Robinson's critique in her *The Economics of Imperfect Competition*. The ground for fresh theorising was opened up as Marshallian occupancy was evicted. These interventions constitute the *second* Cambridge wave of internal critiques of mainstream neoclassical economics and its rendering of the workings of the capitalist economy.

The *third* wave is the Keynesian tsunami from the 1930s, which while still an internal critique of capitalism was profound in demonstrating its inherent systemic instability and the fundamental imperative for state action to ensure macroeconomic balances alongside socially desirable levels of employment. Capitalism needed to be saved from itself, and Keynes, with the *General Theory*, was 'the saviour'; the system could not be left to its own devices, systemic self-correction was a non-starter, and the duties of macro stabilisation of capitalism were the responsibility of the state, with a new international institutional architecture necessary for ensuring global stability. That constituted the Keynesian vision. It turned economic theory, classical and neoclassical, and policy practice based on it in the advanced market economies, upside down; investment led savings; the state led the market; the brave new world had a brave new deal.

If Pigou had pioneered welfare economics with the individual as the unitary social agent, Keynes had used aggregated macroeconomic categories as the basis of diagnostic and policy analysis. But just as Pigou was scripting his internal 'welfare economics' critique, others were constructing an external challenge to capitalism, not just attacking it for inefficiency or instability, but on the fundamental grounds of its key characteristic of class exploitation and alienation; this wasn't something that could be addressed through an application of the Kaldorian 'compensation principle' or Keynesian macroeconomic stabilisation, but called for systemic change in favour of socialism; this was the Marxist and socialist wave, the **fourth**, external, oppositional project that became a reality from 1919; its essence was not reformist but revolutionary—it rejected the capitalist system as a whole.

And then, with the decolonisations at the end of the age of imperialism, new independent nations emerged from centuries of imperialist suppression and underdevelopment to express their development aspirations, to forge new paths to overcome the miserable legacies of colonialism. These nations exhibited various forms of nationalism, and 'socialism' in a spectrum of shades from pale pink to deep red; Oskar Lange had referred to this new emergent group of independent Third-World nations displaying a 'national revolutionary pattern' and collectively, with all their variations, they constituted the arena of development. The terminology was varied: alternative development patterns; non-capitalist development; state-led development; socialistic development; mixed economies; planned economic development.

The lineages of each of these oppositional perspectives and projects have bridges with crossover to the study of development. What is striking is that many of the pioneering contributions in these were made, and were then still active, proximate and readily accessible in Cambridge itself, as building blocks for the emergence of development as a **fifth** oppositional project in its own right. Some of these points of interface would be more in tune with the inherently radical, heterodox orientation of development studies, others less so, but 'negative knowledge' and 'dead-ends', as pedagogical devices, are rich sources of learning in themselves.

11.1.2 Bridges to Development

Cambridge welfare economics had a mixed lineage, from Pigou (1920), there is Kaldor in the 1930s with his 'compensation principle', then the neoclassical microeconomist Johannes de Villiers Graaff with his 1950 PhD published as a celebrated book, *Theoretical Welfare Economics* in 1957, prompting Samuelson (1958: 539) to say "of the many books that are now available on welfare economics, I judge this to be one of the best"; and then there was "Maurice Dobb, who was an astute Marxist economist, ... was one of the few, who to my delight, took welfare economics seriously (and indeed taught a course on it), just as the intensely 'neo-classical' A.C. Pigou had done" (Sen, 1998). Dobb's *Welfare Economics and the Economics of Socialism* was published in 1969; he was still active and lecturing on welfare economics in the early 1970s even after his retirement in 1967, and just prior to his death in 1976.

Maurice Dobb was a profound and greatly under-used resource. A reviewer of his *Welfare Economics* says what is necessary:

> Maurice Dobb is a unique figure. He has been a continuing influence on students of economics in many countries for more than four decades. The range of his reading can seldom have been equalled, in Marxism, economic history, the theory and practice of economic planning, including the original Eastern European sources and the whole range of economic theory from the classical writer to the present day. His systematic critique of orthodox economic theory is unrivalled, and he has made major contributions to the theories of economic development and planning. His scholarship is impeccable, his modesty evident from his style. Yet, no doubt because of a lifelong and unconcealed commitment to the radical cause, he occupies no chair and has no handle to his name. His new study is not about Africa nor indeed is it directly concerned with any part of the underdeveloped world but it is an important and relevant contribution to thinking on economic development. (Ewing, 1971: 332)

Dobb's treatment provided more than just "a critical survey of a complex, somewhat tortuous field, ... more than usually studded with controversy, because of its vital relation to economic policy" (Ewing, 1971: 332). Welfare economics had been used by the liberals to attack both development and socialism and to legitimise capitalism; Dobb puts Pareto, Pigou and all through his sieve to identify the limitations both of welfare economics as well as the critiques of socialism made on its basis.

Other heterodox lineages in Cambridge had been preoccupied exclusively with the case of the mature advanced economy, fully monetised, with universal capitalist relations, with a full separation of the working class from the means of production as the general case. The neo-Ricardians, Sraffa and the Sraffians, the Keynesians and the post-Keynesians were all thus engaged, not to mention the black hole of the cross-Atlantic capital controversies which disproportionately soaked up Joan's energies. Development and the Third World did not figure in these debates, though the heterodox critiques of orthodox theory had obvious general relevance. Development was more concerned with the long term. That said, it is possible to highlight several significant bridges to development theory and policy. As early as 1952, V.K.R.V. Rao had raised the issue of the limitations of the use of the multiplier in an agrarian underdeveloped economy, pointing to structural supply-side constraints in agriculture and the dangers of food price inflation (Rao, 1952). This was a rich line of enquiry with wide-ranging policy implications which continue to remain today, for instance, in the charged debates over the appropriateness a policy of universal basic income grants in India and elsewhere. Gautam Mathur had attempted to adapt Joan Robinson's schema in her *Accumulation of Capital* to make it serviceable in the context of a developing economy such as India. Barring his extended, if sporadic, involvement with Indian issues, Keynes did not directly address the development problematic; nevertheless, there is a very wide interface between Keynes's ideas, expressed over the years, and Keynesianism, and development questions. Excellent commentaries and assessments can be found in Toye (2006) who undertakes a vast 60-year sweep of the Keynesian legacy for development, locating it in relation to strands of development theory and policy thinking after Keynes' death; and in more specific treatments in Chandavarkar (1993) who, going beyond his earlier work Keynes and India (Chandavarkar, 1989), focusses specifically on the issue of Keynes' various writings on the role of the state; and, discursively, in the body of work of Ajit Singh—discussed extensively by Saith (2019: 175–272)—whose theoretical and applied analyses of the international finance, crises, trade and technology, stock markets and the policy imperatives on the Third-World state in the industrialisation process are imbued with the Keynes-Kaldor visions in the national and international frames of reference.[2] Joan Robinson (1979) uses a macro-Keynesian framework for discussing development; and, of course, Michal Kalecki provided typically succinct and sharp analyses of the problems of industrialisation and development in poor agrarian economies, bringing in issues of regressive food price inflation, of the financing issues, and of the constraints imposed by feudal class structures in the countryside. There are multiple bridges between the oeuvres of Keynes, Kalecki, Kaldor and Joan Robinson, and Third-World industrialisation and development. Sukhamoy Chakravarty (1987), in a rare paper, had sifted out the interface between post-Keynesian theory and development, and then had followed it up with a joint paper with Ajit Singh on the question of the optimal forms and degrees of economic openness of developing economies in the context of the IMF-World Bank neoliberal onslaught (Chakravarty & Singh, 1988). And Amiya Bagchi (2004)—while rightly pointing out that Keynes was not an anti-imperialist fighting the corner of the colonies—had offered a sharp

---

[2] These contributions, both in the context of advanced market economies and developing economies, and at national and global levels, are extensively reviewed in Saith (2019: 175–272) under the heading, 'economics as concentrated politics'—reflecting the radical and often iconoclastic nature of Ajit Singh's interventions. As such, these are not listed or reviewed in detail here.

and insightful reflection on the links between Keynes, Kaldor and development economics.[3] Kalecki, easily included in the Cambridge circle, had written extensively on the mixed and developing economies, including especially his classic paper on the financing of economic development (Nuti, 1971). He had written important papers in his involvement with India in the context of the early plans, prior to which he advised the Israeli government in 1950 on immediate economic policy issues. Then, of course, there was the extensive and intensive involvement of some of the modern greats in Indian planning on the invitation and cajolement of Mahalanobis in the 1950s and 1960s (recorded in Rudra (1996) and discussed in Saith (2008)) and taken up later.

Richard Kahn, the exception of his cohort for not having gone to India in the early planning years, had also written a rare paper on "the pace of development", again in the context of his (sustained and close) involvement with Israel as an informal economic adviser (Kahn, 1958).[4] Kahn operated with the theoretical template of the advanced capitalist industrial economy. With his belief system and deep affinity towards Israel, Kahn was a frequent visitor there and offered informal back-room advice on economic policy. In a policy workshop in Jerusalem in 1958, he made almost his sole contribution on economic development; his paper 'The Challenge of Development' made "a plea to the governments of underdeveloped countries to utilise their surplus labour drastically to increase their rate of investment, especially in agriculture" (Kahn & Marcuzzo, 2020: 28; Kahn, 1958). In this, he was in line with the analysis and recommendations of Joan Robinson (based on her earlier learnings from India but also crucially also from Mao's innovative notion of 'labour accumulation' to kick

---

[3] Bagchi (2004: 1): "Their work not only illuminated the issues of turbulence of the capitalist economy but ... also left a conceptual framework for formulating policies for stabilisation and growth both a the global and at the national level ... and can be used to falsify the claim that deregulating financial markets could increase the prosperity of nations. Their writings also demonstrated the importance of stabilizing the commodity markets and the incomes of primary producers for allowing the global economy to grow on a sustained basis." "John Maynard Keynes and Nicholas Kaldor", he laments, "are often treated as economists who have nothing to teach about the problems bedevilling the contemporary global economy"; and he warns that "the deliberate amnesia imposed on the new generations of economists by policy-makers of the neo-liberal persuasion can be enormously harmful for their training."

[4] In the early years after its establishment, Israel, rather like India, had the benefit of external advisors selected to match perceived national needs. Schiffman (2013: 1) provides a listing of "Jewish economists from the Diaspora [who] have played an active role in Israeli economics, on both the academic and policymaking fronts" since the establishment of the State of Israel in 1948. The list is impressive and includes, apart from Richard Kahn's 1957 and 1962 visits: Michal Kalecki (1950), Abba Lerner (1953–1956), Hollis Chenery (1959), Simon Kuznets ("who visited Israel so frequently that he became 'a fixture of the Israeli economics community'" (ibid.), Milton Friedman (five times between 1962 and 1990), Stanley Fischer. The extensive nature of Kahn's involvement in Israeli policy making is evident from his meetings and contacts during these visits as detailed in Appendices B and C; Schiffman concludes, however, that "Ultimately, Israeli policy-makers ignored Kahn's advice ... Kahn was unsuccessful as an advisor, but he was probably successful in the more limited sense of helping government officials attain a greater clarity on economic issues" (ibid.).

start rural development in socialist China); Maurice Dobb (as in his lectures at the Delhi School of Economics); Mahalanobis himself when he blended in the idea of a 'land army' of surplus labour as a countervailing supplementary device to his capital-intensive industrialisation model; Michal Kalecki when he conceptualised the warranted rate of non-inflationary growth in context of Indian planning emphasising the need to overcome the constraints of feudalism on rural investment; and Ragnar Nurkse (1953) with his concept of pulling in the 'slack' through the use of surplus labour for capital formation, resonating again with the converging ideas of these other contributions. Kalecki was also at the same workshop as Kahn in Israel where he also served as an economic advisor, as did Simon Kuznets, who (alongside Richard Stone) also advised the Indian Planning Commission on National Income Accounting in the early 1950s.

Later, looking back, Sukhamoy Chakravarty (1987) provides a typically wide-ranging and insightful analytical review of the interface between post-Keynesian theorising and the theory of economic development, assessing in particular its overlaps and differences with structuralist schools, while pointing out that both of these differed significantly from the neoclassical approach which gave primacy to factor substitution at the margin and to the overriding role it ascribed to the price mechanism as an allocator of resources and determinant of the rate of investment. Chakravarty (1987: 1) refers to "Richard Kahn, who wrote a sadly neglected but important article [Kahn, 1958] which expanded the scope of Keynes' reasoning to include a development dimension." With the (post-) Keynesians, "the causal relationship runs from investment to savings. This is the proposition which was first made by Kahn (Chakravarty, 1987: 2). He extends Kahn's analysis further, bringing into play another proposition "which I think is equally critical to post-Keynesian analysis, which I think is not in Kahn" (Chakravarty, 1987: 3). Citing what Hicks "considered to be a fundamental distinction between the so-called fundists and the materialists in the theory of capital", Chakravarty observes that "according to the post-Keynesians a great deal of confusion in the neo-classical theory of growth and development has been caused by the unwillingness or inability to make a systematic distinction between capital as *a sum of values* and capital as a *concrete stock* of means of production"; he criticises the neoclassical 'malleability assumption' whereby the "initial stock of capital could be spread very thin as it were a kind of putty to employ as many people as you like or as few people as you like. ... the malleability assumption is simply not true ... it has considerable implications ... lack of clarity on this fundamental point can give rise to two misleading conceptions". The first is that aid from one country to another represents usually a transfer of financial funds which do not automatically translate into "the emergence or strengthening of the capital goods sector"; and second, that in view of this, recipient "countries after a little time run into very considerable debt difficulties later" (ibid.: 3–4). Chakravarty's analysis provides clear statements of the areas of agreement and conflict between the neoclassical, followed by an analytical comparison of the post-Keynesian and the structuralist schools (ibid.: 11–13), but then ends by introducing a key new feature which none of these schools adequately considers: "the fact that 70 per cent or more of the population of big countries like India, Indonesia, China, Pakistan and Bangladesh is largely self-employed and for them none of the three theories neoclassical, post-Keynesian or structuralist, applies directly to large segments of the economy. In fact, economics has not adequately dealt with the problem of self-employment. So here on can speak of a fourth type of development theory. In the 'self-employed' sector, the consumption decisions, the investment decision and saving decision are one and the same. They are all combined together in the self-same household" (Ibid.: 14). Intriguingly, Chakravarty sets up the challenge to think afresh and revise and renew received analytical templates.

And finally, and most significantly, was the case of Nicky Kaldor. Though most often cited in development discourse for his extensive advisory work concerning the design of taxation systems in developing countries,[5] his major 'development' contribution lay in his role as the apostle of industrialisation as the strategy for catch-up development. The Kaldorian template of industrialisation provides a critical link between the key contributions of Sraffa and Allyn Young in the 1920s on the role of economies of scale on the one side and the Myrdal–Veblen concept of dynamic cumulative causation on the other; and the formulation interfaces well with Smithian emphasis on the role of the size of the market in influencing the division of labour, and viewed dynamically, the scale of operation, productivity and declining cost curves (which would undermine neoclassical notions of supply–demand equilibrium). The 'new Cambridge' propositions developed by Kaldor and colleagues also gave a crucial driving role to exports, and this laid the basis for what could be regarded as the export-led path of catch-up development as exemplified by the East Asian experience. Kaldor also used his framework to argue against IMF strategies of enforcing devaluations in developing countries, with sharp public conflicts in the Mexican and the Tanzanian cases. This approach provides a clear bridge between the post-Keynesian and the development strands of research in Cambridge and is further reflected in the work on deindustrialisation of the UK economy by Ajit Singh and others, with Ajit explicitly referring to it as his bridge to his subsequent research on industrialisation strategies for the Third World.[6]

Joan became seriously unwell in her final years, but just prior to that, in 1979, she turned her mind and pen towards another lifelong concern, development. She wrote *Aspects of Development and Underdevelopment*. It was not a textbook, but a corrective text. "This small book does not offer a survey of its huge theme", she says. Rather, "it is intended to throw some light upon the question of why a quarter of a century of 'development' has produced results so different from what was proclaimed to be its object." She warns: "there is a certain complacency in mainstream economic teaching which is misleading even in its homeland and cruelly deceptive when transferred to the Third World." This was four years before the moneylenders and debt collectors, IMF and the World Bank, launched their 'get the prices right' and Structural Adjustment Programmes (SAPs, an appropriate acronym) with its mission to push development strategies in the Third World from left to right, from being state- to market-led. "The basic economic theory which seems to me to be useful is a

---

[5] On this aspect of Kaldor's work, see Toye (1989) and Chakravarty (1989).
[6] These aspects are discussed at length in Saith (2019: 175–259).

re-interpretation in post-Keynesian terms of the Classical and Marxian theory of accumulation, distribution and trade" (Robinson, 1979: ix). Joan's book fell between several stools, and ran into some awkward reviews variously from Deng-whateverists and Mao-haters, free marketeers, as well as 'radicals', and in the 1981 edition, Joan felt obliged to insert a qualification on Chinese agricultural development in the light of information available after the death of Mao.[7]

Though there was widespread knowledge and interest in Marxism and socialism, this was not rendered into the curriculum. Sraffa was deeply knowledgeable but not lecturing; Joan was closely engaged, and had running fights with Maurice Dobb on account of her insistence of translating Marxian categories of analysis into Keynesian ones; Dobb was the prime exception, though development was not a major preoccupation for him after the early engagement with planned development, stimulated by his involvement with the Indian experience. Terry Byres (1984: 66) rightly laments: "It is, indeed, a great pity that Maurice Dobb never wrote a full-scale, general text on development. His writing in this field and his strangely neglected Delhi lectures of 1951 suggested the possibility of a truly magisterial work." Dobb's writings on development planning (Dobb, 1951, 1960, 1967) were seminal, and virtually all his other work has a bearing on the theme of non-capitalist paths. Of his 1960 essay on economic growth and planning in developing economies, a reviewer notes: "Mr Dobb's model has the merit of giving full weight to the structural and technological limitations on growth which have tended to become obscured by our long-standing obsession with the motivational aspects of saving and investment" (Seton, 1962: 376). The 'obsession', of course, was a Keynesian phenomenon.

In the same series as Joan's development book, three years later in 1982—a significant cross-roads year for development teaching in Cambridge—came Amiya Bagchi's *The Political Economy of Development*, which answered fully to the description of a textbook, even if eschewing 'a balanced treatment' in favour of a full-blooded Marxist assessment and critique of the discourse on capitalism as the path to development in the Third World. Terry Byres (1984: 75) reviewed it thus:

> Those who are actively seeking a general Marxist text on the 'political economy of underdevelopment' will welcome it most warmly. Here we have no hastily cobbled together lecture notes without unifying structure, no formless eclecticism, no opportunistic compilation. It is a successful exercise in political economy: a closely textured, carefully formulated argument, rich in concrete and historical analysis; at once, coherent, rigorous and sweeping in its range; abjuring empty abstraction; the product of wide reading, prolonged thought and fierce commitment.

Bagchi was at Cambridge in the radical left-dominant heydays in the 1960s. Byres notes the irony that Bagchi's overtly Marxist work appeared in the

---

[7] Joan's *Aspects of Development and Underdevelopment*, as indeed her work on Maoist development strategies in rural China, received unfair and somewhat biased treatment from the reformists (Saith, 2008).

Modern Cambridge Economics Series; he calls it a case of "dialectical justice that the equivalent volume in the old Cambridge Economic Handbooks series, the predecessor to the modern series, was P.T. Bauer and B.S. Yamey, *The Economics of Underdeveloped Countries*, 1957, written from an extreme *laissez-faire* standpoint. Had history repeated itself exactly, I suppose that someone like Deepak Lal, rather than Amiya Bagchi, would have been asked to write the current volume" (ibid.: 66).

At the other end of the spectrum was Peter Bauer who had for a long period been on the staff of the overseas development course in Cambridge teaching young administrators from recently independent ex-colonies that the free market was the best and only route to development. Bauer, a Hayek man, member of the Mont Pelerin Society, later recipient of the first Friedman Prize, and development guru to Thatcher, was elevated by her to a peerage. Deepak Lal, whose diatribe against state-led development in the Third World, *The Poverty of 'Development Economics'* was published in 1983, a year after Bagchi's work, was equally a Hayekian and a Pelerinista, and later president of the Mont Pelerin Society; appropriately his book was published by the Institute of Economic Affairs, the main libertarian Hayekian think tank in the UK and a bulwark of Thatcherism.[8] The 'Devonshire' phase of Cambridge development teaching involved E.A.G Robinson, but also Peter Bauer who was lecturer in economics during 1948–1956, and one can only speculate how the trainees reconciled the teachings of the Keynesian disciple and the Hayekian devotee,[9]

---

[8] Of note here is John Toye's scathing response to Peter Bauer's "disparaging of development economics" in his book (Bauer, 1981; and Toye, 1983). Bauer taught for ten years in the 1950s, in the overseas development course at Cambridge where he was a lecturer in economics; Toye was an Assistant Director Research in the later Diploma on Development Studies (1969–1981) in Cambridge.

[9] Peter Bauer started in Cambridge where he was one of the eighteen supervisees at Gonville and Caius College of an anti-Keynesian John Hicks in his brief Cambridge stay (till 1938). He moved from being a Reader in Agricultural Economics at the University of London (1947–1948) to a lectureship in economics at Cambridge (1948–1956); Bauer taught 'development' to unsuspecting Third-World students who came to Cambridge for a diploma for nearly a decade; there was no prospect of promotion in the Cambridge faculty, and so he moved to LSE where he became a professor in 1960, just at the time that Lionel Robbins left the school. He held strong views simply and vigorously expressed: he was against birth control in the developing countries; rejected the notion that Britain was class-ridden, holding that it was possible to "secure entry into the upper classes through marriage, money, service or official favour"; rejected the idea that imperialism had exploited the colonies; was dead against foreign aid as this would go to the new Third-World elite; against state aid to the poor in UK, except to the utterly indigent—they should solve their own problems; was against Commonwealth leaders imposing sanctions—rather, they should go home and sort out their own problems; and blamed "naïve western intellectuals in the 1930s, like the LSE's Webbs and Harold Laski for the spread of communism". He was a great friend of Friedrich Hayek, a member of his Mont Pelerin Society; subscribed to monetarism à la Friedman; was a great favourite of Margaret Thatcher who elevated him to a peerage in 1982 soon after she took office; she also recommended him for the award of the first Friedman Prize, worth $500,000, from the Cato Institute, in 2002, the year he died. "Markets good, bureaucrats bad, governments worse" could perhaps sum up Bauer's economics; his anti-dirigisme tradition of development was continued by his admirer and fellow MPS colleague, Deepak Lal. The libertarian *Cato Journal*, a prime carrier of the Hayek message, published a fulsome special issue of papers in honour of Peter Bauer

with the former making the case for development interventions while the latter disparaged development economics and its purpose. "Despite my own left-wing inclinations, I realized soon after I arrived in Cambridge that the right-wing Bauer was not only the best teacher of development economics but also the most accomplished thinker on the subject in the university, by a wide margin. Indeed, he was one of the most original development economists in the world, and a lot of what I came to understand about 'how development happens' was the result of our regular conversations. I felt very privileged that Peter befriended me from the time I was a young student and joined me for coffee nearly every week—'to meet and argue' as he used to put it, which was a source of great gain for me. My friendship with Bauer lasted for the rest of his life. The fact that the neo-Keynesians saw little in his work is not, I believe, to their credit" (Sen, 2021, pp. 289–290). Sen's unstinting praise, which matches what Margaret Thatcher showered on Bauer, would chime well with similar tributes from neoclassical and neoliberal quarters, though it might remain puzzling to those of other persuasions in the field of development.

The protagonists of the national planned development paradigm would also have encountered resistance from the camp of anthropologists with their focus on the local, the community, continuities and change in traditions—by its nature hostile to the state as an aggregating force of modernisation 'imposed from the outside' upon 'unwilling' or 'disempowered' or 'unaware' indigenous communities; in this Jack Goody, with his work on the salience of the economic surplus as a force of transformation, might have stood as an exception. Likewise, Third-World socialists or nationalists could not expect even broad agreement from the Cambridge historical school on the question of British imperialism and its role in the colonies. Such divergences would clearly have rendered it more difficult to construct a consistent storyline for the students of the programme who would then need to work through such disagreements on their own—which in itself could have been an instructive exercise.

That said, it is clear that each of the different frameworks identified would have a kernel of relevance to development; the neoclassical obsessive focus on

---

in 1987; contributors included Deepak Lal, Alan Walters, David Gale Johnson, Basil Yamey and Vernon Smith; James Buchanan (2002) wrote a separate appreciation. In his obituary, Andrew Roth (2002) writes: "The usually mild crossbencher Lord Henderson of Brompton commented that when Bauer 'hears the word "development" he salivates like Pavlov's dog and becomes almost rabid'." Amartya Sen, who would have encountered Bauer first in the 1950s in Cambridge and then in the 1970s at the LSE, provides a fairly unequivocal view:

> Bauer is no compromiser ... but Bauer isn't particularly isolated himself. His arguments develop and reinforce deep-seated conservative beliefs. Bauer is, in fact, an eloquent, original, and influential member of the powerful conservative tradition in political economy. He may be facing a multitude of opponents, but he is also leading a large group himself. It is best to get this straight ... If Bauer sees himself as David facing Goliath, then David has come to the battleground on the shoulders of a second Goliath—the one that rules much of the world. Bauer's arguments not only attack widely held views; they also provide justification for some of the most entrenched beliefs underlying official policy in such countries as the United States and Britain. (Sen, 1982)

the market, and the Keynesian premise of market failure and the imperative for state action. The core of the heterodox lineages would provide a flexible political economy framework within which the ideas of List, Gerschenkron, Robinson, Kaldor, Rostow, Prebisch, Lewis, Mandelbaum, Schumpeter, Rosenstein-Rodan, Myrdal, Hirschman, Nurkse, Sweezy, Baran, Streeten, Seers and many others would all form ingredients of modern development theory as another radical oppositional project.[10]

11.2 Evolution of the Teaching Project: Multiple Identities

11.2.1 Timelines

The evolution of the engagement with 'development', in terms of both teaching and research, in Cambridge has to be viewed in the context of their contemporary global contexts and conjunctures; the timeline since the 1920s can be roughly divided into three distinct, though overlapping historical eras: first, the Colonial-Imperial (1920s–1940s); second, Decolonisation, Third World National Development (1950s–1970s); and third, Neoliberal Globalisation (1980s onwards).

The trajectory of formal development teaching can be further profiled by slicing the century, somewhat arbitrarily, into a sequence of six phases, using the objectives and the organisational framework as key markers. Each phase has distinctive features which reflect the political and intellectual imagination, programme objectives and substantive academic orientation, cultural ethos and institutional dimensions within which the demand and supply sides of development teaching were handled.

I	1926–1944	Imperial Business
II	1944–1969	Imperial Hangover
III	1969–1981	Turbulence and Recovery
IV	1982–1995	Recovery and Turbulence
V	1996–2012	Exile to Periphery
VI	2012–	Independence

Phase-I, when development courses begin in Cambridge, is a period of imperial stability, and the objective is to train British colonial officials going out to their assignments in the colonies. This enterprise is taken very seriously at the Cambridge end; the recorded minutes of the meetings of the Committee managing the delivery of the courses demonstrate very high seniority on the Committee, with many professors, several Masters of Colleges and on occasion, the Vice Chancellor. Post-war, Phase-II sees professionalisation and

---

[10] For a critical contemporary, along different axes, of "four phases of development studies" in the decade of the 1960s, see Apthorpe (1971).

vocationalisation with the setting up of the 'Devonshire' courses. The intentions are thwarted as the process of decolonisation proceeds rapidly in Asia in the 1940s, though African colonies do not attain independence till well into the 1960s. This imparts a bi-focality to the course in terms of its objectives, its intake and its orientation. Participants now include administrators from the newly independent Asian countries, alongside British colonial trainees still going out to African destinations. The course is characterised by an imperial hangover with insufficient absorption of the new international conjuncture and its implications for such training. This leads finally to the closure of the Devonshire Courses. In Phase-III, the changed position of the UK in the post-imperial world order induces the launching of an entirely new framework in the form of a Diploma in Development Studies now oriented fully towards the training of administrators from the erstwhile colonies, in development theory and practice; unity is restored with regard to the clientele, and the objectives of the new restyled diploma are managed by an interdepartmental committee of academic staff. The course, leading to the Diploma, survives and recovers from its period of turbulence, though there is a continual reassessment on the part of the Overseas Development Administration (ODA; later transformed into the Department for International Development, DfID) about the utility of such training in the context of rapidly changing economic and political relations between the UK and the ex-colonies; and on the part of the university concerned about standards and profiling and the push towards academic professionalisation in place of the old style 'training' mission increasingly characterised as anachronistic. This leads the university to accept the initiative of younger academic staff, of launching a new M.Phil in Development Studies in the mid-1970s, with funding not from the ODA but the SSRC; the Diploma runs in parallel. Phase III also sees a sharp increase in the intake of doctoral scholars in the Faculty of Economics, focussing on development issues. Phase IV is marked till the mid-1980s by an ascendancy of development teaching, in the Diploma (awarded formally by Land Economy, the MPhil (in the Economics and Politics of Development, awarded by Economics), and in the Faculty's PhD programme in the form of a heavier inflow of doctoral students in development), but then the climate first turns unfriendly, and then hostile, in the Faculty of Economics; the phase ends with the closure, in 1995, of the M.Phil programme started in the Faculty in 1977; development studies is moved out from the Faculty and relocates in the Department of Land Economy. Phase V covers the period of exile to the periphery till 2012, when the final Phase VI, of independence, sees the establishment of the Centre of Development Studies (within the Department of Politics and International Studies) with its own M.Phil and PhD programmes. The timeline in Table 11.1 summarises this complex journey.[11]

---

[11] This timeline is based, for the earlier period, on information from the 'Archives of the Course on Development and earlier and later development studies programmes' covering the period 1925–1982, held at the Cambridge University Archives (GBR/0265/CDEV); and for the subse-

11.2.2 In University Space: The Professionalisation of 'Development Studies'

The Early Years: Fine-tuning Imperial Instruction, 1926–1969
There is a throwback to the preparation of colonial officials for performing their tasks as colonial masters, and prominent here is the role of Thomas 'Pop' Malthus[12] as the Professor of Political Economy and History in the East India College set up in its headquarters in Haileybury in Hertfordshire to train company officials before they set out abroad, mainly to India as recruits into the prized Indian Civil Service, the fabled life-changer which all fresh recruits aspired to enter. Callie Wilkinson (2017) provides an insightful exploration of the charged debates over the nature of such education, and shows how "these disagreements reflected the deeper uncertainties, particularly regarding the ideal relationship to be fostered between the Company, Britain, and India … and highlight the tensions, anxieties, and ambiguities surrounding reform and imperial expansion in the early nineteenth century". The land rent and revenue theories of English political economists were being played out in the harsh realities of Indian fields and farmers, and 'educated' colonial officials were the instrument of such translation and transmission. Theory ruled, even if indirectly. Then there was the question of the most appropriate forms of educating the subjects of colonial rule, and here Macaulay, another Cambridge man, was what Stokes calls "the most representative figure in both England and India, … of English liberalism in its clear, untroubled dawn" (Stokes, 1959: 14). It was Macaulay who had overturned any ambivalence with regard to the instrumental training of minds of Indian elites to convert them into intermediaries, agents and executors of British colonial design in India. It was his doctrines that Lala Hardayal had challenged politically in arguing the case for an Indian nationalist education in a pan-Indian language, Sanskrit, and it was this position that had almost definitely influenced the young Ajit Singh in opting for Sanskrit 'for nationalist reasons' in his university degree in Chandigarh, alongside mathematics and economics.[13] Another Cambridge–India connection, albeit a somewhat circuitous one, is revealed in Keynes's (1924: 326) biographical appreciation of Alfred Marshall, in which he comments on the close equation between Marshall and Dr Jowett, the Master of Balliol, and notes: "on the premature death of Arnold Toynbee in 1883, he [Jowett] invited Marshall to take his place as Fellow of Balliol and Lecturer in Political Economy to the

---

quent period, on information from Dr Ha-Joon Chang, Director of the Centre of Development Studies, University of Cambridge (personal communication).

[12] Malthus got a first class degree in Mathematics, and was later a Fellow at Jesus College Cambridge where he set up the Political Economy Club, though he never held a teaching position there; his portrait would have looked down in recent years on John Toye, Peter Nolan, Shailaja Fennell, all at Jesus, who have had a significant role in the evolution of the teaching of overseas development in its many incarnations. (Geoff Harcourt, though also at Jesus and hugely supportive of the development team, was not personally active in these courses.)

[13] For an elaboration, see Saith (2019: 7–11).

Table 11.1 A century of development teaching—A Cambridge timeline

---

< 1926
Prior to 1927, there had been a short course held in London, but in 1925 the Colonial Office asked Cambridge and Oxford Universities to provide the course and the University set up a supervising committee in November 1926.

1927–1940
The Course on Development began its chequered life as a one-year Course for Colonial Probationers. The course was supervised by the Colonial Service Probationers Committee which reported to the Council of Senate of the University.
All those attending were graduates divided into cadet officers (administrators) and agricultural probationers. The administrators then went on to the University of London for a short period of intensive language instruction at the School of Oriental and African Studies, while the agricultural probationers went to the Imperial College of Tropical Agriculture in Trinidad for a further year. In 1929 the language instruction was transferred to Cambridge and included within the three-term syllabus. Instruction covered practical and academic subjects; examinations were jointly organised with the Colonial Office. A club, the African Services Club, was started to provide a social centre.
In 1940, shortly after the onset of the Second World War, this course stopped.

1947–1953
The Course on Development was revived in 1947 "as the 'Devonshire Courses', as a result of the recommendations of the Devonshire Committee, to provide instruction not only for administrative and agricultural cadets (the First Course), but also for more senior officers (the Second Course)." During 1947–1955, the course was supervised by the Colonial Studies Committee, reporting to the General Board of the University.

1953–1962
From 1953 till 1982 when the course was terminated, it was supervised by the Overseas Studies Committee which reported to the General Board of the University.
In 1953, the name was changed to the Overseas Services Course. "The increasing numbers of locally recruited officers and the approach of self-government for most colonies led to further changes. The First Course became 'Course A' and the Second Course 'Course B'."

1963–1968
"By 1963, more flexible programmes on development economics had been introduced and the name changed to the Course on Development."

1969–1981
In 1969 the lineage of the Devonshire Courses was closed down and replaced by the Diploma in Development Studies (DDS) for overseas administrators at Cambridge, and a one-year programme for overseas diplomats at Oxford. In view of the new post-imperial context, this Diploma programme shifted its catchment area to cohorts of early- to mid-career officers from the administrative services of the recently independent countries. From 1969, course administration was moved to University College, and from 1973 to Wolfson College. The independent project ended with the withdrawal of government funding in 1981.

1972–1973
Especially in these two years, partly to do with the formation of Bangladesh as a new nation, there was an influx of an unusually large cohort of 14 PhD scholars from South Asia, significantly widening the interface of development with regular Faculty and DAE teaching and research, creating a more conducive academic environment for development issues and initiatives through the 1970s; this laid the basis for the launch of an M.Phil in Development Studies with its own clientele and catchment, partly to reduce transaction costs for an entry into the PhD programme. This cohort, including South Asian doctoral researchers already in Cambridge, numbered 15–20 and was strong enough academically and numerically to set up its own South Asian Seminar which met on demand, and in which their ongoing doctoral and other research were put up for collective interrogation.

(*continued*)

Table 11.1 (continued)

1976
A new M.Phil in Economics and Politics of Development was introduced in the Faculty of Economics & Politics, managed by the Development Studies Committee.

1980–1981
ODA terminates its funding for the Diploma in Development Studies managed by the Overseas Studies Committee chaired by Paul Howell; most of the staff scatter; very few stay.

1982
A new Diploma in Development Studies is started and located in the Department of Land Economy; managed by the newly (re-)formed Development Studies Committee which replaced the erstwhile Overseas Studies Committee.

1990
Ha-Joon Chang joins the Faculty of Economics as a lecturer in the position vacated by John Sender.

1995
The M.Phil in Economics and Politics of Development at the Faculty of Economics is terminated.

1996–2010
The Diploma in Development Studies is abolished.
A new M.Phil in Development Studies is started (replacing the closed M.Phil in Economics and Politics of Development which was located in the Faculty of Economics & Politics) and located in the Department of Land Economy.
Paper on Development Economics continued to be taught at the Faculty of Economics (by Ha-Joon Chang, Ajit Singh, Jose Gabriel Palma and Peter Nolan) till 2010, "when the Faculty banned their students from taking it although they allowed their students to take it again a few years ago" (Ha-Joon Chang, personal communication, email dated 2 May 2018).

2007
Professor Ajit Singh retires from the Faculty of Economics; joins Centre for Development Studies (25%), and the Judge Business School (50%).

2011–2020
The Centre for Development Studies (CDS) is set up within POLIS.
The M.Phil in Development Studies is taken over by CDS.
CDS starts its own PhD degree programme in Development Studies.
CDS is chaired by Professor Peter Nolan (who was earlier the Chair of the Development Studies Committee) till his retirement in 2016, after which Dr Ha-Joon Chang takes over as director.

2012
Dr Jose Gabriel Palma retires from the Faculty of Economics; becomes an affiliated lecturer in the Centre for Development Studies.

2016
Professor Peter Nolan retires. Dr Ha-Joon Chang becomes director of the Centre for Development Studies, retaining a 0.2 FTE position in the Faculty of Economics, effectively ending the presence of heterodox economists in the Faculty.

Sources: This timeline is based, for the earlier period, on information from the 'Archives of the Course on Development and earlier and later development studies programmes' covering the period 1925–1982, held at the Cambridge University Archives (GBR/0265/CDEV), and for the subsequent period, on information from Dr Ha-Joon Chang, director of the Centre of Development Studies, University of Cambridge, and from Dr Jose Gabriel Palma (personal communication)

selected candidates for the Indian Civil Service". Balliol College had a long-standing association with the Indian Civil Service. The content of such imperial education did really matter, as is confirmed by Eric Stokes who argues in his classic, *The English Utilitarians in India*, that the Utilitarians should not be understood "solely as abstract moral and political theorists, to the neglect of their practical aims and influence", and he seeks "to show that the nature of these practical aims was deduced logically from their abstract theory, and that both fall into a system whose completeness is more obvious in Indian than in English history" (Stokes, 1959: vi).

But there was more than just the Indian jewel in the crown. In 1926, the Colonial Office arranged for Oxford, Cambridge and (subsequently) LSE to offer a specialised training course for the Tropical African Services (TAS), which in 1932 became the Colonial Administrative Service (CAS) with a wider remit. The year 1926 was marked by more than the launch of the Cambridge training course for its colonial administrators. Away from the sleepy serenity of its spires, much was afoot: Francisco Franco, at 33, became Spain's youngest general; the Italian Great Fascist Council was formed in October; the same month Leon Trotsky was expelled from the Politburo; and a month later, Antonio Gramsci was arrested in Rome; Germany joins the League of Nations, causing Spain to pull out of it; far away in China, Chiang Kai-shek became the national revolutionary supreme commander; and, while a far-sighted industrialist announced the 8-hour, 5-day, working week at the Ford car production plants, at home in UK, there was the General Strike in May in support of the coal miners. And even closer, in the heart of the Faculty of Economics itself, Piero Sraffa, a close friend and comrade of Gramsci's, published his game-changing article in *Economic Journal*. Meanwhile, in the new course, the business of training the next generation of managers of the empire proceeded apace, unfazed by, if not oblivious to, all these external 'disturbances'. Looking ahead, the life of this training programme, till 1940, witnessed in the Great Depression, the rise of Hitler and the Second World War; and in Cambridge itself, the theoretical triumph of Keynesian ideas, and their rapid spread and takeover of the domain of economic policy.

The training courses were halted in 1940, but, as the war ended and new imperatives, and consequently new courses, emerged.

In 1944, with the intention of bringing the training up to speed in terms of the rapidly changing needs of the time, the Devonshire Committee devised a fresh, holistic three-year sandwich training programme, in the form of the 'Devonshire Courses', for all colonial administrative cadres; the new programme ran through till 1969. 1944, like 1926, was another big year in more ways than one: there were the D-Day landings, the march into Rome by the Allies, the breaking of the 880-day siege of Leningrad with 2 million dead on the Soviet side, the rise of Juan Peron in Argentina after the coup d'etat. 1944 was also the year of Keynes and the Bretton Woods Conference and the formation of the IMF and the World Bank; and at home in the UK, the seeding of the welfare state with the UK Education Act 1944 which provided for free secondary education for all. Of course, those devising the revised course, which lasted till 1969, could hardly have foreseen the stepwise conflictual dismantling the British Empire, first in the 1940s in Asia, then in the 1950s and 1960s in Africa. The period also saw Gamal Abdel Nassar shifting the old imperial goal posts and witnessed the British imperial Suez misadventure, the formation and consolidation of Israel and the emergence of 'the Palestinian question'; and of course, the period ushered in the idealism and optimism (in the Global South) and the psychosis of threat and panic (in the USA) unleashed by Castro, Guevara and their Cuban Revolution; with Mao having launched the Great People's Cultural Revolution in 1966, the prospect, or the spectre, of socialism was back centre stage on the political map. Persisting with a unitary 'training' programme that included fundamentally diverse constituencies was a demanding, if not impossible, task—with the mandate of British and local colonial administrators on the one side, and the nationalist aspirations of the intake from the ex-colonies, pulling generally in opposite directions. The UK was a paradox, practicing neo-colonialism overseas and espousing near-socialism at home, with the latter tendency inspiring Friedrich Hayek to write, from the study organised for him at King's College by Keynes himself, his *The Road of Serfdom*, his virulent attack on socialism as well as on the rising welfare state, published in 1944, even as Beveridge published his *Full Employment in a Free Society*. And this was the very year that saw the declaration in India of the 'Bombay Plan' which laid out a blueprint for accelerated industrialisation and planned development through a partnership between the state and the hitherto thwarted ambitions of the nascent Indian capitalist class in India three years in advance of its Independence in 1947.

The Devonshire Courses involved a year at the university, then two years of a supervised apprenticeship in the field, and then back to digest it all, write up and await a posting. This was later collapsed into a one-year training programme covering imperial history, language skills, judiciary and ethnology, and became the Devonshire 'A' course. A second Devonshire 'B' course catered to senior colonial officers who could then take a year's sabbatical-cum-refresher, enjoy and (theoretically) benefit from academic engagement at the university. "In 1953, the increasing numbers of locally-recruited officers and the approach of self-government for most colonies led to further changes. The name changed to the Overseas Services Course. The First Devonshire Course became 'Course A' and the Second Course 'Course B'. By 1963, more flexible programmes in development economics had been introduced, and the name changed to the Course on Development in 1969, the Course administration was moved to University (from 1973, Wolfson) College."[14]

---

[14] Extracted from the brief introduction to the 18 linear metres of archival materials on and around the Course on Development held at the Cambridge University Library (GBR/265/CDEV).

Sarah Stockwell (2018: 95)[15] argues that "over time the courses acquired new epistemologies, focused primarily on development studies. They nevertheless provide striking illustration of how Empire left legacies within the structures of British institutions long after most of the Empire had gone and thus of the colonial roots both of postcolonial development studies and practice."

A 1960s snapshot from the passage of one African student through this Cambridge route provides useful and intriguing texture to the ethos and goings-on of the time. The account draws on the detailed work of Sarah Stockwell on the training of colonial administrators in the post-war years till 1982, when the ODA-funded course was closed down (Stockwell, 2018), and pulls together some observations on the unusual case of one Mr Valentine Musakanya, a Zambian administrator, only one of two black Africans in the cohort of twenty one on the 1961 course. His experience before, during and after the Cambridge course richly embodies some of the novel cultural dimensions and transactions in this 'transfer of knowledge', and the imperial and colonial imaginations of some of the courses

> could create some curious situations, with, for example new elites from emergent states attending lectures on the structure and practices of African societies by leading anthropologists such as Meyer Fortes and Audrey Richards (Cambridge) and E.E. Evans-Pritchard (Oxford). Audrey Richards' regional specialism was the Bemba of Northern Rhodesia. At Cambridge, Musakanya took exception to her analysis, and in 'retaliation' gave his own lecture entitled 'The Sexual Habits of the English Tribe'. It proved popular and was 'convincingly anthropological'.[16] During the 1960s accusations that anthropology characterized Africans as primitive while bolstering the position of colonial rule and traditional elites became common among African intellectuals. For their part, British probationers were sometimes equally perplexed by the orientation of the curriculum, which reflected the preoccupations of the high colonial period rather than the emergence of new disciplines relevant to the probationers and most strikingly omitted analysis of the immediate political contexts to which they would be heading. (Ibid.: 116)

In Musakanya's own words: "It appeared to be the professional practice of anthropologists that in explaining the actions or habits of the so-called primitive peoples, they termed as 'primitive' those which they did not understand, and as 'borrowed' those which approximated to the anthropologists' own customs. In retaliation, I advertised my own lecture entitled 'The Sexual Habits of the English Tribe'. It was well attended and successful: it was convincingly anthropological" (Musakanya, 2010: 26). Larmer (2010a: 26) adds: "he was

---

[15] There is a fine informative resource in the research of Sarah Stockwell's study of the training of colonial administrators in Oxford and Cambridge (Stockwell, 2018), viewed as one dimension of British imperial relations. Its focus is limited by its own purposes, and thus does go much beyond her insightful commentary on the Course on Development which dominates her narrative.

[16] And, according to Musakanya's claim, 'well attended'. He had been "particularly irritated by Audrey Richards' anthropological study, Land and Diet in Northern Rhodesia, and its characterization of Bemba dietary customs as 'primitive'" (Larmer 2010b: 396–397).

equally unimpressed by his Field Engineering training, failing to understand how measuring a cricket pitch with a theodolite would be of practical use in the African bush."

But apart from the public transfer of academic knowledge, there were also apparently surreptitious transfers of other information. "Both Oxford and Cambridge would become known as recruiting grounds for British intelligence, with a network of individuals throughout the colleges spotting talent among the student body ... at least one cadet, Zambian Valentine Musakanya, was 'by all accounts except his own, recruited by the British intelligence services' while based at St Catherine's College Cambridge'" (Stockwell, 2018: 110).[17] Miles Larmer observes: "Unsurprisingly, Musakanya does not mention this in his memoirs, but it seems clear that his subsequent and highly unusual appointment as Consul General in Elizabethville was a reflection of his widely-suspected links to MI6" (Larmer, 2010a: 27). Coincidentally, Larmer (ibid.: 26) notes that "two other Africans, both Tanganyikans, attended the course—both went on to become Tanzanian Cabinet Ministers."

According to Tony Schur, a course mate of Musakanya in the Cambridge course, "He was exceptionally intelligent, always curious, far-seeing, a man of the highest principles and possessed of a delightful sense of humour, much loved" (Schur, 2014: 288).

In 1959, just before coming to Cambridge on the course, Musakanya served as local magistrate also for the mining township of his childhood where he had to judge cases involving his childhood friends—"... there was an indescribably gulf between us ... I felt alienated and with an uneasy sense of having betrayed my class" (quoted in Larmer, 2010b: 396). Larmer writes: "this feeling of personal isolation, the bittersweet result of his education and personal success, is a common theme in Musakanya's autobiography, suggesting a sense of alienation from the excitement and energy that accompanied the struggle for independence that was then dominating public life on the Copperbelt" (ibid.: 396).

Reflecting later on the experience of the Congo, Musakanya laments: "I saw a wonderful and rich country fall to pieces, ravaged by foreigners and its leaders. Ignorant men ... whose greed and hunger for purposeless power were puppets of international politics and insensitive to the rape of their country and the ... misery of their people ... The Congo was a frightening forewarning of what might happen in other parts of the continent, all of which was galloping towards Independence" (quoted in Larmer, 2010b: 397).

With powerful resonance to the then unavailable writings of Franz Fanon—*The Wretched of the Earth* was published in 1961, the same year when Musakanya

---

[17] Larmer (2010b: 396n23) writes that "it was apparently during his time at Cambridge that Musakanya was approached by the British intelligence services. He does no write about his links with MI6, and while these are freely acknowledged by his friends and family, no written evidence is yet available to support he widespread belief that he remained in contact with MI6 agents for some decades."

was in his Cambridge course—Musakanya wrote much later in similar vein about the period of African nationalist struggles leading up to independence:

> Some of the leaders who had travelled [abroad] had not only seen that independence was possible ... they saw prospects of real personal powers and positions impossible for them even under the most liberal colonial Government. As they travelled to independent and self-governing African and other former colonies the budding politicians ... fully appreciate the spoils lying ahead of them after a political 'struggle'. The imprisonment hazards inevitable in the 'struggle' only served to assure one a position in the ... new state. (Musakanya, 2010: 21)

As Larmer (2010a: xix) raises the issue of Musakanya's political "naivete in regard to post-colonial power" and observes: "What Musakanya saw as the development of an efficient and politically neutral civil service was, for many new politicians, the continuation of 'colonial' rule. What was for Musakanya the corrupt patrimonial distortion of government expenditure was, for may UNIP activists, the just reward for their struggle for independence."

Musakanya, and other officers disenchanted with the path being taken by Kaunda and Zambia, formed an informal group, the 'Wednesday lunch club'; Larmer (2010b: 400) observes that "its members became increasingly unhappy with the direction of government policy; they criticized the centralization of power in the presidency and the increasingly authoritarian nature of political life. Some of its members were later accused alongside Musakanya of involvement in the coup attempt."

"Musakanya was later instrumental in establishing his country's civil service, first as Secretary to the Cabinet and then Head of the Civil Service, in which capacities he was a key figure in discussions about sending other Zambian public servants to Britain for training" (ibid.: 140). He came into "conflict with Kaunda's government, especially during a period of political radicalization in Zambia from the late 1960s that culminated in 1972 in the establishment of a one-party state under Kaunda's United National Independence Party ...". Musakanya's Cabinet Office was criticized as being 'colonial'; he was assigned to a several less senior posts, prompting his resignation in 1970. "He was later appointed and then removed from the post of governor of the Bank of Zambia, and in 1980 was probably one of the several instigators of an attempted coup against Kaunda, leading to his arrest although he was eventually acquitted on the grounds that the evidence against him had been extracted under torture" (ibid.: 140–141). It is unlikely that all administrator-alumni on the course had such remarkable careers, though many might have been nudged in the direction of using their local influence in favour of British positions in their home countries and indeed such soft influence was cited as one of the cost-effective benefits that ODA could derive from a continuation of the course.

Musakanya's experience also points to racism of the times, even in such locations of learning as Oxbridge.

Both at Oxford and Cambridge the first appearance of nonwhite and non-Christian students had earlier given rise to tensions, and some colleges had been reluctant to accept students of colonial origin. Even Balliol, notable for its connections to the Indian Civil Service, had operated an 'informal' quota system for Indian students. That as recently as 1938 Cambridge had advised the Colonial Office that 'all colleges were reluctant to accept coloured students and ... all would feel more difficulty in accepting Africans than others', illustrates the prejudice operating within the Oxbridge system. (Stockwell, 2018: 102)

"When Valentine Musakanya and his wife found private landlords unwilling to take a black couple other members of the course rallied round to assist them and, when a fellow student married, Musakanya and another probationer joined them in their new Cambridge house" (ibid.: 113–114).
Then came the decolonisations in Africa. Stockwell (ibid.: 119) observes:

Neither the universities nor Whitehall were well prepared for the breakneck pace at which political change had occurred. As officials scrambled to reconfigure Britain's established colonial development and welfare policies for a new postcolonial age, uncertainty surrounded the future of the Oxbridge training courses. If their survival had been in question in the early 1950s, the odds against now looked overwhelming. Their original constituency—expatriate officers—had become a 'dying species', and with the 'colonial apron-strings' cut, it proved harder to attract recruits to Britain.

The history of the Oxbridge courses in the 1950s and the early 1960s reflects the Janus-faced nature of the later British imperial state. Bits of it were focused on the still-functioning Empire; other elements were concerned more with adjusting to a world *after* Empire. In turn this reflects the protracted nature of British decolonization .... British technical assistance therefore served a dual purpose: it was designed to cater to both Britain's remaining colonies and to recently independent Commonwealth states. The Oxbridge courses saw British probationers trained alongside not just local administrators, but *postcolonial* locals. (Ibid.: 137)

She concludes, overall, that:

by the 1970s ... the needs of emergent nations were changing, and there were also many new sources of technical assistance. The internal institutional motors were also now less significant in part because colonial and Commonwealth studies were increasingly eclipsed by the area studies stimulated by new sources of state funding in the 1960s. Legacies of the earlier activities were left within the institutional structures, but the institutional energy and commitment had gone. (Ibid.: 141)

Turbulence and Transformation: Revising the Mandate, 1969–1982
With periodical restructuring, the 'Devonshire' courses had an extended run till their unworkable anachronistic nature became sufficiently obvious, and in 1969 they were closed down and replaced by a brand-new Diploma in

Development Studies (DDS) for overseas administrators at Cambridge, and a one-year programme for overseas diplomats at Oxford (Kirk-Greene, 1999; see also Kothari, 2005). Paul Howell was appointed the director of the programme with its offerings attuned to the needs of a new clientele, involving a fundamental shift in approach from public administration to planning. Alongside, in view of the new post-imperial context, the diploma shifted its catchment area to cohorts of early- to mid-career officers from the administrative services of the recently independent countries.[18] Over the period, with Asian colonies gaining independence and going their own way, the clientele also shifted perceptibly towards African participants.

> The principal constituency for the course was identified as those responsible for planning and appraising economic and social development, and, in case anyone should be in doubt as to the changes that had occurred, publicity material described the course as 'not a training course in public administration'. Keen to reinforce the message, Howell was aware that they must emphasize that the character of the course was now 'totally changed', being related to 'real needs' rather that starting from the perspective of teaching 'what the natives need to know'. ... Yet, for all that Howell sought to refocus the course on development, he seemed unable to break fully with the earlier traditions. During discussions about the course reform in 1970 its primary purpose was still seen as to 'train the generalist administrator', thus differentiating it from what was on offer at Sussex. Ultimately the continuing purchase of the 'generalist' tradition contributed to the demise of the course. (Stockwell: 133–134)

The troubled course eventually died at the hands of Thatcher's cuts: "Seen as too academic and impractical, the course became an easy target for economies and died after government finance was withdrawn in 1982" (Rosenheim, 1994).

Paul Howell (1917–1994), the Cambridge anthropologist and colonial administrator (in Africa, especially Sudan), served as director of the redeveloped diploma over its chequered and eventually ill-fated lifetime, 1969–1982. Rosenheim (1994) provides a fine sketch of a fine gent of the old guard[19] whose "career paralleled the transition from an era in which British colonial

---

[18] It can be taken as read that though some of these worthies undoubtedly utilised the academic side of the opportunity seriously, many others took it as a leisurely sojourn to take in the atmosphere and air at the hallowed universities and return with a credential and a stamp to show, brag and bore all comers back at home with never-ending re-runs of 'when I was up at Cambridge' stories.

[19] Paul Howell was born posthumously; his father, a brigadier-general fell aged 38 in the Battle of the Somme; his uncles and cousins inculcated in him "a lifelong love for the English countryside, particularly for fishing"; he became "an expert fisherman, both on his beloved Wissey, in Norfolk, and for salmon in Scotland, and was very active promoting the conservation of rivers". Rivers seemed to form the flow of his life. "An early interest in social anthropology took him to the Sudan on a vacation study of the Shilluk of the upper Nile, his first encounter with the river which was to occupy his interest for so much of his life." He retired from the Cambridge fray in 1990, given a meagre ration of four life-years still to enjoy his peaceful riverine pleasures.

power was still exercised to one in which merely influence was sought." Despite serving as ADC to two successive Governor-Generals of Sudan, he was "never himself a colonialist, he was remarkably consistent in his own work as an anthropologist and a government administrator working abroad: his foremost concern was always with the needs of the peoples he worked with and with furthering their control over their political and economic development. He was different from many of his colleagues, and he was less interested in exporting a Westminster concept of government and law than in stimulating the local economy within its traditional social framework." Another obituary observed: "Given his academic background and professional training, Dr Howell was well qualified to address both anthropological and administrative audiences ... A man of great versatility, he was a generalist in the best sense of the word. He was at once a competent administrator, a perceptive development specialist and a distinguished academic" (Deng, 1994: 69). Paul knew about obscure legal systems: his thesis had produced *A Manual of Nuer Law*. But beyond that, he knew about contending Arab tribal systems as his supervisor Evans-Pritchard pointed out, "he has made contributions to our knowledge not only of the other departments of Nuer social life but also of the Shilluk, the Dinka, the Baggara Arabs ..." (quoted in Deng, 1994: 69). For eight years he had headed the Middle East Development Division in Beirut in the difficult 1960s; and in the previous decade (1956–1961), as anthropologist and social administrator in Sudan, he had served as Chairman of the East Africa Nile Waters Coordinating Committee, no social club. But the voluminous archives, surfeit with involuted and convoluted accounts of the struggle first, for the development, and then for the survival, of the course over 1969–1982, reveal that all this was poor preparation for managing the menagerie that constituted the diploma. If anything, Paul Howell was charged by some as being part of the problem, not of the solution.[20] The problem perhaps was that there were too many problems. There seems never to have been a dull day, a case of perennial frictions between

---

[20] An early note, written in the hand of Paul Howell, provides a clue to two dimensions of conflict: interdisciplinary (organised and expressed as inter-departmental), cascading into the interpersonal. Usually, it was a case of economics and economists (in the Faculty of Economics and Politics and/or Department of Land Economy). But interpersonal issues could take bizarre forms. Howell complains, presumably to himself, since the note is not seen to be addressed to any person or address: "For some reason or other [initials of a Land Economy staff member withheld] seems to think I am responsible for encouraging criticism of his activities, that I am opposed to the inclusion of certain aspects he deems important, and for more or less all internal antagonisms which plague his department. He even accused me of promoting a row over the content of examination papers at a meeting I did not attend. Until relatively recently criticisms have confined to faintly ridiculous trivialities—e.g., I deliberately demonstrated my contempt for his subject by giving instructions that all library books covering Lands should be on the lower shelves; by referring 'land' last on the list of options—and so on. Recently, however, antagonism has become more serious and accusations more damaging, ranging on slander, e.g., I am failing in duty to. ... I am neglecting my teaching duties—when I have none. ... That I am personally responsible for deliberately misinterpreting. ... That I am personally responsible for alleged bad relations with the British Council. ..." (Note on File, handwritten by Paul Howell, undated, unaddressed; 3p.)

tribal (read disciplinary, or departmental) factions and fractions. The voluminous files provide, unfortunately, overflowing supportive evidence.

The case for the continuation of the course was fully enunciated by the Overseas Studies Committee in a memorandum containing twelve arguments in its favour (see Appendix). But, coming as it did in the interregnum between the era of the demise of the empire, rapidly lapsing, and the unfolding rise of the Third World, this new diploma suffered, unsurprisingly, from something akin to an identity crisis. While the later, final stretch, spanning especially the 1985–1995 decade, involving the harassment and eventual eviction of 'development' from the Faculty of Economics and Politics was probably the most injurious and traumatic, an immersion into the eighteen linear-metres of archival materials held by the University Library on the Course on Development suggests that the middle period, 1969–1982, was perhaps the most vexatious and management intensive. 'Instructing' or 'teaching' development in the North to students, even if they happened mostly to be administrators, from the South, especially in the era of decolonisation and Third-World economic nationalism, could not have been a smooth ride, especially if one adds into this bubbling cauldron of ingredients the aspects of interdepartmental, interdisciplinary and interpersonal unsolvable simultaneous equations that characterise social sciences in a university setting—and Cambridge was a prime example of such ricocheting adversarial relations, whether bilateral or multilateral. All this had to be negotiated, or muddled through, in steering HMS 'Enterprise Development' through choppy academic and institutional waters. It would have been remarkable if, on the various segments of this criss-crossing voyage, there hadn't been squabbles, quarrels, even attempted mutinies inside the ship itself, rendering the task of the skipper all the more treacherous. There was a plenitude of stakeholders all wanting a piece of the action: the SPS Committee with its constituents; the Department of Social Anthropology; the Department of Archaeology and Anthropology; the Department of Land Economy; the Faculty of Economics and Politics; the staff of the Overseas or Development Studies Committee in its various incarnations; the General Board of the University; various Colleges that housed and hosted the programmes; and the ODA which was the main sponsor and budget holder. And of course, if the consumer is to be the sovereign, there were also the perspectives of the governments and bodies that sent the students, never mind the ultimate consumer, the student himself (and they were indeed almost all males). One could choose to describe this concoction as a principal–agent, or a collective action problem, or wryly as normal institutional life in the university—but it would not change the reality it was; and all this before the first lecture was delivered. The sheer physical evidence of the archives attests to the extremely labour-intensive nature of the institutional process of delivering development instruction to what was, in the end, a relatively small band of students each year. And each year, some wheel or other threatened to fall away from the wagon, making the lives of teachers and administrators all the more 'interesting'.

But apart from these fights between groups of economists in the Faculty and the DAE, the smooth progression of development studies to academic and professional maturity was also hindered by interdepartmental rivalries and contestations over ownership, with resource implications. Archaeology and Anthropology had things to say to Economics; Sociology to Economics; Land Economy had its own agenda, and Social and Political Studies (SPS) and Social Anthropology had minds of their own. Some of this democratic acrimony reflected gestating interpersonal irritations, big egos in small spaces; but other differences arose from differences in subject definitions and knowledge imaginaries of disciplinary prima donnas. There were indeed too many cooks, with the additional complication that each chef was practising a different cuisine, each using its own ingredients and implements, but each describing the final dish on the menu, that is, syllabus, as 'development'—there was perhaps as much chance of authenticity as the British Rail curry concoction.

These interdepartmental and interdisciplinary muddles were further addled by the crosscutting bureaucratic quagmires involving other 'stakeholders', and there were several of those: the General Board of the University which periodically took, or failed to take, decisions in timely or helpful manner, no doubt constrained by wider uncertainties at government or international levels; hosting colleges for the various courses, who had a finger in the resource pie; and the donors, mainly the ODA which had its own distinct perspective. In short, there was a multi-level principal–agent problem involving a hierarchy of 'principals' trying to get multiple agents to prioritise the principal's agendas over their own.[21] Here, it is striking that the case for the continuation of course (beyond 1982) found a consistent support in the ODA, especially through the actions of Bob Porter, though he had often to fight his corner within the ODA,

---

[21] The long-drawn saga of the negotiations between the ODA, the University and the Overseas Studies Committee managing the development courses absorbed an inordinate amount of time and energy over a period as long as four years between 1978 and 1982; this bears testimony to the remarkably circumlocutory and clearly dysfunctional decision-making algorithms at work. This process is documented in painstaking and painful detail by Paul Howell, the Director and Doreen Bennett the administrative secretary; appropriately, the document (dated 14 January 1982) is titled 'Countdown to Doomsday', and it registers, after its final updating, as many as 74 exchanges—running into 10 foolscap pages of text—between the various parties concerning "the lack of negotiation between the O.D.A. and the University since the receipt of the letter from O.D.A. on 22 February 1980 telling us that they would be unable to continue to finance the courses after the end of the current quinquennium in July 1982. Much of 1978 and the whole of 1979 had been spent in an attempt to stave off the withdrawal of O.D.A. support, in the face of changing policies (never announced) and in pressing for a decision on accommodation. ..." Point 72 notes the agreement reached between ODA, the Vice Chancellor and the Secretary General of the Faculties over arrangements for three years; point 73 notes that the proposal was accepted by the General Board; and point 74 records that the "Board of Land Economy and Faculty of Economics and Politics agreed to setting up of proposed new courses and agree to participate in Joint Management Committee"—bringing this part of the saga to a close. This did not preclude a further rather acrimonious run in between the complaining sociologists and anthropologists, who lost turf in the new arrangement, and the university authorities who had essentially gone over their heads in coming to the final agreement.

but then, frustratingly, with the University of Cambridge which should normally have been expected to stand behind the successful programme involving its own staff. The General Board, at the end, became more an obstacle, if not an opponent, to the continuation of the course—a stance that drew reaction from an astonished and disappointed Porter.[22]

In the 1970s, it would appear that the paths of the Diploma in Development Studies delivered in 'university' space by the interdepartmental Development Studies Committee, and that of the narrower offerings on development economics, diverged; the former went into turbulent decline, while the latter could arguably be regarded as being on the ascendant. For instance, in the Faculty of Economics, 1971–1973 saw the numbers of doctoral scholars of South Asian origins alone jump from approximately four to roughly eighteen, with the induction of a dozen scholars from India, Pakistan and the newly independent Bangladesh. The cohort was lively in intellectual terms, and they fairly soon formed a South Asian Seminar which met regularly to discuss each other's work; also, in extra-curricular terms, forming a standing South Asia XI on the cricket field. This implied that an approximately like number of Faculty staff served as supervisors on development themes.

While the demand side for each was strong, there was a wide gap between the academic levels of the Diploma in Development and the PhD cohort, and this vacuum induced the formation of a new M.Phil in development from

---

[22] R.S. Porter, who was a consistent supporter of the DDS, makes his feelings and assessment plain to Nicol, the Secretary-General of the Faculties. "I am naturally very sorry that the Board feel unable to proceed on the basis of the proposals in my earlier letters. We have I believe appreciated through the University's problem and we had gone as far as we could to meet it. While we do of course understand the inherent difficulty over a financial risk in the present climate I cannot but observe that the likelihood of financial embarrassment to the University seems remote in practice given the widespread knowledge of the excellence of the courses and the past and potential enrolment on them. As we have explained previously any possibility of considering continued ODA financial support beyond the 1981/82 Academic Year, even on a tapering basis, would depend on a reasonable expectation that the University would plan to assume full responsibility in 1985, provided there were sufficient suitable applications for enrolment on the courses. However, I am afraid your letter does not provide me with a basis on which I can invite my Minster to reconsider his decision. .... I am bound to say that I find it hard to see a way forward in the light of your letter of 8 August. In these circumstances, though I do not myself have an alternative to offer, I am reluctant finally to close the door to a search for a solution which would resolve the problem within the constraints we face on both sides." As it turned out, the university was not willing even "to express its strong interest in the continuation of the courses" even while refusing to take responsibility for them from 1985, still four years into the future.

(Letter, R.S. Porter, O.D.A, to A.D.I. Nicol, 25 August 1981).

A contemporary record of a 'personal meeting' at the ODA involving Person, Porter, Manning, Perris and Howell provides a confirmation. The record has 14 points. #13, coming from the ODA side notes: "[ODA name withheld] seemed gently annoyed with the Cambridge attitude—referring to the lengths other universities were prepared to go to preserve Development Studies in one form or another; and also point out that ODA were showing willing (sic) to help preserve 3 or 4 jobs over the period. Was the University indifferent to that aspect?" Then, the final #14 notes: "what [ODA] had wanted to see, and had always wanted to see, was a permanent presence of Development Studies in Cambridge on a sound basis. ...."

mid-1976, with the initiative led by Phyllis Deane, then Chair of the interdepartmental Committee for Development Studies.

In the period from the early 1970s and through much of the 1980s, the Faculty had opened the doors to the heavy intakes of PhD candidates from developing countries, and the Faculty Board posed no obstacles for the establishment of a new M.Phil, perhaps also since there was no competing postgraduate degree course in development; if anything, the early resistance to launching the M.Phil in Development Studies came from the University's General Board with its concern over 'academic standards', and Valpy FitzGerald refers to it being 'snobbish' in this regard.[23] Of course, the 1970s were the heyday of the Cambridge greats, and virtually all of them supported the study of Third-World development even if not all were directly involved in it in research or policy advisory capacities. Thus, notwithstanding the termination of the ODA-funded Diploma in 1981, development economics and development studies were flourishing and on the rise in the Faculty and related locations: there was a large cohort of high-level PhD candidates from the early 1970s, and there was the new M.Phil in the Economics and Politics of Development housed in the Faculty of Economics and Politics itself.

From the early 1970s, efforts were building up from academics involved in development teaching, research and PhD research supervision—with a prominent role played by the economists led by Phyllis Deane, Valpy FitzGerald, Suzy Paine, John Wells amongst others—for establishing an M.Phil in Development Studies. The proposal found university approval in 1975, and the programme was launched in 1977; the degree had three options within it, viz., Economics, Sociology and Politics and Lands, each involving the respective departments or faculties. The lead taken by economics can be attributed to the very sharp increase in the intake of PhD candidates working on topics in applied development economics, the majority being from South Asian countries. Many more economics staff were engaged in their supervision, and demand was expected to remain buoyant, while the capacity of Faculty to admit more at the PhD level was finite. This new M.Phil ran alongside two other longstanding related M.Phil programmes: the M.Phil in Economics, and the M.Phil in Land Economy.

---

[23] Valpy FitzGerald observes that "the main driver for change came from us lecturers, pressing for higher academic standards and a student base that was not just the 'mid-career bureaucrats' favoured by the ODA. The prospect of declining subsidy reinforced the argument. The lead for this change in terms of high-level university politics was Phyllis Deane, who was Chair of the Committee for Development Studies. I had some influence because as a PhD student in economics, I had been president of the Cambridge Graduate Students Society" (personal communication; email 11 May 2018). John Toye's reading is that the desired change could have come about within the prevalent structure, and that the real cause of closure lay in the Thatcherite cuts with the university unwilling to pick up the bill to bridge the gap, given their indifference to the subject. It should be recalled that this was a period where external-national and internal-faculty politics began to stack up against groups and causes unacceptable to the orthodox camp.

In the first five years of the new M.Phil, it became quickly apparent that the Economics Option was dominant: in the first year, 1977–1978, there were just three admissions in total, of which two were for the Economics Option, none in the Sociology & Politics Option and one in the Lands Option; in 1979–1980, the numbers were 23 (in total), 10, 8 and 5; by 1981–1982, the total had risen sharply to 35 (from 103 applications), with the Economics now dominating with 26 admissions, with Sociology & Politics, and Lands, declining to just 3 and 4 respectively. Within the Faculty of Economics and Politics, the new M.Phil in Development Studies (Economics Option), with its 26 admissions, had overtaken the Faculty's long-running M.Phil in Economics which had 23 admissions though from a larger pool of applicants in 1981–1982. The new M.Phil in Development Studies (of 1977) was in addition of course to the ongoing ODA-funded Course on Development (COD) which led to the award of the Diploma in Development Studies (DDS), and the divergence in trends between the two over this 5-year period is striking: in 1977–1978, the COD/DDS had a total of 28 admissions, with 13 in COD Economics Options and 4 in COD Sociology & Politics Options; by 1981–1982, the profile had shifted dramatically: the total for COD had wobbled about but came down to 23; that for the COD Economics Options declined steadily to just 6; and that for COD Sociology & Politics kept to roughly the same level, ending at 5. Three conclusions emerge: first, that the M.Phil in Development Studies was proving to be much more attractive than the COD-DDS; second, that economics was dominating the trends; and third, that within Economics, there was a strong shift away from the COD-DDS in favour of the new M.Phil in Development Studies with the Economics Option. Altogether, the pattern reflected the rising demand for an academic professionalisation of the degrees, moving away from what might be perceived as 'training'; and that this pattern was being driven by economics.

But for the COD-DDS, the writing was on the wall. The ODA pronouncement giving notice of complete withdrawal from the DDS in 1982 stirred the latent multi-tribal pot and tensions started building and bubbling up. Against this background, the COD-DDS group, led by Paul Howell, fought a losing battle for survival.[24] In the middle of this period came the ODA announcement of withdrawing completely from the COD-DDS from 1982. While the M.Phil

---

[24] A Battle Group had been formed; at its meeting of 5 December 1980, suggestions were made for "a more aggressive campaign to save the courses than that carried out so far"; the following had been agreed to: "since low profile tactics had not given rapid or positive results a high profile campaign should be adopted. This should include wider representation on the 'Battle Group' from both within and outside the University [persons from outside Cambridge: Michael Lipton, Richard Jolly, Judith Hart, etc.]; political pressures should be applied, e.g. approaches to Members of Parliament [Edward Heath, Robert Rhodes James, Judith Hart, Alex Lyon, Frank Judd, Lord Carrington], letters to the press [The Times, The Guardian, Third World Review, New Statesman, Times Higher Educational Supplement], etc.; staff representation at meetings between the I.D.A. and the University; a meeting between staff and the Secretary-General of the Faculties; representation should be made direct to the U.G.C." (CDEV: OSC.402).

constituency was secured by 'quota' grants from the SSRC, there was no protection for the COD-DDS which had to seek new benefactors, with the university itself digging in and refusing any bail-out, even temporarily for a three-year 'tapering-out' period till 1985, as proposed by the ODA. The group most exposed were the staff hired on ODA monies for the COD-DDS, and by 1981, they had mostly left to seek shelter or fortune in other locations. The ODA-COD-DDS construction duly ended in 1982. The worthy Paul Howell had mounted an honourable and sustained campaign, in the end to no avail—but not entirely without loyal appreciation from some academic[25] and administrative[26] colleagues.

[25] A morning-after letter of contrition to Paul Howell from one of his colleagues expresses the flavour of the time:

Dear Paul,

Showdowns never were my cup of tea—they usually achieve little more than making the parties to these feel wretched. My moan to poor Mrs B was quite out of place and, as regards [D] quite incorrect—for that I apologise without reservation. I was reminded yesterday of your allegory of the pigs biting each other. I think I understand and fully sympathise with the complex problems with which you are confronted, and are tackling with great fortitude. If we differ at all, I suppose it is in that I feel that there are limits to the extent to which our own internal working relationships can absorb the unusual pressures which the outside world brings to bear on us. You, in particular, are alert to the complexities of dealing with that outside world. In trying to diagnose problems, I suppose I have come to the conclusion that our internal organization is neither happily adjusted to expectation of the external agencies on whom we depend. At the moment, I feel that the latter are thoroughly incoherent, and much of our frustration derives from trying to accommodate ourselves to them. If we have to bite at all, I think we should bite, with strategic care, the hand that pokes us. Doubtless you would agree. Internally, the well-worked solution to such dilemmas is inertia, disengagement, disinterest. Although I complain that we opt too often for weak accommodating solutions, and that staff interests do tend to take refuge, centrifugally, elsewhere, the very fact that we generate so much heat indicates that we are alive and kicking. ... Within the small components of the course which we have license to organise, all can be sweetness and light (witness the way in which the soc pol brigade feted [S] for her 'single-handed' efforts). Unfortunately for you, you have only the wider arenas to observe and act in. And those arenas, as we all know, do [not] afford very much pleasure and gratification at the moment. I am sorry you have all these things to worry about when you are feeling ill. I hope the summer's rest will fortify you for the vital roles you have to play, and for which there is much appreciation (albeit rather mute!). (Letter, [R] to Howell, 30 June 1979. 2p.)

[26] With the changing of the guard in Michaelmas Term, 1982, Doreen Bennett, the long-serving, long-suffering administrator of the Overseas Study Committee writes to Paul, her ex-Chairman:

I thought you might be amused if I wrote on the somewhat grandiose notepaper which comes from the small dark room in Silver Street to which I have been consigned! Things carry on in the usual way. Students saying that they can't find the articles and books recommended and staff saying that they are overwhelmed with students asking questions. The Degree Committee office in Economics treat everything we do with great suspicion ... I have taken to the nasty provincial habit of calling Professors 'Profs' since both those concerned with this lot [Development Studies] refer to each other in that way". She refers to the same Land Economy colleague who had a personalised campaign directed at Howell—

The course had fine young economists on the teaching staff, including, amongst other worthies, John Toye, Jose Gabriel Palma, John Sender and Valpy FitzGerald, and they observed it all at close quarters. "The financial support came from the Overseas Development Ministry, changed by Thatcher in 1979 to the Overseas Development Administration. All the academics were on 5-year contracts. The ODA's first step was to insist that everyone's contract expired on the same date. This was presented as mere administrative tidying, but alarm bells should have been ringing because it meant that the whole show could be closed down on the same day in 1981." And so indeed it was. "The University was informed that funding would stop then. Arguments were put by Paul Howell and Ben Farmer in favour of continuing the course on the basis that there was no shortage of fee-paying applicants, but these pleas were to no avail. The university authorities were not interested" (John Toye, personal communication; email 9 May 2018). Valpy FitzGerald recalls that "the ODA had shifted from an annual subsidy from the aid budget which covered all costs to one based on scholarships, which later diminished in numbers" (Valpy FitzGerald, personal communication; email 11 May 2018).

The staff scattered. John Toye: "The Secretary General of the Faculties [A.D.I. Nicol at the time] wrote to me that I could continue on a one-year contract without any University title—to which I replied that I had no intention of staying on such terms" (personal communication); and so John left to use his energies and talents and launch a distinguished career elsewhere, retiring recently as the Director of the Institute of Development Studies (IDS) in Sussex, ranked at the top of the global league of units offering development studies as a programme; Valpy FitzGerald left for a chair at the Institute of Social Studies in The Hague[27]—possibly the oldest academic institution for

> "XYZ finds the whole thing very convenient and is always popping in to see how things are! It is absolutely ironic that the whole thing has turned out in this way. ... Life has changed very much since last July, and Bill says that for the first time since he has known me I don't go out to work each morning looking forward to the day ahead. It is not just the atmosphere of the office itself, but also the mistrust with which I am treated by the Chairman. He behaves as if I was an 18-year old new entrant, not a 50 (next week) year old with more working experience of offices than he has!" Doreen ends her extensive two-page single-spaced letter suitably: "I hope your typewriter is behaving itself"—quite an appropriate concern considering the bashing it had taken at the hands of Paul Howell in the course of accumulating the massive 18 linear-metres archive of the 1969–1982 period. (Letter, Doreen Bennett to Paul Howell, 21 October 1982; extracts)

The anthropologist in Paul would have nodded approval at her field diary of a day recording participant observations on the experience of regime change.

[27] This vacancy was felicitously filled by Jose Gabriel Palma who left his permanent position as senior lecturer at the North London University (then Polytechnic) to accept a 7-month appointment in Cambridge in February 1981 with the possibility of a one-year extension. Palma recalls that times were bad, universities were cutting down jobs, and he was taking a big risk, but "that is how much I wanted to get to Cambridge, then still the Mecca of heterodox economists". At the end of the extension, staffing was cut from Paul Howell, the Director, plus six staff, to three staff (one economist, one from politics and one from Land Economy), and John Sender was retained

development studies in Europe—to return later to Oxford to become Professor of Development Studies at Oxford University; Sandy Robertson, with whom Valpy had been doing joint interdisciplinary research, left for a position in Manchester; David Lehmann went back into SPS; others into Land Economy; some left for their home country; others, tutors in colleges; Sheila Smith went to IDS; Mushtaq Khan, via Land Economy, decided to opt for SOAS, to launch a fine career there in institutional economics leading to a professorship;[28] John Sender also to SOAS, later also to become a professor there; and this gap was filled in 1990 by Ha-Joon Chang, who has since stayed the course in Cambridge, and is presently a Reader in the Faculty of Economics, while serving currently as the Director of the Centre of Development Studies.

The very idea of shutting down development teaching in the early 1980s would appear to be preposterous, considering the explosive highlighting of its salience on the global stage from the 1970s. The first OPEC oil price hike of 1972, followed by the second in 1979, generated the dramatic debt crisis in oil-importing developing economies and marked the demise of the state-led import-substituting industrialisation strategy, replaced, through the ubiquitous and aggressive agency of the IMF and the World Bank, by the roll out, country by country, of their one-size-fits-all Structural Adjustment Programme and attendant conditionalities. And 1979, on the one side, witnessed the Iranian revolution and, on the other, ushered in Margaret Thatcher, joined on the global neoliberal stage in 1981 by her soulmate Ronald Reagan who launched the attack on organised labour with the firing of over 11,000 striking air traffic controllers; and 1981 saw the Elliot Berg *Accelerated Development in Sub-Saharan Africa* ('get-the-prices-right') report from the World Bank setting out the new template for African development policy; 1982 saw the wilful sinking of Admiral Belgrano by a bellicose Thatcher; 1979–1982 saw the massive change in direction away from Maoist high collectivism towards a market economy in China, followed by Vietnam. Thatcher's hostility towards 'charitable' foreign aid was shored up by the trenchant opposition of some of her senior advisors, especially Peter Bauer. But all notwithstanding, there certainly was enough global evidence to underscore the relevance and support the study, in British universities, of contemporary development processes and policies; but government did not budge.

Ironically, against the run of play and in a U-turn on its earlier expressed indifference or opposition to the course, the university suddenly had a change of heart and agreed to a plan, devised in a breakneck rush to meet the deadlines

---

over Gabriel Palma on the basis of seniority, having been appointed a term prior to Palma's appointment. After a year on a research grant, Palma was appointed as lecturer in the Faculty of Economics, to teach econometrics, not development (Personal communication, email dated 22 February 2021).

[28] Mushtaq Khan took a First in the PPE at Oxford, before obtaining his M.Phil and PhD degrees at Cambridge with both dissertations acclaimed in the highest terms by the examiners. Palma observes that the Chang-Khan partnership then "formed the foundations of Development Studies teaching", till the latter's departure for SOAS (ibid.).

of committees and university draftsmen, to restructure teaching in development studies in the form of new diploma and differently structured M.Phil programmes to run from 1982. However, behind a seemingly inexplicable 'change of heart' usually lies an application of mind. Two hypothetical explanations emerge independently from members of staff of that time.

First, John Toye, then very much in the thick of the action, shared his perception of what could perhaps provide albeit a partial explanation of this 'change of heart': "University-level decision-makers apparently did not think highly of some Development staff, and took the opportunity to cut funds to shake them out"; no names were mentioned, but the university's heart seems to have had its reasons (Personal Communication; Conversation on 14 August 2018, Cambridge).

The second potential explanation comes from Jose Gabriel Palma, also a development staff member, and relies on personal observation. It involves and revolves around (later) Sir Francis 'Harry' Hinsley, Master of St. John's College, 1979–1989, and the Vice-Chancellor, 1981–1983, during whose tenure this story unfolded. Harry Hinsley, a First in Part I of the History Tripos never finished his degree, as was recruited into the intelligence duties at Bletchley Park and went on to a distinguished career and a knighthood in 1985; he made International Relations his field, and upon taking up the Vice Chancellorship was very keen to give it a raised academic and institutional presence in the university. He was keen on creating an M.Phil in International Relations "in which by coincidence I was involved", recalls Palma, who also writes that "he [Hinsley] was a fervent proponent of independent centres (like International Relations, and Development) with interdisciplinary M.Phils". He further recollects: "Again, a bit by chance, I could see furious the Secretary General of the University [Faculties]was on being told to reverse the University position on development." Palma's assessment, albeit speculative, was that Development was 'saved' by serving as a cover for legitimising the initiative on International Relations; indeed, but for the persistent opposition of the university bureaucracy which wanted to phase out development, it could well have survived with an even better outcome. So, "the compromise was a big M. Phil. In International Relations and a tiny one in Development (that needed a lot of help from people in Economics, like Ajit [Singh] and later by me) to survive" (Personal communication, email, dated 17 February 2021). A Centre for Development Studies was indeed formed, but for another two decades, in 2012.

Gabriel Palma also provides an explanation of the hostile stance of the university towards Development. Paraphrased, it runs thus: after the Thatcher onslaught, a nasty coalition was formed between the mainstream faction in economics with echelons of sections of the top bureaucracy of the university and a few right-wing senior members of the university "to destroy the heterodox gang of economists at the DAE, Development and in the Faculty". That coalition "wanted to destroy development as the economists there were assigned to the Faculty and could vote in elections. The assault on Development as the precursor of the attack on the DAE." And parts of the top bureaucracy were implicated "up to their neck". In Palma's reading, "had Hinsley not been so interested [in interdisciplinary M.Phils. and Centres] it is unlikely that Development would have survived. That's why the bureaucracy fought a rearguard battle where Development could survive but only with such a small staff contingent that could not really be sustainable." While there are quite a few dots being joined up in these assessments, these hypotheses carry a high degree of credibility and dovetail readily with the narratives of the purges investigated earlier.

The process of implementing the 'change of heart' was somewhat haphazard and drew strong and bitter complaints from the Sociology-Social Anthropology-SPS group that, perhaps rightly, felt that the rushed procedures had passed them by in the process of consultation and that, therefore, they had been cut out from the new offerings; certainly, the shape of the new diploma and degrees suggested that this group had been marginalised from their earlier central position they had traditionally enjoyed. They reacted angrily against both Economics and Land Economy.

In view of the proposed new M.Phil in Economics and Politics of Development to be established in the Faculty of Economics (a modified version of their running M.Phil in Economics of Development), the General Board asked the Department of Social Anthropology to 'disestablish' the running of M.Phil in Development Studies in which it has a major stake. This induced a response from Jack Goody to the Secretary General: "In my view there is room for continuing the long-standing emphasis this Faculty has placed on the social aspects of development, hopefully in collaboration with SPS and other interested groups. I do not think it would be intellectually or administratively wise to leave the teaching of development studies in the hands of economists (either in Economics and Politics or Land Economy). I would therefore ask the Degree Committee to tell the General Board that we wish to retain the M.Phil in Development Studies, with the addition of the words (Social Aspects) in brackets" (Letter, Jack Goody to Secretary General of the Faculties, 16 February 1982).

A week later, Geoffrey Hawthorn, the sociologist, weighs in on the proposed new diploma with his own objections, suggestions and predictions of bad times ahead should these not be followed: "At present, the proposals for the Diploma are not satisfactory. And this ... is what prompts my anger. These are the outcome of haste, of a weak and confused organizing committee and or what might perhaps diplomatically be described as an insensitive energy on the part of one or two Boards and Faculties etc. ... [and then, following his own suggestion] to attempt more now would, I think, create much disarray that the future, not of the courses themselves but of good relations between those who run them, would be jeopardized; but to attempt anything less would be by omission to endorse what is a very unsatisfactory state of affairs" (Letter, Geoffrey Hawthorn to Paul Howell, 25 February 1982).

The diploma which eventually replaced the outgoing ODA DDS was based in the Department of Land Economy whose good fortune at this windfall came with the compliments of the Faculty of Economics and Politics. Paul Howell writes, "One of the principal troubles (apart from the rush) has been the unwillingness of Economics and Politics to assume responsibility for the administration of the Diploma—this for reasons or workload on the part of their Degree Committee Secretary. Hence the switch to Land Economy who (to my way of thinking) assumed a rather arrogant stand; and if you read the rubric of the <u>Diploma</u> Regulations it is apparent that candidates ... are in effect being forced to undergo a lot of the teaching originally contained in the Lands Option—for which there was a specialist but diminishing demand"[29] (Letter, P.P. Howell to R.S. Porter, ODA, 18 March 1982).

A little later down the line, Paul Howell, in a rumination to himself, lodges a rueful grievance, confirming the distance across disciplines in the programme to be jointly delivered between them: "It is worth noting, however, that the new course contents give inadequate scope for the student who wishes to study the social impact and implications of development policies. ... There is a strange almost pathological aversion to the views of those concerned primarily with the sociological aspects; a sort of blanket attribution to them of a particular form of ideology. This is evidence of ignorance of the true nature of the problems facing Third World countries. Any person with genuine experience of the planning, administrative and executive processes of development will know the significance of the human factor, both in putting policies into effect and in the context of the impact of those policies on human beings. There is a certain element of intellectual myopia here, which is, incidentally, not a characteristic of those concerned with assisting developing countries. The significance of the social dimension is fully recognized by the present government in this country—indeed its inclusion int eh new course was a condition of continued support from the ODA, as it on record in these files. It is a dimension which is repeatedly stressed by all major donors, international agencies, and by the World Bank" (P.P. Howell, File Note, 16 October 1982, 'Afterthought').

11.2.3 In Faculty Space: The Disciplining of 'Development Economics'

Running in parallel, though in some ways intertwined, with the teaching on development studies was that on development economics in which there was always a prominent role for the Faculty of Economics and Politics.

The origins of the teaching of development economics can speculatively be assumed to lie in Austin and Joan Robinson's stay in India during 1926–1928,

---

[29] That there was collective tension between the groups of sociologists and anthropologists on the one hand and Land Economy on the other, was something of an open secret, visible from a distance even to the ODA. The record of a personal meeting at the ODA between ODA officials and some of the Cambridge DDS group, including Paul Howell, makes an explicit observation, attributed to the ODA, and to the surprise of the Cambridge persons present, ("who told them??") that ODA "know that there was a schism between Lands on the one hand and the Social Sciences on the other".

when Austin tutored the young Maharaja of Gwalior. In the course of this, while Joan's doodling on the domestic payroll book points in the direction of *The Economics of Imperfect Competition* (1933), Austin was deeply involved with advisory work reviewing primarily the economic relations between the Indian Princes and the British Crown, and wrote up large parts of the review, sometimes with editorial and substantive comments from Joan. She was asked to accompany the group representing the Princes to London to assist with presenting the economic case for the Princes; she stayed back, Austin resigned his job and returned in 1928, and joined Sidney Sussex as a fellow and the Faculty as a lecturer.

The more general course on Development for colonial administrators had already been established in Cambridge (and Oxford and London) in 1926, and for a while in the post-war years, Austin Robinson became part of the organising committee. The close brush with India had obviously left its mark, and the six months that he spent in South Africa when granted leave in 1932 could only have pulled development issues upfront again after being immersed in the heavy Faculty, university and, to be added, 'Pigouvian' duties in the previous years (Cairncross, 1993: 41–42).

Soon thereafter, in **1933**, he delivered a formal course on 'Economic Problems of the British Empire', comprising twelve lectures, of which the first two were on issues of Free Trade and Imperial Preference, the other ten being on South Africa (two), Rhodesia (three), India (two), and one a piece on Central Africa, Australia and Canada. The coverage of the introductory theoretical lectures is summarised in the printed syllabus:[30]

Lecture 1: The Free Trade Ideal
Relation of free trade to the general theory of *laissez-faire*. The gains of international specialisation and exchange. Specialisation dictated by natural resources; by climate; by natural aptitudes; by historical causes; by the advantages of large-scale production. The method by which specialisation is secured under conditions of laissez-faire. The balance of payments.
Lecture 2: Protection, Imperial Preference and the Revolt against Free Trade
Arguments valid and fallacious; that other countries have tariffs; that unemployment exists; that infant or invalid industries need to be protected; that continuity is necessary; that exports ought to exceed imports; that economic arguments are not paramount. Imperial preference. Can the Empire be an economic unit?

Austin Robinson's course, delivered as a 'subsidiary subject', could possibly make a fair claim to be the first on development economics at the university, though it was offered to Cambridge, not overseas, students.

---

[30] University of Cambridge, Subsidiary Subjects, Michaelmas Term, 1933. Syllabus of a Course of Lectures on *Economic Problems of the British Empire*, by E.A.G. Robinson, M.A., Fellow of Sidney Sussex College, Cambridge: Printed at the University Press.

Five years later, in **1938**, the university established the Diploma in Development Economics, based in the Faculty of Economics. That inveterate recorder of the institutional history of Cambridge economics, Austin Robinson, sets out the details of the programme in a note that he circulated in 1960.[31] "It is, perhaps, relevant to remember that in 1938 Cambridge was very much the centre of the Keynesian school of economics and that it was then natural, if over-optimistic to expect a continuing flow of first-class graduates from American and Commonwealth universities." In the one-year course, candidates would have to take three papers from the Tripos, including Economic Principles but excluding the essay; and in addition, submit a thesis of up to 15,000 words; to obtain the diploma, the overall performance would have to meet a 2.1 standard. But the war intervened. The statistical returns on admissions and awards were also disappointing for the post-war period: **between 1947–1948 and 1959–1960**, a total number of just 26 candidates had been accepted, 20 had sat for the examination; just 8 had been awarded the diploma, of which 6 proceeded to a PhD from which 1 withdrew. Robinson observes: "It is doubtful whether in these days what is wanted is a Diploma for first-class men from America, Canada and Australia. They all now take the PhD. The chief need is from those who teach in less developed countries." The orientation and catchment of the diploma need to recognise that "a large proportion of those who teach economics in the less developed countries, and who have most to gain from a Diploma course, are of 2/2 standard, but are none-the-less worth taking trouble over". In Robinson's view, "if there were such a Diploma, it would be much more widely used. There is no question that, if one discusses our Diploma with Professors in the less advanced Commonwealth countries, they regard it as a difficult and dangerous enterprise rather than a helpful one." He proposes to "break the standards-link with the Tripos" and to "make the Thesis the whole test". But he notes that the General Board would then wish to downgrade the title from diploma to certificate, and confesses that "I myself slightly regret the loss of the more dignified name."

Early in **1965**, there is a fully-fledged proposal written up by the Faculty Board for a one-year Certificate in Development Economics with teaching to begin in Michaelmas 1966 with examinations in 1967. Those involved are again Austin Robinson (though he would have retired formally in 1964), but also Phyllis Deane. The proposed certificate would cater to students from less-developed countries, and in cases of exceptional performance, lead on to a registration in the PhD programme. Kenneth Berrill, writing from the Faculty Board, observes that "I had assumed that we were calling this a certificate and not a diploma because the standard was not going to be all that high for those who merely passed. ... As I understood the object of this Certificate it was to give a year's training and be able to give to almost everybody a Certificate at the end of their year" (K.E. Berrill to Miss Deane, cc. Prof Robinson, Letter dated 12 March 1965). Berrill voices a shared sentiment: "we know the

---

[31] EAGR File Tripos/Diploma Reform, 'The Diploma in Economics', 48; dated 11.11.60.

troubles that are caused to candidates from underdeveloped countries when they have to go home labelled a failure and personally I would rather stick to the Certificate because it would enable us to give people their piece of paper at a lower level." The suggested shift from top-drawer young aspirants coming from America to learn about Keynesian economics in its home habitat to less-qualified candidates from the ex-colonies is discrete and significant; the nature of the enterprise had changed character.

While the diploma had evolved, responding to changing external aspirations on the demand side and internal supply-side capacities and constraints, since its establishment in 1938, Kenneth Berrill reported (to the famous *Teaching of Development Economics* Conference in Manchester in 1964):

> that until recently there had been no courses on the economics of underdeveloped countries at Cambridge. They had started in a modest way two years ago [in 1962] when a paper on this subject was introduced which undergraduates could choose as one of their three options in the Part II examinations. The purpose of teaching this subject was purely educational; there was no intention to train planners or people who would go out as economic advisers. It was one out of about a dozen options and there was no requirement for anyone taking it to have particular qualifications. In content, the paper covered both general problems of development of particular areas (mainly India, and to some extent the Mediterranean countries and Africa). Since this was only one of six examination subjects, students could hardly be expected to devote very much time to it. But the paper was fairly popular—it was chosen by about a third of the students in Part II—and having read the scripts in each of the last two years, he [Berrill] felt that the teaching of the subject had been of educational value to the students in that it had widened their horizon. (Martin & Knapp, 1967: 208–209)

In a postscript, Berrill reports that "since the Manchester Conference, the University [of Cambridge] has instituted three area studies centres (South Asia, Africa and Latin America) all of which are concerned with development problems and provide lectures, seminars, publications, and research projects which cut across normal faculty arrangements" (Berrill in Martin and Knapp ibid.: 209). These were significant developments and indicated an explicit acknowledgment by the university which had put resources to walk the talk. It also indicates that the widespread engagements of a considerable number of senior staff from the social sciences, prominently including economics, were coming to constitute some form of mass, if not a network, to induce the formation of these three centres. Development teaching and research was maturing, and there can be little doubt that in this the powerful incremental factor was the demand and interest generated by the independence of erstwhile British colonies, and locally the dense interest in Indian planning amongst the cohort of the Cambridge greats, all involved directly in working on specific planning issues in India. This also accounts for the 'India bias' in the Tripos paper on economic development introduced in 1962, in the period of this intense affair with Indian planning.

At the Manchester Conference, Ken Berrill and Phyllis Deane also share the Cambridge perspective on the new proposal for the Diploma in Development Economics, then under consideration. Expectedly, they point to the very different aspirations, abilities and attitudes of the very distinct clientele from underdeveloped countries who wanted a PhD, but lacked adequate training and "were resistant to taking any kind of qualifying examination, or improve their basic economics and take some Part II examinations; ... it was unavoidable that after three years or more of PhD research some of these PhD candidates had to face the risk of failure; in view of their family responsibilities and their commitments at home this often created very serious personal problems." Hence the proposal for the DDE, as a stepping stone and entry route to the PhD, apart from being a good qualification in itself (ibid.: 209).

What emerges from the in-depth review is a win-win synthesis: the old diploma is refurbished, reburnished and replaced by a new-look stand-alone Diploma in Development Economics which is approved in November 1965 and is launched into the same schedule, in Michaelmas 1966; the link to the Economics Tripos is broken, with candidates sitting for two papers in Principles of Economic Development, and another two in Problems of Economic Development, followed by an Essay. Judging by the examination questions set for the four papers in the opening year, there is no evidence at all of any compromise in the quality or standard of instruction. Indeed, the standard set here is clearly equivalent to that of the Tripos for the corresponding paper; the set of questions for the opening year bears the unmistakable stamp of Brian Reddaway, as several open-ended, think-on-the-spot, work-it-out-for-yourself, applied economics questions, of the legendary 'Reddaway-type' genre[32] confront the candidates. This integrated, deceptively simple, approach was a Cambridge hallmark: testing the ability to deploy appropriate theory for addressing issues of high relevance and working through answers with data which were themselves to be interrogated. The question paper for examining the paper Problems of Economic Development—2 is remarkably challenging, and perhaps would have been found so by a majority of the faculty staff as well. There is detectable resonance to things Indian, as in the question on the estimation of ICORs (incremental capital-output ratios), which was a typically 'Reddaway-type' appendix in his book on the Indian economy (Reddaway, 1962), and the one on the construction of a large dam—K.N. Raj, who employed a similar methodological approach to economic investigation, had grappled with these issues in the context of the Bhakra Nangal Dam project around the same time that Reddaway was in India for his assessment of the consistency of the Third Plan in India (Raj, 1960). This diploma was clearly not just what Berrill had rather disdainfully called 'their piece of paper' to take back home to put up on the wall.

---

[32] See Singh, A. (2008) for another reference to 'Reddaway-type' questions in his appreciation of Brian Reddaway's contributions to economics; here, the example is drawn from a paper in the regular Economics Tripos.

Cairncross (1993: 40–41) provides another wonderful example, this time to do with Austin Robinson who had resumed lecturing to undergraduates in 1929.

> Colin Clark, when he was starting work on *The Conditions of Economic Progress* in the mid-1930s, records 'a casual but profound conversation' with Austin on how to open a lecture course in economics. The right beginning, Austin suggested, was to 'tell your class that per head real income in India was only about a quarter, or at any rate some low fraction ... of per head income in Britain. What were the causes of this situation?' It was a question of abiding interest to Austin and one that was the starting point of Colin Clark's work on the economics of development.

As Austin Robinson later said, "Pigou had taught me that economics was about people and the welfare of people" (Letter, E.A.G. Robinson to Gustav Ranis, 17.4.91).

Forty years later, Dudley Seers poses 'his' fundamental question: what explains the differential growth rates of the advanced and the underdeveloped economies? No less a person than Kaldor, fresh out of having released his *Causes of the Slow Rate of Growth of the UK Economy* the year before (Kaldor, 1966), confesses that he does not have a good enough answer.

Of much relevance here is Dudley Seers's influential and powerfully argued piece, written with "a sense of urgency and some impatience" on 'The Limitations of the Special Case' (1963) and how this translated into the teaching of development economics. Cooper and FitzGerald (1989) note that this article had stirred sufficient interest in the profession, at that stage grappling with the challenge of constructing development teaching for students for underdeveloped economies, to stimulate the organising of the Manchester Conference; the proceedings of the conference (Martin & Knapp, 1967) open with this article. "The whole business is made much more difficult by the widespread practice that authors and lecturers have, of not merely concentrating on the economics of some developed industrial country but presenting it as universally valid" (Seers 1963); Robbins and Bauer are singled out for criticism as prime exemplars of this approach. The social and institutional frameworks of developing economies do not resemble the profiles that form the premise of economic theory derived and applied to advanced industrial economies, whether from the neoclassical or the Keynesian sides. New theoretical frameworks were required that reflect the contrasting profiles of Third-World economies especially to sift through their variations and derive an approximation to a more generally relevant set of propositions that could gravitate, possibly, towards one theory, though not to the exclusion of others. For Seers, Latin American structuralism provided one such template, prompting Tommy Balogh to say that "to aim at a general theory of development was begging for the moon; this was the only point on which he disagreed with Mr Seers" (Martin & Knapp, 1967: 216). But if structuralism was one characterisation of a shared feature of underdevelopment, perhaps Indian planning of the

Nehru-Mahalanobis era, in which the Cambridge economists had closely collaborated, represented one type of hypothetical strategy for overcoming it. John Toye (2006: 989–990), while acknowledging Seers's (and Hirschman's) disagreements with using the case of the advanced industrial economy as a general template, cautions against carrying the argument too far, rendering it untenable.[33] Without going into solutions, Polly Hill and Phyllis Deane (much earlier) had both ploughed this furrow in Cambridge using the West African case, turning the spotlight on the inappropriateness of transplanting social and economic categories that underlay theorising in the advanced industrial economy. The formation of the three area studies centres offered an institutional framework for more meaningful theorising on development and especially for setting up cross-regional conversations on the limits of path dependence in historical terms, and of theoretical generalisation.

In his challenging intervention, Seers (1963: 77–79) has distinguished between three phases in the lifecycle of a theoretical proposition: the 'Hobson' phase—the allusion obviously is to Hobson's early work on imperialism (Hobson, 1902)—where the proponent and the proposition are considered deviant and heretical, and therefore ignored or frowned upon; the 'Kahn' phase, where the relevance and meaningfulness of the new theoretical propositions are sufficiently realised to be absorbed into the discourse, to be tested and developed further; and the 'Keynes' phase, where the new ideas stand fully validated and are welcomed as the new universal theoretical currency displacing the original one. At that point, Seers felt that "we are not even in a position to judge what has to be demolished of the old doctrine, or what can be saved and adapted for further use. This is still somewhere late in the 'Hobson phase', or early in the 'Kahn phase' of development economics" (Seers 1963: 79). Dudley Seers, from a Latin American perspective, credibly nominates Raul Prebisch as his 'Hobson'; the Cambridge seniors, with their up-close and personal experience with Indian planning, might have nominated Mahalanobis; in the China context, a case could be argued for Mao's iconoclastic text, *A Critique of Soviet Economics* (1967); perhaps Nyerere in the African scenario; and there could be

---

[33] "Keynes claimed to have created a more general theory of employment than the classical economists had. Neo- classical economists subsequently reversed this claim, however, arguing that Keynes had invented only a special case of neo-classical theory—the case where the wage level is fixed. Anti-Keynesian development economists on the political left, like Dudley Seers, inverted this argument as follows. All neo-classical economics, including the Keynesian variant, is a special case—the case of smoothly functioning markets in capitalist economies. Thus, a new theory was sought in order to embrace the more general case, the case of the developing countries, whose economies are beset with bottlenecks and rigidities, and where well functioning markets are absent (Seers, 1963: 77–98). Albert Hirschman later changed the general/special distinction into a simple dualism. ... They also share a tendency to emphasise the absoluteness of the distinction between development economics and other branches of the discipline. In this they are following the Keynes legend that deliberately played up the fundamental nature of his quarrel with 'the classics'. However, just as Keynes exaggerated the depth of his quarrel, so Seers and Hirschman are in danger of exaggerating the theoretical gulf between development economics and other sub-disciplines of economics" (Toye 2006: 989–990).

others. The collective search for 'Keynes' and reaching the nirvana of the 'Keynes phase' was what drove the discipline-in-formation at that volatile time.

Over the entire period, it is possible to list seven tracks of teaching in development economics which were based in, or closely linked to, the Faculty of Economics and Politics:

- Austin Robinson's, 1933 Course on the Economic Problems of the British Empire, though there is no ready evidence in the E.A.G. Robinson Papers to suggest a repeat of the course in later years.
- The Diploma in Development Economics started in 1938, and which ran through presumably till 1964 when Austin Robinson retired, probably with a break during the war years.
- A Paper on Economic Development introduced into the Economics Tripos Part II in 1962, with a higher-than-average popularity; this paper ran through till 2010 when it was stopped by the Faculty for some time, before resuming it.
- The new version of the Diploma in Development Economics started in 1966.
- An M.Phil in Development Studies was mooted in 1975 and started in 1977 (managed by the Development Studies Committee) comprising three Options, of which one was in the Economics of Development; this M.Phil was replaced in 1982 by the M.Phil in Economics and Politics of Development (EPD) which had started in 1975, based in the Faculty but managed by the Development Studies Committee; this was 80 per cent 'economics' and 20 per cent a combination of other disciplines; this was abolished in 1995, and restarted in 1996 in a new form as an M.Phil in Development Studies based in the Department of Land Economy; and from the late 1980s till c.1995, an M.Phil in Development Economics ran in parallel comprising a compulsory econometric course from the M.Phil in Economics, alongside optionals from this M.Phil and from the M.Phil in EPD.
- The PhD programme in the Faculty of Economics had periodically admitted candidates from developing economies who had a special interest in development themes; early, pre-War examples are V.K.R.V. Rao and his PhD with Colin Clark on the National Income of India; and earlier, D.R. Gadgil's thesis on The Evolution of the Indian Economy that earned him an M.Phil. Later, in the post-War period, there were successive and substantial cohorts of South Asian PhD scholars from South Asia who worked on development-related themes and went on to eminent careers in the field of development.
- Finally, there was always a small trickle of Third-World candidates in the regular Economic Tripos who later used their skills in the field of development.

All these tracks ran independently of, and in parallel to, the training and teaching on development and development studies to various cohorts of overseas students—practitioners in the earlier years till 1981, and increasingly regular economics students thereafter; the timeline of this development-studies track is provided in Table 11.1.

11.2.4 Against the Mainstream: Subaltern Perspectives

The new Diploma-M.Phil configuration, from 1982, replaced the earlier 'joint' M.Phil in Development Studies with its three Options (running since 1977), with a single M.Phil in Economics and Politics of Development to be firmly located within the Faculty of Economics and Politics; this would absorb some teaching courses on the social aspects of development, but as the sociologists and social anthropologists complained, not enough. This would run in parallel with the two other longstanding, related, M.Phil programmes: the M.Phil in Economics in the Faculty of Economics and Politics; and the M.Phil in Lands located in the Department of Land Economy. The shared diploma was also housed in Land Economy, ostensibly because the Faculty of Economics and Politics decline to host it on the, possibly specious, grounds that it would impose too heavy an administrative burden on its office; more likely they did not wish to run the risk of having to import, alongside the diploma, some of its pre-dating staff into the Faculty proper; possibly, they perceived the diploma to be a lower order activity not worth taking the primary responsibility for. But staff from the Economics Faculty were closely involved with teaching in both the diploma and the M.Phil. This configuration of the DDS and M.Phil (EPD) ran on till 1996, when both were abolished, and the latter reinvented, yet again, as the M.Phil in Development Studies now located in the Department of Land Economy; finally, with the emergence of the Centre of Development Studies (CDS) in 2012, the M.Phil in Development Studies was taken over by the CDS, and ran alongside its new PhD in Development Studies. All stakeholders had gone each their own way. Colonial studies said its prolonged goodbye starting in 1944, died actually in 1969, though last rites were performed only in 1982; Development Studies was expelled from the Faculty of Economics in 1995; and radical academic Development Studies separated from the conservative identity and relationship with Land Economy in 2012, and arrived in a field of its own.

The teaching and research on development issues in Cambridge now have the Centre of Development Studies (CDS) as its primary home, offering "a wide range of opportunities for postgraduate training and research for students looking towards a career in development in the research field, in policy-making, in national and multilateral institutions, and in non-governmental organisations as well as in the private sector and business".[34] Substantively, its general intellectual and ideological orientation could be characterised as being critical

---

[34] https://www.devstudies.cam.ac.uk/welcome.

of the mainstream neoliberal realities of development in the era of untethered finance-capital-led globalisation and the discourses that attempt to legitimise it, whether as the first best, the second best, or the only game in town. With mushrooming incontrovertible evidence that neoliberal globalisation is in itself the problem rather than the solution to meaningful development, this radical interrogative stance in the teaching and research of the CDS is also reflected in the self-selection of a student body that seeks alternatives, made more urgent with every new manifestation or episode of a global crisis, whether financial, environmental, military invasions, displacements, migrants and migration or the quietly rising level of endemic entitlement failures alongside the spectacular explosion of inequalities. It is no longer, if it ever was, appropriate to think of development deficits as a basket comprising the realisation of idiosyncratic risk at the level of individuals; instead, virtually in every dimension, shared, co-variant structural conditions and causes have clearly become overwhelmingly dominant. Alongside, existential risk has become both a profound and an urgent issue. This makes a mockery of approaches to 'development' which prioritise the incremental micro approaches to poverty management through influencing, or nudging, individual behaviour of those in poverty in some one direction or other, based on the claims of some one RCT-approved policy intervention. Recent 'Nobel' Prizes conferred on branded practitioners of this approach tend not so much to give legitimacy to this blinkered approach as much as to question the legitimacy, yet again, of 'the prize' itself. Internal challenges to political stability of these co-existing extremes, of inequality and mass entitlement failures and global crises, have unleased challenges to political stability of elite-controlled regimes which have responded with extended and intensified surveillance and control, of oppression and suppression; there are clear tendencies of democracies, with all their inherent limitations, sliding inexorably into plutocracies, with all their flagrant vulgarities. Partly as strategies of controlling mass oppositions, governing regimes have often instrumentally encouraged, if not created, societal divisions and fractures on the basis of religious or ethnic identity, intensified and instrumentally exploited new and generally fake and toxic narratives of nationalism, thereby weakening the potential for collective opposition to neoliberalism and its 'development strategy'. Such regimes seem, at the present conjuncture, to derive collective strength of their own from one another, sharpening the global divides. Recent exemplars of these tendencies arguably include some of the darlings of neoliberalism, Brazil, India, Turkey, amongst others; but these are dwarfed by the political turn taken in the so-called traditional homes of democracy, the USA and UK. Alongside this is the almost total erosion and atrophy of the authority and capacity of international agencies, especially those concerned with development or with human rights, as they slide into the embrace of dependence on the charity of the new class of global barons displaying their aspirations to buy love, to play god, without any form of public accountability, now reorienting the mandates, research agendas and policy interventions of these development organisations in line with current neoliberal collective thought, or some idiosyncratic personalised variation thereof. The domains of 'development studies' and 'development practice' have never been more contested. This is evident in teaching and research programmes including their staff and students in universities, in internal disagreements between international development agencies, especially the Bretton Woods Institutions versus most of the rest, in the orientation and conditionalities of government aid programmes, in the design and delivery of public policies, and even within the 'community' of billionaire philanthropes.

11.3 Development Research: Ebbs and Flows

At the Faculty of Economics and Politics, as elsewhere in Cambridge, research was an individual's furrow to plough; a prime preoccupation for some or, for others, an optional residual once the demands of lecturing and supervisions were done. Till 1961, when the Faculty building came up at Sidgwick Site, the economists were scattered across colleges, meeting by appointment or in the few seminars, à la the Keynes Political Economy Club—and 'development' was not really a major theme. Yet, on closer scrutiny, it becomes quickly apparent that under this surface of invisibility, the issues of economic development, understood at the time as those concerning the colonies, were quite prominent in the profiles of many Cambridge economists, even if on an unconnected, individual basis. The case of India provides a remarkable, if exceptional exemplar, and conveys the salience of development research as a highly significant parallel if rather independent track to the colonial, and then post-colonial, teaching courses on development. In general, by the time the enterprise enters its later phases with increased academic professionalisation, there is a perceptible convergence between the teaching and research profiles of staff. The Indian case encapsulates the rich if idiosyncratic nature of Cambridge research on economic development, and qualifies for a detailed narration.

11.3.1 Cambridge–India Highway: Cambridge in India[35]

There were rich seams of India interest in Cambridge, and there was a big band of old India hands at the Faculty. Of course, one could dig much deeper and start with two undoubting Thomases of British colonialism, both Cambridge men: Malthus, who trained Company officials at East India College to prepare them for their commercial and colonising work in India (and indeed contemporary classical political economy provided the basis for the design of crucial colonial land revenue policies); and the infamous Macaulay whose colonial education policy was undoubtedly a force, even a century later, propelling the young Cambridge radical Ajit Singh in his choice of reading Sanskrit ("for nationalist reasons") alongside economics in Chandigarh. Leaving that past behind, the trail can be picked up with Keynes's extensive engagement with

---

[35] Sects. 11.3.1 and 11.3.2 draw partially on Saith (2019: 57–63).

India.[36] In fact, there is an active scholarly interest in Indian economic affairs that Marshall sustained all through his career, in particular on matters of Indian currency,[37] a theme inherited by Keynes from his teacher. Joan had been in and out of India since the 1920s when she and Austin Robinson went there, soon after they were married, for him to tutor the ten-year-old Prince of Gwalior, to unknown effect, with Joan picking up and speaking on things Indian.[38] Austin, predictably, was soon deeply engaged with Indian economic affairs, writing advisory notes and research reports,[39] all of which Joan read, commented on, edited and apparently sometimes typed—all this while musing herself on theoretical puzzles to do with imperfect competition, if her doodled diagrams (in notebooks of salary accounts of a retinue of domestic staff) are anything to go by.[40] And when Richard Stone's father was appointed a High Court judge in Madras in 1930, young Richard's headmaster advised the father that "it would be a very good thing if he were to accompany you … he doesn't seem to be doing much good here. So I had a year's break in India between school and university" (Stone, 1984)—possibly the pioneer of the concept of the 'gap year'. Francis Cripps, a rising presence in Cambridge Keynesian economics, and his senior colleague, Wynne Godley, director of the DAE, not only shared the leadership of the Cambridge Economic Policy Group, but both had grandfathers with a strong India interest. Francis was the grandson of Stafford Cripps, the principled left-Labour leader, who led the famous Cripps Mission to India

---

[36] Keynes's Indian interests and interactions were extensive: a blueprint for a central bank in India; wheat imports from India; he was twice the chief guest at the Cambridge Indian Majlis; spoke at the Cambridge Union in support of greater popular government in India; wrote a letter to the *Cambridge Review* in defence of Indian students; all this apart from his well-known official roles in commissions dealing with Indian currency and fiscal affairs; and his very first book, in 1913, on *Indian Currency and Finance*, a topic on which he delivered lectures in the Cambridge Tripos. For a comprehensive treatment of Keynes' extensive interface with people, things and matters Indian, see Chandavarkar (1989).

[37] "Alfred Marshall … interested himself in Indian affairs from a very early period of his life. The contact which he maintained with administrators, many of whom received lessons in economics from him, helped Marshall to retain his interest in Indian affairs until the very last. Moreover, the Commissions which were set up by the Government to enquire into Indian monetary and currency questions turned to Marshall for light and obtained it. That the light which he shed on some many economic questions should not have penetrated the dark chambers of officialdom and also our academic institutions is a pity" (Krishnaswami, 1942: 875).

[38] This was just after E.M. Forster, who had been serving as a private secretary to the Raja of Dewas, had published his celebrated *A Passage to India* in 1924; Forster and Joan were later both honorary Fellows of King's College. Austin's brother Christopher was in India serving as the Rt Hon Bishop of Lucknow—the city that was centre stage of the Indian Rebellion of 1857—then Bishop of Bombay, and finally at (my alma mater) St Stephen's College, Delhi, after he retired.

[39] A major contribution took the form of his detailed report on the economic relations between the Indian Princes and the Colonial Government in India within the framework of the Harcourt Butler Committee, 1927, which was charged with reporting on the relationship between the Princes of the Princely States and Paramount Power in India.

[40] Geoff Harcourt (1998) has provided a nuanced and thoughtful comparative commentary on the contrasting, parallel engagements of Austin and Joan Robinson with development issues over their years.

in 1942.[41] Wynne was a generation older, and his grandfather, Arthur Godley, 1st Baron of Kilbracken had been "the longest serving and probably the most influential Permanent Under Secretary of State for India during 1883–1909", and had argued the case for protection for Indian textiles that were suffering in the face of British imports;[42] Wynne mentions that "he has been the positive inspiration of my life"; he also writes that "he never went to India as he didn't think it necessary" (Godley, 2008); in this, of course, he was following the august example set earlier by James Stuart Mill, the author of three-volume *The History of British India*, who also oversaw official British operations in India from London declaring in his book that "a duly qualified man can gain more knowledge of India in one year in his closet in England than he could obtain in the course of the longest life by the use of his eyes and ears in India", prompting one to wonder why then it took him 12 years to complete his study.

Then, immediately after Indian Independence, Richard Stone,[43] Joan Robinson,[44] Maurice Dobb,[45] Richard Goodwin[46] and others in the 1950s were invited by Mahalanobis, then running the much vaunted Indian Planning

---

[41] I heard the name Sir Stafford Cripps as a child from parental conversations around the dining table at home in Delhi. He came with the offer of a version of home rule for India as a dominion after the war in return for Indian support in the war; but Indian majority, and minority, leaders wanted to get more, Churchill wanted to give less, and so the mission 'failed' and was followed by the Quit India Movement, which eventually fed into full Independence after the war. Incidentally, Stafford Cripps' parliamentary constituency was later inherited by Anthony Wedgwood (Tony) Benn, for whom Francis worked as an economic advisor in the hot decade of the 1970s when Benn was a cabinet minister in the Wilson and Callaghan governments.

[42] This was brought to my attention by Francis Cripps (personal communication, email).

[43] Stone was invited in 1950 to advise the National Income Committee on methods of estimation; Simon Kuznets played a significant role in this work.

[44] When Mahalanobis extended the invitation, Ramachandra Guha reports Joan to have said: "I might be able to knock some sense into the heads of the economists in your country" (Guha, 2007: 215). For a treatment of her awkward relationship with Indian planning, see Saith (2008); Ashok Rudra (1996) provides a discursive, simultaneously incisive and entertaining account of the visits in his volume on P.C. Mahalanobis. When in India, Joan was perpetually frustrated by the lethargy and compromises of Indian planning and often let off steam by haranguing some of her ex-Cambridge Indian students and some other unsuspecting visiting economists, such as Ragnar Frisch, for good measure. India had the problems, China had the solutions, was her general refrain—and of course she had a point. "Wake up, India! Its later than you think!"—she said.

[45] Maurice Dobb, apart from pointing out political problems in the realisation of the Indian planning exercise, also delivered a set of seminal lectures at the Delhi School of Economics on key problems of economic development dealing with the production, mobilisation and utilisation of economic surplus. And, of course, he along with Joan had been engaged in problems of development planning, including especially the choice of techniques on which Amartya Sen wrote his doctoral dissertation.

[46] Vela Velupillai (2015a) has written eloquently about his supervisor Richard Goodwin's "lifelong association with the country", which started with Goodwin's India Decade, beginning from 1954–1955 when Mahalanobis invited him to the Indian Statistical Institute, where he constructed the first Input-Output Table for the Indian economy, alongside Ragnar Frisch (see also Velupillai, 2015b). Velupillai also refers to Goodwin being something of a recluse, with very few connections with the Faculty; apart from the two naturals, Joan Robinson and Geoff Harcourt (as reported by Geoff), the two exceptions he chose to make were Ajit Singh and Prabhat Patnaik.

Commission, under what he referred to as his 'brain irrigation' scheme designed to involve supportive foreign economists in the theoretical exercises underpinning the nascent Indian planning process where they made a series of significant contributions to theory and practice of Indian planning.[47] Nicky Kaldor had been in the 1950s to devise an abortive Expenditure Tax for India—cunning as he was, Nicky didn't know what he was up against in trying to tax slippery rich Indians.[48] Brian Reddaway had just done a typically idiosyncratic and insightful book on the Indian economy (Reddaway, 1962)[49] which contained some rare nuggets in the form of appendices on the methods of estimation of capital/output ratios, and on the significance of gestation lags in planning investment, all with arithmetical illustrations à la Reddaway;[50] this was a theme on which Amit Bhaduri later focussed his doctoral dissertation, though within a technically sophisticated template. There were many other illustrious visiting economists, including Jan Tinbergen, Oskar Lange, Charles Bettelheim, Simon Kuznets and Ragnar Frisch.[51] And one might wish to include Kalecki as 'spiritually Cambridge' since it was in the context of Indian planning that he wrote some of his incisive analytical papers on the financing of non-inflationary devel-

[47] On this, see Ashok Rudra's (1996) biography of P.C. Mahalanobis; see also, Ashwani Saith on Joan Robinson's awkward relationship with Indian planning (Saith, 2008).
[48] Kaldor had made similar forays to Sri Lanka, Mexico, Ghana, Guyana, Turkey, Iran, Venezuela and Chile. John Toye, who continued the Cambridge line of expertise on public finance in developing countries, reviewed Kaldor's efforts and reported that, "Kaldor's own verdict on his efforts was that they 'earned me (and the governments I advised) a lot of unpopularity, without, I fear, always succeeding in making the property-owning classes contribute substantial amounts to the public purse'" (Toye, 1989: 183); a view that is confirmed by Palma and Marcel (1989) with regard to Kaldor's involvement with Chile in the 1950s.
[49] The book was an exercise in checking the consistency and feasibility of the Third Five Year Plan.
[50] In his extensive appreciation of Reddaway's legacy to economics, Ajit (Singh, 2008: 9–11) notes both the critical review by Padma Desai (who complained about the lack of equations in Reddaway's exposition) and Reddaway's robust rebuttal, inter alia providing a succinct statement of his own objections to any *general* necessity of expressing economic reasoning in the form of mathematical reasoning.
[51] Prabhat Patnaik is my source for a Dick Goodwin anecdote that conveys a sense of the ethos and excitement of the pioneering era of planning in India in the 1950s. Amongst several famous economists that Mahalanobis had coaxed and cajoled into spending time in India supporting the work of the Planning Commission was Ragnar Frisch, engaged in work on Indian modelling. He sought an urgent meeting with Nehru, and one was arranged; but Frisch came down with a high fever and was hospitalised and restricted to bed. So, the ever-committed Nehru came to visit him instead, and finding the lifts out of order, had to climb several floors of steps to see him and find out what it was all about; shortly, he came down, fuming and mumbling annoyance under his breath. Ragnar Frisch had wanted to hear from the horse's mouth, the prime minister of democratic India, what precise inter-temporal rate of discount he should use for obtaining the present values of future consumption streams in his model, presumably working this out by establishing what Nehru might regard as equivalences between nominal future levels and their perceived present worth over alternative time periods. One might imagine how the conversation might have gone—Frisch: "Mr Nehru, let us assume that five years from now, India's per capita consumption is 100 units; what would that be worth to you today? And suppose this was ten years from now ...?" Nehru: "Mr Frisch, you are obviously in a deranged and delusional state, and I hope you get well soon. Good day!" (Prabhat Patnaik, personal communication).

opment, edited in two volumes of a selection of his papers, edited by Mario Nuti in 1972. Going south across the Palk Strait, Graham Pyatt was busy constructing the pioneering Social Accounting Matrix for Sri Lanka, an enterprise carried over from the DAE in Cambridge; and moving east, Austin Robinson had edited a volume on a socialist development strategy for an independent Bangladesh. There were also feedback loops that took meaningful ideas back into Cambridge, as is evident from the interaction between Stone and Mahalanobis.[52] And there were other forays, including an international refresher course taught by a remarkable group including the Robinsons, Kaldor and Tarshis, where Joan was in her formidable element.[53]

---

[52] "I have been reading the papers you left with me and have been thinking about the way in which you are now tackling the problem of national income and national accounts estimation in India. I think that without doubt your project is the most interesting thing that is going on at present in national accounts work and that if it succeeds practically it will bring in a new era in this field. As you know I have been campaigning for many years for the introduction of economic and statistical design into national accounts work and while a certain amount of progress has been made in many countries with the former, since this is largely a matter of setting up a reasonable accounting system and adopting clearly stated definitions, very little has been done with regard to the latter at any rate in European countries and in the United States. ... Some changes are of course being made and the scope of purely administrative statistics is being reduced through the undertaking of censuses of production, distribution etc., and through the development of sampling surveys, but even now it is extremely difficult to fit together all the bits of statistical information that have to be pressed into service. There are very serious gaps particularly in the area of capital and financial transactions and the magnitude of the revisions and the general unreliability of the figures are in many cases most disturbing from the standpoint of policy applications. By setting out to integrate the economic information required with a sound method of estimation based on statistical methods in the true sense of the term you are I am sure performing an experiment the interest of which goes far outside the boundaries of India. I am really delighted to assist with this project and am greatly looking forward to my visit to India next December" (Richard Stone to P.C. Mahalanobis, Letter dated 16 May 1950, Richard Stone Papers, King's College Archives, University of Cambridge).

[53] Lorie Tarshis provides an indirect account in a comment about Joan and students: "Her concern—commitment really—for the right was as much a part of her as her intelligence and directness. She had evidently been as a school-girl—so I heard from one what had been at school with her—a person of great courage and strong ideals. I saw this when on a trip with her, the Kaldors and my wife, she led a 'strike' in support of 'the dispossessed'. The role of this Cambridge contingent was to conduct seminars for young instructors in India, Pakistan, Kenya and Malaysia who had not studied in the US or Britain. Joan, my wife and I were put up at a somewhat shabby and very Victorian hotel in Poona; the more junior attendees were housed in barracks at the institution at which the seminars met; and the Kaldors—I say this in admiration—had, through contacts, been invited to stay with a Maharajah. Our meals were tolerable. But Joan heard that the meals served to our young colleagues were inedible, so she persuaded us to join them for lunch from then on. We did and there was a very sudden improvement. And when we were invited to end our visit with a sightseeing trip to the Taj Mahal and Joan learned that this trip was reserved for 'distinguished seniors', she again moved to force a change. She stated clearly that we would not participate unless the trip were opened to the whole group. It was. She *acted* to support her ideals. There were not simply expressions of what she desired" (Tarshis, 1989: 920). A contemporary corroboration adds spice to the curry: "In early 1955, an International Refresher Course was arranged at Pune by Austin Robinson and Vakil. Kaldor, Joan Robinson, Downie and Tarshis came for the course as teachers. ... she accepted the Spartan hospitality, which C.N. Vakil could provide for them at Pune,

One subsequent 'India' engagement which offers rich insights is that of Brian Reddaway's in the period of the Third Plan. Reddaway took a sabbatical year off from his DAE duties in 1959–1960 during which he worked with Pitamber Pant, Head of the Perspective Planning Division of the Indian Planning Commission. His assignment was to study "how the Indian economy worked", and this led to an innovative, typically Reddaway-style book on Indian planning (Reddaway, 1962).[54] Apparently this was Reddaway's initial direct encounter with development issues, but it opened the door subsequently to a continual world-wide engagement as a consultant[55] including some hands-on 'firefighting' assignments as an economist.[56]

The book figures in Ajit Singh's appreciation for Brian Reddaway (Singh, 2008): "The book drew a sharply critical article in *Oxford Economic Papers* from a leading Indian economist, Professor Padma Desai (1963). In response, in the same issue of the journal, the author vigorously defended his position (Reddaway, 1963). Desai argued that the book did not set out a fully specified planning model so that it was difficult to judge whether the plan was efficient or not. She also thought that, from the information given in the book, the model was under-determined, that is, the number of variables to be determined was greater than the number of equations. She further expressed irritation over the fact that Reddaway had not bothered to specify his model in

---

which was just recovering from having been a military-base during the War. Joan Robinson even objected to separate arrangements for food for the scholars from different parts of India etc. and for the Visiting Professors. She sharply told Vakil 'Are we pigs? Why are your discriminating?'" (Sen, 2002: 11–12).

[54] Reddaway (1995: 13) remarks: "I was cheered to find that it was still in widespread academic use a dozen years later, although the statistics had inevitably become outdated." The present author encountered the book in his first year as an undergraduate in 1964, when it was quite up to date, and recalls the pleasure of working through the work-sheet type appendices on gestation lags, on the estimation of the incremental capital-output ratios. The book, and its method, was quite distinct from other contemporary treatments of Indian planning. Unsurprisingly, Reddaway's pragmatic foray into the nitty-gritty of testing the consistency of the Third Plan came under attack from the right flank in the form of a very critical review by Padma Desai (1963), with Reddaway brushing off the critique in a flat response (Reddaway, 1963).

[55] "My work in India led to a whole string of jobs in developing countries, or in international bodies, such as the World Bank, which organised practical work in developing countries. Over the next 25 years I worked in some 20 developing countries, ranging in wealth from Argentina and Saudi Arabia to Bangladesh and Abyssinia [*sic*]; Papua New Guinea and Qatar were amongst the least known, but without exception the work was interesting and worthwhile. The same applied to work inside the World Bank, the IFC, the ILO and as a member of the Committee for the World Development Plan (on which Jan Tinbergen gave such a fine lead)" (Reddaway, 1995: 13).

[56] In the post-War years, Reddaway helped draw up the new index of retail prices, "an activity which led the Colonial Office to send me to Cyprus in 1949, where the inadequacies of the existing index were threatening to produce serious strikes. Fortunately a lot of ingenious common-sense and a careful discussion of problems with all the 'parties' involved led to the smooth introduction of a generally accepted index, and an unofficial statement by an officer 'your's is the first report from an Adviser to be accepted for as long as I can remember'. In 1955 a similar problem arose in Sierra Leone, which led to a riot. It had already been arranged that I should go out in March, and the riot led the Governor to cable 'Send Reddaway quickest'" (Reddaway, 1995: 8–9).

terms of equations, which she regarded as essential to understanding the underlying economic and statistical analysis. In response, Reddaway (1963: 2) observed:

> I saw, and still see, no advantage in expressing the reasoning in the form of mathematical equations. Such equations are a useful device where there is a great deal of mutual dependence of variables, because a verbal description cannot then easily show the interactions and the process of mutual determination; moreover, it is then very laborious to arrive at the solutions which fit the conditions, except by some mathematical process analogous to the solution of simultaneous equations; and one might fall into the trap of not realizing that the system was underdetermined, and arriving by trial and error at a set of figures which fulfilled the conditions but had no superiority over many other sets which would also do so."

Padma Desai, prominently along with Jagdish Bhagwati and T. N. Srinivasan, held positions that were comprehensively antithetical to those of Indian planning and planners and favoured open-market strategies, views they have espoused consistently over time (cf.: Bhagwati & Desai, 1970; Bhagwati & Srinivasan, 1975; Bhagwati & Srinivasan, 1993). Padma Desai's ten-page review concludes with a parting shot, off Reddaway's shoulders, at the Indian planners: [Reddaway] "succeeds in a task which the published Third Five Year Plan document fails to perform—namely a statement of the analytical techniques by which the Plan was (presumably) assembled. It thus begins to be possible to appreciate both the difficulties and the complexities of assembling a Plan and the limitations of the techniques which the Indian planners had managed to acquire and utilize after a decade of planning" (Desai, 1963: 317).

Reddaway who seemed to have become the collateral damage in the crossfire between the anti-planners and the planners was sufficiently annoyed to file in a detailed 15-page a polite but bristling dismissive rebuttal which yielded little ground; he reiterated the limited focus of his exercise—he was not providing a model for the Third Plan, but only checking some key aspects of the consistency of the plan as formulated by the Commission; he also asserted that his model was not underdetermined as charged.[57] His response provides several revealing insights into 'the Reddaway approach' to applied economics, and two specific illustrations concern his eschewing the use of available input-output table, and estimates of the income elasticity of demand.

His reaction to Desai's criticism for not utilising the available I-O tables made by the Indian Statistical Institute[58] is typically 'Reddawayesque' and worth conveying *in extenso*, not least as an exemplar of the practice of his very

---

[57] In their wide-ranging survey of contributions to Indian economic analysis, Bhagwati and Chakravarty (1969: 11) register Desai's criticisms but not Reddaway's responses.

[58] Brian Reddaway would have been well aware that the first Indian I-O tables were constructed with key inputs from his colleague, Richard Goodwin during the latter's assignment with the Indian Planning Commission within the framework of Mahalanobis's so-called brain irrigation scheme of involving external experts in the Indian planning exercise.

idiosyncratic art of practical policy-oriented applied economics; and all the more so as it stood apart as a distinct paradigm within the DAE. Jestfully, but seriously, he cites three reasons:

> If I were feeling cowardly, I might shelter behind the simple fact that I was collaborating with the Delhi branch of that Institute, and was advised by its Head not to use the table, because it would take all the time which I had available (and probably more) to get it on to the basis which would fit in with the rest of the work.
>
> If I were feeling like revealing 'personal secrets', I might say that I have had all too much experience of the tediousness of trying to complete input-output tables on some specified basis, only to find that the usefulness of the table for some later investigation was much less than one might have expected. Moreover, I was anxious to bring to some sort of fruition the enterprise which was suggested by the broad ideas for exploring what was the real logic of the Plan, how far it really did hold together, and whether it could be presented in a more systematic set of national income statistics, if only to make it more intelligible to people who had not been working on it themselves. I even had the thought that the work might reveal some major discrepancy, which would justify trying to get something changed—and for that purpose speed was obviously essential.
>
> In a moment of exceptional frankness I might add to the above that I was moved by the challenge of seeing how far one could get without an input-output table, by using approximate methods on the key problems; and of course I had little idea, before we actually embarked on the exercise, how serious the lack of it would prove. I do not expect Mrs. Desai (or others who like rigidly mathematical equations which can be solved by a computer) to accept my unrepentant views that one can manage surprisingly well with the aid of human intelligence and initiative, which brings in all sorts of incomplete bits of information at the crucial points; but it must be obvious that an exercise which started in February 1960, and yet included the delivery in June 1960 to the Perspective Planning Division of a complete set of tables with preliminary notes on the conclusions to be drawn from them, would have been quite impossible if it had had to start by wrestling with the adaptation of an input-output table to the circumstances of a different base year and a different industrial classification (Reddaway, 1963: 330–331).

He then turns his attention to his non-use of the elasticity estimates: "Mrs. Desai dislikes my approach to this matter, which she would doubtless call 'very crude', though I should prefer to call it 'realistically unambitious'. The trouble is not that there is a lack of Indian estimates of income elasticities of demand— there is a plethora of them, which do not all agree—but rather that there is no particular sanctity about estimates of 'demand' based on an assumption that relative prices remain the same as in some base year. Moreover, tastes may well be changing, as India develops and becomes more urbanized, and there are further complications in the existence of shortages in the base years. A full-scale approach to the problem must therefore be a considerable enterprise, but I should be delighted if someone undertook it. It should—at least in my view—end in a report on how serious the adjustments would have to be in the field of prices (possibly through indirect taxation) or other measures to deal with (or make tolerable) a disequilibrium between supply and demand for particular items. On the basis of such a report, one might, of course, conclude that it would be wise to see whether the Plan could be changed, so as to make such measures unnecessary, but it certainly would not follow automatically that such changes should be made in preference to accepting a change in relative prices, &c." (Reddaway, 1963: 331). So much for mechanically plugging in elasticity estimates into the exercise!

In diverse ways, Austin Robinson, Joan Robinson, Richard Stone, Maurice Dobb, Nicky Kaldor, Richard Goodwin and Brian Reddaway commanded a cumulative expertise on India that could not be matched by any subsequent Cambridge cohort; and though Richard Kahn was not an 'India hand', the work that he did on development (in the context of early Israeli development policy) held significant relevance in general, including contemporary India.

11.3.2 Cambridge–India Highway: India in Cambridge[59]

Traffic on the highway was two-way, and the flow on both sides of the road was heavyweight, though different in one significant respect; while those going out to India were mostly senior academics involved in research initiatives, incoming travellers were of a different category, comprising successive waves of cohorts

---

[59] The Indian seam ran deep in the Cambridge imagination, in particular amongst those of a non-imperial bent of mind. In 1950, there was an extraordinary move within Cambridge to nominate Jawaharlal Nehru for the election as Chancellor of the university, the post falling vacant on the death of Jan Smuts. A swathe of Cambridge academic opinion wished to signal a change of orientation. Sarvepalli Gopal (1979: 111–112), in his biography of Nehru, writes that the proposition "soon derived support from some of the most distinguished figures on the rolls of the University—Bertrand Russell, E.M. Forster, R.A. Butler, Pethick Lawrence, Mountbatten—and eighty nine members of the Senate formally nominated Nehru; ... it was generally recognized that in any election Nehru would carry the majority" (ibid.). Nehru's political judgement, that such a symbolically exalted position in the imperial country, made him firmly withdraw from the contest he had not sought in the first place, managed with a certain degree of confusion through the offices of V. Krishna Menon, the Indian High Commissioner in London. On this episode, Marcuzzo (2008: 64–65) unearths an unusual nugget from the Sraffa papers: apparently in 1950, along with A.S. Besicovitch, E.M. Forster, E. Hobsbawm and J. Needham, "he gave his active support to the candidature ... and contributed financially to the electoral campaign" of the Indian Prime Minister Jawaharlal Nehru (incidentally also a Trinity man, 1907–1910) for the Chancellorship of the university. His rival was Lord Tedder, Marshall of the Royal Air Force and served as Deputy Supreme Commander of Allied Forces under Eisenhower. "However, Nehru stood down, and Lord Tedder was elected. A comment published in the *Spectator* on the eve of the election and conserved by Sraffa in a cutting evokes the climate of the times all too well: 'The supporters of Pandit Nehru [...] are largely younger men of left-wing views [...] The possibility, moreover, cannot be ignored that India may yet separate herself completely from the Commonwealth: Cambridge would hardly wish to have a Chancellor who was a foreigner'" (ibid.).

of young Indian students who came to read economics, mostly for a doctorate, at Cambridge. Four such cohorts may be identified.

The first set, in the inter-war period, is more a pair than a wave, but its massive splash overrides its small numbers. The two are household names in Indian and development economics: Dhananjay Ramchandra Gadgil and the redoubtable V.K.R.V. Rao, affably given the nickname 'Alphabet Rao', as recalled by one of his eminent contemporaries, Hans Singer.[60] D.R. Gadgil's Cambridge dissertation *The Industrial Evolution of India in Recent Times* was published by Oxford University Press (Gadgil, 1924), and set the scene for subsequent work in the field, including the later work of Amiya Bagchi (1976) and Ajit Singh (1977) and colleagues (in the UK context) on deindustrialisation, a theme pioneered by Gadgil in one of the early chapters of his dissertation on the decline of handicrafts in India.[61] Rao's, 1937 PhD dissertation, supervised by Colin Clark,[62] produced his classic work on National Income of India;[63] his subsequent career as a development economist, planner and institution builder is vast and too well known to need even a summary recounting. However, there is a significant, though curiously relatively unknown, early contribution of his that links him closely with his supervisor—a key article on the limits to the applicability of the Keynes–Kahn economic multiplier in the supply-constrained environments of agrarian economies (an early exposé of 'the inflationary barrier')—and with Kalecki's analysis of the non-inflationary warranted rate of growth in a developing economy (Rao, 1952). There was an important latent policy message in that work that the 'food supply constraint', arising from structural and institutional conditions in a poor agrarian economy, needed to be tackled for a sustained industrialisation drive.

Then came the intervention of the Second World War and the momentous arrival of independence in a dismembered South Asia, and with it, the second, post-war, cohort imbued with the liberated aspirations, ambitions and imagination of the new countries. This wave is arguably the highest and most powerful one of all, both for its quality, and the fact that as early birds, its members

---

[60] Hans Singer interviewed by Keith Tribe (Tribe, 2002: 59).

[61] Gadgil was later the founder and first Director of the Gokhale Institute of Economics and Politics in Pune and served as the Vice Chairman of the Indian Planning Commission, apart from being known for the Gadgil Formula which he devised for managing Indian federal finances.

[62] 'Alphabet', aka 'National Income', Rao had Hans Singer as a batch-mate. Singer observes: "Rao developed his dissertation on Indian National Income, also under Colin Clark. If you look at Colin Clark's book *National Income and Outlay* (1937), and his subsequent books, he quotes amply from V.K.R.V. Rao" (Tribe, 2002: 59).

[63] "About fifty years ago, in a meeting of the Planning Commission presided over by Prime Minister Jawaharlal Nehru, Prof. P.C. Mahalanobis, then Statistics Adviser to the Government of India, said that he had invited three distinguished economists from abroad to advise the newly set up National Income Committee on a system of fully articulated national accounts for India. Prof. Mahalanobis had barely mentioned their names—Professors Simon Kuznets, Richard Stone and J.B.D. Derkson—when the Prime Minister asked peremptorily, 'What about Rao?' One of the Commission members asked mildly, 'Which Rao?' The Prime Minister replied with some asperity, 'What do you mean, "Which Rao?" National Income Rao, of course!'" (Krishnaswamy, 2002: 81).

could make a far greater impact on emerging fields, especially pertaining to the objectives of and routes to meaningful development both generally in terms of development theory, and more specifically with respect to their own country. The roll call of names is daunting: I.G. Patel was tutored by Austin Robinson who also supervised his PhD in the years immediately after Indian independence; then there is a remarkable list[64] comprising Amartya Sen, Manmohan Singh, Gautam Mathur, Jagdish Bhagwati and Ashok Desai from India; Lal Jayawardena from Sri Lanka; Mahbub ul Haq from Pakistan; Rehman Sobhan and Swadesh Bose from erstwhile Pakistan, Bangladesh-to-be.

Following half a generation later splashes the third wave that includes Amiya Bagchi, Ajit Singh,[65] Azizur Rahman Khan, Pranab Bardhan and Amit Bhaduri, with the erudite and much remembered Krishna Bharadwaj as a frequent presence; and then the fourth cohort, led by Prabhat Patnaik (who held a Faculty position in Cambridge though his PhD, as a Rhodes Scholar, was from Oxford) and S.K. Rao, and including the first group of Bangladeshi doctoral candidates, Wahiduddin Mahmud, Mahboob Hossain, Iqbal Ahmed, Atiqur Rahman, Muhammed Muqtada, Naeemuddin Chowdhury and Monowor Hossain; Rashid Amjad, Sikander Rahim and Ghazi Mujahid from Pakistan; Stanley 'Sam' Samarasinghe, Piyasiri Wickramasekhara and Vela Velupillai from Sri Lanka; and from India: Ajit Ghose (who had then recently crossed the river from East Pakistan into West Bengal), Satish Mishra, Abhijit Sen, Monojit Chatterjee, Ashwani Saith, and soon thereafter Anjali Kumar, Ruchira Chatterjee, Jayati Ghosh, Ravi Srivastava, Santosh Mehrotra, and later Sukti

---

[64] Amartya Sen, Gautam Mathur and Manmohan Singh each won the coveted Adam Smith Prize. Joan Robinson apparently said Gautam Mathur, whose PhD she had supervised, was the best student that she had ever had; Meghnad Desai (2005) writes "Austin Robinson regarded I.G. Patel as the best tutee he had ever had"; and Geoff Harcourt reports that "Robin Matthews said Manmohan Singh was the brightest undergraduate he ever taught" (personal communication, email dated 16 January 2018); and Manmohan Singh also said with a sense of pride that "Robin Matthews did him the honour of always having one-on-one supervisions for him" (personal communication, in conversation, dated 17 November 2017). Gautam Mathur and Manmohan Singh served in the Department of Economics at Panjab University, Chandigarh, where Ajit was a student.

[65] Notwithstanding the direct involvement of both his two *ustads* Kaldor and Reddaway with Indian economic policy, Ajit looked and went the other way, honing his skills and funnelling all his intellectual energies into massive numerical exercises in applied microeconomics probing the workings of the industrial and corporate cores of advanced market economies. Till the early 1980s, there is virtually no evidence of research or writings on Indian themes, despite the fact that in both the realms of economic policy as well as political events, India was turning as hot as its summers. Intellectually, Ajit was then in another existential zone, perhaps not wishing to be stereotyped and corralled as an economist of the periphery, and thus ipso facto, as a peripheral economist. He wanted to make his mark at the highest levels of the discipline, and that was the mountain he set to climb. He would turn his eye towards development issues later, when these concerns thrust themselves on to the global policy stage after the inflexion points of the oil-price hikes of the 1970s, and the world-wide, neo-imperial imposition of the structural adjustment packages on Third-World economies, thwarting their national development aspirations.

Dasgupta, and Shailaja Fennel.[66] It cannot be gainsaid that these cohorts have made major contributions that have shaped the understanding of development not just in South Asia but more generally.

There was always panoramic India interest and expertise, with statistics, anecdotes and gossip, all at hand among the seniors in the proximate domain of these cohorts of young Indian economists in the making. And there were wider concentric circles of India affinity to explore and engage should a young curious economist find the time and inclination to wander into the contiguous intellectual fields, especially history, at Cambridge.[67]

11.3.3 Not Just India

While India showcases the research interests and strengths of Faculty staff, especially in the senior cohort, development experience and research capacity existed on a far larger scale, covering all regions, with significant work in over twenty developing economies covering a fairly comprehensive spread of development themes, not to mention those tackled at an international or global level of analysis. Also striking is that this large body of researchers also displayed a broad cohesive affinity in their analysis of development problems, thereby implicitly forming a collective critique of contemporary globalisation processes, and of the strategies being promulgated by the Bretton Woods Institutions.

Looking away from South Asia, there was impressive expertise as well. The China field had the likes of Joseph Needham and Joan Robinson with their varied offerings and interpretations of the history, present and future of things Chinese; Ajit Singh and Suzy Paine[68] had developed a research profile on

---

[66] Amiya Bagchi (2019) adds the following names to these lists: G. Uswatte-Aratchi, S.K. Rao, Jitendra Gopal Borpujari and S.M.P. Suriya Aratchi.

[67] Various 'schools' of Indian history were in evidence: "The 'Cambridge school' was founded by Jack Gallagher, co-author with Ronald Robinson of *Africa and the Victorians: The Climax of Imperialism in the Dark Continent* (1961), and early on joined by Anil Seal. In its early years, the later 1960s and 1970s, the school included such figures as Gordon Johnson, Francis Robinson, Christopher Baker, B.R. Tomlinson, and David Washbrook. Christopher Bayly, who was trained at Oxford by Gallagher, among others, only joined Cambridge in 1970" (Dirks, 2001:353); additions are possible, D.K. Fieldhouse, A.G. Hopkins, a.o. Notably standing apart was Eric Stokes who ploughed his own furrow on African and Indian history, with his classic *English Utilitarians in India*, and later *The Peasant and the Raj* which, to tease the anti-Raj, pro-peasantry Indian research students of the time, he would jestfully refer to as 'The Pheasant and the Rat'. On Eric Stokes, see the fine appreciation by Bayly (1998). Then, there was the 'subaltern' school of Indian history due to Ranajit Guha, but this had more visibility and voice in Oxford than Cambridge.

[68] Suzy Paine entered the Faculty from Oxford and quickly became an active member of the younger cohort of left economists there. At Oxford, she had worked on labour markets, employment systems and wage differentials in the Japanese manufacturing sector, ironically, under the 'mainstream' guidance of R.C.O. Matthews (then the Drummond Professor in Oxford), Francis Seton and Christopher Bliss who are all, especially Matthews, much thanked variously for "invaluable advice, assistance and comments", "painstakingly reading and criticizing many versions" etc. in her publications (Paine, 1971: 115; 1971b: 212). Arriving in Cambridge, she took a left turn; in 1973, she accompanied Ajit Singh on a research trip to China, then in the throes of the Cultural

China; and then Peter Nolan had set his own stamp on the field and developed a wide-ranging high-level academic and institutional interface with Chinese economics and economists. Ajit often returned to Chinese themes, on their own or within a global framework, including the global modelling-based work with Francis Cripps and Alex Izurieta. African themes had also been significant, if not as prominent. Of significance was the early work of Phyllis Deane on the construction of national accounts for Northern Rhodesia and Nyasaland, work which caught the attention of Richard Stone who brought her over to the DAE; there was the unusual case of Polly Hill and her research on West Africa;[69] John Sender and Sheila Smith were raising challenging questions about South/ ern African development; also of high significance is the work of Ajit Singh and Brian Van Arkadie on Tanzania in the era of Structural Adjustment; their critique of the Bretton Woods intervention in Tanzania set a template for the analysis of the reruns of the same experience in very many other developing economies. There was a Centre for Latin American Studies, at the time with Brian Van Arkadie as Director; Valpy FitzGerald had worked on various dimensions of the role of the state in Latin America (Fitzgerald, 1978a, 1978b), especially in Peru (Fitzgerald, 1976); Gabriel Palma was a leading authority on economic history, transitions and reforms in Latin America; Ajit Singh, Nicky

Revolution, that seemed to be a transformative experience for her and Ajit who returned to be seen often in Maoist-blue attire. Paine and Singh (1973) followed, based on their research visit to the Shanghai Diesel Factory. She reviewed Hla Myint's (1971) essay collection on Economic Theory and Underdeveloped Countries and chided him for his uncritical adherence to free markets as a recipe for development and for having ignored the experience of China, Soviet Union and Cuba (Paine, 1973). She then worked on Turkey (Paine, 1972) and on international migration taking the case of Turkish workers in Germany (Paine, 1974); moved to writing, unusually, "an introduction to Bhaduri" (Paine, 1977); and produced a stream of papers on Chinese development (Paine, 1976a, 1976b, 1978, 1981) along with some with Peter Nolan where they progressively revised their earlier positive views of Maoist development strategies and elaborated the rationale of the post-1978 rural reforms (Nolan & Paine, 1986a, 1986b; and from Nolan, 1976 to Nolan, 1988); and there were other papers on Vietnam with Adam Fforde, and on Sri Lanka. She became a frontline, and backstage, organiser of the left group in the Faculty working generally under the overall watch of Ajit Singh; she had preceded Robin Matthews in moving from Oxford to a fellowship in Clare College where Matthews became Master in 1975, and she had Brian Reddaway and Charles Feinstein as college colleagues. She would then have found herself increasingly in opposition to Robin Matthews, Frank Hahn and the group of orthodox economists in Faculty politics. At the Faculty, she accumulated a list of impressive PhD students all working on agricultural issues in India and Bangladesh, areas that she had not till then worked on; she (alongside Ajit) extended her support to the self-managed informal South Asian research scholars' seminar which unfortunately stopped functioning when she wanted to formalise it under her tutelage. Sadly, she died in 1985, aged just 40, midway in the process of establishing a firm and steady institutional presence and intellectual reputation.

[69] Joan Robinson supervised the PhD of Polly Hill who later wrote up her high-octane critiques of bad conceptualisations and analysis in the structural context of developing economies, and also her early work on cross-country comparisons across India and Africa; Polly Hill's swingeing critiques of economics came from the right-field, and her research drew from or gave credit to the work of neoclassicals, such as Theodore Schultz, Peter Bauer and Michael Lipton. That she was supervised by Joan could possibly have more to do with family and college obligations than intellectual or ideological affinity.

Kaldor and John Eatwell had engaged closely with Mexican economic policy and Terry Barker had done a joint book on *Oil or Industry?* which included Mexico; Hashem Pesaran had also worked on oil, both as a policy maker and researcher in Iran, a crucial theme in that era for developing countries via the oil-price hikes. Ha-Joon Chang on Korea and East Asia, Gabriel Palma on Latin America and Ajit Singh widely made sustained critical interventions challenging the precepts and policies of neoliberal globalisation. Clearly there would have been credible scope for setting up a centre for the study of development within the Faculty, and all the more so given the potentially supportive role that might have been provided by the DAE.

A substantial body of expertise existed on South Asian agrarian issues; and Satish Mishra had written a fascinating thesis on the regional contrast/paradox of Maharashtra and Punjab under Phyllis Deane. Later scholars significantly extended the list. Two points here: first, that there was technical skill available to support the teaching and research activities of a centre for developing economies; and that the Faculty itself, through involvement in supervisions, was also extending its range of interest and expertise in issues of development economics. Other idiosyncratic links too: Amit Bhaduri's famous article on agricultural backwardness under conditions of semi-feudalism in rural Bengal, carried in *Economic Journal* in 1973, initiated a large literature including contributions from within the Cambridge Faculty by David Newbery, Vani Borooah and a critique by Ajit Ghose and Ashwani Saith. Stepping away from agriculture but staying in South Asia, Wahid Mahmud had done excellent work in the Kaleckian tradition under Dick Goodwin modelling the financing of development in Bangladesh; Rashid Amjad had analysed corporate investment, finance and profitability for Pakistan; and John Toye was an expert on public finance and taxation issues in developing economies.

Noteworthy also is the dense smattering of development themes amongst the Occasional Papers of the DAE.[70] There was early pioneering joint work by

---

[70] A quick scan of the list of the Occasional Papers of the DAE yields the following publications, chronologically ordered, on development-related themes:

Turner, H.A. 1965, Wage Trends, Wage Policies, and Collective Bargaining: The Problems for Underdeveloped Countries;
Reddaway, W.B. in collaboration with S.J. Potter and C.T. Taylor 1968, Effects of U.K. Direct Investment Overseas: Final Report;
Perkins, J.O.N. 1970, The Sterling Area, the Commonwealth and World Economic Growth;
Ellman, Michael 1971, Soviet Planning Today: Proposals for an Optimally Functioning Economic System;
Ward, Michael 1971, The Role of Investment in the Development of Fiji;
Faber, Michael L.O. and J.G. Potter 1971, Towards Economic Independence: Paper on the Nationalisation of the Copper Industry in Zambia;
Rowthorn, Robert in collaboration with Stephen Hymer 1971, International Big Business 1957–1967: A Study of Comparative Growth;
Paine, Suzanne 1974, Exporting Workers: the Turkish Case;
Bharadwaj, Krishna 1974, Production Conditions in Indian Agriculture: A Study Based on Farm Management Surveys;

Bob Rowthorn and Stephen Hymer on multinationals; Suzy Paine's early work on Turkish migration into West Germany; Krishna Bharadwaj's analysis of production conditions in Indian agriculture; Mahmoud Abdel-Fadil's work on land redistribution and reforms in Egypt; the issue of mining in Zambia, by Mike Faber; amongst other research published through the DAE. Those with Harcourtian memory banks would recall that as youngsters Richard Jolly and Dudley Seers were both for a while at DAE; that Phyllis Deane had been working on the conceptual and measurement sides of estimating national income in West African countries; and that Angus Deaton did his PhD when at DAE; the list can readily be extended. There was enough happening in development-related themes at or through DAE to induce a question as to why 'development' did not become a 'proper' project with its own dedicated team and visitors, as in the case of the other macro-modelling teams? Brian Reddaway was very open minded, but the original impulse in this direction from Keynes' preoccupations was lost. Perhaps the frames of vision were different: Keynes was thinking globally within an imperial imagination; in Reddaway's time, the preoccupations were with post-war UK, the new growth and social welfare agendas within the new realities which made for a more inverted gaze. But there was the other side of the coin: the break with explicit and overt development interest in staff profiles, especially at the DAE, reflected the intense engagement with the burning contemporary issues of 'development' relating to the UK economy; and many of these provided frameworks and docking points for research on the Third World, for example, the work on the deindustrialisation of the UK economy and the strategies for reviving manufacturing and industries, problems of lagging regions, issues of employment, labour and incomes, the role of devaluation, the question of exports as the driver of the growth process, the issue of managing higher non-inflationary growth. Thus, while it would be nominally true to note the absence of development-related publications on the CVs of most DAE (and Faculty) staff, many of the ongoing debates in theoretical and especially applied economics had an extensive interface with research of the political economy of development.

The purpose behind this rapid traverse was merely to flash a glimpse of the remarkable accumulated intellectual breadth and depth of development thinkers and thinking connected directly with Cambridge economics over the past century since John Maynard Keynes published his *Indian Currency and Finance* in 1913. While the South Asia connection is truly phenomenal, other countries and regions are also very impressively represented. The study of development has long shed its ghettoised area studies garb and stands at the forefront on the global stage; virtually no economic policy issue can be

Abdel-Fadil, Mahmoud 1975, Development, Income Distribution, and Social Change in Rural Egypt, 1952–1970: A Study in the Political Economy of Agrarian Transition;
FitzGerald, E.V.K. 1976, The State and Economic Development: Peru since 1968;
Abdel-Fadil, Mahmoud 1980, The Political Economy of Nasserism: A Study in Employment and Income Distribution Policies in Urban Egypt, 1952–1972.

considered in isolation from the global dimension, be it trade, technology, capital and finance, the environment, labour and employment, energy, transport, communications and media or culture and politics. Keynes had spotted this, of course, well ahead of time. The decision by the Faculty of Economics to progressively divest itself of this massive asset of historic value, and in particular at a point where it was acquiring first-order academic significance, beggars belief and can legitimately be regarded as a spectacular act of intellectual vandalism, and self-harm, that could only diminish the attraction and reputation of the Faculty. A huge amount of work had been accomplished in and through Cambridge on development themes, and this had occurred in the crucial formative phase of the evolution of the subject; it was a tradition, a living legacy and a firm foundation to build on, not to devalue, dismantle and disenfranchise.

This quick tour brings home a significant if underemphasised reality: while there was enormous interest, expertise and cumulative research output on development issues in Cambridge going back a long way, it somehow remained a sidelined, minor, almost incidental presence in the formal teaching and research profiles as late as the 1970s. And the paradox thereafter is that, while this late entry was compensated for about a decade and 'development' given a profile matching its explosive presence on the global stage, the Faculty of Economics thereafter systematically purged it from its teaching, research and physical environs. As far as the Faculty is concerned, the rising significance of development was blocked and reversed in line with the rising control of the neoclassical axis over the teaching and research offerings of the Faculty of Economics. After 1995 one has to look elsewhere to find Development Studies. The decline in the presence, authority and control of the heterodox group within the Faculty had a direct negative impact on the fate of the study of development there. This atrophy of the subject and the associated staff was part of the process of restoring economics to its imagined pure neoclassical form, within which there is no space for messy development realities and undisciplined questions. Development was whittled down in the Faculty just at a point where it had acquired the intellectual maturity, breadth, professional capacities and global catchment areas, to set up a research centre for the multidisciplinary study of development directly under the Faculty umbrella;[71] just as other uni-

---

[71] One could easily imagine Ajit Singh as its first Director, with the responsibility rotating amongst Peter Nolan, Gabriel Palma, John Sender, Ha-Joon Chang or several others. As an aside, it might be pertinent to note that several of the cohorts of the 1970s and 1980s doctoral scholars in development economics went on later to head institutes or departments of development economics/studies, including Wahiduddin Mahmud at Dhaka University and (the late) Mahboob Hossain at the Bangladesh Institute of Development Studies; Rashid Amjad at the Pakistan Institute of Development Economics, and the Graduate School of Development Studies at the Lahore School of Economics; Massoud Karshenas at the School of Oriental and African Studies, London; Ravi Srivastava, Santosh Mehrotra and Jayati Ghosh at the Jawaharlal University; and Ashwani Saith at the Development Studies Institute (DESTIN) at the London School of Economics, amongst others. John Toye, who was one of the earliest development specialists on the Cambridge Development Diploma, was later Professor and Director of the Institute of Development

versities and departments of economics were busy designing courses, degrees and centres for the study of development, the Faculty of Economics at Cambridge was washing its hands of this source of disciplinary impurity.

11.3.4 Bi-modal Distribution of Development Interest

The distribution of staff interest in development issues was highly skewed. The close interest, though from the distance of Cambridge, of Marshall and Keynes in, say Indian affairs, was absent in Pigou, Shove and Robertson; and if Dobb, Austin, Joan and Nicky were deeply engaged, Sraffa, Meade, Champernowne and Kahn (apart from his existential involvement with Israel) were not, and neither were Neild or Godley; and nor was the Third World on the research map of Luigi Pasinetti or Geoff Harcourt (except indirectly through his students), though Phyllis Deane did have a serious engagement with development in earlier years. While they would certainly not have been indifferent to development concerns, they tended not to sway from their primary area of Keynesian, Robinsonian or other theoretical pursuits, and it was implicitly assumed that Keynesianism did not travel easily to Third-World structures and contexts. And the general equilibrium brigade of that period had never really been interested in development issues in their teaching or research.

Perhaps even more striking is the muted interest amongst the next generation of economists, both on the Faculty as well as the DAE sides. The neoclassicals in general, though with a few exceptions, were preoccupied with general equilibrium and other theoretical and related games, usually indifferent professionally towards to the goings-on in First World outside, let alone that Third World somewhere out there. But more surprisingly, many economists of assorted heterodox persuasions were equally distant from development, and this makes a long list: Harcourt, Marris, Posner, Rowthorn (but for supervising Ha-Joon's PhD thesis and work with Stephen Hymer on transnational firms), Mario Nuti (except indirectly through editing some of Kalecki's essays on the socialist and mixed economies), John Eatwell (except the singular Mexico experience), Alan Hughes, Adrian Wood (while in Cambridge), Ajit Singh (till the late 1970s or even early 1980s apart from the publications emerging from the 1973 China visit). On the mainstream neoclassical side, the overseas courses had Peter Bauer on their staff till he left for LSE; Jim Mirrlees lectured on development as well in the early 1960s;[72] after that, David Newbery and later

---

Studies, and E.V.K. (Valpy) FitzGerald, who was a co-teacher and director of the Cambridge Diploma with John Toye, and had a close hand in setting up the Cambridge M.Phil in Development, was later a professor at the Institute of Social Studies in The Hague, and later still a Professor of Development Economics in Oxford where he was the Director of the Development Economics programme at Queen Elizabeth House. This list would take on enormous proportions if one were to even marginally widen the very narrow markers for inclusion.

[72] "I also lectured on development; that was where I felt there was more scope for creativity, trying to think out what development economics was; I only did it for two years; I must have made most of it up out of my head, I certainly did not have a text book to follow, so my notes actually

Partha Dasgupta were perhaps the sole exceptions: Newbery for his development interest having taught variously on Cambridge development courses spent a couple of years at the World Bank and co-authored books on commodity price stabilisation and the theory of taxation with Stiglitz and Stern, respectively, apart from an early critique of Amit Bhaduri's work on technological change and semi-feudalism; Dasgupta for his work on poverty and nutrition and on the environment; Angus Deaton had not yet set up his shop on development research, and Mervyn King had perhaps just a marginal brush with development issues when at the DAE.

At the DAE, the list, if anything, is longer. Leaving aside the peripheral involvements, then or later, in some specific piece of development research, the list is really very thin for the period into the 1980s: Stone (with the significant exception of India work in the early 1950s), Brown, Godley, Barker (except for work on Mexico and very significantly later on global climate change and environment), Francis Cripps (later work on global finance), Terence Ward, Roger Tarling, Frank Wilkinson, Martin Fetherston, Ken Coutts, Andy Cosh, Jill Rubery (except later work with the ILO), Hashem Pesaran (some work later on Iran oil), John Llewellyn, Geoff Whittington, Michael Landesmann, Vani Borooah (some early, and but then substantial work later), William Peterson, Barry Moore, Graham Pyatt (except through SAMs, e.g., Sri Lanka, but considerable work much later when at the Institute of Social Studies, The Hague). This is perhaps understandable since DAE staff were appointed to projects, and these almost all dealt with aspects of the UK economy. However, despite the open nature of the DAE, especially under Reddaway, there was no major team-based development project at DAE along the lines of the Cambridge Growth Project or later, the Godley-Cripps Cambridge Economic Policy Group. Development seemed to fall between the interstices. This lack of firm rooting of the development research project in the body of staff also meant that when the going got rough in the face of opposition from the orthodox group, there was insufficient numerical staff strength or upfront interest to defend the line. That said, such development-related staff (including those from, say, sociology or economic history, or other applied-economics interests) as remained on the Faculty books could be generally expected to side with the left-oriented heterodox group in Faculty elections. As such, their removal from the Faculty would be on the list of things-to-do of the orthodox group. Thus, with the departure of the senior cohort from the stage, the cutting down of the two DAE macro-modelling teams in the 1980s, and the termination of the ODA-funded Diploma in Development Studies in 1982 and consequent disbanding of that team of development specialists (which included John Toye, Valpy FitzGerald, Sheila Smith, Mushtaq Khan), there was only a relatively small

---

got into the Marshall Library; I would be curious to know whether they are still there; I was delighted when some years later it was reported to me that someone who then worked in developing countries thought that it had been the best course on development economics, and that he had been well prepared" (Mirrlees, 2009).

active group left in the Faculty that had development as a prime area of research interest, prominently Ajit Singh, John Sender, Peter Nolan, Jose Gabriel Palma and Ha-Joon Chang. On the other hand, 'development' was now increasingly being framed within a global matrix of interdependencies and interactions, as for instance in finance and capital flows, labour and migration, environment and cross-border resource-sharing issues, global industrial relocations and so on, and this re-framing effectively widened the contours of those now working on 'development'; Terry Barker, Francis Cripps, Partha Dasgupta would be good exemplars in this regard.

11.4   1996: Divorce and Eviction

[Within the Econ Tribe] the ranking is quite clear. The priestly caste (the Math-Econ) for example, is a higher "field" than either Micro or Macro, while the Devlops just as definitely rank lower. Second, we know that these caste-rankings (where they can be made) are not permanent but may change over time. There is evidence, for example, that both the high rank assigned to the Math-Econ and the low rank of the Devlops are, historically speaking, rather recent phenomena. The rise of the Math-Econ seems to be associated with the previously noted trend among all the Econ towards more ornate, ceremonial modls, while the low rank of the Devlops is due to the fact that this caste, in recent times, has not strictly enforced the taboos against association with the Polscis, Sociogs, and other tribes. Other Econ look upon this with considerable apprehension as endangering the moral fiber of the tribe and suspect the Devlops even of relinquishing modl-making. (Leijonhufvud, 1973: 329)

At Cambridge, so long as the overall character of the Faculty of Economics was heterodox, inclusive of an orthodox strand, there was a potentially viable and potentially productive space for development economics and development studies within its fold. The subsequent elimination of heterodox economics and economists from the Faculty could only have accentuated the antagonistic polarity between orthodox neoclassical economics and heterodox development economics/studies. While one functioned within a historical frame, with structural and institutional rigidities, with discontinuities, prominent roles for the state, with acute market imperfections and class inequalities, the mainstream economics paradigm had a timeless equilibrium framework, which abstracted from all this 'noise', as its default mode. There was virtually no common space, not even a no-man's land in between. The more Cambridge economics self-purified, the greater was the incompatibility. The experience of other universities suggests that development studies and heterodox economics can and do co-exist, interact productively in shared intellectual space, as for instance in SOAS, London, and IDS, Sussex; on the other hand, initiatives for joint postgraduate teaching and degrees between heterodox development and orthodox neoclassical economics at LSE generally floundered. Of course, these two disciplinary fields are not always in opposition, as for instance in Chicago, where the tradition of economics in the 1970s and 1980s was addicted not to the games of general equilibrium but to the adrenalin of hands-on policy intervention, à la the Chicago boys in Chile in the Pinochet era, a paradigm which took over the IMF and World Bank from the 1980s; both 'economics' and 'development' sought and dispensed wisdom from the same Hayek–Friedman bible. This was diametrically opposite to the orientation of development theory and practice in Cambridge when compared with the mainstream economics Faculty. To this has to be added the hostility and 'superiority complex' of orthodox economics to 'sister' social sciences, and the claim of being scientific, as was confirmed by the aggressive position taken by Hahn, Matthews, Newbery and others of the orthodox camp in arguing that stray interlopers from 'vaguely cognate disciplines', viz., sociology and sociologists, be excluded from the citizenship of the Faculty of Economics and the DAE.

With the sudden thinning out of this august senior cohort through multiple retirements and deaths, all concentrated in the 1970s and early- to mid-1980s, and the subsequent rise into full operational dominance of the mainstream orthodox group, the climate took a sharp turn for the worse. Ha-Joon (personal communication) says "the Faculty was getting increasingly hostile" to the presence of development teaching in the Tripos and towards development staff in the Faculty building, and this was manifested in a series of steps all leading out of the Faculty. The year 1996 was a significant point of inflexion. The Diploma in Development, which was already housed in the Department of Land Economy and managed by the interdepartmental Development Studies Committee, was abolished; in view of the increasingly aggressive environment, the small residual group of staff of the M.Phil in Economics and Politics of Development (EPD), which had run in the Faculty, managed by the Development Studies Committee, for two decades till 1995, decided, as Ha-Joon Chang says, "to jump before they were pushed" and proposed to create the new M.Phil in Development Studies, also to be managed by the Development Studies Committee, and based initially in the refuge of Land Economy. Meanwhile, Partha Dasgupta had set up a new mainstream M.Phil in the Economics of Developing Countries (EDC) in the Faculty, sending a clear message that the rival, radically oriented M.Phil in the Economics and Politics of Development, wasn't really 'economics'; EDC was later terminated in the early 2000s. The writing was on the wall, and in large characters: Ha-Joon recalls that "even after that, my Development Economics paper (coordinated by me and taught by Ajit, Gabriel, Peter, and me) was a paper based in the Faculty of Economics until 2010, when the Faculty banned their students from taking it."[73] Alan Hughes pointed out that some of the long-running papers of a more interdisciplinary nature were deleted from the Economics Tripos, for example, the Sociology of Economic Life, Labour, amongst others. The break with the Faculty was completed in 2011 with the setting up of the new Centre of Development Studies, with its own M.Phil and PhD programmes in

---

[73] "The Faculty allowed their students to take it again a few years ago" (personal communication).

Development Studies. Peter Nolan at this point was Sinyi Professor of Chinese Management in the Judge Business School; he had chaired the Development Studies Committee since the late 1990s; now, in 2011, he took over as the first Director of the new Development Studies Centre, and on his retirement Ha-Joon Chang took over in 2017, and handed the reins at the end of Lent Term, 2020–2021 to William Hurst, the new Chong Hua Professor of Chinese Development, a political scientist specialising in issues of labour, land and law in China and Southeast Asia.

And thus, after flourishing in, and outside with the support of, the Faculty since the pre-war decade, teaching on development studies had been exorcised from the Faculty curriculum. The neoclassical Brahmins had shown the door to another bunch of untouchables, and taken another dip in the Ganges to rid themselves of any disciplinary impurities they might have absorbed in the years of rubbing shoulders with lowly development specialists in the Faculty corridors.

There were multiple channels through which development was purged and drained out of the Faculty. Several papers on or related to development themes were dropped from the Tripos; at the level of research degrees, admission and progression criteria were changed to require levels of mathematical or econometric skills that were not really essential for most students wanting to work on development issues but which had the effect of excluding them since their academic backgrounds and qualifications did not match this unnecessarily imposed criterion—to continue with their PhDs, students would have to pass a maths and econometrics exam at the end of the first year; research supervisors had to be agreed to prior to admission, which set a low upper limit for development on account of the small number of staff in this field. The examination process was also oriented in ways to make it more hostile with supervisors excluded at formal and informal levels. Some programmes were closed, like the diploma; or they were shunted out of the Faculty and relocated in Land Economy; staff contracts were not renewed and there were no new hires in development; when a development specialist retired, there was no replacement staff hired with a development profile; and those who were hired had little interest in development issues per se, and certainly not with heterodox perspectives; promotions of development staff were regularly blocked over extended periods; and in general, the atmosphere and Faculty environment were made unwelcoming and unfriendly for staff involved in development, even to the extent of interfering in their entitlements to office space. Research assessments in the form of RAEs and REFs provided further opportunities for haranguing and harassing and generally insulting these staff by branding them sub-standard or mediocre using the criteria set by the orthodox groups. And as the numbers of development staff shrank to a handful, their presence and voice became marginalised and silenced, and the group essentially ghettoised. The frustrating experience of the four long-serving staff[74] involved in development teaching, viz., Ajit Singh, Peter Nolan, Jose Gabriel Palma and Ha-Joon Chang, provides confirmation of such biases and hostility.

Peter Nolan came under pressure to leave, and did, in 1994: walking out upright to a prestigious Sin Yi Professorship in Chinese Management in 1997, and later, in 2012, becoming the Chong Hwa Professor of Chinese Studies at Judge Business School where he set up a high-profile, high-quality and highly successful programme for senior Chinese business leaders and researchers; Peter is widely regarded as one of the leading experts on Chinese economic affairs world-wide, and the author of a string of books tracking the trajectories of China's economy, from the point of the onset of the reforms to the present, and their implications at the global level.

Increasingly from the early 1980s, applied development economics had become Ajit Singh's main line of research, and he amassed an enviable worldwide reputation as one of the leading radical critics of the neoliberal development template imposed by the Bretton Woods Institutions on developing economies, especially after the debt crisis unleashed by the OPEC oil-price hikes. The debilitating impact of Parkinson's Disease notwithstanding, his research productivity actually showed an upward trend, and he became increasingly a central figure in the analysis of the relationship between industrialisation, finance and development, taking over from Kaldor the mantle of being the apostle of Third-World industrialisation—but it was not till 1991 that his application for a promotion for an *ad hominem* readership was approved, and only in 1995 that he became a professor, about 25 years after all the 'nephews' of 'uncle' Hahn—of the same age cohort as Ajit—had been settled in chairs. Ajit was always based in economics; only after his retirement he held a 25 per cent post in the CDS (with another 50 per cent in the JBS, and the remaining 25 per cent in Birmingham).

The redoubtable Gabriel Palma, possibly the leading Latin American economist of the day, was seriously undervalued by the mainstream Faculty, and languished as a senior lecturer till his retirement, unable to lecture on development in the Faculty, and assigned duties to teach econometrics, while remaining remarkably productive in his widely cited research on Latin American issues, and especially on inequality, where his 'Palma Ratio' has entered the lexicon of inequality measures. Gabriel never was formally associated with Development Studies until his retirement a few years ago, after which he was made an affiliated lecturer of CDS.[75]

---

[74] Ajit Singh and Gabriel Palma, at the time, were both Faculty staff members, though they contributed a great deal to the tasks of teaching and supervision in Development Studies including Palma serving as the Economics representative on the Development Studies board. Both maintained this close relationship after their points of retirement from the Faculty.

[75] Jose Gabriel Palma was never promoted to a readership despite his high standing and reputation in the subject. His papers in the Cambridge Working Papers in Economics series were the most downloaded for extended periods, often top ranked and with several papers simultaneously; and for several years was in the top 1 per cent (or better) in the RePec ranks for downloaded

That shifts the spotlight to Ha-Joon Chang, the last surviving member of the development and heterodox clan in the Faculty. Ha-Joon took over from Peter Nolan who retired in 2016 after his long stint as Director. Again, Development Studies as a subject unit performs better in its domain than does Economics in its area; but it remains of course, low caste. Ha-Joon, at present one of the most widely read and cited authors in development economics, is a severe critic of the neoclassical and neoliberal traditions that have captured and distorted development theory and policy, and his pedagogically lucid books are now universal currency in the field, inoculating fresh young minds entering social science against dangerous intellectual fundamentalisms. His books are regularly translated into several languages[76] and he is listed often as a leading world thinker today. Could it be for these attributes that he had his application for an *ad hominem* promotion to a readership declined six years in a row, with an appeal in each of those years also rejected? Perhaps he is a true Gandhian, perennially turning the other cheek; perhaps he was fathoming the depths to which matters could sink; but then, on the seventh—and last permissible—time of asking, he became a reader, when he could probably just ask for a chair, if not a sofa, at most Ivy League universities. His is the last toehold of heterodox economics in the Faculty, quantitatively amounting to 0.2 FTE. "This is why I have said that development economics was the last stronghold of non-neoclassical economics in the Faculty"—perhaps, for 'stronghold', read 'remnant'. Aptly, Ha-Joon describes himself as 'the last Mohican'.

11.5　A Credible Counterfactual

The post-war period was marked by four massive development processes: first, the decolonisations which placed Gerschenkronian state-led accumulation strategies at the heart of the industrialisation drives of the developing economies; second, the Chinese, Cuban and Vietnamese socialist revolutions which brought the contending socialist development strategies to the forefront of discourse and practice, ushering in a countervailing power to old imperialism and neo-colonialism; third, the remarkable explosion of export-led growth of East Asian economies and the debates over its sources and dynamics; and fourth, the great reversal following the Third-World debt crises unleashed by the OPEC oil-price hikes which opened the door to the international

---

papers, along with Hashem Pesaran, being the top ranked members of the Faculty in this regard. But of course, all this did not add up to much for those deciding on promotions; what counted was publications in the core mainstream economics journals.

[76] *Kicking Away the Ladder: Development Strategy in Historical Perspective* (2002) was translated into nine languages; *Reclaiming Development: An Alternative Economic Policy Manual* (2004) obviously did extremely poorly, being translated into only five languages; *Bad Samaritans: Rich Nations, Poor Policies, and the Threat to the Developing World* (2007) went into fifteen languages; and *23 Things They Don't Tell You About Capitalism* (2010) generated much needed employment in the translation industry, going into thirty-three languages; things have gone really downhill after that, since *Economics: The User's Guide* (2014) can be read in only fourteen languages.

moneylenders to step in with their one-size-fits-all structural adjustment programmes that put the developing countries 'back in their place' in the global order. There were surely structural weaknesses in Third-World strategies, but the OPEC-fuelled inflation and the ensuing debt crisis served as the triggers for the reversal of the Third-World development state, just as analogously it led to the rolling back of the welfare state in advanced market economies. Meanwhile, China and Vietnam had reversed their collectivist strategies of development in significant ways. Thus, in the space of just a decade, the three major oppositional projects to raw capitalism as a strategy of development had collapsed: the welfare state, the socialist project and non-capitalist development in the Third World. Indeed, a variation on the theme of John Reed's, 1919 classic, *Ten Days that Shook the World*—the ten years did fly past as ten days, with the storyline running in reverse.

The dismantling of this architecture of multiple alternatives also revealed in full force the power of capital on a global stage, soon permeating, even overtaking, the role of governments and international development agencies. This open connectedness unleashed new opportunities for capital and capitalists, and for big mobile money and finance rentiers generating unprecedented levels of intra- and inter-country inequalities.[77] Rapacious footloose finance capital inevitably generated instability and financial breakdowns, on top of the environmental and health crises and various mass entitlement failures emanating from jobless, or what K.P. Kannan has recently called job-loss growth, which in turn fuelled intense pressures creating massive flows of migrants, augmented by flows of refugees from multiple wars and other dislocations. With the weakening, or non-existence, of multilateral rule making and governance in virtually all domains, 'development' had escaped its ghettoisation in 'area studies' and arrived as a central dimension of globalisation. This alarming sketch serves as an approximation to the global state of play from c.1980.

---

[77] "Some researchers argue that in the globalisation era, levels of global income inequality have declined somewhat, if country borders and intra-country inequalities are not taken into account. This paradoxical result arises, of course, from the increase in the average per capita income of China and India. This poses the Chindian paradox: what is the intrinsic value of claiming that global inequality has diminished when, within a large majority of countries, inequality has actually increased over the same period? And all the more so, when inequality has increased dramatically within both China and India, the two countries whose rapid growth of average incomes is the basis for opposite result at the global level? Subjective perceptions arise from one's sense of identity. Does an Indian or a Chinese national regard himself essentially in global terms without noticing that he was born in India, will probably live and die there without leaving its borders? Will she perceive and calibrate her relative societal and economic position in comparison with some imagined global median person or against her neighbour, her employer and the high profile plutocrats who control the economy and country. This is clearly a class issue. The global perspective might well be gaining greater relevance as a referential frame for the widening imaginations and aspirations of the rising new elite and middle classes; but for the common wo/man, such an assumption surely would be untenable. Most Indians and Chinese are likely to directly perceive and react to the inequalities they know and experience in their daily lives, and are perhaps unlikely to be impressed by a methodological interpretation which tells them they should not perceive or be experiencing what they do" (Saith, 2011: 73–74).

Development themes emerged centre stage in terms of policy, research and teaching, and this was reflected in an across-the-board reorientation and expansion in universities, and also in international agencies, corporates and banks, and the non-government sector. To put it one way, there was a discrete outward shift in the demand curve, and everywhere it induced, with variable lags, a significant supply response, as new courses, departments, centres and institutes of development studies/economics sprang up, not only in the northwest, but also in the south-east. Both at intellectual and commercial levels, a massive market had opened up.

How did all this play out for development teaching and research in Cambridge; how did these tectonic shifts reflect in the Faculty of Economics? It is striking that it was precisely at the time, from the early 1980s, when the study of development issues was becoming central in national and global theoretical and applied policy analysis, that the study of development went into decline at the Faculty of Economics and Politics, with increasing hostility from the mid-1980s as the orthodox mainstream took control of the Faculty. This all the more remarkable in view of (the then) recent trajectory of the subject: although the ODA, under Thatcher rules, had shut down the Diploma in Development Studies, a new diploma had been launched from 1982; and from the mid-1970s, there was a viable new M.Phil in Development Studies that had been started; further, the 1970s had witnessed a boom in the inflow of research scholars for the PhD programme focussing on topics on development economics. Against this backdrop, the negative response of the Faculty appears all the more inexplicable, and unsound; as seen, this led inexorably to the departure of development studies altogether from the Faculty by 1995, when the M.Phil programme was terminated, and relocated in the Department of Land Economy. This outcome can only be understood as being the outcome of a process of orthodox purification of 'economics' within the Faculty, and politically in terms of the expulsion of staff of heterodox intellectual leanings who generally stood in opposition to the orthodox camp in Faculty decision-making and elections.

A sharp contrast can be observed with the pattern of response in some other leading universities. At the London School of Economics, the Director, I.G. Patel, himself a leading practitioner of development, had set up a new interdepartmental Development Studies Institute (DESTIN) during his 1984–1990 term with Meghnad Desai, Professor of Economics, as the first head of the institute and about thirty students and about three full-time staff; Desai returned to the Department of Economics in 1994. There ensued a dramatic transitional period, initiated by the next Director of DESTIN, in the decade from 1995 which saw a spectacular increase both from the demand side, with applications to DESTIN running at over 1200 a year for about 120 places; and the supply side, with the development of multiple post-graduate degrees on Development Practice and various joint degrees with gender, or environment, or anthropology; core staff at DESTIN rose to between ten and twelve, with many others involved in related departments. In 1995, the precise year that the Faculty of Economics and Politics in Cambridge closed down its development studies programme, the first Chair in Development Studies was advertised, with the chair also to serve as the head of DESTIN. Research programmes in development studies incubated and flourished at DESTIN. Nearby, SOAS mirrored these LSE initiatives, and also set up their first Professorship in Development Studies, leading to a dynamic and expanding enterprise; IDS, Sussex, also witnessed a boom, and other universities rapidly entered the 'market'. These trends were reflected also elsewhere in Europe.

Cambridge, meanwhile, had gone its own perverse way and step-by-step shut down what it had.[78] The staff at the Faculty dealing with development teaching included several (mostly) mainstream practitioners variously engaged with specific development questions, but the radical, non-neoclassical contingent had been whittled down to four, all senior stalwarts in the field: Ajit Singh, Peter Nolan, Jose Gabriel Palma and Ha-Joon Chang, who had joined in place of John Sender in 1990. Ha-Joon says, "Ajit of course was the towering figure, but he was not alone. We all worked closely with him, and kept Development as the last stronghold of non-mainstream economics in Cambridge Economics Faculty. And we are still carrying the torch in the Centre of Development Studies" (personal communication). The Centre for Development Studies was housed in 2012, not in the Faculty of Economics, but as a semi-autonomous unit in the Department of Politics and International Studies.

The development phoenix seems to be flourishing on the periphery and flying high—seemingly higher than economics at the centre. Since its formation in 2011, the Centre of Development Studies has steadily gained strength and established a reputation for excellence and relevance in development studies, significantly including the pedagogical level. Cambridge development studies was fifth in the 2019 QS global subject rankings, when Cambridge economics was ranked tenth; Cambridge social sciences, and Cambridge University overall were both placed sixth. The M.Phil and the PhD in Development Studies programmes are hugely oversubscribed and rank amongst the most popular in the university in terms of the demand for admissions. Staff are overworked, no doubt, meeting the huge demand at high-quality levels of delivery, but they do not suffer the continual haranguing and hostility of old from mainstream economists who, by their own ascription, had claimed a superior Brahmanical status for themselves. An intrinsically and strategically significant intellectual opportunity had been lost in the path not taken at the Faculty of Economics.

---

[78] In 1995, I joined LSE as the Chair of Development Studies and Head of the Development Studies Institute and was directly involved in all the developments described. On joining, I was invited to serve as the external examiner for the Cambridge M.Phil in Development Studies then in its nomadic days; I recall being struck by the contrast between trajectories at the two institutions.

Appendix 11.1: Arguments in Support of Continuation of Development Studies Course in Cambridge

1. The Cambridge courses have played an important part in relationships with developing countries; initially in the training of British administrative and agricultural officials and more recently in training government officers, university teachers and researchers and some private sector employees from developing countries in the wider field of development studies. The connection goes back to 1925, and in 1969 at the specific request of the ODA the courses were reviewed, restructured and new staff were appointed.
2. In 1977 the M.Phil course was established, the content and structure having been discussed at great length with the ODA and received their approval. The Course on Development continues to be provided in parallel with the M.Phil for the time being.
3. The courses continue to receive increasing interest and recognition over a wide range of potential candidates overseas and their employers and sponsors.[79] Communications from past students suggest that a high proportion regard the courses as valuable and relevant. Many occupy posts of considerable importance and have expressed dismay that there is a prospect that the courses may cease after 1982.
4. Recognition of the academic excellence of the courses within the university has grown, and this was reflected in the establishment of the M.Phil. In the last two years several students have proceeded from the courses to further degrees, for example, in the Faculty of Economics and Politics, where the entry requirements are known to be highly competitive. The courses have replaced the Diploma in Development Economics as the principal means by which students from developing countries are admitted for the PhD in Economics.
5. Moreover the S.S.R.C. has awarded the M.Phil in Development Studies 'quota' status in circumstances in which this has only been given for courses regarded as being of quite exceptional merit in view of the Council's limited finance. Staff have also contributed a substantial number of research publications related to development, and the *Journal of Development Studies*, one of the foremost academic journals in this field, has been edited from Cambridge by members of the course staff for a number of years.
6. For the overseas student, working in government service of higher educational institutions concerned with development training and research, the courses:

---

[79] On average over the last ten years 37 students have been enrolled in the courses each year. For the academical year 1980–1981 there were 137 applicants, 64 being qualified and offered admission, though numbers fell back to 36.

(a) Provide an interdisciplinary structure in which students are encouraged to think for themselves, a theoretical framework and wide spectrum for study, while also providing teaching of a specialist nature in each component discipline;
(b) Enable students to review problems and policies in their countries in the perspective of distance, and to do so in a situation in which the student complement being drawn from so many countries and many sources provides a comparative dimension;
(c) Provide the opportunity for study in a major university where they are able to make use of outstanding resources over the wide range of subjects of their choice. The supervision system in Cambridge also ensures that students receive close personal attention and intellectual stimulus in an outstanding academic environment.

7. Cambridge as one of the leading universities of the world has an international reputation, and this alone, in the interests of Britain, justifies the investment of very modest sums in the promotion in this university of interest in developing countries and their problems as well as resources to enable us to offer appropriate facilities for those concerned with development both from within this country and overseas. The courses on Development have in the past made a major intellectual and practical contribution to the work of several other University Departments in Cambridge, thereby stimulating and enhancing their contribution to effective research and teaching in fields related to development in the interests of the Third World.

8. The continuance of Cambridge as a centre for the study of the problems of developing countries is dependent, in various ways, on the existence of the courses on development. The courses, and the staff and students on these, provide a very important focus for the promotion of understanding of problems of developing countries among members of the university, especially among undergraduates. This results from contacts made within the Area Studies Centres, personal contacts and contacts through undergraduate societies.[80] Development studies in Cambridge is more formally enhanced by the contribution which the staff make to lecturing and supervision in Faculties, Departments and the Areas Studies Centres, as well as by the access which all members of the university have to the lectures provided by the Overseas Studies Committee.

9. The international economic environment is characterised by growing economic interdependence between, on the one hand, the newly industrialised countries, the primary commodity exporters and a wide range of developing counties whose demand for imports of technology-intensive inputs is rapidly expanding, and, on the other hand, the indus-

---

[80] For Example The Development Society, Third World First, Africa Society.

trialised economies whose future economic performance depends upon the establishment of mutually beneficial trade and investment relationship with those developing countries. The competitiveness of the UK in this environment is likely to depend upon the degree to which Britain maintains its comparative expertise in detailed understanding of the political, economic and sociological realities of developing countries. If the experience and knowledge of developing countries at present available in Cambridge are not sustained, then the long-run ability of British entrepreneurial management, both in the private and in the public sectors, to take advantage of marketing and investment opportunities in the developing countries will be proportionately lessened as compared to that of our competitors.

10. It is not possible for Cambridge to obtain U.G.C. financing for these courses in isolation from other university commitments and priorities, even if it proves possible to obtain finance for new needs at all in 1981. The university does, however, already make a contribution to the financial viability of the course on Development:

   (a) The cost of overheads in the form of library services, lecture rooms, seminar rooms and central administration and so on;
   (b) Teaching inputs from a number of faculties and Departments (Economic and Politics, Social Anthropology, Social and Political Sciences, Land economy, Geography, Applied Biology) as well as the Area Studies Centres.

   It should be possible to run the courses on a bare and maintenance basis with parallel economies in secretarial services and other charges amounting to about 25 per cent of the present total ODA contribution. In addition, it is anticipated that in the years 1982–1985 the fees from students participating in the courses should provide a substantial inflow of revenue.

11. Response to the facilities on offer in the form of students from overseas with adequate finance is clearly difficult to predict in present circumstances. It seems unlikely that many candidates till be supported to the extent of meeting fees based on the unit costs of teaching an administration (at present GBP 3250 and likely to be in the region of GBP 3500 for 1981–1982, plus college fees). Given student numbers at present levels and fees charged at the standard rate of GBP 2000 there seems likely to be a shortfall of around GBP 45,000 (or the costs of about three posts at maximum point in the scale) which represents the measure of subside required. This is a conservative calculation and the shortfall colugo be much reduced if more students with adequate funds can be found. The university will also require some form of underwriting against further subsidy requirements if staff are to be employed as University Teaching Officers.

12. Given the importance to Britain's political interests and possibly commercial objectives, the amount of money needed to ensure continuation of the courses is modest. These courses have a long background and the knowledge and understanding of Third-World problems thus generated in Cambridge are, among like institutions, a national asset. The standard of excellence of the courses and the range of needs and interests they meet could only be re-established with great difficulty if the continuity is once broken.

[OSC.404] undated; circa 1980

References

Apthorpe, R. (1971). The new generalism: Four phases in development studies in the first development decade. *Development and Change, 3*(1), 62–75.

Bagchi, A. K. (1976). Deindustrialization in India in the nineteenth century: Some theoretical implications. *Journal of Development Studies, 12*(2), 135–164.

Bagchi, A. K. (2004). *Keynes, Kaldor and development economics.* Occasional Paper No. 1. Institute of Development Studies.

Bagchi, A. K. (2019, September 13). The practical economist. *Frontline.*

Bauer, P. T. (1981). *Equality, the third world and economic delusion.* Methuen University Paperbacks.

Bhagwati, J. N., & Chakravarty, S. (1969). Contributions to Indian economic analysis: A survey. *American Economic Review, 59*(4, Part 2, supplement), 1–73.

Bhagwati, J. N., & Desai, P. (1970). *India: Planning for industrialization; industrialization and trade policies since 1951.* Oxford University Press, on behalf of OECD.

Bhagwati, J., & Srinivasan, T. N. (1975). *Foreign trade regimes and economic development: India.* National Bureau of Economic Research.

Bhagwati, J., & Srinivasan, T. N. (1993). *Report: India's economic reforms.* Associated Chambers of Commerce and Industry of India.

Buchanan, J. (2002). The sayer of truth: A personal tribute to Peter Bauer. *Public Choice, 112*(3–4), 233.

Byres, T. J. (1984). Amiya Bagchi and the political economy of underdevelopment. *Social Scientist, 12*(132), 64–75.

Cairncross, A. (1993). *The life of an economic adviser.* Palgrave Macmillan.

Chakravarty, S. (1987). *Post-Keynesian theorists and the theory of economic development.* Working Paper No. 23. WIDER-UNU.

Chakravarty, S. (1989). Nicholas Kaldor on Indian economic problems. *Cambridge Journal of Economics, 13*(1), 237–244. Retrieved June 1, 2021, from http://www.jstor.org/stable/23598159

Chakravarty, S., & Singh, A. (1988, July). *The desirable forms of economic openness in the South.* Unpublished paper, First Draft, 53p.

Chandavarkar, A. (1989). *Keynes and India: A study in economics and biography.* Macmillan.

Chandavarkar, A. (1993). Keynes and the role of the state in developing countries. In D. Crabtree & A. P. Thirlwall (Eds.), *Keynes and the role of the state* (Keynes Seminars) (pp. 126–160). Palgrave Macmillan. https://doi.org/10.1007/978-1-349-22708-2_9

Cooper, C., & FitzGerald, E. V. K. (Eds.). (1989). *Development studies revisited: Twenty-five years of the Journal of Development Studies*. Frank Cass.

Deng, A. (1994). Obituary: Paul Philip Howell, D.Phil, CMG, OBE. *The Cambridge Journal of Anthropology, 17*(I), 69–71.

Desai, P. (1963). The development of the Indian economy. An exercise in economic planning. *Oxford Economic Papers, 15*(3), 308–317.

Desai, M. (2005, July 20). I. G. Patel: Economic statesman and director of LSE. *The Independent*.

Dirks, N. B. (2001). *Castes of mind: Colonialism and the making of modern India*. Princeton University Press.

Dobb, M. (1951). *Some aspects of economic development*. Ranjit Printers and Publishers. (Reprinted in M. Dobb 1967).

Dobb, M. (1960). *An essay on economic growth and planning*. Routledge and Kegan Paul.

Dobb, M. (1967). *Papers on capitalism, development and planning*. Routledge and Kegan Paul.

Ewing, A. F. (1971). Review of *Welfare economics and the economics of socialism: Towards a common-sense critique*, Cambridge: Cambridge University Press. *Journal of Modern African Studies, 9*(2), 332–333.

Fitzgerald, E. V. K. (1976). *The state and economic development: Peru since 1968*. Cambridge University Press.

Fitzgerald, E. V. K. (1978a). The fiscal crisis of the Latin American state. In J. F. J. Toye (Ed.), *Taxation and economic development: Twelve critical studies*. Frank Cass.

Fitzgerald, E. V. K. (1978b). *Public sector investment for developing countries*. Macmillan.

Gadgil, D. R. (1924). *The industrial evolution of India in recent times*. Oxford University Press.

Godley, W. (2008, May 16). Interview with Wynne Godley. In S. Harrison & A. Macfarlane, *Encounter with economics*. Interviews filmed by A. Macfarlane and edited by S. Harrison. University of Cambridge. http://sms.cam.ac.uk/collection/1092396

Gopal, S. (1979). *Jawaharlal Nehru: A biography, volume 2, 1947–1956*. Random House.

Guha, R. (2007). *India after Gandhi: The history of the world's largest democracy*. Harper Collins.

Harcourt, G. C. (1998). Two views on development: Austin and Joan Robinson. *Cambridge Journal of Economics, 22*(3), 367–377.

Hobson, J. A. (1902). *Imperialism*. James Pott & Co.

Kahn, R. (1958). The pace of development. In A. Bonne (Ed.), *The challenge of development: Papers of a symposium held in Jerusalem* (pp. 153–191). Eliezer Kaplan School of Economics and Social Science, Hebrew University of Jerusalem.

Kahn, R., & Marcuzzo, M. C. (2020). Richard Kahn: A disciple of Keynes. *History of Economics Review*, 57p. https://doi.org/10.1080/10370196.2020.1767930

Keynes, J. M. (1924). Alfred Marshall, 1842–1924. *The Economic Journal, 34*(135), 311–372.

Kirk-Greene, A. (1999, May). The colonial service training courses: Professionalizing the colonial service. *Overseas Service Pensioners' Association (OSPA) Journal, 77*. https://www.britishempire.co.uk/ospa.htm

Kothari, U. (2005). From colonial administration to development studies: A postcolonial critique of the history of development studies. In U. Kothari (Ed.), *A radical history of development studies: Individuals, institutions and ideologies* (pp. 47–66). Zed Books.

Krishnaswami, A. (1942). Marshall's contribution to Indian economics. *Indian Journal of Economics, 22*, 875–897.

Krishnaswamy, K. S. (2002). V.K.R.V. Rao on some macroeconomic relationships. *Journal of Social and Economic Development, 4*(1), 81–87. http://webcache.googleusercontent.com/search?q=cache:MxfhZYX4cHUJ:http://www.isec.ac.in/JSED/JSED_V4_I1_81-87.pdf%2Bvkrv+rao+multiplier+agricultural&client=safari&rls=en&hl=en&ct=clnk

Larmer, M. (Ed.). (2010a). *The Musakanya papers: The autobiographical writings of Valentine Musakanya.* Lembani Trust. https://books.google.nl/books?id=o4r6nOBcD9AC&pg=PA22&source=gbs_toc_r&cad=3#v=onepage&q&f=false

Larmer, M. (2010b). Chronicle of a coup foretold: Valentine Musakanya and the 1980 coup attempt in Zambia. *Journal of African History, 51*(3), 391–409.

Leijonhufvud, A. (1973). Life among the econ. *Economic Inquiry, 11*(3), 327–337.

Marcuzzo, M. C. (2008). Piero Sraffa at the University of Cambridge. In H. D. Kurz, L. Pasinetti, & N. Salvadori (Eds.), *Piero Sraffa: The man and the scholar. Exploring his unpublished papers* (pp. 51–77). Routledge.

Martin, K., & Knapp, J. (Eds.). (1967). *The teaching of development economics. Its position in the present state of knowledge. The proceedings of the Manchester Conference on teaching economic development, April 1964.* Routledge.

Mirrlees, J. (2009). *Interview of Sir James Mirrlees, Nobel laureate in economics, covering aspects of his life and work.* Interview on 21 September 2009 filmed by Alan Macfarlane and edited by Sarah Harrison. https://www.sms.cam.ac.uk/media/1126590

Musakanya, V. (2010). *The Musakanya Papers: The autobiographical writings of Valentine Musakanya.* Edited by M. Larmer. Lembani Trust. https://books.google.nl/books?id=o4r6nOBcD9AC&pg=PA22&source=gbs_toc_r&cad=3#v=onepage&q&f=false

Nolan, P. (1976). Collectivization in China: Some comparisons with the USSR. *Journal of Peasant Studies, 3*(2), 192–220.

Nolan, P. (1988). *The political economy of collective farms: An analysis of China's post-Mao rural reforms.* Routledge.

Nolan, P., & Paine, S. (1986a). Towards an appraisal of the impact of rural reform in China, 1978–85. *Cambridge Journal of Economics, 10*(1), 83–99.

Nolan, P., & Paine, S. (1986b). *Rethinking socialist economics: A new agenda for Britain.* St. Martin's Press.

Nurkse, R. (1953). *Problems of capital formation in underdeveloped countries.* Basil Blackwell.

Nuti, D. M. (1971). 'Vulgar Economy' in the theory of income distribution. *Science and Society, 35*(1), 27–33.

Paine, S. (1971). Lessons for LDCs from Japan's experience with labour commitment and subcontracting in the manufacturing sector. *Bulletin of the Oxford Institute of Economics and Statistics, 33*(2), 115–133.

Paine, S. (1972). Turkey's first five-year development plan (FFYDP) 1963–67: A different assessment. *Economic Journal, 82*(326), 693–699.

Paine, S. (1973). Review of *Economic theory and the underdeveloped countries* by Hla Myint. *Modern Asian Studies, 7*(2), 311–313.

Paine, S. (1974). *Exporting workers: The Turkish case.* Occasional Paper 41, Department of Applied Economics, Cambridge University Press.

Paine, S. (1976a). Balanced development: Maoist conception and Chinese practice. *World Development, 4*(4), 277–304.

Paine, S. (1976b). Development with growth: A quarter century of socialist transformation in China. *Economic and Political Weekly, 11*(31/33), 1349–1382.

Paine, S. (1977). Agricultural development in less developed countries (particularly South Asia): An introduction to Bhaduri. *Cambridge Journal of Economics, 1*(4), 335–339.

Paine, S. (1978). Some reflections on the presence of 'rural' or of 'urban bias' in China's development policies, 1949–1976. *World Development, 6*(5), 693–707.

Paine, S. (1981). Spatial aspect of Chinese development: Issues, outcomes and policies, 1949–1979. *Journal of Development Studies, 17*(2), 133–195.

Paine, S., & Singh, A. (1973). The Shanghai diesel engine factory. *The Cambridge Review, 94*.

Palma, J. G., & Marcel, M. (1989). Kaldor on the 'discreet charm' of the Chilean bourgeoisie. *Cambridge Journal of Economics, 13*(1), 245–272.

Pigou, A. C. (1920). *The economics of welfare*. Macmillan.

Raj, K. N. (1960). *Some economic aspects of the Bhakra Nangal project: A preliminary analysis of selected investment criteria*. Asia Publishing House.

Rao, V. K. R. V. (1937). *The national income of British India, 1931–32*. PhD Dissertation, Faculty of Economics and Politics, University of Cambridge, UK.

Rao, V. K. R. V. (1952, February). Investment, income and the multiplier in an underdeveloped economy. *The Indian Economic Review*.

Reddaway, B. (1962). *The development of the Indian economy*. George Allen and Unwin.

Reddaway, W. B. (1963). The development of the Indian economy: The objects of the exercise restated. *Oxford Economic Papers, 15*(3), 318–332.

Reddaway, W. B. (1995). Recollections of a lucky economist. *BNL Quarterly Review, 192*, 3–16.

Reed, J. (1919). *Ten days that shook the world*. Boni and Liveright, Inc.

Robinson, J. (1933). *The economics of imperfect competition*. Macmillan.

Robinson, J. (1979). *Aspects of development and underdevelopment*. Cambridge University Press.

Rosenheim, A. (1994, April 9). Obituary: Paul Howell. *The Independent*.

Roth, A. (2002, May 6). Obituary: Lord Bauer – Thatcher's rightwing economist opposed to third world aid. *The Guardian*.

Rudra, A. (1996). *Prasanta Chandra Mahalanobis: A biography*. Indian Statistical Institute; Oxford University Press.

Saith, A. (2008). Joan Robinson and Indian planning: An awkward relationship. *Development and Change, 39*(6), 1115–1134.

Saith, A. (2011). Inequality, imbalance, instability: Reflections on a structural crisis. *Development and Change, 42*(1), 70–86.

Saith, A. (2019). *Ajit Singh of Cambridge and Chandigarh: An intellectual biography of the radical Sikh economist*. Palgrave Macmillan.

Samuelson, P. A. (1958). Review: *Theoretical welfare economics*, by J. de V. Graaff. *Economic Journal, 68*(271), 539–541.

Schiffman, D. (2013). *Richard Kahn and Israeli economic policy, 1957 and 1962*. Ariel University. https://ssrn.com/abstract=2373517

Schur, T. (Ed.). (2014). *From the Cam to the Zambezi: Colonial service and the path to new Zambia*. I. B. Taurus.

Seers, D. (1963). The limitations of the special case. *Bulletin of the Oxford Institute of Economics and Statistics, 25*(2), 77–98.

Sen, A. (1982, March 4). Just deserts. Review of *Equality, the third world, and economic delusion*, Harvard University Press. *The New York Review of Books*.
Sen, A. (1998). *Amartya Sen – Biographical*. https://www.nobelprize.org/prizes/economic-sciences/1998/sen/biographical/
Sen, A. (2021). *Home in the world: A memoir*. Allen Lane and Penguin Random House.
Sen, R. K. (2002). On Professor P. R. Brahmananda and his writings. In R. K. Sen & C. Biswajit (Eds.), *Indian economy agenda for the 21st century: Essays in honour of Professor P. R. Brahmananda* (pp. 1–45). Deep and Deep Publications.
Seton, F. (1962). Review: *An essay on economic growth and planning* by M.H. Dobb. *Economic Journal*, 72(286), 376–379.
Singh, A. (1977). UK industry and the world economy: A case of de-industrialisation? *Cambridge Journal of Economics*, 1, 113–136.
Singh, A. (2008). *Better to be rough and relevant than to be precise and irrelevant: Reddaway's legacy to economics*. Working Paper No. 379. Cambridge University Centre for Business Research. www.cbr.cam.ac.uk/fileadmin/user_upload/centre-for-business-research/downloads/working-papers/wp379.pdf
Stockwell, S. (2018). *The British end of the British empire*. Cambridge University Press.
Stokes, E. T. (1959). *The English utilitarians in India*. Clarendon Press.
Stone, J. R. N. (1984). Richard Stone: Biographical. *The Nobel Prize*. https://www.nobelprize.org/prizes/economics/1984/stone/auto-biography/
Tarshis, L. (1989). Remembering Joan Robinson. In G. R. Feiwel (Ed.), *Joan Robinson and modern economic theory* (pp. 918–920). Palgrave Macmillan.
Toye, J. F. J. (1983). The disparaging of development economics. *Journal of Development Studies*, 20(1), 87–107.
Toye, J. (1989). Nicholas Kaldor and tax reform in developing countries. *Cambridge Journal of Economics*, 13(2), 183–200.
Toye, J. (2006). Keynes and development economics: A sixty-year perspective. *Journal of International Development*, 18(7), 983–995.
Tribe, K. (2002). *Economic careers: Economics and economists in Britain, 1930–1970*. Routledge Taylor & Francis.
Velupillai, K. V. (2015a). Richard Goodwin: The Indian connection. *Economic and Political Weekly*, 50(15), 80–84.
Velupillai, K. V. (2015b). Perspectives on the contributions of Richard Goodwin. *Cambridge Journal of Economics*, 39(6). Special Issue: *Perspectives on the contributions of Richard Goodwin*, 1485–1496.
Wilkinson, C. (2017). The East India College debate and the fashioning of imperial officials, 1806–1858. *The Historical Journal*, 60(4), 943–969.

CHAPTER 12

From Riches to Rags? Economic History Becomes History at the Faculty of Economics

Abstract This traverse through the rich career and contributions of the economic historians, first in the Department of Applied Economics and subsequently in the Faculty of Economics, serves to highlight the wide interface and intrinsic value embodied in the intertwining of discourses on economic theory, economic history and economic policy through facilitating border-crossings between disciplines, methods and divergent spatial and temporal contexts. Certainly, and at the least, for the heterodox lineages of Cambridge economics, the presence of economic history and economic historians in the Faculty represented a constant marker of the discontinuities and disequilibrium inherent in historical processes, of time being history, and of Joan's binary, "history versus equilibrium", or in Kaldor's pithy dismissal of neoclassicism, "the irrelevance of equilibrium economics". Also investigated are the potential links, whether positive, antagonistic or just missing, in the interactions between the practice of economic history in Faculty of Economics, and in parallel in the Faculty of History—in specific, through the bridging position of the professorship in economic history formally located in the latter. On the side of Economics, the path of economic history reveals an inverted U-curve the apogee of which is marked by the foundational work of the historical statisticians in the DAE, after which that interest wanes, while additional tracks of research evolve, including significantly one on the gendered study of industrial revolutions, and another continuing in the wake of the DAE's applied macro-Keynesian tradition. However, well over a century after the time when Alfred Marshall had worked hard to wean the rising discipline of Economics away from History and from Moral Sciences, the study of economic history, with all the vicissitudes en route in its trajectory, has arrived at a point where the Faculty of Economics has scarcely any economic historian left standing in its ranks. By a combination of default and design, neoclassical economics seems to have achieved the agenda of the founder of its tradition in Cambridge, at least for the time being.

© The Author(s), under exclusive license to Springer Nature Switzerland AG 2022
A. Saith, *Cambridge Economics in the Post-Keynesian Era*, Palgrave Studies in the History of Economic Thought,
https://doi.org/10.1007/978-3-030-93019-6_12

12.1 Introduction: Economics and Economic History

In his thoughtful survey of the practice of economic history in Cambridge, Martin Daunton, holder of the Chair of Economic History in the Faculty of History over nearly two decades (1997–2015), observes that locally the subject had several legs to stand on. "The strength of economic history in Cambridge arises from the fact that there was never a separate department. It has been able to connect with many different types of history and economics, as well as with colleagues in geography and law. It escaped from the sense of failure in other British universities where separate departments were closed in the 1980s as a result of cuts to university budgets and intellectual crisis with the rise of cliometrics, the marginalisation of Marxist approaches, and the widening of the agenda of many traditional history degrees. In most cases, economic historians moved into departments of history, with the potential danger that posts would be transferred into the more flourishing fields of social and cultural history. ... In Cambridge, UK, ... economic history was a requirement both in the History and Economics Triposes, and academic posts were accordingly protected. The subject could look both ways, towards history and towards economics, with the prospect of continued collaboration from somewhat different perspectives" (Daunton, 2017a, p. 180). An additional resource, dealing with early years of the establishment of economic history as an independent and permanent enterprise, is provided by G. Kitson Clark (1973) in his essay on a century of history teaching at Cambridge covering the vast and varied terrain from 1873 to 1973, in the course of which he helpfully devotes a couple of pages to the early life of economic history.

The present piece is narrower in scope and is focussed primarily on the place of economic history in the Faculty of Economics and Politics, including the Department of Applied Economics, a domain which, while included in Daunton's list of the Cambridge sites of the subject, understandably receives relatively marginal treatment from his vantage point in the Faculty of History. Regardless, his treatment of the evolution of the discipline, viewed primarily through the perspectives of the string of holders of the chair of economic history,[1] provides an extremely valuable contextual framing for the narrower

---

[1] Since its inception in 1928, there have been 8 holders of the chair over 94 years. Leaving out the present incumbent, Gareth Austin, David Joslin who died after just five years into his tenure that could have run for another 22 years, and Tony Wrigley, who hit retirement age four years after appointment, the other five holders had an average tenure of 16 years apiece.

John Clapham (1873–1946)	1928–1937
MM 'Munia' Postan (1899–1981)	1938–1965
David Joslin (1925–1970)	1965–1970 (died in 1970)
Donald Coleman (1920–1995)	1971–1981 (took early retirement in 1981)
Barry Supple (1930–)	1981–1993
Tony Wrigley (1931–)	1994–1997
Martin Daunton (1949–)	1997–2015
Gareth Austin	2016–

project at hand. While it would appear natural to focus on such a bilateral dialogue, especially in view of the intertwined roots in Marshallian times, it is necessary to accept that doing so would exclude a good deal of the work of other economic historians in the Faculty of History. This loss in the field of vision could be considerable for specific regions or fields of study.

12.2 The Pre-War Period: 1939, Marshallian

12.2.1 At the Faculty of History

Cunningham to Clapham via Marshall
Economic history as taught at Cambridge was the child of William Cunningham. For a variety of reasons Cunningham came early to the opinion that what were then generally believed to be the immutable unchallengeable laws of economics were not laws at all and did not fully explain the working and structure of society at *every stage*, indeed in his later thought he believed at *any* stage, of its economic development. This conclusion was probably endorsed for him by his contact with Trade Unionists, which began when he was at Liverpool, and probably by his interest in co-operation; it was certainly confirmed by a visit to India in 1881 where he studied Indian village communities, in which economic life did not seem to conform to the principles enunciated by Ricardo. He therefore believed that the way to approach economic history was not first to reassert economic principles, and then to rough-hew the facts so that they should fit the required pattern, but rather first to discover the facts and then to spell out the lessons they might teach. He based his lectures on this principle, and while Fawcett, who was an eminent politician, indeed from 1880 to 1884 Postmaster General, was Professor of Political Economy, he was able to follow his bent. When, however, in 1884 Marshall succeeded Fawcett there was trouble. Marshall wished Cunningham to devote one term's lectures to theory before he turned to history. This Cunningham, who was a pugnacious Scott, did not feel that he could conscientiously do, and there was friction, which was so serious that Cunningham resigned his University lectureship in 1888, when appointment to a College Lectureship by Trinity made this financially possible for him. However, in spite of this opposition Cunningham was able to build up his own subject in his own way. In 1882 he published the first version of his *Growth of English Industry and Commerce*, which constantly extended, became required reading for Cambridge historians. In 1885 English Economic History entered the Tripos as a separate paper distinct from Political Economy and thereafter it consolidated its position. (Clark, 1973, pp. 545–546)

There was disagreement between Cunningham[2] on the one side and Marshall supported by Sidgwick on the other, when the former "objected to the regulation which allowed the substitution of Political Philosophy for Metaphysics in the case of Economic students who took up the second part of the Tripos" for the reason that "there was a large part of Political Economy which must deal with socialistic difficulties and behind all these lay the question, 'What is meant by an individual?' How far an individual was to be considered as a sort of monad, or as itself formed by social surrounding, were most important problems in relation to the whole controversy of socialism" for which a study of Metaphysics was essential. Further, "a great many of the burning questions in modern Economics related to the appropriate method of study, and they could not be thoroughly treated without trenching on metaphysical problems as to the nature of knowledge. The same was true with regard to the attack which was commonly made on Political Economy as not forming an independent science" (Whitaker, 1996, p. 363). "Marshall rejected the idea that Metaphysics contributed to questions of scientific method; and as to the question whether a man was to be regarded as a monad, that must indeed come before all students of Ethics and Economics in some way or other; he did not object to anybody treating it as a metaphysical question, but he should prefer not to treat it so; and he objected to making its metaphysical treatment compulsory" (364). And Marshall refers to the three alternatives before the Board as possible substitutes for Metaphysics: a paper on Economic History; or "a paper on Advanced Scientific Method with special regard to statistics, in order that they might be worked at by mathematicians who take up the study of Economics after their degrees"; or, a paper on Political Philosophy—and Marshall's preference was in that order.[3] (Whitaker, 1996, p. 365).

Robin Matthews and Barry Supple (1991) provide an insightful reflection on Marshall and the early institutional and disciplinary tensions between 'economics' and 'history' in Cambridge. "Marshall explicitly played down history's place in the study of economics for undergraduates, especially in his Inaugural Lecture (1885) and in some of his other writings and his correspondence. The

---

[2] "Cunningham, William (1849–1919). Economic historian and churchman. Senior Moralist in 1872. He combined teaching, first in Cambridge extension lecturing and then as a College or University Lecturer in Cambridge, where he was associated with Trinity, with active churchmanship, rising in the latter to the rank of archdeacon. Although an early student of Marshall's, Cunningham soon became something of a thorn in his side. The two differed on methodology, on curricular reform, and on economic policy, Cunningham being a staunch opponent of free trade and anything smacking of laissez-faire, as well as a proponent of empire. He is best known for his influential *The Growth of English Industry and Commerce* (1882). In addition to his other activities, Cunningham served as Tooke Professor at King's College, London, from 1891. He was, over the years after 1885, the most vocal opponent of Marshall's schemes for the reform of economics teaching in Cambridge" (Whitaker, 1996, p. 363).

[3] Extracts from Whitaker (1996, pp. 363–366) Appendix IV: The 1889 Debate on Reform of the Moral Sciences Tripos.

context must be remembered here. In 1890 economics was not well established in Cambridge. It was studies either as part of the History Tripos or as part of the Moral Sciences Tripos. Things were no different in Oxford. The issue was whether there was a place for economics as a separate discipline at all, rather than whether economics should be enriched by historical insights. The establishment of a separate Economics Tripos in Cambridge in 1903 was agreed only in the face of opposition; it was carried by 103 votes to 76. Many of Marshall's remarks in apparent disparagement of the importance of earlier history for economic study have to be read as part of an effort to emancipate the study of economics in Cambridge from the study of history. As such, they were the result of the professionalization of academic study" (Matthews & Supple, 1991).

Clapham to Postan via Power
"Cunningham had a worthy successor in John Clapham", says Clark (1973, p. 546); and "If certain reports are to be trusted, Alfred Marshall regarded him as his favourite pupil and wanted him to devote himself to economics" (Postan, 1946, p. 57). Clapham became the first Professor of Economic History in 1928, and "was formally assigned to the Faculty of History, but was also an ex officio member of the Board of the Faculty of Economics, a dual identity that well suited Clapham's intellectual formation as a protégé of Lord Acton, the Regius Professor of Modern History, and of Alfred Marshall" (Daunton, 2017b, p. 423).

From his student days, Hobsbawm (2002, p. 107) recalls "the impressive and craggy John Clapham, just retired from the chair of economic history, author of that rarest of products of history in interwar Cambridge, a major work on a major topic, namely the three volumes of his *Economic History of Modern Britain (1926–1938)*" (Hobsbawm, 2002, p. 107). Clark (1973, p. 546) writes: "Clapham with his huge mask-like face, his formidable body and his still more formidable command of his subject lecturing to crowded audiences in the lecture theatre at the Arts School was one of the most notable figures in Cambridge between the wars." Maxine Berg (1996, p. 167n86) adds that he "was a central figure in Cambridge, indeed a rival with Keynes for the provostship of King's". "His tradition was continued by John Saltmarsh, and the distinguished successor to Clapham's Chair, Professor Postan, gave it new dimensions and complicated it. … But the subject [economic history] has remained, and remains, an important and characteristic component of Cambridge historical studies, important for its own sake, and important because its presence tends to prevent Cambridge history from developing that bonelessness which normally characterizes history which is taught or written without reference to its economic background" (Clark, 1973, p. 546). Postan, in his obituary, pays him a rather complex compliment: "He was a pioneer in the sense in which all men who colonize virgin lands are pioneers; there were beasts and even men in the field before him, but he was the first to live and to build in a civilized way. 'On the ground on which Dr Clapham has worked and still works he found a mass of half knowledge, overgrown with picturesque and stubborn weeds. This ground he not only cleared, but in his own inimitable, lapidary way, has covered with a structure of facts as hard and certain as granite.' Thus wrote, in 1938, Clapham's successor the Cambridge Chair, and to this he can now add but little" (Postan, 1946, p. 57).

Daunton (2017b, pp. 448–449) writes that Clapham's work was embedded with "a strong implicit ideology. His emphasis on economic forces as natural and superior to government action could lead to accusations that his work was an apologia for free-market capitalism As Postan pointed out, Clapham had 'an admiring appreciation of the self-adjusting action of the economic mechanism, and a horror of sudden and dramatic change' (Postan, 1946, p. 56). [Clapham's] account of development of the British economy in the nineteenth century avoided the moral outrage at capitalism that had been expressed by Engels, Toynbee, or the Hammonds, and left-wing critics found him to be complacent"; Clapham himself wrote that "a Christian nation in the real sense of the word would certainly come very near to the socialist ideal" (Clapham, quoted in Daunton, ibid., p. 449).

"In politics he was officially a Liberal, but his liberalism had nothing of the latter-day radicalism in it. He had an admiring appreciation of the self-adjusting action of the economic mechanism and a belief in the capitalist order (he did not like to hear it described as such). No wonder his work won unstinted praise from the economists of the London School of Economics. He was in fact the economic historian they respected most, and this affection he greatly reciprocated" (Postan, 1946, p. 56). Postan's reference is to the LSE at the height of the Robbins-Hayek era. Clapham's was clearly a sufficiently safe pair of hands to have been invited to write the two-volume history of the Bank of England to mark its 250th anniversary.

And it was through his connection with Bank of England that Clapham helped to raise funds for the founding meeting of Hayek's Mont Pelerin Society in 1947, which took place a year after Clapham died,[4] and at which meeting Hayek noted his absence and acknowledged his contribution through a rich tribute in his opening statement expressing his regret that "two men with whom I had most fully discussed the plan for this meeting both have not lived to see its realisation"—the two were Henry Simons (from Chicago) and John Clapham.

John Clapham was succeeded in the chair by M. M. 'Munia' Postan, who held the longest tenure over the position from 1937 to 1965, and whose legacy has left a lasting mark, directly on the subject in the Faculty of History, and perhaps indirectly in the Faculty of Economics as well. The manner of his appointment to the chair is an episode that teasingly tempts counterfactual hypothesising. 1937 was a big year for Postan: he got elevated to the

---

[4] Clapham supported Hayek's initiative; see Chap. 3, pp. 22, 34, 79.

prestigious chair of Professor of Economic History at Cambridge; he got married to the eminent historian, Eileen Power; and the two life events were intimately intertwined.

Eileen Edna Le Poer Power (1889–1940), much respected as an economic historian, and a feminist, studied the history of medieval women, and rose to become Professor of Economic History at the London School of Economics. Munia Postan, then at the LSE, was first her student, then appointed as her research assistant in 1926 (Flinn & Mathias, 1982), then her colleague and from 1937, her husband.

Writing about interactions with economics and economists at the LSE, Maxine Berg, perhaps as a proxy for Power, writes: "it was perfectly true that economic historians often mistook the nature of some of their problems through an inadequate knowledge of economic theory. But economics as a deductive science had gone too far; obsessed with formalism, it had become too much like medieval scholasticism to comment on the 'dusty realm of reality'. Elsewhere Power denounced the turn taken by economics at the School; under Robbins and Hayek it had turned to neo-Austrian marginalism and *laissez-faire* market models. ... She described Allyn Young as 'one of the wisest men who ever taught in this School'" (Berg, 1996, p. 165, and sources cited therein). Nicholas Kaldor was a student at LSE at the time and wrote later about how he was enthralled by the lectures of Allyn Young; and Thirlwall, Kaldor's biographer, records that "in his first year at LSE in 1927, Kaldor was supervised by Eileen Power 'whom he held in high regard'" (Thirlwall, 1987b, p. 522.)

> A number of economists she was close to—Dalton, Gaitskell and Durbin—were socialists, of more or less moderate persuasion. Tawney's socialism was ethical not Marxist, and Postan, now lapsed from his radical socialist youth, was widely conversant with Marx's writings, but no longer a Marxist. Eileen Power who saw herself as a socialist faced the problem of just how far she would take Marxist positions and methodologies in the writing of history. In a lecture on the Marxian interpretation of history she praised the insights Marx had brought to historical writing. She was attracted by the emphasis Marxism brought to the historical process .... (Berg, 1996, p. 163)

"Clapham was close to Eileen Power; she was a friend of the family from the time she had taught in Girton." On the basis of an interview with Barbara Clapham, Berg writes that Mrs. Clapham and Eileen "shared a common pleasure in the French language and literature. She stayed frequently at the Clapham home in Storeys End on trips back to Cambridge, and was friendly with Clapham's daughters and his son ... Mrs. Clapham and her daughters loved talking about the fashions with Eileen until she was summoned away by Clapham with, 'Now, Eileen, enough Ladies Page, it's time to talk economic history'" (Berg, 1996, p. 167).

Writing the obituary for the much younger Eileen Power, Clapham writes: "... when the new Chair of Economic History in Cambridge was to fall vacant, she knew very well that, if she cared to stand, hers would be a very strong candidature. There is an elder statesman of conservative leanings at Cambridge who let me know, with statesmanlike caution, that as chairs were now open to women, why, that was the sort of woman we wanted. I did my best to persuade her to stand, but in the end, she decided not to let her name go forward. Cambridge appointed her working partner as she had wished" (Clapham, 1940, p. 358).

Postan's election in 1938 to the Cambridge professorship was "a post that Power had in mind for him as early as 1931", writes Martin Daunton (holder of the Cambridge chair from 1997 till 2015), who quotes from her declaration to Postan: "It is a snag that you are not a Cambridge man; but as far as I can see there aren't going to be any Cambridge men available, for Clapham has failed to train up any successor of the right calibre ... I shall never say this to anyone but you, because it would be most unsafe, but I have had it for some time in my mind. It depends entirely on how big a reputation you can amass in the next 7 years, & on how we manage Clapham" (Daunton, 2017a, p. 160).

> Power valued her independence, and for most of her life was opposed to marriage as an institution, convinced that domestic binds were incompatible with a woman's public ambitions. The ideal wife, she suspected, 'should endeavour to model herself on a judicious mixture of a cow, a muffler, a shadow, a mirror.' When in 1937 she finally decided to marry her former student and LSE colleague Michael Postan, ten years her junior, it was a balance of head and heart. Sadly, just three years later she died suddenly of a heart attack, aged just 51. (Smith, A. K., 2020)

Had she allowed herself to contend for the Cambridge professorship instead of projecting her husband into the position, it could be conjectured that there could well have been a rather different, more intellectually interactive and professionally productive, equation between the economic historians at the Faculty of History, and the rising radical post-Keynesian, Marxist and heterodox group of economists at the Faculty of Economics during that period. That did not come to pass; instead, Postan arrived in Cambridge economic history with a different disciplinary agenda and with little affinity for the intellectual perspectives of the economists at the Faculty of Economics.

12.2.2 At the Faculty of Economics and Politics

Maurice Dobb, 1900–1976
Maurice Dobb got First in both parts of the Economics Tripos; joined the Communist Party in 1921; became a lecturer in the Faculty of Economics and Politics in 1924, remained in that position for the next 35 years (Table 12.1). Apropos the hostile political climate of the 1920s, Eric Hobsbawm writes that "for several years, Dobb was virtually the only Communist in either university

Table 12.1 Economic historians at the Faculty of Economics and Politics, 1924–2021

	MD	CC[a]	RS	HJH	PB[a]	RM	PD	MC	CHF	BM	NVT	JR[a]	MW[a]	JE[a]	JH	MK[a]	SS	SH	SO	TA
	1900	1905	1913	1915	1915	1927	1918	1921	1932	1929	1943	1951	1955	1943[b]	1948	n.a.	1957[b]	1962	1958	1969
1924	F–L																			
1931	F–L	F–L																		
1932	F–L	F–L																		
1933	F–L	F–L																		
1934	F–L	F–L																		
1935	F–L	F–L																		
1936	F–L	F–L																		
1937	F–L	F–L																		
1945	F–L		DAE–D																	
1946	F–L		DAE–D	F–L																
1947	F–L		DAE–D	F–L																
1948	F–L		DAE–D	F–L	F–L															
1949	F–L		DAE–D	F–L	F–L	F–L														
1950	F–L		DAE–D	F–L	F–L	F–L	DAE													
1951	F–L		DAE–D	F–L	F–L	F–L	DAE													
1952	F–L		DAE–D	F–L	F–L	F–L	DAE–S													
1953	F–L		DAE–D	F–L	F–L	F–L	DAE–S													

(continued)

Table 12.1 (continued)

	MD	CC[a]	RS	HJH	PB[a]	RM	PD	MC	CHF	BM	NVT	JR[a]	MW[a]	JE[a]	JH	MK[a]	SS	SH	SO	TA
	1900	1905	1913	1915	1915	1927	1918	1921	1932	1929	1943	1951	1955	1943[b]	1948	n.a.	1957[b]	1962	1958	1969
1954	F–L		DAE–D			F–L	DAE–S													
1955	F–L		DAE/F–D		F–L	F–L	DAE–S	DAE–O												
1956	F–L		F–P		F–L	F–L	DAE–S	DAE–O												
1957	F–L		F–P			F–L	DAE–S	DAE–O												
1958	F–L		F–P			F–L	DAE–S	DAE–O	DAE–R											
1959	F–R		F–P			F–L	DAE–S	DAE–O	DAE–R											
1960	F–R		F–P			F–L	DAE–S		DAE–R	DAE–O										
1961	F–R		F–P			F–L	DAE–S		DAE–R	DAE–O										
1962	F–R		F–P			F–L	DAE/F–S		DAE–R	DAE–O										
1963	F–R		F–P			F–L	F–L		DAE/F	DAE–O										
1964	F–R		F–P			F–L	F–L		F–AL	DAE–O										
1965	F–R		F–P				F–L		F–L	DAE–O										
1966	F–R		F–P				F–L		F–L	DAE–O										
1967	F–R		F–P				F–L		F–L	DAE–O										

1968	F–P	F–L						
1969	F–P	F–L		F–L				
1970	F–P	F–L		F–L				
1971	F–P	F–R		F–L	DAE/F			
1972	F–P	F–R		F–L	F–L			
1973	F–P	F–R		F–L	F–L			
1974	F–P	F–R		F–L	F–L			
1975	F–P	F–R		F–L	F–L			
1976	F–P	F–R		F–L	F–L	DAE-A		
1977	F–P	F–R		F–L	F–L	DAE-A		
1978	F–P	F–R		F–L	F–L	DAE-J		
1979	F–P	F–R		F–L		DAE-R	DAE–J F	
1980	F–P	F–R	F–P	F–L		DAE-R	DAE–J F	F–L
1981		F–R	F–P	F–L		DAE-R	DAE–J F	F–L
1982		F–P	F–P	F–L		DAE-R	DAE–J F	F–L
1983			F–P	F–L		DAE-R	DAE–J F	F–L DAE—J
1984			F–P	F–L		DAE-R	DAE–J F	F–L DAE—J
1985			F–P			DAE-R	DAE— F	F–L DAE— F— J AL
1986			F–P			DAE-S	DAE— F	F–L DAE— F— J AL

(continued)

Table 12.1 (continued)

	MD	CC[a]	RS	HJH	PB[a]	RM	PD	MC	CHF	BM	NVT	JR[a]	MW[a]	JE[a]	JH	MK[a]	SS	SH	SO	TA
	1900	1905	1913	1915	1915	1927	1918	1921	1932	1929	1943	1951	1955	1943[b]	1948	n.a.	1957[b]	1962	1958	1969
1987						F–P						DAE–S	DAE/F	F	F–L	DAE–R	F–AL	DAE–A		
1988						F–P						DAE–S	F–AL	F	F–L	DAE–R	F–AL	DAE–A		
1989						F–P						DAE–S	F–AL	F	F–L	DAE–R	F–L	DAE–A	F–AL	
1990						F–P							F–L	F	F–L	DAE–R	F–L	DAE–R	F–AL	
1991						F–P							F–L	F	F–L	DAE–R	F–L	DAE–R	F–AL	
1992													F–L	F	F–L	DAE–R	F–L	DAE/F	F–L	
1993													F–L	F	F–L	DAE–R	F–L	F–AL	F–L	
1994													F–L	F	F–L	DAE–R	F–L	F–AL	F–L	
1995													F–L	F	F–R	DAE–R	F–L	F–L	F–L	
1996														F	F–R	DAE–R	F–L	F–L	F–L	
1997														F	F–R	DAE–R	F–L	F–L	F–L	
1998														F	F–R	DAE–R	F–L	F–L	F–L	F–L
1999														F			F–L	F–L	F–R	F–L
2000														F			F–SL	F–SL	F–R	F–L
2001														F			F–SL	F–SL	F–R	F–L
2002														F			F–SL	F–SL	F–R	F–L
2003														F			F–SL	F–SL	F–R	F–L

Year					
2004	F	F–SL	F–SL	F–P	F–L
2005	F	F–SL	F–SL	F–P	F–L
2006	F	F–SL	F–SL	F–P	F–L
2007	F	F–SL	F–SL	F–P	F–SL
2008	F	F–SL	F–SL	F–P	F–SL
2009	F	F–R	F–SL	F–P	F–SL
2010	F–R	F–R	F–SL	F–P	F–SL
2011		F–R	F–SL	F–P	F–SL
2012		F–R	F–SL	F–P	F–SL
2013		F–R	F–SL	F–P	F–SL
2014		F–R	F–SL	F–P	F–SL
2015		F–R	F–SL	F–P	F–SL
2016		F–R	F–SL	F–P	F–R
2017		F–R	F–SL	F–P	F–R
2018		F–R	F–SL	F–P	F–R
2019		F–R	F–R	F–P	F–R
2020		F–R			F–R
2021		F–R			F–R

MD, Maurice Dobb; CC, Colin Clark; RS, Richard Stone; HH, Hrothgar 'John' Habakkuk; PB, Peter Bauer; RM, Robin Matthews; PD, Phyllis Deane; MC, W.A. 'Max' Cole; CHF, Charles Feinstein; BM, Brian Mitchell; NVT, Nicholas Von Tunzelmann; JR, Jill Rubery; MW, Martin Weale; JE, Jeremey Edwards; JH, Jane Humphries; MK, Michael Kitson; SS, Solomou Solomos; SH, Sara Horrell; SO, Sheilagh Ogilvie; TA, Toke Aidt
DAE, Department of Applied Economics; F, Faculty of Economics and Politics; A, Research Associate; J, Junior Research Officer; O, Research Officer; S, Senior Research Officer; AL, Assistant Lecturer; L, Lecturer; SL, Senior Lecturer; R, Reader; P, Professor; D, Director

[a] Indicates a secondary involvement in economic history and/or with other economic historians
[b] Indicates estimated

or city." (Hobsbawm, 1967, p. 4). "Within Cambridge he soon came to occupy the characteristic position which he has retained ever since, totally isolated as a Marxist in his faculty for so long ..." (ibid., p. 5). Dobb was promoted to a readership in 1959, and there he remained till his retirement.[5] Hobsbawm refers to "the casual dismissal of Marxism" then says that "his very existence as a Marxist academic was itself an achievement. It is not easy to recall the Siberian climate in which the plant of intellectual Marxism then attempted to put out its feeble shoots in the country." He wrote his first significant book in 1925, *Capitalist Enterprise and Social Progress*, followed by his *Russian Economic Development since the Revolution* in 1928. It appears now to be a text of economic history, but was nothing like it when published in the hot wake of the rise of the Soviet Union. His stature as a Marxist economic historian arises from his *Studies in the Development of Capitalism* in 1946, which, as John Eatwell (1977, p. 2) wrote in his obituary in the first issue of the first volume of CJE, "inspired a major historical debate [the Sweezy-Dobb exchange, 1950, amongst others] on the interpretation of the transition from feudalism to capitalism, even though, as Maurice Dobb himself acknowledged, he was rather an amateur historian. ... The bold sweep of historical analysis in *Studies in the Development of Capitalism* is a courageous application of theory to the interpretation of reality." Perhaps John Eatwell should not have taken Dobb at his word.[6] The continually self-effacing Maurice Dobb was far from being an 'amateur' historian. As Ronald Meek (1978, p. 343) wrote in his appreciation, "few who can match him in his great modesty and humanity..."; and he goes on to quote Eric Hobsbawm's description of how Maurice Dobb would be remembered by his friends: "sitting in his armchair, rosy-faced, still elegant in an informal but carefully colour-checked shirt and disclaiming, against all probability, any special competence on any subject under discussion, diffidently intervening in conversation, with a natural deep-seated courtesy ..." (ibid., p. 340). Meek (1978, p. 338)) quotes from Dobb's preface to *Studies* where he states his "obstinate belief that economic analysis only makes sense and can only bear fruit if it is joined to a study of historical development, and that the economists concerned with present-day problems has certain question of his

---

[5] Hobsbawm writes that Joan Robinson and Nicky Kaldor were also made readers at the same time, but this is not accurate: Joan was promoted to a readership in 1959, but Thirlwall (1987b, p. 537) records that Kaldor was promoted to a readership much earlier in 1952. Then, Thirlwall (ibid.) writes that both Joan and Nicky were elevated to professorships in 1966; this seems inaccurate for Joan, who was promoted (over a disgruntled Nicky) to the chair held by Austin Robinson when he retired in 1965, and Nicky was promoted to a personal chair the following year; Joan was 3 years, and Nicky 8 years, younger than Maurice who had also held a Faculty lectureship since 1924—Joan since 1937, and Nicky since 1949.

[6] Eatwell (1977, p. 1) himself refers to Dobb's legendary modesty: "How many of us have received those long, carefully written comments, of which the first paragraph was devoted to a denial of any particular competence to comment on the topic in hand, and of which the second paragraph would begin 'However, ...'?"

own to put to historical data". And, with his close and youthful encounters as a student, and then a Fellow at Trinity, Amartya Sen (1990, p. 141) calls him "undoubtedly one of the outstanding political economists of this century". "These two fields—economic theory and economic history—were intimately connected in Dobb's approach to economics." Eatwell (1977, p. 2) is entirely right in saying that "his openness was an inspiration to progressive students everywhere", though when lamenting "that the magnitude of his contribution is more widely acknowledged in Italy, Poland, Latin America and Japan that it is in England"; missing from the list is India where Dobb made important contributions and enjoyed a wide following amongst all shades of red and pink.

Dobb's "critique of the economic orthodoxy of the time ran parallel to the more influential Keynesian one, but hardly touched it except perhaps in the common rejection of both of theories whose refinement was bought at the cost of gross unrealism. Nor did either side make much effort to approach the other. The Keynesian pre-occupation with controlling economic fluctuations within the capitalist economy was one which Marxists in the 1930s were not likely to share, and conversely, Dobb's argument, intellectually able as it unquestionably was, seemed quite remote from the practical policy questions which British economists, always potential Treasury advisers at heart, sought to influence" (Hobsbawm, 1967, p. 7). In 1925, the year before Keynes published his pamphlet against *laissez-faire*, Dobb wrote: "Keynes is certainly departing from the assumptions of orthodoxy sufficiently to be anti-*laissez-faire* (quite the fashion now in Camb.) to wish to displace anarchic by *controlled* economic operations—but with the class basis of the whole thing still untouched. If you told him that he is neglecting this, he will simply misunderstand you, or else say that you are introducing 'sentimental' considerations which do not concern him and do not seem to him important" (quoted in Hobsbawm, 1967, pp. 3–4).

Meek (1978, p. 334) refers to a letter written in the difficult 1920s where Dobb expresses his distaste at "teaching embryo exploiters how to exploit workers in the most up-to-date and humane way"; that notwithstanding, all writers of appreciations or obituaries of Maurice Dobb have underscored his complete dedication to his students and teaching. "Economics students knew him as a devoted supervisor and lecturer, initially on any and every subject required by the syllabus—even, at one stage, Public Finance—later increasingly on the congenial topics of the history of economic thought and on social problems.[7] They did not know, and could not appreciate, the immense care and

---

[7] While all these plaudits are entirely justified, the author might humbly confess to a sense of puzzlement, tinged with disappointment, when, sitting in for the first time in Dobb's lectures in 1972, he encountered not what he expected, viz., a rousing lecture from a firebrand—based on a study of Dobb's books in Delhi before arriving in Cambridge—but instead a rather flat almost dull somewhat conventional, albeit crystal clear, lecture on welfare economics from a gown-clad, three-piece tweed suited country gentleman type of person; others, including Michael Ellman, have recalled an almost identical experience of their first exposure to Dobb in the lecture hall.

trouble he brought to his teaching, which made him into the most painstaking and sympathetic of examiners" (Hobsbawm, 1967, p. 5). Hobsbawm recalls his "punctilious refusal to use his position as a teacher for political purposes[8] ... [confining] his contacts with the student Marxists to the extra-curricular ...at summer schools during vacations. He probably taught us more about Marx's analysis on such occasions than we ever learned in an equally brief space of time before or since."

With his continuous stream of writings, many of them classics of political economy or of the history of economic thought, Maurice Dobb was the permanent, and revered, Marxist presence in the Faculty of Economic and Politics, though his influence beyond was infinitely greater. The affection and respect, indeed admiration, in which he was held was reflected in the list of contributors to the Festschrift presented to him in 1967 (Feinstein, 1967).

12.3 Post-War Period-I, 1945–1980s: Post-Keynesian

12.3.1 At the Faculty of Economics and Politics

'Marshall' yielded to 'Keynes'; Geoff Harcourt (2012b, p. 333) rightly notes that "an important aspect of Keynes's influence is the seminal contributions of economic historians—Phyllis Deane, Charles Feinstein, W.J. ('Iain') MacPherson and Brian Mitchell [the list is only indicative and can be considerably extended]—to our understanding of the first Industrial Revolution and to development generally, including in Phyllis's case, the evolution of economic ideas." The ball was indeed set rolling by Keynes during the war years when he got Richard Stone and James Meade working on the construction of British national income, and then through the prominence given to data collection and economic history in the research programme of the DAE in its early phase under Stone. In the Stone era, there was a strong focus on the compilation of time-series of data and statistics, as these were essential for the rest of the applied research to proceed. Likewise, tests of inference and econometric techniques evolved out of, or were devised specifically, for serving the needs of empirical analysis. Over time, there was a steady erosion in the interest, time and resources devoted to these up- and downstream needs, and the work came to be focussed primarily on modelling the process of structural change in the British economy. In the Reddaway years, the overall research 'programme' was an eclectic conglomeration of diverse projects of policy-oriented applied economics, generally not reliant on historical data; and in the Godley period, the focus was primarily on contemporary policy issues and socio-economic structures and processes, and the pursuit of economic history, panoramic or partial,

---

[8] In this regard, see Chap. 2, pp. 14–15, for Amartya Sen's entertaining anecdote about Dobb, Robertson and the 'blowing up' of the Trinity College Chapel.

steadily evanesced as the DAE economic historians either shifted into positions in the Faculty, or took up college fellowships, or left Cambridge altogether.

On the DAE Side

Stone, Historical Statistics and National Accounts
Even as Colin Clark was the carrier of the quantitative spirit into Cambridge economics, the DAE itself was the brainchild of Keynes who knew the necessity and value of its mandate. As Austin Robinson puts it, "We were old-fashioned logical non-quantitative model makers with little evidence other than guesswork of the size or importance of the things we were talking about. [W]e had what I believe was then the strongest faculty anywhere in the world. But we were, as I say, non-quantitative. Colin, considerably, but not wholeheartedly encouraged by Keynes (remember his review of Tinbergen), set out to make us quantitative" and the message "gradually penetrated our non-quantitative heads". The rest is history, or more accurately, the historical statistics and national accounting projects of the DAE which in their first two decades are acknowledged to have laid the quantitative foundations for the study of modern British economic history, using national accounting for the rigorous analysis of structural change, and company accounts for applied industrial economics. Equally remarkably, in the following two decades, the project of economic history evanesced from the DAE; a dramatic arrival was followed by a silent slipping away, leaving few traces other than a handful of iconic books, some fond obituaries and a patchy institutional memory of its instrumental treatment by its senior sibling, economics

As is apparent in the first 'annual' report of the DAE (for 1946–1948), the initial focus of 'economic history' was really limited to the systematic construction of data sets of historical statistics. "The Department's research programme has been conceived as a group of interrelated investigations which should yield results along each of these main lines of activity [viz., theory-data-testing]. As, however, the most pressing problems of applied economics today turn on the inadequacy of suitable data and methods of analysis, our first attention has been given to these. Accordingly, a number of the projects are concerned with building up systematic bodies of data for the British economy" (DAE Report, 1946–1948, p. 4). "There is great scope for the development of new methods of collecting economic data which will incorporate as far as possible those contemporary ideas of statistical design which have led to such remarkable achievements in other fields, notably in biology and agriculture" (ibid., pp. 3–4).

Especially in view of Keynes's death in 1946, the promulgation of the lineage of economic history in the DAE could be attributed, to a significant extent, to Keynes's eye for spotting, and matching, intellectual talent to research needs as he perceived them. It was through Richard Stone, as the first Director, that the ship of economic history was launched, closely piloted in the first decade by himself, and then into the 1960s by his successor Brian Reddaway who was equally a supporter of the enterprise.

In offering a legitimation of the change in identity and direction of the DAE after 1988, David Newbery (1998) tends to a selective reductionism in highlighting Stone's early personal contributions and the DAE's research objectives primarily in the fields of theoretical econometrics and methods of testing and inference. This was undoubtedly a major strand, and it is widely acknowledged that the pioneering work in the 1950s marked a highpoint of creativity in the then nascent field of econometrics. But it would be distortionary to let this valid perception obscure the phenomenal breadth of Stone's interests, especially as they evolved in the following decades. In fact, Stone was profoundly interested in projects of generating usable data sets; in developing the SNA system of national accounts; in comparative conceptual and statistical work in the underdeveloped countries; in social demography; in setting up the method of social accounting matrices for analytical and policy use; in the construction of social indicators well before the UNDP 'discovered' the human development index; in work in setting up Indian statistics to support planning; in exchanges with Mahalanobis with his innovative development of national sampling frames to overcome major data gaps; many of these interests were manifest from the early days, and the list can surely be extended. Fundamentally, the DAE was about applied economics focussing on national policy issues, at macro, sector and micro levels. The range of Stone's contributions affirms this width of vision, illustrated tellingly in his Raffaele Mattioli Lectures in 1986 where he resurrected the contributions of a dozen British empiricists from 1650 with William Petty—eleven men, and Florence Nightingale (Stone, 1997). Phyllis Deane, one of his proteges at the DAE, and discussants at the Lectures, observed, "He is now the leading English political arithmetician, arguably the most distinguished of those who have followed the tradition started by Sir William Petty…" (Deane in Stone, 1997, p. 389).[9]

However, notwithstanding the huge intrinsic worth, wide recognition and sustained impact of the early work on historical data and related themes in the DAE, economic history failed to find a permanent home there after its initial purple period; successive Annual Reports indicate an inverted-U and testify to its fading visibility in the DAE research profile. In the first 'Annual Report' of the DAE, covering the years 1946–1948, the description of research activities includes a section on 'National Income, Product and Social Accounting Projects'; for the following three reports covering the period till 1957, the label changes to 'The Collection of Data'; the report for the period 1958–1964 has a section for research projects on 'Studies in Economic History'; then through till 1972–1973, the section is called 'Economics and Economic

---

[9] A similar assessment and sentiment is expressed later by Hashem Pesaran and Geoff Harcourt (Pesaran, 1991; Pesaran & Harcourt, 2000); and Angus Deaton who described his doctoral supervisor as "the inheritor of the British empiricist tradition in economics that saw its first flowering among the 'political arithmeticians' of the English Restoration, men such as William Petty, Gregory King and Charles Davenant" (Deaton, 2008, pp. 1–2).

History'; finally, for the period 1973–1974 to 1975–1976, the label is 'Economic History' and the list thins out, with the Charles Feinstein's 'Capital Accumulation' project the only survivor. Thereafter, from 1976–1977, 'economic history' disappears altogether from the listing of the DAE's research projects, as does the names of its economic historians who are then no longer connected with the DAE, even though they held positions in the Faculty.

The location of the small band of economic historians parallels this trajectory. Leaving aside Maurice Dobb, as economic historian, in the Faculty, Colin Clark, who had long left seeking other pastures, Richard Stone (with his interest primarily focussed on methodology and historical statistics), and Robin Matthews (who held a consistent if side interest in modern, near-contemporary economic history), in the early 1950s there were several researchers at the DAE engaged in work on economic history, historical statistics or on national accounting systems; but numbers soon thinned out. Phyllis Deane, the senior most of the next generation, spent the longest period at the DAE, from 1950 through till 1962, when she moved to the Faculty, first as a lecturer, then reader (in 1971), and finally as a professor (in 1981), retiring in 1982; her co-researcher W.A. 'Max' Cole worked with her during 1955–1959, and then left Cambridge;[10] Charles Feinstein[11] was at the DAE between 1958 and 1963,

---

[10] William Alan (Max) Cole arrived at Peterhouse, Cambridge, in 1943. Owing to wartime and post-war National Service he did not complete his undergraduate work until 1950, and then remained at Cambridge for a PhD in History (1955). He was Research Officer in the Department of Applied Economics, Cambridge, 1955–1959. In his schooldays, he had once been asked to produce a paper on a Soviet writer; he wrote and talked about the only one he knew, Gorky, and forever came to be called Max, for Maxim (Cole, 2007, p. 154). Max Cole was a Bevin Boy, in that he worked underground on the coal face in the Gedling Colliery near Nottingham, and was discharged in November 1945 from the mines on medical grounds. Influenced by Maurice Dobb, a foundation member of the British Communist Party, "I joined the student branch of the Communist Party almost immediately after my arrival in Cambridge in October 1943 and remained a member for 15 years. I had been a communist in all but name for two or three years before I became eligible for party membership and a socialist of sorts ever since I was old enough to think about the world around me." Influenced in this by John Strachey's *The Theory and Practice of Socialism* (1936); and 'the titanic struggle' of Russia against the Germans, which Churchill dubbed "the Russian glory"; this "had such a profound effect on a highly impressionable teenager (I was 15 at the time) that I became determined to join the Communist Party as soon as I was eligible to do so" (ibid., p. 150). Following the Soviet invasion of Hungary, Max, "after two years of prevarication, resigned from the CP and little later jointed the Labour Party instead. ... This was not in my case a matter of a God that failed, because the Communist Party was never my God, nor did I ever regard the writings of Marx and Engels as Holy Writ. But a Marxian socialist I became early in life, and a Marxian socialist I remain" (ibid., p. 150).

[11] The DAE had two vacancies around the time when Feinstein was completing his PhD: he got one of these in 1958, to complete Maywald's work on domestic capital formation (which led to *Domestic Capital Formation in the United Kingdom* in 1965); the other one went to Brian Mitchell in 1960 to work with Phyllis Deane and Max Cole on the *Abstract of British Historical Statistics*. Stone had launched the project on the retrospective national accounts: his own work on consumers' expenditure was the first volume, followed by the works of Stone and Prest [both on Consumer

after which he followed Phyllis Deane to the Faculty side of the building till 1978, when he left to a chair at York; Brian Mitchell[12] joined DAE to work with Phyllis in 1960, worked on assorted projects till 1968, when he too shifted to a lectureship in the Faculty till 1972. The Faculty already had Maurice

---

Expenditure], Utting [on Income and Expenditure of Public Authorities], Chapman [on Wages and Salaries], and Feinstein-Maywald [Domestic Asset Formation]. This opened the opportunity for him to "pull it all together and provide the key series for GDP; so I went to Stone and Reddaway and said I would like to do this" (Feinstein, 2007, p. 290); and this resulted in his much acclaimed *National Income, Expenditure and Output of the United Kingdom, 1855–1965*, published in 1972. Feinstein had shifted to a university assistant lectureship in economic history in the Faculty position in 1963 and remained there till 1978, when he shifted base to a professorship at the university in York. His close association with Robin Matthews was manifested in their jointly authored book, along with Odling-Smee, *British Economic Growth, 1856–1973: The Post-War Period in Historical Perspective*, which "incorporates the Solow neoclassical production-function growth model as the base of its total factor productivity calculation" (Offer, 2008, p. 13); it was published in 1982, by which time Charles had already been in York for four years. Charles was apparently something of a Marxist in South Africa where he was identified with taking anti-apartheid positions. He had invested three years in chartered accountancy prior to Cambridge; then took the one-year Diploma in Economics at Cambridge where he did well enough to be inducted into PhD research. He moved away from Marxism (from 1956) after arriving in Cambridge, this despite his devotion to Maurice Dobb from the early years. In Faculty politics, soon, he was, and remained, closely allied to the orthodox Hahn-Matthews axis and at a considerable distance from the left-Keynesian and radical groups in the DAE and the Faculty. According to one knowledgeable contemporary, "the Faculty Left regarded him as a renegade and were hostile to him, an attitude that he reciprocated." For an extended reflection, see Chap. 2, pp. 58–64.

[12] Born in 1929, Brian Mitchell first arrived in Cambridge in February 1952, at Peterhouse. "It didn't take me long to decide that his was where I'd like to live out my days." After finishing the PhD, he landed a post at DAE—a two-year appointment "to compile a volume of British historical statistics to accompany the great pioneering work of quantitative economic history being produced by Phyllis Deane and Max Cole." Three further two-year appointments, "mostly working with Phyllis Deane and Charles Feinstein on making estimates of British capital formation in the long 19th century ... led to a large contribution to Charles Feinstein's monumental work on British national accounts—something which he gave me full credit for, but which others have generally failed to appreciate" (Mitchell, 2009). As the capital formation project was ending, Mitchell wanted to shift from the DAE cycle of two-year project assignments to a tenured post. "But economic history lectureships didn't normally come up all that frequently—I think there have only been five or six in the last forty years—and Phyllis Deane and Charles Feinstein had each been appointed quite recently; so I was extraordinarily lucky when another one was advertised in 1967 and I got it" (ibid.). Subsequently, he shifted from CUP to the "much more commercially driven" Macmillan, produced *European Historical Statistics*, and then another two massive volumes of *International Historical Statistics* which ran into second and third editions—"so most of the rest of my life until retirement and, in fact, well beyond, was taken up with that at times I referred to as a work of academic prostitution, for though I didn't receive *poule de luxe* rates, they were quite lucrative" (ibid.). If his DAE contemporary Max Cole was a lifelong 'Marxian socialist', Mitchell, despite the proximity and interactions with Maurice Dobb, was on the other side of the barricades: "I was involved with in the usual stint on committees—as chairman of the Degree Committee; on the Faculty Board, where I was a Council of the Senate appointee to provide a semblance of a counterweight to the controlling Marxist faction."

Dobb[13] (from 1924 till retirement in 1967) and Robin Matthews (in positions in Cambridge, at the Faculty and/or Clare College during 1949–1965 and 1975–1993) with (contrasting) interests and expertise in economic history; and finally, Jane Humphries provided more than just an illuminating flicker of the dying flame of the subject within the Faculty where, after the retirement in 1982 of her much respected and admired Newnham teacher and colleague Phyllis Deane, Jane effectively became the worthy inheritor of her tradition and the sole torch bearer for economic history *per se*—she served as a lecturer (1980–1995) and then as reader till 1998 when, it is said, in the face of the proverbial glass ceiling and pompous hostility from key power honchos of the new regime, she opted for Oxford, bequeathing the tradition to her accomplished student (and subsequently research collaborator) Sara Horrell.

The 1950s and 1960s formed "the heroic phase of historical national accounting" (Offer, 2008, p. 11); "a golden age for the study of trends in the Victorian economy, a good deal of it in Cambridge" (ibid., p. 5). 'National accounts', 'Data collection', 'historical statistics', 'social accounting', 'economic history' and related lines of work accumulated pioneering research output and legendary reputations for the individual researchers and for the DAE as a whole. It is remarkable then to discover, on closer scrutiny, that this edifice was built primarily by a small group of researchers who were based at the DAE really for quite limited periods of time. Leaving aside Dick Stone and Alan Prest,[14] the longest serving researcher was Phyllis Deane who was based at the DAE between 1950 till 1962; her research collaborator Max Cole was at the DAE only during 1955–1959; Charles Feinstein during 1958–1963; and Brian Mitchell between 1960 and 1968; pulling all these years together in a string still adds up to no more than 30 years, still a decade short of a single full pension! DAE projects were time bound, and Stone's 'retrospective' historical statistics project was instrumental, in that it filled a huge gap, and also set the stage for the remarkable uses to which the data series were put through the development and application of customised econometric methods. So, the historical data hunters and gatherers scattered, in a trickle to the Faculty, or elsewhere. But then at the Faculty, there was little scope for a career motivated both by a desire and an impatience, for promotions; only the modest and self-effacing Phyllis stayed the course. It is striking that such a vibrant and accomplished lineage of research steadily atrophied and eventually disappeared from

---

[13] Dobb published his classic *Studies in the Development of Capitalism* in 1946, followed in 1948 by his *Soviet Economic Development since 1917* which followed his original *Russian Economic Development since the Revolution* published in 1928.

[14] Alan Richards Prest was a part-timer at the DAE for the early years but his research was fully financed by the Colonial Office; as such, his name does not appear in the list of research staff appended to any of the DAE annual reports for those years. There were significant contributions in the economic history projects in the early DAE years from, amongst others, A.A. Adams, Agatha Chapman, Dorothy Cole, Karl Maywald and J.E.G. Utting.

academic and intellectual profile of the Faculty of Economics and the DAE. Culpability for this demise must be shared by the DAE that was not able to creatively sustain innovative research in economic history within its domain beyond the early 1960s, and the Faculty which showed altogether minimal affinity and lesser support in maintaining and expanding such research capacity in the body of staff. Perhaps Charles Feinstein was too much the chartered accountant of historical statistics, but Phyllis Deane had a vast interface with the evolution of economics, with the experience of industrialisation, with gendered development issues in underdeveloped economies that went well beyond counting and accounting. The induction of Jane Humphries promised to nurture and extend this broad tradition, but with hindsight it becomes clear that this was too optimistic an expectation; if the heterodox groups could not clear more space for economic history, the orthodox neoclassical camp had even lesser inclination to do so, and this was manifest in the lack of institutional support and welcome that led her, virtually the last serious practitioner in that lineage—barring the exception of her illustrious student Sara Horrell—to leave Cambridge. In relocating to Oxford, she was following an exit path trod earlier by Charles Feinstein, when locally facing the barrier to upward mobility, he took the lateral route, moving first to a chair at York, and then to the Chichele Professorship in Oxford. Avner Offer, his student, and successor to that position, wrote a fine appreciation for Charles: "Theories came and went, good data endured: 'I think that the assets I construct are more likely to prove durable if I do one type of work rather than another. It might be more exciting and more intellectually demanding to try and do more speculative and theoretical research, but I doubt that it would make a lasting or worthwhile contribution'" (quotation from Feinstein, 2007, as cited in Offer, 2008, pp. 14–15).

Perhaps of pertinence here is the changing professional and political imagination of the Cambridge practitioners of applied economics, with the war forming something of a divide. The neoclassicals didn't really even have much time or space for economic history or the history of economics, except perhaps as extra-curricular reading, and possibly even then not. But even within the heterodox, post-Keynesian frame of reference, issues of contemporary policy dominated to an extent that squeezed out resources, in terms of time, finance or inclination, to delve systematically into the patterns of the past; there was not so much any hostility, as might have been the case with the neoclassicals, as a form of passive or benign neglect. It was as if economic history was always there and would remain, whereas economic policy was here and now, and had to be done; arguably such an orientation enveloped the DAE as well as the Faculty in the cut-and-thrust of ideologically turbo-charged policy debates especially from the 1970s, and the tools of applied economics needed to serve this demanding master. The country was forward looking, locked in economic battle. Priorities shifted from constructing statistical timelines of the past, to developing methods for projecting conditional trajectories into the future, whether in short, medium or longer terms. Feinstein (2007, p. 290) ruefully laments that "by the 1960s, [Stone] had lost interest in the project [of 'retrospective national accounts'] and moved on to other things." The main 'other thing' would be the iconic Cambridge Growth Project, launched by Stone and Brown in 1960—a commitment which epitomised the shift of focus and priority into applied modelling frames directly relevant to policy analysis for the medium and longer terms. And, subsequently, with Wynne Godley, Francis Cripps and the Cambridge Economic Policy Group constituted in 1970, the purposes of modelling became even more sharply focussed on the live policy issues of the short term, generating know-how for the here-and-now. In between, there was the brilliant 'back-of-the-envelope' common-sense economics of Brian Reddaway which, while fully mindful of theory and history, sacrificed all theoretical and econometric sophistry in favour of meaningful policy relevance; the bible then was the annual *National Accounts 'Blue Book'*, and later, from 1970, also *Social Trends*. Looking at 'the past' became more truncated and instrumentalised as temporal extensions serving immediate arguments between opposing theoretical and policy camps[15]; and the grand theorists, with Kaldor as a prime example, conveniently condensed the accumulated wisdom of economic history into 'stylised facts' that could assist in distilling the abstractions of Cambridge 'grand theory'. The past was in the archives, the future was on the anvil.

Analogous tendencies could be detected in contiguous disciplines: in sociology, for instance, Geoffrey Hawthorn was harking after ethnographies of the British working classes, but the field was being overtaken, even swamped, by the search for understandings of the new modernity, à la Tony Giddens, embracing Britain and the rich world. And the imperatives Third World development were displacing the antiquated, anachronistic colonial narratives of anthropologists researching the primitive others; this trend was manifest and immediately visible, for instance, in the Cambridge Course on Development sponsored by the ODA but taught, for Cambridge qualifications, by Cambridge academics. Likewise, erstwhile imperial narratives of apology and defence of colonialism were yielding to the onslaught of a wave of nationalist writing from the South, even as the imperialist camp constructed new discourses to subvert the rising economic nationalism in the South. Radical development thinking aligned itself largely with the project of accelerated planned industrialisation in newly independent countries under the aegis of the state; this enthusiasm infected Cambridge economists as well, with many seniors participating in laying the foundations of Indian planning, with inspiration drawn from Soviet planning models and methods; the interface with the work of Maurice Dobb

---

[15] See, for instance, the diverging assessments of post-War growth in the United Kingdom and in Europe by R.C.O. Matthews's rejection of the Keynesian "fiscal explanation" for "why has Britain had full employment since the War?" (Matthews, 1968); Francis Cripps's broader (1973) analysis of the growth process in advanced capitalist economies; and Glyn et al. 's (1988) substantial piece on the rise and fall of the 'golden age' of capitalism in Europe in the three post-War decades—the latter two contributions very much in the Keynes-Kaldor tradition.

on planning techniques is immediate. The dismal stories of colonialism were being overtaken by the forward-looking perspectives drawn variously from Marx, Gerschenkron, Schumpeter, Kuznets, Kalecki, Kaldor and, for the misguided, Rostow. Thus, it is arguable that the economic historians of the DAE and the Faculty were distanced to an extent both from the 'proper' historians in the History Faculty (as was perceived by Charles Feinstein (2007)), and from both sides of the ideological divide within the Faculty of Economics, and conditions were therefore uncongenial for establishing and asserting the continued relevance of the historical and national statistics projects to the new perceived imperatives of politics and policy. To an extent, this strait-jacketed vision distorted a balanced appreciation of the permanent relevance of economic history within any Faculty of Economics. Feinstein could find affinity only with those in his own Faculty that had an interest in economic history, and he singles out Robin Matthews in this regard. But perhaps the problem lay also in the narrowness of the research agenda and interests of the national and historical statisticians: on the one side they were naturally distanced from historians doing other kinds of history; and further, the statisticians were overwhelmingly focussed on the British economy, and this extreme specialisation would surely also preclude cross-boundary interactions across departments and faculties. India, again, provides a convenient illustration. Cambridge at the time boasted the active presence of a bevy of established and rising historians of empire, enough for identifying multiple schools of imperial and Indian history within them.[16] Feinstein moved from the DAE to the Faculty in 1963; just two years later, in 1965, Amiya Bagchi was appointed as a lecturer in the Faculty. While Bagchi's doctoral work was a statistical compilation of a time series of investment in the Indian economy, his own interests interfaced much more widely with themes of Indian economic history, as for instance, the question of the deindustrialisation of the Indian economy under colonial conditions. When Bagchi returned to India, the vacant lectureship was occupied by Prabhat Patnaik who also researched private investment in the Indian economy for his doctoral dissertation. Earlier groundwork had been provided in Cambridge by the work of D.R. Gadgil in the 1920s on Indian industry, and by V.K.R.V. Rao in the 1930s with his pioneering work on the estimation of the national income of India. It is arguable credibly, then, that it was not necessarily, or exclusively, the narrowness or lack of interest of the historians outside the DAE and Faculty, but rather the extreme narrowness of focus of the DAE

---

[16] Imperial historians of Africa and India (and Japan) were well represented by Jack Gallagher, Ronald Robinson, W.J. MacPherson, amongst others; Eric Stokes, on Africa and India, stood at a discrete distance and ploughed his own furrow. A younger cohort of followers included B.R. Tomlinson, Chris Bayly, Anil Seal, amongst others; there were other divergent non-historians about, such as Peter Bauer and Polly Hill. There was also Joseph Needham's panoramic standalone research enterprise on Chinese history. However, at the DAE or in the Faculty of Economics, the economics and legacies of Empire, constituting the initial conditions of subsequent national development agendas, had little systematic presence; the DAE and the Faculty's research agenda of 'economic history' was UK-centric to the point of being insular.

national statisticians that made wider conversations and interactions infructuous if not impossible.

Brian Mitchell (2009) has observed that the productivity of the economic historians on the Faculty suffered on account of effectively being reduced to teaching mules carrying huge supervision loads,[17] albeit a counterfactual hypothesis he casually floated on a sample of one, himself. Economic history remained very much part of the undergraduate teaching shop, and no doubt college supervisions were demanding, but expanding the sample from one to two, to include Phyllis Deane, or to three, to further include the highly productive Jane Humphries, reduces the hypothesis largely to an alibi for a community of worthy fellows who taught a lot but researched a little. Here, Jane puts in a corrective word for college supervisors, especially those, unlike Mitchell at Trinity, from the poorer, particularly women's colleges where there were few resources for relief or compensating financial support in the form of research assistance.[18]

---

[17] Brian Mitchell was at Trinity for 40 years, during which he produced one monograph and two or three articles, apart from his statistical abstracts. "That it isn't more is partly ... down to the amount of teaching I've done. All the economic historians who've stayed in the Cambridge Economics Faculty for any length of time have published less that they might have done because there have been so few of us to cover the teaching of twenty-plus colleges. I used to teach regularly for five or six, with another one or two thrown in when someone was on leave. That meant between forty and fifty pupils a year, and amounted to a regular seven to nine hours a week" (Mitchell, 2009).

[18] Kitson Clark (1973) ends his account of a century of the teaching of history at Cambridge, from 1873 to 1973, with an ode, to the unsung college supervisors of students of history, and his tribute deserves to be reproduced to throw the spotlight on the unglamorous foundations of the impressive edifice, as also on those that sustain them.

> Active research and fresh historical thought are necessary to keep a history school and its teaching alive; but equally necessary is the realization that the teaching of history is as honourable, as useful, as arduous, a task as historical research and the writing of history books. To realize this it is, I believe, necessary also to realize that the object of teaching is not only to impart historical knowledge, but also to impart what Adolphus Ward defined, in the controversies which took place when the Tripos was being established, as 'historical power'. 'Historical power', he said, 'as I understand it means the power of applying to the original treatment of historical questions, historical knowledge which has been accumulated by reading, which has been sifted by criticism and which has been invested in literary form by composition.' He was right to value this power. It is of great value to the man or woman employed not only on what is recorded in history books but also on what is reported day by day in the news and is rapidly turning into history. But I do not think that this power is likely to be gained from books alone, I think it is more likely to be imparted by living teaching. This has been given with unstinted generosity at Cambridge and the success of the hundred years of history teaching has been at least as much due to those who have served all their working lives as supervisors and directors of studies and lecturers as to those who have had the good fortune to become Readers or Professors. My final word therefore will be to honour those who have tended 'the homely slighted shepherd's trade'. (Clark, 1973, pp. 552–553).

Phyllis Deane

Phyllis Deane[19] represented, perhaps, the golden mean[20]: the inquisitive, innovative and incorrigible statistician of national income in the challenging contexts both of the past of a developed economy and the present of developing economies; arguably an early feminist economist; an analytical interpreter of the British industrial revolution and the carrier of its decoded complexities into the undergraduate imagination in a readily comprehensible and readable style; a thoughtful interlocutor of the evolution of economic ideas, locating the state and economic system in the history of political economy[21]; a brilliant intellectual biographer; a fine editor in perhaps the best team to have run *Economic Journal*; an institutional stalwart, both in Cambridge—where she made vital contributions, unfortunately generally overlooked, to the professionalisation of development teaching in the University and then in the Faculty—and in the wider discipline, serving as president of the Royal Economic Society, amongst other institutional 'chores' on which she delivered—and all this apart, of course, from duties at her Newnham College, not to mention all that supervision and teaching; and, to boot, she was a fine PhD supervisor. In her obituary, Negley Harte (2012) writes, "she unassumingly made an impact on the national mind for a good half-century."

At the DAE, she produced, separately with W.A. Max Cole and Brian Mitchell, some outstanding work in historical statistics: with W.A. 'Max' Cole came *British Economic Growth: 1688–1959*; and with Brian Mitchell, *Abstract of British Historical Statistics*, both works published in 1962, the year she shifted base from the DAE to the Faculty side of the building, where she produced her acclaimed *The First Industrial Revolution* in 1965. "For a generation, these were the central works in a tradition going back to Gregory King and Adam Smith ... these mark the beginning of the high point of British economic history as a discipline" (Harte, 2012). It was a tradition in which she was equally a partner as her mentor and Director, Richard Stone. In opening

---

[19] Born 1918 in Hong Kong; National Institute of Economic and Social Research, 1941–1945; UK Colonial Office 1947–1949; Senior Research Officer, DAE, Cambridge, 1950–1962; 1962–1983 Faculty of Economics & Politics, Cambridge, as Lecturer (1962), Reader (1971), Professor (1981); retired 1983.

[20] Apart from her stellar work in economic history, which her fellow economic historian of the following generation, Jane Humphries (quoted in Bortis, 2017, p. 890), refers to as "a seismic shift in the tectonic plates of economic history", finely perceptive appreciations of her later books (Deane, 1978, 1988a) on the evolution of economic ideas, and on the history of political economy can be found in Bortis (2010, 2017); her outstanding biography of J.N. Keynes (Deane, 2001) was described by Harcourt as "one of the finest jewels in the crown of our profession; Phyllis much admired Neville Keynes for his integrity, hard work and good sense, like calling to like, I think" (Harcourt, 2012a, p. 19); on her own typically modest commentary on her J.N. Keynes biography while the text was still on her anvil, see Deane (2007, pp. 144–145).

[21] Bortis (2017, p. 889), in his appreciation, observes: "only a political economist like Deane, being *simultaneously* an excellent economic historian and an outstanding historian of economic ideas, could bring the issue *political economy* and *economic science* into sharp focus."

her remarks as a discussant of Stone's Mattioli Lectures, Phyllis Deane says: "it will surprise no one who has had the good fortune to collaborate with Dick Stone that the work on Gregory King's national income estimates to which he has referred in his first lecture as 'Professor Deane's work' is as much due to him as to me" (Deane in Stone, 1997, p. 389).

She is unstinting in acknowledging her debts to her seniors. First, came Austin Robinson when she was at the NIESR and the Colonial Office: "I was very fortunate in having Austin Robinson as a supervisor. Many well-known economists were working in Whitehall for the war effort, including Austin Robinson, Richard Stone, James Meade, and Arthur Lewis, the last three of who subsequently became Nobel Prize winners. They used regularly to come over to the National Institute to have a sandwich lunch with me and advise me on my work. So I started out with an advantage that very few research students have. I had interested attention from people who found it a break from their daily grind and were glad to assist me" (Deane, 2007, p. 134). And what 'people', one might exclaim!

And then, to Richard Stone when she joined the DAE in Cambridge: "He was one of the research advisers who first set me to work in that area four and a half decades ago. It was then that I began to apply to underdeveloped countries the system of social accounting which Richard Stone and James Meade had devised for the United Kingdom economy under the inspiration of J.M. Keynes. After the war when I joined the Cambridge Department of Applied Economics ... he was again my mentor and the most fertile source of stimulating research ideas" (Deane, in Stone, 1997, p. 389).

At the DAE, Stone and colleagues were developing their standardised system of national accounts, a statistical-analytical template that would permit meaningful comparisons over time and across countries. In parallel, what they wanted "was to apply this system to a completely different economy than the UK, for example, to colonial territories. So I sat in London through most of the War using the Colonial Office library and other such sources trying to work out national income for Northern Rhodesia and Jamaica and to see whether I could set the results into a system of social accounts." (She was later also involved closely as an adviser on the project—wholly financed by the Colonial Office—on the estimation of the national income of Nigeria.[22]) Her 1948 work on colonial national incomes was the outcome. Then, "at the end of the War, as soon as the seas were open again, I wanted to go to developing countries to find out what it was like on the ground[23] because I had so far worked with

---

[22] "The inquiry provides a valuable opportunity for a reconsideration of the conceptual problems relating to national income and its components in underdeveloped territories, in the very practical setting of a compilation of estimates which will both fit the conceptual framework and yield useful new information on the economy of the Colony." The project was advised by a committee which included, amongst others, Peter Bauer, Phyllis Deane and Alan Prest, with Austin Robinson as chairman (DAE, Second Report, 1948–1951, p. 17). See also: Prest, A. R. & Stewart, I. G. (1953).

[23] Phyllis was born in Hong Kong; her father was an engineer in the Admiralty and was posted in locations all over the British empire.

documentary evidence only. So in 1946–1947 I went to Northern Rhodesia and Nyasaland and produced national income accounts for them." What transpired "was what one of my colleagues once called the 'perpetual invention' method. I had to make estimates all along the line on the basis of what little data, experimenting all the time with the kind of data I could find. It ranged from actually sitting down in African villages and taking family budget studies to visiting copper companies, finding out what their accounts meant … I was also fortunate enough to be allowed into the census office in Lusaka … the returns included some income data, and I was allowed to work through the originals … I did not know how accurate the information was … it was an eye-opener as to how uninformative such aggregates [as the income of copper companies, or agricultural yields] are and how important it is to analyse the components. There were a lot of interesting questions that arose as to what the concept of national income meant in a country like that and what uses it might serve" (ibid., p. 134).

The shift from colonial accounting in Northern Rhodesia and Nyasaland to Gregory King's national income estimates for England and Wales was less of a break than might be imagined. In his assessment of her work, Heinrich Bortis (2017, p. 875) comes to the conclusion that "almost certainly, the experience gained through her work on colonial accounts enabled Deane to fully and ingeniously put to use the data collected by King to set up a system of social accounts for England and Wales in 1688. This is typical of her research: later work grew out of former work, always with a view to broadening and deepening knowledge on socio-economic and political matters."

She was head-hunted by Dick Stone and brought over to the DAE, from where she made her subsequent major academic contributions that put British economic history on the contemporary intellectual map. What perhaps most attracted Stone was her pioneering in assembling using a variety of statistical ingredients for the construction of social and national accounts in Northern Rhodesia, Nyasaland and Jamaica. All this interfaced productively with Stone's own efforts at constructing universal systems of national income accounting at the DAE. Stone had a specific interest in testing the interface between his standard system of national accounting with the social and economic realities of underdeveloped economies with their distinct pre-modern structures and activities. (A commentary on her Africa engagement is provided in Appendix 2.)

Richard Stone's SNA template for the UN excluded unwaged labour from national income estimates. However, "Deane continued to research ways to quantify women's work, including even the elusive firewood collection and crop transport", as Macekura (2018) notes, "with an eye towards social reform, as she believed in order to address distributional concerns, the economic contributions of all producers and consumers, including subsistence producers and women, should be counted". As Harte (2012) points out, "she was attracted by research, by the careful finding-out of things; …the increasingly econometric fussiness of 'the new economic history' did not appeal to her. She did not like empty economic boxes. She liked them filled with human variety."

Stephen Macekura (2018) and especially Luke Messac (2016) have provided valuable additional insights into the pioneering questions she raised in her work on national income estimation but, perhaps, they go too far in concluding, as Macekura states, that "in the end, Deane ended up scoffing at the goal Robinson had originally laid out: a clear and comparable framework for accounting in colonial territories." Any implication that Phyllis Deane and her supervisor Austin Robinson, and by implication Richard Stone, were working at cross purposes is strictly untenable. If anything, the seniors were consistently supportive of her work and highly appreciative of its intrinsic value-addition to the overall project of national income accounting. Phyllis had much guidance from them in her work based at the National Institute and in the Colonial Office; and indeed, it was the recognition of the worth of this work that prompted Stone to invite her into the DAE team.[24]

Phyllis Deane's eclectic methodological approach to researching rural realities in Africa immediately conjures up the image of her Cambridge contemporary, Polly Hill the economic anthropologist, and an intriguing prospect of a crossing of their paths.[25] Polly Hill, described as "an academic outsider" (Serra, 2018, p. 94), and as a "deflator of theories rather than a builder of theories" (Manning, 1971, p. 156), "carved spaces of intersection between economics and anthropology" generally fighting for the inductive epistemological approach of the latter against the generalising and aggregating methodologies of economists; if Polly Hill hunted and gathered in this no-woman's land between the disciplines, so did Phyllis Deane who realised the imperative of anthropological observational and assessment methods in coming to any deductions about the scale and value of local activities that needed to be included in any estimate of the national income. The disciplinary upbringing of economists stood in the way of such creative, explorative induction; Serra (2018, p. 95) quotes W. Arthur Lewis: "the economist who studies the non-market economy must abandon most of what he has learnt and adopt the techniques of the anthropologist." Indeed, in her work on Zambia, Deane utilised the knowledge and assistance of anthropologists in surveying village economies in Zambia. But if Hill cast herself in the role of the iconoclast smashing the misguided conceptualisations and generalisations of economists, Deane, fully sensitive to the same problem and coming from the same direction, was

---

[24] "When Dick and James had completed their work on the British national income, I was anxious to see whether their methods would help one with the impossibly difficult task of calculating colonial national incomes. This was a problem that I had run across when working myself on African problems. We started in the National Institute a study of the national incomes of three colonial countries and we hired, with the help of Cairncross, Phyllis Deane to do the work. We had a small committee of Dick and Feodora, Phyllis herself, myself and Arthur Lewis. This was Dick's first involvement in work on countries other than U.K." (Robinson, E.A.G., Letter to Angus Deaton, dated 8 May 1992).

[25] Of course, their paths intersected at various points: a closeness to Joan Robinson (who was Polly Hill's supervisor), whereas Phyllis Deane's work was supervised in the early years by Austin Robinson; later, Phyllis and Joan were both editors of the Modern Cambridge Economics series; and Phyllis Deane wrote the highly acclaimed biography of John Neville Keynes, Polly Hill's maternal grandfather; in one manner or other, for decades they would have shared the general intellectual environment and social ecology of Cambridge economics.

the builder, seeking to develop national income aggregations constructed from meaningful building blocks that reflected the local social frameworks underlying economic activity; as an economist, 'knowing' and 'finding out' about African rural realities that did not fit the standard national income template was not enough, she wanted to understand and capture them, howsoever knowingly imperfectly, to make them useful for the economic analysis of economic development processes. It can be speculated that somewhere along this traverse, the two might conceivably have parted company.

Phyllis Deane was an unlabelled feminist economist before the times of formal feminist economics: in her earliest works she identified the paradox of the ubiquitous presence of women's economic and reproductive activities in rural Africa on the one side, and their virtual invisibility in statistical and accounting systems on the other. She assiduously began to set this right: she worked out methods for estimating the imputed values of women's work in the home in milling grain; initially excluded, she returned also to the vexed issue of the quantifying and valorising the unwaged labour of rural women this time incorporating firewood collection and crop transport (Macekura, 2018). Feminist economists opened up this battlefront later though, as Macekura rightly observes, "in many ways, Deane's work for the NIESR presaged all these valuable critiques"—which, incidentally, remained applicable in several regards to the national income templates developed by Stone. There are two issues at stake. First, estimating imputed values for non-monetised items that were included in the national accounts; the question was how to obtain prices at which such items were to be valued, and this task had a high nuisance value. The second was a more fundamental issue: where was the so-called production boundary to be drawn—what should be counted and included, say, of all the products and services generated by women's work inside the household; this was both a conceptual and statistical issue that goes to the heart of what is deemed to constitute value for society.[26]

---

[26] Arguably, Phyllis Deane's pioneering work on these issues had ripple effects. Anecdotally speaking, I recall the induction seminar given by Graham Pyatt, one of the earliest cohorts of young quantitative economists working with Stone at the DAE, as part of the process of his professorial appointment at the Institute of Social Studies in The Hague around the late 1980s. The Institute was an institutional pioneer in gender teaching and research, and it was refreshing to hear Graham rising to the challenge and speaking on time-use patterns and issues in the valuation of time, all oriented towards the invisibility of women's work in economic accounting. And indeed, on distant memory, he grappled both with the issue of imputing values for non-priced goods and services, as well as on the vexed issue of 'production boundary' in the estimation of national income. In his paper on accounting for time use (Pyatt, 1990), he "discusses how statistics on time use can be integrated into a social accounting matrix representation of economic activity. Time use data are presented as an extended manpower matrix and related to Stone's basic dynamic framework for social statistics. The valuation of time and methods of imputation are then discussed in relation to the choice of production boundary. It is argued that any imputations of labour income must be balanced by valuing goods consumed at their user cost and that there is a case for imputing value to all uses of time." Phyllis Deane, his colleague of old—between the late-1950s and early 1960s—at the DAE, would surely have been delighted, even if somewhat disappointed that the world was still some distance from a full recognition of women's work.

After university, Phyllis had firmly wished not to be a civil servant—and a two-year immersion in that role confirmed this aversion; and not to be a teacher—"but teaching in Cambridge I found rather attractive because I started supervising, which involves an exchange between equals, rather than pontificating. I started lecturing in the 1960s … it was not difficult, but it was an advantage to have done research because it gave one something to communicate. … if you are lecturing to small groups of people …you can create a discussion." And there was a positive kickback into research: "I think it helped the research. It certainly forced me to concentrate on putting my findings into an interesting form" (ibid., p. 139). Referring to *The First Industrial Revolution*, she says: "what I wanted to do most of all was to … use economists' methods of analysis and bring in enough economic theory to fit economic history into a first-year course for students working towards a degree in economics" (ibid., pp. 139–140). And in doing so, she was trying also to build bridges to development economics, which she was then teaching to graduate students.

She was "terrifically good and efficient at organizing anything she thought worthwhile", and Harte (2012) rightly lists her editorship of *Economic Journal*, serving as president of the Royal Economic Society, her being a Fellow of the British Academy and working for her Newnham College. What could have been further added was her steady and effective support for the institutional embedding of the teaching of development studies and development economics both at the University and the Faculty levels, navigating the complex and often treacherous interdepartmental and interdisciplinary waters, calmly negotiating the usual diversity of disagreeing academics on the one side, and the bureaucratese of University authorities on the other.

This brief traverse through the rich career and contributions of Phyllis Deane serves to highlight the wide interface and intrinsic value embodied in the presence of an eminent economic historian, through facilitating border-crossings between disciplines, methods and divergent spatial and temporal contexts. Certainly, and at the least, for the heterodox lineages of Cambridge economics, the presence of economic history and economic historians in the Faculty would be a constant marker of the discontinuities and disequilibrium inherent in historical processes, of time being history, and of Joan's binary, 'history versus equilibrium'.

On the Faculty Side[27]

John Hrothgar Habakkuk, 1915–2002
If anything, John Hrothgar Habakkuk's intellectual affinities and polarities were not attuned to those dominant in the Faculty of Economics and Politics

---

[27] The case of Maurice Dobb, who retired in 1967 and remained active till his death in 1976, figures in the earlier section; and that of Jane Humphries, who joined the Faculty in 1980, appears in a later section.

in the immediate post-War period, when he held the position of lecturer in economics between 1946 and 1950, before taking up the Chichele Chair in Oxford at the age of 35. As a student reading history (1933–1936) at Cambridge, he had attended the 'exhilarating' lectures by Clapham, and then the first lectures delivered by his successor Postan, finding these 'electrifying' (Harte, 2002); Postan presented "an entirely fresh vision of economic history", he said in his address at the memorial service for Postan in 1981 (Thompson, 2004, p. 95) he "recalled the sheer ebullience and intellectual excitement of Munia Postan's lectures, darting about from nineteenth-century movements of capital and labour to fourteenth-century agrarian crises, and grounded in the latest continental teachings of figures—Sombart and Bloch, for example—who were virtually unknown in Cambridge." Hrothgar fell "entirely under the almost hypnotic influence of Postan's supremely confident and exuberant pronouncements" (ibid., pp. 95,96). John Clapham was his supervisor,[28] but he was Postan's man. It was Postan who pushed Habakkuk into his famous work (Habakkuk, 1940a) on (the Postanian theme of) English landownership, 1680–1740, that established his reputation and academic stature; the article was published in *Economic History Review* in 1940, in which year he joined Postan as a joint editor of the journal on the cusp of "a period of seminal expansion for the next decade" (Harte, 2002).

In keeping with the charged political climate of 'red Cambridge' of the 1930s, "Hrothgar, already a teenage socialist who had been active in the school debating society, spent much time as a Cambridge undergraduate discussing politics, and went to many meetings with Bryan Hopkin—whose friendship doubtless kept him abreast, also, of the new economics of Keynes and Joan Robinson. Hrothgar was strongly anti-communist, having been greatly impressed by a talk in the local chapel early in 1933, given by Gareth Jones (son of headmaster Edgar Jones) who had just spent the winter in the Ukraine: he spoke of the catastrophic famine caused by forcible collectivisation that he had seen at first hand. Hrothgar was also influenced by his dock-side conversations with his step grandfather, who greatly disliked the local communists and thought they were dishonest rogues. At Cambridge he used to argue with his brilliant contemporary John Cornford, the communist poet and womaniser later killed in the Spanish Civil War, whose irresponsibility shocked Hrothgar almost as much as his politics. 'What I most hated about the communists,' he wrote in the last month of his life, 'was their millenarian element—the belief that a million or so deaths were well worth the coming of the age of prosperity and peace which they would inevitably bring about. I used to argue with Cornford whom I now think was much less sensible and well informed than my father's stepfather'" (Thompson, 2004, pp. 94–95).

---

[28] He had never registered for a PhD, "it not being the done thing at that time for high flyers" (Thompson, 2004, p. 95).

Like many other Cambridge contemporaries, Hrothgar did a two-year codebreaking stint at Bletchley (1940–1942); though he was at the Board of Trade for much of the war, Daunton (2017a, p. 167) writes, "to assist in drafting papers on international financial negotiations leading to Bretton Woods"; this was followed by a return to Pembroke College as director of studies in history and, alongside, as university lecturer in economics[29] during 1946–1950; "his lectures on British economic history being directed at both economists and historians" (Thompson, 2004, p. 101). Thompson refers to Habakkuk's "intensely active postwar period in Cambridge" in the course of which "he shared with Postan a Special Subject on the 'British Economy, 1886–1938', a virtually contemporary subject well-suited to the home of Marshallian and Keynesian economics and a reminder that Hrothgar, as well as Postan, had no narrow chronological limits to his interests" (ibid., pp. 101–102). This engagement is striking: Colin Clark, who was at the Faculty of Economics and Politics between 1931 and 1937, before leaving for Australia, had been laying the foundations of a quantitative analysis of the British economy through his series of books (Clark, 1932, 1937, 1938, 1940); and in 1945, just the year prior to Habakkuk taking up his economics lectureship, the Department of Applied Economics (mooted before the war) was launched under Keynes's eye and Stone's directorship. Was there any dialogue between the two traditions, or were these ships crossing in the night? The latter, it would seem: there is no mention at all in the annual reports of the DAE of the period to Habakkuk in any capacity; of course, his work on American and British technology was still in the future, but he had published a substantial piece on free trade and commercial expansion in the 1853–1870 period (Habakkuk, 1940b). It appears likely that while his lectureship might have been based in the Faculty of Economics and Politics, his substantial academic interests and activities continued to remain in the Faculty of History working closely with Postan; while at the DAE, the main body of research on the compilation of historical series had not yet taken off, and the main thrust was on quantitative methods and techniques.

By 1950, Habakkuk had published just three articles, but as Negley Harte (2002) observes, "it was very perceptive of Oxford to identify his potential" and appoint him to the Chichele Chair.

Thompson (2004, p. 102) recalls: "He introduced the practice of having a full minute of each seminar paper and discussion, and as his first graduate student and seminar secretary I found this exercise an invaluable way of getting to grips with the take-off into self-sustained growth, trade cycle theory, Kontratiev (*sic*) cycles, and other mysteries. He continued to build his reputation in the Postan manner, through a string of articles, rather than through writing the large books favoured by his initial supervisor, Clapham; but it was the

---

[29] It needs confirmation whether this lectureship was formally located in the Faculty of Economics & Politics or elsewhere in the university.

publication of his first book, in 1962, *American and British Technology in the Nineteenth Century*, which not only consolidated his position as one of the leading figures on the international stage." The range of teaching, and the book, confirms his diversification into modern economic history.

Two visits to the United States, in 1954–1955 to Harvard and in 1962–1963 to Berkeley, led to his first significant book on American and British Technology in the Nineteenth Century (Habakkuk, 1962) which explored the impact of relative factor endowments—especially the high cost of unskilled labour in the USA attributable to an open land fronter—on the choice of techniques and degrees of automation comparing Britain and America. Thompson (2004, p. 103) observes that "it remains the most brilliant example of Hrothgar's historiographical methodology, the 'marriage of history and theory' expressed in the elegant prose of a master of the logical deduction of theoretical explanations from concrete empirical observations."

Harte writes that "in Habakkuk's hands the marriage of history and theory was a successful one, but history was evidently the dominant partner ... by the 1970s, perhaps too much theory was entering economic history" and Habakkuk was not enthusiastic about this turn. "Already faintly alarmed by the rise of cliometrics, Temin's 1966 article 'Labor Scarcity and the Problem of American Industrial Efficiency in the 1850s'—which contained a formal theoretical presentation of Habakkuk's argument and a highly algebraic appendix that mounted a mathematical proof of inconsistencies and paradoxes in the Habakkuk treatment of labour scarcity—convinced Hrothgar that the practice of economic history, at least in the United States, had moved beyond his intellectual reach. Reflecting in old age, he claimed that the invitation in 1967 to become Principal of Jesus College came in the nick of time to prevent a serious collapse in his self-confidence as an economic historian" (Thompson, 2004, p. 104); he remained in that post till his retirement in 1984. In the interim (1973–1977), he also served as Vice Chancellor of Oxford University. Negley Harte (2002) describes him as "a trim figure with a silver tongue, an elegant hand and, above all, a great mind". But it is highly significant that in the face of the new direction taken by economic historians, he chose to give up perhaps the most prestigious chair at the age of 53, a long way short of its normal tenure to retirement age.

The work on technology was not sustained, and his research returned to his original focus on population, demography and household formation, and on the issue of landed estates. His return to this topic—with his 1994 tome (Habakkuk, 1994) of nearly 700 pages and over 50 pages of notes—was in sharp contrast to his 1940 work and revealed how far he had travelled from his original methods. "He had moved a long way from the days when the 'marriage of history and theory' had been the touchstone of his research. There is precious little theory in this book, except of lawyers' theory on the interpretation and impact of legal instruments.... It is in a sense more of a lawyer's book that a social or economic historian's book ... It is also true that Hrothgar's pronounced distrust of econometrics and quantification meant that he declined to do any counting and produced no tables or graphs, so that the evidence is presented in a literary rather than a statistical framework. What had happened was that in the historian's continual tension between being a 'lumper' or a 'splitter' the accumulation of evidence had pushed Hrothgar more and more into the splitters' camp. What the evidence indicated was the great diversity of the experiences, and the behaviour, of landed families in their marriages, their children, heirs, and heiresses, their debts, their extravagances and economies, their purchases and sales of lands, and their good or bad luck. The certainties which he had seen in 1940 had been dissolved by his increasingly detailed knowledge of the workings of the estate system. The 'diversity of experience', he had come to feel, 'makes the identification of representative behaviour and of dominant trends particularly difficult.'" Gone were the generalisations enabled by an overarching theory or hypothesis. Instead, "the result was a triumphant demonstration of the strengths of a perhaps somewhat old-fashioned historical empiricism, worthy of his original supervisor, Clapham" (Thompson, 2004). His biographer writes that "the seminal landownership article marked both a lifelong interest and the starting point for a group of followers who have developed the modern history of the subject in the same way that followers of Postan developed the history of medieval landownership and tenure" (Thompson, 2004, p. 98); now, the 1994 return had confirmed the Postanian influence by withdrawing from any tendency to generalise in favour of an emphasis on complexity and diversity.

Nick Von Tunzelmann, 1943–2019

Though of a later generation, Nicholas von Tunzelmann's coordinates in the Faculty of Economics and Politics are perhaps best located here in view of his intellectual and professional affinities with the work of John Habakkuk and Robin Matthews on technology and economic growth. 'Nick' von Tunzelmann got an MA at the University of Canterbury, New Zealand, followed by a D.Phil. at Oxford, and then began a career as an economic historian at the University of Canterbury, New Zealand. In 1970, he became a lecturer in economic history at the Faculty of Economics and Politics; 14 years later, with little prospect of upward career mobility in Cambridge, he moved out in 1984, joining SPRU at the University of Sussex, first a Reader, and then from 2005, the R.M. Phillips Professor. "Nick has called his time at SPRU a 'reincarnation', suggesting that he had two careers. The first one, as a classical economic historian, stemmed from his doctorate and his highly cited 1978 book on *Steam Power and British Industrialisation to 1860*. The second one as an economist of innovation, a precursor of later studies in the field, and central to the training of young scholars."[30] The two incarnations are embodied in his two books. In the first

---

[30] Memorial notice posted on behalf of Yuki Kikuchi, University of Sussex Business School. http://www.sussex.ac.uk/broadcast/read/48771

(Cambridge) book, his "aim was 'to combine economics, engineering and history to reassess the contribution of the steam engine to British economic growth during the industrial revolution'" (Bruland, 2004, p. 143). While some of his methods remained open to critique, "the underlying empirical basis of his work, which demonstrates rather limited diffusion of steam relative to other poser sources, has not been challenged, and his critique of the alleged backward and forward linkages of steam also remains unchallenged. What we can conclude here—in what is after all one of the very few detailed empirical examinations of a critical technology—is that the claims made for stead as a driving force for growth are seriously overdone." Such advantages as there were of steam power, Bruland concludes, "do not necessarily add up to support for the extreme views of those who advocate a steam-driven view of industrialisation" (ibid., p. 145).

In the second (SPRU) book, he used a much broader frame, in theory and empirics, and in space and time, to explore explanations of the rate and direction of technological change and its interconnections with other determinants of economic growth and development. Here, he used his historian's toolkit for a comparative examination of the experience of countries that had been the leaders of industrialisation: Britain in the eighteenth century, USA in the nineteenth and Japan in the twentieth centuries, and going on, using approaches from evolutionary economics, to investigate the transfer of historical patterns to later industrialising economies of the 1990s; in this, he linked the micro-level, individual firms and specific technologies, to macroeconomic factors and outcomes. Le Bas (2019) highlights two key features of his later work that he regards as his intellectual legacy. The first is 'the original idea' of 'time-saving innovations' and their distinction from 'labour-saving innovations'. "The introduction of time-saving innovations allowed households—and household members—to change their activity patterns and reallocate their time to other (perhaps new) activities, which have important economic consequence (on energy use in particular but also on structural change). ... As a result, time allocation is profoundly affected, as is the way of life" (ibid.). The second key feature of his later work was his work on innovations in large low-tech industries emphasising the role of new markets, quality upgrading and catering to new tastes; his significant conclusion here was that "associating Low-Tech industries with low innovation, is misleading" (ibid.).

If Tunzelmann's first Cambridge incarnation was in the frame of the classical economic historian, somewhat standing apart amidst economists, his second SPRU avatar stood at the crossroads of various intersections. His ideas on time- and labour-saving technologies and the link to the labour market and intra-household labour allocations suggest wide potential interface with some of the areas of work thoroughly developed by Jane Humphries and Sara Horrell in the Faculty of Economics in Cambridge; and his ideas on innovations in major low-tech industries dovetail on the one side with the wider ongoing work on the evolution and development of technological capabilities, as in the oeuvre of Sanjaya Lall, and his exploration of the determinants and implications of innovation and technological change at the firm- and macro-levels could place his interests and ideas squarely in the domain of Alan Hughes's Centre for Business Research at the Judge Business School in Cambridge.

12.3.2 At the Faculty of History

'Munia' Postan

Vision and Approach
"Postan's approach was unlike Clapham's cautious unwillingness to adopt a position." Rather, he displayed, according to Edward Miller, "a taste for speculative thought not altogether common among historians, even economic historians" (Daunton, 2017a, p. 162). Martin Daunton provides a distillation of the Postan perspective: "Postan wanted an approach on the lines of his analysis of capital, not as an abstract, uniform concept but through understanding its nature in precise social and institutional settings. What was needed was a concern for the 'whole combination of social forces' that was irreducible to mathematical formulae, 'an interrelation so multiple as to make the work of abstraction impossible and undesirable'" (Daunton, 2017a, p. 165, with citations to Postan (1939) therein). If Postan challenged the systemic generalisations of economics and economists, he defended his approach which focussed on localised diversities and specificities. "Unlike a sociologist he [the historian] refuses to ask universal questions or try to formulate general laws" (Postan, 1939, p. 32). Instead, "the economic historian should make 'microscopic problems of historical research' into 'microcosmic'—capable of reflecting worlds larger than themselves. It is in this reflected flicker of truth, the revelations of the general in the particular, that the contribution of the historical method so social sciences will be found" (Postan, 1939, pp. 32, 34) (Daunton, 2017a, p. 165). For him, history was too complex for simple generalisations, a stance he maintained over the decades.[31] There is a difficulty here, in that if generalisations are to be eschewed in the first place, how would the micro-focussed economic historian find in his or her 'flicker of truth' a revelation of the general? Postan resolves this thus: "their preference must be for generalizations which are not formulated but merely implied. They would imply the existence of underlying social laws by showing how a seemingly concrete phenomenon is shaped by the actions of general forces; they could make a unique phenomenon reflect the laws of society by presenting it as a microcosm—a particle of a universe and of a flow of event much wider than itself" (Postan,

---

[31] Flinn and Mathias (1982, p. v) seem to take a differently nuanced view of Postan's stance on generalisations: "throughout his career his work was informed by his insistence on the exact application of proper economic concepts to the interpretation of economic history, on the need to keep track of long-run trends, and on finding some common explanation of similar developments in different countries or regions."

writing in 1968, quoted by Daunton, 2017a, p. 165). In Martin Daunton's opinion expressed in 2017, "Postan's credo is still one that most Cambridge economic historians could accept" (Daunton, 2017a, p. 165). This revelatory assessment carries significance, as it comes from the recent holder of the same chair over the extended period from 1997 till 2014. It could be conjectured that, within the Faculty of Economics, Postan might have well approved of the methodological approach of Sheilagh Ogilvie, digging deep into medieval European history to interrogate spatial and temporal rigidities of narratives and interpretation, to expose variations and diversities, and using these to challenge generalised propositions about any hypothesised uniformity of patterns in historical processes.

Hostility Towards Cambridge Economists
"At the end of 1919, finding himself out of sympathy with events following the 1917 revolution, he left Russia in circumstances of some risk to himself" (Flinn & Mathias, 1982, p. iv). For a while before Postan left the Soviet Russia, "he was involved with radical socialism and the Jewish autonomy movement in the Ukraine, … though his Jewish identity was not subsequently of any importance" (Daunton, 2017a, p. 159). Maxine Berg, writing about his years at the LSE, observes: "Postan, now lapsed from his radical socialist youth, was widely conversant with Marx's writings, but no longer a Marxist" (Berg, 1996, p. 163). "His early years in Russia shaped some of his later career. John Habakkuk pointed out that 'there were many perceptions about peasant society and early industrialization which came naturally to someone educated in Russia before 1918'—and Postan was sceptical about Marxist interpretations of history and apologists for the Soviet Union.[32] … He was influenced by both the transformations in Russia and the Soviet Union—the emancipation of the serfs in Tsarist Russia and the destruction of the kulaks by Stalin formed an undercurrent in his thinking" (Daunton, 2017a, pp. 159, 162, and sources cited therein). Significantly for the subject at hand, Daunton (ibid., p. 162) notes: "neither was [Postan] sympathetic to the Marxist interpretation of a

---

[32] Keynes would easily qualify going just on the last paragraph of his reflection on his short visit to Russia in 1925: "Russia will never matter seriously to the rest of us, unless it be as a moral force. So, now the deeds are done and there is no going back, I should like to give Russia her chance; to help and not to hinder. For how much rather, even after allowing for everything, if I were a Russian, would I contribute my quota of activity to Soviet Russia than to Tsarist Russia! I could not subscribe to the new official faith any more than to the old. I should detest the actions of the new tyrants not less than those of the old. But I should feel that my eyes were turned towards, and no longer away from, the possibilities of things; that out of the cruelty and stupidity of Old Russia nothing could ever emerge, but that beneath the cruelty and stupidity of New Russia some speck of the ideal may lie hid" (Keynes, 1925). Then, the other usual suspects: Dobb would be on the top of Postan's list with his analysis of the Russian economy in the revolutionary phase (Dobb, 1928); and not far behind would be Joan Robinson and probably Nicky Kaldor for their positive allusions to Soviet planning in the context of their interventions in the war years about the reconstruction of Britain after the war.

transition from feudalism to capitalism that was propounded by Maurice Dobb in the Faculty of Economics at Cambridge, a man who inspired a post-war generation of Marxist economic history." Dobb's 1946 book, *Studies in the Development of Capitalism*, was greatly praised, especially by historians not predisposed to hostility towards Marxism, but, unsurprisingly, not by Postan who, as editor of the *Economic History Review* refused to carry reviews of it in the journal—"Dobb's class interpretation differed radically from Postan's Malthusian model in which different levels of agrarian society were affected by demographic variables" (Daunton, 2017a, p. 163); he also attacked the Marxian concept of primitive accumulation and its position in the development of capitalism. Daunton (ibid., p. 164) points out that "Postan's approach to capital did not rest on a Marxist account of exploitation of labour by capital or a conflict of classes, but on changing institutional patterns with a concern about the stultifying effect of the demise of personal ownership of capital." Flinn and Mathias (1982, p. v) report that Postan "for many years gave important lectures on Marxism at Cambridge", perhaps as a preemptive act of inoculating the young against the revolutionary virus. In terms of the many and complex dividing lines within the Faculty of Economics over the period, such visceral antipathy would probably not have made him warmly welcome in heterodox or radical circles within the Faculty. Martin Daunton (2017a, p. 159n1) writes: "personal knowledge of Chimen Abramsky and Anna Abulafia suggests that Postan was older and that he was a Menshevik."

Though for differing reasons, Munia Postan explicitly directed his ire at his Cambridge contemporaries and neighbours, notably Keynes and especially Kaldor. The Keynesians were attacked frontally in his inaugural lecture in 1939; and the tendency persisted all through, and Kaldor was (attempted to be) savaged in obviously ill-tempered, and arguably ill-judged, articles in *Encounter* in 1968, shortly after his retirement. Economists tended to theoretical generalisations which were derived by abstracting from the diversity of varied social realities. One can imagine that his complaint would be directed at devices such as the representative case or an average which ironed out the wrinkles of such local and deeper social variations which could potentially nullify the grand generalisation. Daunton extracts Postan's treatment of aspect of the *General Theory*, then hot off the press, from the inaugural lecture where he takes the discipline to task with respect to their understanding of key concepts and variables such as employment, interest, consumption and savings, liquidity preference: "How much do the economists know about them? Do they know or have they explained the complex social process which throughout history has determined the employment of income and its allocation to consumption or rather to consuming classes, or have they tried to discover what social forces lurk behind liquidity preferences?" (Postan, 1939, p. 23, quoted in Daunton, 2017a, p. 164). The ink had barely dried on the economics-testament according to Keynes, vetted and validated by his illustrious band of apostles of the Cambridge Circus; and here was a medieval historian audaciously firing off salvos of rudeness across the disciplinary divide.

For good measure, Postan widened the contours of his assault also to target Colin Clark and Nicky Kaldor on the basis of another, related, methodological complaint, viz., the sectoral classification of national income. Amusingly, the attack is triggered by an epiphanic experience at the Reform Club in London, and Munia Postan tells how: "Recently a company of officials and economists, taking their coffee at the Reform Club, were provoked by the sight of a group of government economists, filing out of the luncheon room, to try and fit them with a collective noun."[33] Naturally enough 'a pride of professors', 'a school of specialists', 'a gaggle of experts' were suggested. But the collective noun which found most support was 'a plague of economists'. And off went Postan and wrote up a stinging article with the same title, carried by *Encounter* (Postan, 1968a); it seems like a seamless continuation of the critiques he had launched three decades earlier in his inaugural lecture; it was an opening volley fired on arrival, this one was a parting valedictory shot.

"In my view the implied opprobrium is excessive. ... 'a catarrh of economists' is perhaps a better appellation"; but then Postan weighs in, regardless (Postan, 1968a, p. 47). He starts with a kind word of condescension: "many an economist in government service is ... able to do good simply by being sensible in a non-professional way", presumably so long as they do not open their disciplinary toolbox; but the trouble with them is that they "try to solve the largest number of problems from the least possible knowledge". He had already dispensed his critique of the macro tendencies towards aggregates and averages. Now it was the turn of the micro level to come under Postan's cosh. "The main vices of the few avowedly specific and micro-economic measures inspired by economists, come not from the aggregative and holistic preoccupations of economic theoreticians, but from the classificatory devices favoured by statisticians. Since the very early days of statistics as a social science, statisticians have adopted a 'sectoral' classification of economic activities [primary, secondary, tertiary] which has not become sanctified with academic usage. ... On the eve of the war this classification of economic sectors was given great publicity by Colin Clark's famous *Conditions of Economic Progress* (1940). In Clark's formulation the tripartite order of sectors was transformed from a mere classification into an itinerary of economic progress. The lesson he taught was that economic progress had been achieved in the past and was to be achieved in the future by transferring resources first from primary occupations to secondary ones and, finally, from secondary to tertiary ones. This sectoral itinerary is not out-of-date" (Postan, 1968a, p. 45).

---

[33] The scenario is not apocryphal: Wilfred Beckerman narrates how, in the late 1960s, government economists many of whom were members of the Reform Club had set up what he refers variably as the Treasury Cafeteria, or a dining club, or a Political Economy Club, that would meet once a month for lunch at the Reform Club; someone would introduce a topic, which would be seriously discussed after lunch. See Chap. 6, pp. 18–19, n13.

The origin of this particular doctrine and its justification are largely historical: a badly understood lesson of England's Industrial Revolution. In its popular version, the lesson postulates that all that happened to Britain's economy in the 18th and 19th centuries was industrialisation: a process whereby manufactures grew at the expense of agriculture. This piece of historical misconstruction—it neglects the immense development of British agriculture both before and during the Industrial Revolution—has inspired a recipe for the economic growth of underdeveloped territories in which growth has been similarly identified with industrialization. The country first to accept the recipe, unmitigated and undiluted, was Stalin's Russia, and under Russian inspiration it has now become the sovereign remedy Communists prescribe for all backward countries. But it is not so much the Communist example as the advice of the economists which has been responsible for the same recipe being applied equally universally and equally undiluted to India and other countries of Asia and Africa. For all their lip-service to agriculture and rural industries, the Indian planners, until very recently, devoted to industrial projects the lion's share of the country's scarce capital flow and almost the whole of its supply of intellectual and administrative talent. As a result, India has now equipped herself with a number of the most up-to-date and immensely costly (even if under-used) steel complexes and sophisticated engineering and electro-technical industries, while its agriculture remains unreformed, the country periodically undernourished, its villages poverty-stricken, and untold millions of its rural population unemployed or under-employed. (Postan, 1968a, p. 46)

The Indian pre-1966 example has been reproduced and Indian penalties have been paid in a number of other countries. [Apart from Mexico] most of the other under-developed countries continue to follow the Economist-Communist route. Needless to say, their failure to develop faster than they have done can be put down to a number of unfavourable factors, such as the insufficiency of foreign aid, the ruinous cost of armaments, the low prices for the commodities underdeveloped countries produce for export. But the misuse of their meagre supplies of indigenous capital and of the capital aid they received on over-ambitious, premature, and capital-intensive industrial projects is one of the main reasons why the poverty of the poor nations still remains largely unrelieved. And for this misuse, the sectoral fallacy is largely to blame. (Postan, 1968a, p. 46)

Postan's assessment of the Indian experience requires consideration. Between 1950–1951 and 1967–1968, real GDP grew at 3.6 per cent per year; stopping short of the Indo-Pak War of 1965 and the famines the following two years, the rate was 4.1 per cent per year. This has to be contrasted with virtual economic stagnation under British imperialist rule. The slower rate of increase of per capita was on account of a relatively high, and as Bhagwati and Srinivasan (1975, Table 1.1) point out, an accelerating, rate of growth of population between 1950–1951 into the 1960s. Postan's attribution of the persistence of poverty to the industrialisation strategies of the communist economies. Bhagwati and Srinivasan, as also several other mainstream economists, favoured an export-oriented, labour-intensive industrialisation path but, while the agrarian constraint was acknowledged by all, there was general consensus on the imperative of industrialisation. Postan wishes to ignore the positive experience of Japan and the negative experience of Latin America, and his complaint appears rather disingenuous in the absence of any recognition of the impact of the two centuries of colonisation. And before attacking industrialisation per se, he could have reflected on the role it played, at the least, in the production of the materials for the Soviet Army that kept Nazi Germany at bay. Subsequent pathways, be it Communist China or capitalist East Asian tigers, further validated the power of industrialisation. For larger countries, China and India, there was a question of a possibly delayed switch point from an inward, internal demand-oriented strategy towards a more export-led industrialisation path, but nothing in the experience of the Third World supports Postan's remarkable criticism of industrialisation, to his linking it to any misreading of the British industrial revolution, and even less to his critique of the Smith-Clark-Kuznets template of sectoral structural change underlying and propelling economic development. Many of the senior economists in the Faculty of Economics and the DAE had been directly involved in technically supporting Indian planning exercises, including Joan Robinson, Maurice Dobb, Richard Stone, Richard Goodwin, Brian Reddaway and Nicky Kaldor, during the 1950s and 1960s,[34] the period about which Postan makes his complaint. Ajit Singh, who called Nicky Kaldor the apostle of Third-World industrialisation, "tells how, when he first went to Cambridge, Nicholas Kaldor taught him three things: first, the only way for a country to develop is to industrialise; second, the only way for a country to industrialise so to protect itself; and third, anyone who says otherwise is being dishonest!"[35] A couple of years before Postan's tirade, Kaldor had published one of his classics on the causes of the slow rate of growth of the UK economy (Kaldor, 1996); a year later, he had extended the case for industrialisation to the developing economies in his treatment of strategic factors in economic development (Kaldor, 1967), a study of which might have been instructive and punctured some of the reductionisms of Postan's charges. Sukhamoy Chakravarty (1989, p. 239) shares his reading of Kaldor's policy position on the interactions between agriculture and industry: "he strongly emphasised the vital necessity for an effective land tax both for increasing the efficiency of land use, as well as for mopping up the agricultural surplus for productive investment outside agriculture. … Kaldor did not believe in a 'squeeze agriculture' thesis; what he was emphasising was the necessity for siphoning off a considerable part of the agricultural surplus which went into satisfying merely 'rentier' consumption, in order to sustain additional wage payments in industry. He believed that a two-way relationship between industry and agriculture could be mutually self-propelling in an upward direction. The argument is stated most succinctly in his Cornell Lectures 'Strategic factors in economic

---

[34] This is discussed in some detail in Chap. 11.
[35] Thirlwall, quoted in Saith (2019, p. 193) with original citation.

development' (Kaldor, 1967), although it appears in several other places as well. Kaldor's basic perception on this point would appear to me to be fundamentally valid for Indian economy even today." A friendly meeting with Sukhamoy Chakravarty, the erudite and vastly learned Indian economist, might have proven instructive.

Then he shifts aim and sets about Kaldor's Selective Employment Tax (S.E.T.).

> Other examples of sectoral fallacy will be found at home. None of them is more blatant or more familiar to the public than the Selective Employment Tax. Its underlying presuppositions and its avowed objects betray all the "realist" illusions of sectoral classification and all the irrelevancies of theoretical aggregates. Its authors have apparently assumed that services, taken together, possess economic characteristics and have effects on the economy which are sufficiently common and *sui generis* clearly to differentiate them from manufacturing occupations. Yet, while in this respect the authors of S.E.T. follow the letter of Colin Clark's scheme, they have in other respects run counter to its very philosophy. For it is contrary to that philosophy to conclude that the economy would prosper more and grow faster if its services were prevented from expanding. The authors of S.E.T. also believe that services—all services—contribute less to exports than manufacturing industries, that they are also less productive, or less able to increase their productivity by investment and technological improvements. These beliefs find no support in either experience or sense. The relative contribution which such services as the hotel industry, or City finance, make to current trade balances is greater than the relative contributions of such manufacturing industries as electrical appliances, bricks, or even coal and steel. As for productivities, it has recently been argued (by Professor Matthews and Mr. Feinstein, with much evidence to support them) that the increases of productivity per head in the United Kingdom since the War could be largely accounted for by the increasing productivity of labour in the services. In respect of both exports and productivities some services and manufactures have performed better than other services and manufactures; and in all of them, some individual firms performed better than others. To group, for purposes of legislative encouragement and punishment, all services apart from all industries is to be guilty of the worst crimes of irrelevant classification. S.E.T.'s errors of excessive aggregation are equally blatant. In the first place, it assumes that factors of production (including manpower) are wholly general and unspecific, so that by reducing the employment of labour in some occupations it would automatically augment the supply of labour to other occupations. In actual fact the reservoirs of manpower available to such services as the retail trade or banking are largely self-contained and uncommunicating—with the result that the labour released from offices and shops would not easily and spontaneously flow to engineering works and building sites. But what is most surprising is that the economists, of all people, should have taken so little account of the differing elasticities of the demand for labour in different industries. So inelastic has been the demand for labour, as well as the demand for services, in the retail trade and catering and hotel business, that the sole response to S.E.T. has been to pass on to the consumer the higher costs of the labour these businesses employ and to continue to employ that labour in the same numbers as before. However, S.E.T. is only one

instance of statistical concepts misapplied. Other instances, not so well known and not so generally disliked, could be cited by the dozen. So can also be the instances of the harm done by irrelevant economic aggregations. (Postan, 1968a, pp. 46–47)

There is scant engagement in Postan's complaint with the deeper structural malaise underlying UK economic decline manifest in what the emerging left-oriented Cambridge economists characterised as a process of premature deindustrialisation with sharp falls in the importance of manufacturing in the national economy. Kaldor's perspective was not an example in the form of a Keynesian short-term intervention, but rather an alternative long-term growth strategy as conveyed in two major books published in the previous two years (Kaldor, 1996, 1967). Kaldor, following Allyn Young and Gunnar Myrdal, amongst others, had crystallised a vision of the growth process where the key lay in increasing returns, dynamic economies of scale and a process of cumulative causation that diffused the externalities of the growth process into the economy; in turn, after a protected period of incubation, as appropriate, this industrial engine of growth would lead to an export-driven growth process, which in turn would take the pressure off any domestic measures to reduce or avoid budgetary deficits. He did not deem devaluation, a one-off price correction, as being sufficient for overcoming the structural roots of the loss of competitiveness of British manufacturing partly due to its historical pioneering role, and also due to running into a labour constraint as surplus labour ran out in agriculture, and wages in agriculture and industry converged towards near parity. This modern Cambridge paradigm provided the template for a desirable policy framework, which included the S.E.T. designed to ease the labour constraint deemed to be acting as a constraint on the growth of manufacturing.

S.E.T. might have had its problems as a policy instrument, but the Kaldorian perspective neither rests on it, nor falls with it; a contemporary review on its impact helps in assessing Postan's criticism. S.E.T. was introduced in 1966 by the first Harold Wilson Labour government, the rate increased in 1968 and again in 1969; it was halved in 1971, and abolished by the Edward Heath Conservative government, 1970–1974. It was regarded as the brainchild of Nicky Kaldor. In view of its significance and controversial nature, in early 1968 the Treasury asked Professor W. B. Reddaway, in his capacity as Director of the DAE, to set up into an enquiry into the impact of S.E.T. on prices, margins and productivity. This 5-year 'independent and strictly impartial' exercise[36] was a fearful task given the 'appalling' state of basic data on the SET paying sectors. Robin Marris, who carried out a review of the first report of the Reddaway enquiry (Marris, 1971), calls it "an outstanding example of economics applied to fiscal policy, marked by statistical thoroughness and ingenuity" (Marris, 1971, p. 393). He observes that "a more general report on the economic

---

[36] Marris notes that Reddaway "was evidently excellently served by his assistants, who are names as C. F. Pratten, P. M. Croxford, J. S. O'Donnell, C. H. Fletcher and T. S. Ward".

consequences of the tax can no longer be expected, presumably because a government already committed to abolishing S.E.T is not interested in whether it is good or bad" (ibid.). Reddaway asked "how the tax was borne, as between prices, service and profits; whether it increased labour productivity; whether it changed the type of labour employed and finally, what market mechanisms were responsible for such changes as were observed." The overall effect "was to reduce gross margins as compares with their long run trend by *more* than the effect of the increase in productivity, so that not only was the tax no passed on but profits were reduced and the consumer gained at the expense of the retailer" (Marris, 1971, p. 395). There was indeed a final report in 1973, where Reddaway felt "bound to record that our efforts leave me with the rather strong impression that SET probably did have some upward effect on productivity ... but I do not feel able to put a figure on it"; Allsopp (1973, p. 1284), in his review of the final report, observes that "those who disbelieve on *a priori* grounds the conclusion that, at least in some sectors, S.E.T. improved productivity have a lot of work to do". It is the prerogative of the reader to decide whether to travel with Postan's *ex ante* presumptions or Reddaway's *ex post* reports, though on a fair examination, Postan's full-blooded critiques of Keynesian and Kaldorian economics seem to be anaemic and misdirected.

Postan's 'plague' provoked a flurry of reactions[37] from diverse quarters, some widening the breach, others defending it—each with its own axe to grind. Harry Johnson downgrades the malaise from a plague to merely a catarrh. Apropos Postan's lurching criticism that economists deal systemically with aggregates and averages, with policies applied to the totality without regard to the diversity of its constituent units, that is, industries, firms, individuals, Harry Johnson's response is equally dismissive: "to ask the economist to predict the behaviour of the individual unit in the system, and even more demandingly to recommend policies to alter that behaviour to something more satisfactory, is to ... argue that a life assurance company is improperly managed if it cannot predict the precise day and hour at which each one of its policy-holders will die, and does not attempt to furnish each with a personal survival-maximisation programme" (Johnson, 1968b, p. 51). Johnson rejects Postan's approach "anti-scientific and pro-judgmental in the extreme" (Johnson, 1968b, p. 53) and fears that Postan "really believes in priestly magic rather than science" (ibid., p. 51). But this notwithstanding, Johnson predictably stretches Postan's critique of Keynesian methods into a full-scale attack on the Keynesian policy paradigm; and similarly following his own agenda, Beloff targets Cambridge economists, highjacking Postan's words to his own ends.

---

[37] *Times Literary Supplement* (24 May 1968), *New Statesman* and *Financial Times* devoted many pages of discussion on Postan's article. Notable reactions come from Harry Johnson, Max Beloff, Peter Wiles, Michael Stewart and "the author of the leading article in the *TLS*".

Max Beloff, soon to join the Thatcher camp and be elevated by her to a knighthood in 1980 and for good measure to be made a life peer a year later, wrote teasingly to draw Postan away from all qualifications in criticising Keynesian economists. "Professor Kaldor who is generally credited with being the brain behind S.E.T. is characterized as having qualities of 'near genius'. It is as though one said of some Harley Street oracle that his medical skill is superb—what a pity all his patients die!" "Historically the record of economists since the discipline became a recognized one has been almost uniformly dismal"; "Keynes himself ... was woefully at sea on many matters of the highest practical importance, particularly in the international field"; "he was probably never so harmlessly occupied as when pursuing his homosexual amours as so entertainingly presented by Mr. Michael Holroyd in his recent biography of Lytton Strachey"; "some economists are sensitive, thoughtful, and skilful human beings. Of course it is possible for an economist to be intelligent in the same way as it is possible for a 'starlet' to be chaste. It is just very difficult" (Beloff, 1968, p. 91).

Michael Stewart, author of *Keynes and After* (1967), and incidentally, Nicky Kaldor's son-in-law, responded from Kenya, where he was then stationed on an advisory assignment, with a thoughtful and colourful critique of Postan's critique. Reading Postan's piece, Stewart says, "reminded me of that Renoir film in which the house-party sallies forth on Sunday morning and shoots every bird and rabbit for miles around. Bang! Bang! Bang! Goes Professor Postan, and down they crash. Aggregates, economists, Corporation Tax, existing statistical classifications, macro-economics, industrialisation in the developing countries, S.E.T.—before long the landscape is littered with their corpses." Stewart continues, "but closer inspection of this scene of indiscriminate slaughter raises doubts. Are the victims of Professor Postan's marksmanship really dead? Are they, indeed, even wounded?" (Stewart, 1968, p. 54). Stewart proceeds then to demolish Postan's propositions and concludes: "Professor Postan's real trouble is simply that he has got things upside down. The economy has not got into a mess because there has been too little micro-economic intervention by economists. It has got into a mess because the economists' advice on *macroeconomics* (emphasis in the original) has not been listened to. If the correct Keynesian macroeconomic remedies had been applied to the economy in recent years, the economy would not be in a mess. But they were not applied; and they were not applied because they did not suit the politicians. ... A plague of economists? Come, come, Professor Postan, be fair. Surely what you mean is a plague of politicians" (ibid., p. 56).

It is possible to elicit several points from Postan's response to his piece (Postan 1968b). First, he reacts to "the author of the leading article in the *Times Literary Supplement* of 24 May ... [who] obviously belongs to the same chapel of worshippers of *laissez-faire* as Morgenstern or Hayek or Jewkes, and like them has nothing but contempt for all attempts to interfere with the works of economic Providence. It is therefore not surprising that he should find the true causes of Britain's predicament in socialist meddling with economic processes …; few economic historians, however, will agree with him." Postan explicitly distances himself from this ideological stance. Second: "he prises himself out of Beloff's unwanted embrace: "I must, above all, disassociate myself from the point of view represented by my friend Professor Max Beloff. The uninitiated may easily mistake him for a supporter of mine, albeit an extreme one. This he certainly is not. We may be co-belligerents but we are not allies. Professor Beloff holds the entire occupation of economists in contempt and wants governments to reject their counsel root and branch. Whereas I, for all my strictures, regard the economists with the greatest respect." Postan thus seems to distance himself from the embryonic Thatcherite wing of politics. Third: after picking on the criticisms by Harry Johnson and Michael Stewart, Postan restates his essential message, this time in more temperate and substantially qualified terms:

> The criticisms in my article were largely directed at the narrowly economic range of economic advice of the public debate of economic problems. In my view the advice of the economists and their contribution to the debate do not draw fully enough upon the specialized knowledge of other social sciences of men of affairs. But the contention I pressed hardest was that within their own, purely economic, range the services of economists were excessively concerned with national aggregates and insufficiently informed with ideas about the separate components of the economy, its structural and institutional problems. My recommendations were to match. What was necessary was not to do away with the services of the economists, but to back them with the cognate expertise of other sciences and to infuse them with a larger dose of micro-economic understanding, i.e., with ideas about the influence affecting the individual factors of production, labour, capital and management, or the factors shaping the structure and behaviour of individual industries and firms. (Postan, 1968b, pp. 85–86)

With all these fresh qualifications and acknowledgements, there is hardly much left of Postan's original critique; and "the contention he pressed hardest" would also have dissolved almost entirely should Postan have visited the establishment, research projects and annual reports of the Department of Applied Economics. When all this is picked away, what seems to remain is an attitude of visceral animosity towards Keynesian and Kaldorian theoretical framing and policy approaches. If such an orientation characterised Postan over the duration of his lengthy tenure (stretching from 1938 till 1965) as the Chief Whip of the economic historians at the Faculty of History, there would perhaps not be much intellectual enthusiasm or personal bridges to build collaborations with the Faculty of Economics and the DAE in areas of common interest and potential benefit. This would perhaps explain Charles Feinstein's observation that he felt greater affinity amongst the economists at the Faculty of Economics and Politics than with the economic historians at the Faculty of History. Postan had held steady with his criticisms of economists from the time of occupying the Chair to the time of vacating it; Daunton observes that the same constancy also applied to Postan's own historical method.

That a personality clash between two charismatic, Irrepressible and Incorrigible prima donnas might have contributed to Postan's vitriol perhaps cannot be ruled out. Eric Hobsbawm's recollection of Postan from his student days is evocative: "Looking somewhat like a red-haired Neanderthal survivor and speaking through a heavy Russian accent, he was nevertheless so brilliant and compelling a lecturer that he filled Mill Lane at nine o'clock in the morning … Everyone of his lectures—intellectual-rhetorical dramas in which a historical thesis was first expounded, then utterly dismantled, and finally replaced by his own version—was a holiday from interwar Cambridge insularity" (quoted in Daunton, 2017a, p. 159). And Flinn and Mathias (1982, p. vi) add: "He could project an epithet like an arrow, glinting in the sun before it struck." On the other side, there are the accounts of Nicky Kaldor. His biographer, Thirlwall (1987b, p. 519), refers to his "intellect and passion; dominant and controversial; style, charm and sense of fun which made it impossible not to listen to what he had to say; rare charisma and magnetic quality which made it difficult not to fall under his spell; captivating power of the ju-ju magicians; ender his audience by the heavily accented flow of English prose; more English than the English; the image of a rotund and jovial medieval monk holding forth in intellectual discourse fits him perfectly." For Geoff Harcourt (2001, p. 349), Nicky was "a larger-than-life figure: a completely honest and ultimately lovable man who always said what he thought, who loved and lived life to the full"; for Bob Rowthorn (who incidentally had a very public spat with him in print over Kaldor's 'laws'), "he was a brilliant economist and not in this school at all, not defensive, too interested in creating new ideas; a jolly person, full of life, a wonderful man" (Rowthorn, 2008); Wynne Godley (2008) characterised him as "a Falstaffian intellect who thought with his gut; he emanated genius, was very persuasive and would never give up" (Godley, 2008). Then, Thirlwall points to Kaldor being "a life-long socialist"; and to "his view of economics as a moral science—a branch of ethics in the Cambridge tradition" (Thirlwall, 1987b, p. 519). To all this might be added Kaldor's propensity to work his hypotheses, theories and laws, using 'stylised facts' which represented the compressed bottom-line structural features of complex historical processes and trends—a proclivity towards abstracting from and reducing complexities into manageable generalisations that were diametrically opposed to Postan's method.

The Turn to Business Studies-I, David Joslin 1965–1970
Post-Postan, the Chair of Economic History changes direction and focus, with three subsequent appointments in succession of business historians. David Joslin's tenure, which could potentially have been a very lengthy one, was sadly brief, cut short when he died suddenly in 1970, aged 45, just five years after assuming the chair. Like Clapham, he wrote, on invitation, a substantial 'centenary' history of a bank, Bank of London and South America (Joslin, 1963), but further studies on Latin America remained still in outline form. It may be speculated, from the vantage point of Cambridge economics, that such a

specialist on modern Latin American economic history might have created a wide interface of potential interaction, especially as Latin American economies were then on the cusp of turbulent periods of economic and political upheavals. Following the Report on Latin American Studies by the J. H. Parry Parliamentary Committee, five 'Parry Centres' had been established in Oxford, London, Cambridge, Glasgow and Liverpool; the Centre of Latin American Studies (CLAS)[38] in Cambridge was formed in 1966, the year after Joslin began his tenure at the Faculty of History.

At the Faculty of Economics, till Jose Gabriel Palma settled into the Faculty, there had been only a slim presence of this region in the profiles of Faculty staff limited mainly to John Wells and his research on the complexities of the then ongoing Brazilian 'miracle', though there was another significant link through the presence of the economist E. V. K. 'Valpy' FitzGerald who was on the staff of the Course on Development in the 1970s and had a serious specialisation in Latin American economics, especially Peru; and another connection via the sociologist David Lehmann, Director of the Centre for 1990–2000, who had run a research project in Chile, based in the DAE in an earlier period.[39]

But, in the brief years that Joslin held the Chair, there was a prospect, even if speculative, of catalysing the study of Latin American economies in the SPS Committee and in the Faculty of Economics. For one, "the Parry Committee had been set up in 1962, with the initiative coming primarily from the Foreign Office ... [which was essentially concerned about British business and the decline of British trade in Latin America, as well as the lack of academic research on the region in Britain. That was the impetus for the Parry Committee, and it chose the model of multi-disciplinary area studies centres concentrating on postgraduate studies and research" (Miller, 2016). "Development economics was just getting under way in the 1960s and one of the things that you continually read in the Parry Committee minutes on their visits to different universities was that Latin America was of key interest to economists then because of inflation of the kind experienced in Argentina or Chile or Brazil in the 1950s and early 1960s. ... Cambridge had very few researchers in sociology and

---

[38] CLAS celebrated its 50th Anniversary in 2016, and a Symposium organised for the occasion offers a rich spectrum of recollections and assessments of the past and present of the experience of Latin American studies in Cambridge; of particular relevance in the present context would be the presentations of Rory Miller, PhD student 1970–1973; David Brading, CLAS Director, 1973–1990; David Lehmann, CLAS Director, 1990–2000, and Joanna Page, then the Director of CLAS. http://www.latin-american.cam.ac.uk/news/50th-anniversary-1966-2016, http://www.latin-american.cam.ac.uk/latest-news-and-events/50-years-media/memories-reflections-clas

[39] After Christopher Platt, Director during 1969–1972, Brian Van Arkadie filled in as Director till David Brading began his lengthy tenure in 1973. Brian was an economist, as Rory Miller notes "not really a Latin Americanist"; he was a Fellow, as was Platt, in Queens' College; he served as Director of Studies in economics in Queens and lectured in the development courses in Cambridge, though he was not on the staff of the Faculty of Economics and Politics. Van Arkadie's tenure was too short to develop any firm links between CLAS and the Faculty of Economics and Politics.

contemporary politics in Latin America until the Social and Political Sciences degree was established." Thus, it could be surmised that Economics and SPS, alongside economic history, could well have had an inside track in Cambridge.

Rory Miller, an early PhD from the CLAS, writes that "when the Parry Committee visited Cambridge in 1963/1964, they talked to around 13 people who all had interests in Latin American studies from different perspectives", with apparently little representation from economics; "three Cambridge scholars were heavily involved … Jack Street, who was a member of the Parry Committee and then the first Director of the Cambridge Centre; Clifford Smith, who later Director of the Centre for Latin American Studies in Liverpool; and David Joslin, who … became fascinated with the economic history of the region. These three—Street, Joslin and Smith—were probably the driving forces at the time the Parry Committee came to Cambridge. … In the 1960s … Cambridge University Press also became very interested in Latin American Studies. … Cambridge University Press was beginning to establish area studies journals … As of 1964/1965, CUP was already talking about a 'Journal of Latin American Studies' It eventually began publication in 1969. … David Joslin was one of the first two editors … but he died suddenly the following year. Cambridge University Press also started publishing its Latin American monographs series in 1967 with David Joslin and Jack Street as the editors. The Centre certainly had a bumpy ride in the first few years, with momentum being lost as Directors moved on (Brian van Arkadie, who was not really a Latin Americanist, replaced Platt in 1972), but then the appointment of David Brading and David Lehmann meant more sustained activity and continuity from the mid-1970s."[40] Lehmann recalls: "I arrived in 1973, but initially I was in Development Studies. For people like me, the Centre was a point of reference, a place to go and feel at home … There was a lot of enthusiasm around Latin America which was thought to be the next great hope for social revolution" (Lehmann, 2016).

He recalls an event in 1976. "There had been a coup in Brazil in 1964, a coup in Argentina in 1966, and another creeping coup from about 1972 in Argentina with the full seizure of power in 1976. Pinochet came to power in 1973, and there was Uruguay as well; those really were very dark days: it seemed that some sort of fascism had installed itself definitively. So we had this idea that we would do a seminar on the state and economic development in Latin America and it turned into a big event with about 150 people. It was just a series of lectures but all the top people were there: Fernando Henrique Cardoso, Guillermo O'Donnell, Ernesto Laclau. It had been planned as a small seminar but mushroomed into a series of big lectures. That event had a big effect on Latin American Studies in the UK." David Joslin would probably been at the centre of all that, and given the special interest in Latin American

---

[40] Extracted from Miller (2016).

economics, some Cambridge economists as well; but his early death preempted such possibilities.

The Turn to Business Studies-II, Donald Coleman 1971–1981
Donald Cuthbert Coleman (1920–1995) was the fourth holder of the Chair during 1971–1981, and "the interface between economics and history was his milieu" (Harte, 1995). He enrolled at LSE in 1939, but began only in 1946 after service in the war; "In early 1946 ... Donald was appointed to manage the Hotel Tramontano in Sorrento, which was an officers' rest camp, and he went straight from there to LSE in the autumn of 1946" (Mathias & Thompson, 2002, p. 171). There, he informed his tutor, Nicky Kaldor, that "he did not now need to learn economics, he informed his tutor Nicky Kaldor, having done so while running a chain of requisitioned hotels in Italy and he turned instead to economic history ..."(Harte, ibid.).

In 1951 he was appointed lecturer in industrial history "as part of a scheme to inject some civilizing influences from the humanities into the curriculum of engineering students from Imperial College" (Mathias & Thompson, 2002, p. 173). He wrote a 'magisterial' multi-volume history of Courtaulds (Coleman, 1969a, b, 1980), and later "a short but highly perceptive account of History and the Economic Past (1987), which he called 'the rise and fall of economic history in Britain'" (Harte, ibid.).

"These were the guiding principles of Coleman's scholarship: no history without theory; no simply descriptive writing, which was mere antiquarianism; and also, no ideological manipulation of the evidence. On occasion, when being dismissive of both mindless story-telling and arid number-crunching, he referred to his style as being 'analytical narrative'" (Mathias & Thompson, 2002, p. 170). Coleman, an iconoclast, "was recognized as a star and an irritant at both LSE and Cambridge" (Harte, ibid.), and became "the scourge of such intellectual red herrings as 'industrial revolution', 1966; 'mercantilism', 1969; and 'proto-industrialization' 1983" (Farnie & Tweedale, 2009, p. 60).

Mercantilism[41] was dismissed "with a trenchant side-swipe as 'that misleading and cumbersome portmanteau, that unnecessary piece of historical baggage'" (Mathias & Thompson, 2002, p. 175); "the economy which Coleman [in his 'Labour in the English Economy of the Seventeenth Century', 1946] described, with its necessarily considerable dependence on child labour because of the demographic structure, its inherent features of irregularity and seasonality of employment with long intervals of idleness, and strong leisure preferences induced by the extremely limited array of consumer goods, except for beer, on which any increased money income might be spent, was in marked

---

[41] Incidentally, across Sidgwick Site, 'The New Mercantilism' was the title of Joan Robinson's Inaugural Lecture in 1966 (Robinson J., 1966).

contrast to the received wisdom of an economy shaped by laws and regulations which reflected adherence to some nebulous concept of a 'mercantilist system'. In his 'Industrial Growth and Industrial Revolutions'—incidentally, a paper read first at Professor Postan's seminar in Cambridge in November 1953—Coleman attacked "the indiscriminate proliferation of 'industrial revolutions' in the academic literature"; he asks: "may it not be that the term has achieved its wide application at the expense of losing its true significance?" (Coleman, 1956, p. 1). Significantly (in view of the subsequent cliometrics revisions), Mathias and Thompson (2002, p. 177) comment: "presciently, he observed that diligent number-crunching might produce an 'index in which even the classical industrial revolution can be made if not quite to disappear at least to appear as no more than a small change in the industrial growth rate' [Coleman, 'Industrial Growth and Industrial Revolutions', *Economica*, 1956]. Then, a couple of years after retirement, his ire fixed on 'proto-industrialization', when he "rather more pointedly deflated a new concept 'rattling around in the corridors of economic history' in his trenchant article on 'Proto-industrialization: A Concept Too Many', in which this new-fangled and half-baked theory that domestic, putting-out, industry flourished in harsh mountainous regions and paved the way for the transition from feudalism to capitalism by stimulating real mechanised industrialisation was dismissed as an exercise in which 'the familiar findings of various scholars [are] dressed up in long words and sociological finery' [Coleman, "Proto-industrialization: A Concept Too Many", *Economic History Review*, 1983]. Subjected to empirical testing the concept simply disintegrated: many industries never had a 'putting-out' phase; some were capitalistic from the start; many regions once prominent in 'proto-industrial development' never moved on, but subsequently de-industrialised and reverted to agricultural economies. It was a devastating critique, although a few proto-industrial believers refused to renounce their faith" [42] (Mathias & Thompson, 2002, p. 177).

He came to be increasingly disenchanted at LSE with what he saw as poor management, administration and policy: "He had detected increasing alienation of staff from students in the 1960s, for which he blamed the administration's policy of allowing lecturers to opt out of first-year teaching and making promotion entirely dependent on publications, sending off a blistering letter in 1965 denouncing the School's rulers for deliberately disparaging the prime

---

[42] "One of his principal objections to 'proto-industrialisation' theory was that it brought such conceptual confusion, as he saw it, to the pre-eighteenth century debate ('industrialisation before industrialisation'), while so much use of the same term had added to terminological and conceptual confusion both chronologically and in different contexts—the industrial revolution 'of the late bronze age', that of the thirteenth century, of the period 1540–1640, the second, and subsequent industrial revolutions et al.—their profusion flourishing in inverse proportion to their conceptual specification. Popularising the term spelled 'dangerous multiplicity'. This was, at heart, a vigorous defence of the empirical and historiographical identity of the English Industrial Revolution" (Mathias & Thompson, 2002, pp. 182–183).

purpose of university teaching. In turn, he alienated the School's Director by daring to write to *The Times* without seeking permission; he quarrelled rather publicly with the School's Librarian; and he became disillusioned with the lack of leadership and downright incompetence of his mentor, Jack Fisher" (Mathias & Thompson, 2002, pp. 180–181). Cambridge beckoned (again) when the incumbent David Joslin, aged 45, died suddenly in 1970, and Donald Coleman was installed as the Professor of Economic History.

In the Cambridge years, Mathias and Thompson (2002, pp. 189–190) well capture Coleman's unhappiness over the rising tendencies in the practice of the discipline of economic history:

> Already in his inaugural lecture at Cambridge in 1972 he showed his disquiet over 'What has happened to Economic History?' (the title of the lecture), giving a statistical demonstration of the rise and fall of its popularity as a school and undergraduate subject since 1945, and attributing its declining appeal to the then recent fashion for reducing all economic history to the sophisticated number-crunching of the econometric historians and their mathematical models borrowed from economics. In 1987 he elaborated on this theme with his history of economic history, *History and the Economic Past. An account of the Rise and Decline of Economic History in Britain*. A dispassionate analytical narrative of the founding fathers of economic history as a distinct discipline, this progressed into a passionate exposure of what Donald saw as its decline from the point at which … in 1970, the econometricians attempted a quantitative take-over of the subject, and the craze for social history captured many journals and university departments, a subject which had become 'a meaningless catch-all term' embracing labour history, demographic history, psycho-history, family history, women's history, magic history, mentalités, crowds, sports, crime, literacy, and children, and offering exciting and seductive articles on witchcraft, musical taste, menstruation, and rituals, in contrast to the 'unexciting offerings typically to be found in the pages of the *Economic History Review*'.

Mathias and Thompson (2002, p. 183) refer to his "withering scorn for more recent attempts to promote an enterprise culture by invoking the 'values' of the Industrial Revolution and the myth of Adam Smith's supposedly unequivocal support of the free market". "At the root of long-term business success, he saw human effort. It was fashionable at the time the book was being written to decry 'entrepreneurship', excluded almost by definition from a perfectly competitive economy (as current neo-classical theory assumed), but to those seeking to understand enterprise in the real world it was different. 'The entrepreneur', concluded Donald Coleman, 'having been exorcised by abstractions, has reappeared through the back door. He insists upon intruding into the model.'" (Mathias & Thompson, 2002, p. 186; Coleman is quoted from the third volume of his study of Courtaulds.)[43]

---

[43] This paradoxical, if not bizarre, disappearance of the core driver of capitalism, the entrepreneur, from neoclassical models is ruefully acknowledged in the conversation between Tony Atkinson and Nick Stern (Atkinson & Stern, 2017); see Chap. 14, of the present work.

One can wonder what choice of invective Coleman might have employed in relation to the Walrasian tradition of neoclassicism and its variants installed by Frank Hahn in the Faculty of Economics and Politics—though it is not difficult to imagine lively cross-boundary interdisciplinary discussions with the likes of Nicky Kaldor over the history and future of British manufacturing, perhaps with expositions of Verdoornian and Kaldorian 'laws' of capitalist dynamics, cumulative causation spirals etc. For Coleman, as business historian, there is a clear sense of Schumpeterian processes of the creative destruction unleashed by the first industrial revolution. "'In a context of unprecedented population growth', he wrote, '…in spite of the dislocation of labour which it involved, in spite of the hardship to many, a vast amount of far more regular employment came into being in the course of the nineteenth century than had ever been known amongst the unemployed masses of the pre-industrial world. New jobs came into being, new categories of employment opened up, new skills replaced old skills. The skilled mechanic did not "survive" the industrial revolution, he was created by it.' In his view social and intellectual changes were integral to the transformation—a 'vital conjunction of changes in which population growth, large-scale and extensive industrial investment and the remarkably pervasive effects of the application of science to industry'" (Mathias and Thompson, 2002, p. 184; quotations within text from Coleman (1956), as cited therein). The Industrial Revolution was more than a catalogue of social disaster.

Negley Harte (1995) wrote that "he took early retirement from his chair in 1981, before such activity became enforcedly fashionable, largely to escape the administration he conspicuously found irksome, and to concentrate on a life of productive scholarship."

12.4 Post-War Period-II, 1980s: Unravelling and Divergence

12.4.1 At the Faculty of History

The Turn to Business Studies-III, Barry Supple 1981–1993
It seemed that the position of Professor of Economic History in the Faculty of History had become the province of business history; Barry Supple was the third in the line of such historians to occupy the chair; his tenure lasted from 1981 to 1993. The work that established Barry Supple's credentials as an economic historian, the commercial crisis in England in the mid-seventeenth century (Supple, 1964) and the long-sweep study of the Royal Exchange Assurance since 1720 (Supple, 1970) would not offer any docking points with the research interests in the Faculty of Economics as then constituted, and even

less bearing in mind the campaign for a return to theoretical orthodoxy.[44] That said, Supple had one firm link with the Faculty of Economics, through his association with Robin Matthews with whom he had been a co-author, including on a paper on mainly on Marshall's stance on the relation between economic history and economics. Paradoxically, this partnership with Matthews could offer one explanation for Barry Supple being given the crucial position of disciplinary specialist on the first-stage committee appointment by the General Board of the University to conduct the very controversial, and seemingly motivated, Review of the Department of Applied Economics—the process, allegedly instigated by Robin Matthews and Frank Hahn in their campaign against the local groups of economists of heterodox persuasions.[45] As such, this tenure could not be regarded as one of lost opportunities of partnership between the two disciplinary branches, as none were really created. Unlike the earlier tenures of Joslin and Coleman, there wasn't much potential dissipated since arguably there wasn't much in the first place.

Modern Times: Martin Daunton 1997–2015
In an interview, Martin Daunton (2008) opens a window on some of his early experiences and influences that shaped his career. He went to a grammar school in Barry, in South Wales; the school had also produced David Joslin and Sir John Habakkuk. Of the "people whom I was reading when I was a student, the people I admired then and still do. It was Michael Postan, the Middle Ages and thinking about the constant balancing between resources and population"; "always greatly admired his [Tony Wrigley's] work" and which had "a huge influence"—still in the domain of the interactions between resources and population. On the other side, he mentions two left-oriented historians: "a person I read a lot when I was student, and now would not see as such a great influence was E. P. Thompson. I always found intellectual problems with the interpretation of the class-conscious proletariat and so on; I would now be much more critical of his interpretation"; and, Eric Hobsbawm, "whose work again had a big impact when I was a student. Again, I would be much more critical of his approach now, but reading his early essays on labouring men and primitive rebels again I found very interesting and provocative." He kept away from the quantitative side, but he "very greatly admires" the work of "very great scholars like Charles Feinstein … that provides a basis for a lot of other things". And he "never accepted the approach of the cliometricians, of counter-factual

---

[44] Supple's third work on the history of the British coal industry over the years of the two Wars (Supple, 1987) could have held potential interest, though by the time it appeared, those battles had been fought and won or lost in the coalmines, in Thatcherite Government corridors, and the main groups that would have had an interest in this research had been purged from the DAE, in part due to the DAE Review in which Supple had played a role in the early stages.
[45] Ironically, that Supple was at hand was partly owing to the circumstance that Dd Coleman had decided to take early retirement well short of the mandatory retirement age, probably one of several who took up the 'opportunity' offered by Thatcher's cuts on university budgets.

history, which always seemed to me—seeing the work of Donald and Deirdre McCloskey—to assume markets function without asking how markets were created, and how they differ between different societies, and vary over time"; it would be revealing to learn how, in Daunton's framework, the market, say for labour, was created. He wished to be part of "a wider history faculty", but then cites his experience at UCL where a collaborative degree between the historians and the economists on account of "its tensions because the economists wanted a highly mathematical intellectual formation for the students, which the students didn't have. And in the end that joint degree was abandoned, and I then moved much more into history itself." But, speaking in 2008, he strikes a note of optimism: "Now there are also in Cambridge economic historians within the faculty of economics who will have a different approach, will be much more attuned to economic theory, but we can behave in a way which is complementary, so there does not need to be a tension. And I think what is now happening is that there is a coming together ... The work that I've done myself recently on taxation for example will use some of the terminology from the economics field. From game theory, about credible commitment and so on, but trying to understand all that historically by using archives. So I think it is perfectly possible to bring these things together" (ibid.). The somewhat unusual and seemingly one-off illustration he might have in mind, notwithstanding his rejection of cliometrics, is his joint research and co-authored article with two mainstream economists from the Faculty of Economics, Jayasri Dutta, an applied econometrician, and Toke Aidt, the latter styling his title as 'political economics'. The choice of approach and method in their modelling and testing of the "the retrenchment hypothesis and the extension of franchise in England and Wales" indicates Daunton's acquiescence to the epistemology and methodology of mainstream applied economics (Aidt, Daunton and Dutta, 2010).

Apart from the regulation period treatment of British economic and social history in two volumes covering the entire period since 1750 (Daunton, Progress and Poverty in 1995, and Wealth and Welfare in 2007), his specialisation has been taxes and public finance, with the scope of the agenda conveyed in an early paper his chosen title—"How to pay for the War: state, society and taxation in Britain, 1917–1924"—resonates with Keynes's famous work. "It is over the Budget ... that Parliaments for some time to come will find the fundamental party cleavage ... involving, as it must, in the society of today, the sharpest issues between class and class—between those who, whether by hand or by brain, live by producing and those who live by merely owning—[that] will presently dominate our politics" (Daunton, 1996, p. 882). The ramifications of the central theme are explored in another pair of volumes—Trusting Leviathan, and Just Taxes—covering the long period from 1799 to 1979 (Daunton, 2001, 2002) with another work that extends the analysis for the period since 1970s (Buggeln, Daunton and Nutzenadel et al., 2017).

About himself, Martin Daunton sums it up in saying "[I] pursued a somewhat eclectic approach which brought together several of the strands mentioned above" [pursued by previous holders of the chair]. He confirmed that all holders of the chair had broadly followed Postan's method, presumably including himself in this. The temporal and geographical spread of his intellectual interests and concerns—as visible on his webpage—brings to the fore the potential for what he calls 'a coming together' between Cambridge economists and Cambridge historians, emphasising 'complementarities' over 'tensions' that dog the equation.[46] Realising this objective, intrinsically desirable as it is, would require overcoming serious obstacles. Both houses are internally divided, and that makes generalisations problematic. Cliometrically minded economic historians might find it viable to cross the bridge to mainstream applied economists and econometricians, just as more classically oriented economic historians might find it intellectually congenial to collaborate with quantitative heterodox economists; but not all cross-combinations are likely to be feasible. For instance, in the joint work with his mainstream economist co-authors, Daunton would willy nilly have to buy into the mainstream route and thought map of the theoretical, epistemological and methodological approach of contemporary mainstream economics, belying what would otherwise appear to be the affinities of his body of work with heterodox, rather than neoclassical, approaches.

And commendably (in principle) again, Martin Daunton "is particularly concerned to engage with policy makers and practitioners with an interest in the historical background to current issues",[47] a proclivity that he seems to share with Sheilagh Ogivlie, whom Daunton alludes to as Postanian in approach. But, especially for Postanians, could this practice of "drawing of lessons from [the] history" of others not pose a contradiction? Ogilvie is ostensibly rather more flighty in this regard with spectacular leaps from medieval Germany to contemporary developing economies, defying Postan's strictures against historical generalisation, and his strong attacks on economists, who are inherently generalisers, for not following this tenet. An awkward balance then has to be found on the tightrope between a postulate of extreme path

---

[46] The Professor of Economic History at the Faculty of History held an ex-officio membership of the Faculty Board in Economics, though as a general rule there was little presence or participation in this regard. Patterns of attendance might have varied with different chair holders, but the economic historian from history was a rare sighting on the economics terrain; in the earlier decades at least, there seemed to be few transactions between the two spaces—for instance, Phyllis Deane had little to do with the Faculty of History, and likewise, Charles Feinstein found his intellectual environment in Economics much more congenial and productive and did not stray across. Jane Humphries was on the Faculty Board during the 1990s and recalls that the professors of economic history from the History side were almost never present at the Board's meetings, though Barry Supple attended occasionally (perhaps in view of his role as a member of the committee set up by the General Board for the controversial Review of the Department of Applied Economics, a process widely thought in Economics to have been instigated by Supple's economic-historian friend Robin Matthews and Frank Hahn; see Chap. 9).

[47] http://www.martindaunton.co.uk/

dependence, with the risk of a slide into post-modern nihilism or silo-ism, and presumption of generalisability. Making deep history travel to very different and distant current contexts might require packing a bag of assumptions whose weight might render the journey not worth embarking on.

12.4.2 At the Faculty of Economics: Turbulence, Transitions and Affinities

The 1980s witnessed the launch of the full-scale campaign by the mainstream group of economists, led by Frank Hahn and Robin Matthews, to gain control over the Faculty and purge heterodox lineages from it. It also constitutes the decade of kaleidoscopic transition for economic history, with the dissolution of some of the older teams and interests through closures, retirements and departures and the emergence of new formations through an inflow of fresh arrivals. Once the foundations of historical statistics had been laid for the downstream analysis of structural change and economic policy, the DAE's historians dispersed. Apart from the specialist historical statisticians, there were several others in the DAE with interests in the proximate historical dimensions of contemporary issues of economic policy. With the big changes at the DAE after the closure of the CEPG and CGP and the impact of the DAE Review culminating in the takeover of DAE management by the orthodox group of economists, those in this disparate group fashioned their own paths: Phyllis Deane retired in 1982; Nick von Tunzelmann moved away to Sussex in 1984; Jill Rubery left in 1989 for Manchester to build her very impressive subsequent career there; Martin Weale, always with a deep interest and proficiency in the interrogation and use of numbers for policy purposes, relocated from the DAE when the CGP was shut down and joined the Faculty as a lecturer in 1988 till 1995 when he leapfrogged to the position of Director of the NIESR; Michael Kitson continued at the DAE, part of the Alan Hughes's team on industrial economics and business research; and the appointment to Faculty positions of Solomos Solomou in 1985, and Sheilagh Ogilvie in 1989; with Sara Horrell, who had started in the Labour Studies group in the DAE also relocating later in 1992 to a Faculty position; and Toke Aidt being recruited in 1998. The erstwhile cohesive and unitary DAE project of economic history focussed on the setting up of the foundations for historical national accounts and accounting systems lapsed; there followed an unravelling and separations into disparate and mostly independent strands, with some inherent polarisations in substantive interests and methodological approach. While there were no formal subgroups or teams, it is possible tentatively to suggest four different combinations of staff with interests (though not exclusively) in economic history: Jane Humphries and Sara Horrell, with an overlap perhaps with Phyllis Deane, though not for long; Michael Kitson, Solomos Solomou and Martin Weale; Sheilagh Ogilvie and Jeremy Edwards; and Toke Aidt in a group all to himself; such a grouping emerges using the criterion of shared authorships in publications.

Cluster 1: Humphries—Horrell

Jane Humphries
A couple of years prior to Phyllis Deane's retirement, the Faculty made an inspired appointment which promised to widen the field of vision with regard to manner in which economic history might be perceived in the Faculty, looking into the future. Jane Humphries[48] entered the Faculty in 1980 as a lecturer, on the cusp of the turbulent decade that witnessed the purge of heterodox traditions and lineages from the subject and the staff, and she left in 1998 as a reader, having seen and experienced those upheavals up close and all around her. She came in just as Phyllis Deane was elected President of the Royal Economic Society in 1980, but at the end of her term in 1982, Phyllis, made a professor that year, retired three years early, cutting short Jane's overlapping years to two. Jane got a First-Class in both parts of the Tripos (1968, 1970), and then took an MA and a PhD from Cornell University, where her dissertation was on the role of manufacturing in economic development, a theme then central to the agenda of the heterodox groups—in the Faculty and in the DAE—that she was entering. During her years in Cambridge, she, like Phyllis, was a Fellow of Newnham. "Phyllis Deane was a pioneering scholar, inspirational teacher, caring mentor, and warm friend. It was wonderful to come up to Newnham and see Phyllis's work included in all the required reading lists. [And her] research represented a seismic shift in the tectonic plates of economic history. After her book [with Max Cole], British Economic Growth 1688—1959 (1962), the discipline was on a different development path. Phyllis [also] was an excellent supervisor: critical but constructive, encouraging but with the highest standards" (Humphries, 2012). Jane was a worthy inheritor of that mantle.

Half a century after Dobb got his double-first in economics, so did Jane Humphries, supervised by none other than Dobb himself; she well remembers that experience. Phyllis was good friends with Maurice Dobb, and she arranged for Jane—her charge at Newnham—to be supervised by him in her third year. She got along extremely well with Maurice, and reminisces with affection about his thoughtfulness, politeness, his famously special, country-squire, sartorial style and his niceness, as she said, to this young girl from a working-class background from the North; above all she emphasised the quality of her learning experience with Dobb as "a caring and inspiring teacher. Both Dobb, and Phyllis, were not comfortable lecturing but they were very good supervisors—much more their forte. Maurice Dobb's supervision embodied everything that

---

[48] Jane Humphries (1948-): BA 1968, 1st class, 1970 1st class; MA, PhD Cornell 1973 ('The Role of the Manufacturing Sector in Economic Development'); University Lecturer in Economics 1980-1995, and Fellow of Newnham; Reader Economics, 1995-1998; Editorial Board, *Cambridge Journal of Economics* 1983-1998; Reader, Economic History, Oxford, 1998-2004; Professor of Economic History, Oxford, 2004—; Centennial Professor, LSE, 2018—.

supervisions were supposed to be about." When Jane's result was announced, Maurice penned his 'warm congratulations' for her 'very well-deserved' First in a letter, in his inimitable medieval copper-engraving handwriting, to Jane, and that testament to Dobb's dedication as a caring teacher and a person remains a cherished possession of Jane's.[49]

Phyllis Deane's and Maurice Dobb's efforts were wonderfully rewarded in the results Jane achieved in Parts I and II. A special letter from a doting Phyllis to a favourite student:

> *Dear Jane,*
> *By the time this reaches you the notice will have been posted on the Senate noticeboard telling the world that you have go a First in Part I. Many congratulations! I expected it, in spite of your forebodings, but it is still a special pleasure to have one's predictions confirmed.*
> *I should not be telling you even as much as this before the results have been processed by the Registry, but I cannot resist going one stage further and telling you that two of the examiners separately and independently and without my even asking have told me that yours was an outstandingly good result in an unusually good year.*
> *I hope therefore that you will not be tempted to change from Economics!*
> *Have a good holiday,*
> *With all good wishes,*
> *Yours,*
> *Phyllis Deane.*

Then, after Part II, further well-deserved commendations and congratulations: the letter from Dobb; a telegram from Phyllis, and then an airletter to Jane when she had landed in Cornell.

> *Dear Jane,*
> *… I hope you have enjoyed the interval between one way of life and the next and that you have not filled it with dreary things like work. And I very much hope that you will find Cornell a challenge and a pleasure. You should have learnt some solid self-confidence and some healthy self-knowledge in Cambridge to make the new experience a happiness.*
> *But don't be too seduced by the American way of life. I am looking forward to seeing you back in Cambridge one day as a colleague. Perhaps one day, not too far ahead, you will follow me in Mary Marshall's footsteps. …*
> *Good luck and enjoy yourself!*
> *With all good wishes*
> *Yours sincerely,*
> *Phyllis Deane.*

---

[49] Personal communications, including email dated 29 August 2021.

Jane spent the decade of the 1970s in the USA: first an MA and then a PhD (in 1973) from Cornell followed by an Assistant Professorship at the University of Massachusetts at Amherst (1973–1979) with a promotion to Associate Professorship in 1979–1980, at which point she fulfilled the fond wish and prediction of her mentor Phyllis, by returning to a lectureship in Cambridge in 1980 and taking up a Fellowship at Newnham, following indeed in the footsteps of Mary Paley Marshall and Phyllis Deane—no doubt giving Phyllis the satisfaction of another of her predictions proven correct.

In Cambridge, it was Pigou (1920)—whom Jane held in high esteem—who had famously set the ball rolling with his remark that "if a man marries his housekeeper of cook the national dividend is diminished". However, after highlighting a wide range of striking 'paradoxes' or contradictions between valued human activity and its recording, or not, in the national dividend, Pigou found it 'preferable' to follow the now conventional prescription "in accordance with the precedent set by Marshall", his mentor.[50] And it was Phyllis Deane in her pioneering feminist critique and work on colonial accounts who had widening this breach and challenged these national income measurement protocols being developed by her Cambridge mentors. Ironically, Alfred and Mary Marshall left Cambridge for Bristol as college fellows were not allowed to marry; Marshall became Principal of University College Bristol and the Professor of Political Economy, with Mary becoming a university lecturer in economics; but despite Bristol's high position as a vanguard in promoting women's equality in higher education, Mary Marshall's salary was drawn out of her husband's pay, so clearly while the national knowledge quotient would have registered a perceptible improvement, the national dividend would have remained unchanged. Mary, who had taken the Moral Sciences Tripos in 1874, but not allowed to graduate, became a Fellow of Newnham College in 1875 and the first teacher of economics at the University; and it was her money, after Alfred's death, that contributed to the setting up of the Marshall Library, where she worked for a couple of decades till ill health and her doctors intervened.[51] It was a measure of Phyllis's assessment of Jane that she placed her in the Newnham line running through Mary Marshall and herself.

Jane Humphries completed her PhD (at Cornell) in 1973, the year that Nancy Folbre started hers in Amherst, where Jane joined that year as Assistant Lecturer. Jane was a member of Nancy's dissertation committee; Nancy completed her doctorate (working on Patriarchy and Capitalism in New England,

---

[50] Pigou goes on to expand this paradox into areas directly researched later by Jane. "These things are paradoxes. It is a paradox also that, when Poor Law or Factory Regulations divert women workers from factory work or paid home-work to unpaid home-work, in attendance on their children, preparation of the family meals, repair of the family clothes thoughtful expenditure of housekeeping money, and so on, the national dividend, on our definition, suffers a loss against which there is to be set no compensating gain" (Pigou, 1920: Chapter 3).

[51] For an insightful discussion of the persistence of gender inequalities rooted in patriarchal gender norms as espoused by Alfred Marshall, see Rohini Pande and Helena Roy (2021).

1622–1900) in 1979 (Razavi, 2011), the year that Humphries became an Associate Professor prior to shifting back to Cambridge in 1980. Recalling that early interaction, Jane observes "Nancy was already clearly an outstanding scholar".[52] Later, in 2002, Nancy succeeded Jane as the President of the International Association for Feminist Economics.

Jane Humphries was recruited as an economist with an interest and expertise in economic history, but not as an economic historian *per se*. She came also with an identifiable Marxist intellectual orientation, which would have made her welcome to those on this side, or unwelcome, to those on the other side, of the barricades dividing the heterodox and the orthodox groups in the Faculty. Before she came, she had announced herself in a string of papers published in the emerging academic journals of the left: "Class struggle and the persistence of the working class family" in the first volume of the *Cambridge Journal of Economics* (where was one of the editors between 1983 and her departure in 1998); "Women, scapegoats and safety valves in the Great Depression" in *Review of Radical Political Economy*; and "From the latent to the floating: the 'emancipation' of women in the 1970s and 1980s" in *Capital and Class*. Just these confirm the temporal spread of her interests and capacities in interrogating dialogues between past and present. Predictably, there was an ideological struggle over the position which the mainstream power brokers managed to delay, but not to successfully block.

Her research has been a sustained project of the recovery of occluded histories of subaltern labour, lurking relatively unremarked and unplumbed in the depths of archives and in a wide range of other sources, on not just the long-term improvements in welfare indices, but also the blood, sweat and tears of women and child workers, congealed in the building blocks that form the constituent elements of the statistics of the industrial revolution, or for that matter, of the Keynesian macro aggregates of output, investment, consumption so carefully compiled by earlier work of the economic historians and statisticians in the DAE, including prominently Phyllis Deane, and Charles Feinstein whom she later joined in Oxford.

Her work in the area of the labour market and industrialisation broke out in fresh directions with her specialist focus on the dynamic interface between the family and the economy, on the history of women's work, leading to a major contribution on working-class childhood in the British industrial revolution (Humphries, 2010). Epistemologically and methodologically innovative, her research used "innovative quantitative and qualitative methodology to illuminate aspects of children's lives which are inaccessible on the basis of more conventional sources". The book describes itself: "This is a unique account of working-class childhood during the British industrial revolution, using more than 600 autobiographies written by working men of the eighteenth and nineteenth centuries Jane Humphries illuminates working-class childhood in contexts untouched by conventional sources and facilitates estimates of age at

---

[52] Personal communication, email dated 5 September 2021.

starting work, social mobility, the extent of apprenticeship and the duration of schooling. The classic era of industrialisation, 1790–1850, apparently saw an upsurge in child labour. While the memoirs implicate mechanisation and the division of labour in this increase, they also show that fatherlessness and large subsets, common in these turbulent, high-mortality and high-fertility times, often cast children as partners and supports for mothers struggling to hold families together. The book offers unprecedented insights into child labour, family life, careers and schooling. Its images of suffering, stoicism and occasional childish pleasures put the humanity back into economic history and the trauma back into the industrial revolution" (Humphries, 2010).[53]

---

[53] Professor John Clapham was not anything but a conservative economic historian; Munia Postan describes him as one with "a head that was shrewd and cool, an outlook which was wholly unsentimental, and a rule of life disciplined to the point of being hard." (Postan, 1946, p. 56). This makes a reading of the first and last paragraphs of his 1949 book all the more interesting. Opening his book, Clapham pronounces: "Of all varieties of history the economic is the most fundamental. Not the most important: foundations exist to carry better things. How a man lives with his family, his tribe or his fellow-citizens; the songs he sings; what he feels and thinks when he looks at the sunset; the prayers he raises—all these are more important than the nature of his tools, his trick of swapping things with his neighbours, the way he holds and tills his fields, his inventions and their consequences, his money—when he has learnt to use it—his savings and what he does with them. Economic advance is not the same thing as human progress. The man with a motor-car may have less imagination, and perhaps a baser religion, than the men who frequented Stonehenge" (Clapham, 1949, p. 18). It is not difficult to applaud his clear separation between economic advance and human progress, though his lyrical prose embodies rather a man-vision, though perhaps not much out of place for its times.

A jump to the closing paragraph finds Clapham, again unusually, displaying emotion over the plight of the boys and girls of the underclass, alluding to the underside of "the drift to Town, … there was Gin Lane and all the marshy insanitary ground by the waterside … full of old tumble-down timber houses …" with a reluctant and grudging Parish overseeing the plight of young apprenticing boys and girls "for whom they could not deny responsibility"; "there was misery enough in the system at its best, apart from the far too numerous cases that came in to the courts of criminal ill-treatment of apprentices. The courts did what they could. When … gross neglect or ill-treatment was proved, they would discharge the apprentice from his obligation to remain and serve a bad master, or if a girl, to stay with a mistress who starved her. But what proportion of the cases of neglect and ill-treatment that was not quite criminal, or even of those that were, ever got into court, in the ill-governed and imperfectly-supervised London of the eighteenth century? What became of the girls apprenticed into 'literal slavery' until the age of twenty-one with the milk-sellers? They were not often those charming young persons in bright frock cut low at the neck who appear in coloured prints of 'the Cries of London'. Theirs would be other crying" (Clapham, 1949, pp. 304–305).

However, those led by these sentiments and looking in the book of a gendered treatment of the history of the times would be disappointed: the words girl (or boy), women or female do not find an entry in the index or in any chapter or section heading, the works of Mayhew, Dickens, Engels, Booth, Rowntree, notwithstanding.

The holder of Clapham's chair in the year that Humphries joined the Faculty, Donald Coleman, fine historian that he surely was, focussed on the propelling power of entrepreneurs and business; for him, the Industrial Revolution was not a catalogue of social disaster. That indeed might have been so, but it did have its underside, and Humphries follows in a line of eminent feminist historians of British economic history, including Ivy Pinchbeck and Eileen Power, "putting trauma back into the industrial revolution".

During and after Cambridge, a substantial block of her research was in partnership with her younger Cambridge colleague Sara Horrell, and they state the fundamental motivation and premises underlying their analyses on women, children and the family (Horrell & Humphries, 1995a): "We must establish why it is important to study the effects of industrialization on women's work and family lives. Women deserve attention as historic actors whose experiences were not the same as men's", but also "because without it major historical misreadings go unchallenged" (89). "What happened to the standard of living of the working class during industrialization ... is based on trends in indices of the real wages of adult males ... [which] implicitly assumes that the same number of people were dependent on the male wage through time, that non-wage inputs into welfare did not decline, and that the earning opportunities of women and children were unaltered. Yet it is in just these areas that industrialization is argued to have brought significant changes"—a dimension which, they point out, had not gone unnoticed by Deane and Cole in their classic study (ibid., p. 90n5). Further, "if women's and children's labour input varied over the course of the industrial revolution, estimates of productivity growth are likely to be inaccurate" (ibid., p. 90). Horrell and Humphries then proceed with their investigation of the economic activity of women and children during the industrial revolution, drawing "from 59 sources including contemporary social commentators, Parliamentary Papers, local archives, provincial record offices, and working-class autobiographies; some of the sources are well known and widely quoted; others unpublished and unused" (ibid.). The significance of the cumulative body of their individually or jointly authored work can hardly be overstated.[54]

The breadth and nature of the work potentially offered a wide interface with economics, with history, with development, sociology and social anthropology, in particular with labour, gender and child studies interweaving economic theory with a range of sources, research materials and methodologies that potentially opened up fresh subaltern perspectives on the structural processes and lived experiences of the industrial revolution. And, both Humphries[55] and

---

[54] See, for instance: Horrell and Humphries (1995a, 1995b, 1997, 2019), Horrell et al. (1992b, c), Horrell et al. (2015), and Horrell et al. (1998), Humphries and Rubery (1984), Humphries in Rubery ed. (1988).

[55] For instance, the introduction to her Ellen McArthur Lectures delivered in February 2016 in Cambridge, though in the Faculty of History, begins: "Women from all times and regions will be seen about their daily lives, at work and at home, in these 4 lectures." In the third lecture, she "builds on earlier work, in this case using working-class autobiographies to uncover the experiences of families which lived through the industrial revolution. My 2010 book used proletarian life writing to uncover aspects of work and family life inaccessible through conventional historical sources. But all 600 plus accounts were authored by men and so presented an exclusively male perspective. In the lecture I will draw on women's stories to provide female reflections on childhood, child labour, schooling, parenting and family life, looking particularly at the ways in which experience was gendered and speculating about its implications for our understanding of the division of labour and the cultural power of gender in post-industrial society." http://www.econsoc.hist.cam.ac.uk/podcast-humphries.html

Horrell have consistently displayed a lively research engagement—in several partnerships, significantly with Jill Rubery, and Deborah Oxley—on the interface with historical and current contexts in UK, in Europe or globally, including especially the developing economies.

Jane did not change from economics, as indeed Phyllis Deane had once exhorted, but she did move from her interest in development economics: "I was married, had a family, and therefore could not do fieldwork, and so I switched into economic history." She shared with Phyllis that development economics and economic history had close natural links, but not everyone around her thought so. She recalls attending a conference in Cambridge in 2001 on Economic History and Development Economics, and she narrated two strong memories: first that 9/11 occurred during the conference period; and second, that at the conference Tony Wrigley and Richard Smith vehemently expressed diametrically opposite positions on the interface between development economics and economic history, with the former asserting that there was no connection of significance between the two, and the latter arguing the converse view. In her assessment, Richard Smith, from CAMPOP, stood out as the exception amongst the economic historians (in CAMPOP and the Faculty of History) in being seriously interested in developing connections between the two disciplines, and he was in general very helpful in making links between the two, both at CAMPOP, but also through his involvement in seminars at the Faculty. Of course, to make good sense, it is necessary to bear in mind the intra-discipline conflicts over what made for 'good' development economics, or 'good' economic history; thus, Wrigley might not agree with Smith; nor did Postan with Dobb; neither North with Deane; nor, for that matter, Ogilvie with Humphries.

Soon after Jane Humphries took up her appointment, the process of regime change, from the heterodox and radical, to the orthodox and mainstream, picked up pace in the Faculty; her profile would hardly have matched what the new masters would deem desirable; selective hostility and career blocks eventually took their toll and induced a shift away to Oxford and to a flourishing career thereon.[56] Her submission for promotion to reader was blocked twice by

---

[56] Curiously, at Oxford, Jane Humphries did not graduate into the Chichele Professorship when it fell vacant; and thereby there might hang some folklore, again involving the hostility of some senior mainstream economist/s who held the reins of influence over this high-profile appointment based at All Souls, the institutional home of the Chichele Professor.

> An early exponent of computable general equilibrium in economic history was Jeffrey G. Williamson, at Wisconsin and later at Harvard. His first study appeared in 1974, and in 1986 he published *Did British Capitalism breed Inequality?* This tested a famous Kuznets hypothesis, namely that in the long-run course of economic growth, inequality would first increase, before it began to decline once again. ... Charles accepted the book for review with few prior expectations, and his article eventually occupied thirty pages in the *Journal of Economic History*. He was not familiar with computable general equilibrium, but no one had a more intimate knowledge of British historical statistics. He criticized both the data and the model. (Offer, 2008, p. 14)

the neoclassical power holders and brokers in the Faculty, and it was well understood in faculty circles where the roadblocks had come from; she succeeded on the third attempt with the roadblockers then disingenuously wanting to claim credit and control for her having broken through the opposition. And so, soon after, she was recruited by an enthusiastic Charles Feinstein to join the Faculty in Oxford. Jane points out that Charles was very supportive of her and her career[57]; indeed, she shared the feeling that her path in Oxford could have evolved rather differently had Charles not passed away, only 72, in 2004, the year that she was promoted to a personal professorship that was soon converted into a statutory position. Mainstream economists might have obstructed her path, first in Cambridge and then in Oxford (in connection with the Chichele chair), but they couldn't hold her back from a career replete with peer respect and recognition manifest in a continuous string of high-profile professional positions, editorships of major professional journals, prestigious named lectures, fellowships and honours, including prizes and awards, including most recently the Royal Economic Society Prize for her 2019 article in *Economic Journal* (jointly authored with Jacob Weisdorf) 'Unreal Wages? Real Income and Economic Growth in England, 1260–1850' which is reorienting discourse on the Industrial Revolution. Maurice Dobb and Phyllis Deane had got it right.

At the time of writing the appreciation for Charles Feinstein, Avner Offer was the Chichele Professor at All Souls in Oxford, and one of his colleagues was Jane Humphries who had given up a readership in Cambridge to come across to Oxford, a move which Charles, also ex- of Cambridge, was said to have welcomed and enabled. There was a fair expectation that after Offer vacated the chair in 2010, Jane Humphries would be its next occupant. Ironically, as it happened, the choice fell on a cliometrician, Kevin O'Rourke—whose PhD dissertation 'Agricultural Change and Rural Depopulation 1845–1876' was based on computable general equilibrium modelling, supervised by none other than Jeffrey Williamson; the two had written several papers together in the tradition and methodology that Charles had so critically reviewed, including a prize-winning book *Globalisation and History*.

Avner Offer writes, "Charles hoped that the dust-up with Williamson left few lingering resentments [—perhaps a forlorn wish?—] and that it encouraged respect for data integrity. It is still a focal point for a methodological divide that remains charged. It confirmed Charles in his convictions. Theories came and went, good data endured: 'I think that the assets I construct are more likely to prove durable if I do one type of work rather than another. It might be more exciting and more intellectually demanding to try and do more speculative and theoretical research, but I doubt that it would make a lasting or worthwhile contribution'" (quotation from Feinstein, 2007, as cited in Offer, 2008, pp. 14–15). But had that dust-up perhaps indirectly inflicted its own collateral damage? But perhaps it reflected the momentum of the tidal wave of mainstream cliometrics then redefining and incorporating large swathes of economic history as provinces of neoclassical economics.

[57] Folklore handed down offers an amusing, perhaps apocryphal, snippet. By the time Jane Humphries sat for her final year exams, the assessment system had moved to anonymised scripts. Apparently, in a marking meeting, Charles vehemently talked up a script that, on the basis of the handwriting, he thought was that of the daughter of a known senior historian, but in reality, the script was that of Jane's; the misidentification notwithstanding, Charles was clearly a keen scout spotting quality early.

Sara Horrell

Sara Horrell was born in 1962 the year that Phyllis Deane shifted from the DAE to the Faculty, and after a 1st Class BA from Bath in 1983, the year after Phyllis retired, and an M.Phil in Economics at Cambridge in 1985, she entered the DAE in 1987, just as the dust was settling down on the trilogy of purges at the DAE. She was immediately involved in the new ESRC-funded countrywide, multidisciplinary project, "Social change and Economic Life" project with the DAE assigned the Northampton Labour Market (to) study.[58] In 1991, she obtained her Ph.D. while at Trinity College with a thesis on 'Working Wife Households—Inside and Outside the Home', supervised by Jane Humphries. After a productive five-year stretch in the DAE,[59] she followed on the same track other economic historians, viz., Brian Mitchell and Charles Feinstein, had also taken earlier from the DAE to the Faculty. She became University Assistant Lecturer in Economic History in the Faculty in 1992, lecturer in 1995, Senior Lecturer in 2000, becoming Reader in 2019 and leaving almost immediately thereafter to take up a professorship in economic history at the London School of Economics—becoming the third Cambridge Reader in Economic History (after Feinstein and Humphries) who had to move out from Cambridge to a Chair elsewhere.

While Sara Horrell follows on directly in the line of descent from Phyllis Deane and especially Jane Humphries, with the most powerful thrust of her research being on the gendering of the economic history of the British industrial revolution, she has significant work in other fields also in a contemporary time frame. There is also much evidence of rich research partnerships in these diverse lines of research.

An attempt to investigate the changing structure of the British economy in the industrialisation process was an exercise in the DAE-Stone genre. Another noteworthy spinoff a couple of years later is Sara Horrell's article on 'home demand and British industrialisation' (Horrell, 1996). Then there is an unusual partnership with Martin Weale and Jane Humphries to produce an Input-Output Table for UK for 1841[60] (Horrell et al., 1994). And there are further papers on the British economy, contemporary or historical (Begg & Horrell, 2002; Horrell, 1999).

---

[58] "John Devereux and Sara Horrell, research students linked to the project, have access to the data and are using parts of the set in their research" (DAE Annual Report, 1986–1987, p. 16); for details of the project, see DAE Annual Report 1985–1986, pp. 22–26.

[59] She was at the DAE first as a Research Assistant (1987–1989) and then as a Research Officer (1990–1992); during 1989–1990 she was Director of Studies in Economics at New Hall, having taken over the position from Jill Rubery; she served in this role for twenty years till 2009.

[60] An opening footnote acknowledges Robin Matthews, Charles Feinstein and Phyllis Deane; another mentions that "an entry by entry commentary on the sources used and assumptions made to construct the input-output table is available in S. Horrell, "Notes on construction of an input-output table for the UK economy in 1841", Department of Applied Economics, University of Cambridge, mimeo."

A second, though seemingly not a major, strand pertains to contemporary development issues: there is work, done in partnerships, on poverty and productivity in female-headed households in Zimbabwe with Pamela Krishnan (Horrell & Krishnan, 2007); on aid, the public sector and the market in LDCs (Horrell et al., 1992a), and a book-length work on work, female empowerment and economic development (Horrell et al., 2008).

A third, more weighty, line evolves from the DAE's multidisciplinary project on Social Change and Economic Life and involves close partnerships with the Labour Studies group of the DAE, especially Jill Rubery and Frank Wilkinson (amongst others),[61] and with DAE sociologists on gendered analyses of labour markets, jobs, work time, skills, pay and work inequalities (Burchell et al., 1989, 1990; Horrell & Rubery, 1991, 1992/93), with the research subsequently extended to the EU, this time in partnership with Jill Rubery and Jane Humphries with a gendered analysis of women's employment in various industries (Horrell et al., 1992b, c).

Over her tenure at the DAE, Jill Rubery, not an economic historian per se, but an economist specialising on gender and labour markets, worked on a range of the projects in the Labour Studies group in the DAE, starting as a Research Associate, then becoming Junior Research Officer (1978), Research Officer (1979) and Senior Research Officer (1986); obtained her PhD at Cambridge in 1987; and left in 1989 for the Manchester School of Management (UMIST) almost immediately in the hostile aftermath of the DAE Review and subsequent change of the DAE directorship. There she rose to a professorship and served first as the Deputy Director of the Alliance Manchester Business School (2007–2013), and then as Director of its Work and Equalities Institute.[62] She has developed a major standing in theoretical and policy-oriented research with a specialisation on gender and labour markets, nationally, in the EU, within specialised international agencies, and globally; in this, she has relocated and evolved her work in the Labour Studies Group of the DAE. Her extensive research partnerships, in particular with Jane Humphries and Sara Horrell, set up meaningful historical and contemporary cross-country dialogues concerned with the gendered impact of contemporary economic processes and policies. Jill Rubery has been a prolific scholar with a high level of productivity sustained throughout her career.[63] She highlights two main collaborations with Jane Humphries from the time they were both in Cambridge. "The first is our joint lecture course on women and the labour market, which led for both one of our most highly cited articles (Humphries & Rubery, 1984) that effectively provides an historically-based account of how social norms change and help to

---

[61] Others included: Roger Tarling (in the early stages), Ray Jobling, Colin Fraser, Cathy Marsh and Brendan Burchell.

[62] https://www.research.manchester.ac.uk/portal/jill.rubery.html

[63] For the bibliometrically inclined, Google Scholar lists 44 research papers with more than 100 citations.

convert temporary and contingent participation in employment into more permanent attachment.[64] The second collaboration was on the *Women and Recession* book[65] (Rubery, 1988), where Jane played a major part, providing a chapter on the U.S. labour market but also working together on the common methodology for the comparisons between the U.K., the U.S. France and Italy, researched in the book. Again, it reflects contemporary and historical interests in how the specifics of women's position in the labour market shapes the gender impact of crises and business cycles."[66]

Sara Horrell's work takes off from her doctoral thesis, and is on gendered economic history, much of it done in partnership with Jane Humphries, as described earlier. The cumulative body of their individual and joint work represents a major intervention in revising received understandings and interpretations of the industrial revolution prompted by their disruptive interrogations and insights, and this is visible in recent bibliometric analyses of research in economic history as published since 2000 in eight major academic journals (Galofre-Vila, 2019). Apart from these joint works, Horrell has another productive partnership with Deborah Oxley,[67] the Australian economic historian whose work challenges hegemonic narratives across a wide interface of historical oppressions embedded in the Industrial Revolution and in European Imperialism, dissecting these from the 'other' side, be it gender, health and inequality, children and childhood; or, coerced, convict and unfree labour. She constructs "a somatic history of the industrial revolution … measuring the biological consequences of European imperialism", using an anthropometric approach that deals with the body as evidence. She declares her interest in the "micro-economics of the household; but diametrically different from the standard neoclassical theoretical frame".[68] Based at All Souls College, Oxford, till recently as Professor of Social Science History, she returned to Australia when

---

[64] Jane Humphries delivered the Ellen McArthur lectures on this theme, which has been the leitmotif of her research, in Cambridge in 2016.

[65] Jill Rubery points out that Roger Tarling was also involved in this work.

[66] This work, and the follow-up book, *Women and Austerity* (Karamessini & Rubery, 2013), "was also the basis for me taking over the coordination of the EU's gender and employment expert group for about 14 years between 1992 and 2007. So again there was a legacy as the gender network and the IWPLMS were very much the key foundations for my comparative research career, but both have their origins in these earlier Cambridge collaborations" (Personal communication: email dated 29 November 2021).

[67] See, for instance: Horrell and Oxley (1999) on intra-household resource allocation and the male breadwinner model in Victorian Britain; Horrell et al. (2009) on the measurement/s of body mass for the London poor in the Victorian era; and Horrell and Oxley (2016) on investigating gender bias in nineteenth-century England via evidence on factory children.

[68] https://www.history.ox.ac.uk/people/professor-deborah-oxley#/

Listed as research interests are: "penal transportation to Australia; coercive labour systems; colonial Australian development; crime and punishment in Great Britain and Ireland; convict Australia: coercions and freedoms in Australian penal colonies; and the history of childhood and education."

she was overlooked for the Chichele Chair after O'Rourke retired in 2019. It would be a fair speculation that Oxley might have had the support and endorsement of Jane Humphries who, meanwhile, had retired from her professorship in economic history in the Faculty of History in Oxford and relocated to LSE where she had become a Centennial Professor. In 2011 when O'Rourke was appointed, it was the radical Jane Humphries who had been bypassed; this time, the position went to Sheilagh Ogilvie, an exponent of economic history in the tradition of Postan and, so for a second time of asking, radical subaltern gendered perspectives on modern history were declined apparently due to a similar constellation of orthodoxy prominently including mainstream economists.

Cluster 2: Kitson—Solomou—Weale
The second grouping comprises Solomos Solomou, who had been appointed to the Faculty in 1985; Martin Weale, who had joined the CGP in 1979 and after its closure shifted to the Faculty in 1988; and Michael Kitson, who joined the DAE as a JRO in 1983 and stayed till he moved with Alan Hughes's industrial-economics team to the Judge Institute at the end of the 1990s.

Solomos Solomou
Apart from the extensive joint work with Michael Kitson and Martin Weale, Solomou's prime body of individual research was on Kondratieff long waves and Kuznets swings in economic growth in the world economy, rooted in his PhD dissertation, done in 1983 (Solomou, 1986a, 1986b, 1990). Andrew Tylecote, reviewing the work in the *Economic Journal*, writes: "this book is of great importance. For the whole of the period for which adequate statistics are available, it confronts the main theories of fluctuations in economic growth, with the evidence. The result is fascinating, and at times devastating" (Tylecote, 1988, p. 855). "Solomou's achievement in this terse and clear book of 170-odd pages is remarkable. His handling of the main statistical series on growth is masterly; as to the multitude of possible explanatory factors, his knowledge of the secondary sources is clearly encyclopaedic … Anyone interested in the recent economic history of the major Western economies, or the world economy, should read and re-read Solomou; so should economists interested in growth. Most particularly, all *afficionados* of the longwave should think long about this book" (Tylecote, 1988, pp. 855–856).

There are other noteworthy lines of research: Ristuccia and Solomou (2014) investigate the question, "does the concept of general-purpose technologies help explain periods of faster and slower productivity advance" and use a new comparative dataset on electricity usage in the early twentieth century in the manufacturing sectors of the USA, Britain, France, Germany and Japan, coming to a negative conclusion about the power of GPTs to predict aggregate or sectoral growth.

A third strand pursues issues of finance, banking and crises (Kitson & Solomou, 1989, 1990, 1991; Kitson et al., 1991), including a

Cambridge-INET Symposium in Economics and History, 'Financial Crises: Lessons from History' in 2015, where Bruno Rocha and Solomos Solomou (2015) examine "the time-profile of the impact of systemic banking crises on GDP and industrial production using a panel of 24 countries over the inter-war period and compare this to the post-war experience of these countries" showing, within a broader systematic intertemporal comparison, that "the short term macroeconomic impact effects are much larger in the post-war period, suggesting that the propagation channels of shocks operate at a faster pace in the recent period" (ibid., p. 35). A research sideline in earlier years has been a statistical analysis of the impact of climatic factors on agricultural output.

Martin Weale
Martin Weale (1955–) was at Clare College and graduated with a First in Part 2 Economics from Cambridge in 1977; as an ODI Fellow, went as a statistician to Malawi for two years,[69] returning in 1979 to join the Stone-Barker CGP team in the DAE in Cambridge as a Junior Research Officer, combining it with a Fellowship in Clare College from 1981 till 1995, when at the young age of 40, he became the Director of the NIESR, a post he held till 2010, when he was appointed an external member, till 2016, of the Monetary Policy Committee; in 1999, he was honoured with a CBE for services to economics. He did not do a standard PhD but later obtained an Sc. D. in Economics at Cambridge in 2006. During 1990–1998, he was a member of the HM Treasury Academic Panel; during 1995–1997 he was a member of the HM Treasury's Panel of Independent Forecasters (the so-called Wise Men which had Wynne Godley as a member). In the CGP and the DAE, Weale graduated from an apprentice to a master of number-craft, a cross-product of the traditions of Stone and Reddaway. His research curiosity and expertise grew wider to include macroeconomic policy, economic forecasting, life-cycle behaviour, health and well-being and pensions and saving, providing a very broad interface with the key areas of government policy. Perhaps classifiable as a moderate Keynesian— he was closely associated with James Meade in the latter's later years—his impressive career bears a sustained affinity with Clare College, the CLARE Group and with the LibDems-SDP groupings.

Later, when Director of the NIESR, reflecting his wide and eclectic interests, Weale co-authored papers with Partha Dasgupta, the scourge of the leftgroups in the Cambridge Faculty, generally defending the GDP as a measure of the quality of life (Dasgupta & Weale 2002, published in *World Development*; another with Hashem Pesaran in 2006; and a paper in 2006 with James A. Sefton on the concept of income in general equilibrium, published in the *Review of Economic Studies*). It is striking that when DAE research staff

---

[69] https://www.odi.org/blogs/3586-life-fellow-dr-martin-weale, https://www.odi.org/sites/odi.org.uk/files/odi-assets/publications-opinion-files/4701.pdf

dispersed after the closure of the CGP, and the installation of David Newbery as the new Director of the DAE, only a select few were absorbed into the Faculty; one of these was William Peterson, who had been a signatory of the Hahn-Dasgupta-Newbery (and others) letter to the DAE Review Committee; another was Martin Weale, who had close relations with Matthews and Hahn, and came across from the DAE into the Faculty in 1987.[70]

Martin Weale was an accomplished and highly productive applied economist, and he carried across part of his research portfolio from the defunct CGP into his Faculty position, and from his publications it is evident that he had the capability for striking up collaborations across a wide spectrum of topics and colleagues. What is pertinent here are his lines of research on themes under the broad rubric of quantitative, though not cliometric, economic history mostly (though not exclusively) relating to the twentieth century.

Michael Kitson
Michael Kitson's webpage at the Judge Business School confirms his sustained research interest and publication in historical dimensions of economic policy, usually with dialogues between episodes, or conundrums, in the present and in the proximate past. This body of research pertains to his later years in the DAE (till 1999), and then at the Centre for Business Research at the JBS, where his research focus shifted away progressively towards issues of "new developments in innovation policy and analysing knowledge exchange between academics and private, public and third sectors" (https://michaelkitson.org/). In addition to the jointly authored articles with Solomon Solomou, his historically oriented papers significantly include: Harcourt and Kitson (1993) on 'Fifty Years of Economic Measurement: A Cambridge View'; 'The Deindustrial Revolution: The Rise and Fall of UK Manufacturing, 1870–2010' (Kitson, 2012); 'Trade and Growth: An Historical Perspective' (Kitson & Michie, 1995); 'Recession and Economic Revival in Britain: The Role of Policy in the 1930s and 1980s' (Kitson, 1999).

Solomou, Weale, Kitson
Kitson and Solomou (1989) focus on a controversial aspect of the raging debates over macroeconomic policy in the 1970s and 1980s, the issue of protection; they investigate "whether the policy shift to protection in 1931/32 *contributed significantly* to ... cyclical and trend economic recovery. Our perspective is a Kaldorian one, incorporating the Harrod foreign trade multiplier" (ibid., p. 156). The radical, left-Keynesian schools in Cambridge argued strongly in favour of protection for manufacturing industry—instead of the non-selective instrument of devaluation—on multiple grounds. Within the New Cambridge Godley-Cripps framework, tariffs would curb imports and

---

[70] From 'the other side', Ken Coutts also came across on to the Faculty side, but as an Assistant Director of Research, not as a regular lecturer.

improve the trade balance, taking pressure off the alternative of austerity measures for cutting the fiscal deficit; in parallel, Kaldor argued effectively in favour of a manufacturing sector export-led strategy based on protection, since in his view devaluation, that is, price adjustments, would be unable to address the structural factors holding back British industry—here protection would be part of a wider set of policies aimed at restoring British industrial competitiveness and expand exports in order to reap the benefits of economies of scale, and catalyse a virtuous process of cumulative causation.[71] With due qualifications, they conclude the "protection in 1932 benefited the British economy by generating a major fall in the manufacturing sector's import propensity", and that alongside other policies and factors, tariffs were "a major source of recovery which has been underemphasised in the past".

Their work is thoroughly embedded in the post-Keynesian macroeconomic policy analytics of the DAE, and also connects with other Cambridge economists and economic historians, including Von Tunzelmann's (1982) work on structural change and leading sectors in the British economy; with Matthews et al. (1982); Jane Humphries (1987); and extensively with Kaldor; and relies on Mitchell's (1980, 1982, 1983) compilations of European historical statistics. "Much of this paper is based on research funded by the ESRC ... and directed by the late Lord Kaldor. His involvement was immense and is sadly missed" (ibid., p. 155n1). The paper leads to a book-length study (Kitson & Solomou, 1990) exploring the crucial policy issue more generally for the inter-war British economy; and then there is a follow-up on the question of trade policy and manufacturing import performance in inter-War Britain (Kitson & Solomou, 1991), and another on related issues also involving Martin Weale (Kitson et al., 1991). As a by-product of these policy-oriented papers on proximate economic history, there is a slew of papers co-authored by Solomou and Weale—in the first half of the 1990s, till the latter left Cambridge to take up the Directorship of the NIESR—on aspects of the estimates of UK GDP and personal sector wealth variously over the 1870s–1950s period (Solomou & Weale, 1997), including econometric investigation of the implications of measurement errors; work on monthly and quarterly GDP estimates for inter-War Britain (Mitchell et al., 2012; also, Solomou and Weale, 2010) on unemployment and real wages in the Great Depression. A look across their profiles reveals that Solomos Solomou co-authored eight papers with Michael Kitson, and another six papers with Martin Weale—though there is no record of a jointly authored paper by Kitson and Weale; clearly Solomou was the middle link in this chain of partnerships; tentatively, the titles are suggestive of a 'Stone-type' agenda for the Solomou-Weale partnership, in contrast to a 'Kaldor-type' frame for the Solomou-Kitson pairing. Collectively, there is a substantial body of

---

[71] Kitson and Solomou (1989, p. 157n1) observe that "although Kaldor's perspective influenced the Cambridge Economic Policy Group (CEPG) in the 1970s the two approaches are rather different."

cumulative research focussed on the inter-war policy issues, and on the construction and use of national accounts data within an extended Stone-DAE template. From all this emerges Solomou's textbook for students of economic history analysis, a set of sharply posed policy-oriented questions concerning the performance of the British economy in the 1919–1939 period (Solomou, 1996).

Cluster 3: Ogilvie[72]—Edwards
The third strand is Sheilagh Ogilvie's sustained accumulation of work and publications based on her doctoral and subsequent research on protoindustrialisation and related themes in early medieval Germany. After schooling in Canada, she took a first-class degree in modern history and English at St. Andrews, and then switched to medieval German history and wrote her doctoral dissertation at Cambridge on 'Corporatism and regulation in rural industry: woollen weaving in Wurttemberg, 1590–1749', completed in 1985. It was with that deep specialisation, prima facie standing at a discrete distance from the bread-and-butter teaching and research preoccupations of the Faculty of Economics, that she became an assistant lecturer there in 1989. Unusually, she then completed an MA in social science (economics) at Chicago in 1992 and was promoted to a lectureship.

In contrast to the challenges experienced by many others, including Jane Humphries, in their career trajectories at the Faculty, Sheilagh Ogilvie progressed steadily and unobstructed through the ranks with virtually metronomic regularity, her work and quality apparently finding strong support from Robin Matthews and Partha Dasgupta amongst the Faculty seniors. Ten years younger than Jane, she completed her PhD in 1985 as a Research Fellow at Trinity College, five years after Jane had taken up her lectureship at the Faculty of Economics. Sheilagh became an assistant lecturer at the Faculty in 1989; three years later in 1992 was promoted to a lectureship; and seven years after, in 1999, to a readership in economic history, to be followed five years subsequently with an elevation to an ad hominem professorship in 2004. She had moved from the lowest to the highest rung in double quick time. In earlier years, to reach a professorship, economic historians at the Faculty of Economics and Politics had to pack their bags and look elsewhere: Charles Feinstein first to a chair in York, then to a readership in Oxford leading on to the prestigious

---

[72] Sheila Ogilvie (1958–): 1984–1988 Research Fellow, Trinity College, Cambridge; 1985 PhD completed with a thesis on 'Corporatism and regulation in rural industry: woollen weaving in Wurttemberg, 1590–1749'; 1989 appointed Assistant Lecturer in Economic History in the Faculty of Economics and Politics; 1992 completed MA in Social Sciences (Economics) at University of Chicago, a choice that would have seemed remarkably odd in heterodox circles, but one that might have sat well with the orthodox group then in control of the Faculty, and also one that could have reflected her own preference for the Chicago approach to economic theory and policy; also in 1992, promoted to Lecturer; 1999 promoted to Reader; 2004 promoted to Professor of Economic History; 2020 Chichele Professor of Economic History, Oxford; taught in Cambridge for 31 years.

Chichele Chair at All Souls; and later two decades later in 1995 Jane Humphries hit her head against the same ceiling and took the straight road to join Feinstein in Oxford as a reader, becoming professor of economic history in 2004 till she retired there in 2015, and then took up a Centennial Chair[73] at the London School of Economics in 2018. 2004 was a big year for women economic historians: at Oxford, Jane Humphries became professor of economic history, and in Cambridge, Sheilagh Ogilvie joined the rare club of women professors at the Faculty of Economics in Cambridge, promoted to an ad hominem professorship in Economic History, a position she held till 2020, when she, after 31 years of teaching in Cambridge, opted for the Chichele Chair in Oxford over her Cambridge professorship.[74]

"I explore the lives of ordinary people in the past and try to explain how poor economies get richer and improve human well-being. I'm particularly interested in how social institutions—the formal and informal constraints on economic activity—shaped economic development in Europe between the Middle Ages and the present day. In recent years my publications have analysed guilds, serfdom, communities, the family, gender, human capital investment, consumption, and state capacity."[75] Through her deep study of roots and process of German industrialisation, Ogilvie, in Postanian style, challenged several

---

[73] 'Centennial Chairs' were created at the LSE under the watch of Tony Giddens in his avatar of brilliant academic and institutional entrepreneur; these free-wheeling chairs were appointments made at School level and allowed Giddens and the School to cast a roving predatory eye over broad areas and attract senior talent to the LSE; and these provided an intellectual fillip and public visibility to the department to which the professor was attached, and of course to the School as a whole. They were also proof, if such were needed, that at the conventional age of retirement, usually 65 but 67 for Oxbridge with its inherent elitist premium, high performing academics, far from being over the top, were at the peak of their powers. These were ad hominem appointments. Only a cynic would regard these appointments as expedients in the competitive era of the Research Assessment Exercises and accompanying beauty parades of university rankings; with less envy from red-tape-bound universities, Giddens's initiative could be seen as a bold break to capture public intellectual space potentially with powerful backward linkages not just into the hosting department but also to the School as a whole. BBC was (then) across the road from the LSE, which was a stone's throw from Westminster and within shouting distance of Fleet Street; LSE was ever adept at working those angles for public effect and institutional advantage.

[74] Cambridge historians appeared to have an informal lien over Chichele professorships in Oxford: John Habakkuk jumped from lecturer in economic history in the Faculty of Economics in Cambridge in 1950, then aged just 35 years, to the Chichele professorship in economic history, holding the position till 1967; he handed over to another eminent Cambridge historian, Peter Mathias who remained in the Chichele Chair till 1987; then it was the turn of Charles Feinstein in 1989. Avner Offer, of Oxford—but still with the vestiges of a 'Cambridge' link in the form of being Charles's doctoral student, took over that Chair during 2000–2010; and then, after the exception to prove the rule of Cambridge—in the person of Kevin O'Rourke, 2011–2019—the Chichele Chair in Economic History returned to a Cambridge incumbent in 2020 as Sheilagh Ogilvie took over. The sequence could accidentally convey the casual impression that over the past 70 years, while Oxford could not produce economic historians of the necessary stature, Cambridge could not retain the ones it had produced.

[75] https://www.history.ox.ac.uk/people/professor-sheilagh-ogilvie#/

received or contemporary generalisations about the place of protoindustrialisation, hypothesised European marriage patterns, about the nature and role of guilds and social capital, and social and political institutions in stymieing or stimulating economic growth; illustrations from the German experience are used as counter examples to question the generalisability of earlier propositions. The bottom line of Martin Daunton's assessment of Ogilvie's oeuvre is that "Ogilvie is pursuing Postan's approach of microcosmic history—a concern for the concrete and real without losing sight of the general" (Daunton, 2017a, p. 176); Postan might have been tickled by the vision of a Postanian cuckoo in the erstwhile Kaldorian nest. [76]

While the study of the German industrial revolution should arouse as much intrinsic interest as the British case, the overwhelming concentration of the body of research on this, and the Russian pre-industrial, experience does place it in a rather special niche in the context of the overall research profile of a department of economics, let alone of a mainstream orthodox kind. There is a great deal of research in partnership, but the co-researchers and co-authors are mainly external to the Faculty as well as to the University, and indeed the country.[77] Strikingly, there is little evidence from a massive list of publications[78] of cross-fertilisation across to the equally substantial body of work on connected, though not identical, themes by Jane Humphries and Sara Horrell on labour, nutrition, children gender, women, family and households, on early industrialisation; cross-referencing is mutually invisible, suggesting a possible lack of connectivity or affinity. The somewhat extreme degree of specialisation on a theme ostensibly quite distant from the research concerns of the Faculty begs the question if this body of work might not have been more 'at home' in the neighbouring building housing the large, diverse and accomplished Faculty of History where both medieval and German history were listed specialisms. Also of pertinence could be the opportunity cost of a possible silo effect, arising from the discrete distance from the research of colleagues and thus the possible limitation on a role of academic leadership, interaction or guidance for younger colleagues with research profiles and academic careers to develop in economic history. All this notwithstanding, there is much evidence of a sustained effort

---

[76] Daunton (2017a, pp. 175–177) for a distillation of the import of Ogilvie's work in this area.

[77] Almost the solitary exception is Jeremy Edwards with whom there is a substantial list of co-authored papers starting from 1996 and continuing till well after his retirement. Apart from this, the only visible of linkages to Faculty economists are in acknowledgements or occasional references to, or in, the work of Partha Dasgupta on social capital, a side theme of his in (Dasgupta, 1995, cited as 1993 in Dasgupta, 2002). In a later work on social capital and economic performance in the context of development, Dasgupta argues in favour of formal markets over informal institutions: and, in support of this position, chooses—somewhat curiously given the substantial literature on these aspects in development discourse—to cite Ogilvie (1997) [presumably Ogilvie (1997)] "for a chilling portrait of life constrained by communitarian rules in the Black Forests of Wurttemberg in the early-Modern period, and persisting until the nineteenth century" (Dasgupta, 2002, p. 5n3).

[78] Full list of publications till 2020 from Faculty of Economics website.
https://www.econ.cam.ac.uk/people/faculty/sco2/publications

to use the spotlight of the experience of protoindustrialisation and related themes in medieval German, Russian or Czech history to illuminate contemporary policy issues of poverty and human development, the role of institutions in economic development, aid policy and so on.

Thirty years ago, Ogilvie discovered the inventories in the archives of two German communities "a vast number of observations in a huge database on the lives of southwest German villagers between 1600 and 1900; ... the database includes court records, guild ledgers, parish registers, village censuses, tax lists and—the most recent addition—9,000 handwritten inventories listing over a million personal possessions belonging to ordinary women and men across three centuries. Since 2009, Ogilvie and her team have been building the vast database of material possessions on top of their full demographic reconstruction of the people who lived in these two communities. 'We can follow the same people—and their descendants—across 300 years of educational and economic change,' she says. The inventories Ogilvie is analysing listed the belongings of women and men at marriage, remarriage and death. From badger skins to Bibles, dung barrows to dried apple slices, sewing machines to scarlet bodices—the villagers' entire worldly goods were listed. Inventories of agricultural equipment and craft tools revealed economic activities; ownership of books and education-related objects like pens and slates suggested how people learned. In addition, tax lists recorded the value of farms, workshops, assets and debts; signatures and people's estimates of their age indicated literacy and numeracy levels; ... 'previous studies usually had just one proxy for linking education with economic growth—the presence of schools and printing presses, perhaps, or school enrolment, or the ability to sign names. This database gives us multiple indicators for the same individuals,' she explains. 'I began to realise that, for the first time ever, it was possible to link literacy, numeracy, wealth, industriousness, innovative behaviour and participation in the cash economy and credit markets—for individual women and men, rich and poor, over the very long term.' Individual lives have unfolded before their eyes."[79] Ogilvie has utilised this data set to offer her solutions to contemporary development problems.

Of note also is her collaborations with Tracy Dennison whose specialisation, analogous to Ogilvie's for medieval Germany, is medieval Russia; she investigates a similar range of issues in a similar iconoclastic style and seems to follow a parallel track in also challenging various historical generalisations about Russia, for example, the established presumptions about village societies and communitarian, redistributive institutions in rural Russia; in particular, the demography of A. V. Chayanov on the persistence of a peasantry; their joint work analyses serfdom and social capital, the European marriage pattern, the

---

[79] https://www.cam.ac.uk/research/features/how-9000-lists-written-over-300-years-are-helping-to-test-theories-of-economic-growth

relationships between institutions, demography and economic growth (Dennison & Ogilvie, 2007, 2014, 2016). Dennison obtained her BA in USA, her M.Phil in Oxford, her PhD in Cambridge in 2004, held a postdoctoral post at the Centre for History and Economics in Cambridge, lectured in Russian History and the Department of Slavonic Studies of Faculty of Medieval and Modern Languages in Cambridge, before relocating to the California Institute of Technology where she is a Professor of Social Science History.[80]

In an interview with a students' magazine in Cambridge in 2012, Emma Rothschild, amongst other positions the Joint Director of the Centre for History and Economics, was posed a question: "Historically, Cambridge has had a tradition of world-leading research in the field of economics. Is the university still a leader in the subject? If not why not?" Her response singled out Sheilagh Ogilvie: "I think in general, US research universities at MIT and Harvard particularly have come to the forefront of economics worldwide over the last generation, and all UK universities have been affected by that to the extent that it matters what world rankings say. But there are wonderful economists at this university and just a few days ago I heard a marvellous talk by Professor Sheila Ogilvie who is one of the leading economic historians in the world and is a member of the economics faculty here. She is someone who really does speak to both historians as well as economists."[81]

As a fresh Fellow of the British Academy, she responds to a question about "the challenges and opportunities they see for their subjects over the next decade". Economists need to learn from economic historians, is her message: "I hope economics in the 2020s will work out how societies can change their institutions. Recent research has found that institutions—the 'rules of the game' that shape human interaction—are fundamental, if poor societies hope to improve growth and well-being. Thanks to close cooperation between economists and economic historians, we've discovered that it's not a single magic bullet, but a whole interconnected cluster of institutions that support well-functioning markets and impartial governments. But we don't know how to get from where we are now to an institutional cluster that's friendlier to growth. To change institutions, we need to understand them better. This needs economists and economic historians to work together—even more closely than we already do."[82]

---

[80] https://divisions-prod.s3.amazonaws.com/hss/people/Dennison_CV_May_2020.pdf
[81] Interview: Emma Rothschild, *The Cambridge Student*, 2 July 2012.
https://www.tcs.cam.ac.uk/interview-emma-rothschild/
[82] https://www.thebritishacademy.ac.uk/blog/nine-fellows-british-academy-humanities-social-sciences-shape-2020s/

Sheilagh Ogilvie's apparent mission to make deep, even silo, economic history fit for purpose for guiding, or 'drawing lessons', for contemporary policies, including especially problems of poverty, human development and economic growth in less developed economies, does not stop with these conversations between economists and economic historians. Ogilvie published her book *The European Guilds: An Economic Analysis* in March 2019, and the following year appears as a blur of multi-media promotional dissemination, in Cambridge, in UK and on the Continent, significantly including a rather unusual event: a Thought Experiment Lecture at the Cabinet Office for officials from the Cabinet Office, HM Treasury and Number 10 on 'Institutions and Economic Growth: Cautionary Tales from History' on October 18, "emphasizing, on the bias of European economic history, that policymakers should regard institutions as an integrated system rather than a menu from which one or two items can be chosen", with three separate videos recorded on the messages she thinks policy makers can draw from economic history; and then on 29 January 2020, another message delivered via the British Academy, shortly after taking up the Chichele professorship in Oxford.[83]

While the motivation to seek modern global lessons from medieval German history is remarkable and laudable, it does raise a question of whether it isn't a bridge too far, especially for a Postanian who is expected to shun generalisations. One could legitimately query how well lessons drawn from the medieval silo of her research might travel into the contemporary open field of economic development in poor economies; at best, such 'lessons' would be tenuous and contingent to a degree that could render them almost irrelevant. Such a concern has not prevented Ogilvie from using the specificities of the German medieval experience as ammunition to take aim at a wide range of development-related propositions, for example, pertaining to the social capital, to the link between education and economic growth,[84] to formality and informality of

---

[83] https://www.econ.cam.ac.uk/news-tag?tag=Economic%20History

[84] Ogilvie believes that this statistical archive of medieval Germany "may hold the answer to a conundrum that has long puzzled economists: the lack of evidence for a causal link between education and a country's growth and development." "It might sound as if this is a no-brainer," explains Ogilvie. "Education helps us to work more productively, invent better technology, earn more, have fewer children and invest more in them—surely it must be critical for economic growth? But, if you look back through history, there's no evidence that having a high literacy rate made a country industrialise earlier." "German-speaking central Europe is an excellent laboratory for testing theories of economic growth," she explains. "We know that literacy rates and book ownership were high and yet the region remained poor. We also know that local guilds and merchant associations were powerful and resisted changes that threatened their monopolies. Entrenched village oligarchies opposed disruptive innovations and blocked labour migration." "Early findings suggest that the potential benefits of education for the economy can be held back by other barriers, and this has implications for today," she says. "Huge amounts are spent improving education in developing countries but this spending can fail to deliver economic growth if restrictions block people—especially women and the poor—from using their education in economically productive ways. If economic institutions are poorly set up, for instance, education can't lead to growth."

https://www.cam.ac.uk/research/features/how-9000-lists-written-over-300-years-are-helping-to-test-theories-of-economic-growth

markets, to the role of institutions and governance,[85] no doubt amongst other dimensions. Does Ogilvie set up strawmen in such scripted exchanges between past and present?

Cluster 4: Toke Aidt

The fourth grouping comprises Toke Aidt, whose body of research is suggestive at best only of a tenuous link with the lineages of classical economic history practiced in the Faculty over the decades. He describes his research interests as 'political economics', not to be confused with 'political economy' that was once the standard fare of the Faculty; his research groups as 'empirical microeconomics' and 'economic history'; and his expertise as 'corruption'. The scope and substance of his published research (mostly) with co-authors from outside the Faculty, all tend to indicate weak affinities and linkages with other staff in the Faculty, which, a few years after his appointment, had decided to drop the reference to 'politics' even from its title—as the General Board of the University then stated, "in order to reflect more accurately the research interests that would be represented in the integrated Faculty" (Cambridge Reporter, 21 July 2004).

Toke Aidt's research output displays a staggering range of themes revealing him as an academic with a wide-angled research curiosity and matching proclivity for joint work,[86] but as it happens, with both the research and the

---

[85] "Economic history is widely supposed to support the idea that successful economies do not require public order institutions—those associated with formal authorities such as states, rulers, and legal systems—because private order institutions—those formed through informal collective action by individuals—can substitute for them. This is taken to imply that modern poor economies can achieve sustained growth without well-functioning governments or legal systems, since private-order substitutes have a successful historical record of supporting growth [Ogilvie cites references, e.g. World Bank, 2002; Dasgupta, 2000; Helpman, 2004; Dixit, 2004, 2009]. These claims are arresting, but the facts tell a different tale." "A vocal set of economists argue that economies can succeed in the absence of strong state and public institutions. This column looks to the 'Champagne fairs' of medieval Europe for lessons in how important public institutions can be. Public authorities are crucial—for good or for ill. When rulers provided these as generalised institutional services to everyone, the Champagne fairs flourished. When they granted them to privileged groups only, trade declined and business moved elsewhere" (ibid.). One can wonder which group of 'vocal economists' would hold such views rejecting the need for well-functioning governments or legal systems, and how and why the experience of the Champagne fairs from medieval times should be prioritised over learnings from the contemporary or historical experience of the context at the receiving end of the lessons from Champagne.

Ogilvie, S. (2015). Medieval Champagne fairs: lessons for development.
https://voxeu.org/article/medieval-champagne-fairs-lessons-development

[86] Rent seeking and corruption (Aidt, 2016); riots and democracy in sub-Saharan Africa (Aidt and Leon, 2016); fiscal federalism (Aidt & Dutta, 2017); government ideology and sustainable development (Aidt, Castro and Martins, 2018); oligarchic elites and democratisation processes from the Great Reform Act of 1832 (Aidt & Franck, 2019); collective action and the Swing riots (Aidt, Leon and Satchell., 2021); ballots and vote buying (Aidt & Jensen, 2017); immediate themes such as 'breaking the Brexit impasse' (Aidt, Chadha and Sabourian, 2019); political regimes and foreign interventions (Aidt & Albornoz, 2011); and then, some intriguing titles such as 'the golden hello and political transitions' (Aidt, Albornoz and Gassebner, 2017), and 'the big five personality traits and partisanship in England' (Aidt & Rauh, 2018); from another drawer on 'are prices enough? The economics of material demand reduction' (Aidt, Lili and Low, 2017); and then a project in collaboration with colleagues in Belgium, studying 'democratic purges in post-World War II France'.

partnerships generally falling outside the domain of the Faculty. And clearly, 'economic history' is not quite dominant in the profile of publications (though mention has been made of a joint paper in 2010 with Professor Jayasri Dutta, then of the Faculty of Economics, and Martin Daunton, the Professor of Economic History in the Faculty of History); and arguably, the substantive content of his work could blend in perhaps better in a department of politics where potentially there could be greater intellectual affinities than in economics. On the other hand, what might connect better with economics—in the manner in which it is practised at the Faculty—would be his general methodological approach that involves asking specific questions about a specific phenomenon—which in substance could be contemporary or historical, economic or sociological or political—assembling a data set, and then testing the formulated axiomatic hypothesis using optimising behavioural models based on utility maximisation by all agents; it is such a universal neoclassical toolkit that is usually carried to the diverse items in the wide array of his research papers which are thus united not by thematic unities as by this reliance on the opportunistic application of a shared methodological approach. As such, this genre is located at a discrete distance from the perspectives and methodologies of classical economic history, though the potential bridges to cliometrics are immediately apparent.

How the choice of epistemological and methodological approach potentially creates polarities is illustrated by the work on corruption, a field surveyed both by Aidt Toke (2003, p. F632) and Mushtaq Khan (1996). Mushtaq Khan sets up typologies of corrupt transactions, evaluating alternative theoretical constructions from economists. "Economic theory has attempted to identify the conditions under which corruption has particularly harmful effects. This article evaluates these theories and argues that the classifications offered are misleading. Very successful interventionist states have suffered from corruption just as much as very unsuccessful ones. Policy responses to corruption require an understanding of the effects of corruption and the determinants of these effects. The fact which appears to have a strong effect in determining the harmfulness of corruption is the balance of power between the state and its clients. An alternative classification of the effects of corruption is suggested on this basis" Khan, M. (1996, p. 12). In Toke's contribution, "a theoretical as opposed to a practical or an empirical angle in chosen to differentiate this survey [on corruption] from existing ones" (Toke, 2003, p. F632); Toke's wide-ranging survey covers a list of references pushing a hundred but—notwithstanding the albeit lapsed Cambridge connection—seems to entirely exclude the substantial body of work on corruption-related themes of Mushtaq Khan, one of the leading theoreticians and analysts in this field at both theoretical and empirical levels, though his methodological approach, rooted in political economy, is quite distinct from that of Toke.

12.5　C.2020, HERE, TO WHERE?

Martin Daunton provides an overarching reading on the trajectory economic history over the long sweep in Cambridge:

> Economic history in Cambridge developed its own particular characteristics as a result of five intellectual and institutional factors: a concern for the relationship between population and resources that goes back to Malthus; the work of the Department of Applied Economics of the Faculty of Economics in the creation of long-run national income data; the influence of the Cambridge school of the history of thought; a concern for political and institutional influences on markets and economic life; and connections with the history of imperialism. As a result, disciplinary boundaries were blurred and economic history was more widely diffused, with a greater range of influences and questions. (Daunton, 2017a, pp. 179–180)

"The application of econometric analysis to the past was a challenge to economic historians in Britain. In many universities, separate departments were closed and posts lost."[87] But in Daunton's judgement, "Cambridge was different, for economic history was taught within both the Faculty of History and the Faculty of Economics, and it continued to flourish in part through the continuation of Postan's focus on the relationship between population and resources rather than the use of econometrics" (Daunton, 2017a, p. 167). This could be a fair assessment of the past decades in the Faculty of History, but how well might this sanguine reflection apply to the experience of economic history in the Faculty of Economics?

12.5.1　*Economic History at the Faculty of Economics: Full Stop?*

An important attribute of any individual research profile is its embeddedness in teamwork where collaborations generate synergies and externalities through scale and scope effects, building a collective body of work where the cumulative impact exceeds a simple summation of its individual components. This applies all the more when large data sets need processing and analysis, requiring multiple qualitative and quantitative methodologies, and in tasks of generating research funding, report-writing, seminars, conferences, institutional networking, public dissemination, etc. Such collective capacities also enable the viability of thematic teaching and doctoral research programmes and, overall, can achieve far greater impact both on the discipline as well as in wider public

---

[87] Daunton writes that "In the USA, economic history survived within departments of economics, largely by adopting the techniques of the economics profession and applying theory to the past, sometimes producing real insight and sometimes provoking mutterings about empty economic boxes" (Daunton, 2017a, p. 180). At the Faculty of Economics, this space seems to be occupied, solely perhaps, by Toke Aidt.

policy discourse. Viewed from a departmental perspective, the benefits are all the greater if these synergies and linkages are developed within its domain, but while it takes time for coherent and cohesive research identities of teams to evolve and gain recognition, sustainability is often fragile and subject to the idiosyncrasies of individual careers and departmental decisions[88] especially when the teams are relatively small. Again, from an institutional perspective, individual or team research has to have pertinence and salience within the substantive research and teaching rubric of the department or faculty. A productive individual outlier might score high, say, in research assessment exercises but not contribute equivalently to the mandate of its host unit.

Viewed through such a prism, the four clusters of researchers and research in economic history in the Faculty seem to display perceptible differences. The Solomou-Kitson-Weale cluster clearly conveys genetic affinity with the bread-and-butter business of the erstwhile research teams of the DAE: there appears to be continuity in terms of a careful focus on the necessary data bases to make them fit for the purpose of analysing significant, generally macroeconomic, questions with a strong interface with policy. The Humphries-Horrell cluster conveys both continuity and development: on the one side, fundamental questions are posed to received narratives of the industrial revolution within a gendered theoretical and quantitative approach, and here, there is a clear backward linkage with the oeuvre of both Phyllis Deane and of Charles Feinstein; but there is also a very significant departure in the systematic treatment of economic history from a gendered perspective, potentially erecting a scaffolding for a permanent institutional intervention—a potential dissipated rather than realised by Faculty decision-makers. Given the fact that both were trained as economists, there was also considerable possibility of productive research interactions not just with other economists, but also with sociologists and development economists—this, especially in view of their command over diverse epistemological and methodological treatments. The third cluster, Ogilvie-Edwards, is again highly productive at the individual level, but arguably tends to fall short on the criterion of productive salience and articulation within Faculty research interests; indeed, the deep degree of specialisation is such as to raise a question about whether the Faculty offered the best home for it. And the fourth 'cluster' reflects mostly the idiosyncratic research agenda of an individual academic. Considering the period as a whole, an inverted U-curve could well depict the trajectory of economic history in the DAE and the Faculty, with

---

[88] These aspects were much in evidence within the DAE where most research was done within teams, though Faculty staff with their individual research projects were always encouraged and accommodated. That said, the impact on the academic discipline and on the wider policy discourse was achieved by teams: the Cambridge Growth Project, the Cambridge Economic Policy Group, the Labour Studies team, the Sociology Group, the Business research team; and there were the earlier teams of historical statisticians constructing systematic time series of national accounts, and other data sets for the UK and European economies.

the apogee in the decade of the mid-1980s to the mid-1990s, and fraying and a slide down the other side thereafter. Notably, unlike in other places, culpability for the atrophy cannot be pinned on the displacement effect associated with the arrival of cliometrics, simply because this did not happen within the Faculty of Economics and Politics.

Quite recently as 2014, in its submission to the REF2014, the Faculty of Economics was able to post the following description of its work on economic history: "The Economic History Research Group uses economic approaches to investigate the past and historical expertise to analyze how economies work. Our research interests include—but are not limited to—business cycles, climate, consumption, the environment, fertility, financial markets, guilds, human capital, inequality, living standards, market integration, property rights, serfdom, technological innovation, trade, women's work, and the economics of institutions and government. Our research spans more than 1,000 years, from the late tenth century to the early twenty-first. We maintain strong interdisciplinary links, which extend from economics into demography, geography, history, and political science."[89]

This length and range of specialisations are somewhat bewildering bearing in mind the size of the 'team' then comprising four Faculty staff members each ploughing her or his individual furrow. A Centre for Quantitative Economic History is mentioned, but it is unclear how well it thrived or how long it survived. Regardless of the somewhat exaggerated spread of offerings listed in 2014, such claims have probably become even more untenable now with the departure in 2019/20 of Sheilagh Ogilvie, a Postanian practitioner, to the Chichele Professorship in Oxford, and the migration of Sara Horrell, of the mould of the classical quantitative economic history, to a professorship at the LSE, leaving Solomos Solomou—with a few years to retirement—and Toke Aidt as the remaining economic historians in the Faculty. It would appear then that the fate of economic history in the Faculty of Economics is converging with that experienced by the subject elsewhere: displacement by cliometrics and new economic history merged with economics; relocation into departments of history with social and cultural labels; or disappearance and demise, with this being the most likely outcome at the moment, barring a major turn of fortune.

At the height of his authority over economics in Cambridge and UK, Frank Hahn (1989, p. 899) had another gratuitous go at Joan Robinson, who had died six years earlier: apropos general equilibrium: "she tried her best, but she never managed … she never got there. …She was very hostile to equilibrium because in her (just as Nicky) common sense kept breaking through. They saw the economy in a much more Schumpeterian way, perhaps in a Marxian way, much more historically based …)." A few global crises down the line, Nicky's assertion of the 'irrelevance of equilibrium economics' didn't seem much of an

---

[89] https://www.econ.cam.ac.uk/research/research-groups/hist

exaggeration; the trouble for Hahn, the general equilibrium man, was that 'history' as reality kept breaking through. William Janeway supervised by Richard Kahn for his PhD, major donor (with his wife) to Cambridge economics, and co-founder of the Institute for New Economic Thinking (INET), lists four pillars as markers of new economic thinking, of which the fourth is: "taking history seriously: 'thick' history that reaches beyond quantitative data to take account of the evolution of the social and political and cultural contexts which condition economic and financial experience" (Janeway, 2015).

"A generation ago, Cliometrics proposed to bring rigor to economic history by embedding historical data in the neoclassical production function, thereby imposing on history the radical counterfactuals that at all times resources are fully employed and optimally allocated. Far from honouring historical experience, it produced a travesty of it." Required are explorations of economic development over the past 250 years, involving the impact of technological innovation and its creative destruction. "New economic thinking means reading old economics books", Janeway quotes Mark Thoma with approval: "indeed he was right. Recognition that there is much to learn from past efforts to comprehend the dynamics of production and growth, employment and consumption, savings and investment, price discovery and price fixing—and the roles of the state with respect to all—is a marker not only of new economic thinking, but of the maturity of the discipline itself" (Janeway, 2015). Will donor dollars and direction make the wheel take a full circle, reverse the decades of wilful attrition of the cumulative capacity and restore the meaningful study of economic history into the intellectual frame of Faculty economics? Has the wheel taken a full circle? Janeway, even with his deep pockets, faces an uphill struggle, as indicated by the progressive disappearance of economic history as a discipline from universities in the USA and Europe.

Peter Temin (2013) provides a sobering requiem for the demise of economic history at MIT, its fate sealed by the tribe of the econometricians throwing their lot with the economic theoreticians, leaving classical economic historians in the lurch. Avner Offer writes: "In the 1960s, a new approach to the past emerged in the USA which came to be known as the 'new economic history', or 'cliometrics'. It premised that individual rationality and market equilibrium provided a good explanatory framework for the economic past. It typically postulated a causal mechanism suggested by deductive economic theory, and sought to measure it by means of a statistical test of the explanatory power of each of a cluster of quantitative variables on the 'dependent variable' to be explained. Identifying the relative importance of labour and capital as independent sources of economic growth also followed this procedure…" (Offer, 2008, p. 12). Clearly, in its epistemological framing and techniques, cliometrics converted 'economic history', as indeed Janeway himself notes, into an applied field of mainstream neoclassical economics, and so 'economic history' aka 'cliometrics' migrated into a subordinate zone in departments of economics. Economic history lost its identity and space to cultural, social and other exotic forms of history, missing the core of political economy. And all quantitative economic history had to be cliometric or be ascribed as being deficient in theory or technique.

Somewhat he plaintively asks: "What is the cost of not having economic history at M.I.T.?" He offers a thoughtful wide-ranging answer to his rhetorical question, but then proceeds to illustrate it by taking a scalpel to dissect the blind spots and misreadings of a widely lauded work of economic history, conducted in his own neighbourhood, in the cliometric tradition. "This is a loss to the department because economic history … adds to our understanding of economic growth in several ways. Most importantly, economic history contains a sense of time. … In addition, politics and economics are intertwined in the economic history. Nations make choices, even if only by default, and these choices affect growth. Demography and resources affect economic growth, but they do not determine it. … And the study of history can expand the insights of formal economics … into a narrative of people and choices. In particular, … it can acknowledge that history is not always monotonic. The classic account of modern economic history is of a sequence of leading economies, which have taken their turn at the world's center stage, … Spain, Holland, Britain and the United States in successive centuries. … The reasons for the decline of some countries and the rise of others… provide a sense of possibilities that are excluded by what economic historians call Whig history, that is, monotonic progress."

> What is the cost of not having economic history at MIT? It can be seen in Acemoglu and Robinson, *Why Nations Fail* (2012). This is a deservedly successful popular book, making a simple and strong point … The book is not however good economic history. It is an example of Whig history in which good policies make for progress and bad policies preclude it. Only transitions from bad to good are considered in this colorful but still monotonic story. The clear implication is that if countries can copy the policies of English-speaking countries, they will prosper. … They ignore the gorilla on the basketball court: the United States. The United States is in danger of becoming a failed state … The distributions of income and wealth have been getting worse since the 1970s, and political power has been concentrating more and more in the very wealthy … This process has gone on for a generation … The election of 2000 went Republican because citizens who have completed prison sentences are not permitted to vote in Florida. There were enough disenfranchised felons in 2000 that the state would have gone Democratic if voting had been a universal right. … More recently, the Supreme Court decided … that corporations are people with full political rights, even though people who have passed through the criminal judicial system are not. … The United States government is barely functioning at the moment, and it is a very interesting question whether the United States could become a failed state in the near future. It is a shame that Acemoglu and Robinson did not use their erudition to confront what may be the most important question of how nations fail today. … the book itself presents a picture of an Olympian America looking down on a multitude of failed states. … The United States is not the only advanced country in trouble at the moment. … the United States is joining Britain in self- inflicted austerity. The countries of southern Europe are deflating in response to pressures to save the euro. The resulting strains on the fabric of

society led to political problems in the immediate aftermath of the First World War and again in the early 1930s. Economic history would help policy makers today if we recalled it to them, as no one wants to see democratic governments in trouble or the rise of something like fascism in Southern Europe. (Temin, 2013, pp. 11–17).

12.5.2 *At the Faculty of History: New Turnings*

The narratives that engaged most of the string of holders of the chair of economic history share the feature of projecting the stories from a vantage point of dominance. Land ownership and family estates focus on the transmission of rights of owners; were there no other classes? Narratives of the industrial revolution, as spun by the historians of business, tend to become the stories of businessmen; were there no workers? And they tend not to worry overly about the role of empire, an abstraction or distraction shared with the CAMPOP school of thought; and when imperialism is discussed (by other historians), these are all too often renditions from the perspectives of those who hold and execute imperial power rather than those at the other end of the imperial gun. It was as if India, China, Africa, Latin America, were not even part players in their script of the drama of British social and economic change. Cambridge economics has often been accused of intellectual insularity, but this seems to be well matched with the nationally introverted imaginaries that seem to characterise many if not most of these economic historians, all eminent in their own right. This background brings into sharper relief, even if by default, the uphill trajectories of historians (Dobb, Hobsbawm, Humphries, Oxley) who interrogate such hierarchical narratives and dig out perspectives as viewed from the (under)side of the 'others'. Against this, albeit caricaturised simplification, there appears to be a turning point at the Faculty of History with the appointment, in 2016, as Professor of Economic History, of Gareth Austin who is in the vanguard of what he and Stephen Broadberry (Austin and Broadberry 2014) call "the renaissance of African economic history".

Gareth Austin's Inaugural Lecture (Austin, 2017, 20 October) demarcates "three 'revolutions' in the study of economic history since the days of Clapham: (1) the cliometric revolution of the 1960s, which applied neoclassical theory and analytical statistics to the economic past; (2) the emergence in the 1950s–1980s of the systematic and continuous study of the economic history of the non-Western world, what may be called 'The Other Economic History'; and (3) the attempt, essentially in the present century, reciprocally to integrate the economic history of the West and the Rest, using quantitative and other methods." His work locates him firmly in the second and third genres; he cautions: "we have a lot still to do to achieve a genuinely global economic history, based on the principle of reciprocal comparison."

The appointment of Gareth Austin runs against the flow of all earlier appointments (except David Joslin), in that he is not a specialist in some aspect of British economic history; this pulls into the frame not just the salience of colonialism, especially through his specialisation of African economic history, but also of global studies on a level field of study. In a landmark special issue of *Economic History Review* devoted unusually to mentioned 'renaissance', Austin and Broadberry, as editors, observe: "Until a few years ago, the most important outlets for African economic history continued to be the Journal of African History and the African Studies series of various book presses. Africanists tended to assume that Europeanists were uninterested in their work. Conversely, economic historians of the West perhaps tended to assume that the source constraints on African economic history were even greater than they actually are, and that the study of African economies was so interwoven with anthropology as to be indecipherable in terms familiar to economic historian, especially those trained in economics" (Austin & Broadberry, 2014, p. 898). "[T]he relationship between African economic history and the Western-centred core of the economic history discipline remained an example of the segmentation of the market for knowledge … The recent resurgence of interest in Africa's economic past has been accompanied by a markedly greater integration of such markets" (Austin & Broadberry, 2014, p. 899).

Austin and Broadberry (2014, pp. 893–894) list different conceptual frameworks used in addressing African economic history: the polarity between Polanyi's depictions of markets in precolonial economies where market transactions were governed by reciprocity and administration, and Hopkins's more conventional view of market functioning and price formation; the "shift of analytical focus from individual calculus to the structures conditioning economic behaviour". French Marxists highlighted the colonial extraction of surplus from pre-capitalist African economies; dependency theory promoted the centre-periphery paradigm where imperialism invested capital for extraction but not for productive reinvestment for local development; dependency theory was "subjected to a coruscating critique from historically minded economists more impressed with Marx's view of imperialism as spreading capitalism worldwide and pointing to the continuing growth of wage labour";[90] the shift to a

---

[90] Austin has in mind here *Imperialism, Pioneer of Capitalism*, the iconoclastic and hugely controversial work of Bill Warren edited by John Sender after Warren died; and the follow-up joint work purporting to flesh out Warren's thesis for Africa, in *The Development of Capitalism in Africa* (Sender & Smith, 1986). John Sender and Sheila Smith were both teaching development courses in Cambridge. Worth mentioning here is review of this intervention by Thandika Mkandawire (1987). If Sender and Smith were 'coruscating', Mkandawire's rebuttal is excoriating. This is how Thandika closes:

> The significance of this book lies not in its scientific value (which is meagre) but in the fact that it is part of a genre of current writing on Africa that is intended to unburden the erstwhile colonial masters of any sense of guilt they may have felt about the pain, suffering and dehumanization they inflicted in their past doings on the rest of humanity. In this new spirit nationalism is discredited as simply obscurantist and the venality of some of the purveyors of this nationalism is used to completely absolve the object against which this nationalism was directed—imperialism. The book is part of the cultural and intellectual atmosphere which sustains nostalgic films about the colonial past, nourishes laudatory accounts of the economic role and civilizing mission of colonial rule and makes bashing of "nationalism" à la rigueur. It is the economist's version of 'Out of Africa'. (Mkandawire, 1987, p. 170)

composite framework which combined "the economic rationality of indigenous farmers with the neo-marxist insistence on the importance of coercive state intervention, to argue that the settler economies of Africa had seen first the emergence of small-scale production for the market, and then its repression as states sought to drive Africans into the labour market, supplying make migrant labour to European employers"[91]; and finally, Robert Bates and rational choice perspective and new institutional economics. Generously, and resonating with the earlier assessment of Martin Daunton, they remark that "we need to combine the best insights from the cliometric and other traditions of economic history, respecting the different approaches which historians and economists take to determining causality. Economic History needs to re-affirm its position as the intersection set of the disciplines of History and Economics"—a position that Gareth Austin reiterated in his Inaugural Lecture in 2017. Of course, a prior requirement giving meaning and substance to this wish would be a specification of 'which economics' and 'which history' it was intended to combine. In a recent book *Teaching Economics with Economic History*, one of the editors, Matthias Fluckiger (2018, p. 55), claims: "Economic historians speak the same language as economists. They share a common disciplinary core, and they employ similar research approaches to address related questions." This is a type of untenable reductionist one-eyed claim that protagonists of multidisciplinary research might wish to be careful to side-step.

Gareth Austin's agenda, with its global canvas, clearly marks a perceptible break with the earlier introverted UK-focussed imaginaries, with David Joslin—the other non-UK specialist—as a previous exception. Thus, at the present, there appear to be multiple crosscurrents and potential articulations with other disciplines. The potential links to development studies and development economics and politics are immediately obvious. The contents of the 'African renaissance' special issue of the *EHR* are also striking in their wide interface with contiguous disciplines, and there is also a throwback, across a time barrier, to the early work on national and historical accounting done in the DAE in the Stone and Reddaway eras—for instance, the articles by Morten Jerven and Hanaan Marwah on the construction time series for GDP, and investment, respectively, resonate with this early heroic phase of historical statisticians in the DAE, including work not just on UK, but also on developing national income accounts for African colonies, work that was overseen by the likes of Austin Robinson, Richard Stone and W. Arthur Lewis and carried out by a young Phyllis Deane in her pioneering studies—as discussed earlier. Austin and Broadberry also observe that "it is fitting that this special issue on Africa should follow the previous issue of the *Economic History Review* on the *Great Divergence*" (with a mention of Kenneth Pomeranz (2001) though not of the

---

[91] The pertinent contemporary reference here is to the group of economic historians working at Queen Elizabeth House and the Institute of Commonwealth Studies in Oxford in the late 1970s and 1980s, in particular Stanley Trapido, Coilin Bundy, William Beinart and Robin Palmer.

earlier *ReOrient* by Andre Gunder Frank (1998) which sketched a fresh vision for the place of China and Asia in historical and global perspectives). Such a widening of the gaze was long overdue. And regrettably, the possibilities that this might have released in earlier times have also long lapsed, there being virtually no one there at present with manifest interest of expertise to team up with. The Stone-Reddaway type of applied economics is all in the distant past; development studies and development economics were also eased out a long while back. So as with the earlier case of David Joslin and Latin American Studies, natural partnerships and affinities would be found now in the units within the Centre for Development Studies, the Judge Institute or other institutional locations.

Well over a century after the time when Alfred Marshall had worked hard to wean the rising discipline of Economics away from History and from Moral Sciences, the study of economic history, with all the vicissitudes en route in its trajectory, has arrived at a point where the Faculty of Economics has scarcely any economic historian left standing in its ranks. By a combination of default and design, neoclassical economics seems to have achieved the agenda of the founder of its tradition in Cambridge, at least for the time being.

Appendix 12.1: Economic History and Accounting at the DAE

While the mainline activity of constructing long-term series of the constituents of national accounts, and of national income itself, slowly dissolved at the DAE as the focus of research shifted into the use of these data sets for the analytical purposes for which they were intended, this genre of foundational work continued through the efforts of Martin Weale and Solomos Solomou after the former relocated there from the DAE in 1987, and also later from the NIESR after Martin Weale moved there from the Faculty as the Director.[92] A pair of comprehensive reviews of 'measurement' and 'national income accounting' in Cambridge economics, each covering 50 years, and both coincidentally published in the same year, are provided respectively by Geoff Harcourt and Michael Kitson (1993), and Martin Weale (1993).

Geoff Meeks (2017, pp. 192–193) discusses in some detail the range, substance and contributions of the empirical analyses of company accounts in pursuing important issues of industrial concentration and organisation, the relationship between company size and profitability, takeovers and mergers. Much of this work produced influential papers on a range of interrelated themes that provided a strong empirical platform for a critique of neoclassical theoretical propositions and for superior understandings of this important field of industrial economics with macro ramifications. "This stream of research …

---

[92] See, for instance, Solomou and Weale (1996, 1997) and Sefton and Weale (1995).

on these themes developed into a division of the new Centre for Business Research (CBR) at Cambridge, directed by Hughes, which, although housed in the Business School, welcomed disciplines from across the University, including economics, engineering, and law." Most significantly, Meeks points out, "this diversification into cognate disciplines coincided with a period in which the Faculty was withdrawing from sister fields such as accounting, development studies, finance, politics, and sociology. It was warmly welcomed and funded by the ESRC, which praised the CBR's 'first class programme of interdisciplinary research', especially 'first class contributions to the analysis of corporate governance and the growth performance of small and medium sized enterprises'" (ibid.).

Further, on the teaching side as well, accounts and accounting, in one form or another, entered Faculty courses, not least due to the 'Reddaway' approach that was then legal tender. "National income accounts were for decades an important part of the regular diet in applied economics for Tripos students: the Blue Book was a required purchase when I joined the Tripos in 1969" (Meeks, 2017, p. 200n21). Here, a personal recollection is pertinent. When scholarship money ran out, for a couple of years in the 1970s I served as the Faculty Assistant in Research, the lowest rung on the ladder, and slave work as it was, it was, at least in some respects, also a remarkable learning experience. Apart of doing disparate statistical jobs supporting individual professorial research, there was the task of producing the drafts of some of the tables that Brian Reddaway and Ajit Singh used in the handouts they used for their lectures in the Applied Statistics course in the Tripos. And then there was another penny-earning sideline activity, undergraduate supervisions, that provided the thin layer of jam on top of the wages of necessity. Inevitably, there were questions to set and essays to read on applied statistics, which is where I became a master of the remarkable Reddaway method of decomposing time series data into its constituent trend, cyclical, seasonal and random elements without recourse to a computer or calculator, and inflicted the pain, or conveyed the pleasure, of capability-building learning to unsuspecting students. In Reddaway-Singh fashion, I set up essay questions from the hot debates of the times: one asked students to extract the seasonal effect on death rates in the 'winter of discontent' with the 'Heath' coal strikes; and for another, I drew on an excellent paper, then very recently published, by Geoff Meeks, then almost a neighbour on the upper floor of the DAE wing of the Faculty Building. Geoff's article was 'Profit Illusion', and it served as the key resource for students to answer his question: "are profits being squeezed", then a big question between the left and the right. This was another 'Reddaway-type' question, and it demanded the detailed understanding and use of the Blue Book; for good measure, whenever students used some numbers from it, they were required to refer also to an appendix there which provided a tabular summary of the degree of reliability ascribed to that particular series. All this was ground-breaking learning experience for the students, and I dare say teachers as well, a wonderful way of entering the field of applied economics. I take the liberty, even if as a retro indulgence, to reproduce the opening paragraph of the Geoff Meeks's article in the *Oxford Bulletin of Economics and Statistics*, a well-thumbed copy of which must still be buried in some one other box of teaching materials.

> Are profits being squeezed? Drawing data from the same basic source, two sets of observers reach quite opposite conclusions. On the one hand, Glyn and Sutcliffe ... maintain that the sixties witnessed a severe decline in profitability; whilst, on the other, Panic and Close ... object that 'after 1960 there is simply no evidence of a significant decline in the pr-tax profitability of UK industry'. And that 'the inclusion of investment grants would probably eliminate completely the downward trend in post-tax profitability between 1961 and1969'. More recent work shows that such contradictory opinions result from different profit measures. It is the aim of this paper to pursue this theme, suggesting that different measures of profit may be appropriate for different issues. It is argued that a single measure, giving clear answer, is appropriate for one of the issues with which both sides were much concerned: whether companies' ability to finance investment from internal sources has been curtailed. (Meeks, 1974)

One might add, that apart from the *Blue Book*, another resource with rich seams of numbers for setting puzzling and rewarding exercises was *Social Trends*.

The national accounts estimations fed into the construction, originally by Richard Stone and Alan Brown, of the Cambridge growth model which subsequently evolved with its continual development by the team under Stone and Terry Barker: through teamwork, the model was made dynamic, and significantly disaggregated. The 1986 version included "about 8000 variables compared with about 1000 variables in the next largest, the Treasury model".[93] Stone (1984), in his 'Nobel' Prize 'bio', had mentioned that "this model can also be used for purposes other than forecasting"; and Meeks (2017, p. 190) points out that "this innovative disaggregation of the economy, to the industry level, lent itself to two unusual accounting extensions: accounting for environmental externalities associated with climate change; and a joint venture with financial accounting to integrate company accounts into the macro framework."[94] This observation has acute pertinence in that it shows the woeful lack of expertise and/or judgement of the ESRC experts and the Consortium that criticised the CGP's disaggregation approach when switching off the team's

---

[93] Barker and Peterson (1987, p. 23); cited by Meeks, who also highlights Weale (1985) and Sefton and Weale (1995).

[94] As with so many other lines of work, this thread too goes back to Stone: The very first Annual Report of the DAE for 1946–1948 states: "Mr Sewell Bray and Mr Stone are working on a study of the accounting basis for the measurement of aggregates of transactions. The aim of the project as a whole is to provide a common meeting place for the theoretical requirements of the economist and practical possibilities set by business records and accounting technique. At present work is concentrated on the accounting aspects of a system of social accounting designed to bridge the gap between national income statistics and accounting records. The first results have been embodied in

funding.[95] Richard Stone, then a recent 'Nobel' Prize winner, had complained, bitterly muttering comparing such behaviour to a 'banana republic', but to no avail.[96]

Meeks provides a thoughtful semi-Darwinian assessment on the life, while it lasted, of accounting in the Faculty of Economics: "There are few traces of accounting now left in the Faculty. In the process of departmental fission by which Cambridge tends to evolve (economics out of moral sciences, sociology out of economics, etc.) much of accounting has moved into the new (in Cambridge time) Business School. But it survived longer than in most economics departments elsewhere, and this chapter suggests some reasons for this. First, in contrast with some universities, there was a very indistinct frontier between accounting and economics for much of the Faculty's first century. People were comfortable straying over the frontier in both directions as their current research problem demanded. Second, as I have tried to illustrate, the activity delivered results, recognised by academic peers, and the outside world. Third, the participants were not identified with a particular single faction in the Faculty's feuds, and the activity was often seen as worthy, but boring, and no threat to the glamorous high theorists or policy maestros. So the participants in accounting were allowed to continue quietly with their measurement activities[97] ..." (ibid., p. 201). But what Meeks refers to as a process of departmental

---

a book by Mr Sewell Bray entitled *Social Accounts and the Business Enterprise Sector of the National Economy*, which is now in the Press (Bray, 1949). As time permits similar investigations will be made for other sectors of the economy. Arising out of this work Messrs Bray and Stone recently contributed an article to *Accounting Research* on 'The Presentation of the Central Government Accounts'" (Bray & Stone, 1948) (DAE Annual Report 1946–1948, #30, 31; p. 12). The second report, for 1948–1951, registers the progress made in this initiative: "Mr Sewell ... has since continued his work on the definition of the empirical correlates of certain important economic magnitudes and on the study of accounting statements appropriate to various sectors of the economy for recording transactions in a way which will be useful to the economist and, in particular, which will facilitate the collection of social accounting data. He is planning a comprehensive work on the problems involved and the treatment of various items in the accounts. He has also had under consideration the problem of whether it is possible to measure social costs in a way which would enable them to be incorporated into a social accounting system" (DAE, Annual Report 1948–1951, p. 10).

[95] The ESRC decision is fully discussed in Chap. 8 which investigates the case of the Cambridge Growth Model.

[96] This is discussed in some detail in Chap. 8.

[97] Thus, apart from the work of Ajit Singh, Alan Hughes and Andy Cosh, Meeks here also cites other major contributors: "Stone was a central figure in the construction of the UK's, and then the world's, national accounts. Whittington was a central figure in the overhaul and reconstruction of first the UK's, and then the world's, business accounts. Barker, with Peterson, led the way in engaging big business—companies such as IBM and ICI—in modelling and forecasting disaggregated national accounts; and Barker played a lead role at the IPCC. Dasgupta has been a leader in developing Green National Accounts for India" (Meeks, 2017, p. 200). Early classics in the genre of the exploration of theoretical questions through rigorous analysis of large data bases prominently include Singh, A. (1971) and Singh, A. and Whittington, G. (1968). It is noteworthy that, in the course of the hostile University Review of the DAE, one external expert, none other than

fission eventually produced the new purified species of economics in the Faculty, with accounting shifting the locus of its own existence to the environment of the CBR in the JBS.

Appendix 12.2: Locating Phyllis Deane in National Accounting and Feminist Discourse: A Supplementary Note[98]

An apposite point of entry is provided by the review by a highly knowledgeable peer, Peter Ady, of the two pioneering works of Phyllis Deane that effectively launched subsequent debates, *The Measurement of Colonial National Incomes* (Deane, 1948a) and *Colonial Social Accounting* (1953)—the work of a Cambridge female economist working in eastern Africa assessed by an Oxford female economist working in West Africa roughly on a similar enquiry at about the same time.

Peter Ady (1954, p. 174) concludes her review by emphasising that "these books are most valuable, and they remain … reference works of the highest importance for economists and administrator in the colonial field", but she carries her 'disappointment' that Phyllis Deane, in her second book, inexplicably held back from her promise of providing a consistent integrated set of social accounts for which—barring the limitation that her capital formation estimates were derived exclusively from savings estimates with all their known problems of reliability—she had set up all the necessary elements, controlled the required methodology of double-entry tabulation, and amply possessed the 'skill in

---

Michael Posner, attacked the DAE as an overgrown garden of weeds, but singled out this work on industrial economics as being of the highest international quality (See, Chap. 9). Also to be mentioned is the prior contribution of Robin Marris on managerial capitalism. In the 1950s, Geoff Harcourt began in Cambridge, and wanted to work on the macroeconomic implications of firms in oligopolistic structures in a Keynesian framework, and was sent [by his supervisor Ron Henderson] to the NIESR where they were setting up balance sheets and fund statements for the whole British quoted company sector" (Harcourt, 2007). "You are to write two reports for them, using the new accounted data that are coming out", he instructed Geoff. "Thus I was the first person to use those consolidated profit-and-loss accounts, funds statements and balance sheets for the whole population of British quoted companies. I wrote two reports, one on the chemical industry, and one on the woollen and worsted industry" (Harcourt & King, 1995, p. 169; see also Tew and Henderson (ed.) 1959).

[98] This note supplements the commentary on Phyllis Deane in Chap. 12, and should be read alongside that text. It is intended for readers with a special interest in these aspects of her work, or in the complexities of the early work on developing meaningful templates for national accounting which were sensitive to the complexity of societies and economies distinct from advanced market economies and societies. Reliance is placed upon very informative and thoughtful works by Luke Messac (2016) and Robert Ross (2013), and on the original report on the Ashanti Survey by Fortes et al. (1947) for shedding light on different aspects of the field contexts in which Phyllis Deane (and others) conducted their pioneering research.

exposition'. "To have completed a set of social accounts proper would have provided the final and most valuable cross-check upon the accounts as a whole. It would have provided an even more useful guide to the structure of these economies ... [and] finally a discussion of the advantages and otherwise of the current trend towards social and sector accounting and away from isolated national income estimates." Ady's lament is the absence, "despite the title, ... of a system of interlocking and integrated accounts showing the main money-flows throughout the economy". Developing such a system of social accounts, in Ady's view, would have been the crowning glory. Be that as it may, what Ady sought from Deane's second volume was a direction which was being pioneered at the DAE under the guidance of her mentor Dick Stone who, between the time of the volume and Ady's lament over the second, had brought Phyllis Deane over to join his band of national and social accounts statisticians at the DAE.

The undiluted appreciation from Peter Ady[99] carries special significance, since she was a peer researcher in her own right who, coincidentally, was engaged in a similar though independent research exercise to measure the national income of Gold Coast on the other side of the African continent, focussing on the Ashanti. Thus, while Phyllis was deep into her extended visit to Nyasaland and Northern Rhodesia in 1946, Peter was fully engaged in the Ashanti Survey of 1945–1946, contending with a similar set of economic accounting and estimation issues at the household and village levels again focussing on the vexed issues of valuation of a wide array of non-monetised products and activities, and of demarcating the 'production boundary'. And inevitably, the fieldwork extended into anthropological territory, with the Pandora's box of conceptual, definitional, measurement and data availability and generation issues ranging from accounting for and valuing bits and pieces of time, of documenting activities 'productive' and 'unproductive', of who does what, quantities of outputs and inputs, recording intra-, inter- and other transfer gifts and incomes, and all this accumulated across widely fluctuating seasons of the year, and for the diversity of units of production and consumption. Underlying it all was the simple, yet confounding, question: what is the household? "Her discussion of the difficulties of defining the economic unit in these Central African territories and her methods of handling these problems statistically are of interest of economists an anthropologist alike" (ibid., p. 173).

---

[99] "Both these volumes are of the greatest interest and value to any student of colonial economic problems, whether trained economist or layman. They are written in the most lucid manner, explaining at each stage the concepts used, and avoiding all use of jargon. The introductory chapters of the first book contain a specially simple and clear exposition of the concepts of national accounting and the logic of the fundamental tables. These chapters form an excellent beginner's guide to national accounting practice: in addition, they provide a unique collection of material for these colonies, together with an excellent discussion of the basis of all the figures used and the significance which can be attached to them" (ibid., p. 173).

Robert Ross (2013), the historian of South and Southern Africa, provides a valuable collation and analytical commentary on the politics of household budget research in Colonial Central Africa, in the course of which he sheds light on the political and institutional motivations underlying these pioneering research investigations, which had involved scholars with Cambridge links, then or subsequently. Questioning the ostensible neutrality of statistics, Ross emphasises the political framework of governmentality within which the early work was launched and records the catalytic role played by E. A. G. Robinson in undertaking the earliest studies in the 1930s on the wages of the Roan Antelope miners in the Northern Rhodesian Copperbelt; in the politically charged context, this provided sufficient legitimation for the Governor, Hubert Young, to push through his own favoured project of setting up a research institution for focussing on social issues in the colony—and thus the Rhodes-Livingstone Institute (RLI) was created (ibid., p. 8).

"During and after World War II, the British state began to look for ways of increasing its revenue from its African colonies, and generally began to set about 'developing' them." Following the passing of the Colonial Development and Welfare Act by the British Parliament in 1940, and especially after the end of the war, "the British implemented actively interventionist policies with regard to agriculture and stock-keeping, which have been described as 'the Second Colonial Occupation', an invasion of the daily practices of African farmers and cattle herders by agriculturalists, veterinary surgeons, and the like. The resentment this produced was often at the heart of early nationalist agitation. However, alongside such actions, it was also considered necessary to increase the knowledge that the government had of what was going on in its territory. Equally, a series of strikes, particularly in the docks and on the railways, meant that the intervention of government in the relations between employers and their employees began to increase. There is thus the sense in which the activities of the social scientist in collecting information about the Africans' way of life was as much a part of the Second Colonial Occupation as were the dealings of an agricultural officer" (Ross, 2013, p. 9). Ross locates the RLI "as part of the colonial offensive in the immediate post-war Africa, even if many of those who worked for the RLI might have hated the thought. Ethnography, whether rural or urban, was a way in which the colonial rulers, whether in Africa or in London, could acquire information about their subjects. It may not always have been the information which they wanted to receive, or that met their prejudices, but it was sufficiently appreciated for the funding of the RLI to be maintained for many years" (ibid.).

Ross (2013, p. 7) shows a nuanced appreciation of the varying political perspectives that might be embedded in the project of statistics. "There are questions as to where the research should be done, and to what questions it is hoped to provide evidence in answer. The sort of research involved is likely to be costly, both as regards time and money, with the consequence that the enthusiasm for it will generally depend on the perceived need of fund-givers, particularly governments, to acquire information on some subject, and this can never be considered a neutral act. Statistics are collected, inter alia, to provide rulers with information about their subject population, in order to tax them and to control them. Indeed, the whole history of statistical practice emphasises the degree to which statistics and statecraft were, and remain, intertwined.1 But states, of course, are never monolithic. There is always some form of internal tension, and political argument. As a result, statistics can be, and have been used, to argue for varying positions within a state's political life."

This recognition of multiple agendas acknowledges the varying motivations of the researchers themselves. For instance, Austin Robinson, who was a deeply religious, practicing Christian who generally blended his values into his economics albeit within the political context of the times, had gone to Africa during June–November 1932 on an International Missionary Council Commission to look at the effects of industrialisation in the Copper Belt of Northern Rhodesia, and in the course of his 20-week stay wrote 43 'long descriptive letters' to Joan Robinson in Cambridge—and later in 1942, he selected 22 of these and wrote an introduction in a typescript version of 'African Letters'.[100]

The RLI also served as a base station for anthropologists of central and southern Africa, who while benefiting from the opportunities and resources made available by the RLI could not really be classified as card-carrying members of the colonial development project. One of these was the young John Barnes, a Research Officer at the RLI during 1946–1948, working on the Ngoni in Northern Rhodesia, before returning to Oxford to write up his PhD. (obtained in 1951) for which his supervisors, in sequence, were Max Gluckman, Meyer Fortes and E. E. Evans-Pritchard (Barnard, 2011, pp. 31–32); a couple of decades later he was to become the first holder of the chair of sociology in Cambridge, but at the time a doctoral scholar. "John Barnes and Clyde Mitchell in the rural hinterland of the Copperbelt conducted the first budget studies under the RLI. The primary purpose of this research was to train the neophyte researchers in the techniques of fieldwork, above all, according to the director, Max Gluckman, the collection of genealogies and the taking of a census. Their interest in household budgets came, it was noted, as the result of a direct request from the department of agriculture. But it was all part of the project of making the colony better known, and thus more easily governable" (Ross, 2013, p. 10). Rightly, or perhaps more likely wrongly, Ross seems to locate Phyllis Deane within the rubric of the 'second colonial occupation'. "This was even more clearly the case with the research carried out by Phyllis Deane, in conjunction with the RLI, although she was not on the Institute's pay roll. Deane was a trained economist who was well at home in the new economic world of planning and of, as she noted, 'the great increase in the accepted responsibilities of government, which characterised the post-war world'. In

---

[100] 'Box 10: African Letters, 1932', in *Austin Robinson Papers*, held in the Archives of the Marshall Library of Economics in Cambridge, UK.

essence, her project was to work out ways to construct national accounts in the circumstances of a colonial state, where there was both a vast quantity of economic activity that went on outside the cash nexus, and in which the sources of information on even that part of the economy that used cash were fragmentary and of poor quality. It was a heroic task, and one that entailed working together with the RLI's anthropologists, notably Barnes, Elizabeth Colson, and Gluckman, to gain some insight into the economic structure of African farming households. These allowed her to produce information sufficient to give 'a series of articulated but necessarily incomplete social accounts', but not of the quality which would have formed the basis for 'detailed national budgeting'. The quantities of local level data that she would have needed were simply not available to her. Nevertheless, from the point of view of this paper it is clear that the work on the budgets of farming communities was a part of the process whereby colonial governments attempted to strengthen their grip on the societies of Northern Rhodesia and Nyasaland. Her information at a local level derived exclusively from Northern Rhodesia. There were at that stage no budget studies for Nyasaland, and her estimates of production and consumption derived entirely from agricultural surveys. At the very least, her work would have increased the 'legibility', to the state, of the colonial population. Further, the colonial government would be able to use the results of such a survey to determine, at least in part, its economic policy, with all the attendant consequences of that. State intervention requires the information that Phyllis Deane attempted to provide. She did not manage to do so to her own satisfaction, but in the process, obviously, she showed what more was needed" (Ross, 2013, p. 10).

Ross seems somehow to overlook the fact that Phyllis Deane's agenda was not to support colonial development in academic, statistical or political terms; instead, her project was rooted in the Cambridge initiative—led by Richard Stone but also involving several others including Austin Robinson—to develop a standardised international template for the measurement of national income; she was testing and adapting that template in order to make it fit-for-purpose in the structural and social configurations of a rural developing economy where a large swathe of economic activity was not monetised, or took a form that was not even recognised as being 'productive' for the purpose of inclusion in national income. Deane was clear in her belief that a meaningful system of social and national accounts would be helpful for development—but holding such a belief hardly conflates with being a statistical enabler of the colonial development politics of the imperial country.[101]

---

[101] Newly designed 'Devonshire Courses' for British colonial officials, largely directed at African colonies, were launched in 1944, with Cambridge as one of the selected centres for this training, and later overseas development courses evolved out of these efforts at keeping such training relevant for the British imperial mission and mandate. See Kirk-Greene (1999); and Chap. 12 for a discussion.

Leaving this aside, what is striking is the extent to which she went to interact with and learn from rural anthropologists in getting to grips her own recognition and measurement issues in theory and in the field. The inherent nature of the questions she asked effectively pushed her into forms of multidisciplinarity in dealing with the conceptualisation of 'the household' and of understanding production and consumption within and across units. While she interacted with Max Gluckman, Elizabeth Colson and John Barnes (her future Cambridge colleague to be), a similar collaborative multidisciplinary 'field experiment' was ongoing within the Ashanti Survey team engaged in broadly similar research in West Africa, where the research team comprised an economist, Peter Ady,[102] faced with conceptual and measurement challenges rather like Phyllis Deane's; a geographer, R. W. Steel, and Meyer Fortes who was one of supervisors of John Barnes's doctoral research and who would later also be his colleague in Cambridge. Doing meaningful social and national accounts was clearly inevitably and unavoidably a multidisciplinary project, an imperative underscored by each of the specialists on the Ashanti Survey. In closing her 'economics' section, Peter Ady remarks: "I hope that enough has been said to show the interdependence of our field-work. It seems clear that the fields of study cannot be separately defined without loss. Research in these areas should be considered at the level of human ecology, with increasing returns to be gained from skillful integration of field investigations" (Fortes, Steel and Ady, 1947, p. 177). Meyer Fortes reinforces the significance of "the scope and methods of the Ashanti Survey and of the ways in which the ecological, economic, and sociological factors interact in modern Ashanti" (ibid., p. 171).

Some prime lessons emerge from the brilliant expositions by Meyer Fortes and Peter Ady of the complexity of Ashanti ground realities in the economic and social domains; of course, to the local population, these 'complexities' would be known to all as the humdrum universally understood simple facts of daily ordinary life. This is the difficult terrain that Phyllis Deane would have had to negotiate earlier in her fieldwork in Nyasaland and Northern Rhodesia, and it is fruitful to track Peter Ady's and Meyer Fortes's illuminating elaborations of their respective trails and travails in the field.

> During my recent visit to the Gold Coast, which had as its aim a National Income Study of the whole colony, I was invited by the Ashanti Social Survey team, consisting of Dr Fortes, and Mr. Steel, to conduct my own field investigations in collaboration with theirs. Although this meant giving more time to Ashanti that its size warranted, it was an excellent opportunity of seeing what light would be

---

[102] Born in Rangoon, Peter Ady was an Oxford development economist who constructed the first set of integrated social accounts for Burma in 1951, covering the 1945–1950 period. She lectured and wrote extensively on development issues. Both she and Phyllis Deane were participants in the landmark conference on the teaching of development economics in Britain, held in Manchester in 1964, leading to the breakthrough publication edited by Kurt Martin and John Knapp (1967) (see Chap. 11, 30–34). See also Dudley Seers (1979) for a revisit of the first conference, and his lament that not much had changed in the interim years.

thrown upon my own field problems by examination from these other viewpoints. Of the time actually spent in the field surveys more than half was devoted to Ashanti; and it was time well spent. The advantages of collaboration between geography and economics ae obvious since both are concerned with the production and distribution of wealth. The usefulness of anthropology to the economist is perhaps less obvious. It is to this aspect of my field-work, the gain from collaboration, that I shall restrict myself today. (Peter Ady, in Fortes et al., 1947, p. 171)

Three aspects, of many possible, are elicited to highlight the degrees of complexity and consequent difficulty in obtaining information readily usable for constructing national or social accounts. If sample surveys consumption and family budgets could throw up per capita consumption levels, or household incomes, these could be scaled up to the total population to make national estimates. In reality, this was much more easily said than done.

The first element concerns the key variable of estimating the population through a census, a seemingly simple task (for developed-economy contexts) which was confounded by the nature of social structure of rural African society compounded by the complexities of the matriliny, the fact that men might have several wives living separately, and the very high degree of the mobility of the population, especially seasonally. The task of census taking was far from straightforward, and any unique number would come with several qualifications. It could be educative for unsuspecting downstream users of such statistics to read in detail the problems confronting the surveyor.

Peter Ady cautions that "the task of census-taking presented difficulties which were largely the result of economic factors and it is appropriate and instructive to reflect on her elaboration." During a census in Great Britain the householder is required to state on the form provided the names of all persons spending the night selected under his roof. This method, which is impossible in a country where only one in a thousand could fill in the form, obviates all sorts of difficulties since in theory at least everyone is recorded once and once only. In the Gold Coast, an enumerator would have to call at each house to make out the required list, and if all records were to be related to the same date a multitude of such officials would be required. Yet, to compile a record over a period of time would leave open all sorts of loopholes. The population of the villages is extremely fluid in its composition, because of the nature of its economic activities. Most of the rural population lives in villages, and from them the men and women go out by day to their farms, sometimes 5 miles or more away, often remaining at the farm for a night or more and sometimes migrating to the farmstead for weeks or months at a time. Cocoa labour, both labourers proper and caretakers, may live on the farm throughout the cocoa season. Furthermore, the men often leave a village for months at a time to go on a hunting trip or to inspect their cocoa farms elsewhere; the women go away for long periods to trade, setting out with forest produce such as peppers, onions, palm oil or snails, and returning later with cloths, trade goods such as matches and candles, or fish for local consumption. Visits of long duration are paid to relations in distant villages; sick persons go far afield in search of treatment; and superimposed upon this shifting population is the steady stream of migrating labour, chiefly that from the north bound for the mines and for the centres of government employment. There is also a slow turnover of cocoa labour; and the semi-skilled tradesmen of the Ashanti community itself, the carpenters, masons and tailors, move from village to village in search of new contracts. Lastly there are the emigrant women who return to their native villages for confinements or when sick, to leave it again when the emergency is over. If the census cannot be carried through on one date (and this is clearly impossible with farmstead huts and isolated hunter's camps scattered through the bush, even if it could be managed in villages), the task of listing individuals must be related to some stable unit of society which defines membership and makes it possible to avoid both double counting and omissions. This unit cannot be the 'family', for the word is too widely used in this society and covers groups, some of whose members are only remotely related to the head. The 'household' too is not a very clear unit, because on the one hand persons living under the same roof may constitute separate household units; on the other, and this is a much more serious difficulty, it is the common custom for a man and his wife to live in different houses, each in groups of their own blood-relatives, the children of the union living either with the mother or with the father according to their age and sex. Since either man or woman may have been married before and may therefore have the children of these earlier unions still under their care, and since the man sometimes has more than one wife at a time, the spreading and intermingling of household ties make this unit of society unreliable for census work."

And that wasn't all. "The final complication is the extremely limited range of names. First names are day names, seven in number and even surnames are relatively few, so that it is quite common to find in each village four or five persons with the same pair of common Ashanti names. All foreigners tend to be called, and so refer to themselves, by their places of origin: John Lagos, Mumuni Mossi, Bukari Grunshi or worse still, Tongo Fra-Fra where the first name is the man's village and the second his tribe, no individual name i remaining" (Ady, 1947, pp. 176–177). Fortes had encountered similar issues: "Comparing the records made in October 1945 in the course of my fertility census in Agogo with those made by Miss Ady three months later, I found that an appreciable number of domestic groups were different in their make-up on the two occasions" (Fortes, 1947, p. 168). And such differences emerged not just across, but within surveys conducted by the same researcher: "The shortcomings of even the most carefully conducted, first enumeration are revealed later when a second list is made for some other purpose, as I found when the sample families were re-enumerated for later studies. The reason ... above all, is the lack of a clearly definable unit of structure in the community" (Ady, 1947, p. 177).

The second example pertains to the seemingly simple exercise of tabulating family budgets and consumption. Fortes (1947, p. 168) provides a quick glimpse into how 'simple' this task might be on the ground. "Each adult member of the domestic group earns his or her own living, and perhaps owns is or her own cocoa and food farms. Thus there is no community of production under the leadership of the family head, as is the case in many peasant societies. But a man generally helps his wife either with money to pay labourers or with his own labour to start a new food farm; and a man's wife and unmarried children usually help him with his cocoa farm if he farms it himself, whether or not they live together as a patrilocal family. A man must provide his wife and children with food every day and with clothes at certain times of the year, and she must cook for him and the children, adding her self-grown foodstuffs to the meals. Every evening, in large villages, and even in Kumasi, one sees young girls carrying dishes of food from their mothers' to their fathers' houses. Food thus passes, in a two-way traffic, between matrilineal households along lines of marriage connections. But the food that thus enters a matrilineal household is not consumed only by the recipient. It is shares with other members of the unit. This makes the study of family budgets a task requiring mush patience and ingenuity, as Miss Ady's material shows."

Additionally, Ady (1947, p. 175) provides her account of the difficulty of recording daily consumption: "Budget records must necessarily relate to groups of persons, and this raises a host of problems in a matrilineal society such as that of the Akan peoples of the Gold Coast. In these village communities it is customary for a man and his wife or wives to live under different roofs. In any household unit, all the adult women cook every day, and most of the food each prepares is shared as soon as it is ready with all those members of the household who happen to be present, including the other women who are cooking. Some of the food cooked however may go to people not living in the same house; for example, a dish of food is sent each day by each married woman to her husband. At the same time, male members of the household with wives living elsewhere receive food daily from them. This pattern makes the task of food accounting very complex. ... Besides questioning every adult woman about her contribution to the common food supply, it is necessary to ask every member of the household in person whether any food has been eaten outside the house, that is, on the farm or elsewhere. This is particularly important in the case of the adults. Further, it is essential to check each day the numbers who have actually partaken of each meal served, this being an extremely variable quantity. Visitors are frequently present, while, on the other hand, there are frequently absentees from the household. If these variations are not taken into account, quite nonsensical values of food intake may result. When taking the records of non-food expenditure, the complexity is even greater, since its boundaries cut across those of the household."

A third example shows how the economist needs to turn anthropologist in estimating the sources, amount and distribution of incomes. Fortes writes about "the most dangerous feature of the [Ashanti matrilineal] system ... witchcraft occurs principally within the lineage. It is one of the major factors of instability in the whole social organisation, affecting all classes and ranks, educated folk and illiterate people, Christians and pagan alike. There is not a village in Ashanti that lacks a witch-finding fetish, and one of the most profitable industries in the country is running these cults. Miss Ady's data will, I think, show that the owners of witch-finding cults come into high income groups" (1947, p. 170). Clearly, Peter Ady had her job out for her—not hunting down 'witches' but identifying the structure and stakeholders in witch-finding cults, and then interrogating them over the costs and returns of this service industry.

In Deane's case, she had the great benefit of the earlier body of detailed fieldwork data on consumption gathered within the rubric of the Nyasaland Nutritional Survey conducted by Dr Benjamin Platt and his multidisciplinary team of six specialists over a ten-month period during 1938–1939. In his fine, wide-ranging review of the lively interface between national income accounting and feminist economics, Luke Messac (2016) writes about this survey, pioneering in the African context, using amongst other sources, the research of Veronica Berry and Celia Petty (1992) and Cynthia Brantley (2002). "The Nyasaland Nutritional Survey began in three villages in Nkhotakota district in September 1938, under the leadership of Benjamin Stanley Platt. Though only in his mid- thirties, Platt was already [a] physician and biochemist of considerable repute. He had spent the previous six years in Shanghai, where he had conducted controlled trials and published findings the links between thiamine (Vitamin B1) deficiency, rice preparation, and the symptoms of beriberi. The survey team included another doctor, HG Fitzmaurice, who had been the medical officer stationed in Nkhotakota for two years [before] the survey began. Fitzmaurice and his successor, WTC Berry, were tasked with examining all the adults in the three villages using Platt's 10-page-long examination form, and periodically weighing the infants and young children. For the team's nutritionist, Platt chose Jessie Barker, a young researcher who had worked on nutrition surveys in the UK. Her job was to record the weight of all food before cooking and as consumed, and to pack samples to be sent to a laboratory in Aberdeen for biochemical analysis. Barker's nickname in the villages was *Mwadya chiyani* (Chichewa for 'What have you eaten') due to the frequency with which she asked the question. The team's anthropologist, Margaret Read, was to study the impact of social organization on nutrition. Richard Kettlewell, an official in Nyasaland's Department of Agriculture, was the team's agriculturalist. The final expert on the survey team was Geoffrey Herklots, an economic biologist whom Platt had met at the University of Hong Kong. For their part, the Africans in the three villages that were to be the focus of the study had been promised exemption from the hut tax for the duration of the study" (Messac, 2016, pp. 6–7).

While this survey disappointed Platt in not providing evidence of any quick-fix link between micronutrient nutritional deficiencies as the root of health and specific disease (as had been the case in his Shanghai research—where "Platt's studies of beriberi had shown that simple nutritional supplements, or slight alterations in the preparation of rice, could ameliorate biochemical deficiencies" (ibid., p. 7))—the survey accumulated a rich body of disaggregated statistics by age and sex over the time period of the survey. "This trove proved sufficient to establish that although the villagers did not exhibit florid deficiencies of any particular micronutrient, many suffered from what one physician on the team called 'seasonal semi-starvation'; ... Platt's dreams of another silver-bullet nutritional cure—along the lines of the thiamine supplementation for beriberi he helped develop in Shanghai—would go unrealized" (ibid., pp. 7–8). But there were endemic health issues nevertheless, as Messac (2016, p. 10n18), relying on the social anthropologist Lucy Mair (1944, pp. 95–96), reports that "expert opinion said these deficiency states exacerbated all manner of disease (including ulcers, leprosy, tuberculosis, hookworm disease, malaria), and increased the rates of maternal and infant mortality". The intensive Nyasaland Nutritional Survey had provided a mine of statistics and indicators that directly reflected on the physical quality of life, health and well-being of the surveyed population. Platt papers were held at the London School of Hygiene and Tropical Medicine[103] and used by Phyllis Deane in constructing her estimates of rural subsistence production, consumption and incomes. The Nyasaland Survey, as conducted by Platt's team, revealed the realities of rural lived life in ways that no national income data could; there was a wide gap between the two approaches. But the Cambridge NIESR Colonial Office projects had other objectives, and this line was not pursued much further. The Survey did provide some basis for Deane to make estimates of production and consumption of the rural population, based the sample data, bravely generalised with assumptions for this purpose. As Austin Robinson pointed out, Nyasaland was selected precisely because Platt's survey provided potentially useful baseline information for extrapolations on to a national level.

The fundamental issue which emerges from this narrative of the complexity of social organisation and economic life in rural Africa is whether all this information could or should be coaxed or forced, with a variety of expedient assumptions and adjustments, into the standardised SNA template applicable in general to advanced industrialised capitalist economies. This was the crux of what could be called 'the accounting question'. But there was a second crucial dimension embedded within this: 'the gender question' lodged in choice of which 'production boundary' was used for reckoning incomes. This took varying concrete forms and significance in different contexts, but the basic point was the same: the vast proportion of the work and income which would get included or excluded, depending on the choice of the production boundary, was conducted by women. The three illustrations of difficulties discussed earlier are merely the tip of the iceberg of conceptual, survey and data gathering constraints to be surmounted before even arriving at the threshold of making a choice about the production boundary. The choice of production boundary also then served as the line of division between the 'exclusionary' national accountants of the SNA school, à la Richard Stone, and the 'inclusionary' social

---

[103] Not all the papers, though! "Some of the clinical survey data was lost when, while Platt was driving to Zomba with survey papers in 1940, the door of his car burst open and scattered onto the muddy road and in the bushes" (Messac, 2016, p. 7n15), citing Berry and Petty (1992, p. 13).

accountants who wished to ensure the visibility of the vast volumes of work done and outputs produced by women, and to have this properly incorporated as productive activity in national accounts; Phyllis Deane pitched her tent in this contested no-(wo)man's land, and it was then almost entirely a field of her own.[104]

Phyllis Deane became acutely aware of the limitations and the herculean leaps this involved. In the field, she supplemented and conducted her own rural surveys through collaboration with the team anthropologists at the Rhodes-Livingstone Institute (Deane, 1946, 1947, 1948a, 1948b, 1949). With a broad brush her findings could be regarded as a proxy for wider rural realities. But she was fully cognisant of the dangers of generalisations based on small sample surveys in a national context of vast diversities in social structures and ecological environments, as was also apparent from the field assessments of Peter Ady for Ashanti. Samples were acceptable at best for very approximate profiling and generating some macro estimates with relatively low degrees of confidence—but it would be questionable, methodologically, to translate all these systematically or reliably into a national accounting template, à la Stone's SNA, even if the conceptual issue of where to draw the production boundary was settled more in keeping with Deane's exhortation. Stone was focussed on developing an internationally comparable statistical template, and so SNA was restricted to the doable and the measurable; on the other hand, Deane wished the boundary to render visible and countable a large excluded area of work and production, mostly involving women. The two aims were incompatible, not in conceptual terms, but more pragmatically in terms of the possibility of assembling or estimating the necessary statistics country by country. In this regard, perhaps there is a degree of unwarranted speculation about a supposed disagreement or divergence between Phyllis Deane and her mentors Richard Stone and Austin Robinson. The young research was fully aware of the impossibility, at the time, of meeting the statistical requirements for a full adaptation of the SNA to a wider more inclusive production boundary, a pragmatic constraint that she recognised and accepted on grounds of realism.

On the other hand, Marilyn Waring, later, took a far more uncompromising position, declaring (as Luke Messac (2016, p. 30, 30n84): "the UNSNA is an essential tool of the male economic system … When international reports and writers refer to women as statistically or economically invisible, it is the UNSNA that has made it so" (Waring, 1999, p. 639). There are no grounds for arguing that Stone was opposed to the wider production boundary in principle or in intrinsic conceptual terms; the issue was data availability. It is also pertinent to point out the Phyllis Deane remained very close to Richard Stone throughout

---

[104] Messac (2016, pp. 13–14) writes: "the wartime mobilization had generated a demand for trained economists, lowering (at least temporarily) the barriers women faced in securing important posts in economic research institutions: another young female investigator, Phyllis [*sic*] Ady, held a fellowship from the Colonial Research Council to measure the national income of the Gold Coast."

the years in Cambridge and held him in very high regard personally and especially as a statistician. The rightful demand for visibility did induce action, and satellite accounts were developed to supplement the SNA, also for the other invisible elephant in the SNA schema, the environmental dimension. Messac (2016, pp. 32–33) points out that "Waring later recanted her own recommendation to expand the production boundary"; she did not wish women's work to be placed, with equal status and significance, alongside such undesirable elements as armaments, depleting environmental resources, etc. Luke Messac summarises Waring's perspective: "By advocating the inclusion of women's unpaid work in national income, she feared that she and other feminists risked advancing the idea that GDP maximization should remain the central focus of economic policy. Waring sought a new epistemology, one that did not convert every measure into monetary units. She sought instead to enthrone a new measure of welfare: time. Time was 'the common denominator of exchange' and 'the one investment we all have to make.' It was, she argued, a far more useful piece of information than the single aggregate of GDP. Time-use surveys could demonstrate, among other things, 'which sex gets the menial, boring, low-status, and unpaid invisible work', as well as 'the interdependence of the activities of household members, and of how paid work, caring work, housework, community work, leisure, and time spent on personal care are interrelated'. Analysis of this data would show, for instance, how cuts in social spending increased women's burdens of work, or lessened their opportunities for education and leisure. The data would, in short, allow for a less ambiguous and contested evaluation of the benefit or harm wrought by policy than the imputation of values to unpaid labor" (ibid., p. 33).

Looking ahead[105] from the pioneering work of Phyllis Deane, the subsequent rich imbricated seams of gendered research on the conceptual, measurement and statistical dimensions of 'economic' and 'non-economic' work highlight the key issues of the value of time, and of the nature of the division of labour between men and women in paid and unpaid work, and work outside and within the household, as exemplified in the extensive contributions of Luisella Goldschmidt-Clermont (1990, 1993), also jointly with Elisabett Pagnossin-Aligisakis (Goldschmidt-Clermont & Pagnossin-Aligisakis, 1995,

---

[105] Looking back from Phyllis Deane's work, it is also possible to spot earlier contributions emphasising the significance of 'invisible' female non-waged work and labour. A special issue on Women in the Modern World in the *Annals of the American Academy of Political and Social Science* in 1929 contains no less than 36 contributions, some of these quite remarkable, on women's work, labour, wages, trade unions, time-use, capabilities and aspirations. Hildegard Kneeland (1929a, 1929b, 1929c) provides a powerful empirical analysis of women's substantial work on the farm and in the home; while Elsa Voorhees (1929) vehemently argues the case for the strengthening of women's 'choices of satisfactions' through a widening of their capabilities, arguing in terms that bear a direct resonance with the capability analysis of Sen—though Voorhees seems to have a blissful suburban American life in mind, with no allusion to issues of race, colour, class, ethnicity or religion; nor strikingly are there any notable allusions to the role of patriarchy and male power within private or public domains.

2005). Goldschmidt-Clermont rhetorically asks: "Is it really necessary to measure non-market household production? Research data indicate that in the industrialised countries this unrecorded production absorbs *about as much labour time as all combined activities in the recorded sectors of the economy ... They also indicate that the unrecorded household product may amount to some 30 to 50 per cent of the measure gross domestic product (GDP).* Broadly similar results are observed in developing countries" (Goldschmidt-Clermont, 1990, p. 281). She argues further: "It is easy to imagine the dramatic slowing down that agriculture, industry, transport, etc., would undergo if domestic activities suddenly ceased to be performed under the present social arrangements. How, for instance, could a factory worker clock in on time *and* see to it that the baby is fed every four hours, that food is available at mealtimes, that small children are met from school, and so on? Other forms of social organisation can be conceived for meeting the needs presently met mainly by domestic activities, but these needs have to be met, one way or another, if the economy is to function effectively" (Goldschmidt-Clermont, 1990, p. 281). In turn, this pulls in the issue of decision-making structures of authority and control that determine the allocation of such tasks between male and female members of families and households, including crucially the question of the freedom and volition in the formation and exercise of 'choice' by individual household members, in particular men and women.

Had the wheel turned a full circle? Messac (ibid., pp. 33–34) rightly points out: "Though she did not mention the history of social science research methods, Waring was calling for a return to some of the surveys used by Margaret Read during the Nyasaland Nutrition Survey and the social anthropologists of the Rhodes-Livingstone Institute. Waring's favored measures recapitulated the multifactorial and intensive methods of the nutrition surveys that had served as the substrate for Phyllis Deane's calculations of colonial national income. Women's work figured prominently in both Deane's critique of the production boundary and Waring's more totalizing denunciation of the primacy of national income. Both Deane and Waring considered intensive field research crucial to rendering women's work legible to policymakers."

This was not the end of the list of problems with the meaningfulness of the SNA approach, more specifically with the concept of GDP itself, as a true indicator of the well-being or quality of life of the population. The direction of subsequent discourse, and accounting practices, has been bipolar. While SNA was universally adopted as the gold standard, there were rising feminist and philosophical movements that challenged this ascendancy. This strong refrain was also increasingly voiced from development circles: in 1969, Dudley Seers trenchantly asked "what is the meaning of development"; in 1972, he raised another question, "what are we trying to measure" and provided his answer to both: "development means creating the conditions for the realization of human personality" (Seers, 1969, 1972). At UNRISD, there was sustained work ongoing by Jan Drewnowski (from the 1960s), Donald McGranahan and others on composite social indicators and direct measures of well-being; in 1979,

Morris D. Morris introduced his 'physical quality of life' (PQLI) indicator; before Haq-Sen monopolised the bandwidth and airwaves with the UNDP's institutional product of the 'human development index' (HDI), followed very soon by a slew of indicators that focussed on gender dimensions, or others that styled themselves as 'capability' measures à la Sen. Alongside these initiatives on the track of 'direct' measures were other epistemological with their distinct methodological approaches: the predating measure of poverty; the new ones based on subjective assessments of people themselves, linking with Robert Chambers's institutionalised instrumental participatory approach—a distant deviant of the original wider and intrinsically more meaningful epistemology and imaginary of participation introduced by Paulo Freire in his books in 1967 and especially his *Pedagogy of the Oppressed* in 1968.

The very Cambridge origins of some of the major strands in this discourse are striking. Richard Stone, Austin Robinson (and to an extent Arthur Lewis) set the frame that launched Phyllis Deane's interrogations of the SNA—aided in the field by John Barnes, her future Cambridge anthropologist colleague—highlighting other indicators en route; later Amartya Sen bundled it all in the human development and capability approach; and in Cambridge, Partha Dasgupta ran with the baton in his interdisciplinary *An Inquiry into Well-being and Destitution* (Dasgupta, 1995). In parallel, there is another Cambridge chain linking Phyllis Deane to the gendered work of her student and successor Jane Humphries, alongside the joint work with Sara Horrell, a student of Jane's, on the industrial revolution in Britain, demonstrating how gender invisibility erodes the validity of several conventional interpretations of the industrial revolution as experienced by the working classes.[106] Around this are several significant connections: to the work of Sara Horrell and Jane Humphries with Deborah Oxley with their gendered analyses of using long-term direct, anthropometric indicators, and have also viewed the gender question through Amartya Sen's prism of capabilities, but within historical frameworks that highlight the role of imperial power over colonies and indigenous peoples. And then there is an indication of some convergence in perspectives as expressed in Agarwal et al. (2004) on gender and capabilities in the work of Amartya Sen. It is but a short hop from Sen to Pigou with regard to the problems with using GNP as an indicator. Pigou knew all the limitations, but nevertheless settled for a qualified acceptance. He did though put in a warning: "…there is no guarantee that the effects produced on the part of welfare that can be brought into relation with the measuring-rod of money may not be cancelled by effects of a contrary kind brought about in other parts, or aspects of welfare… The real objection then is, not that economic welfare is a bad index of total welfare, but that an economic cause may affect non-economic welfare in ways that cancels its effect on economic welfare."[107] But ways of doing are not independent of the ways of

---

[106] A direct connection can also be made between Jane Humphries and Nancy Folbre on whose thesis committee Jane served in University of Massachusetts, Amherst.

[107] Cited in Beckerman (1968, p. 40).

seeing, and in this sense, it is readily arguable that the invisibilities definitionally embedded in the SNA concept could only have damaged the need and case for more just and sustainable forms and patterns of growth. So a bad index could, and probably would, legitimise bad policies. That was also the problem that bothered Phyllis Deane's problem.

Phyllis did not directly participate—at least not in the form of academic publications—in these later debates many of which were ongoing around her in Cambridge; but her early work in Africa stood at the intersection of several of these themes and laid some of their analytical and methodological foundations. She prised open the Pandora's box that was the standard SNA approach, and released a swarm of epistemological, methodological and ultimately political questions into the ether; as such she was one of the pioneers of subsequent gendered approaches to the recognition and measurement of incomes, time-use, well-being and quality of life, and the gendered power structures underlying observed outcomes in these domains. This early deep immersion into unruly rural realities laid a solid foundation for an understanding of development issues and this was manifest in her longstanding role, extending over decades, in the academic and institutional trajectory of teaching and research on development economics and development studies in Cambridge.

References

Ady, P. (1947). *Peter Ady's special section*. In: Fortes, Steel and Ady (1947).

Ady, P. (1954). Review of books: The measurement of colonial national incomes, 1948, and *Colonial Social Accounting, 1953*. *Africa, 24*(2), 173–174.

Agarwal, B., Humphries, J., & Robeyns, I. (2004). *Capabilities, freedom, and equality: Amartya Sen's work from a gender perspective*. Oxford University Press.

Aidt, T. (2003). Economic analysis of corruption: A survey. *Economic Journal, 113*(491), F632–F652.

Aidt, T. S. (2016). Rent seeking and the economics of corruption. *Constitutional Political Economy, 27,* 142–157.

Aidt, T. S., & Albornoz, F. (2011). Political regimes and foreign intervention. *Journal of Development Economics, 94*(2), 192–201.

Aidt, T. S., & Dutta, J. (2017). Fiscal federalism and electoral accountability. *Journal of Public Economic Theory, 19*(1), 38–58.

Aidt, T. S., & Franck, R. (2019). What motivates an oligarchic elite to democratize? Evidence from the roll call vote on the Great Reform Act of 1832. *Journal of Economic History, 79*(3), 773–825.

Aidt, T. S., & Jensen, P. S. (2017). From open to secret ballot: Vote buying and modernization. *Comparative Political Studies, 50*(5), 555–593.

Aidt, T. S., & Leon, G. (2016). The democratic window of opportunity: Evidence from riots in sub-Saharan Africa. *Journal of Conflict Resolution, 60*(4), 694–717.

Aidt, T. S., & Rauh, C. (2018). The big five personality traits and partisanship in England. *Electoral Studies, 54,* 1–21.

Aidt, T. S., Albornoz, F., & Gassebner, M. (2017). The golden hello and political transitions. *Journal of Comparative Economics, 46*(1), 157–173.

Aidt, T. S., Castro, V., & Martins, R. (2018). Shades of red and blue: Government ideology and sustainable development. *Public Choice, 175*, 303–323.

Aidt, T. S., Chadha, J. S., & Sabourian, H. (2019). Breaking the Brexit impasse: Achieving a fair, legitimate and democratic outcome. *National Institute Economic Review*, February, F4–F11.

Aidt, T. S., Daunton, M., & Dutta, J. (2010). The retrenchment hypothesis and the extension of the franchise in England and Wales. *Economic Journal, 120*(547), 990–1020.

Aidt, T. S., Leon, G., & Satchell, M. (2021). The social dynamics of collective action: Evidence from the diffusion of the Swing riots. *The Journal of Politics* (ahead of print version).

Aidt, T. S., Lili, J., & Low, H. (2017). Are prices enough? The economics of material demand reduction. *Philosophical Transactions of the Royal Society A: Mathematical, Physical and Engineering Sciences, 375*(2095).

Allsopp, C. J. (1973). Effects of the selective employment tax. Final report, Review by C. J. Allsopp. *Economic Journal, 83*(332), 1282–1284.

Atkinson, A. B., & Stern, N. (2017). Tony Atkinson on poverty, inequality, and public policy: The work and life of a great economist. *Annual Review of Economics, 9*, 1–20. https://doi.org/10.1146/annurev-economics-110216-100949

Austin, G. (2017, October 20). *Inaugural lecture. Three revolutions in economic history*. University of Cambridge. https://www.econsoc.hist.cam.ac.uk/podcasts.html

Austin, G., & Broadberry, S. (2014). Introduction: The renaissance of African economic history. *Economic History Review, 67*(4), 893–906.

Barker, T., & Peterson, W. (Eds.). (1987). *The Cambridge multisectoral dynamic model of the British economy*. Cambridge University Press.

Barnard, A. (2011). John Arundel Barnes, 1918–2010. *Proceedings of the British Academy, 172*, 27–45.

Beckerman, W. (1968). *An introduction to national income analysis*. Weidenfeld & Nicolson.

Begg, I., & Horrell, S. (2002). UK banking and other financial services and the euro. In A. El-Agraa (Ed.), *The Euro and Britain* (pp. 277–303). Prentice Hall.

Beloff, M. (1968, March). A plague of economists? *Encounter*, Letters, 91.

Berg, M. (1996). *A woman in history: Eileen Power, 1889–1940*. Cambridge University Press.

Berry, V., & Petty, C. (1992). *The Nyasaland survey papers 1938–1943, agriculture, food and health*. Academy Press.

Bhagwati, J., & Srinivasan, T. N. (1975). *Foreign trade regimes and economic development: India*. National Bureau of Economic Research.

Bortis, H. (2010). Political economy and economic science: The work of Phyllis Deane. *Journal of Economic Analysis, 1*(1), 49–77.

Bortis, H. (2017). Phyllis Deane (1918–2012). In R. Cord (Ed.), *The Palgrave companion to Cambridge economics* (pp. 871–892). Palgrave Macmillan.

Brantley, C. (2002). *Feeding families: African realities and British ideas of nutrition and development in early colonial Africa*. Heinemann.

Bray, F. S. (1949). *Social accounts and the business enterprise sector of the national economy*. Cambridge University Press.

Bray, F. S., & Stone, R. (1948). The presentation of the central government accounts. *Accounting Research, 1*(1).

Bruland, K. (2004). Industrialisation and technological change. In R. Floud & P. Johnson (Eds.), *The Cambridge economic history of modern Britain* (Industrialisation, 1700–1860) (Vol. 1, pp. 117–146). Cambridge University Press.

Buggeln, M., Daunton, M., & Nutzenadel, A. (2017). *The political economy of public finance: Taxation, state spending and debt since the 1970s*. Cambridge University Press.

Burchell, B., Horrell, S., & Rubery, J. (1989). Unequal jobs or unequal pay? *Industrial Relations Journal, 20*(3), 176–191.

Burchell, B., Horrell, S., & Rubery, J. (1990). Gender and skills. *Work, Employment and Society, 4*(2) Reprinted in *Gender and Economics*, J. Humphries (ed.), Edward Elgar, 1994.

Chakravarty, S. (1989). Nicholas Kaldor on Indian economic problems. *Cambridge Journal of Economics, 13*(1), 237–244. Retrieved June 1, 2021, from http://www.jstor.org/stable/23598159

Clapham, J. (1940). Eileen Power, 1889–1940. *Economica, New Series, 7*(28), 351–359.

Clapham, J. (1949/1957). *A concise economic history of Britain from earlier times to 1750* (1st ed./3rd ed.). Cambridge University Press. [Prepared by John Saltmarsh after the death of John Clapham].

Clark, C. (1932). *The national income 1924–31*. Macmillan & Co.

Clark, C. (1937). *National income and outlay*. Macmillan & Co.

Clark, C. (1938). Determination of the multiplier from national income statistics. *Economic Journal, 48*(191), 435–448.

Clark, C. (1940). *The conditions of economic progress*. Macmillan & Co.

Clark, G. K. (1973). A hundred years of the teaching of history at Cambridge, 1873–1973. *Historical Journal, 16*(3), 535–553.

Cole, W. A. (2007). W. A. Cole interviewed by A. J. H. Latham. In J. S. Lyons, L. P. Cain, & S. H. Williamson (Eds.), *Reflections on the cliometric revolution: Conversations with economic historians* (pp. 146–154). Routledge. Interview on 17 April 1998 at University of Wales, Swansea, by A.J.H. Latham.

Coleman, D. C. (1956). Industrial growth and industrial revolutions. *Economica, 23*(89), 1–22.

Coleman, D. C. (1969a). *Courtaulds: An economic and social history: Volume 1 – Rope and silk*. Clarendon Press.

Coleman, D. C. (1969b). *Courtaulds: An economic and social history: Volume 2 – Rayon*. Clarendon Press.

Coleman, D. C. (1980). *Courtaulds: An economic and social history: Volume 3 – Crisis and change*. Clarendon Press.

Cripps, F. (1973). *Growth in advanced capitalist economies, 1950–70*. Department of Applied Economics, Occasional Paper No. 40. Cambridge University Press.

Dasgupta, P. (1995). *An inquiry into wellbeing and destitution*. Clarendon Press.

Dasgupta, P. (2000). Economic progress and the idea of social capital. In P. Dasgupta & I. Serageldin (Eds.), *Social capital: A multifaceted perspective* (pp. 325–424). World Bank.

Dasgupta, P. (2002). *Social capital and economic performance: Analytics*. https://citeseerx.ist.psu.edu/viewdoc/download?doi=10.1.1.127.8067&rep=rep1&type=pdf. To appear in: Ostrom, Elinor, & Ahn, T. K. (Ed.). (2003). *Foundations of social capital*. Edward Elgar.

Daunton, M. J. (1996). How to pay for the War: State, society and taxation in Britain, 1917–24. *The English Historical Review, CXI*(443), 882–919.

Daunton, M. (2001). *Trusting Leviathan: The politics of taxation in Britain, 1799–1914*. Cambridge University Press.

Daunton, M. (2002). *Just taxes: The politics of taxation in Britain, 1914–1979*. Cambridge University Press.
Daunton, M. (2008). Interview with Professor Martin Daunton interviewed by Danny Millum. *Making history: The discipline in perspective*. https://archives.history.ac.uk/makinghistory/resources/interviews/Daunton_Martin.html
Daunton, M. (2017a). Cambridge and economic history. In R. A. Cord (Ed.), *The Palgrave companion to Cambridge economics, Volume I* (pp. 157–186). Palgrave Macmillan.
Daunton, M. (2017b). John Harold Clapham (1873–1946). In R. A. Cord (Ed.), *The Palgrave companion to Cambridge economics, Volume I* (pp. 423–454). Palgrave Macmillan.
Deane, P. (1946). Measuring national income in Colonial Territories. In *Studies in Income and Wealth* (pp. 145–174). National Bureau on Economic Research.
Deane, P. (1947). National income: Problems in social accounting in Central Africa. *Human Problems in British Central Africa: The Rhodes-Livingstone Journal, 5*, 24–43.
Deane, P. (1948a). *The measurement of colonial national incomes: An experiment*. N.I.E.S.R. Occasional Papers XII. Cambridge University Press.
Deane, P. (1948b). *Village economic surveying in Central Africa*. Colonial Research Fellowships, Plans and Reports of Miss PM Deane, October 28, 1948, CO 927/17/5, UK National Archives.
Deane, P. (1949). Problems of surveying village economies. *Human Problems in British Central Africa: The Rhodes-Livingstone Journal, 8*, 42–49.
Deane, P. (1978). *The evolution of economic ideas*. Cambridge University Press.
Deane, P. (1988a). *The state and the economic system: Introduction to the history of political economy*. Oxford University Press.
Deane, P. (2001). *The life and times of J. Neville Keynes: A beacon in the tempest*. Edward Elgar.
Deane, P. (2007). Phyllis Deane interviewed by Nicholas F. R. Crafts. In J. S. Lyons, L. P. Cain, & S. H. Williamson (Eds.), *Reflections on the cliometric revolution: Conversations with economic historians* (pp. 132–145). Routledge. Interview conducted in Spring, 1993.
Deaton, A. (2008). Stone, John Richard Nicholas (1913–1991). In S. N. Durlauf & L. E. Blume (Eds.), *The new Palgrave dictionary of economics* (2nd ed.). Palgrave Macmillan. https://www.princeton.edu/~deaton/downloads/Deaton_STONE_JOHN_RICHARD.pdf
Dennison, T., & Ogilvie, S. (2007). Serfdom and social capital in Bohemia and Russia. *Economic History Review, 60*(3), 513–544.
Dennison, T., & Ogilvie, S. (2014). Does the European marriage pattern explain economic growth? *The Journal of Economic History, 74*(3), 651–693.
Dennison, T. K., & Ogilvie, S. (2016). Institutions, demography, and economic growth. *The Journal of Economic History, 76*(1), 205–217.
Dobb, M. (1928). *Russian economic development since the revolution*. George Routledge & Sons.
Dobb, M. (1946). *Studies in the development of capitalism*. Routledge.
Eatwell, J. (1977). Maurice Dobb. *Cambridge Journal of Economics, 1*(1), 1–3.
Farnie, D. A., & Tweedale, G. (2009). *A bio-bibliography of economic and social history* (5th ed.) https://www.yumpu.com/en/document/read/9266699/a-bio-bibliography-of-economic-history-society

Feinstein, C. H. (Ed.). (1967). *Socialism, capitalism and economic growth: Essays presented to Maurice Dobb*. Cambridge University Press.
Feinstein, C. H. (2007). Charles H. Feinstein interviewed by Mark Thomas. In J. S. Lyons, L. P. Cain, & S. H. Williamson (Eds.), *Reflections on the cliometric revolution: Conversations with economic historians* (pp. 286–300). Routledge. Interviewed by Mark Thomas on 2 August 2002 at All Souls, Oxford.
Flinn, M. W., & Mathias, P. (1982). Obituary: Sir Michael Moissey Postan, 1899–1981. *Economic History Review, 35*(1), iv–vi.
Fluckiger, M. (2018). Teaching economics with economic history. In M. Blum & C. Colvin (Eds.), *An economist's guide to economic history* (pp. 55–59). Palgrave Macmillan.
Fortes, M. (1947). *Meyer Fortes's special section*. In: Fortes, Steel and Ady (1947).
Fortes, M., Steel, R. W., & Ady, P. (1947). Ashanti Survey, 1945–46: An experiment in social research. *The Geographical Journal, 110*(4/6), 149–177. https://doi.org/10.2307/1789946
Frank, A. G. (1998). *ReOrient: Global economy in the Asian Age*. University of California Press.
Galofre-Vila, G. (2019, May). *The past's long shadow. A systematic review and network analysis of cliometrics or the new economic history*. EDES Working Paper No: 154. University of Bocconi, 18p. http://ehes.org/EHES_154.pdf
Glyn, A., Hughes, A., Lipietz, A., & Singh, A. (1988). *The rise and fall of the golden age*. UNU-WIDER Working Paper No. 43. UNU-WIDER.
Godley, W. (2008, May 16). Interview with Wynne Godley. In S. Harrison & A. Macfarlane, *Encounter with economics*. Interviews filmed by A. Macfarlane and edited by S. Harrison. University of Cambridge. http://sms.cam.ac.uk/collection/1092396
Goldschmidt-Clermont, L. (1990). Economic measurement of non-market household activities: Is it useful and feasible? *International Labour Review, 129*(3), 279–299. https://www.proquest.com/docview/224019616/fulltextPDF/D6BDE500E5134DACPQ/12?accountid=13598
Goldschmidt-Clermont, L. (1993). Monetary valuation of non-market productive time: Methodological considerations. *Review of Income and Wealth, 39*(4), 419–433.
Goldschmidt-Clermont, L., & Pagnossin-Aligisakis, E. (1995). *Measures of unrecorded economic activities in fourteen countries*. https://core.ac.uk/reader/6248730
Goldschmidt-Clermont, L., & Pagnossin-Aligisakis, E. (2005). Households' non-SNA production: Labour time, value of labour and of product, and contribution to extended private consumption. *Review of Income and Wealth, 45*(4), 519–529.
Habakkuk, H. J. (1940a). English landownership, 1680–1740. *Economic History Review, 10*.
Habakkuk, H. J. (1940b). Free trade and commercial expansion, 1853–1870. In J. H. Rose, A. P. Newton, & E. Benians (Eds.), *Cambridge history of the British empire* (The new empire, 1783–1870) (Vol. 2, pp. 751–805). Cambridge.
Habakkuk, H. J. (1962). *American and British technology in the nineteenth century: The search for labour-saving inventions*. Cambridge University Press.
Habakkuk, H. J. (1994). *Marriage, debt, and the estates system: English landownership, 1650–1950*. Oxford University Press.
Harcourt, G. C. (2001). *Fifty years a Keynesian and other essays*. Palgrave Macmillan.
Harcourt, G. C. (2007). Interview with Geoffrey Harcourt 15th May 2007. In S. Harrison & A. Macfarlane, *Encounter with economics*. Film interviews with leading

thinkers, filmed by A. Macfarlane and edited by S. Harrison. University of Cambridge; Created 28 March 2011. http://sms.cam.ac.uk/collection/1092396

Harcourt, G. C. (2012a, October). Phyllis Deane. *Royal Economic Society Newsletter, 159*.

Harcourt, G. C. (2012b). *On Skidelsky's Keynes and other essays: Selected essays of G. C. Harcourt*. Palgrave Macmillan.

Harcourt, G. C., & King, J. (1995). Talking about Joan Robinson: Geoff Harcourt in conversation with John King. In J. E. King (Ed.), *Conversations with post Keynesians* (pp. 168–186). Palgrave Macmillan. Also in: *Review of Social Economy, 53*(1), 31–64.

Harcourt, G. C., & Kitson, M. (1993). Fifty years of measurement: A Cambridge view. *Review of Income and Wealth, 39*(4), 435–447.

Harte, N. (1995, September 8). Obituary: Professor D. C. Coleman. *The Independent*. https://www.independent.co.uk/news/people/obituary-professor-d-c-coleman-1600207.html

Harte, N. (2002, November 14). Sir John Habakkuk. *The Guardian*. https://www.theguardian.com/news/2002/nov/14/guardianobituaries.highereducation

Harte, N. (2012, October 1). Professor Phyllis Deane: Leading and influential figure in the field of economic history. *The Independent*.

Hobsbawm, E. (1967). Maurice Dobb. In C. H. Feinstein (Ed.), *Socialism, capitalism and economic growth: Essays presented to Maurice Dobb* (pp. 1–12). Cambridge University Press.

Hobsbawm, E. (2002). *Interesting times: A twentieth-century life*. Knopf Doubleday Publishing Group.

Horrell, S. (1996, September). Home demand and British industrialisation. *Journal of Economic History, 56*, 561–604.

Horrell, S. (1999). Economic history: Great Britain. In J. Peterson & M. Lewis (Eds.), *The Elgar Companion to feminist economics* (pp. 193–201). Edward Elgar.

Horrell, S., & Humphries, J. (1995a). Women's labour force participation and the transition to the male-breadwinner family, 1790–1865. *Economic History Review, 48*(1), 89–117.

Horrell, S., & Humphries, J. (1995b, October). The exploitation of little children: Child labor and the family economy in the Industrial Revolution. *Explorations in Economic History, 32*, 485–516.

Horrell, S., & Humphries, J. (1997). The origins and expansion of the male breadwinner family: The case of nineteenth-century Britain. *International Review of Social History, 42*, 25–64.

Horrell, S., & Humphries, J. (2019). Children's work and wages in Britain, 1280–1860. *Explorations in Economic History*.

Horrell, S., & Krishnan, P. (2007, November). Poverty and productivity in female-headed households in Zimbabwe. *Journal of Development Studies, 43*, 1351–1380.

Horrell, S., & Oxley, D. (1999). Crust or crumb?: Intrahousehold resource allocation and male breadwinning in late Victorian Britain. *Economic History Review, LII*, 494–522.

Horrell, S., & Oxley, D. (2016). Gender bias in nineteenth-century England: Evidence from factory children. *Economics and Human Biology, 22*, 47–64.

Horrell, S., & Rubery, J. (1991). Gender and working time: An analysis of employers' working-time policies. *Cambridge Journal of Economics, 15*(4), 373–391.

Horrell, S., & Rubery, J. (1992/93). The 'new competition' and working time. *Human Resource Management Journal, 3*(2), 1–13.

Horrell, S., Hudson, J., & Mosley, P. (1992a). Aid, the public sector and the market in less developed countries: A return to the scene of the crime. *Journal of International Development, 4*(2), 139–150.

Horrell, S., Humphries, J., & Rubery, J. (1992b). Women's employment in textiles and clothing. In R. Lindley (Ed.), *Women's employment: Britain in the single European market* (pp. 81–100). HMSO.

Horrell, S., Humphries, J., & Rubery, J. (1992c). The SEM and employment in the banking sector. In R. Lindley (Ed.), *Women's employment: Britain in the single European market* (pp. 126–140). HMSO.

Horrell, S., Humphries, J., & Weale, M. (1994, August). An input-output table for 1841. *Economic History Review, XLVII*, 546–567.

Horrell, S., Humphries, J., & Voth, H.-J. (1998, May). Stature and relative deprivation: Fatherless children in early industrial Britain. *Continuity and Change, 13*, 73–115.

Horrell, S., Johnson, H., & Mosley, P. (2008). *Work, female empowerment and economic development*. Routledge.

Horrell, S., Meredith, D., & Oxley, D. (2009). Measuring misery: Body mass among Victorian London's poor. *Explorations in Economic History, 46*, 93–119.

Horrell, S., Humphries, J., & Sneath, K. (2015). Consumption conundrums unravelled. *Economic History Review, 68*, 830–857.

Humphries, J. (1987). Inter-war house building, cheap money and building societies: The housing boom revisited. *Business History, XXIX*(3).

Humphries, J. (2010). *Childhood and child labour in the British industrial revolution*. Cambridge University Press.

Humphries, J. (2012). Inspiration passes from generation to generation. In *Inspiring future generations of economists: The creation of the Phyllis Deane fund at Newnham to support teaching in economics*. http://www.newn.cam.ac.uk/sites/www.newnham.local/uploads/files/After-Newnham/Giving%20to%20Newnham/Economics%20Fund%20Leaflet%202.pdf

Humphries, J., & Rubery, J. (1984). The reconstitution of the supply side of the labour market: The relative autonomy of social reproduction. *Cambridge Journal of Economics, 8*(4), 331–346.

Janeway, W. (2015, April 14). *How to recognize new economic thinking*. Institute for New Economic Thinking. https://www.ineteconomics.org/perspectives/blog/how-to-recognize-new-economic-thinking

Johnson, H. G. (1968b, May). A catarrh of economists? From Keynes to Postan. *Encounter*, 50–54.

Joslin, D. (1963). *A century of banking in Latin America*. Oxford University Press.

Kaldor, N. (1967). *Strategic factors in economic development*. New York State School of Industrial and Labor Relations, Cornell University.

Kaldor, N. (1996). *Causes of Growth and Stagnation in the World Economy. The Raffaele Mattioli Lectures delivered in 1984*. Cambridge: Cambridge University Press.

Karamessini, M., & Rubery, J. (Eds.). (2013). *Women and austerity: The economic crisis and the future for gender equality*. Routledge.

Keynes, J. M. (1925). A short view of Russia. In J. M. Keynes (Ed.), *Essays in Persuasion. The collected writings of John Maynard Keynes* (Essays in Persuasion) (Vol. IX). Royal Economic Society, Palgrave Macmillan, 1972.

Khan, M. H. (1996). A typology of corrupt transactions in developing countries. *IDS Bulletin, 27*(2), 12–21.

Kirk-Greene, A. (1999, May). The colonial service training courses: Professionalizing the colonial service. *Overseas Service Pensioners' Association (OSPA) Journal, 77.* https://www.britishempire.co.uk/ospa.htm

Kitson, M. (1999). Recession and economic revival in Britain: The role of policy in the 1930s and 1980s. *Journal of Contemporary European History, 8*(1), 1–27.

Kitson, M. (2012). Britain's withdrawal from the gold standard: The end of an epoch. In R. Parker & R. Whaples (Eds.), *Handbook of major events in economic history*. Palgrave.

Kitson, M., & Michie, J. (1995). Trade and growth: An historical perspective. In J. Michie & J. Grieve Smith (Eds.), *Managing the global economy*. Oxford University Press.

Kitson, M., & Michie, J. (2014). The deindustrial revolution: The rise and fall of UK manufacturing, 1870–2010. In R. Floud & P. Johnson (Eds.), *The Cambridge economic history of modern Britain, Volume 2* (pp. 302–329). Cambridge University Press.

Kitson, M., & Solomou, S. (1989). The macroeconomics of protectionism: The case of Britain in the 1930s. *Cambridge Journal of Economics, 13*(1), 155–169. Retrieved June 1, 2021, from http://www.jstor.org/stable/23598154

Kitson, M., & Solomou, S. (1990). *Protectionism and economic revival*. Cambridge University Press.

Kitson, M., & Solomou, S. (1991). Trade policy and the regionalization of imports in interwar Britain. *Bulletin of Economic Research, 43*(2), 151–168.

Kitson, M., Solomou, S., & Weale, M. (1991). Effective protection and economic recovery in the United Kingdom during the 1930s. *Economic History Review, 44*(2), 328–338.

Kneeland, H. (1929a). Women on farms average sixty-three hours work weekly in survey of seven hundred homes. In *US Department of Agriculture, Yearbook of Agriculture, 1928*. Government Printing Office.

Kneeland, H. (1929b). Is the modern housewife a lady of leisure? *Survey, 62*.

Kneeland, H. (1929c). Woman's economic contribution in the home. *Annals of the American Academy of Political and Social Science, 143*, 33–40.

Le Bas, C. (2019). Towards a deepening of knowledge in the economics of innovation: The intellectual legacy of Nick Von Tunzelmann. *Journal of Innovation Economics & Management, 3*(30), 235–238.

Lehmann, D. (2016). *Interview with David Lehmann*. 50th Anniversary Symposium, Centre of Latin American Studies, University of Cambridge. http://www.latin-american.cam.ac.uk/latest-news-and-events/50-years-media/memories-reflections-clas/interview-dr-david-lehmann

Macekura, S. (2018, May 30). *Phyllis Deane and the limits of national accounting*. National Institute of Economic and Social Research, blog. https://www.niesr.ac.uk/blog/phyllis-deane-and-limits-national-accounting

Mair, L. (1944). *Welfare in the British Colonies*. Royal Institute of International Affairs.

Manning, P. (1971). Review of *Studies in rural capitalism in West Africa* by Polly Hill. *African Historical Studies, 4*(1), 156–157.

Marris, R. (1971). *Effects of the selective employment tax. First report*, review by R. Marris. Her Majesty's Stationery Office. *Economic Journal, 81*(322), 393–395.

Martin, K., & Knapp, J. (Eds.). (1967). *The teaching of development economics. Its position in the present state of knowledge. The proceedings of the Manchester Conference on teaching economic development, April 1964*. Routledge.

Mathias, P., & Thompson, F. M. L. (2002). Donald Cuthbert Coleman, 1920–1995. *Proceedings of the British Academy, 115*, 169–191.

Matthews, R. C. O. (1968). Why has Britain had full employment since the war? *Economic Journal, 78*(311), 555–569.

Matthews, R. C. O., Feinstein, C. F., & Odling-Smee, J. (1982). *British economic growth 1856–1973: The post-war period in historical perspective.* Oxford University Press.

Matthews, R. C. O., & Supple, B. (1991). The ordeal of economic freedom: Marshall on economic history. *Quaderni di Storia dell'Economia Politica, 9*(2–3), 189–213. Also available as a typescript in E.A.G. Robinson Papers, Marshall Library Archives, University of Cambridge, EAGR 6/4/16, 23p.

Meeks, G. (1974). Profit illusion. *Oxford Bulletin of Economics and Statistics, 36*(4), 267–285.

Meek, R. (1978). Maurice Herbert Dobb, 1900–1976. *Proceedings of the British Academy, 63*, 332–344. https://www.thebritishacademy.ac.uk/publishing/memoirs/pba-63/dobb-maurice-herbert-1900-1976/

Meeks, G. (2017). Theories came and went, good data endured: Accounting at Cambridge. In R. A. Cord (Ed.), *The Palgrave Companion to Cambridge economics* (pp. 187–205).

Messac, L. M. (2016). *What is an economy? Women's work and feminist economics in the construction and critique of national income accounting.* Earlier version of paper presented at the New York Area African History Workshop. https://www.ineteconomics.org/uploads/papers/June-Messac_What-is-an-economy.pdf

Miller, R. (2016). *The centre in the early years.* Presentation on the occasion of the 50th anniversary of the Centre of Latin American Studies, University of Cambridge. http://www.latin-american.cam.ac.uk/latest-news-and-events/50-years-media/memories-reflections-clas/early-years-dr-rory-miller

Mitchell, B. R. (1980). *European historical statistics 1750–1970.* Macmillan.

Mitchell, B. R. (1982). *International historical statistics: Africa and Asia.* Macmillan.

Mitchell, B. R. (1983). *International historical statistics: The Americas and Australasia.* Macmillan.

Mitchell, B. (2009). *Dr Brian Mitchell celebrated his eightieth birthday on 20 September 2009.* https://www.trin.cam.ac.uk/wp-content/uploads/mitchell_brian_80th_Birthday.pdf

Mitchell, J., Solomou, S., & Weale, M. (2012). Monthly GDP estimates for inter-war Britain. *Explorations in Economic History, Elsevier, 49*(4), 543–556.

Mkandawire, T. (1987). Review: *The development of capitalism in Africa*, by John Sender and Sheila Smith. *Africa Development, 12*(2), 166–170. Published by CODESRIA.

Newbery, D. (1998). Foreword. In I. Begg & S. G. B. Henry (Eds.), *Applied economics and public policy* (pp. xix–xxii). Cambridge University Press.

Offer, A. (2008). *Charles Feinstein (1932–2004), and British Historical National Accounts.* Discussion papers in Economic and Social History No. 70. University of Oxford.

Ogilvie, S. (1997). *State Corporatism and Proto-Industry: The Wurttemberg Black Forest 1580–1797.* Cambridge University Press.

Pande, R., & Roy, H. (2021). *"If you compete with us, we shan't marry you"* – *The (Mary Paley and) Alfred Marshall lecture*. Working Paper 29481. National Bureau of Economic Research, 33p.

Pesaran, M. H. (1991). The ET interview: Professor Sir Richard Stone. *Econometric Theory, 7*(1), 85–123.

Pesaran, M. H., & Harcourt, G. C. (2000). Life and work of John Richard Nicholas Stone 1913–1991. *The Economic Journal, 110*, F146–F165.

Pigou, A. C. (1920). *The economics of welfare*. Macmillan.

Pomeranz, K. (2001). *The great divergence: China, Europe and the making of the modern world economy*. Princeton University Press.

Postan, M. M. (1939). *The historical method in social science: An inaugural lecture*. Cambridge University Press.

Postan, M. M. (1946). Obituary notice: Sir John Clapham. *Economic History Review, 16*(1), 56–59.

Postan, M. M. (1968a). A plague of economists? On some current myths, errors, and fallacies. *Encounter, 30*(1), 42–47.

Postan, M. M. (1968b). The uses and abuses of economics. *Encounter, 31*(3), 85–90.

Pyatt, G. (1990). Accounting for time use. *Review of Income and Wealth, 36*(1), 33–52.

Razavi, S. (2011). Nancy Folbre: Interviewed by Shahra Razavi. *Development and Change, 42*(1), 315–329.

Ristuccia, C. A., & Solomou, S. (2014). Can general purpose technology theory explain economic growth? Electrical power as a case study. *European Review of Economic History, 18*(3), 227–247.

Robinson, J. (1966). *The new mercantilism: An inaugural lecture*. Cambridge University Press.

Rocha, B., & Solomos Solomou, S. (2015). The effects of systemic banking crises in the inter-war period. *Journal of International Money and Finance, 54*, 35–49.

Ross, R. (2013). The politics of household budget research in colonial Central Africa. *Zambia Social Science Journal, 4*(1), Article 4. http://scholarship.law.cornell.edu/zssj/vol4/iss1/4

Rowthorn, R. (2008). Interview with Bob Rowthorn 13th June 2008. In I. S. Harrison & A. Macfarlane (Eds.), *Encounter with economics*. Interviews filmed by A. Macfarlane and edited by S. Harrison. University of Cambridge. http://sms.cam.ac.uk/collection/1092396

Rubery, J. (Ed.). (1988). *Women and recession*. Routledge and Kegan Paul.

Saith, A. (2019). *Ajit Singh of Cambridge and Chandigarh: An intellectual biography of the radical Sikh economist*. Palgrave Macmillan.

Seers, D. (1969). The meaning of development. *IDS Communications Series, 44*.

Seers, D. (1972). What are we trying to measure? *Journal of Development Studies, 8*(3), 21–36.

Seers, D. (1979). The birth, life and death of development economics: Revisiting a Manchester conference. *Development and Change, 10*(4), 707–719.

Sefton, J., & Weale, M. (1995). *Reconciliation of national income and expenditure: Balanced estimates of national income for the United Kingdom, 1920–1990*. Cambridge University Press.

Sen, A. (1990). Maurice Herbert Dobb. In J. Eatwell, M. Milgate, & P. Newman (Eds.), *Marxian economics. The new Palgrave* (pp. 141–147). Palgrave Macmillan.

Sender, J., & Smith, S. (1986). *The development of capitalism in Africa*. Methuen.

Serra, G. (2018). Pleas for fieldwork: Polly Hill on observation and induction, 1966–1982. In F. Fiorito, S. Scheall, & C. E. Suprinyak (Eds.), *Research in the his-

tory of economic thought and methodology. Including a symposium on Mary Morgan: Curiosity, imagination, and surprise (pp. 93–108). Emerald Publishing.
Singh, A. (1971). *Take-overs: Their relevance to the stock market and the theory of the firm.* Cambridge University Press.
Singh, A., & Whittington, G. (1968). *Growth, profitability and valuation: A study of United Kingdom quoted companies.* Cambridge University Press.
Smith, A. K. (2020, January 19). *Women at Cambridge: Eileen Power.* https://akennedysmith.com/tag/eileen-power/
Solomou, S. (1986a). Non-balanced growth and Kondratieff waves in the world economy, 1850–1913. *Journal of Economic History, 46*(1), 165–169.
Solomou, S. (1986b). Innovation cluster and Kondratieff long waves in economic growth. *Cambridge Journal of Economics, 10*(2), 101–112.
Solomou, S. (1990). *Phases of economic growth, 1850–1973.* Cambridge University Press.
Solomou, S. (1996). *Themes in macroeconomic history.* Cambridge University Press.
Solomou, S., & Weale, M. (1996). UK national income, 1920–1938: The implications of balanced estimates. *Economic History Review, 49*(1), 101–115.
Solomou, S., & Weale, M. (1997). Personal sector wealth in the United Kingdom, 1920–56. *Review of Income and Wealth, 43*(3), 297–318.
Solomou, S., & Weale, M. (2010). Unemployment and real wages in the great depression. *National Institute Economic Review, 214*(1), 51–61.
Stewart, M. (1967). *Keynes and after.* Penguin Books.
Stewart, M. (1968, May). A plague of politicians. *Encounter*, 54–56.
Stone, J. R. N. (1984). Richard Stone: Biographical. *The Nobel Prize.* https://www.nobelprize.org/prizes/economics/1984/stone/auto-biography/
Stone, J. R. N. (1997). Some British empiricists in the social sciences, 1650–1900. In A. M. Cardani & G. Stone (Eds.), *Raffaele Mattioli lectures 1986.* Cambridge University Press.
Supple, B. (1964). *Commercial crisis and change in England, 1600–1642.* Cambridge University Press.
Supple, B. (1970). *The royal exchange assurance: A history of British insurance, 1720–1970.* Cambridge University Press.
Supple, B. (1987). *The history of the British coal industry. Volume 4: 1914–1946, The political economy of decline.* Clarendon Press.
Temin, P. (2013, June 5). *The rise and fall of economic history at MIT.* Working Paper 13-11. Department of Economics, M.I.T.
Tew, B., & Henderson, R. F. (Eds.). (1959). *Studies in company finance: A symposium on the economic analysis and interpretation of British company accounts.* Cambridge University Press.
Thirlwall, A. (1987b). Nicholas Kaldor 1908–1986. *Proceedings of the British Academy, LXXIII*, 517–566.
Thompson, F. M. L. (2004). Hrothgar John Habakkuk, 1915–2002. *Proceedings of The British Academy, 124*, 91–114. https://www.thebritishacademy.ac.uk/documents/1779/124p091.pdf
Tylecote, A. (1988). Review of *Phases of economic growth: 1850–1973: Kondratieff Waves and Kuznets Swings*, by Solomos Solomou. *Economic Journal, 98*(392), 855–857.
Von Tunzelmann, G. N. (1982). Structural change and leading sectors in British manufacturing 1907–68. In Kindleberger & di Telia (Eds.), *Economics in the long view* (Vol. III). Macmillan.

Voorhees, E. D. (1929). Emotional adjustment of women in the modern world and the choice of satisfactions. *Annals of the American Academy of Political and Social Science, 143*, 368–373. http://www.jstor.org/stable/1017216

Waring, M. (1999). *Counting for nothing: What men value and what women are worth* (2nd ed.). University of Toronto Press, Scholarly Publishing Division.

Weale, M. (1985). Testing linear hypotheses on national account data. *Review of Economics and Statistics, 67*(4), 685–689.

Weale, M. (1993). Fifty years of national income accounting. *Economic Notes, 22*(2), 178–199.

Whitaker, J. K. (Ed.). (1996). *The correspondence of Alfred Marshall, economist* (Climbing, 1681–1890) (Vol. 1). Royal Economic Society Publication. Cambridge University Press.

CHAPTER 13

Research Assessment Exercises: Exorcising Heterodox Apostasy from 'Economics'

Abstract The origins of the Research Assessment Exercises lay in politicians and mandarins wanting 'value for money' for the research grants they were dispensing. Viewed from Cambridge, however, the RAEs offered the orthodox economists an effective device to extend and intensify their ongoing campaign against the heterodox groups in the Faculty and the DAE. Cambridge economics, as the original habitat of heterodox economics, unsurprisingly had the highest concentration of heterodox economists compared to other UK departments of economics. One obituary candidly observed that "Hahn had been unable to affect changes in the way the Economics Faculty was run because he didn't have the required tools. Those became available with the establishment of the Research Assessment Exercise and were used to bring about the necessary changes some years later" (Dasgupta, Obituary: Frank Hahn. *Royal Economic Society Newsletter, 161*, 2013). From his controlling position as President of the Royal Economic Society at the apex of the profession, Hahn could shape and instrumentalise the RAE process to suit his dual ends: to spread the gospel of neoclassical mathematical economics and simultaneously to clear out heterodoxy from Cambridge economics. The time frame of the early exercises dovetailed seamlessly with the ongoing Hahn-Matthews assault on Cambridge heterodox economics: in 1982, CEPG had been closed down; over the 1984–1987 period, the same fate befell the CGP; over the 1983–1987 period, in two phases, the DAE Review was the instrument that handed managerial control to the Hahn group, including the directorship of the DAE, adding to the recruitment of one of the 'nephews' from Uncle Frank's 'academy' to a Cambridge professorship in 1985. This set the stage for initiating the final

---

Successively labelled: Research Selectivity Exercise, Research Assessment Exercise and Research Excellence Framework.

© The Author(s), under exclusive license to Springer Nature Switzerland AG 2022
A. Saith, *Cambridge Economics in the Post-Keynesian Era*, Palgrave Studies in the History of Economic Thought,
https://doi.org/10.1007/978-3-030-93019-6_13

965

phase of the orthodox campaign, viz., of exorcising heterodox apostates, from the Faculty and leading Cambridge economics to the pristine purity of mathematical neoclassicism led by the other Cambridge. The chapter assesses the inherent biases and negative impacts of the RAEs and REFs and highlights how the Cambridge orthodox group came to exercise disproportionate decision-making influence over the exercises, effectively gaining the authority to decide what constituted 'economics', therefore who was an 'economist', what constituted 'quality' of research, how this was to be measured and certifying the practitioners who would pronounce on these issues. This orthodox stranglehold over RES-CHUDE-RAE decision-making—initiated by Hahn during his RES Presidency during 1986–1989, with preparatory groundwork in the preceding presidency of his partner Matthews during 1984–1986—was fully in evidence in the 1992, 2001, 2008 and 2014 rounds and visible in the RAE Economics Panels. The RAEs and REFs became an effective instrument for doctrinal control by orthodox mainstream economists working in tandem with departmental and university resource managers, not just in Cambridge but in the UK as a whole. In this, the controlling orthodox camp in the UK was imitating the methods of their American peers and principals who had already cleaned out their own 'cesspool', to borrow Dasgupta's infelicitous term, of heterodoxy.

13.1 The Agenda

I was bewildered when I first arrived here, the Great and Good of the University appeared to believe all those faculty members in economics were professionally just as able as Hahn and Matthews; external credentials didn't seem to matter in Cambridge; in comparison, LSE was a dream place; as it was my first appointment, I was protected there by my senior colleagues for several years, among whom were Peter Bauer, Terence Gorman, Harry Johnson, Michio Morishima, Denis Sargan, and Amartya Sen; that's a galaxy of stars; they differed politically but seemed to be united over what constitutes original work; so I knew something about the way academic excellence can be realised in a department; the Cambridge Faculty of Economics and the allied Department of Applied Economics in contrast resembled a failed Court of early-Modern times; on the rare occasion I managed to squeeze in the right appointment, I had to take recourse to underhand practice; I hated that, it was corrupting; matters changed once the Research Assessment Exercise was instituted by the government; the Faculty of Economics scored a 4, which concentrated the minds of the university authorities; I guess over time I gained the confidence of colleagues in the university; I was Chairman for five years and enjoyed that greatly; today my Chairman is an outstanding theorist, someone I managed to slip through an unsuspecting appointments committee a couple of years after I had arrived here; a failing Department of Applied Economics has been shut down, which has helped the

Faculty to get a lot better; but ruining a department is easy, rebuilding it is extremely hard; it's taken more than a decade to make us look attractive. (Partha Dasgupta, 2010)

Further, Dasgupta notes in his obituary for Frank Hahn: "Hahn had been unable to affect changes in the way the Economics Faculty was run because he didn't have the required tools. Those became available with the establishment of the Research Assessment Exercise and were used to bring about the necessary changes some years later" (Dasgupta, 2013).

The RAE stick was used by the neoclassical group to beat the Faculty practitioners of heterodox traditions. Dasgupta (2010) is fairly explicit: the neoclassical professors could develop a doomsday scenario and frighten unknowing University-level decision makers into taking timely action to stem the rot, the slide into, what Dasgupta had described as the 'cesspool', and save Cambridge from public embarrassment and from the loss of its historical reputation as the most powerful and creative centre for economics in the UK, and arguably the world. On closer inspection, the scary spectre of such an apocalyptic scenario turns out to be little more than a bogey, a mask hiding other realities. But it worked; and once the RAE was adopted nationally, it became an effective instrument for doctrinal control by the mainstream, not just in Cambridge but in the UK as a whole.

At the Faculty, the Hahn-Matthews duo had been strengthened in 1985 by the appointment of Hahn's junior, Partha Dasgupta, from LSE, as professor; and further in 1988 with the rapid promotions of another member of Hahn's 'academy', David Newbery, from lecturer to reader to the new Professorship in Applied Economics, a post held simultaneously with the directorship of the DAE. The DAE itself had already been slashed with the successive terminations of its two celebrated macroeconomic modelling teams, the Stone-Barker Cambridge Growth Project (CPG) and the Godley-Cripps Cambridge Economic Policy Group (CEPG), the closures effected significantly by the external decision-making networks influenced, if not controlled, by Hahn and Matthews. Then followed the surprise University Review of the DAE, instigated it was widely believed by the same neoclassical gang leaders; the Review was used as an instrument by Hahn and Matthews to enforce the changes in structure and management of the DAE, including control over the process through which appointments were to be made, including that of the new director, leading in due course to the appointment to the joint professorship and directorship. These victories of the orthodox group also had the effect of significantly diminishing the numerical strength of the heterodox group in voting for positions on the all-important Faculty Board. Along with the DAE's applied macroeconomic modellers, the group of sociologists based in the DAE were also summarily shown the door; they had an inherent intellectual affinity with the heterodox group of economists whom they tended to support in Faculty matters, and their continued presence was deemed both an impurity and an anomaly by the orthodox economics group; and at the end of the DAE Review process, this group of sociologists were relocated, lock, stock and barrel.

This set the stage for initiating the next phase of the orthodox campaign, viz., of exorcising the heterodox economists, the apostates, from the Faculty and restoring Cambridge economics to the purity of mathematical neoclassicism, as preached and practised by the other Cambridge that was the vanguard of Samuelson's third and fourth revolutions in economics, that is mathematisation and econometrification. The introduction of the RAE into the British university system provided a most opportune instrument for pursuing this next stage of the orthodox campaign in Cambridge; the timing was also perfect and made for a seamless continuation of the orthodox assault on Cambridge heterodox economics. The RAEs, and the REFs, have been well investigated at a UK-wide level over their cycles, and their inherent biases and negative impacts have been identified by various analysts focussing on the exercise as a whole, or on specific disciplines, including and especially economics. The purpose here is to highlight the manner in which the Cambridge orthodox group came to exercise disproportionate decision-making power in the crucial questions of defining the subject and certifying its practitioners; viz., in deciding what was 'economics', and who was an 'economist'. Having obtained control over this process, the RAE apparatus was used as a strategic instrumental device to reshape the Faculty—its teaching and research, its staff and student selection and reward systems, and its valuation systems.

Donald Gillies (2012) has provided a devastating commentary on the RAE and economics, taking 2008 as the focus. The instruments of control, of disciplining the discipline, designed to maximise mainstream purity as a religious form, have been identified and analysed extensively by (the late) Frederic Lee and his colleagues (see, amongst others, Lee, 2007; Lee & Harley, 1998); and recently, about the 2014 round, by Engelbert Stockhammer et al. (2017). The key criteria driving the RAE were imported from the US mainstream; once installed in the RAE, they quickly captured decision-making processes with regard to Faculty appointments and promotions. Dasgupta (2010) is right in pointing to the RAE as an instrument for capturing power in the Faculty of Economics in Cambridge, but was it a power for good?

13.2 The Teaching Body: Unification, Hierarchy, Control

It is useful to start at the beginning with a dose of organisational history, from a time when there was no association of the teachers of economics.

The Royal Economic Society (RES) was formed in 1890,[1] and its *Economic Journal* in 1891, but there was no professional association of economists till

---

[1] Coats and Coats (1970: 79) dig into the history of the origins and early years, 1890–1915, of the RES to look for the roots of economics as a profession, but come up in the end with this rather inconsequential conclusion: "Thus, although in a general sense it is clear that the period 1890–1915 marked an important phase in the development of British economics, one in which the basis was laid for the subsequent expansion in numbers and influence of those with academic qualifications

the Association of Teachers of Economics (ATE) was formed through the efforts of William Beveridge of the LSE in the early 1920s, in time for its inaugural conference to be held at Balliol College Oxford (with Beveridge as Chairman), in his alma mater, in January 1924. "The Association attempted to challenge the cliquish nature of existing academic bodies such as the Royal Economic Society and Keynes's Political Economy Club. Initially, it was open to a relatively diverse membership ... to teachers of economics, economic history, sociology, commerce and 'kindred' subjects" (Komine, 2018: 250–251). At the time, its other officers included T. S. Ashton, R. F. Harrod and E. A. G. Robinson. For the first five years, Beveridge tried, as he did at the LSE, to use it as a device to open up the core discipline of economics to contiguous subjects; and, not so coincidentally, "the main academic subjects referred to in the AUTE's constitution were similar to those contained in LSE's curriculum" (ibid.: 251). But "Beveridge's efforts petered out".

There was professional polarisation within the organisation: the original Association of Teachers of Economics subsequently restyled itself as the Association of University Teachers of Economics, thus introducing a division and a hierarchy of status between University and non-University teachers (ibid.: 250). In 1931, "the constitution of the Association was amended to put university teachers at a slight advantage over others. In 1932, the organisation was renamed the AUTE ... young economists such as Robbins, Robertson, Henderson, Kaldor [then still in his LSE incarnation] and others became more active.[2] Therefore, not only at LSE but also at AUTE, Beveridge found that he could not stand in the way of more 'academic' economists, who oriented themselves more towards the 'purification' of the subject" (ibid.: 251). As Komine observes, confirmed in Susan Howson's massive intellectual biography of Lionel Robbins (Howson, 2011), Beveridge "laid the foundations of an international intellectual group at LSE, differentiated from the Cambridge School", an agenda close to, if not at, the heart of Lionel Robbins. But paradoxically,

---

in economics, it would be unwise to attempt too precise an identification of the beginnings of the economics profession."

[2] Bernard Corry had been asked to write a short history of the AUTE. He had "fairly detailed notes of conferences post 1946 and a rather skimpy minute book that dates back to 1932". He asks Austin Robinson for information about "its origin and early days". He notes a reference in the EJ to a meeting in 1924. This last meeting could only have been a meeting not of the AUTE, which was formed in 1932—which is why the skimpy minute book only went back till that year—but to the formation meeting at Balliol College, Oxford of its predecessor, the Association of the Teachers of Economics (ATE) in 1924 (Bernard Corry to E. A. G. Robinson, Letter, 12 September 1989, No. 352; Correspondence, E. A. G. Robinson Papers, Marshall Library Archives, Cambridge). Austin Robinson replies: "I have no papers and no worthwhile memories. Such memories as I have of the existence and importance only begin after the war and I was never a member. My reason was perhaps a silly one. I was by then chairman of the faculty here and the A.U.T.E. came very near to being a trade union disputing with the employers, and I was inadvertently an employer as much as a worker, so I thought I ought not to join when I should have done" (E. A. G. Robinson to Bernard Corry, Letter, 12 December 1989, No. 3; Correspondence, E. A. G. Robinson Papers, Marshall Library Archives, Cambridge).

instead of succeeding in his project of promoting (what now would be called) multidisciplinarity, his brainchild, the ATE, had mutated into the AUTE which evolved into the instrument of the purification of economics as a 'science'. An illustration of this was that Social Biology (the subject and the Chair which Beveridge had created in the hope of making cross-disciplinary intellectual links), "was completely removed from LSE immediately after Beveridge left the School. In this sense, his attempt to make economics an inductive science had failed" (Komine, 2018: 249–250).

Later, in a further development, the Association of Polytechnic Teachers of Economics (APTE) was formed in 1972, and ran till 1992; in 1977, it established the *British Review of Economic Issues* with Thanos Skouras as the editor during 1997–1984, and Philip Arestis taking over for 1985–1988; the *Review* had a distinctly post-Keynesian heterodox identity Lee (2009: 137). Cyril Smith, writing in 1991, observes that "although there have been moves to establish associations for professionals, so far there is no single body. Different sectors have their own groupings such as the Association of University Teachers of Economics, the APTE for those in polytechnics, the Society for Business Economists, and so on. Insofar as economists have needed to organize to protect their interests, they have looked to the relevant trade unions" (Smith, 1991: 140). Backhouse (2000: 31) also notes the birth of APTE as "echoing the divide between the two sectors in higher education". The APTE's orientation was clearly more heterodox than that of the AUTE which remained nominally open to all comers.

Between the Robbins Report of 1963, and the Amendment of the Education Reform Act in 1992, there was a massive expansion in the numbers of university teachers of economics. This occurred in two steps. First, the Robbins intervention led to the creation of many new, red-brick universities including Warwick, York, Essex, Sussex, Bristol and Southampton; many employed substantial numbers of economists: York, 61; Warwick, 53; and Sussex, 49; the big 3, LSE, Oxford and Cambridge, had 122, 80 and 60 respectively in 1988. According to a survey done that year, there were 1116 economists in university departments of economics, and another 1044 in research units of other departments or polytechnics (Blaug & Towse, 1988: 51, cited in Backhouse, 1996: 40). The RES, and Frank Hahn as its president, were now dealing with very large numbers.

Then the 1992 legislation bestowed the status of being a university on polytechnics, thereby increasing the number of universities by thirty-five. As a consequence, APTE became redundant and its membership automatically merged with that of AUTE; there was constitutional equality between the two merged strands, though perceptions of caste and status hierarchies surely persisted as they all competed for intellectual space and resources on an officially level playing field. As AUTE and APTE merged, and polytechnics and universities came under the same funding body, the approximately doubled, and most had departments of economics. The teaching body expanded massively, unified and consolidated, and came under the purview of the RES for all matters to do with the teaching of the discipline.

Hahn retired from the Faculty in 1992, the year of the merger, passing on the baton to the trusted team following him, viz., Jim Mirrlees as the new RES President, David Hendry as the Vice President, Alistair Ulph as the President of CHUDE (the Conference of Heads of University Departments of Economics) and Tony Atkinson as the Chair of the Economics Panel for the RAE of 1992; thus a continuity of perspective, purpose and control was guaranteed.

The RES has been described by Partha Dasgupta as being a moribund organisation (till the time that his seniors and peers took over, that is): "for most of its history ... the RES did relatively little.[3] Annual conferences were organized not by the RES but by the Association of University Teachers of Economics (AUTE), established for this purpose in the 1920s" (Backhouse, 2000: 31).[4] Conferences were held annually excluding the war years, though Parkin and Nobay (1975: iii) note that their *Proceedings of the Warwick Conference of 1973* is only "the second of what is intended to be an annual publication". The conference was open to full-time researchers in industry and government, visiting academics and to teachers from other branches of higher education. Parkin and Nobay write: "The Association has played a key role in the development of professional standards in the economics profession in this country" (ibid.). Of the contributors to the *Proceedings* volume of just this conference alone, there is an extended group, many of whom have strong links, then and/or later, to the Hahn-Matthews network: M. J. Artis, J. S. Flemming, R. A. Hart, Geoffrey Heal and J. R. Sargent, R. Layard, C. J. Bliss, B. J. McCormick, I. C. R. Byatt, Marcus H. Miller; and several others on the AUTE Executive Committee in 1975.

Frank Hahn had been an active participant in the AUTE conferences—witness his rousing call-to-arms "I am John the Baptist" speech heralding the arrival of general-equilibrium-with-money recalled by Meghnad Desai and David Newbery (see Chap. 2). Upon taking over the presidency of the RES in 1986, Frank Hahn displayed his characteristic purpose and gusto and set about implementing his vision and agenda for shaping the teaching, and teaching departments, of economics. He was on a mission to universalise the mainstream mathematical economics approach in the UK, along the US lines, already initiated from the 1960s at the LSE by him, Gorman, Sargan and others. This would require control over the AUTE. Backhouse (2000: 31) notes

---

[3] This view possibly reflects the anti-Oxbridge sentiment of historians, including for instance A. W. 'Bob' Coats and others, who wish to highlight the divide between the elite universities and the rest, with RES very much a bastion of the former. For other perspectives, see Hey and Winch (1990). Austin Robinson, who was closely involved with the evolution of the RES, might not have accepted such a sweeping critique applied over such a long period. But every new leader often starts by denigrating the performance of the predecessors in the earlier 'lost' years or decades.

[4] Komine points out that the original ATE, formed in 1924, changed its name (and constituency) to AUTE only in 1932.

that "it was only in the 1980s that the role of the RES expanded. The society became more democratic, electing the President and members of the governing body by a postal ballot of all members."[5] Hahn and his active group of followers had long been placed in senior positions in many rising universities as professors and heads of departments of economics. Alongside, "the annual conference came to be jointly organized by the RES and AUTE, and eventually the AUTE disappeared altogether". In 1989, Hahn created a new body, more responsive to (his) RES leadership in the form of the CHUDE, the Conference of the Heads of Departments of Economics in UK universities. AUTE, in any case, was well under Hahn's control already: the Chairman of AUTE when Hahn took over the RES Presidency in 1986 was none other than Jim Mirrlees, part of his inner circle. In a letter to Austin Robinson, dated 16 October 1987, Aubrey Silberston, then Secretary General of the RES, notes "another possible name [for President of RES after Hahn] of course is that of Jim Mirrlees. He has now stopped being Chairman of AUTE, and might be willing to do this at some time." Duly, Mirrlees became RES President in 1989 for the three-year term following his senior, Frank Hahn. CHUDE then served as the liaison between the RES President and the university teachers of economics who were under the charge of their respective heads of department.

Backhouse (2000: 31) observes, "when higher education came under pressure in the 1980s, the RES was instrumental in defending the interests of the subject, convening a regular meeting of the heads of all university economics departments for this purpose"; "the RES carried out an analysis of the RAE assessment, and sought to mitigate changes in research council policy that were perceived as damaging to the profession" (ibid.: 37, n21). This interpretation seems somewhat short of content. Hahn certainly succeeded in building a unified and active organisation with a structure responsive to the RES (headed by himself); however, this begs the question about what "the interests of the subject" were interpreted to be, or what was to be "perceived as damaging to the profession". That was the crux of the matter; if Hahn wanted to enact organisational reforms at RES and AUTE, it was not because he had the imagination of an administrator but because he wanted the revamped organisation to be fit for his purpose of bringing the neoclassical general equilibrium revolution to the door, and into the curricula, of economics teaching on a country-wide level. What was 'good' economics, indeed what was 'economics' in the first place and how was it to be codified in teaching and research; how was 'good' research to be identified, measured, incentivised; how was 'deadwood' of earlier generations of literary style economists, aka Dasgupta's 'cesspool', to be cleared out of departments and replaced by bright, bushy-eyed 'properly trained' young economists that were the vanguard of the new revolution; how was all this to be achieved, that was the question, and the imperative could be called the orthodox revolutionaries.

---

[5] Backhouse (2000: 37, n20) informs that "prior to this, elections had simply been at the Annual General Meeting, often very poorly attended".

13.3　1986: SWINNERTON-DYER AND THE GENESIS OF THE RAE

Sir Peter Swinnerton-Dyer,[6] the Cambridge mathematician who was Chair of the University Grants Commission from 1983 to 1991, devised the first RAE, called the Research Selectivity Exercise (RSE) in 1986, and then implemented the first full-blown RAE in 1989.[7] "Universities were spending money

---

[6] Sir Peter Swinnerton-Dyer was something of a polymath. His sympathies did not seem to lie with the radical student causes of the 1970s: he was present when the student activists arrived at The Old Schools in the Sit-in of February 1972, and went out to shoo them off; and earlier in the 'Greek week' of February 1970 had not approved of the student protests at the Garden House Hotel against the Greek dictators being entertained there; he said later he was quite fond of Margaret Thatcher and quite liked her, though he did not have much to do with her; she made him Chair of the UGC, for which services he was knighted. He was Master of St Catherine's between 1973 and 1983, during which period he served a term (1981–1983) as the Vice Chancellor of Cambridge University, after which he left to become Chair of the UGC, staying on till 1991—a period that covered the early Research Selectivity/Assessment Exercises of 1986 and 1989. His successor as Master of St Catherine's was Barry Supple, an economic historian from Oxford. It would not at all be surprising if Robin Matthews was the matchmaker. Matthews and Supple had been close collaborators; both were economic historians and had co-authored research papers. Matthews had been Drummond Professor of Political Economy in Oxford from 1965 till 1975, when he gave up the chair of economics for the seat of Master of Clare College in Cambridge, staying in the post till 1993. Swinnerton-Dyer was a mathematician, who gained fame early for setting the Birch-Swinnerton-Dyer problem in number theory in 1965—with a $1m prize, announced in 1999, for a solution; a bridge player who represented England in the 1953 European Championship in Helsinki, coming second to France; he followed his father as the 16th Baronet, but also as an accomplished chess player. Matthews was Master of Clare, but also an international master chess problematist, specialising in three-move endings; he had written books about this and was said to have felt that he was better at this than at economics. Their tenures as Masters of their respective Colleges overlapped by eight years and they would have sat across many a High Table; Swinnerton-Dyer might have reminded Matthews that he held bragging rights when he sat across him on Board 5, and beat him, at the Varsity Chess Championships in 1947. No slouch, Swinnerton-Dyer apparently merited a couple of mentions in the 1965 edition of *Modern Chess Openings* (p. 118). "In a [bridge] tournament, Swinnerton-Dyer once scuttled his opponents' grand slam by bidding eight clubs; the rules at the time invalidated an impossible bid made by mistake or oversight so he first informed the tournament director that his bid was intentional. The rules of bridge were subsequently revised to prevent this" (Reid, 2019). This might have gone down well with Matthews, who took no hostages and would not mind winning by hook or by crook. In the context of his long tenure as Master of Clare College, "one shrewd Fellow observed that [Robin] will not be remembered as an impartial Chair", but as one who pondered his responsibilities and high principles, and then "fought his corner with all the expedients he had learned during his stint with the SSRC and ... long term as Master" (quoted in Harcourt, 2017a: 972). So, the chess and college masters had much in common. In this context, it is perhaps worth noting that Partha Dasgupta returned to Cambridge as a professor in 1985, a year before Swinnerton-Dyer's RSE of 1986. "I was at Trinity; Peter Swinnerton-Dyer was one of my supervisors and was also Dean of College; ... I got to know him well even as an undergraduate and now see him pretty regularly" (Dasgupta, 2010: 63).

[7] William Waldegrave said that "I was responsible for appointing Peter Swinnerton-Dyer to the U. G. C. because he believed that the cuts should be shaped, and excellence attempted to be preserved ... I became a junior Minster in the Education Department in 1981, with Keith Joseph; I was responsible for higher education at a time when university spending growth was to be cur-

wastefully", he said looking back in a later interview, "so ... the [RAE] was essentially invented by me and was instituted so money would be divided up in a fair way" (Grove, 2013, April 8). He is clearly an admirer of Margaret Thatcher: "She was a great prime minister and she did much to change the atmosphere of higher education", and in that he was surely quite right. And then confirming his gender credentials: "the instinct of a woman is to spring-clean and this country needed spring-cleaning, not least the university sector" (ibid.).

Kogan and Hanney (2000: 97–98) reproduce "a vivid account of the RAE's genesis" in the words of Christopher Ball:

> Peter Swinnerton-Dyer, David Phillips and I used to have dinner together, and plan our ... strategy. One evening, Peter said, 'I have a problem ... I can no longer defend the funding of universities through my leg of the dual support system without real accountability to government.' Some universities were apparently getting huge funds and no one knew how effectively these were being used; on the other side some others were producing excellent research without any serious funding; so 'why does the university system need all these unspecific research funds?' So we discussed it and I suppose at that dinner we invented the research selectivity exercise. Peter said: 'I think I know how to do it for science, technology and medicine, the bigger worry for me is social science and the arts.' I said: 'I don't think you should do it in these areas at all, the funds there are relatively little. What you need to account for is the massive medical and engineering spends. ... So don't do it [the research selectivity exercise] for these disciplines. The cost will be so enormous, it won't be justified by the redistribution of funds that will result.' A month later, when I met him again, he said, 'I liked your advice but I am not going to follow it. I have been to the heads of the disciplinary groups in social studies and arts, and they said if there is going to be a selective exercise, arts and social studies can't be left out. It would appear to the public that our research is unimportant. The dons want it. What do you say to that?' I said, 'They are bloody fools, and they will live to regret it.' (Christopher Ball has added that his memory tends to dramatize events in retrospect—but he believes the gist of this account to be true.)

Details of the Research Selectivity Exercise (RSE) introduced by Peter Swinnerton-Dyer are scarce and not written up online, but Paul Jump (2013b), even within the constraints of a write-up of an interview with Swinnerton-Dyer in 2013, has filled this gap admirably. The scientist stood outside the contestations of social science, but was very clear that while he could recognise, and so also fairly appropriately, though approximately, measure, the 'quality' of research in the sciences, he could not transplant the same model to the social sciences, where several other considerations came into play, undermining the

---

tailed—which Shirley Williams in the previous Government had warned was inevitable—and there was a most tremendous uproar wherever I went" (Waldegrave, 2013). Shirley Williams had appointed Michael Posner as Chairman of the Social Science Research Council months before the fall of the Callaghan Labour government.

basic, defensible assumptions applicable to the sciences. He was also clear that what was sought was a fair criterion for the allocation of research funds, and there would be several parameters feeding into this determination, and that this was distinct from the measurement of research 'quality' which would be but one criterion—should it be measurable in the first instance in the social sciences. A transparent algorithm was deemed necessary for the allocation of research funding especially in view of the Thatcher budgetary cuts, and the rising competition across universities. Prior to Swinnerton-Dyer's intervention with his RSE allocations were made on an ad hoc basis, showing a high degree of path dependence: "I think they looked at last year's grant and adjusted it for [recent] circumstances", and the case for adjustment rested on demonstrating "some new development". In any case, much of the grant depended predominantly on the numbers of students and related dimensions. Paul Jump spoke with Swinnerton-Dyer in 2013 just when the submissions deadline for the 2014 REF was about to close. According to one analyst of the process, remarking on the simplicity of the RSE 1986 "by today's standards this looks a laughably amateurish process" (Sayer, 2015: 19). The thirty-seven Subject Sub-committees of the UGC were charged with making the determination, based on an optional four-page (maximum) write-up where a department could show off its strengths and a total of five research outputs from the previous five years on which it would be "content for its total output to be assessed". Swinnerton-Dyer observed, "we didn't say 'best outputs' because that would have led to all sorts of disputes from philosophers"—and one can safely add, economists. His logic was simple—if the five outputs were good, it would be fairly safe to surmise that the overall output of the unit would also be roughly 'good', and that was all that was needed. He was against using the total output of the department as an indicator of strength, as this would "only encourage the production of low quality papers"; and he was against individual assessments, as this would place an enormous, unconscionable burden on individual staff. "I don't think you can run an assessment of individuals without an intolerable level of work", he said to Paul Jump.

This procedure passed for 1986, but by 1989, when Frank Hahn was into his third (extended) year as President of the RES with hands-on responsibility for inputs for shaping the upcoming RAE, Swinnerton-Dyer's simple scheme was a thing of the past. Then, a department like LSE with a staff strength of say 100, would have submitted five outputs; in 1989, two were required of each, 200 in all; for the next RAE, the number doubled to four per staff, as the focus of the exercise shifted fundamentally to enabling the leaders of the subject, both at the 'local' level of the individual department but also at the level of the profession as a whole, now managed by Frank Hahn and his RES team, to control the composition of the teaching and research staff and to bring it in line with the US-led mathematical revolution in economics. For this and his purpose, a focus on sifting out the heterodox and other chaff from the orthodox grain was imperative; hence the change in parameters towards individual staff research assessment matched the needs and intent of the Hahn camp in Cambridge, indeed as explicitly declared by Dasgupta, though these applied not just to economics but across the board.

13.4   1986–1989: Frank Hahn and the Orthodox Capture of the RES

Frank Hahn's purpose, zeal and alacrity perhaps fall into perspective if it is noted that after the first, tentative, RSE under Peter Swinnerton-Dyer in 1986, it was known that the following full-scale exercise, with teeth, was on the anvil to be implemented in 1989. It is to be noted that Hahn became President of the RES in 1986; in his obituary of Frank Hahn, Partha Dasgupta (2013) writes: "When elected President of the Royal Economic Society for the customary two-year period, Hahn took over a moribund institution; but with the then Secretary General Aubrey Silberston's help transformed it into the hugely influential body it is today. In order to enable Hahn to oversee the changes, the Statutes were altered to the current one where Presidents serve for three years."[8]

So in his transformative mission, Hahn was aided by Silberston, another old Cambridge hand and a long-term friend, and member of their common friend, Robin Matthews's CLARE Group. Another Cambridge (and DAE) contemporary, John Beath who also served later as the Secretary General of the RES, writes, in the obituary of his predecessor:

> In 1979 Aubrey was approached by Richard Stone, then President of the RES, asking if he would take on the role of Secretary-General. He was delighted by this and readily accepted. At Imperial he only had a handful of fellow economists but holding the meetings of the RES Council and Executive Committee there ensured he remained fully integrated into the economics profession at large. His period as Secretary-General saw an increase in the Society's activities facilitated by the income from the large investment fund that had been built up during Tad Rybczynski's Treasurership. Two important structural changes were joining up with the Association of University Teachers of Economics (AUTE) and the formation of CHUDE. The AUTE had established an annual conference that was the main gathering for economists in the UK to present their research and exchange ideas. RES also ran conferences, but these were infrequent, on specific

---

[8] In October 1987, Aubrey Silberston, as Secretary General of the Royal Economic Society, writes to Austin Robinson to say, "I would very much welcome your raising the question of what ought to be the tenure of the President. I think it is true of the two Presidents before Frank Hahn, i.e., David Worswick and Robin Matthews, that each would have benefitted from a further year. It would, I think, be possible to elect Frank Hahn for a further two years, even if no long-term change is made to increase the tenure of the President. It seems to me that the by-laws give us the authority that we would need for this. If Frankie does not go on. … Charles Feinstein seems to me an obvious President one day. Another possible name of course is that of Jim Mirrlees. He has now stopped being Chairman of the AUTE, and might be willing to do this at some time."

Aubrey Silberston to EAG Robinson, dated 16 October 1987.

topics and hence were relatively small and somewhat selective. The union of the RES and the AUTE meant that the annual gathering became the RES Annual Conference that we know today. CHUDE was an important innovation because it led to more continuous and closer links between the Society and UK university departments. CHUDE is now an important forum for the critical discussion of key issues and the exchange of ideas. (Beath, 2015: 18)

Thus, another strategic space captured was the Presidency of the Royal Economic Society. It is worth recording that the President for 1974–1976 was Nicky Kaldor and Cambridge (and ex-Cambridge) seniors of various heterodox persuasions provided the next four incumbents till 1982: Alan Brown, Dick Stone and Phyllis Deane. Then the presidency shifts solidly to the Hahn-Matthews-Gorman camp: R. C. O. Matthews becomes President in 1984–1986, followed crucially, by his collaborator Frank Hahn for the pivotal 1986–1989 period. The baton then passes on to their queuing 'juniors', an unbroken succession of Hahn-Gorman boys: Jim Mirrlees, followed by David Hendry, followed by Tony Atkinson, followed by Partha Dasgupta, followed by Stephen Nickell, through till 2004; and then by other followers of varying rank—J. Sutton, J. Vickers, R. Blundell, C. Bean, P. Neary and most recently, with retro nostalgia, Nick Stern.

The position provides stature, a stamp of authority, but also the capacity to influence strategic outcomes in the professional practice of the discipline within the UK. This was demonstrated dramatically by Frank Hahn during his term of office during 1986–1989. The Presidency of the RES, prior to Hahn, was indeed perhaps the highest, but rather passive, official marker of professional prestige and status; Hahn lapped that up, but carried on with urgency to convert and use it as a strategic, instrumental platform for interventions to reshape the contours and content of teaching and researching economics in the UK. Along with and through his team, he could control the definition, recognition and production of 'knowledge' in economics, as he saw it.

This he could achieve through the 'facipulation'—that is facilitation with manipulation—of the new Research Assessment Exercise (RAE), which was the third commanding height captured by the orthodox neoclassical school. As noted, the first RAE had been conducted for the UGC by Swinnerton-Dyer in 1986 and was a quick, rather opaque, rough and ready affair (the specific details of which were never really divulged in full), without significant impact on the pattern of official research funding across universities and departments. This was just like a beauty contest—there were serious prizes and penalties involved, measured in hard cash for research; and at the level of individual staff, there were serious consequences for the assessment of their work and for their prospects for promotion. The current and future fate of staff and units were at stake.

There were three fundamental issues: first, what constituted 'beauty'? Second, how was this 'beauty' to be measured in units that would make it comparable? And third, whose eyes would judge this beauty parade? Well, beauty was definitely not deemed to lie in the eye of any old beholder: beauty was as

Hahn, the one with the beautiful mind, saw it: mathematical mainstream economics, what else. The quantity and quality of your beauty could be measured by the journals in which you published, and only those that subscribed to this specification of beauty really counted; and for quick reckoning, conveniently at hand was A. M. Diamond (1989) to provide his eponymous list of 'core' economics journals that really mattered. And finally, the vital issue of the jury that was to look 'beauty' up and down and take the vital measurements of each contender with the prescribed measuring tapes; a jury which also made the exercise look participatory and democratic, even though it was really a load-sharing device, since by using the set definitions and criteria, jury members could be expected to provide converging judgements and rankings. Still it was good to have a full firing squad; at the very least, 'collective responsibility' would protect every member from any charge of bias. That said, it wouldn't do to have a jury comprising economists who were not singing from the Hahn hymn sheet.

Famously, in his talk 'The End of Laissez-faire' in 1926, Keynes played the clairvoyant predicting the demise of laissez-faire. "The disposition towards public affairs, which we conveniently sum up as individualism and *laissez-faire*, drew its sustenance from many different rivulets of thought and springs of feeling. For more than a hundred years our philosophers ruled us because, by a miracle, they nearly all agreed or seem to agree on this one thing. We do not dance even yet to a new tune. But a change is in the air. We hear but indistinctly what were once the clearest and most distinguishable voices which have ever instructed political mankind. The orchestra of diverse instruments, the chorus of articulate sound, is receding at last into the distance" (Keynes, 1926). But less than twenty years later, the same unvarnished, unqualified doctrine had been reborn and dispensed as a substitute for mother's milk—Friedrich Hayek had written his *The Road to Serfdom* (1944). Once again, Keynes, this time with his *General Theory*, despatched laissez-faire into the long grass. And yet again, less than thirty years later, the doctrine was back centre field, this time with Frank Hahn playing neoclassical orthodox soothsayer predicting the imminent integration of money into Walrasian general equilibrium (Newbery, 2017: 500).

Hahn was already presiding over the AUTE; now, in 1987, through the RES he set up a Conference of the Heads of Departments of Economics (CHUDE) which was the body through which the RES liaised with the community of economics teachers in the country, and provided a range of professional services. But crucially, it was also the consultative mechanism for obtaining recommendations from the body of teachers for the constitution of the RAE panels for each unit of assessment, such as economics and econometrics. In his personal and presidential capacity, Hahn exercised huge sway over this process, including the inputs from his extensive network across the country. His term of office as President would have ended, as per the standing rules till then, in 1998, that is a year before the RAE was to take place, but as Dasgupta informs us, the tenure was extended by a year by a change of Statutes in order to allow Hahn to carry through his reforms—surely including the preparation and management of the structure, design and staffing of the RAE economics panel and its Chair. Even without the measuring, or spanking, rod of the RAE, Hahn had imposed his vision and standards. Newbery (2017: 499–500) notes, "Hahn arrived at the LSE in 1967 like a whirlwind" and quotes Richard Jackman, an old Churchill hand: "Hahn and the other newly appointed professors [Gorman, Johnson, Walters] set about imposing serious academic standards with traumatic consequences. Several junior lecturers were denied tenure on the grounds, which seemed extraordinary at the time, that they hadn't published anything." Now, two decades down the line, he and his group which had risen to the top of departments, could be equally ruthless in using this new measuring rod to beat anyone not loyal to the faith. And all this would be done 'objectively' without any 'subjective' bias getting in the way. As Dasgupta (2013) significantly revealed, it had not been possible for Frank Hahn to reshape the Cambridge Economics Faculty into his preferred form because he lacked the institutional instruments to enforce these changes, till the time the Research Assessment Exercise was imposed on the system thereby providing him with the requisite means and powers.

AUTE dissolved and merged with the RES; CHUDE was formed with its Steering Committee which liaised with RES on the matter of panel selections for the RAE; and in 1988 Aubrey Silberston wrote the original constitution of CHUDE.[9] RES and Hahn ruled over British economics. RES Council members had a role too in discussing, advising and stamping decisions; members served for five years and a cohort of five new members was elected each year to replace an outgoing cohort that had completed its term. Table 13.1 provides the names of these cohorts and it is apparent that in the vital period where RES came to be controlled by Frank Hahn, the clear majority of those s/elected were of the 'Hahn' persuasion. The stranglehold was comprehensive.

With strategic synchronicity, Frank Hahn became President of the Royal Economic Society (RES) in 1986, and had his term extended for an additional year to 1989 to allow him to implement his agenda of reforms for teaching and research in economics; he had taken over from his Cambridge partner Robin Matthews, and set about his business with typical gusto.

> The leadership of the Society acted quickly to capture the process by which assessors were appointed to the economics panel. In particular, the Society actively supported the establishment of CHUDE [the Conference of Heads of University Departments of Economics] in 1987, whose most important activity was the selection of RES-acceptable candidates for the economics panels. Consequently,

[9] "John Beath, at a meeting of the CHUDE Steering Committee in 2010, explained that the original CHUDE constitution, written by Aubrey Silberston in 1988, had been located. The actual practice of CHUDE has evolved somewhat differently from the constitution so there is a need to revise it. A revision is also timely given the changes to the RES governance procedures" (Beath, 2010). Aubrey Silberston was Secretary General of the Royal Economic Society during 1979–1993 and was followed by Richard Portes of the London Business School for the 1993–2008 period.

Table 13.1 Presidents and council members of the Royal Economic Society, 1975–2019

Year	President	Council members elected to serve 5-year term					
1975	N. Kaldor	R. J. Ball	K. Berrill	P. M. Deane	P. J. Hammond	A. G. Hines	C. M. Kennedy
1976	N. Kaldor	J. C. R. Dow	H. F. Lydall	E. Penrose	W. B. Reddaway	J. R. S. Revell	A. K. Sen
1977	A. J. Brown	M. J. Artis	J. Black	R. D. C. Black	P. Kay	M. C. Kaser	J. A. Parkinson
1978	A. J. Brown	A. B. Atkinson	F. T. Blackaby	S. S. Daniel	G. McCrone	R. C. O. Matthews	M. Zinkin
	J. R. N. STONE						
1979	J. R. N. Stone	A. D. Bain	E. Bennathan	D. F. Hendry	D. P. O'Brien	M. H. Peston	S. J. Prais
1980	J. R. N. Stone	K. Berrill	K. G. Cowling	C. H. Feinstein	A. G. Hines	A. P. I. Minford	A. P. Thirlwall
	P. M. Deane						
1981	P. M. Deane	F. Cairncross	J. S. Flemming	K. D. George	F. H. Hahn	P. E. Hart	A. K. Sen
1982	P. M. Deane	D. Hague	J. P. Hutton	K. Kaser	M. A. King	B. J. Loasry	M. V. Posner
	G. D. Worswick						
1983	G. D. Worswick	A. J. C. Britton	I. C. R. Byatt	J. A. Mirrlees	A. S. Skinner	A. Skouras	M. J. C. Surrey
1984	G. D. Worswick	J. D. Dribbin	M. Jones-Lee	A. I. MacBean	A. R. Nobay	M. F. G. Scott	D. K. Stout
	R. C. O. Matthews						
1985	R. C. O. Matthews	C. H. Feinstein	J. P. Neary	D. M. G. Newbery	S. J. Nickell	F. Steward	A. P. Thirlwall
1986	R. C. O. Matthews	M. C. Casson	J. S. Flemming	M. B. Gregory	S. Hogg	I. G. Patel	A. K. Sen
	F. Hahn						
1987	F. Hahn	M. J. Artis	T. Burns	C. A. E. Goodhart	D. Hague	J. D. Hey	R. Portes
1988	F. Hahn	I. C. R. Byatt	K. D. George	C. Johnson	H. H. Liesner	J. A. Mirrlees	J. R. Shackleton
1989	J. A. Mirrlees	A. Budd	P. Dasgupta	G. Davies	M. Desai	J. Odling-Smee	D. Vines

1990	J. A. Mirrlees	R. Blundell	C. H. Feinstein	R. Freeman	J. R. Lomax	S. J. Nickell	K. F. Wallis
1991	J. A. Mirrlees	A. B. Atkinson	W. Beckerman	D. Currie	D. Greenaway	G. C. Harcourt	A. M. Ulph
1992	J. A. Mirrlees	V. Chick	C. Crook	R. Portes	N. H. Stern	L. A. Winters	M. Wolf
1993	D. F. Hendry[a]	P. Arestis	H. Joshi	D. Julius	M. King	J. P. Neary	J. Sutton
1994	D. F. Hendry[a]	C. Bean	A. Dilnot	C. Huhne	M. Miller	M. Morgan	R. O'Brien
1995	D. F. Hendry[a]	K. Barker	K. Burdett	S. Dow	Malcomson	D. de Meza	D. Osborn
1996	A. B. Atkinson	R. Lea	M. Mayer	D. Ulph	A. J. Venables	A. Wood	P. Rowlatt
1997	A. B. Atkinson	P. A. David	H. Dixon	P. Geroski	S. Hogg	M. Muellbauer	P. Sinclair
1998	A. B. Atkinson	E. Balls	K. Binmore	A. Booth	W. Buiter	C. Mayer	S. Page
1999	P. Dasgupta[a]	C. Pissarides	D. Coyle	J. Humphries	C. Mayer	S. Wren-Lewis	M. Sawyer
2000	P. Dasgupta[a]	J. Beath	A. Chesher	J. H. Moore	A. Kaletsky	R. Kelly	M. Weale
2001	P. Dasgupta[a]	W. Arulampalam	C. Bliss	T. Besley	J. Driffill	C. Propper	A. Robinson
2002	S. Nickell[a]	E. Davis	R. Disney	P. Klemperer	A. Oswald	G. O'Donnell	J. Vickers
2003	S. Nickell[a]	C. Butler	A. Carruth	V. Pryce	A. Muscatelli	A. Sibert	M. Taylor
2004	S. Nickell[a]						
2005	J. Sutton[a]						
2006	J. Sutton[a]						
2007	J. Sutton[a]						
2008	J. Vickers[a]						
2009	J. Vickers[a]						
2010	J Vickers[a]						
2011	R. Blundell[a]						
2012	R. Blundell[a]						
2013	R. Blundell[a]						
2014	C. Bean[a]						

(continued)

Table 13.1 (continued)

Year	President	Council members elected to serve 5-year term
2015	C. Bean[a]	
	J. H. Moore[a]	
2016	J. H. Moore[a]	
	A. Chesher[a]	
2017	A. Chesher[a]	
	P. Neary	
2018	P. Neary	
	N. Stern	
2019	N. Stern	
	t.b.a.	

[a]Also "Life Vice-Presidents of the Royal Economic Society"

the assessors appointed to the 1989 and 1992 panels had the common characteristics of being mainstream economists and of holding a significant position within the RES, such as a member of the Council or Executive Committee, Treasurer, or President, being on the editorial board of *The Economic Journal*, and/or being a member of the CHUDE Standing Committee. With the capture of the economics panel, the RES obtained the power to cleanse economics departments of non-mainstream economists. … Since the paradigm-bound view, that the quality of non-mainstream research was inferior to mainstream research, was largely accepted by the assessors, the two panels financially rewarded departments who did mainstream research and published in core mainstream journals and generally damned those who did not. The real threat of financial sanction by the economics panel, in light of the declining financial support for universities and research, drove British economic departments to discriminate against non-mainstream research and the hiring of non-mainstream economists as well as to restrict if not eliminate the teaching of non-mainstream economics to students. For example, evidence from our survey suggests that when a member of an economics department who took particular interest in teaching a non-mainstream course left, effort was generally not made to retain the course by hiring a suitable replacement. (Lee & Harley, 1998: 42–43; see also Lee, 2009; Lee et al., 2012a, 2012b)

It is not known if and to what extent Frank Hahn or Robin Matthews, or some of their mainstream proxies, were involved in the generic redesigning of the overall template of the RAE of 1989 as it applied across all academic disciplines. But at whatever distance they might have stood from the general RAE template, the emphasis on the volume and especially the quality of 'research productivity' would provide them with the desired sticks (for some) and carrots (for others) to manipulate and reorient the discipline of economics—and this would apply not only to the full gamut of economics teaching and research in UK universities, but also to their own Faculty in Cambridge. While CHUDE provided the institutional management instrument for this disciplining of the discipline across the UK, in Cambridge itself, the Hahn-Matthews axis was now in full authority in the Faculty: they dominated the professoriate, with Hahn, Matthews, Dasgupta, Brown and Newbery; and they occupied the Chair of the Faculty Board: as of 1989, this crucial chair also changed hands, passing from Alan Hughes to Frank Hahn himself—and it subsequently seated a string of economists of that grouping, a profile that was also visible in the presidency, council or other strategic offices of the Royal Economic Society.

13.5 Through the RES: Controlling Panel Selection

The make-up of the 1989 panel consisted of two appointments by the UGC, four economists recommended by the Royal Economic Society (RES), one economist recommended by the Scottish Economic Society, two non-economists, and two observers from other panels. The economists appointed by the UGC were Charles Feinstein and Leonard Nicholson. In Feinstein's case, the UGC asked the RES to nominate someone for the chair of the economics panel and the Society proposed Feinstein. As for the other five economists, four were selected from a list of five

> names sent to the UGC by the RES. To obtain the five names, the Society solicited nominations from members of its standing committee of the Conference of Heads of University Departments of Economics (CHUDE). The CHUDE Steering Committee considered all the nominations that came in and recommended to the RES Executive Committee what it thought to be a balanced slate of five names for transmission to the UGC. The five names put forward by the RES were Meghnad Desai, John Flemming, Kenneth George, James Mirrlees, and Alan Winters. Of these Desai, Flemming, Mirrlees, and Winters were selected by the UGC for the panel. The fifth economist on the panel, Peter Sloane, was nominated by the Scottish Economic Society and supported by the CHUDE Steering Committee. The names of the panel assessors were not made public until after the exercise was completed. (Lee, 2009: 156)

The orthodox stranglehold over RES-CHUDE-RAE decision-making, initiated by Hahn during his RES Presidency during 1986–1989—and planned and prepared for, no doubt, in the preceding Presidency of his partner Matthews during 1984–1986—was fully in evidence in the 1992, 2001, 2008 and 2014 rounds and visible in the RAE Economics Panels where a markedly high proportion of the members held positions in the RES, or had editorships in the *Economic Journal*, both domains effectively controlled by Hahn and the orthodox group (see Table 13.2).[10]

In turn, these Panels—dominated by the orthodox group—used quality criteria and measurement parameters that were drawn from their school of mainstream neoclassical mathematical economics, using the journal in which the article was published as a proxy for its quality. This approach was imported from their parent neoclassical tradition from the USA.

> Lee et al. (2013) argue that these standards were initially set by a small group of economists who belonged to elite institutions and the process of peer review (where the panel would judge work according to its own judgements about quality) further reinforced them. Thus, while the elite schools maintained and reinforced these standards, the middle rank universities also started to follow them to sustain themselves. In particular, the so-called 'Diamond' list played an important role in this process since it was the unofficial key guide for departments and RAE economics panels as a measure for research quality. … Lee et al. (2013) argue that this has resulted in the elimination of heterodox economics from UK economics, the concentration and homogenization of mainstream economics research and the dominance of a small group of economics departments, even though the initial research assessment exercises may not have intended to homogenize the discipline. (Stockhammer et al., 2017: 5)

The anti-heterodox bias built into the RAE process become apparent from the orientation of the publications of the selected members of the early RAE

---

[10] For 2001, there were thirteen instances out of a possible maximum of twenty, or 65 per cent, in this category; 45 per cent in 2008 and 38 per cent in 2008; if memberships of CHUDE were to be added, an even higher percentage of the panels would display this attribute.

Table 13.2 RAE panels 1989, 1992, 1996

RAE round	1989	1992	1996	Remarks
RES President	Frank Hahn 1986–1989 James Mirrlees 1989–1992	James Mirrlees 1989–1992 David Hendry 1992–1995	David Hendry 1992–1995 Tony Atkinson 1995–1998	
RES Council	Served until 1989 C. H. Feinstein; J. P. Neary; D. M. G. Newbery; S. J. Nickell; F. Steward; A. P. Thirlwall	Served until 1992 I. C. R. Byatt K. D. George C. Johnson H. H. Liesner J. A. Mirrlees J. R. Shackleton	Served until 1996 V. Chick C. Crook R. Portes N. H. Stern L. A. Winters M. Wolf	
CHUDE President	Frank Hahn?	Alistair Ulph	David Greenaway	
Economics Panel Chair	Charles Feinstein	Tony Atkinson	David Hendry	
Panel members		Michael Artis	Philip Arestis John Beath Anne Booth	
	Meghnad Desai John Flemming		Kenneth George Charles Goodhart David Greenaway	
		David Hendry James Malcomson (replacing Frank Hahn)	James Malcomson	
	James Mirrlees Leonard Nicholson			
	Peter Sloane	Ted Podolski Peter Sloane Max Steuer (replacing Nicholas Stern)	Peter Sloane	
	Alan Winters	Alan Winters		

Sources: (1) RES Website; (2) Lee (2009: 155–157)

panels. The painstaking compilation of some relevant data by Frederic Lee and his research associates provides a confirmation. Table 13.3 gives the profile of the publications of the members of each of the 1989, 1992 and 1996 rounds—in which journals was their work published? The statistics incontrovertibly reveal that with perhaps just one exception, Philip Arestis (entering possibly through the erstwhile APTE/Post-Keynesian constituency) in 1996, there is virtually nothing published in heterodox journals: 3–4 per cent in the first two rounds, rising to 10 per cent in 1996 but almost entirely due to the inclusion of the committed and productive heterodox economist Philip Arestis. This picture is further confirmed in Table 13.4, which shows that again with

Table 13.3 Journal publications of members of RAE Economics Panels 1989–1996

Panel members	Number of journal publications	Percentage of journal publications in Mainstream journals	Heterodox journals
In 1989			
M. J. Desai	22	55	5
C. H. Feinstein	1	0	0
J. M. Flemming	17	100	0
J. Mirrlees	21	95	0
J. L. Nicholson	3	67	0
P. Sloane	14	57	14
L. A. Winters	15	80	7
TOTAL	93	76	4
In 1992			
M. Artis	13	62	0
A. B. Atkinson	42	74	2
D. Hendry	39	82	3
J. Malcomson	22	100	0
T. M. Podolski	0	0	0
P. Sloane	17	59	12
M. Steuer	2	50	0
L. A. Winter	27	70	4
TOTAL	162	76	3
In 1996			
P. Arestis	27	26	59
J. Beath	4	75	0
A. Booth	15	0	0
K. D. George	9	89	0
C. Goodhart	26	69	8
D. Greenaway	58	67	5
D. Hendry	47	79	2
J. Malcomson	28	100	0
P. Sloane	21	62	10
TOTAL	235	65	10

Source: Lee, 2009: 159

Number of Journal Publications: for 1989, as listed in SSCI Source Index for 1966–1988

Number of Journal Publications: for 1992, as listed in SSCI Source Index for 1971–1992

Number of Journal Publications: for 1989, as listed in SSCI Source Index for 1971–1994

exception of Arestis (and to a lesser extent Desai), the vast majority of the other 90 per cent of the panellists for the three rounds had under 2 per cent of their references (in their publications) to core heterodox or other non-mainstream journals; nine had under 0.5 per cent. This would confirm that there was neither interest in engaging, nor expertise in assessing the work of heterodox economists. It would be impossible for those working in this long-standing tradition of economics, especially in the UK, to be fairly treated by such 'fixed' juries.

Table 13.4 References in publications of members of Economics Panels, 1989, 1992, 1996

Panel member	Total number of references listed in articles	Percentage of references to articles published in: Core mainstream journals	Core heterodox and other non-mainstream journals
P. Arestis	697	25	36.4
M. Artis	230	27	0.4
A. B. Atkinson	915	39	0.3
J. Beath	43	60	2.3
A. Booth	417	2	0.5
M. J. Desai	265	45	10.0
C. H. Feinstein	50	14	0.0
J. M. Flemming	167	54	1.8
K. D. George	290	43	8.3
C. Goodhart	770	28	1.3
D. Greenaway	1099	36	0.9
D. Hendry	2011	46	0.4
J. Malcomson	466	67	0.4
J. Mirrlees	175	59	0.6
J. L. Nicholson	26	23	0.0
T. M. Podolski	0	0	0.0
P. Sloane	580	30	1.4
M. Steuer	25	4	0.0
L. A. Winters	424	30	1.7
TOTAL	8650	36	4.2

Source: Lee, 2009: 160

The number of references includes journals, books, chapters in books, government publications, unpublished papers, archive material and miscellaneous material

Data on the research and institutional profiles of the members of the Economics Panels of the last three REFs—2001, 2008 and 2014—suggest that the drive towards the control and domination of orthodoxy has intensified. Three summary indicators support this deduction. First, the submissions of these members to Diamond-list journals: in RAE/REF-2001, of the ten members, three had none; the other seven had a total of eighteen; the average was 1.8 such submissions per panel member; in RAE/REF-2008, again there were ten members and two recorded a 'zero', the other eight had a total of twenty-one, making an average of 2.1; in the RAE/REF-2014, there were fifteen members, and all made at least one submission to a Diamond-list journal; the total number of such submissions was forty-one, an average of 2.7.[11] Second, the incidence of leadership positions in the RES and/or on the Steering

---

[11] The numbers for submissions to the RAE/REF-2014 are from the 2008 exercise. It could be fairly expected that the publications performance might have improved by 2014, so the outcome

Committee of CHUDE; these could be regarded as representative, as against strict academic, authority. Here, in 2001, nine of the ten members had RES leadership positions, and five were on the CHUDE Steering Committee, so that these panel members brought the full organisational weight of the profession to the table; the average is 1.4 such positions per panel member and every member has one or other role; this average drops to 0.8 in the 2008 round, with three members not having a senior role in the RES or CHUDE; for the last, 2014 round, the average for the fifteen panel members is 0.6, with six members having a role neither in the RES nor in CHUDE. Third, while organisational representation declines, academic credentials are clearly increasingly visible, using the indicator of an editorship of one of the Diamond-list journals (including *Economic Journal*). In 2001, five of the ten did not have any such editorship; of the five who did, four were with the *Economic Journal* of the RES itself, and one member, not an *EJ* editor, had three other editorships; the average number of journal editorships per panel member was 0.7. In 2008, there are four on the *EJ*, of whom two also have other editorships; and the average editorships per member rises to 1.0. By 2014, there is a sharp change: of the fifteen members, five are on *EJ*, four of whom also have other Diamond-list editorships; the top two, Peter Neary and Tim Besley, have twelve editorships between them covering ten Diamond-list journals. Of the fifteen, six, or 40 per cent, do not have any such editorship, a lower rate than the earlier rounds; the total number of such editorships is twenty-two, at an average of 1.5 per panel member. It is clear from these snapshots that composition of the Panels has moved increasingly towards orthodox economics, and that the balance has shifted perceptibly towards academic status and away from organisational position, though three of the four members with multiple editorships also held senior RES leadership positions.

This homogenised mainstream lived within the confines of its own abstractions, far removed from the world outside their assumptions, and they were readily found out when they were obliged to step out of their ivory towers to provide answers to the urgent public policy questions of the day—as was made obvious by the dithering confusion which met the Queen at the LSE when she asked why no one had seen the 2007 financial crisis coming. Mainstream economics and economists had no sensible response to the 'Queen's Question'; only dissembling deflection in vague self-justifying generalities. But several heterodox economists did sound the alarm well before the crisis struck; and significantly, these economists did not show up as regular authors in the Diamond list of journals (Bezemer, 2011). If, say India, China and Malaysia were protected from the extreme impact of the financial crisis, it was due to the understanding and interventions of non-mainstream economists whose toolkit and theoretical approach bore no resemblance to the fanciful and futile dynamic stochastic general equilibrium modelling produced and autoregressively reproduced

for this year understates the increased rate of submissions to Diamond-list journals over the three cycles. The data for all three indicators are estimated from Lee et al. (2012b: Appendix 10).

mechanically, not with a view to dealing with real world issues, but driven by filling up CVs with Diamond-list publications. The monodisciplinary mainstream approach is inherently incapable of posing fundamental global problems in meaningful forms and it is a non-starter when it comes to designing integrated strategic and policy responses to these complex issues. But this remarkable, and incontrovertible, failure of mainstream economics has not dislodged it from its apex position, begging the question of its intrinsic utility, or futility.

13.6 Outcomes

First, consider the record. Dasgupta entered the Faculty in 1985, by which time the external and internal campaign and attacks were in full flow, with Hahn and Dasgupta providing hostile advisory inputs, the former from within Cambridge, the latter, prior to 1985, from the LSE as an external referee. However, the initial RAE exercise was conducted in 1986, and so its outcome could not have legitimised these attacks on the alleged poor quality of the Cambridge heterodox economists. In fact, the 1986 RAE results placed Cambridge economics in the highest, 'outstanding' category of research quality. This should have buried the bogey and silenced the bogeymen. But mysteriously, In the following RAE of 1989 when the economics assessment process is dominated by Hahn and his group, with Charles Feinstein as Chair of the Panel with Jim Mirrlees (amongst others) in support, Cambridge economics drops a star—for reasons not readily understandable; but whatever the cause, this would give Hahn & Co. the stick to beat the heterodox economics and economists within the Faculty. (Strikingly, there are three 'new' universities in the top category in 1986, four in 1989 and five in 1992 [Backhouse, 1996: Table 1]; the economics departments of all these universities were dominated, almost exclusively, by orthodox appointments from the beginning, when their first professors or heads had come from Hahn's Cambridge orthodox stable.) Then in 1992, it recovers and returns to the top category, temporarily it turns out as it drops into the second category in each of the exercises in 1996, 2001 and 2008, and remains in fourth place in 2014. This lagged and persistent trend can hardly be blamed on the apostasy of the heterodox clans of earlier decades—it is disingenuous to point fingers in that direction; the fault would more credibly seem to lie with the quality of orthodox research in Cambridge, as judged by their equally orthodox peers.

Second, it is worth following the heterodox staff, as they were effectively purged out of the Faculty, to their new academic homes in Cambridge—what havoc did their alleged low research capability wreak on the reputation of their new institutional homes? Using the same 'gold standard' of the RAE, recent results offer an indication.

A good number of heterodox economists went away from Cambridge, and comparisons are not possible here. But there was a significant cohort that shifted from the DAE and the Faculty to the new Judge Business School (JBS) and set up their applied research projects there, notably the applied economics team at the Centre for Business Research built up and led by Alan Hughes; other researchers worked on corporate and global finance. These moves took place from the end of the 1990s, and as such comparisons are possible only from 1992, by which time things were more settled and JBS researchers could potentially have their work evaluated in the Business and Management Studies (BMS) unit of assessment; this allows a summary comparison to be made between the scores received by Cambridge Economics and the JBS BMS research groups for the five subsequent cycles, 1992, 1996, 2001, 2008 and 2014 (Table 13.5).

Table 13.5 Standing of Cambridge economics in successive RAEs and REFs

1986	1st 'Research Selectivity Exercise' conducted by the UGC; 37 'cost centres' (or units of assessment) of which Economics was one; each university asked to submit in all five outputs, and a maximum of four pages of general description of the department's research profile and quality. Units assessed on a 4-point scale, from 'below average' to 'outstanding'. Cambridge economics is adjudged to be in the 'outstanding' category. The Department of Business and Management Studies was not yet formed.
1992	
Economics	10 departments score the top 5; Cambridge is one of them.
BMS	6 departments score the top 5; Cambridge is not one of them.
1996	
Economics	3 departments score a top 5*; 10 departments score a 5, and Cambridge is one of them; thus, Cambridge is in joint 4th place along with 9 others.
BMS	3 departments score 5*; 6 departments score a 5; 16 departments score a 4, including Cambridge; thus, Cambridge is joint 10th along with 15 others.
2001	
Economics	4 departments score a 5*; 9 departments score a 5, and Cambridge is one of them; thus, Cambridge is joint 5th along with 8 others.
BMS	3 departments score a 5*; 10 departments score 5 and Cambridge is one of them; thus, Cambridge is joint 4th along with 9 others.
[In 2008, the maximum score is 4*, and there is a percentage distribution of department staff in different scoring categories.]	
2008	
Economics	5 departments have more than 30% staff scoring 4* and Cambridge is not one of these; 4 departments have 30% staff scoring 4*, and Cambridge is one of them; thus, Cambridge is joint 6th along with 3 others.
BMS	only 1 department has more than 35% staff scoring 4*; 3 departments have 30% staff scoring 4*, and Cambridge is one of these; thus, Cambridge is joint 2nd along with 2 others.
[In 2014, there are ranks scored on four criteria: 'output'; 'impact'; 'environment' and 'overall'. The 'environment' criterion is shared by the two Units of Assessment and hence left out below.]	
2014	
Economics	ranks 2nd on output; 6th on impact; and 4th overall.
BMS	ranks 6th on output; 1st on impact; and 2nd overall.

Such rough and ready comparisons that are reasonably possible thus show a steady improvement in the scores and ranks of the Judge Business and Management Studies over the five cycles from 1992, when it entered the RAE, till 2014, the most recent round. Further, the numerical profiles show that for each of the last three cycles, 2001, 2008 and 2014, Business and Management Studies at the Judge Institute outperformed the Economics Faculty. This provides a simple refutation of the allegations by the orthodox group that the heterodox economists of the DAE and others in the Faculty, were of inferior quality and tarnishing the reputation of Cambridge economics. Indeed, judging by the high-quality professional career tracks of those DAE economists that left Cambridge when the CEPG and the CGP were forced to close, the performance of the DAE applied heterodox economists' cohort of the 1980s might have posted even better scores. And all this, even in the face of research measurement yardsticks that were heavily biased against non-orthodox, non-neoclassical non-mathematical economics. This must remain an indirect deduction, since a direct comparison between CBR and other ex-DAE/Faculty economists who shifted to the Judge Institute, with the Faculty is not possible with the available data.

Finally, it is pertinent to record an observation made by the DAE Review Committee set up by the General Board in 2004, at the end-point of David Newbery's directorship. The Review Committee paid tribute to David Newbery as "an outstanding Director who had done much for the DAE". But it went on: "However, they also concluded that urgent action should be given to … measures to enable the Faculty and Department to pursue research which meets overall the criteria for international excellence"; the Review Committee "noted that the Faculty's ratings in recent Research Assessment Exercises (1992: 5, 1996: 5, 2001: 5) showed scope for improvement. In addition, the Review Committee reported their impression that the relationship between the two institutions was not working as well as it should" (Cambridge University General Board, 2004). Given that the orthodox group had been in effective control both of the DAE as well as the Faculty for the 15 years prior to this Review, the critique speaks for itself.

13.7 Consequences and Critiques

There is now a vast literature of assessments and critiques of the metrification of quality assessment in higher education, and especially in economics. Each fresh cycle attempts to respond, in reality or in rhetoric, to the catalogue of criticisms of the previous round, and then attracts its own list of complaints over biased or blind methodologies. A selection of these is sufficient to undermine the utility of this paradigm of quality assessment in the social sciences, including especially economics, where disciplinary, methodological and ideological contestations preclude any form of consensus across traditions.

13.7.1 Gaming

The evaluation of the quality of research at a national level has become increasingly common. The UK has been at the forefront of this trend having undertaken many assessments since 1986, the latest being the 'Research Excellence Framework' in 2014. The argument of this paper is that, whatever the intended results in terms of evaluating and improving research, there have been many, presumably unintended, results that are highly undesirable for research and the university community more generally. We situate our analysis using Bourdieu's theory of cultural reproduction and then focus on the peculiarities of the 2008 RAE and the 2014 REF, the rules of which allowed for, and indeed encouraged, significant game-playing on the part of striving universities. We conclude with practical recommendations to maintain the general intention of research assessment without the undesirable side-effects. (Mingers & White, 2015)

John Mingers and Leroy White (2015: 27) refer to an "extreme example" of the deleterious impact of RAE culture and gaming practices on the quality of academic life with little advantage to balance the sacrifice of collegiality, autonomy and creativity. They cite "the changes that have occurred at Warwick Business School (WBS) since a (relatively) poor result in the 2008 RAE":

> WBS has always been one of the UK's leading business schools, seen as research intensive, innovative, and engaged with industry. It had been in the top 3 schools in all the assessments until 2008 when it appeared to be in ninth position in the league tables (actually joint fifth with five other schools). This was seen as a disaster by the University and a new Dean was quickly parachuted in with little or no consultation or discussion. He set about transforming WBS in order to prepare for the 2014 REF. Within a few years, a large proportion of the academics, even the best researchers, had moved to other institutions and the OR/MS group, one of the top two in the country, was decimated. These were replaced with staff, many from overseas, whose main quality was that they had 4* publications, especially in US journals. Their fit, or teaching contribution, did not matter that much.

In the event, these measures did not help much—WBS came only twelfth on GPA, worse than before having been more selective in their staff submission.

But gaming goes on in an environment of incomplete information, with managers often shooting in the dark. An explanation comes from the indologist Richard Gombrich, scholar of Sanskrit, Pali and Buddhism and the Boden Professor of Sanskrit at Oxford from 1976 till 2004. In 2000, he delivered a lecture in Tokyo on British higher education policy since Margaret Thatcher had taken over as Prime Minister, and subtitled it: "the murder of a profession" (Gombrich, 2000). In the course of his devastating critique, he refers to the element of competition in the algorithms of the RAE. "Let me describe the system as it operated in 1996, when I was an assessor for the second time":

> "Individual researchers are assessed at one of five grades, from A to E. Their departments, which submit their names and publications, are assessed at one of

six grades: the top is 5*, the rest go down from 5 to 1. A complicated formula is prescribed to the assessors for converting a department's set of individual grades into a single joint grade. The individual grades remain secret; the joint grades are published and determine the department's level of research funding until the next RAE. How is this calculated? The HEFCE assigns a sum of money to each joint grade from 5* to 1. Let us call these unknown figures u, v, w, x, y and z. (I suspect that z has a value of zero.) The values of these figures are not announced until the assessment is complete, nor is the total sum of money available for distribution. The money awarded to the department is then the value corresponding to its joint grade multiplied by the number of names submitted. Let me give an example. Prof. P. heads a department of 9 academic staff, 5 of whom he knows to publish good research, even though he cannot be sure how good the assessors will think it. Another 2 of the staff have published nothing worth mentioning, so he is disinclined to submit their names at all. There are however also two who have published research in the relevant period but he finds their work undistinguished. If he submits their names, his department will probably get a lower joint grade than if he left them out. He guesses that without them his department will get a 5 and so be at level v; with them, he expects a 4 and level w. So if their names do not go forward he expects to get v x 5 pounds, with them w x 7 pounds. The trouble is that he has no idea of the values of v and w, so even if he is clever (and lucky) enough to predict the ranking correctly, he cannot calculate his better tactic, but has to guess. In the end it might even turn out, to his frustration, that he should have submitted all 9 names, because even though the other two pull the joint grade down to a 3, x x 9 pounds turns out to be the biggest of the three sums." Gombrich asks: "Is this a serious way of funding academic research, or a kind of sadistic party game?" (Gombrich, 2000)

13.7.2 Competition and Conflict: Managerialism

"Perhaps naively, we would argue that the academic community was, once, a community—a group of people interested in and committed to the discovery and transmission of knowledge. Whilst there were, of course, rivalries and disputes between research groups and disciplines there was common ground that research should be relatively unfettered, up to the interest and expertise of the individual; that academics should undertake a range of activities—teaching, research and administration; that departments should be relatively autonomous and self-governing; and that the highest values were integrity and innovative thinking. Successive research assessments have significantly changed this, shifting the balance from collegiality to managerialism" (Mingers & White, 2015: 25).[12] From a Cambridge vantage point, this rather idyllic utopian 'original state' had possibly not existed ever, and serious rifts and divisions are known to have fractured the Faculty since the 1920s. As such, the impact of the RAE as an instrument in Cambridge could be expected to, and did, intensify the frictions between groups. A second Cambridge 'difference' would be that in a self-managing Faculty of economics, the 'managers' would be academics

---

[12] In this quotation, Mingers and White cite Yokoyama (2006).

themselves, thus adding a sharper edge to the conflicts between groups in the context of the RAE exercises.

The result in this competitive environment is that departmental managers, and only some of them might be academics, make calls on which staff to put up and which to exclude; which unit of assessments to make their submissions, and different staff could be asked to submit to different units; and at the other end, there are decisions, equally arbitrary and idiosyncratic, on what elite academics to poach and lure into their department from elsewhere with promises of golden deals.

Gombrich seems to give expression to the Buddhist middle path: "One does not have to be a social Darwinist, as I think Mrs. Thatcher was, to agree that competition has value in many areas of human life. Academics naturally compete to make discoveries and to impress their peers and students. It is possible (though untestable) that the British university system for a long time profited from being bicephalous: the friendly rivalry between Oxford and Cambridge is harmless and may be beneficial. However, competition for limited resources ... is another matter, and in many cases seems an insane way of running the university system: co-operation would be both pleasanter and far more efficient" (Gombrich, 2000).

Coming from a scholar of Sanskrit and Buddhism, recourse to terms, such as 'murder', 'sadistic', 'insane', 'unmitigated catastrophe', suggests that Margaret Thatcher might have seriously depleted his reserves of endurance. Mark Harrison, the noted economic historian of the Soviet Union, shares his autobiographical musing on "my economic history: from revolutions to routines" (Harrison, 2001). "The only thing that spoils the practice of economic history for me now", he confides, "is that, although the Soviet Union has gone, its habits are being continually recreated in British higher education by ever more burdensome regulation and inspection and proliferating performance indicators that are screwed ever tighter as people get better at fulfilling them and increased in number as people learn ways around them; in a Soviet context we called this mechanism the 'ratchet'. At heart I am still a utopian. I look forward to a future society of material abundance in which the state has withered away, taking with it the HEFCE, the ESRC, the AHRB, the RAE and the QAA. Humanity's chief want will be to have fun, and we will all be able to do economic history to our hearts' content, for no reward but the sheer pleasure of it" (Harrison, 2001: 5–6). Yes, indeed, when the moon is Brechtian blue cheese, a cynic might mutter.[13]

---

[13] Gombrich extends his critique of measurable performance indicators adopted by managerialism to the case of research students. "If one is lucky enough to be among the very few students who get a state grant to pursue research in the humanities, that grant is given for three, or in very few cases for four years of study. If the student studies for longer, it is entirely at her own expense: she costs the State nothing, and the marginal cost of her presence at the university is incalculably small. Nevertheless, any department in the humanities or social sciences in which students are taking over four years to complete their doctorates is penalized by no longer being allowed to take research students who are on state funding. The reason for delay is irrelevant: whether the student

13.7.3 Individual Stress

The tendency towards and the process of the selection of potential 4* staff for RAE submissions divides staff, but also generates huge psychological stress on the individual staff who might be in the running but miss the cut, or who are deemed 'not good enough' to be put forward. The exercise demeans individuals on the one side and creates a pampered research elite on the other, replicating in the university the tendencies towards extreme inequality and exclusion on display in the world outside. Mingers and White point out: "top researchers can command very significant salaries, and other inducements, to move to a competitor, and if their current institution wants to keep them, they will have to match or exceed the offer—promotions, light teaching loads, large research funds and high salaries have become the norm. None of this actually improves overall research at all—there in only a limited supply—it just pushes up the price" (ibid.: 26). As competition between universities stiffens, a transfer market, rather like in football, comes into play especially close to the time of the upcoming REF; the richer universities, like the richer clubs, gain at the expense of the rest, leading to further market polarisation. "Those who struggle for one reason or another, get less resource, more teaching and general opprobrium. They then have to become 'teaching fellows' or indeed are encouraged to move elsewhere" (ibid.).[14] "Overall", they conclude, "the culture of academia has moved from one of collegiality to one of conflict and antagonism between researchers and teachers, and the managers ... and the managed. And this is not a recent occurrence" (ibid.: 27). That would indeed be the case in Cambridge economics which would display virtually all the negative effects that the literature on the RAEs documents.

A particularly perverse tendency needs explicit recognition. Often, these negative effects are referred to as being the 'unintended consequences' of the exercise. But this need not be so. As made clear by Frank Hahn and Partha Dasgupta in Cambridge, the RAE was to be used purposively and systematically to clean out what *they* regarded as unproductive staff or low-quality

was ill, employed, or fulfilling family responsibilities makes no difference to the operation of the policy. One of the first departments to be hit was economics at Cambridge. This is, or certainly was, the most distinguished economics department in Britain. Its research students tended to be employed, before finishing their doctorates, at such prestigious institutions as the World bank and IMF. So the department's four-year completion rate was poor, and soon it found itself with only foreign research students, plus perhaps the rare British student rich enough to pay the fees from his own pocket" (Gombrich, 2000).

[14] A recent study by Johnston and Reeves (2018) reveals the socio-geographic fragmentation of the economics discipline in the UK as a result of the RAE/REF/REE in the UK. It is revealed that "the marriage of economics teaching and research is now limited to elite institutions located mainly in the south of the UK. None of the UK's new (post-1992) universities submitted to the Economics and Econometrics (E&E) unit of assessment (UOA) in 2014, the UK's most recent research evaluation exercise (REE). Lower REE scores are shown to be associated with higher withdrawal rates from the next E&E UOA and subsequent undergraduate economics programme closure. Universities that exit the E&E UOA moving to the Business and Management (B&M) UOA appear to benefit in the form of higher REE scores" (Johnston & Reeves, 2018: 589).

research. The 'consequences' then would be fully intended, and pressure is consciously brought to bear on 'undesirable' staff in unconscionable and unbearable ways, often leading to serious distress. The case of the suicide of the economist John Wells in Cambridge in 1999 is sometimes mentioned in this context. Recently, Dr Liz Morrish (2019) has drawn attention to "the epidemic of poor mental health among higher education staff", citing a 2018 study which found that 43 per cent of academic staff had "exhibited symptoms of at least a mild mental disorder, … nearly twice the prevalence of mental disorders in the general population". Apart from the usual suspects of massive workloads destroying work–life balance, the research regime is highlighted as the culprit. "Academics are also evaluated by an assortment of research metrics: citation counts, the impact factor of the journal in which it is published, and the amount of research grant money obtained. These are all poor proxy measures of research quality, but they are easy to track. Despite the obvious limitations, academics are forced to accept that metrics have become the currency of performance management in universities. To work there means giving yourself over to forensic surveillance, and also being willing to have your closest friends and colleagues scrutinize your work, in both teaching and research. That pressure is cumulative and to many, the university has become an 'anxiety machine'."

At the point of origin of the RAE, the creator of the RSE had only sought five top submissions—not per staff member but from the entire unit—judging that the quality of these pieces would stand as a reliable proxy for the quality of the unit. He had also explicitly argued then, and later, against individual submissions and then more strongly against increasing the number of individual submissions required, on the grounds that this would place individual staff under high and unnecessary pressure, while simply increasing the volume of research without adding value in terms of its quality. Yet, this is the path taken by the RAEs. Perhaps the reason lies in the fact that the managers of the process and those that set the measuring rods of quality, viz., Hahn & Co. for economics and econometrics, were less interested in the RAE as a signifier of the overall quality of the department—they were more focussed on using the RAE as an instrument, as a stick, to wield at an individual level within the department to cleanse and purge it of staff who were not welcome members of their ideological lineage, as for instance, all heterodox economists of various descriptions.

Mingers and White (2015) discuss various other forms of collateral damage unleashed by the RAE phenomenon: the suppression of innovation as standardisation takes hold in the recognition and measurement of quality; the "destruction of the journal ecosystem" through the negative impact on journals not placed in the top echelon as their supply of submissions is diverted away by the biases of the RAE; the avoidance of large projects in favour of smaller piecemeal ones that can yield a quicker flow of measurable individual output; the reduction of interdisciplinary research as it falls between various stools; the marginalisation of practical and applied research as 'pure' theory takes the throne.

13.7.4 Medium Over Message: Diamonds for Ever

With regard to the 2014 REF, Stockhammer et al. (2017: 21) come to a startling finding. They point out that while the REF's peer-review process and its documentation clearly states that outputs should be assessed independently of where they have been published, they find that journal ratings and journal impact factors explain around 90 per cent of the variation in the REF's output and total evaluations for the Economics Unit of Assessment "without having read the relevant outputs or knowing what they are about, but merely by knowing where they were published. The significance of this finding can hardly be overstated."

On the basis of their empirical analysis, Heckman and Moktan (2020) come to the conclusion that: "the Top Five has a large impact on tenure decisions within the top 35 US departments of economics, dwarfing the impact of publications in non-Top Five journals. There are many consequences of the discipline's reliance on the Top Five. It subverts the essential process of assessing and rewarding original research. Using the Top Five to screen the next generation of economists incentivises professional incest and creates clientele effects whereby career-oriented authors appeal to the tastes of editors and biases of journals. It diverts their attention away from basic research toward strategising about formats, lines of research, and favoured topics of journal editors, many with long tenures. It raises the entry costs for new ideas and persons outside the orbits of the journals and their editors. An over-emphasis on Top Five publications perversely incentivises scholars to pursue follow-up and replication work at the expense of creative pioneering research, since follow-up work is easier to judge, is more likely to result in clean publishable results, and is hence more likely to be published.[2] This behaviour is consistent with basic common sense: you get what you incentivise."[15]

Another likely exclusionary side-effect is the marginalisation of applied policy work in the 'top' journals which deal primarily with theoretical topics; or when occasionally with policy questions, these tend to relate to the US economy which, by sheer scale, dominates the interests of the readership.

Heterodox economics is a clear loser. "There seems to be a catch-22 situation for heterodox departments when submitting to the REF. On the one hand universities refrain from making heterodox submissions to the Economics UOA [Unit of Assessment] of the REF and hence even if the REF's Economics sub-panel was heterodox-open, heterodox economics research is marginalized. On the other hand, the evaluation of Economics UOA in the REF 2014 is highly consistent with journal rating and impact factor lists, and many of these ranking lists are biased against heterodox economics journals. The effects of this on heterodox economics have been quite devastating. … This poses an

---

[15] Aistleitner, Kapeller and Steinerberger (2018: 832) confirm the impact of citation metrics in France where a formal scoring system was adopted in 2005. "Parallel to the introduction of the scoring system, the relative amount of heterodox economists newly appointed in France fell from almost 18 percent in the period for 2000 to 2004 to 5 percent in the period from 2005 to 2011."

existential threat to heterodox economics and impoverished economics as a discipline" (Stockhammer et al., 2017: 22). The REF "has further narrowed economics research in a time when public dissatisfaction with the economics mainstream is high".

Heckman and Moktan (2020) point out that "a proper solution to the tyranny will likely involve more than a simple redefinition of the Top Five to include a handful of additional influential journals. A better solution will need to address the flaw that is inherent in the practice of judging a scholar's potential for innovative work based on a track record of publications in a handful of select journals. The appropriate solution requires a significant shift from the current publications-based system of deciding tenure to a system that emphasises departmental peer review of a candidate's work. Such a system would give serious consideration to unpublished working papers and to the quality and integrity of a scholar's work. By closely reading published and unpublished papers rather than counting placements of publications, departments would signal that they both acknowledge and adequately account for the greater risk associated with scholars working at the frontiers of the discipline."

A recent study investigating "the power of scientometrics and the development of economics" confirms the exclusionary biases operating against heterodox economics and research that challenges the mainstream neoclassical orthodoxy (Aistleitner et al., 2018: 831): "It shows that heterodox journals exhibit a quite balanced citation pattern (heterodox and mainstream journals are cited equally), while the citation behavior of mainstream journals is drastically in favor of other mainstream journals. In this view, heterodoxy is more open or pluralist, whereas orthodoxy is relatively closed or monistic." The study also confirms the closed inbred nature of the mainstream neoclassical paradigm: "while it is beyond question that economic research has changed in some ways in response to the recent crisis", the authors argue that these changes have not to "an increased reception of alternative economic approaches in mainstream outlets"; rather, "this reaction follows a Kuhnian pattern of an 'internal' adaptation of existing models". The analysis confirms that "evaluative scientometrics significantly contributes to the stabilization of a dominant economic paradigm and limits the influence of alternative or critical approaches in the scientific discourse" (ibid.: 833); in coming to this conclusion, the authors also make reference the experience of heterodox economics in the UK.

13.7.5 Unethical Research Practices and Shaky Quality Proxies

This blind acceptance of proxies for research quality, such as the Diamond list of journals, is hardly without problems, as the task of quality assessments is implicitly passed on by the UoA assessors to editors of favoured journals, though such faith may not be justified even on conventional technical matters. Ajit Singh (2008: 15), registering a critique due to Brian Reddaway, had cited the much earlier report by McCloskey and Ziliak (1996) "who show, from a survey of 137 papers in the *American Economic Review* in the 1990s, that 82 per cent 'mistook a merely statistically significant finding for an economically significant finding', presuming that 'looking at the sign of a coefficient rather that its magnitude was adequate from an economic perspective'". Ajit felt that the race to publication was partly responsible for this, with prospective authors (rightly) double-guessing that referees shared this one-eyed approach to understanding 'significance', which reflected "normal econometric practice for not distinguishing statistical from economic significance". This is a simple point, and one might think that it would apply only to a small minority of poor practitioners and would disappear over time: except that it does not seem to have done. Ioannidis, Stanley and Doucoudliagos (2017: F236) "investigate two critical dimensions of the credibility of empirical economics research: statistical power and bias. We survey 159 empirical economics literatures that draw upon 64,076 estimates of economic parameters reported in more than 6700 empirical studies. Half of the research areas have nearly 90% of their results underpowered. The median statistical power is 18%, or less. A simple weighted average of those reported results that are adequately powered (power ≥ 80%) reveals that nearly 80% of the reported effects in these empirical economics literatures are exaggerated; typically, by a factor of two and with one-third inflated by a factor of four or more."

> Necker (2014) argues that science as a winner-take-all market and the publish-or-perish culture, which has been cultivated as a result of the competitive environment in academia, have resulted in the increase of scientific misbehaviour in Economics. In a survey conducted among members of the European Economic Association, she found that 20–59% of the participants agreed to different questionable research practices, such as copying without citing or fabricating and excluding data due to publishing pressures. Replicability of research results on the other hand is a basic requirement for progress in science. Economics performs poorly in this respect. Chang and Li (2015) tried to replicate 67 papers with author provided data and codes from 13 well regarded journals such as the *American Economic Review*, *Econometrica* and the *Economic Journal*. They were able to successfully replicate only 49% of these papers. Thus, it does not seem that the competitive milieu in academia today is a guarantee for high quality scientific research. (Quoted in Stockhammer et al., 2017: 5–6)

Other questionable practices are cited by Baccini et al. (2019) who report on the impact of performance evaluation metrics on the instrumental use of citations. Using an Italian case study, they demonstrate that "scientists are *quickly responsive* to the system of incentives they are exposed to" (emphasis in the original) "[which] actively interact and quickly shape the behavior of the evaluated researchers, especially when [these impact] key career steps". In response to a change in the criteria employed, "there was a spectacular increase in authors' self-citations and a rise in the number of citations exchanged within citation-clubs formed by Italian scholars; this reflects a strategy clearly aimed at boosting bibliometric indicators set by the governmental agency". They refer to this 'anomalous behaviour' as 'pathological inwardness'.[16]

13.7.6   The Atrophy of Collective Research Traditions and Environments

Austin Robinson (quoted in Marcuzzo, 2012: 18–19) reminds all of the Cambridge tradition of the collective, not individual, ownership of ideas: "When a small group is constantly arguing together, arguing with their pupils and arguing with others outside, one seldom knows exactly who was initially responsible for which elements in the collective thinking, and any one person may be transmitting collective rather than individual ideas."

Schumpeter (1954: 1152) describes Richard Kahn and Gerald Shove as "scholars of a type that Cambridge produces much more readily than the other centres of scientific economics or rather of science in general. They throw their ideas into a common pool. By critical and positive suggestion, they help other people's ideas into definite existence, and they exert anonymous influence—influence as leaders—far beyond anything that can be definitely credited to them from their publications" (quoted by Pasinetti, 1991: 435). And Paul Samuelson (1994: 55) drew attention to the invisibility of Richard Kahn "who got acknowledged in Pigou, Keynes, and Joan Robinson footnotes as the *eminence vert* who kept them from error and provided generalised proofs".

This tradition continued well into the 1970s—for example, as Francis Cripps pointed out in the context of the development of the research on the deindustrialisation of the UK economy, there was individual and collective work being done by several scholars and teams, all of which would share and test the hypotheses and empirics freely in the corridors, common rooms and seminars—so that while specific papers might carry the name/s of one or a few authors, the published work was in a real sense a reflection of the collective thinking of the group of collaborating like-minded researchers both in the Faculty and the DAE. Specifically, with reference to deindustrialisation, Ajit Singh led the pack with his 1977 paper on the deindustrialisation of the UK economy, but then there was variational work by Bob Rowthorn and John Wells; and all the while, this theme was quite central to the work of the two big macroeconomic teams, with CEPG looking at the phenomenon with a

---

[16] Baccini (2018) provides a similarly dismal picture for the sciences; and Horton (2015, cited in Baccini, 2018) writing about medicine in *The Lancet*, sounds a warning: "The apparent endemicity of bad research behaviour is alarming. We aid and abet the worst behaviours. Our acquiescence to the impact factor fuels an unhealthy competition to win a place in a select few journals. Journals are not the only miscreants. Universities are in a perpetual struggle for money and talent, endpoints that foster reductive metrics, such as high-impact publication. National assessment procedures, such as the Research Excellence Framework, incentivize bad practices. And individual scientists, including their most senior leaders, do little to alter a research culture that occasionally veers close to misconduct."

short-term policy frame, and the CGP considering the more structural aspects of medium- and longer-term evolution of the industrial sector.

This proclivity towards collective research made the work of a team much greater than the simple sum of the research of the individuals, through dynamic externalities and cross fertilisation. This ingrained Cambridge tradition—of those times—contrasts rather sharply with the reference of Tony Lawson, when he first arrived in Cambridge, to the stifling secretiveness at the LSE from where he had come. He singled out his memory and appreciation of refreshing Cambridge openness in intellectual exchange. At LSE, individual researchers held their work close to their chest lest it be stolen; they were good examples of their own methodology, individual utility maximisers in a competitive world.

In Cambridge such collective production of ideas was quite compatible with an awareness and unspoken acknowledgment of the significance of individual contributions;[17] reputation building could and did happen within the loose collective, though without being dominated by egotistical competition. This logic was not compatible, of course, with the individual bibliometrics of the Research Assessment Exercises which incentivised individual maximisation as measured in publications in numerically rated and ranked outlets. The very rationale and design of the RAE intervention was aimed at ranking and sifting individuals by giving department heads the objective, resource incentive, and authority to influence hiring and firing of staff. The tradition of collective, interactive research was a casualty, collateral damage of an inherently flawed exercise.

13.7.7 *The Loss of Intrinsic Values*

These cumulative critiques, new ones heaped on many persisting from earlier rounds, of the methodologies of the successive RAE/REF rounds, come to be scanned through rapidly to get to the bottom line, the status and resource outcomes for the different departments. These urgent concerns distract attention from the elephant in the room, from what is important—the loss of intrinsic values in the conduct of research in the social sciences, concerns that seem to fall between the cracks and become invisible. First, to use Joan Robinson's simple words, 'What are the questions?'. There is nowhere in the RAE/REFs any serious attention paid to the question of the societal relevance of research being assessed—this is implicitly taken for granted, or converted into quite problematic methods of the measurement of the 'social impact' of specific research works. Second, there is no acknowledgment of the fact that divisions in societies are mirrored in the ways that societies are analysed in the social

---

[17] Of course, collective research is a different commodity from collaborative research, and Cambridge had more than its fair share of both, as for instance in the case of Geoff Harcourt, who apart from his vast array of inputs into the work of others, also managed, till 2017 with numbers steadily rising, to collaborate 92 times with 104 collaborators (Harcourt, 2017: 183). On the intrinsic joys and worth of collaborative research, see Szenberg and Ramrattan (2017).

sciences, and economics is far from being an exception notwithstanding orthodox claims of being 'scientific'. This calls for a plurality of approaches, but there is no recognition of this. Third, the complexity of societies calls for integrated interdisciplinary approaches for social science research. Major all-embracing exercises such as the RAE/REF have the capacity, through their sheer scale and link to resources, to influence the orientation and direction of the research enterprise meaningfully—in reality, the opposite has been the case. Fourth, the need for plurality, the imperative of interdisciplinarity and the complexity of the increasing manifestation of global crises make collective, team work critically important. Here again, the inbuilt orientation of the assessment exercises reflects the philosophical premises and prejudices of orthodoxy which has the individual optimiser as its unitary agent. The method of the RAE/REF ensures a loss of meaning. Fifth, even apart from the value of serendipity, most frontier, innovative research inherently demands time and does not necessarily guarantee the time-bound measurable outputs that resource managers demand. Sixth, by betting on the strong, the entire process intensifies historically embedded inequalities which, apart from being socially undesirable (though not to orthodoxy), have the long-term effect of weakening overall research capacity through their exclusionary effects.

13.7.8 Undervaluation of Undergraduate Teaching

In an interview, Martin Daunton, (then) Professor of Economic History at the Faculty of History in Cambridge, reflects on the changing relationship between research and teaching. "The attitude at Cambridge is that one's teaching is inspired by research. ... The rule at Cambridge is that special subjects are normally taught for five years and then they stop. But what most people do is they teach for five years and write the book, and move on. It's what I'm going to do myself. I've just signed the contract with Penguin for the book on my current special subject. And so that very much is the continued intersection of the two. Of course one can be criticised for being rather self-indulgent. That perhaps this is not the way to do it for undergraduates, perhaps it's not starting from what their needs are but from what our career objectives might be. And that of course is a huge danger with the RAE, because the RAE gives universities funding for research, but does not give additional funding for teaching. So I think there is a danger in some places that you can appoint very very good people to positions (I won't name any universities), where they hold research professorships, where they don't need to do the teaching. ... It can also lead to something which is unfortunate, which is the chasing of RAE points, and then to a concern about the undergraduate teaching. It might then be that too much of the undergraduate teaching is being done by a more casualised staff—by research students, or temporary teachers, who then don't really have the opportunity to write their own books. So I think there are dangers" (Daunton, 2008). The risk is of a progressive polarisation between vanguard research and lowly tasks of undergraduate teaching and research; the RAE could well be intensifying tendencies which have generally pervaded the top universities, though often the main core course lectures are often retained by the professoriate to ensure that the undergraduates are imparted their chosen perspectives (and prejudices) from the start, while supervisory, tutorial and marking tasks are delegated to the lower ranks and cadres of apprentices; Cambridge economics would generally resemble this profile.

13.8 THE SUPPRESSION OF HETERODOX ECONOMICS AND ECONOMISTS

Going beyond the abuse of the RAE by the neoclassicals in assembling support from non-economists and senior administrators at university level, it is necessary to scrutinise the validity of the RAE as a gold standard. Considerable systematic research is now available which clearly demonstrates the powerful intellectual lobotomising impact that the imposition of extremely narrow inward-looking disciplinary standards, criteria and measurement indicators have had on the practice of economics, a negative effect which is multiplied by the gaming practices of universities and departments in the transfer and purchases of potentially high-scoring economists. The result has been the encouragement of an inbred monoculture, and the devaluation of all work within non-mainstream traditions and work that crosses academically arbitrary but institutionally rigid disciplinary borders.[18] The negative impact has been internally acknowledged, as is explicitly evidenced in the Stern Review of the RAE/REF experience.[19]

Cambridge was perhaps the university most affected by the assault on heterodox economics as it was the original habitat of these traditions, and over time had accumulated the highest concentrations of such economists and such work, in terms of both teaching and research. A cumulative internal diversity

---

[18] Also worth recording is a critical reflection from an SSRC/ESRC 'insider', Chris Caswill who had a 33-year career at SSRC/ESRC, starting at the SSRC from 1971, retiring in 2003 as ESRC Director of Research. "No comment on the incentives for interaction with those outside the academic community can be complete without reference to the Research Assessment Exercise (RAE). Defenders of the RAE are at pains to point out that complex systems are in place to give recognition to the generation of knowledge outside the established journals of the established (and splendidly distant) academic disciplines. These assertions are greeted by a great deal of scepticism. According to a study commissioned (but not often quoted) by the RAE's parents, the Funding Councils themselves (Evaluation Associates, 1999), social scientists are amongst those who most strongly suspect the RAE of being inimical to work and publication outside the conventional frameworks. We would only add that we cannot see which aspects of the RAE positively encourage the practice of ISS [interactive social science]" (Caswill & Shove, 2000: 156). Caswill and Shove use the definition of ISS as in Scott et al. (1999): "a style of activity where researchers, funding agencies and 'user groups' interact throughout the entire research process, including the definition of the research agenda, project selection, project execution and the application of research insights".

[19] Stern (2016). The independent review was commissioned by the Minister of Universities and Science, Jo Johnson, in November 2015, and reported in July 2016. See also Jump (2013a, 2013b).

was the unmistakable hallmark of the intellectual ecology of the habitat of Cambridge heterodox economics. Available evidence all tends to establish that the great intrinsic value of these interactively evolving traditions was systematically eroded by the monocultural weedicides applied by the neoclassical camp to get rid of all 'other' varieties—an ideological act the intellectual vacuity of which has become increasingly apparent over time. Each successive tidal wave of global challenges attests to the need for holistic, interconnected, synergetic research that synthesises various relevant disciplines from the social and the natural sciences, all demanding intellectual and professional capacities, approaches and methods that have been treated by the mainstream economists as untouchables, not allowed entry into the pure disciplinary spaces of orthodox neoclassicism. Hahn, Dasgupta & Co. might have successfully sold the RAE dummy to gullible non-economists, but their so-called gold standard is widely regarded as a fake currency, regrettably still in circulation as legal tender as it gives academic high priests and professionalised academic managers a wider remit and control over knowledge-production structures and processes, that is, over the intellectual class comprising teachers, researchers and students. And in Cambridge, this power was utilised, as conveyed by Dasgupta, to clean out what he regarded as a 'cesspool' of mediocrity.

Lee and his research colleagues have done (one part of) the profession a sterling service by their detailed, 'evidence-based' investigation of the structures, procedures and outcomes of successive rounds of the RSE, RAE, REFs, revealing their embedded 'revealed preferences', that is biases and sectional agendas, and the practices through which these were implemented. The speed and scale of this ideological cleansing were astonishing, as the UK hurtled mindlessly into a monocultural academic environment that suppressed diversity and pluralism, discouraged innovation and out-of-the-box thinking through its drive for standardisation and homogenisation in belief and practice, devalued collective research environments in favour of competitive individual maximisation of scores that converted ideas into private property, and forced researchers away from pursuing open-ended, complex, multi-disciplinary, policy-oriented research that was increasingly and most visibly becoming an imperative at a global level—whether to do with inequalities or financial and environmental crises. Professor Hahn and his choirboys, and they *were* almost all lads, kept on singing odes to general equilibrium in its many incarnations; their worry was not the role of money as was plain to the blind in the real world, but the stratospheric abstract game of integrating money into general equilibrium. Hahn had claimed in Aberystwyth that he had seen the future, and it was general equilibrium with money; and now, like all revolutionaries, he sought to convert his daydreams into reality as he found the weapons that he and his group could swing to realise it.

Table 13.6 provides some markers on the elimination of heterodox economists and economics in the course of the REFs of 1992, 2001 and 2008, tracking the percentage of university economics departments with no heterodox economists at all, and the percentage of heterodox submissions made in the

Table 13.6 Elimination of heterodox economists and economics from 'economics': RAEs 1992, 2001, 2008

Year	Top two rating categories		Bottom two rating categories	
	% of universities with no heterodox economists	% of heterodox economics submissions in total economics submissions	% of universities with no heterodox economists	% of heterodox economics submissions in total economics submissions
1992	21.1	1.5	7.7	16.7
2001	53.8	2.0	55.0	3.5
2008	69.2	0.5	53.3	1.9

Source: Derived from data in Lee et al. (2012b, Appendix VII, pp. 22–26)

REF as a percentage of the total economics submissions; both indicators are provided separately for two groups, the top two and the bottom two rating categories. The numbers show that even by 1989, at the top end, 21.1 per cent of departments had no heterodox economists compared with 7.7 per cent for the bottom two rating categories. In 2001, these numbers rise dramatically to 53.8 and 55 per cent respectively; and in 2008 to 69.2 and 53.3 per cent. Thus, the majority of economics departments had no heterodox economists at all, and their numbers were declining dramatically—they do not disappear since heterodox economists hired before 1987, and having tenure, might have suffered the arrows and slingshots and stayed the course, in whatever downgraded capacity in their departments. The data on heterodox submissions is even more alarming: even in 1992, submissions by heterodox economists accounted for a miniscule 1.5 per cent of all economics submissions in the top two rating groups, and 16.7 per cent for the bottom two groups; for 2001, the numbers were 2.0 per cent for the top and 3.5 per cent for the lowest two groups, showing a big drop as the lowest two groups began to conform and start gaming the new rules of the exercise; for 2008, the respective incidence was 0.5 per cent (or 1 in 200) for the top two categories, and 1.9 per cent (or 2 per 100) for the lowest two. Were the heterodox economists not researching and writing papers at all? The answer of course is that they were as engaged and productive as ever, though far less secure and with inferior career prospects and visibility for their work within 'economics'; they were being jostled and pushed into making their research submissions increasingly within other Units of Assessment, for example Politics, Sociology and Development Studies, varying with each round. It is clear that the pattern had already been more or less established by 1992, based on the assessment parameters and metrics instituted by the apex decision makers in 1989 when Frank Hahn had 'revolutionised' the system; what followed was a series of variations and refinements to optimise and speed up the process of purification.

Against this background, and knowledge of the not-so-secret agenda, indeed mission, of Hahn both in Cambridge and at the RES, it is all the more remarkable to read Frederic Lee's account of an exchange with Tony Atkinson, who had chaired the Economics Panel in the 1992 round, and then took over as President of the RES, in which capacity he was answering questions being put to him by anxious economists:

> At the 1994 Royal Economic Society Annual Conference a special session was held at which the chairman of the economics panel for the 1992 RAE, Anthony Atkinson, gave his view of what the panel did and also received questions from the floor. One question asked was how did the panel regard economic research that fell outside the domain of mainstream economics. The answer was, in part, that the assessors did not discriminate against heterodox research and that the RAE exercise should not be used by economic departments to discriminate against heterodox research. Atkinson went on to add that he did not believe British economists would actively discriminate against heterodox economists and their research. (Lee, 2009: 154)

The response from Atkinson, prima facie, could be ascribed by some to an amalgam of goodness and gullibility, or read by others as dissembling or diversionary, or (worse) as misleading and misinforming, because by that time, the inbuilt biases were so obvious on the ground that they could not be sweet-talked away. Lee adds:

> However, at the same conference a flyer appeared which announced that the University of Manchester was in the market for nine economists who would raise the School of Economic Studies research profile in mainstream economics (see *Guardian* March 29, 1994). ... Advertisements for posts in other institutions subsequently appeared that similarly specified that applicants must be working within mainstream economics and linked this explicitly to either maintaining or improving their ranking in the assessment exercise. ... Therefore, it seemed that economics departments were, in their hiring practices, discriminating positively towards mainstream economists and their research as a way to maintain and/or enhance their rating in the 1996 RAE; and that such practices implied a discriminatory attitude towards heterodox economists. (Lee, 2009: 154)

The place, of course, on which Hahn's gaze was especially fixed was Cambridge itself, the den of heterodoxy, and that was the lion whose beard he wanted to singe, almost as an existential compulsion. The impact on heterodox economics more broadly was indeed devastating, but it was felt the most in Cambridge itself, the epicentre of the UK heterodox economics, but at the same time, the domain of Hahn, Matthews, Dasgupta and Newbery, the prime architects, in the UK, of the mainstream revolution in economics—even if this 'revolution' really reduced essentially and eventually to following their American leaders in the other Cambridge. Cambridge economics, both at the Faculty and especially the DAE, was arguably the original habitat of heterodox economics and unsurprisingly had the highest concentrations of such economists in comparison with the rest of the UK departments of economics.

This density of heterodoxy in Cambridge was 'the problem'. Robin Matthews had worked out his own stock-flow algorithm and come to the conclusion that even if the orthodox group controlled fresh appointments, if he relied exclusively on natural wastage of the tenured heterodox staff, it would take far too many years for this fresh inflow, presumably all mainstream, to shift the overall balance significantly in favour of orthodoxy. The Education Reform Act of 1988, which had done away with conventional tenure, helped by adding to the power of the managers to hire, but then fire those hired if they did not quickly line up and measure up. Nevertheless, time was at a premium, and other direct measures needed to be devised to short-circuit the process of transformation. From other universities, including in the United States, there was an inventory of such mechanisms: relocations and exits; closures; migrations to other units; hounding, harassing and haranguing 'undesirable' individual staff to 'encourage' them to take early retirement or to move out. The RAE/REF intervention potentially served as one such instrument.

Lee et al. (2012b: Appendix VIII) provide some information on the location of heterodox economists in universities in England over the period 1992–2012 and list twenty-six names for Cambridge; its heterodox partner SOAS registers seventeen; the mainstream schools, LSE, Warwick, Surrey, Essex each have one. It has to be noted here that the density of heterodox economists in Cambridge would have been much higher but for the earlier dismantling of the two DAE macroeconomic modelling teams, the Cambridge Growth Model and the Cambridge Economic Policy Group, in the 1980s, through interventions from the orthodox gang. This strength was reflected in 1981, before the CEPG was shut down, in the Hahn-Neild letter (signed by 364 economists from 42 units across the country) against Thatcher's monetarism: at the time, despite the fact that many well-known names of heterodox economists, for example Ajit Singh and Bob Rowthorn amongst others, were missing from the Cambridge list of signatories (due to the timing and short turnaround period of the letter), Cambridge again had the maximum number of names, at fifty-four—as many as six London universities put together—with Oxford, LSE, Birkbeck, Bristol and UCL all in the ten to fifteen range. As estimated by Frederic Lee for 2012, their number had dwindled to just twelve; and at present, Ha-Joon Chang would appear to be the only remaining heterodox economist on the Faculty list; "I am the last Mohican", he is wont to saying.

13.9   Follow Big Brother: Elimination of Heterodoxy in USA

In his history of heterodox economics, Frederic Lee discusses in some detail "the contested landscape of American economics in the 1965–1980 period and provides information on the managed elimination of heterodoxy from economics departments country-wide, especially in lower ranked departments that want to move up the ladder" (Lee, 2009: 66). Many methods were used.

Perhaps the most widely used tactic to eliminate or reduce the heterodoxy in a graduate program was simply to deny the material resources needed to maintain it. One approach was to deny tenure to the heterodox professors teaching the heterodox components, which directly resulted in the demise of heterodoxy at Yale in 1980 and contributed to the demise of heterodoxy at Rutgers by 1987. A second was to remove heterodox economists from important positions in the department and eliminate the heterodox course offerings while a third approach was not to replace heterodox professors who taught the heterodox components when they leave or retire, which contributed to the demise at Texas (1980), Oklahoma (1985), UC-Berkeley (mid-1990s), Tennessee (1990s), Stanford (1990), Michigan (1992), Rutgers (1987), and Maryland (late 1980s). ... An underlying current that tended to reinforce both tactics was the ranking of departments in terms of their adherence to and exposition of neoclassical theory. For example, at Texas, the combination of retirements and deans wanting a high-quality, that is high-ranking, department meant that perspective [prospective] faculty members must have doctorates from the top doctoral programs and be neoclassical economists as well. Consequently, the hires from the 1970s onwards were nearly all neoclassical economists from top programs: so that by 2002, 82 percent of the faculty had doctoral degrees from top programs. (ibid.: 76)

By 1970 there were over 15,000 American economists, most of whom were neoclassical economists and belonged to the AEA. Because of the repressive dominance of neoclassical economists and because of the pre- and post-war repression of heterodox economics and economists, neoclassical economists shared membership in a tightly knit hierarchically arranged community. This community accepted a single relatively homogeneous body of ideas or theories, shared the same set of standards—theoretical, technical, and empirical—for evaluating research and hierarchically ranking publications, engaged in a network of inter-institutional and interpersonal ties that promoted communication, reciprocated employment and conference participation opportunities, and rejected or suppressed all else. Clearly, the neoclassical community circa 2000 institutionalized the anti-pluralism, red scare-repression, and the McCarthyism values of the previous seventy years. But it did more; it institutionalized what can be called 'thinking like an economist'. That is, to think like an economist is to use chains of deductive reasoning in conjunction with neoclassical models to help understand economic phenomena. It includes identifying trade-offs in the context of constraints, tracing the behavioural implications of some change while abstracting from other aspects of reality, explaining the consequences of aggregation, and using equilibrium as a theoretical organizing concept. To violate this neoclassical creed, to not think like a neoclassical economist, is not be an economist at all. (ibid.: 66)

Moreover, they believed that neoclassical economic theory and its applications to the real world should be accepted by students without question or discussion. However, some students found it sterile and innately conservative. So they doubted and questioned the theory only to be slapped down by the professor with denigrating phrases, such 'perhaps you should study neoclassical theory and learn it thoroughly before you criticize it' or 'if you continue to have these doubts about the theory, perhaps you should drop out of economics'. (ibid.: 68)

It is fairly obvious from this description of the strategies followed by neoclassical mainstream departments for the elimination of heterodox economics and economists in American universities from the 1970s, that a very similar process was adopted in UK universities as the neoclassical group managed to acquire domination in decision-making at the levels of the department, university and professional bodies and associations.[20] In the UK, the switch point was 1989, when Frank Hahn became the President of the Royal Economic Society and gained operational control of the representative associations of economics teachers on the one side, and the management of the first major Research Assessment Exercise (in 1989) on the other. The observed processes and results mirrored the strategies and outcomes of their American counterparts—whether in terms of the course content, research orientation, quality metrics, appointment and promotion criteria, rankings of journals, of departments, and individual economists, the UK body of mainstream economists systematically imitated their 'superior' American counterparts. Hahn & Co. had rendered British economics generally, and Sidgwick Site in specific, an arid outpost of American neoclassical orthodoxy, flattering its masters through imitation, and always losing out in comparison, destined to play second fiddle. As Backhouse showed, Americanisation had been creeping into UK economics through various channels: the percentage of Americans in a sample of British economics departments had stood at about 1 per cent in 1960, and then risen steadily, though not dramatically till the early 1990s; LSE stood out as an exception, with a jump to 15 per cent by 1970 with the level remaining over 10 per cent since (Backhouse, 1996: 47, Fig. 3). With respect to US-educated staff in the sample, the trends, again starting from 2–3 per cent levels in the 1950s, are similar; once again LSE is an extreme outlier, with a huge jump from 3 per cent in 1960 shooting up to 25 per cent by 1970, and rising to about 45 per cent by the end of the period in 1994. What stands out is the outlier status of the economics department at LSE, leading the Americanisation process with a sharp upward jump in the 1960–1970 period. It is no surprise that this coincides with the simultaneous arrival at the LSE of the gang of the revolutionaries

---

[20] A personal reflection on the Canadian context comes from Marc Lavoie: "Something somewhat similar happened in our department at the University of Ottawa, where there was at least a one-third heterodox representation among the staff, when I started my career in 1979. Now, there is zero heterodox economics! At some point, the chair and the dean proposed that three of us be moved to Political Science (my name was mentioned as a possible fourth, but I was using more math than the other three). We collectively turned down the offer, thinking that we were bona fide economists, as our mainstream colleagues. Retrospectively, this was perhaps a mistake: we could perhaps have built a political stream and control recruitment there." Citing other parallels, he ruefully continues: "All this makes for depressing memories, and like some of your former colleagues in Cambridge, I try to avoid thinking about all this. In fact, here, as in Cambridge, the relations between heterodox and mainstream economists turned sour in the early 1980s, whereas before it seemed nobody cared what we believed or taught. Also, what you tell about the development field and exams being taken over by mainstream colleagues who had no clue what development was besides some equations, also happened here" (Personal communication, email dated 22 December 2021).

of US-style neoclassical mathematical economics in teaching and research: Frank Hahn, Terence Gorman, Harry Johnson and Alan Walters. Further, Backhouse (1996: 41) points out: "research assessment and internationalization are linked. Assessments of research quality are influenced, at least in part, by where the research is published, and in economics many of the most prestigious journals are U.S. based. Diamond's, 1989 list of 'core journals' was widely discussed in the context of the 1989 exercise. Of the journals included in it, 14 are published in the United States, 8 in the Netherlands (North-Holland/Elsevier), 4 in the U.K., and 1 in Canada"; and it can be added that all these journals are thoroughbreds of the mainstream stable. Hahn, Gorman and Sargan, amongst a few others, kick-started Samuelson's third and fourth revolutions, viz., mathematisation and econometrification, in the UK in the 1960s, and the LSE was then, and remains, the bastion.

Francis Cripps saw and resisted, the neoclassical takeover of Cambridge economics from the 1970s as a leading member of the radical Cambridge Economic Policy Group that was one of the heterodox lineages purged by the orthodox campaign, and his reflection on the dynamics of the processes of takeover is insightful:

> I thought at the time in the 1970s and still tend to believe that the main reason for the sea-change in economics as a rationalisation of public policy (which is why we had all signed up) was the war-time disintegration of Europe and rise of the US. European economists had an institutional understanding of economic behaviour. The new, more radical economics from the US was a pseudo-science relying on unrealistic abstract axioms such as "existence of general equilibrium"; and increasingly absurd postulates that came after, in combination with econometrics as a supposedly scientific method for validating and calibrating theory with statistical evidence. Equilibrium theory and econometrics allowed mathematicians to get scholarships and jobs without institutional and historically-dependent knowledge of real-life economies. US hegemony was manifested in scholarships and positions for W European and UK economists who were starting out or ready to jump ship (e.g. Hahn and Malinvaud) who formed a transatlantic club. Now as US hegemony recedes, more historically and institutionally rooted analysis is coming back but given the conservative nature of universities, another generation may have to pass in the US, Europe and much of the rest of the world before equilibrium economics fades away. Econometrics may survive even longer by morphing into AI (it is an excellent tool for MPhil and PhD students and younger researchers, allowing them to skate over the complex realities underlying increasingly voluminous statistical datasets). I guess this is what Keynes anticipated and Kaldor was afraid of. (Personal communication, email dated 16 January 2020)

One might ask: What 'backward' impact did the accumulation of wide-ranging critiques of the RAEs and REFs have on their objectives, design and use? Not much, it would appear, judging by the assessment of the outgoing Secretary General of the Royal Economic Society, Richard Portes, at the end of his tenure from 1992 till 2008, the longest stretch since Keynes. He had come in "succeeding the extremely capable Aubrey Silberston ... following the major renewal of the Society inspired by Frank Hahn" (Portes, 2008: 5). The RES had served as the engine room from where the mainstream template had been propelled into UK economics by Hahn and his associates; hence his reflections would be insightful. Portes greatly emphasised the beneficial impact of the introduction of competition and incentives into the measurement, valuation and rewards research in economics; he also decried criticisms and counter actions that spoke in favour of multidisciplinarity or heterodoxy as would be evident from some of the bottom lines that can be elicited from his forceful elaboration.

"Whatever the objections to the RAE, however, there is no doubt it has effected a remarkable change in incentives. The stimulus of competition is strong, even if imposed from above in a heavily regulated environment rather than developing from below with light regulation. ... Competition is not the universal solution. It is, however, the best weapon we have against institutional rigidities, and we have seen the very positive results in the UK university sector." To make what kind of competition he has in mind for the universities, Portes provides "an example from recent research on transparency in European and American corporate bond markets. ... We are often told that the US capital markets are the deepest, broadest, most liquid and most efficient in the world. We fancy ourselves to believe that the UK is not far behind. In fact, however, on a conventional measure of efficiency, the bid-ask spread, we found that spreads were actually lower in the euro-denominated corporate bond markets than either the US or the UK. Why? Our conjecture is simple: competition."

Then he takes aim at the bureaucrats: "Research programmes are often dictated by funders in a top-down manner. This is perhaps more frequent and blatant in the social sciences, because administrators and politicians think they understand these disciplines, which also have overtly political dimensions (whereas they cannot pretend to understand high-energy physics). So administrators, who may not have deep disciplinary backgrounds, nevertheless impose their own views rather than deferring to professional standards. We see this at the EU level in prescribed research topics, criteria for evaluating proposals, the choice of evaluators, and enforced multi-disciplinarity."

The next target is heterodoxy: "We also often find deep distrust of 'orthodox, mainstream economic thought'. ... Mediocrity is rationalised on the grounds that it is hard for the 'heterodox' to publish in top journals—despite the examples of Joseph Stiglitz, Amartya Sen, Herbert Simon, Samuel Bowles, Herbert Gintis, and many others."

Then comes the solution: "What we clearly needed was a European Research Council like the US National Science Foundation. We need not so much more but better funding, awarded on the basis of serious competition. And we now have it. The ERC now exists, it has made an auspicious start, and it is good to know that soon the distinguished economist Andreu Mas-Colell will become its Secretary General" (Portes, 2008: 4–5). Presumably, the new Council will inter alia excise heterodoxy in favour of orthodoxy, and eliminate the multidisciplinarity in favour of monodisciplinarity. The remarks of Portes leave little room for doubt.

13.10 1662, Deja Vu

About Peter Swinnerton-Dyer's 1986 RSE, Sayer observes that "by today's standards this looks a laughably amateurish process" (Sayer, 2015: 19), but the mathematician had seen little advantage in pressing for the total number of publications from departments, or individual submissions to assess staff quality, as he judged that the former would "only encourage the production of low-quality papers" and the latter would impose "an absolutely intolerable level of work"; in his view, asking for "the 5 best publications" from each department was "adequate for getting the estimates roughly right"—he reasoned that "if the best five elements are good, the overall quality is probably good as well"; he did not see the necessity or the validity of trying to make it into rocket science. But with the high stakes involved, bureaucracy felt the need for greater transparency, and legally defensible, 'transparency' was deemed essential, thus inducing increasing complexity and demands from departments and individuals. The 1989 RAE, where Hahn was effectively in control of the process, ignored Swinnerton-Dyer's robust rationale and focussed on assessing research quality on the basis of individual assessments. What Swinnerton-Dyer had overlooked was that while his own procedure was sufficiently sturdy for making generally fair allocations of research funds across aggregated units (thereby protecting individual staff from stress and distress), Hahn & Co. had a very different agenda whereby the RAE could be used to differentiate between the research performance of individual staff on the basis of their chosen measuring rods—which in economics, were drawn from their ideologically narrow, almost fundamentalist view of what constituted economics and its methods. Arguably, Hahn would be more interested in being able to wield a discriminating tool to include or exclude individual staff, and much less interested in the algorithms determining overall departmental allocations. Swinnerton-Dyer wanted a method for allocation; Hahn, a weapon for purification.

Two accompanying changes in the institutional environment were important: first, in 1988, the Education Reform Act abolished tenure for academic staff hired after a specified cut-off date in 1987; then an Amendment in 1992 converted thirty-five polytechnics into fully fledged universities. Both raised the levels of competition and the stakes across and within departments and led inexorably to ever greater reliance on 'objective' bibliometrics with a diminishing role for the exercise of holistic judgement through peer-review processes. Economics was ahead of the game, since Hahn & Co. had already linked quality assessment to publication in 'Diamond list' journals, thus embedding mainstream criteria even more firmly into the process. Their 'rules of the game'—and it was a game even if more of a blood sport—extended their sway over all economics teaching in the country; and all new staff could be assessed, disciplined and re-hired or fired depending on whether they would swear an oath, and could recite appropriately from the mainstream economics testament according to St Frank.

Keith Joseph, Secretary of State for Education under Margaret Thatcher, was a devotee of Karl Popper (amongst other idols), and Richard Gombrich, in voicing his dismay over "British higher education policy [which] over the last twenty years has been an unmitigated catastrophe", refers to an informal meeting of Sir Keith Joseph, and scientists at Oxford, where he reportedly told them: "if you want to do research, my advice to you is to emigrate". Gombrich (2000) confronts the devotee with the words of his guru: "The holistic planner overlooks the fact that it is easy to centralize power but impossible to centralize all knowledge which is distributed over many individual minds, and whose centralization would be necessary for the wise wielding of centralized power. But this fact has far-reaching consequences. Unable to ascertain what is in the minds of many individuals, he must try to control and stereotype interests and beliefs by education and propaganda. But this attempt to exercise power over minds must destroy the last possibility of finding out what people really think, for it is clearly incompatible with the free expression of thought, especially of critical thought. Ultimately it must destroy knowledge; and the greater the gain in power, the greater will be the loss of knowledge" (Karl Popper, quoted in Gombrich, 2000).

On 24 August 1662 Charles II enacted the Act of Uniformity,[21] which made it mandatory in the Church of England to follow the forms of worship prescribed in the new edition of the Book of Common Prayer. This royal edict unleashed an upheaval and led to the Great Ejection when more than 2500 clergy rejected the required oath of conformity to the established church. There was to be only the one god and the one gospel, one prayer book—which the Act required "to be truly and exactly translated in the British or Welsh tongue"—and not swearing total allegiance meant, among other exclusions and punishments, that non-conformists could not study and get degrees from Cambridge or Oxford, then the only two universities in England; they scattered to pursue their studies at Glasgow, Edinburgh, Leiden and Utrecht; they could not hold civil or military office and were forced to resign their livings; they were forbidden from teaching in schools; could not hold assemblies of more than five persons who were not from the same households, thereby preventing non-conformists from worship; and with the Five Mile Act, they were forbidden to come within five miles of incorporated towns or the location of their former residence. The exclusions enforced by the 1662 Act remained in force till 1872 when they were partially amended or revoked; and a few sections of the Act were still in force in 2010. The Book of Common Prayer was universalised; conformism was the rule; an oath of loyalty had to be taken to the King; Oxford enforced tests at the point of admission, and Cambridge before it awarded a degree, to ensure conformity. There are canny parallels here with the suppression of all heterodox economics traditions by the mainstream orthodox faith in the UK, USA and globally. Cambridge provides a prime

[21] Act of Uniformity 1662 https://en.wikipedia.org/wiki/Act_of_Uniformity_1662; https://en.wikipedia.org/wiki/Great_Ejection; https://en.wikipedia.org/wiki/1662_in_England.

illustration of this phenomenon policed by Frank Hahn—now multi-tasking as Charles II—his gang-of-four, and loyal minions and myriad dependents. "If Austin Robinson could speak from his place of rest, he might well ask for the Faculty Building on Sidgwick Site to remove his name from its entrance; he had intended it to be a congenial interactive space for open intellectual exchange, not a fortress of ideological narrow-mindedness or a laboratory of lobotomization."[22]

The origins of the RAEs lay in the politicians and mandarins wanting value for money for their research grants and could be seen as an independent phenomenon. Viewed from Cambridge, however, the RAEs offered the orthodox economists an effective device to extend and intensify their ongoing campaign against the heterodox groups in the Faculty and the DAE. From his controlling RES position at the apex of the profession, Hahn could shape and instrumentalise the RAE process to suit his dual ends: to spread the word and realise the prediction of John the Baptist, and simultaneously to clear out heterodoxy from Cambridge economics. The time frame of the early exercises dovetailed perfectly with the ongoing campaign: in 1982, CEPG had been closed down; over the 1984–1987 period, the same fate befell the CGP; over the 1983–1987 period, in two phases, the DAE Review was the instrument that handed managerial control to the Hahn group, including the directorship of the DAE; and fitting in with these attacks running in Cambridge came, in parallel, the force of the RAEs from the late 1980s—the final move in the endgame.

References

Aistleitner, M., Kapeller, J., & Steinerberger, S. (2018). The power of scientometrics and the development of economics. *Journal of Economic Issues, 52*(3), 816–834. https://doi.org/10.1080/00213624.2018.1498721

Baccini, A. (2018). *Performance-based incentives, research evaluation systems and the trickle-down of bad science.* https://www.ineteconomics.org/uploads/papers/Baccini-Value-for-money-Berlin-final.pdf

Baccini, A., De Nicolao, G., & Petrovich, E. (2019). *How performance evaluation metrics corrupt researchers.* https://www.ineteconomics.org/perspectives/blog/how-performance-evaluation-metrics-corrupt-researchers

Backhouse, R. E. (1996). The changing character of British economics. In A. W. Coats (Ed.), *The post-1945 internationalization of economics*, Annual Supplement to volume 28, *History of political economy* (pp. 33–60). Duke University Press.

Backhouse, R. E. (2000). Economics in mid-Atlantic: British economics, 1945–95. In A. W. Coats (Ed.), *The development of economics in Western Europe since 1945* (pp. 19–39). Routledge.

Beath, J. (2010). Comments recorded in the minutes of CHUDE Steering Committee Meeting of 26th March 2010, Item 5.2. Royal Economic Society Conference of Heads of Departments of Economics at the University of Surrey. https://www.google.com/url?sa=t&rct=j&q=&esrc=s&source=web&cd=13&ved=2ahUKEwjM

---

[22] Saith (2019: 138–139).

rpeskPnjAhVH26QKHSNRAEQQFjAMegQIBxAC&url=https%3A%2F%2Fwww.
jiscmail.ac.uk%2Fcgi-bin%2Fwebadmin%3FA3%3Dind1011%26L%3DCHUDE
%26E%3Dbase64%26P%3D5048%26B%3D%2D%2D%253D_3fd5r5o4aeng%26T
%3Dapplication%252Fpdf%3B%2520name%3D%2522chudeagendapapers061110.
pdf%2522%26N%3Dchudeagendapapers061110.pdf%26attachment%3Dq&usg=A
OvVaw0qi1hy_FArteCVhSF4cQHt

Beath, J. (2015). Obituary: Aubrey Silberston (1922–2015). *Royal Economic Society Newsletter, 171*, 17–18.

Bezemer, D. (2011). The credit crisis and recession as a paradigm test. *Journal of Economic Issues, 45*(1), 1–18.

Blaug, M., & Towse, R. (1988). *The current state of the British economics profession*. Royal Economic Society.

Cambridge University General Board. (2004, July 21). Report of the General Board on the Faculty of Economics and Politics and the Department of Applied Economics. *Cambridge Reporter*.

Caswill, C., & Shove, E. (2000). Introducing interactive social science. *Science and Public Policy, 27*(3), 154–157.

Chang, A. C., & Li, P. (2015). *Is economics research replicable? Sixty published papers from thirteen journals say 'usually not'*. Finance and Economics Discussion Series, 2015-083. Board of Governors of the Federal Reserve System.

Coats, A. W., & Coats, S. E. (1970). The social composition of the Royal Economic Society and the beginnings of the British economics 'profession', 1890–1915. *British Journal of Sociology, 21*, 75–85.

Dasgupta, P. (2010). Interview with Partha Dasgupta 6th April 2010. In S. Harrison & A. Macfarlane, *Encounter with economics*. Interviews filmed by A. Macfarlane and edited by S. Harrison. University of Cambridge. http://sms.cam.ac.uk/collection/1092396

Dasgupta, P. (2013). Obituary: Frank Hahn. *Royal Economic Society Newsletter, 161*(April).

Daunton, M. (2008). Interview with Professor Martin Daunton interviewed by Danny Millum. *Making history: The discipline in perspective*. https://archives.history.ac.uk/makinghistory/resources/interviews/Daunton_Martin.html

Diamond, A. M. (1989). The core journals of economics. *Current Contents, 21*(1), 4–11.

Evaluation Associates. (1999). *Interdisciplinary research and the research assessment exercise: A report by Evaluation Associates Ltd*. Higher Education Funding Council for England.

Gillies, D. (2012). Economics and research assessment systems. *Economic Thought, 1*(1), 23–47. http://et.worldeconomicsassociation.org/files/ETGillies_1_1.pdf

Gombrich, R. F. (2000, January 7). *British higher education policy in the last twenty years: The murder of a profession*. Lecture delivered at the Graduate Institute of Policy Studies, Tokyo. http://www.damtp.cam.ac.uk/user/mem/papers/LHCE/uk-higher-education.html

Grove, J. (2013, April 8). Thatcher had 'immense impact' on higher education. *Times Higher Education*. https://www.timeshighereducation.com/news/thatcher-had-immense-impact-on-higher-education/2003059.article

Harcourt, G. C. (2017). Robert Charles Oliver (Robin) Matthews (1927–2010). In R. A. Cord (Ed.), *The Palgrave Companion to Cambridge economics* (pp. 955–978). Palgrave Macmillan.

Harrison, M. (2001). *My economic history: From revolutions to routines*. https://warwick.ac.uk/fac/soc/economics/staff/mharrison/comment/econhist.pdf

Heckman, J. J., & Moktan, S. (2020). *Publishing and promotion in economics: The tyranny of the Top Five.* https://voxeu.org/article/publishing-and-promotion-economics-tyranny-top-five. Published later as: *Journal of Economic Literature, 58*(2), June.

Hey, J. D., & Winch, D. (Eds.). (1990). *A century of economics: 100 years of the Royal Economic Society and the Economic Journal.* Blackwell.

Howson, S. (2011). *Lionel Robbins.* Cambridge University Press.

Ioannidis, J. P. A., Stanley, T. D., & Doucouliagos, H. (2017). The power of bias in economics research. *Economic Journal, 127*(605), F236–F265.

Johnston, J., & Reeves, A. (2018). An investigation into the role played by research assessment in the socio-geographic fragmentation of undergraduate economics education in the UK. *Higher Education, 76*(4), 589–614.

Jump, P. (2013a, July 10). REF 'risks narrowing economics'. *Times Higher Education.* https://www.timeshighereducation.com/news/ref-risks-narrowing-economics/2005673.article

Jump, P. (2013b, October 17). Evolution of the REF. *Times Higher Education.* https://www.timeshighereducation.com/features/evolution-of-the-ref/2008100.article

Keynes, J. M. (1926). The end of laissez-faire. Hogarth Press (pamphlet). In *The collected writings of John Maynard Keynes* (Essays in Persuasion) (Vol. IX). Royal Economic Society, Palgrave Macmillan, 1972.

Kogan, M., & Hanney, S. (2000). *Reforming higher education.* Jessica Kingsley Publishers.

Komine, A. (2018). William Henry Beveridge (1879–1963). In R. Cord (Ed.), *The Palgrave Companion to LSE economics* (pp. 239–262). Palgrave Macmillan.

Lee, F. (2007). The Research Assessment Exercise, the state and the dominance of mainstream economics in British universities. *Cambridge Journal of Economics, 31*(2), 309–325.

Lee, F. (2009). *A history of heterodox economics: Challenging the mainstream in the twentieth century.* Routledge.

Lee, F., & Harley, S. (1998). Peer review, the Research Assessment Exercise and the demise of non-mainstream economics. *Capital and Class, 22*(3), 23–51.

Lee, F. S., Pham, X., & Gu, G. (2012a). *The UK Research Assessment Exercise and the narrowing of UK economics.* MPRA Paper No. 41842. https://mpra.ub.uni-muenchen.de/41842/1/MPRA_paper_41842.pdf

Lee, F. S., Pham, X., & Gu, G. (2012b, October 9). *The UK Research Assessment Exercise and the narrowing of UK economics – Appendices.* https://hetecon.net/documents/ResearchAssessment/UKRAE-Narrowing-Appendix.pdf

Lee, F. S., Pham, X., & Gu, G. (2013). The UK Research Assessment Exercise and the narrowing of UK economics. *Cambridge Journal of Economics, 37*(4), 693–717.

Marcuzzo, M. C. (2012). *Fighting market failure: Collected essays in the Cambridge tradition of economics.* Routledge.

McCloskey, D. N., & Ziliak, S. T. (1996). The standard error of regressions. *Journal of Economic Literature, 34*(1), 97–114.

Mingers, J., & White, L. (2015). *Throwing out the baby with the bathwater: The undesirable effects of National Research Assessment Exercises on research.* https://arxiv.org/ftp/arxiv/papers/1502/1502.00658.pdf

Morrish, L. (2019, May 23). *The university has become an anxiety machine.* Guest blog contribution, Higher Education Policy Institute. https://www.hepi.ac.uk/2019/05/23/the-university-has-become-an-anxiety-machine/

Necker, S. (2014). Scientific misbehaviour in economics. *Research Policy, 43*(10), 1747–1759.
Newbery, D. (2017). Frank Horace Hahn 1925–2013. *Biographical Memoirs of Fellows of the British Academy, XVI*, 485–525. https://www.britac.ac.uk/sites/default/files/23 Hahn 1837 9_11_17.pdf
Parkin, M., & Nobay, A. R. (Eds.). (1975). *Contemporary issues in economics: Proceedings of the conference of the Association of University Teachers of Economics, Warwick, 1973*. Manchester University Press.
Pasinetti, L. L. (1991). Richard Ferdinand Kahn, 1905–1989. *Proceedings of the British Academy, 76*, 423–443.
Portes, R. (2008, July). The annual report of the Secretary-General. *Royal Economic Society Newsletter*, No. 142.
Reid, M. (2019, January 9). Peter Swinnerton-Dyer: Obituary. *The Guardian*.https://www.theguardian.com/science/2019/jan/09/sir-peter-swinnerton-dyer-obituary
Saith, A. (2019). *Ajit Singh of Cambridge and Chandigarh: An intellectual biography of the radical Sikh economist*. Palgrave Macmillan.
Samuelson, P. A. (1994). Richard Kahn: His welfare economics and lifetime achievement. *Cambridge Journal of Economics, 18*(1), 55–72.
Sayer, D. (2015). *Rank hypocrisies: The insult of the REF*. Sage Swifts.
Scott, A., Skea, J., Robinson, J., & Shove, E. (1999). *Designing 'interactive' environmental research for wider social relevance*. ESRC Global Environmental Change Programme, Special Briefing no 4, May.
Schumpeter, J. A. (1954). *History of economic analysis*. Oxford University Press.
Singh, A. (2008). *Better to be rough and relevant than to be precise and irrelevant: Reddaway's legacy to economics*. Working Paper No. 379. Cambridge University Centre for Business Research. www.cbr.cam.ac.uk/fileadmin/user_upload/centre-for-business-research/downloads/working-papers/wp379.pdf
Smith, C. S. (1991). Networks of influence: The social sciences in the United Kingdom since the war. In P. Wagner et al. (Eds.), *Social sciences and modern states: National experiences and theoretical crossroads* (pp. 131–147). Cambridge University Press.
Stern, N. (2016). *Building on success and learning from experience: An independent review of the Research Excellence Framework*. https://assets.publishing.service.gov.uk/government/uploads/system/uploads/attachment_data/file/541338/ind-16-9-ref-stern-review.pdf
Stockhammer, E., Dammerer, Q., & Kapur, S. (2017, October). *The research excellence framework 2014, journal ratings and the marginalization of heterodox economics*. Working Paper No. PKWP1715, Post Keynesian Economics Society (PKES). Version 1.05.
Szenberg, M., & Ramrattan, L. B. (2017). *Collaborative research in economics: The wisdom of working together*. Palgrave Macmillan.
Waldegrave, W. (2013). *William Waldegrave interviewed by Alan Macfarlane*. Film interviews with leading thinkers. University of Cambridge. https://www.sms.cam.ac.uk/media/1901304
White, L. H. (2015). Susan Howson, *Lionel Robbins*. Book review. *Oeconomia, 5-3*, 419–422. https://journals.openedition.org/oeconomia/2104#quotation
Yokoyama, K. (2006). The effect of the research assessment exercise on organizational culture in English universities: Collegiality versus managerialism. *Tertiary Education and Management, 12*, 311–322.

CHAPTER 14

Reincarnations

Abstract The great banyan tree of Cambridge heterodox traditions extended its roots and branches, and flourished for over a half century from the landmark year of 1926 which saw Piero Sraffa's iconoclastic article in the *Economic Journal*, and John Maynard Keynes's dramatic pronouncement heralding the death of laissez-faire. Then, within the short space of about 15 years from the mid-1970s, these lineages and most of their practitioners evanesced or were essentially purged from the Faculty of Economics and the Department of Applied Economics—the turnaround occurring as a result of a sustained campaign by the orthodox mainstream camp in Cambridge, enabled by the sea change in national and global politics from state-led or state-managed Keynesian or state-capitalist development strategies in the North and South, towards raw 'free-market' neoliberalism on a global scale. The Hahn-Matthews-led campaign, through a series of battles, had won its local Cambridge war and purged virtually all vestiges of heterodox economics, as well as related disciplines, from its midst; it had attained its objective of sanskritised neoclassical disciplinary purity. What then transpired the day after the battle was done, what came of the victors and what fate befell the various vanquished tribes of heterodox apostates? This chapter follows these trajectories and uncovers some expected and several counter-intuitive outcomes both within the Faculty core, which tended to lose rank in its chosen orthodox world, and on the periphery where the diverse 'purged' groups reincarnated themselves and rebuilt productive institutional lives, and flourishing reputations that, by many 'objective' measures, exceed those achieved by the orthodox economists at the core. Widely recorded student satisfaction and appreciation at the periphery contrasted with student protest campaigning against the reductionist mono-disciplinary

© The Author(s), under exclusive license to Springer Nature Switzerland AG 2022
A. Saith, *Cambridge Economics in the Post-Keynesian Era*, Palgrave Studies in the History of Economic Thought,
https://doi.org/10.1007/978-3-030-93019-6_14

approach of mainstream economics within the Faculty. The chapter notes also some recent developments reflecting the preferences of major donors to Cambridge economics; ironically, these donations, and nudges for a change of direction again towards regenerated forms of heterodox economics, come from some famously successful Cambridge alumni who were supervised in their Cambridge years by leading heterodox economists, and who later made their fortunes in the whirlpool world of global finance, a resonance to Keynes that is unmissable.

14.1   In a Nutshell, à la Joan

Paul Samuelson (1988: 328)—notwithstanding all their competitive battles—in speaking about "the incomparable Joan", remarks: "when Diogenes reached Joan, he could douse his lamp and end his search". In "What Are the Questions?", another of her frequent frontal challenges in 1977 to mainstream economics, a battle-weary but unbending Joan Robinson[1] decries the lack of progress since the high-theory era of the 1930s:

> "The movement of the thirties was an attempt to bring analysis to bear on actual problems. Discussion of an actual problem cannot avoid the question of what should be done about it; questions of policy involve politics (*laissez-faire* is just as much a policy as any other). Politics involves ideology; there is no such thing as a 'purely economic' problem that can be settled by purely economic logic; political interests and political prejudice are involved in every discussion of actual questions. The participants in every controversy divide into schools—conservative or radical—and ideology is apt to seep into logic. In economics, arguments are largely devoted, as in theology, to supporting doctrines rather than testing hypotheses. Here, the radicals have the easier case to make. They have only to point to the discrepancy between the operation of a modern economy and the ideals by which it is supposed to be judged, while the conservatives have the well-nigh impossible task of demonstrating that this is the best of all *possible* worlds. For the same reason, however, the conservatives are compensated by occupying

---

[1] For Lorie Tarshis too, as indeed for so very many others, Joan was "an absolutely admirable person—and a person so committed to pursuing her own ideals, that she sometimes created ill-will in place of the good-will (towards others) that she intended" (Tarshis, 1989: 918) "She took stands that were her own, no matter how strong was the opposition, she set a wonderful example. Unfortunately, humans, being no better than human, often resented it and she accumulated far more enmity than she deserved." Contrast this with Frank Hahn's banter just ten pages earlier in the same volume: "What I liked about Joan—something that most people do not realize—was that she was cast in the tradition of the upper-class Englishwoman. In another age she would have been on a camel, riding through the desert. She was that sort of person. ... One of the most amusing things about Joan was her thinking of herself as a proletarian, when, in point of fact, she was totally a heterodox upper-class Englishwoman—a type that has been thoroughly described through history. I rather liked that about her! I enjoyed it!" Hahn (1989: 907). It would not be fair to accuse Frank Hahn of not being able to rise above the human.

positions of power, which they use to keep criticism in check" (Robinson, 1977: 1318, emphasis in the original).

How is this done, how is this power used to suppress opposition? Joan elaborates, favourably citing Benjamin Ward[2]:

> The power inherent in this system of quality control within the economics profession is obviously very great. The discipline's censors occupy leading posts in economics departments at the major institutions. ... The lion's share of appointment and dismissal power has been vested in the departments themselves at those institutions. Any economist with serious hopes of obtaining a tenured position in one of these departments will soon be made aware of the criteria by which he is to be judged ... the entire academic program, beginning usually at the undergraduate level but certainly at the graduate, consists of indoctrination in the ideas and techniques of the science. ... These inside instruments of control are accompanied by outside instruments exercised by members of the larger society. Probably the most important of these is control of funds for research and, to a lesser extent, teaching ... (Ward, 1972: 29–30). Consciences are not much troubled by such practices because economics has mixed its ideology into the subject so well that the ideologically unconventional usually appear to appointment committees to be scientifically incompetent. (ibid.: 250)

And there we have it, in 1977, more or less in a nutshell, Joan-style, an aphoristic distillation of the neoclassical campaign to purge all heterodox traditions from Cambridge economics, launched precisely around the time that Joan makes these pithy observations—embodying as much prescience as prediction; there was surely a foreboding sense of something Greek in the air.

14.2 Purges and Purification

The Purges constituted a relentless process of assault and attrition. The crunch period was the decade of the 1980s though there was a build-up before and follow-up later. The starting point could be pegged to the year 1972 when the Trojan horse bearing Frank Hahn was pulled into the Faculty by the unlikely trio of Nicky Kaldor, Richard Kahn and Brian Reddaway, or to 1976, when the flagship of Cambridge economics, *Economic Journal*, was relocated from its long-term address into the Oxford neoclassical camp; and notably, Robin Matthews had given up his Drummond Chair in Oxford in 1975 and returned to Cambridge as Master of Clare College, forming the Hahn-Matthews team. The campaign begins to unfold from 1980, and its second visible manifestation is the closure of the Cambridge Economic Policy Group (CEPG) in 1982. The

---

[2] Benjamin Ward was at Berkeley for over three decades from the early 1960s when he did his graduate studies, and PhD there; as such, he was surely the Berkeley contemporary of Ajit Singh before Ajit came over to Cambridge and effectively became the political commissar of the radical and heterodox lineages in the Faculty of Economics and the Chief Whip of their struggles against the rising power of the mainstream led and controlled by Frank Hahn and Robin Matthews.

third assault is on the Cambridge Growth Project (CGP) of the DAE, which is shut down in 1987, both through the termination of funding from the SSRC/ESRC through committees arguably dominated by orthodox opposition groups strongly under the influence of Hahn and/or Matthews. This axis is strengthened in 1985 by the induction of Partha Dasgupta from the LSE, and further, in de facto terms, by the strategic support, or the tactical absence of opposition, from Willy Brown, appointed to a professorship in the Faculty in the same year. Meanwhile the axis had contrived to instigate a University Review of the DAE, a process which lasted four years, and culminated in 1987 in a restructuring virtually designed by the mainstream group; this resulted in due course in the appointment of a fourth member of the orthodox group to a professorship and to the directorship of the DAE, in place of Wynne Godley, in 1988, adding to the mainstream dominance of decision-making in the Faculty. The fifth element of the campaign followed through the instrumental design and use of the Research Assessment Exercises (RAEs) which take place under the watch of Frank Hahn as the President of the Royal Economic Society during 1986–1989. By the end of the decade, the damage is done and the orthodox victory is complete, barring the post-war follow-up and mopping up of the heterodox apostates from the Faculty, to be deposited beyond the now purified precincts of the Faculty, purged of all vestiges of the lineages of heterodox economics that dominated it for half a century from the 1920s through till the 1970s. What came next, what were the spoils of victory? What happened to the vanquished? Did they all become discouraged workers, give up the tools of professional economics, and switch to some menial, manual trade?

From sampling the folklore, and from various personal accounts—and there were many—these campaigns were frequently characterised by much negativity: visceral vitriol, ideological venom, egotistical polarities, institutional and political animosities, rivalries and competition; long-standing grudges all dressed in professional disciplinary lexicon and jargon, all through carefully set-up committees with chosen members. There was much red on the battlefield; it was no tea party.

In terms of their own agenda, G4 had won their battles and were installed in a strong position of authority in the Faculty, unconstrained at the professorial level; from 1988 they had control over the DAE and from 1989 they effectively took over the position of Faculty Chair. What came next? First, there were the purification campaigns to complete. Here, the content and forms of teaching were easier to chop and change than the staff contracts. The Tripos was reshaped—there was no room for the fabled Reddaway-type questions which actually made students think and respond to tough open-ended questions that revealed their command in articulating theory, method, data and policy; new technique-oriented fashion was in; courses such as Ha-Joon Chang's on Development Economics got kicked out (though later reinstated); the research degree programmes became technique- and training-oriented, away from the big free-thinking projects earlier, and mathematical and econometric preconditions were set that precluded the entry of scholars with a heterodox bent of mind; interdisciplinarity was a funny word, replaced by disciplinary deepening but only in the neoclassical silo. Of course staff with tenure could not be kicked out, though sustained unpleasant pressure was brought to bear on various staff (including Ajit Singh) to leave or take early retirement, and some found the situation sufficiently uncongenial to take up one of those options. Amongst others, John Wells, Peter Nolan, Gabriel Palma, Jane Humphries, Ha-Joon Chang, John Sender, Tony Lawson were all made generally, or very specifically, unwelcome. The G4 also enjoyed a controlling influence on the selection of the panels for the RAEs and REFs, and these were used to isolate heterodox economists. The main change in staffing patterns came about through filling vacancies, and there were several of those in the transitions. And in 2004, the DAE disappeared into the folds of the Faculty. In the same year, the Faculty of Economics and Politics dropped the lower-caste signifier 'and Politics' and with it, the Faculty had completed the rituals of sanskritisation, barring a collective dip in the holy Ganges at the *ghats* of Banaras. The trouble with sanskritisation is that it is an exercise for self-promotion in the ranking order of caste; but there are sub-caste differentiations and jostling even within castes, including Brahmins; only those of acknowledged twice-born pedigree at the top have no more rungs to climb. The Cambridge self-promotees depended on acceptance by association and imitation.

14.3 Triumphalism

This evolution was marked by declaring open season on the Keynesian paradigm. Anti-Keynesian sniggering became a genre.

For three post-war decades Keynesianism had dominated teaching in the universities and policy making in governments. Alan Blinder (1988: 278–279) points out that "by about 1980, it was hard to find an American macroeconomist under the age of forty who professed to be a Keynesian; that was an astonishing intellectual turnabout in less than a decade, an intellectual revolution for sure". Skrabec (2014: 16) continues: "At major universities the only group that would sit at the lunch table with the Keynesians was visiting creationists". Friedman and Hayek, and the Mont Pelerin Society, had a huge influence in this turn, and they were now lauded in the USA, and were welcomed with admiration, if not outright adulation, in Downing Street. At the outset, Hayek had predicted it would take two or more decades to gain traction; now, "after roaming in the wilderness for thirty years, Hayekians had overcome Keynes' (sic) influence" (Wapshott, 2011: 269); Hayek had come in from the cold. And Robert Lucas (1980) made one of his premature pronouncements on the death of Keynesianism: "Keynesian economics is dead … I don't know exactly when this happened but it is true today and it wasn't true two years ago. … You cannot find a good, under-40 economist who identifies himself and his work as 'Keynesian'. Indeed, people even take offense if referred to in this way. At research seminars, people don't take Keynesian theorizing seriously any more—the audience starts to whisper and giggle to one another. Leading journals aren't getting Keynesian papers submitted any more." Lucas went on: "True, there are still leading Keynesians—in academics and government circles—so Keynesian economics is alive in this sense—but this is transient, because there is no fresh source of supply. Only way to produce a sixty year old Keynesian is to produce a thirty year old Keynesian, and wait thirty years" (Lucas, 1980, cited in De Vroey, 2010: 10).[3] De Vroey (2010: 9) also provides Solow's collation of Lucas's earlier Keynesianism-bashing, jointly with Sargent, drawn from a 1978 paper (Lucas Jr. & Sargent, 1994/1978). In De Vroey's account: "Solow ... found Lucas and Sargent's 'polemical vocabulary reminiscent of Spiro Agnew' and he (Solow) found the following phrases offensive: 'wildly incorrect', 'fundamentally flawed', 'wreckage', 'failure', 'fatal', 'of no value', 'dire implications', 'failure on a grand scale', 'spectacular recent failure', 'no hope'". It may be recalled that Solow was a self-declared "Keynesian" in the short run.

The orthodox mainstream, in its variational forms, was comprehensively dominant; the end of theory was nigh, all that remained was for the world outside to conform to its postulates. On cue, Robert Solow's student Alan Blinder had bugled his own version of triumphalism atop a pedestal. Like life imitating art, the real world was reshaping itself to conform to the free-markets theoretical model, he proclaimed. Blinder was described (in America) as one of the most brilliant minds of his generation; in his address on the occasion of being awarded the Adam Smith Prize in 1999, he made the extraordinary hubristic claim that "a convergence of forces is driving economies and their individual actors closer to the classical microeconomic model" (Blinder, 2000: 16). His statement offers a rare and elaborate insight into the modes of thought of the neoclassical school at the time and as such is worth an extended exposure, since it charts the contours and the depth of the malaise in the orthodox perspective.

"Over the years, economists have spent much effort to modify the capitalist, perfect-competition, profit-maximizing model of classical microeconomics to fit reality. Thus, it is ironic that in recent times reality has been approaching the classical model" (ibid.). After the standard qualifications—to which due lip-service is paid—he carries on unperturbed: "However, I *do* perceive a general pattern, and it is an ironic one. One might have assumed that economists would have to adjust their models to fit reality, rather than the other way around. That's certainly the way it works in the natural sciences. Germs did not change their behavior to accommodate Pasteur's theory, nor was Mercury's

---

[3] De Vroey (2010: 10) offers an account of the provenance of the in/famous Lucas anti-Keynesian quotation, observing that "getting hold of the full paper proved to be difficult. My requests to the people who had posted the passage for a copy of it were always met with the answer that they had none! Lucas gave me a similar answer. So the passage, cut loose from the rest of the paper, achieved a life of its own." De Vroey suggests that Lucas was attacking "the middle ground" in Keynes as much as in the Samuelsonian neoclassical synthesis.

orbit perturbed so that Einstein wouldn't be. But economists appear to have bent reality (at least somewhat) to fit their models. That's quite a feat." (ibid.)

He lists a series of forces underlying this "reversion to the classical model"; "the failure of socialism, alignment of managerial and shareholder interests, focus on shareholder value, decline of labor union power, changes in financial markets, global competition, and changes in regulatory practice". This is a breath-taking reading of the equation, including its direction, between 'theory' and 'reality'.

He provides elaborations of these factors. On the environment, he observes: "tradable carbon emissions permits and variants thereon are also central elements in the US government's policy toward global climate change—though, unfortunately, they are not so central to the policy recommendations of many other nations". And on another major policy concern, social security, Blinder has an offer: "if social security is privatized, that will mark one more step back toward the pure economic model" (ibid.: 17–18).

On financial markets: "our canonical models envision markets that are efficient in the strong sense (all known information is embodied in the price), highly competitive, and pretty much 'complete'—meaning that you can buy or sell futures on just about anything. In the rarified heights of general equilibrium theory, a full menu of Arrow-Debreu securities—defined by date, place, and 'state of nature'—is assumed to exist. The real world is not quite like this, of course, but it seems to be moving rapidly in that direction."

> The proliferation of futures contracts, options and other derivatives, and the 'securitization' of seemingly everything have greatly broadened the available asset menu in recent years, bringing it closer to the full set of Arrow-Debreu securities. It would be a gross exaggeration to say that investors can now buy 'contingent commodities', but newly-created assets have greatly expanded the possibilities for both hedging and gambling. You can now buy bonds whose payments are tied to the occurrence of hurricanes or to the receipts of rock stars. The basic theoretical insights into finance originally contributed by Markowitz's (1952) portfolio selection model, Sharpe's (1964) capital asset pricing model, and others have been so thoroughly incorporated into contemporary financial practice that they are now considered commonplace. Reports on stock that you receive from investment advisers routinely include the company's 'beta' and 'Sharpe ratio'. Options pricing has gone even further and now accords extraordinarily well with the Black-Scholes (1973) theory, which is based on exactly the sort of no-arbitrage condition which is the mother's milk of economic theory. Once options traders acted on intuition and hunches; now they carry hand-held computers programmed with the Black-Scholes formula. When prices deviate from this theoretical benchmark, money moves quickly to arbitrage away any differences. Indeed, the theory is so universally accepted that, rather than using price data to test it, financial experts now routinely assume the validity of the Black-Scholes formula and use it to 'back out' the market's implied estimates of volatility. (ibid.: 20–21)

On labour, Blinder poses a rhetorical question, but with a sting in its tail.

In the academy, we have a special subdiscipline of economics called 'labor economics'. But there are no subjects called 'equipment economics' or 'ball-bearing economics'. Why not? ... Many economists of earlier generations refused to accept the idea that the market for labor should be treated just like any other input market—with an upward-sloping supply curve, a downward-sloping demand curve, and equilibrium where the two curves cross. Instead, there was a long and deep tradition of *institutional* labor economics ... while marginal productivity theory insists that labor is always paid its marginal revenue product, astute observers of labor markets thought they saw something different ... the institutionalists are all but gone today. Look at what's happening in labor markets now. Unions are on the decline—down from 36 percent of American workers in 1945 to just 14 percent today. Slack is being squeezed out as firms strive more single-mindedly to maximize profits. Long-term relationships between firms and their employees are under siege. Jobs are being outsourced both to reduce benefits and to rid firms of the burdens of long-term relationships. Temporary and contingent work, though still small shares of total US employment, are growing rapidly. In brief, labor is increasingly being treated as 'just another commodity' to be bought and sold on a spot market. Thus the real world, though still far from the simple economic model, is again moving closer to it. ... Here too, [neoclassical] economists' ideas did play an indirect role, I believe. Specifically, the greater concentration on profit maximization carried a stark corollary for the labor market: slack had to be squeezed out. Thus economic logic may have played a supporting role in creating the harsher climate that labor now faces. (ibid.: 20)

Blinder (ibid.: 18) turns his gaze to social security which is "the government's largest tax-and-transfer program but also its main tool for income redistribution".

Standard economic theory offers little justification for a government program that not only compels saving for retirement but regulates both its volume and form. Rational individuals should make such decision for themselves; in dynamic optimization models, they do so all the time! So why is this seemingly-private function placed squarely in public hands? The main reasons, I believe, are 'non-economic' in the sense that they are based on the belief that *homo sapiens* behave differently than *homo economicus*. In particular, real people are likely to be short-sighted and therefore to underprovide for their old age. *Social Security forces them to do something (save for their retirement) that makes them better off.* That is *not* the normal perspective of economics, whose image of man is a rational, self-interested calculating machine. Thus, if Social Security is privatized, that will mark one more step back toward the pure economic model. Has the recent interest in privatizing Social Security been driven by economists' ideas? I think it is fair to answer: yes. But it has also benefited mightily from the support of vested interests who envision large fees from millions of new accounts to manage. Adam Smith would have understood that, too. (Blinder ibid.: 17–18)[4]

---

[4] Yes, Alan, Adam would have understood, but would he have agreed? (see, for instance, Rothschild, 1996).

Blinder goes to discuss several other factors that make economic life imitate neoclassical art. Each is cited with a sense of approval and satisfaction, and towards the end there is a listing of outstanding items of recalcitrant reality which still need a nudge in the direction of what the model assumes and desires them to be. He attributes the convergence partly to shifts in reality driven by forces independent of the neoclassical economic model, and often to the force of its theoretical propositions which act as forces of change in their own right through driving policy or the behaviour of economic agents.

His conclusion is unambiguous: "Decades ago, Paul Samuelson wrote of a 'neoclassical synthesis' in which proper application of macroeconomic stabilization policy would create the full-employment conditions necessary to validate neoclassical microeconomics. Well, to a first approximation, we have now achieved that neoclassical synthesis in the United States. Thus did the intellectual descendants of John Maynard Keynes pave the way for the worldwide comeback of Adam Smith" (ibid.: 24).

It is possible to offer an alternative: that the selective and twisted interpretation of Adam Smith, and the subsequent evolution of neoclassical theory, based on assumptions about reality including the nature of human beings, has come both to provide the legitimation of these trends described by Blinder and also the vested interests that drive them, leading in the end to the Frankenstein economies, with mass entitlement deficits and failures, with endemic global crises, and extreme inequalities creating a mutation of constitutional democracy into predatory plutocracy.

Each of the elements has profound problems, but perhaps the most spectacular component is the detailed exposé on financialisation which appears to come from the trading floor. Blinder was not alone, of course, but speaking for the tribe. Consider the acuity of Robert Lucas, rewarded for the rational expectations paradigm with the bankers' Nobel Prize in 1995:

> "I am sceptical about the argument that the subprime mortgage problem will contaminate the whole mortgage market, that housing construction will come to a halt, and that the economy will slip into a recession. Every step in this chain is questionable and none has been quantified. If we have learned anything from the past 20 years it is that there is a lot of stability built into the real economy" (Lucas, 2007). Four days short of a year later, Lehman Brothers filed for bankruptcy, the largest case in history. USD 639b in assets and USD 619b in debt. Lucas had a coming out moment: "I guess everyone is a Keynesian in a foxhole". Richard Nixon, one second-hand car dealer, had beaten him to it by 38 years: "we are all Keynesians now" he had famously said in 1971.

The spectacular nature of the before-after contrast is perhaps best caught by switching channels and tuning in to the iconic case of the weather forecast by the BBC's Michael Fish:

> 'Earlier on today apparently a woman rang the BBC and said she had heard a hurricane was on the way.' So began the most infamous weather bulletin in British

history on the lunchtime news 30 years ago. 'Well I can assure people watching', smirked weather forecaster Michael Fish, 'don't worry, there isn't'. Just a few hours following that fateful broadcast in the early hours of October 16, 1987, the south coast of England was battered by the greatest storm witnessed in nearly three centuries. Gales reaching 115mph caused utter devastation across the southern half of the country, leaving 18 people dead, 15 million trees flattened, and a repair bill totalling £2bn. (Shute, 2017)

For Michael Fish, read Robert Lucas?

Of course, from the outset, the Cambridge heterodox tribes had a very different view of the rational expectations hypothesis—they could not decide whether to laugh or to cry. Says Tony Lawson (Dunn, 2009: 483): "In the mid 1970s Cambridge was a very lively place and the battles were fought everywhere, not least in the coffee room of the top floor of the Economics Faculty. The debates covered policy and economic understanding. I remember, too, the fortnightly Queens Seminar (which still goes on, although less regularly) where there were lots of arguments going on." "I remember a first time when the idea of rational expectations was talked about at the Queens Seminar. Probably it was the only time. I forget the name of the non-local speaker. But I do remember Kaldor being in the audience, because after the speaker had defined rational expectations, Kaldor stuck his hand up and said something like 'Did I understand you to be saying the following ...' and repeated the definition of rational expectations. The speaker replied 'Yes' and then Kaldor just started laughing. And you know what Kaldor looked like? Massive. His whole frame was shaking and he was giggling and it was so infectious the whole audience fell about laughing too. And this was happening at a time when much of the rest of the economics profession was already well on its way to being taken over by this really quite daft idea" (ibid.).[5]

14.4 A Royal Mess: The Queen's Question

Then came something not in the script: Her Majesty the Queen put in a gracious guest appearance. In September 2007, Robert Lucas disdainfully dismissed any possibility of a recession, or a general crisis in the mortgage market arising from the sub-prime problem—his analytical judgement and foresight soon appeared laughable, and he was not alone amongst mainstream economists to hold such a position. Exactly a year later, in September 2008, Lehmann Brothers filed for the largest bankruptcy in history. Two months later, in November 2008, with global markets in utter turmoil, the Queen inaugurated the new economics building at LSE, and innocently, but cannily, sought enlightenment: she gently posed what has come to be known as 'The Queen's Question': if these things were so large, how come everyone missed them? A

---

[5] A part of this quotation is also used in Chap. 4 in the context of Ajit Singh's Political Economy Seminar at Queens' College.

month later, the RAE 2008 results were posted; economics and econometrics was highlighted as the top-scoring discipline by far across both natural and social sciences, and within economics, LSE was by some distance the highest scorer. Yet, these wizards had not only not seen the crisis coming, they were in dismissive denial prior to, and well into, the crisis, and had not much of a policy clue how to respond from their mainstream theoretical toolkit, which comprised a single multi-purpose universal spanner, and it did not seem to fit. The discipline had been there before; that was when Keynesian economics was born. So the savvy Queen was posing the right question at the right time at the right place to the right people of the right discipline.

But Keynesian and other heterodox schools had been systematically squeezed out of business, aided crucially by the RAE's measurements carried out by mainstream criteria and instruments, a process carefully dissected and diagnosed by Gillies. These other schools, in the words of Weintraub (quoted by Gillies, 2012: 30), "are regarded by mainstream neoclassical economists as defenders of lost causes or as kooks, misguided critics, and antiscientific oddballs. The status of non-neoclassical economics in the economics departments in English-speaking universities is similar to that of flat-earthers in geography departments: it is safer to voice such opinions after one has tenure, if at all." Gillies (ibid.) refers to another Lucas observation: "at research seminars, people don't take Keynesian theorizing seriously any more, the audience starts to whisper and giggle to one another".[6] It leaves one wondering who and how many the gigglers were in the silence following the Queen's question. The silence lasted until July 2009 when two LSE professors, Tim Besley and Peter Hennessy, attempted an answer in a letter which is a fine example of deflection—no 'mea culpa' or munching of humble pie in evidence—and this induced annoyance and further letters to the Queen, prominently including one from a group of ten economists (including Sheila Dow, Geoff Harcourt and Geoffrey Hodgson) which effectively shredded the dissembling and side-stepping in the letter from the LSE professors, directly pointing the finger at the negative and profoundly damaging influences introduced into economics teaching and research by the mainstream orthodox tradition (Dow et al., 2009).[7] A second

---

[6] It is especially striking that this Lucas comment was apparently made in 1980, when Cambridge economics seemed to be flourishing and not under any immediate existential threat.

[7] "We believe that the narrow training of economists—which concentrates on mathematical techniques and the building of empirically uncontrolled formal models—has been a major reason for this failure in our profession. This defect is enhanced by the pursuit of mathematical technique for its own sake in many leading academic journals and departments of economics. There is a species of judgment, attainable through immersion in a literature or a history that cannot be adequately expressed in formal mathematical models. It's an essential part of a serious education in economics, but has been stripped out of most leading graduate programmes in economics in the world, including in the leading economics departments in the United Kingdom. Models and techniques are important. But given the complexity of the global economy, what is needed is a broader range of models and techniques governed by a far greater respect for substance, and much more attention to historical, institutional, psychological and other highly relevant factors" (Dow et al., 2009). The LSE had been in the forefront of the orthodox movement from the 1960s.

letter came from Thomas Palley, who took umbrage at Besley and Hennessy telling the Queen that the crisis had not been spotted due to what they had called a "failure of collective imagination". Palley (2009) warns the Queen: "that claim is tendentious and will mislead you". "The failure was due to the sociology of the economics profession. This failure was a long time in the making and was the product of the profession becoming increasingly arrogant, narrow, and closed minded. One was compelled to adhere to the dominant ideological construction of economics or face exclusion. That was the mindset of the IMF and the World Bank with their 'Washington Consensus', and it was the mindset of central bankers (including your own Bank of England) with their thinking about the sufficiency of inflation targeting and hostility to regulation." And Palley provides another correction: "the crisis was predictable and was predicted"; he provides the Queen with a reading list, and of the three papers cited, kindly with URL links, two are from the Levy Institute, dating from April and June 2006, being Godley and Zezza (2006), and Palley (2006). "Professors Besley and Hennessy's letter is another example of the economics profession's complete inability to come to grips with its sociological failure which produced massive intellectual failure with huge costs for society ... we will all continue to pay the costs as long as it is unaddressed" (Palley, 2009). There was enough in these letters perhaps to make the Queen wonder if she had done the right thing in opening another facility at LSE instead of closing one down. Embarrassingly, the neoclassical mainstream emperors of the profession had lined up naked to welcome the Queen, and there was no fig tree in sight.

Damage limitation followed the denial and dissembling. With alacrity, a round table was organised at a British Academy Forum "to provide the basis of an 'unofficial command paper' that attempted to answer this question" and a summary of the discussion was communicated by Besley and Hennessy (2009) to the Queen on July 2009. This summary—as suggested above—is remarkable for its dissembling, deflections and questionable conclusions and consensus at the discussion between a large mixed group including many of those in the dock. A second Forum was convened on 15 December 2009 with the purpose of considering means for 'financial and economic horizon-scanning'—a kind of 'land ahoy', or more 'storm ahoy' capacity; so follows another missive from the LSE duo to the monarch, though this time the bottom line is not so promising as earlier. "To be candid, Your Majesty, your Ministerial servants were seen by some as an extra cause of anxiety. It was often very hard to persuade them to become properly involved in horizon-scanning. Some found it too gloomy; others saw the contingencies covered to be too remote ... not all were keen to devote time to these ... attracting and retaining their attention ... remains a perennial problem. Nobody volunteered either individually or institutionally to lead this task and there was scepticism. ... So, we end with a modest proposal. If you, Your Majesty, were to ask for a monthly economic and financial horizon-scanning summary from, say, the Cabinet Office, it could hardly be refused. It might take a form comparable to the Joint Intelligence

Committee's 'Red Book', which you received each week from 1952 until 2008 when it was abandoned. And, if this were to happen, the spirit of your LSE question would suffuse still more those of your Crown servants tasked to defend, preserve and enhance the economic well-being of your country" (Besley & Hennessy, 2010). Many might think that the professors were barking up the wrong tree, or playing the old game of passing the buck. The show was more a naive exercise in attention seeking gone astray.

14.5 Students Speak Up

In making a case for pluralism in the teaching of economics, Alan Freeman pronounces on mainstream economics:

> 'Economics' ... is an institution. It is a material entity, sustained by an unholy combination of state, academic, and financial sources, which employs upwards of 50,000 diligent intellectuals worldwide, principally in occupations in which job security consists ... of toeing the line. The principal function of this institution is to provide justifications for the policies that its financiers wish to implement. However, it has a secondary function which is to set limits on the imprudent social consequences of an over-enthusiastic implementation of these same policies. The institution has a residual instinct for survival, however suicidal its recommendations have been for some time. The question is whether this instinct will be sufficient to offer some kind of resistance to the abusive practices its patrons have successfully imposed upon it. The prospects are not bright. ... However, the line itself is drawn by material forces. Even those who finance the institution of economics are keenly aware of their love child's limitations and, like all good risk-taking capitalists, recognise the need for a plan B. (Freeman, 2020: 26)

Drawing a parallel with the practice of health and medicine, Freeman treats pluralism in teaching as a right of the learner, equivalent to the right to a second opinion; and the responsibility and obligation of the teacher. "Teaching and learning can then be organised around the principle that the economist, analogously with the health practitioner, has a duty to reduce the risk of harm" (ibid.: 13).

14.5.1 In Cambridge

But in Cambridge after the mid-1980s, plurality and choice were getting scarce if not invisible and there was a lock-in without much meaningful choice of alternative perspectives on the subject, and no second opinions. While the purged and scattered branches of the various unwanted heterodox lineages had taken root and begun to flourish at the periphery, there were troubles at the core in the House of Hahn, at the dipped-in-the-Ganges Faculty of purified orthodox economics. Part of ritual of sanskritisation was the acquisition and bearing of mathematical stripes on the forehead, and this precondition for graduate entry effectively ruled out applicants from most other disciplines and worldly intellectual curiosities. It turned out that their students didn't much care to be thus theoretically and methodologically excluded and limited. Dissatisfaction in the ranks began to bubble and boil over the brim. In June 2001, 27 PhD scholars of the Faculty of Economics took the courageous step to write an Open Letter of Protest demanding a more open and inclusive pedagogical approach to research methodology about the pedagogical approach of the Faculty of Economics and Politics in Cambridge, then as now, firmly under the monopolistic authority of the orthodox mainstream that had carried the mathematisation and econometrification revolutions to Cambridge. The tenor of the letter was far less confrontational than its content and import. The heart of the trouble was that people did not want to be fiddling and faffing with general equilibrium fairy tales and games while real economies were up in flames in multiple crises. They wanted to understand, analyse and respond—but had found that the neoclassical larder was, as ever, entirely bare and had little remotely sensible to offer in return (Appendix).

The Cambridge protest was significant: the Letter of Protest went viral—judged in contemporary terms—and the list of signatories spiralled to 797 before it was closed, a significant number of them being staff, including a raft of professors and many heads of department and directors of institutes from UK universities and beyond (Cambridge Graduate Students, 2001). There was notable support from Cambridge heterodox economists, signing from the various spots to which they had scattered; but there was no signatory at all, needless to say, from the Faculty of Economics and Politics, where, the Chairman of the Faculty Board was none other than Hahn's faithful lieutenant and local inheritor of his mantle, Partha Dasgupta, while David Newbery was still the Director the DAE. Newbery was not a signatory either, though there were many ex-DAE research staff who were, including one Wynne Godley. Ajit Singh was still on the Faculty, one of the few remaining survivors of the culling of the heterodox apostates, and one wonders if the protesting students learnt about earlier such episodes in the Faculty, with the difference that the Faculty and its Board, with Ajit (and, then, Bob Rowthorn) in the lead, were then standing four-square behind the students' demands for better pedagogical practices.[8]

14.5.2 Elsewhere

Marc Lavoie (2015: 1) draws attention to an earlier momentous protest:

---

[8] An example of this is provided by Backhouse (1996: 46) with respect to the MPhil Economics as a formal route to entering the PhD: "Cambridge followed this pattern only a decade later [after Bristol, Essex and other departments] with the establishment, in the mid-1970s, of its M.Phil. there was a compulsory theory paper right from the start, but divisions among the economists meant that there was no common core. Students might take neoclassical micro theory with Hahn, or they could opt for a less orthodox, left-wing alternative taught by an economist such as. Bob Rowthorn. It is only recently that a master's by coursework has become a prerequisite for Ph.D. registration."

In 2000, in downtown Paris, a group of students from the École Normale SupÉrieure, one of France's Élite schools, wrote a petition asking economics teaching to be devoted to the study of real-world problems, with an instrumental use of mathematics rather than to the description of imaginary worlds based on meaningless formalizations. The students also asked for a greater amount of pluralism in the way economics was being approached. They claimed that they no longer wanted to have 'an autistic science' being imposed upon them, as a result of which the group got called the post-autistic movement in economics. The petition made a big splash at the time, with a few other student groups internationally making the same complaint. A large number of university professors supported the student demands. An inquiry was called by the French minister of Education, led by no less an economist than Jean-Paul Fitoussi, and in England the French movement induced the creation of the 'post-autistic economics newsletter', run by Edward Fullbrook ... which eventually became the *Real-world Economics Review* with the constitution of a World Economics Association, along with a couple of sister electronic journals.

Following the Cambridge protest in 2001, there were others, including the PEPS-Economie—(For a Pluralist Teaching in Economics)—in 2010, "which was at the origin of the manifesto endorsed by more than 60 student organizations throughout the world. This was the May 2014 International Student Initiative for Pluralism in Economics (ISIPE 2014), which called for a triple kind of pluralism: pluralism in methods, pluralism in schools of thought and an integration of other sciences or social sciences—disciplinary pluralism" (Lavoie, 2015: 2); and the Rethinking Economics Group originating from Germany in 2012 which spread to other parts of Europe and to the rest of the world. Thomas Piketty joined in:

> To put it bluntly, the discipline of economics has yet to get over its childish passion for mathematics and for purely theoretical and often highly ideological speculation, at the expense of historical research and collaboration with the other social sciences. Economists are all too often preoccupied with petty mathematical problems of interest only to themselves. This obsession with mathematics is an easy way of acquiring the appearance of scientificity without having to answer the far more complex questions posed by the world we live in. (Piketty, 2014: 32, quoted by Lavoie, 2015: 2–3)

14.6   Faculty Performance: A Summary Report Card

Student assessments of teachers usually don't count for much, and are generally brushed aside, except when students quietly nail them up on the noticeboards, or write them up collectively as in the Cambridge students' letter of protest. What does impact on reputations and resources are the so-called objective metrics of 'quality' and 'performance', variously gauged by external agencies which compare subjects/departments across universities and countries. The RAEs and the REFs within the UK, and the global ranking lists by subject, are generally used for drawing comparisons. Indeed, the Hahn group had made instrumental use of such metrics, using variables they had themselves devised, in their strategy to reorient the Faculty away from heterodox economics. So there would be special interest in sneaking a peek at their own report cards. The relative positions of Cambridge submissions to three REF units of assessment are compared: economics; business and management studies; and development studies

14.6.1 *Global Ranks*

The QS World University Rankings offered not much joy, with Cambridge far from the top, and slipping rank besides. Following the other Cambridge, flattery by imitation, but not successful enough to have a seat at the top table. A comparison of world rankings of three relevant subject areas provides one, now widely used, type of 'reputational' snapshot, howsoever rough and arbitrary it might well be—though it is unlikely to militate especially for or against any particular subject area. Indeed, some of the University-wide indicators would be common to all three, so perhaps the differences in ranks could well understate subject-specific differences between the three Cambridge units.

Table 14.1 tells a simple story: the two subject groups effectively expelled from the erstwhile Faculty of Economics and Politics have better ranks than Economics, and further, their ranks have improved over the period, whereas that of Economics has slid a couple of notches; in 2018, Development Studies is ranked in fifth place, Business Studies in seventh place, and Economics in eleventh place. Business Studies and Development Studies are relatively better at what they do than is Economics at what it does, and the distance between them has widened; and further, Economics performs relatively worse when comparing the different unit ranks with those for Cambridge social sciences or the University as a whole. Yes, one can hear a murmur: 'aren't you comparing apples and oranges'; the answer simply is that the orange growers are growing better quality oranges than the apple growers, whose apples are relatively inferior in quality on the 'apple' scale. Business Studies and Development Studies might have won a bronze each in their respective events, but Economics hasn't made it to the podium in its own event. No bragging rights then for the sanskritised Faculty of Economics on this count.

14.6.2 *RAEs, REFs*

The RAE report card wasn't one to crow about either. Relevant comparative data are summarised in Chap. 13, Table 13.5, and the information for the REF-2014 is extracted below for two Units of Assessment in the REF, viz., Economics & Econometrics (E&E) and Business & Management Studies (BMS). In 2014, there were three broad criteria: 'output', 'impact' and 'environment'—generating an 'overall' score. On this basis, in 2014, E&E ranks

Table 14.1 QS global ranks of selected Cambridge units, 2013–2019

Category →	Economics and Econometrics	Business and Management Studies	Development Studies	Politics and International Studies	Sociology	Social Sciences	Cambridge University
YEAR							
2013	9	n/a	n/a				
2014	10	n/a	n/a				
2015	9	13	8				
2016	10	7	6	5	8	4	4
2017	11	8	4	5	8	4	4
2018	11	7	5	6	6	4	5
2019	10	7	5	5	6	6	6
2020	10	8	5	6	6	5	7
Four-year average rank 2016–2019	10.5	7.25	5.0	5.25	7.0	4.5	4.75
Five-year average rank 2016–2020	10.4	7.4	5.0	5.4	6.6	4.6	5.2

Source: QS Global University Rankings Website, various years.

2nd on output, 6th on impact and 4th overall, amongst all units in its category; in comparison, BMS ranks 6th, 1st and 2nd, respectively, within its own category.[9]

"In last year's Research Excellence Framework the Faculty performed very well in terms of the world-class quality of its research output, but the number of its researchers was substantially fewer than were entered by the other universities at the top of the British league table. This matters not only in terms of research; it matters for research training" (Brown & Cockerill, 2015: 2). Twenty-five years down the line from 1989 when Hahn-Matthews-Dasgupta used the RAE broom to start sweeping out 'mediocrity', it is difficult to cite heterodoxy as a reason for being ranked fourth overall and sixth on 'impact' in the UK; the comparison with the relatively new domain of Business and Management Studies, an amalgam of specialist and heterodox identities, is telling.

14.7 Exiles and Reincarnations

What happened then, the day after, when Frank Hahn, Robin Matthews and their adjutant Partha Dasgupta, had cleared out, in their terminology, the "cesspool" of heterodox economics, various "vaguely cognate disciplines", and all mediocrity resembling "a failed Court of early Modern times", performed the necessary ablutions, conducted the prescribed sanskritisation rituals and restored the pristine Brahmanical purity of neoclassicism—from Marshallian partial analysis to Walrasian general equilibrium (with money). What happened to all that filth shovelled out—did it get flushed down the pipes, into the oceans and feed seaweed? The old village clearly contained a lot of impure castes, whether as groups or individuals. For any historian of the subaltern, it is a pertinent, even compulsory, question: what was the fate of the purged, where did they all go? Perhaps they introspected, pleaded guilty as charged, gave up economics and retrained?

---

[9] 'Business and Management Studies' was Unit of Assessment 19 while Economics and Econometrics was UoA 18. In this comparison, a general assumption is being made that—given the intellectual and disciplinary affinities between the JBS offerings and the CBR—the scores for UoA-19 could be used as a rough quality proxy for CBR staff as well, though CBR staff made submissions from several UoAs (including a couple also from B&MS); there was a strong overlap in the research themes mentioned by the JBS research staff and those for CBR. The comparison should be interpreted as reflecting Economics relative to B&MS as UoAs, and not a direct comparison of Economics with CBR staff. It could well be argued that CBR staff—if taken as a group in their own right—might have scored better than the overall B&MS UoA given their excellent record of publications (output), or fund-raising (environment), or policy interactions (impact). The high performance of CBR over the years would tend to support such a broad, though speculative, reading.

14.7.1 The DAE Flagships: CGP and CEPG

Consider the two macroeconomic modelling flagship units: the famous Growth Project, and the equally in/famous Economic Policy Group. The first to be shown out in 1982 was the Cambridge Economic Policy Group of Wynne Godley and Francis Cripps. Next in line to be shut down, in 1987, was the Cambridge Growth Project team headed, after Richard Stone's retirement in 1980, by Terry Barker. For both teams, each comprising about ten research staff, there are two questions to ask: what happened to the researchers? And, what happened to those terrible macroeconomic models of theirs; were the equations dismantled, variables untangled, the raw data on a compost heap, recycled? In reality, as noted, both initiatives were reconstituted in new forms elsewhere, and have had highly productive lives thereafter, making some marked contributions to the policy-oriented analysis of key global issues, including real-financial economy imbalances, and climate change issues. A striking feature of the charged and often confused public debates in Britain over the Brexit decision has been the paucity of reliable empirical analysis that provided some reasonably reliable simulations of alternative scenarios at international, national and regional levels; and then also by different sectors of the economy; for the likely impact on employment also by region; it cannot be gainsaid that this kind of research with an immediate and critical public purpose had been the central preoccupations of the two macroeconomic teams of the DAE. But these had been silenced, and thus when the financial crisis broke, or when key environmental issues had to be analysed quantitatively, or when the spectre of Brexit arose, there was indeed generally silence from Faculty economics. Not just the macroeconomic teams, but the DAE itself had long gone. Notably, these units, in their new incarnations, persisted, as for instance the work of Wynne Godley and his co-researchers on the rising threat of financial meltdowns, and of Terry Barker and his team on climate change.

Here, it is appropriate to emphasise the influence of Cambridge post-Keynesian economics, including the SFC approach on ecological macroeconomics. Marc Lavoie (2022, forthcoming, Chap. 9) demonstrates this in a wide-ranging analytical survey of this very active theoretical and methodological interface, pointing out that "the main *macro-econometric* models dealing with energy use, materials consumption and greenhouse gas emissions are post-Keynesian in approach. Of particular interest is the E3MG (E3 Model at the Global level) run by Cambridge Econometrics, and developed by the Cambridge Centre for Climate Change Mitigation Research (4CMR), sited at the Department of Land Economy, where Philip Arestis and John McCombie are located. E3MG arose from the work of Terry Barker within the Department of Applied Economics, as part of the Cambridge Growth Project (CGP) launched by Richard Stone, a purpose of which was to create an alternative to computable general equilibrium based on SAM. The post-Keynesian pedigree of E3MG is no surprise since the other research group at the Department of Applied Economics was the Cambridge Economic Policy Group with Wynne

Godley at its helm, as previously noted." Complementing this is Servaas Storm's rigorously argued policy mapping of the debates and the alternatives, the dead ends, cul-de-sacs and possible ways ahead in addressing the crisis of climate change. "Climate change is a quintessential 'global public bad', because the incremental impact of one ton of GHG on climate change is independent of where in the world it is emitted. Hence, warming can only be stopped by *global collective action* to prevent leakage and free riding" (Storm, 2009). There are sweeping policy imperatives: "This means a much broader agenda for the climate movement (going beyond carbon trading and technocratic discussion of mitigation options). What is needed for climate stability is a systemic transformation based on growth scepticism, a planned transition to a non-fossil fuel economy, democratic reform, climate justice, and changed global knowledge and corporate and financial power structures" (ibid.). These structural theoretical, applied and policy approaches stand in virtually diametric opposition to orthodox diagnoses and prescriptions. That these heterodox approaches survived and revived after the mainstream onslaught confirms the dedication of their researchers on the one side, while testifying to the continued, indeed dramatically increased, relevance of their work in addressing the rampant multiple crises for which much culpability attaches to the practitioners of mainstream economics.

14.7.2 DAE Industrial Economics: Alan Hughes and the CBR

Attention shifts then to the work within the DAE on industrial economics where Ajit had made major contributions, and where his younger co-researcher Alan Hughes had created the Centre for Business Research (CBR), while he retained a lectureship in the Faculty. The CBR, and its pilot Alan Hughes, were flying high: even while nominally a lecturer in the Faculty, Alan held a professorial salary as Director of the ESRC-funded CBR, and in 1998 he won the open competition, outside the Faculty, for the newly created Margaret Thatcher Professorship, with the CBR thereafter shifting base to the new Judge Business School. The CBR has flourished and has established a high reputation on the global stage.

14.7.3 Judge Business School

The arrival of the Judge Business School (JBS) provided a second congenial space, adding to the open institutional camping site provided by the Department of Land Economy to the migration of Development teaching from the Faculty of Economics. For Development, the arrangement with Land Economy was an interim expedient, a temporary marriage of institutional convenience. For instance, Land Economy with its association with the management of landed estates could hardly resonate with the economic and political issues of productive and redistributive land reforms in the Third World; and Development was a lot more besides. In contrast, the JBS provided an institutionally stable and permanent space for several lines of theoretical and applied economics, and these interlocked naturally with the academic mandate and intellectual research and teaching agendas within the JBS. Of course, the main macroeconomic modelling units of the DAE had been suppressed in the orthodox campaign, but there was a good deal more applied economics and political economy research, both inside the DAE but also the Faculty that still remained after the dust settled on the DAE Review and the change of guard and directorship at the DAE. For the controlling orthodox group, most of these heterodox economists were, to different degrees, unwanted, and the message was conveyed in a variety of forms, both direct and indirect. Approximately over the period 1999–2010, there was a regular flow of relocations of heterodox and/or applied economics groups to the JBS, including to newly established chairs in JBS.

The University of Cambridge Judge Business School started life in 1990 as the Judge Institute of Management Studies (JIMS) on the strength of an endowment of 8 million pounds from Paul Rupert Judge, an alumnus of Trinity College, and later a Director-General of the Conservative Party; he was knighted in 1996. The first director, Stephen Watson, played a crucial role in the foundation of JBS. Leading the process of extricating Management from Engineering and obtaining the core foundation funding from Paul Judge. The Judge, and Monument Trust, donations enabled the construction of the building for JIMS which was officially opened by Queen Elizabeth II in 1995 when Sandra Dawson took over as the Director of JIMS till 2006. In 2005, JIMS was renamed the Judge Business School (JBS); then in November 2010 it became the Cambridge Judge Business School, and finally to dispel any doubts about its official standing, it was named the University of Cambridge Judge Business School.

Building on Stephen Watson's pioneering role, Sandra Dawson made a huge contribution to the development of JBS during her tenure (from 1995 to 2006), the crucial formative years of the JBS. Videler (2011) picks up some insights from a talk given by Sandra Dawson on leadership: "you don't need a strict plan to stick to but take opportunities that come along"; "always assume a solution can be found and work to find it"; "a lot of decision making and getting things to happen come through committees and boards—learn how these work"; and "don't get too 'tram-tracked'—explore the relationships and interfaces between subjects"; the REF obliges academics "to tunnel their interests while they get established because of the overriding importance attached to REF, publications, etc. which she thought was a shame as she had enjoyed an 'eclectic' start to her research career". These tips seem to demarcate a personal philosophy and intellectual orientation to the development of academic institutions that in some crucial ways could appear as a mirror opposite of the general manifest in the purifying Faculty of Economics with its uncompromising and exclusionary focus on mainstream economics. It is also possible to see all these ingredients coming together in the manner in which, during her tenure, the JBS evolved as a welcoming, fluid and dynamic space for absorbing various initiatives emanating from the loose network of Cambridge heterodox economists who, for diverse reasons, migrated from their original location in the DAE and the Faculty of Economics to the JBS where they developed a mutually productive presence, as exemplified by Alan Hughes's Centre for Business Research, and the Cambridge Endowment for Research on Finance which underwrote a variety of teaching and research initiatives at JBS.

Peter Nolan perhaps served as the pathfinder. Much respected internationally (and within China) as a wide-ranging and deeply knowledgeable sinologist and development expert, he was sensitive to the orthodox pressure to leave the Faculty, did not overstay his welcome and in 1997 shifted to a prestigious position, becoming the Sin Yi Professorship in Chinese Studies, and later the Chong Hwa Professor of Chinese Studies at Judge Business School. At CERF (within JBS) he set up a very successful programme for business leaders and researchers drawn from the top echelons of the Chinese government and corporate sectors under the aegis of the Chinese Executive Leadership Programme (CELP). Peter has researched and published extensively tracking the trajectories of China's economy and their complex implications at the global level. Peter left for the JBS in the mid-1990s; he also served later as the Chair of the Development Studies Committee, and then as the Director of the Centre for Development Studies (CDS) when it was formed in 2012 (within the Department of Politics and International Studies, POLIS), and which quickly became the thriving space for development economics and development studies in the University. In teaching, a collaboration emerged between JBS and CDS in the form of the MPhil in Development Studies. Additionally, the development niche in JBS also was enlarged through the presence of Ajit Singh, renowned (also) as a development specialist, in the JBS after his retirement in 2007.

The main linkage from Economics to JBS, however, has taken the form of the relocation of the flourishing CBR of Alan Hughes from the DAE to the Judge Business School, following on from his appointment in 1999 to the new Margaret Thatcher Chair of Enterprise Studies to be held at JBS and the subsequent success of a joint JBS-CBR bid to obtain a million pounds in external funding to complete the construction of the top floor of the JBS building as purpose-built research accommodation into which the CBR could move from its original home in the DAE. 1999 was also the year when Sandra Dawson was appointed the (first female) Master of Sidney Sussex, a position she held till 2009; she also served later as a Deputy Vice Chancellor of the University and was created a Dame Commander of the Order of the British Empire DBE in 2004.

Sidney Sussex College was also, coincidentally, Alan Hughes's academic home, where he had held an official fellowship from 1973, being made Life Fellow in 2013. In Alan's own words: "I held the Margaret Thatcher Chair of Enterprise Studies at the Judge Business School Cambridge from 1999–2013. I held this Chair simultaneously with the Directorship of the Centre for Business Research (CBR). I was Director of the CBR from its establishment as a University Department in 1994 to 2013. The CBR is an interdisciplinary centre of excellence. It brings together economists, engineers, geographers, lawyers, management scientists and sociologists to study the determinants of the organisation and competitive success of nations, industries and enterprises. In 2013 I was appointed to a Life Fellowship at Sidney Sussex College, Cambridge. As Director of the CBR I had overall responsibility for the direction of the Centre's research programme which involved management of a research budget of £900k per year, around a dozen equivalent research and administrative staff and 40 research associates worldwide. I was from 2004–2013 a member of the UK Prime Minister's Council for Science and Technology (CST), the UK government's top-level advisory body on science and technology policy issues. From 2009 to 2013 I was also Director of the UK Innovation Research Centre (UK-IRC), a joint venture between the CBR and Imperial College Business School" (Personal communication; extract from Alan Hughes's *Curriculum Vitae*). He is currently Professor of Innovation at Imperial College Business School and Distinguished Visiting Professor at Lancaster University. The CBR has been a flourishing enterprise and built an enviable stature as a top echelon applied research unit on industrial and corporate themes; the reputation, rooted in the industrial economics research conducted by successive research teams inside the DAE from the 1960s through the 1980s, has been sustained under the directorship of Simon Deakin—a top drawer legal expert straddling corporate, finance and labour concerns—who took over the reins of CBR after Alan Hughes retired in 2013. Alan Hughes singled out the supportive role played by Sandra Dawson, Director of the JBS, during the 1995–2006 period which saw the development of significant interconnections between JBS and heterodox economics and economists.

Apart from the CBR, the JBS also housed the newly created unit of the Cambridge Endowment for Research on Finance (CERF), set up with external funds donated by William and Weslie Janeway; it was run by John Eatwell, Professor at CERF/JBS, but for whose theoretical economics[10]—in several heterodox lineages—there was no room in the purified Faculty, where his lectureship in macroeconomics was reportedly replaced by one in game theory. CBR and CERF were host to a wide range of teaching and research degree programmes, as well as research that has made a significant impact on the study of finance in relation to the real economy; and its long-stay members have included the rejuvenated Wynne Godley, his young co-researcher Alex Izurieta,[11] and of course, Ajit Singh for whom JBS, with CBR and CERF, was

---

[10] See, for instance, his recent authoritative treatment on the fall and rise of Keynesian economics (Eatwell & Milgate, 2011).

[11] Alex Izurieta has served as Senior Researcher at the Cambridge Endowment for Research on Finance (CERF), University of Cambridge and Research Scholar at the Levy Economics Institute of Bard College, New York. He is presently a Senior Economist in the Division on Globalization and Development Strategies (GDS) of UNCTAD. His specialist expertise is on macroeconomic and global models for the evaluation of alternative policy models within ongoing global economic developments, seeking potentially better ways of doing things. His professional career was launched

a new research home after his retirement; Ajit was a Senior Research Fellow at JBS, and Director of Research (2007–2009) at CERF; Geoff Meeks moved from the Faculty to a Chair in Financial Accounting at JBS in 2003; and, over the years, several senior researchers from the old DAE and its research network moved productively to the JBS, viz., Peter Nolan, Alan Hughes, Frank Wilkinson, Ajit Singh, Michael Kitson, Andy Cosh, John Eatwell and Simon Deakin, and no doubt several others.

There can be little doubt that the institutionally and intellectually congenial space offered by the Judge Business School has been a critical factor in the survival and sustenance of various heterodox strands of economics that were otherwise expunged from the DAE and the Faculty of Economics as a result of the hostile campaign mounted by the group of orthodox economists.

14.7.4 The Economic Historians

What, then, came of the economic historians at the DAE who had done all that painstaking work statistically recording and analysing the industrialisation of Britain, did they lengthen the time horizon, stretch the breadth of vision at the Faculty—did they deservedly acquire to stellar status and progress to honourable careers in the Faculty? No, would have to be the single syllable answer. The initial investment in historical statistics and related economic history faded at the DAE and yielded rapidly to more immediate policy-oriented applied research focussing primarily on the post-War period, looking ahead, speculatively, rather than back, definitively. There was no tenure at DAE, so some of the economic historians shifted, in single file, to positions in the Faculty; those who couldn't, went to fellowships in the colleges or to high positions in other universities. But few who did enter the Faculty quickly, or rather slowly, discovered that the higher echelons of that wing of the building were closed off to them; promotions were well-nigh impossible, projected waiting times would need to be reckoned in decades, not years. And so after varying experiences of

---

from his pathbreaking PhD obtained in 2000 at the International Institute of Social Studies, The Hague, titled *Crowding-out or Bailing-out? Fiscal Deficits and Private Wealth in Ecuador, 1971–99*. From there he went to work with Wynne Godley, Francis Cripps, Ajit Singh for many years, focussing on comprehensive analyses of aspects of global imbalances (Cripps et al., 2011) using the Global UN Policy Model (Cripps & Izurieta, 2014) and on key global policy issues, such as the implications of the fast growth of China and India for the US and global economy (Izurieta & Singh, 2010), work still ongoing with Francis and others. Recently, in one of his interventions on the utility of UNCTAD's demand-side Global Policy Model and futility of the global macroeconomic models produced by the IMF, the OECD and the European Commission, he offers a sobering reflection on the costs of getting it wrong: "It is a truism of modern times that when an enterprise fails, it pays all it can and goes bankrupt. Large financial institutions are exceptions to this rule but that is well known and widely critiqued. Less discussed is the fact that when an economic model fails, it is reality that pays the bills while the model remains unscathed—especially if it carries the stamp of an influential international organization" (Izurieta, 2017). He has been deeply entrenched in the macroeconomic and global modelling research in the Cambridge tradition.

frustration, freely expressed or stoically suppressed, these few also moved on to pursue more fulfilling careers elsewhere; Charles Feinstein left in 1978 to become a professor at York, then as reader to Oxford before occupying the Chichele Chair there; the unsung Phyllis Deane, who stayed the course in Cambridge, was indeed granted a professorship (but only in 1981), a parting smile guiltily flashed virtually at the end of time, a year prior to her retirement (in 1982). The Faculty, then still solidly influenced by the heterodox radical and left groups, did make an inspired appointment in Jane Humphries in 1980, whose shoulders in time would carry her much respected and admired supervisor and Newnham colleague Phyllis Deane's mantle, to be passed on to her own accomplished student Sara Horrell; she built an exceptional reputation in her long stint in Cambridge, becoming a reader eventually in 1995[12]. By then, times had changed, not for the better, under the new regime; if earlier there might have been collegial benign neglect, with the new orthodox gang this was replaced by perceived malign sentiment; Jane Humphries upped sticks in 1998 and pitched her tent afresh in the more congenial terrain of Oxford historians, where she has held a professorship since 2004, heads the department, is a Fellow of the British Academy, lately a CBE, a Centennial Professor at the London School of Economics. And with the recent departures of Sheilagh Ogilvie to the Chichele professorship in Oxford, and of Sara Horrell, again to a professorship at LSE, economic history within the body of the Faculty, as earlier in the DAE, is well on its way to becoming history.

14.7.5 Sociology: That 'Vaguely Cognate Discipline'

Sociology found a new home in an independent department; the heterodox group of economists, down to the last, had been strongly in favour of keeping the partnership going within the DAE and the Faculty, but not the Hahn-Matthews-Dasgupta-Newbery Gang-of-Four which had wanted these 'anomalies', 'relics' of times past, 'vaguely cognate disciplines' out. And so they went, following their leader who was one Tony Giddens who had been a lecturer in the Faculty who felt that the new discipline "was sneered at"; just a few years ahead he was a full professor, had founded Polity Press (and kept its wheels rolling almost by his books), and now is the most widely read sociologist on the planet.

14.7.6 Development

Then there is the case of Development which, paradoxically, was steadily eased out from precisely the period that it became profoundly important on a global scale. The vicissitudes in the life of Development and Development Studies within the Faculty have been recounted earlier, ending with the outright

---

[12] She was apparently only the third female reader in the history of the Faculty, the others being no less than Joan Robinson in 1956, and Phyllis Deane in 1971.

shifting of the enterprise, with its courses and degrees and all, outside the Faculty. Development, inherently a heterodox field, was effectively excised from the Tripos, with its leading, and renowned, practitioners shifting out, or languishing in disempowered spaces within the Faculty. Jose Gabriel Palma, one of the most highly regarded economists of Latin America, hit a hard promotional ceiling at the level of senior lecturer; he was also unable to lecture on development in the Tripos, and assigned duties to teach econometrics, while remaining remarkably productive in his widely cited research on Latin American issues, and on inequality, where his 'Palma Ratio' has recently entered the lexicon of inequality measures; John Sender departed from Cambridge and was welcomed in London as Professor at the School of Oriental and African Studies, London; another rising Latin Americanist, John Wells, felt so hounded that he resigned his lectureship—and took his own life the same year under difficult personal and professional circumstances. That brings one to the last surviving member of the development and heterodox clan surviving in the Faculty: Ha-Joon Chang.[13] Development regrouped at the now flourishing Centre for Development Studies, and Ha-Joon took over from Peter Nolan after the latter's long stint as Director. Again, Development Studies as a subject unit performs better in its domain than does Economics in its area; but it remains of course, low caste. Ha-Joon, at present one of the most widely read and cited authors in development economics, is a severe critic of the neoclassical and neoliberal traditions that have captured and distorted development theory and policy, and his pedagogically lucid books are now universal currency in the field, inoculating fresh young minds entering social science against dangerous intellectual fundamentalisms. His books are regularly translated into several languages[14] and he is listed often as a leading world thinker today. Could it be for these attributes that he had his application for an *ad hominem* promotion to a Readership declined six years in a row, with an appeal in each of those years, also rejected? Perhaps he is a true Gandhian; perhaps he was taking soundings of the depths to which matters could sink; but then, on the seventh—and last permissible—time of asking, he became a Reader, when he could probably just ask for a chair, if not a sofa, at most Ivy League universities. His is the last toe-hold of heterodox economics in the Faculty, quantitatively amounting to 0.2 FTE.

---

[13] This paragraph is shared with Chap. 11.
[14] Kicking Away the Ladder: Development Strategy in Historical Perspective (2002) was translated into 9 languages; Reclaiming Development—An Alternative Economic Manual (2004) obviously did extremely poorly, being translated into only 5 languages; Bad Samaritans—Rich Nations, Poor Policies, and the Threat to the Developing World (2007) went into 15 languages; and 23 Things They Don't Tell You About Capitalism (2010) generated much-needed employment in the translation industry, going into 33 languages; things have gone really downhill after that, since Economics: The User's Guide (2014) can be read in only 14 languages.

14.8 Reluctant Regrets

What is new and striking though, is how some of the leading lights of the orthodox clan come to look back and reflect on consequences of their victory and the subsequent purges they unleashed against virtually any and all heterodox apostasy and apostates. There are fleeting glimpses, if not of remorse and regret, of partial recognition and acceptance that their triumph, and subsequent vindictive retributions, had only gone on to highlight the utter inadequacy of the neoclassical camp to acknowledge, let alone address, the screaming problems that 'free-market' globalisation had unleashed or intensified.

Orthodox economics was a part of the problem, stood in the way of solutions, and virtually all but the orthodox economists themselves have long been acutely aware of this assessment; the avalanche of interconnected complex global crises has rightly intensified frustration against the discipline in its contemporary mainstream incarnation, and the constant barrage of evidence-based criticism has perhaps begun to permeate the thickest of orthodox skins and skulls.

The obfuscating reply from the LSE professors to the Queen should perhaps be contrasted with the honest—but far too belated—self-critical lament of Tony Atkinson (another prime follower of the Frank Hahn general equilibrium tradition) shortly before he died, in which he confesses that they got it wrong, and that young entrants into the profession are now receiving narrow, counterproductive training which takes them away from the purposes of economics (Atkinson & Stern, 2017). Perhaps if he, and others of his tribe, had thought thus 35 years earlier, the discipline and possibly the world might have been somewhat better for it.

In the years of Keynes, or later, Hayek never changed his stance, but Lionel Robbins did, and explicitly acknowledged his conversion to the Keynesian doctrine, certainly for short-run macroeconomic management.

14.8.1 Robin Matthews

Geoff Harcourt (2017: 973, 973n7), friendly with Robin Matthews from across the Faculty battle lines, writes that "I use to tease Robin on the basis of his limited success in 'reforming' the Cambridge Faculty. ... In retrospect he came to think that the attempted reforms were misguided, to some extent anyway." In the obituary Harcourt (2010) wrote, he tells us that in his later years Robin Matthews had come to question his earlier orthodox faith: "As he ruefully was to admit, his attempts to reshape the ways in which that faction-benighted Faculty went about its business were not successful. Moreover, in retrospect, he felt that his aims in this regard were probably mistaken anyway and that his own comparative advantage lay much more with scholarship than with attempting to change administrative structures; ... his teaching, research and administrative duties over the years made him more and more aware of the inadequacies [in Matthews's own words] of 'the conventional model of rational individualistic utility maximisation [so that increasingly his] interests moved toward the institutional and psychological underpinnings of economic behaviour'."[15] It is difficult to see how faith in the Lucasian rational expectations framework could have survived even after the 2007 meltdown.

14.8.2 Frank Hahn

The high priest of the faith was Frank Hahn, of course, and the holy grail of orthodoxy was general equilibrium with money. That had been his passionate preoccupation after he had moved supervisors from Kaldor to Robbins, and then teamed up with his economist soulmate Terry Gorman at Birmingham. Mathematical maps were the key to finding the trail to the Grail. The world outside was forgotten in the ecstasy of the mission. Of those years, Hutchinson (in Tribe, 2002: 138) writes: "Alan Walters at least had an interest in the real world. I suppose Hahn and Gorman *thought* they had an interest in the real world, but they didn't realise it *wasn't the real world* up on the blackboard which they were manipulating so magnificently." What came of it? Partha Dasgupta (2013), in his insightful and personal obituary for Frank Hahn, remarks that "over time he saw less and less in the point of economics, even theoretical economics"; "Frank often said if had his life all over again he would have chosen to be a cosmologist. The subject's grandeur was a factor of course, but speculation over possible worlds attracted him; and if speculation could be disciplined with mathematical precision so as to meet the test of coherence, so very much the better. The beautiful, austere features of general equilibrium of economic systems drew him to their study." "The purpose of economic theory was to test the logical coherence of social thinking, or so he often said and occasionally wrote. In that attitude to theoretical musings he resided in Classical Greece and the centuries of the Talmud. When I once remarked to him that his sense of the purpose of theoretical discourse resembled that of logicians in Sanskritic India, he said so much the better for that lost world."

But what, apart from admiring this stark precision, coherence and beauty, could be done with this construction; what might be some social purposes to which it might be deployed? Or was it a self-contained exercise in intellectual aesthetics, replete in itself? Dasgupta continues: "his views on the uses to which economic theory could be put were unusual by contemporary standard. He was suspicious of computable general equilibrium models; simulation exercises weren't suggestive to him; and he couldn't but look astonished at attempts to put general equilibrium models to use in deriving practical policy. The purpose of economic theory was to test the logical coherence of social thinking."

How is this distance between his theoretical imagination, and his periodic passionate engagement with immediate policy issues—as for instance in the

---

[15] Geoff's assessment is that "he [Matthews] changed his mind and regretted much of what he had done, coming around to think that Ajit [Singh] was on the right track" (Personal communication, email dated 28 March 2019).

famous letter against monetarism—to be squared? Were these interventions in 'policy' not based in economic theory other than general equilibrium economics which he had himself ruled to be out of court for policy purposes? Yet, throughout his career he fought consistently and with all his intellectual and political resources to install his definition of pure theoretical economics in every corner of the discipline in terms of teaching and research, to the systematic exclusion of all other lineages of economic theorising that saw the social purposes of economic theory in a very different light. Was it an empty victory ending with a realisation of the futility of the endeavour?

14.8.3   David Newbery

David Newbery shares his realisation that "an increased awareness of the importance of institutions, laws and customs of society, informed by game theory and the recognition that agents interact over time under incomplete information, has made us more receptive to the other social sciences, leading to increased collaboration across subject boundaries" (Newbery, 1998: xxi). Could this be the same theorist who argued at length for the expulsion of sociology and sociologists from the Faculty of Economics and Politics in 1986 during the University Review of the DAE? Newbery finds it possible to reconcile these two positions: "problems of informational asymmetry and incompleteness were recognised by me and many economists I worked with, from Stiglitz and Akerlof in the late 1960s, and constituted a core motivation for the *Risk Project* under Hahn located in the DAE. ... The relevant social science was not at that time to be found among the sociologists in the faculty and DAE." This raises the question of the limited instrumental meaning that mainstream neoclassical economics might attach to this notional widening of the contours of 'economics' to interact with other social science disciplines. For instance, the recent turn in orthodoxy towards incorporating behavioural economics has been widely criticised by philosophers, sociologists, development and other heterodox economists; as has the tendency, especially following Schultz, to look for an utility optimisation choice framework for reductionist explanations of a wide range of social behaviour, customs and institutions (especially pertaining to gender issues), again a trend that has been widely questioned outside orthodoxy. There is also the issue that while the neoclassical economists might not have found joy in the kinds of sociology practised by the DAE or Faculty sociologists at the time, the presence and work of these groups was strongly and widely appreciated and endorsed by virtually all other DAE and Faculty economists with several of them working closely in interdisciplinary projects. Newbery's had referred to the sociologists as "stray colleagues in a vaguely cognate discipline"—but this pejorative ascription would not have been accepted by the heterodox groups in the DAE or the Faculty. Clearly, multidisciplinarity carries different meanings for the orthodox and heterodox lineages. That said, "the increased awareness" that Newbery refers to suggests a realisation that the subject as earlier delimited was wanting in critical respects, even by its own internal criteria.

14.8.4 Tony Atkinson

Shortly before he died, Tony Atkinson was interviewed by his old friend and colleague Nick Stern (Atkinson & Stern, 2017), and changes in the discipline are well captured anecdotally in this frank conversation between two reflective members of that lineage. Several insights can be elicited from this informative and illuminating interview.[16]

Atkinson provides clues to the unusual combination of influences that has framed his work: on the one hand, general equilibrium economics, and careful empirical applied economics on the other; and then a third, distributional concerns, which are usually not high on the priority list of the orthodox neoclassical. He speaks of the excitement radiated by Hahn as his Director of Studies at Churchill College—"he taught a wide range of fields, but the sort of general equilibrium approach I have to economics is very much how Frank thought". Then, he enthusiastically refers to the meticulous attention paid by Brian Reddaway whom he calls "a masterful applied economist". "From him, I learned about taking data seriously and asking, 'Where'd that number come from?' and 'Who actually wrote that number on a piece of paper?'". And Stern adds: Was it Brian that said, "Unless you've plotted the points on the graph paper yourselves, you don't really understand the data"? Atkinson's concern is amplified later in the interview when speaking of "the explosion of data and fancy data-handling techniques"; Atkinson refers to a comparative study: "we discovered that about half the difference in the recorded growth rates between the UK and the US was due to this difference in method"; Stern adds: "there was some fancy econometrics trying to bring all sorts of theories into that difference, when actually it was a data issue, which you could only understand if you got into the data". Atkinson agrees: yes, and it affected political perceptions. The US growth rates were faster in part because you made up the numbers differently (ibid.: 17–18). The third influence reflects his commitment to social justice, influenced by early readings of Peter Townsend and Abel-Smith, and James Meade's small 1964 book, *Efficiency, Equality and the Ownership of Property*. And this was the aspect came to dominate over time—this set the question that theory and data were meant to answer.

Most of Atkinson's early work was framed within a general equilibrium paradigm. He refers to his early joint book with Stiglitz on public economics and frankly admits: "First, a *mea culpa*, because Joe Stiglitz and I wrote this textbook on public economics (Atkinson & Stiglitz 1980), and in some ways, I think we probably set the wrong agenda. Because, under the influence of our

---

[16] The lengthy interview runs into 20 pages and traverses a wide range of issues dealing both with the content and profession of economics; in the selective collation used here, the focus is on Atkinson's (and Stern's) rethinking, looking over their shoulders into their experience.

early training, we were thinking of the starting point as being competitive general equilibrium, which, after all, was an innovation compared to, say, the old public finance literature, which was black-letter law and verbal reasoning. There was no formal theory, apart from a few notable exceptions, until Peter Diamond, Jim Mirrlees, and the rest of us began to take theory seriously in public economics. With a few exceptions, there wasn't any proper theoretical discussion. Arnold Harberger did good work on general equilibrium tax incentives; that was an innovation, but one that, in retrospect, gives rise to the attitude you've just described: You start with a world in which the government can only make things worse." Stern agrees: "It locked in a lot of the assumptions about perfectly functioning markets that should've been at the root of many discussions of policy itself" (ibid.: 13).

Atkinson continues: "as we say in our new introduction to [the second edition of] the book ... we wouldn't start from there, we'd start from a world in which there's monopolistic competition, imperfect information, search behaviour, and all sorts of things, taking account of what's happening in behavioural economics and several other things. I think that matters not just because each of them is important but because, when several of them are taken together, you then get to a very different position than if you just use one on its own" (ibid.: 13).

And then there is an acknowledgment of vacuums in the general equilibrium approach. Atkinson: "I think that economists have rediscovered institutions in some sense. But I think, in a way, it can also be put the other way around: They forgot about institutions." Stern confesses: "the testimony of theories of search behaviour and of institutions, which have no content in a perfectly competitive perfectly functioning world, have increasing centrality to understanding how badly we got it wrong before". Atkinson joins in: "Yes. I can remember the lecture given by Jacques Dreze, called 'the firm in general equilibrium theory'. He said, 'How do you get the firm into general equilibrium theory? Well, you blow up a paper bag, and then you puncture it.' And so you let all the air out. The firm has no real existence" (ibid.: 14).

Then comes another joint confession; this time with regard to the role of the state.

> *Stern*: The period of the 1980s into the mid-1990s was rather peculiar in our subject; at least I hope it was peculiar.
> *Atkinson*: It was, yes. I think we took a wrong turn.
> *Stern:* And you wrote about that at the time.
> *Atkinson*: Yes. It fell on deaf ears, largely.
> *Stern:* Yes, I tried, too, but with the same result.
> *Atkinson*: I think it happened to a different extent in different areas, but I think it affected most areas. It affected development economics as well, it felt like.
> *Stern:* Yes, it did. There was a notion that governments trying to do things would just create problems, and the most beneficent government was the one that got out of the way. And markets would work very well, provided governments didn't interfere. (ibid.: 13)

The exchange finally shifts to the key question of the reproduction of the profession. "Are we really helping create the all-around economist in a way that, perhaps, came more naturally earlier?" They highlight four concerns: over specialisation leading to fragmentation; a loss of capability in dealing properly with data; the pressure and incentivisation to publish, and particularly in top theory journals; and being pushed off their preferred course by the demands of employability in the profession.

> *Atkinson*: When you and I were students, we could actually read the major journals—there were probably, at most, a dozen—and one could at least cast one's eye down and see what was going on. They were all a lot less fat than they are today, too....
> The subject is partly the victim of its success. The profession is so much bigger, and there's so much more research going on. But I think this has come at a cost. We have become too specialized, and people define themselves as being specialized economists, whereas I just think of myself as an economist. Now, if you meet people, they'll say, 'I'm a labour economist', or, 'I'm an IO [industrial organization] economist', as if they belong to that tribe. I think that's fine, but of course you then get seminars taking place on labour economics, which actually would've benefited enormously from the seminar on industrial organization that happened at the same time. And people just don't talk to each other, and I think that's a loss; at least all my cohorts had an appreciation of what was going on elsewhere.
> *Stern*: So, behavioural economics and institutional economics [took] us beyond the narrowness of the 1980s in ways that really matter. Another huge advance that has occurred in the time that we've been economists, is the increase in the availability and use of data. Do you think that now, with the explosion of data and fancy data-handling techniques, people perhaps don't start with the questions as strongly as they should?
> *Atkinson*: I do indeed think that's the case. Whenever I talk to a would-be graduate student, I say, 'What is it you want to know?' Not having an answer to that question is a weakness, and, in some way, it's partly due to the professionalization. People are doing economics as a profession rather than because they're really interested in the answers. I think the other thing is that our understanding of data on the more macro side is much inferior to what it was. In the early days of national accounts, they were constructed by people who did macroeconomics, as well, people like Richard Stone, Paul Samuelson, James Meade, and so on. They were doing work on constructing national accounts, so they knew perfectly well what they were using. Keynes, for example, knew how his younger colleagues were making up those numbers. I fear that, today, that's one of the areas where people just don't understand what they're using, and the origin of the numbers should not just be a footnote point.
> *Atkinson*: I think the position of young economists is actually very difficult at the moment, at least as far as the academic sphere is concerned, because we've now moved to a pretty unforgiving judgement based on journal publication. This means they're under great pressure, which ... affects the choice of subject matter and the style of economics. It's much easier to publish, I suspect, theoretical than applied economics in major journals; it is certainly easier to publish theory than applied economics concerned with countries other than the US. I think that

young economists are being pressured into a very difficult situation where their academic careers are related to things that are often quite opposed to what they want to do. If you ask them what the question is that they want an answer to, many of them have a very good response: They're doing economics because there is something they really want to find out, they're really concerned about some particular issue, or they've read something that really inspired them and that they want to follow up. I often find it very difficult to advise them. My instinct is to say, 'Follow your instincts', but, on the other hand, they may never get jobs.

Stern: I've just finished writing a review (Stern, 2016) of the Research Excellence Framework in the UK. We were very concerned by those kinds of perverse incentives. Going beyond the details of how you evaluate students and put incentives in place for them, isn't it also about the behaviour of more senior members of the profession?

Atkinson: I think it's certainly an issue of how the profession is defining itself, which, largely, is the choice of the senior members. It is defining itself in really quite a narrow way. There are … certain excursions you can make, into psychology, for example, or behavioural economics, that have somehow been legitimized. It's probably all right to work with law, and economic history sometimes manages to be accepted, but, basically, there's a pretty clear view of what economics is; this is not a very catholic view. It's a view that doesn't recognize that there are all sorts of issues that straddle the borders between economics and other social sciences. I think that's why people quite often get driven out of economics into adjacent subjects. (ibid.: 19)

For its candour, its breadth and its informed thoughtfulness, this is a remarkable exchange which traverses the turbulent years that their careers spanned. It would probably be fair to take away the impression that they started off in the straitjacketed imagination of the general equilibrium paradigm and broadened out, through pursuing their chosen questions, into wider more eclectic theoretical frameworks and methods over their careers. In the process the weaknesses of the mainstream approach then, and now, are exposed. There are some paradoxes: first, Atkinson was and remained a radical redistributionist neoclassical, which would be an oxymoronic term but for his predecessor, James Meade. Second, Atkinson is very forthright in his critical responses to the way that the control of the subject is distorting careers through perverse incentivisation, not least through the route of the Research Assessment Exercises or Research Excellence Frameworks, and how the boundaries of the subject are being narrowed down by the seniors. Yet, Tony Atkinson was one of the key players on a long list of committees, in the SSRC, ESRC, RES, RAE/REF, University Review of the DAE and others, that consistently pushed these trends. Taking Tony Atkinson's integrity as a firm given, the explanation has to lie in the evolution of his own thinking and agency; he was a fellow traveller in the Hahn caravan and campaign in the 1980s and 1990s, what they called "the peculiar period" where the subject took "wrong turns". Frederic Lee (2009: 154) points out that it was Atkinson as Chairman of the Economics Panel that assured anxious academics that there would be no discrimination against heterodox economics and economists; the reality that imminently followed was clearly the opposite. Only a later change of perspective could explain what otherwise appear as inconsistencies; perhaps there was also gullibility in taking what some of his fellow travellers might have been telling him then at face value. For the present moment, there is little in this insightful exchange to suggest that the subject, in the UK, has broken out of its orthodox lock-down, except at patrolled edges.

14.8.5   *Francois Bourguignon*

Francois Bourguignon was the Chief Economist at the World Bank leading up to 2007 when the financial crisis broke. The Bank and the Fund were part of the problem, not of the solution; in an interview (Bourguignon, 2012),[17] he reflects on the state of economics in relation to the state of the world it is meant to study. Some take-aways can be elicited:

How did we get here? He blames the dominant theory of the times: "We got here because the theory underlying those conclusions was faulty. It was based most notably on the key assumption of 'rational expectations'". The theory persisted because "empirical observation led to an underestimation of the possibility of significant slippage. The observed stability has somehow been considered an *a posteriori* justification of the choice of assumptions, like that of rational expectations, and therefore also of their conclusions as to the efficiency of the markets, the need for deregulation, etc." "Since everything appeared to be working well, and it became the prevailing discourse." Were the economists pushing these positions culpable, complicit? "I do not think that these people acted in bad faith any more than I think they were taking orders from traders to reproduce this discourse. It's not the same as the tobacco industry paying scientists to develop scientific research to show that cigarettes are harmless! The finance industry did not 'buy' the economic community so that there would be a cover-up of certain things. A good economist is someone who has a general understanding of economic systems in all their complexity. They will also have understood that there are few universal rules—and hence few ideologies—in the way economic policy is conducted, because it depends a lot on specific circumstances. It is nevertheless regrettable that the careers of economists are now marked by relatively narrow specializations, with less global perspective. To advance professionally, young researchers must show an ability to formulate new ideas, and it is easier to innovate on a specific topic. One can only hope that, over time, they will expand their scope of thought. The most important thing is to show the rationality of the economic agents is more limited or complex than that suggested by economists' models. But that's when the problems start, because there are an infinite number of ways not to be

---

[17] This account comprises a series of excerpts from answers to different questions; care has been taken to convey as accurate a sense of the answers as possible and to avoid any misleading impressions.

economically rational. ... As soon as we move away from the rational expectations hypothesis, which is clearly unsatisfactory in the financial markets, there is no longer a simple representation of the interactions between those involved. In recent years, economics has experienced an increasingly open and welcome approach toward other social sciences. Luckily, it is no longer a question of everything from marriage to suicide being explained by the behaviour of the *homo economicus*, but rather about being open to psychology, sociology, history, etc. This more open approach can only be beneficial. ... But I don't see economists completely abandoning the assumption of a certain rationality of agents. They would lose the analytical tool which they use to try and understand the world." So, going back to the opening question about the role of dominant theory, the question arises about the impact of the crisis on economic thinking—is there any change? "I don't get that impression, at the moment. Maybe someone will quickly offer a great idea for doing without it, or maybe we will have to wait a hundred and fifty years!"

14.8.6 *Alan Blinder*

Alan Blinder's reflections on his learning curve after the financial meltdown make quite a contrast with his triumphalist, doubt-free pronouncements in 1999 that the economic world was moving to converge to the assumptions about it in the neoclassical model. In Blinder (2014), he drew ten lessons for fellow economists, listed below in his words:

 (1) It can happen here.
 (2) Minsky was basically right.
 (3) Reinhart-Rogoff recessions are worse than Keynesian recessions.
 (4) Self-regulation is oxymoronic.
 (5) Fraud and near-fraud can rise to attain macroeconomic significance.
 (6) Excessive complexity is not just anti-competitive, it's dangerous.
 (7) Go-for-broke incentives will induce traders to go for broke.
 (8) Illiquidity closely resembles insolvency.
 (9) Moral hazard isn't a show-stopper, it's a trade-off.
(10) Economic illiteracy can really hurt.

He then proceeds to a series of seven lessons for teaching economics, listed below in his words:

1) We need to teach basic Keynesian economics better.
2) Models with one interest rate won't do any longer.
3) We must deal with unconventional monetary policies.
4) Bubbles can cause trouble.
5) Leverage is a double-edged sword.
6) How much financial complexity?
7) Systemic risk, too big to fail, and moral hazard?

Blinder (b. 1945), Diamond (b. 1940); both Solow PhD products. Solow declared he was Keynesian in the short run, neoclassical in the long run, and undecided in between.

Blinder has an epiphany: "we economists have learned quite a lot from the financial crisis, the Great Recession that followed, and the pathetic recovery we've had since. Some of this material needs to seep into our curricula, including at the principles level" (Blinder, 2014: 21). Better late than never, but will the message stick? Incidentally, there is no reference in this 'lessons learnt' article to the earlier 2000 proclamation on the economy inexorably converging to 'the model'; and allegiance to the rational expectations model is not explicitly referred to at all in the 17 points listed. On the whole, Blinder manages to make a safe descent from the high perch he had occupied in 1999.

14.8.7   Peter Diamond

Consider the comments of Peter Diamond, 'Nobel' prize winner in 2010, as written up by his interlocutor, Tony Cockerill, on a visit to Cambridge in 2012 to deliver the Marshall Lecture:

> Diamond notes here that search theory, which helps to explain how certain market forms adjust and which has formed a large part of his research interest and output, has contributed only a limited amount to this analysis. It works best for labour markets and, to a lesser extent, for housing markets. But it has contributed very little to understanding adjustment through consumer markets in the economy as a whole. Reflecting on the current global recession and the slow adaptation of the US economy, Diamond stresses that the failure to reduce structural and secular unemployment imposes a high price on society through the harm done to building human capital, particularly among those hoping to enter the labour market: experience is lost and lifetime earnings' expectations are damaged. He looks to government to ease this problem, emphasising the importance of first stabilising and then maintaining the flow of aggregate spending in the economy in the short-to-medium term, whilst at the same time putting measures in place for the longer term to deal with budget imbalance. Seeking fiscal balance ahead of reducing unemployment is, he argues, to get things precisely the wrong way round. (Cockerill, 2012: 5)

Was Diamond laying on the Keynesianism in its Cambridge home? Perhaps he was following his mentor Solow's formula of being a neoclassical in the long run but a Keynesian in the short term; whichever, there isn't much orthodox drumbeating here.

14.8.8   Partha Dasgupta via Robert Neild

Another expression of belated half-hearted regret might possibly be detected in Partha Dasgupta's appreciation for Robert Neild, both Fellows of Trinity College. Dasgupta (2010) castigated Joan Robinson, Nicky Kaldor and Richard

Kahn who "had wanted to protect Cambridge economics from the increased post-War use in the US of maths and stats; they conducted a secret economics seminar to which only chosen colleagues were invited; that they used ideology to determine an economic argument was bad enough, but they also mistook technical tools for ideology"; they "established an intellectual tone ... that their immediate successors in the professoriate were at pains to follow; but the successors had few intellectual credentials, and right through the 1970s they encouraged the appointment of mediocrities so long as they in turn showed a disdain toward modern economics; this was common knowledge in other universities of course, a matter of satisfaction there because it meant Cambridge wasn't competing in economics." Who might be these successors? (see Table 2.1). Kaldor's was a personal professorship which lapsed with his retirement in 1976; Richard Kahn's professorship went to Frank Hahn, so Dasgupta would surely not be referring to him; and Joan's professorship was awarded amidst much controversy to Robert Neild, so Dasgupta's derogatory remarks made in 2010 could presumably apply to him. In his appreciation for Frank Hahn, David Newbery expands on the issue of these appointments[18] and refers to the 'outrage' at Robert Neild's appointment.

Partha Dasgupta's obituary of Robert Neild is rightly generous and appreciative, though in some ways a trifle dissembling. Neild is first promoted, alongside Brian Reddaway and Wynne Godley, into "a triumvirate that shaped the intellectual climate of economics at Cambridge in the 1970s. That influence lasted for over two decades" (Dasgupta, in Trinity College Colleagues, 2019). Neild had many fine qualities and was steadily evolving his institutional approach to economics and to the study of society, but few contemporaries might elevate him to such an exalted pedestal of influence and power over the discipline in Cambridge. What these three did share, individually, were two beliefs: first, a dedication to making economics useful for policy purposes; and second, a recognition of the futility of the mathematical general equilibrium type economics practised by Frank Hahn and his youth academy; one could add that all three were hands-on practitioners of an eclectic post-Keynesian theoretical frame and tool kit customised to address macro and related policy questions. Dasgupta acknowledges that "in modern economics [a euphemism for mathematical general equilibrium theorising] policy is often kept at a distance. In contrast, the approach that Robert favoured insisted on a tight and

---

[18] "The Appointments Committee started making doubtful appointments that sometimes seemed based more on whether the candidate signed up to the Kahn–Robinson line than whether they were potentially outstanding. Kaldor manoeuvred the Electoral Board to appoint Robert Neild as Joan Robinson's replacement when she retired from her professorship in order to keep Hahn out, even though Kaldor and Hahn lived in Adams Road and continued to see each other. Silberston (Faculty Chairman) had a terrific row with Kaldor over Neild's appointment, because by then Kaldor had become anti-mathematical and also anti-Hahn. Apparently, Neild's appointment in preference to Hahn caused so much outrage that when Richard Kahn retired eighteen months later, Hahn was elected to Kahn's chair in Economics in 1972, and to a professorial fellowship at Churchill" (Newbery, 2017: 501).

constant link between analysis and policy; so much so that the separation between analysis and policy was wafer-thin."

"In retrospect, I believe it was socially a good thing that the Faculty of Economics at Cambridge offered students and professionals an approach to economics that was in sharp contrast to the growing uniformity of instructions and practice elsewhere. [19] ... Robert however stood out among his peers at Cambridge because his dislike of modern economics was tempered by doubt about how the subject should be taught and practised. I think his wide experience in Government House Economics and Peace Studies, allied to an enquiring and generous mind would have made him an ideal mentor for developing a blend of economics teaching and research at Cambridge that would draw on high quality analysis to inform policy. Unfortunately, that wasn't to be. ... There is no one here now with his intellectual blend. It's our loss." All this might have been more convincing had the early retirement taken by Neild had not been due to the nasty Faculty environment at the peak of the campaign that Frank Hahn and party were running against the likes of post-Keynesian, left and other heterodox economists, very much including Robert Neild, in Cambridge—even though Hahn had joined Neild in writing an open letter against Thatcherite monetarism reflecting the Cambridge consensus. In 2013, Neild wrote a frontal attack on neoclassical economics in his "Economics in Disgrace: The Need for a Reformation"; in 2017, he followed it up developing this critique into a case for evolutionary, institutional economics. Could Dasgupta's lament—"it's our loss", "there is no one here now with his intellectual blend" and so on—then be read as an oblique "mea-culpa" statement of belated regret tinged with a hint of self-reflection? Perhaps.

14.8.9 Another Snowflake Moment?

Memories of crises are short, they melt and disappear like snowflakes and the world returns to a new cycle of business as usual. There are few grounds for believing that the last crisis was any different, and indeed much evidence that it was not. The neoliberal thought collective still rules the waves; plutarchy is more evident today than a couple of decades ago; regulation is weaker and more vulnerable to capture by the oligarchs; inequalities are as rampant as ever; there is no evidence of any viable global financial architecture; financialisation is as explosive as it was prior to the last crisis; the bonus culture is alive and well having come out stronger from the crisis. In the discipline, despite the cathartic beating that mainstream economics had to take after the crisis, it has not been knocked off its perch, the profession is run to its dictates as before, the caste system in academic publication is no different, and heterodox economics and

---

[19] Dasgupta could perhaps be retrospecting on the campaign launched by Cambridge graduate students in their letter of protest, discussed earlier, against the absence of methodological diversity; Dasgupta happened to be Chair of the Faculty Board at the time. (See: Cambridge Graduate Students (2001).)

multidisciplinarity are kept at arm's length and occasionally allowed in on set and specific terms. If there were qualifications and critiques of the mainstream, these have mostly been incorporated without threatening the core. There seems to be an ever-greater disjuncture between mainstream theory and the state of the world. And even at points where positive change might have been effected, there are indications of a creeping return of the bad old ways.[20]

14.9 Donors: Leveraging a Reboot?

While the Queen had merely sought an answer to her simple question, others have called for a change of direction in Cambridge economics, linking it again in very many significant ways to the Post-Keynesian, heterodox lineages, restoring the salience of related disciplines such as economic history, philosophy, sociology, psychology, applied economics based on team work, emphasis on statistics and empirical methods, macroeconomic research linking the real and the financial economies, policy relevance—and in doing so, eschewing the blinkered theoretical and methodological perspectives of orthodox mainstream economics. Usually, the orthodox camp might have been expected to turn a deaf ear to such pronouncements, even thinking this was a replay of an old Joan or Ajit recording; but in the recent Cambridge scenario, they have been listening carefully to such loud-and-clear messages, even if only because they come attached to large cheques from engaged donors who would like the Faculty pipers to change their orthodox tune.

Using the Hahn years as a benchmark, the shift in orientation of the Faculty, if still well short of a volte face, is astonishing. Faculty newsletters provide information on a series of significant benefactions, most of them explicitly mandating areas of research that require such a change. *Cambridge Economics* (2012: 1) reveals that "a number of exciting initiatives in Applied Economics are under development in the Faculty. Newly launched following a generous benefaction, the Keynes Fund for Applied Economics will provide grants for research, fellowships and teaching at the intersection of financial markets with the real economy. The Faculty is also engaged in discussions with the New York-based Institute for New Economic Thinking to undertake a fundamental research programme in economics at Cambridge. The initial focus will involve the themes: Networks, Crowds and Markets; Transmission Mechanisms and Economic Policy; Information, Uncertainty and Incentives; and Empirical

---

[20] For instance, with regard to the Assessment Reports (ARs) of the International Panel on Climate Change, "Terry Barker asserts that the economics behind the projections in AR5, Mitigation of Climate Change, 2014, appear scientific but are the outcome of ideological assumptions about the economy, typically based only on one year's data. The economic models used all involve General Equilibrium. Many are based on the premise that the global economy is in long-term optimal equilibrium, such that any deviation from that equilibrium, e.g. in the form of regulations and/or carbon taxes, will ipso facto lead to economic costs. Terry Barker will assess this and other aspects of this approach and the implications for the costs of radical cuts in emissions." https://www.politicaleconomy.group.cam.ac.uk/events/TerryBarker2020

Analysis of Financial Markets. The Faculty also wishes to establish a Chair in Applied Economics." This professorship, originally created specifically for David Newbery (till retirement) when he was appointed Director of the DAE in 1988, had lapsed in 2010; Dasgupta had retired a year earlier in 2009, and with him the hands-on influence of the Hahn-Matthews axis. In this context, it is particularly relevant to take cognisance of the statement of objectives and focus of the Keynes Fund; its non-mainstream orientation is obvious.[21] Information is provided on projects and research outputs; both number over 30, and it is striking that only a very small fraction of the projects, and a small fraction of outputs, involve theoretical work on inference, or on pure mathematical economics; as groups, both are squarely in the realm of applied economics on themes of policy significance.

Bill and Weslie Janeway had already funded the establishment of CERF, the Cambridge Endowment for Research on Finance, at the Judge Business School in 2001, and this had provided the institutional and financial support for much valuable research, including prominently the work of Ajit Singh, John Eatwell, Wynne Godley, Alex Izurieta and many others. In its year of establishment, the Chairman of the Faculty Board was Partha Dasgupta, and the endowment came a couple of years after Alan Hughes, who had moved his Centre for Business Research to the JBS, was appointed to the Margaret Thatcher Professorship.

Two of the major thrusts of Faculty research are institutionally promoted by the externally funded Cambridge-INET Institute and The Keynes Fund for Applied Economics. "In 2011, the Keynes Fund for Applied Economics was established by a GBP 5 million donation to further support research within the Faculty ... it provides grants for research, fellowship and teaching at the intersection of financial markets with the real economy; it actively encourages collaboration between economics and other disciplines such as psychology, history, anthropology and biology, and supports academics in extending the frontiers of traditional economics" (p. 7). Further, The Keynes Fund is intended as the key "to create a key presence for Faculty research in the global debate on the interaction between the macroeconomy and financial markets. This was motivated by the market failures and policy failures in the recent crisis and a vision

---

[21] "The focus of the teaching and research supported by the Fund shall be the sources and consequences of failure of market efficiency, particularly but not exclusively as a result of Agency costs. In particular the income of the Fund shall be used to encourage research into: capital market mispricing; the design of incentive systems and mechanisms to reduce the incidence and significance of institutional or general economic failure as well as into responsive public policies. The scope of work to be funded shall include interactions between the financial markets and the real economy. The Managers of the Fund shall encourage research based on empirical observation of the behaviour of market participants, drawing as appropriate on relevant work in the other social sciences, biology and history. They shall also encourage academics to extend the frontiers of traditional economics in order to raise Cambridge's profile in the critical area between economic theory, best private sector practice and public policy, with a bias towards promoting long-term thinking, dampened pro-cyclicality, improved economic growth and reduced income/wealth disparities." http://www.keynesfund.econ.cam.ac.uk/

of moving Cambridge to the forefront of research on the crisis" (p. 3). Included in its three 'external managers' are William Janeway and Lord Adair Turner[22], both publicly professed critics of the mainstream economics and its inherent incapacity to deal meaningfully, at conceptual and policy levels, with the macroeconomic crises at global level.

Following this, "in 2012, in collaboration with the New York-based Institute for New Economic Thinking, the Faculty set up the Cambridge-INET (C-INET) to cut across Research Groups and to support fundamental research in economics ... its interdisciplinary focus maximizes interaction of Faculty researchers with colleagues and visitors". "For the next 5 years, the Faculty has already obtained external funding commitments of GBP6.4 million, including the funding of C-INET to the tune of $750,000 annually for five years from the Soros Foundation and the Cambridge Endowment for Research in Finance, amongst others."[23]

Then came two massive donations. One, to the tune of $25 million, came from Mohamed El-Erian, an alumnus of Queens' College, and who has recently been elected as College President after the departure of John Eatwell (who was another of Ajit Singh's admiring students); the funding was to be shared between the Faculty of Economics and Queens' College. Mohamed El-Erian has had an illustrious career with several high-profile positions of leadership in global finance. In making the benefaction, Mohamed explicitly cited Ajit Singh and Andy Cosh as the teachers at Queens' who inspired him and taught him "not what to think, but how to think". Gabriel Palma told me how much he respected Ajit for having the stamina and dedication to his calling when he put

---

[22] Baron Adair Turner is hugely experienced on both sides of the line, with hands-on senior responsibilities in the worlds of industry and finance leading up to the crisis, and then, à la the Keynes aphorism, being persuaded by the new realities to become a vocal critic of mainstream economics. He is no stranger to Cambridge, where he took a double first in economics and history, was Chairman of the Conservative Association, joining the new SDP in 1981, aged 26. A passage through BP, Chase Manhattan Bank (1979–1982), McKinsey & Co. (1982–1994) and Merrill Lynch Europe (in the years, 2000–2006, leading up to financial crash) was interspersed with by high appointments including Director-General of the Confederation of British Industry (1995–1999), Chairman of the ESRC from 2007, Chair of the ODI's Council, and the first Chairman of the UK Government's Committee on Climate Change (2008–2012), and alongside Chairman of the controversial Financial Services Authority till it was abolished (2008–2013). Made a peer in the Blair years, he was elected to an Honorary Fellowship of the Royal Society in 2016. Perhaps seeing it all from the inside provided the epiphanous revelations and the push to cross the line, switching roles from a hands-on doer to a critic. A supporter of the Tobin tax, he joined George Soros's INET as a senior research fellow in 2013; converted lectures delivered the LSE in 2010 into a book *Economics After the Crisis* published by MIT Press in 2012; wrote *Between Debt and the Devil: Money, Credit and Fixing Global Finance* published by Princeton University Press in 2016; was Chairman of INET till January 2019; chairs the Energy Transitions Commission; and has written a copious flow of papers and commentaries on critical economic and environmental policy issues. https://www.ineteconomics.org/research/experts/aturner/p4?tab=more-from-this-expert&tab=more-from-this-expert&tab=more-from-this-expert#more-from-this-expert

[23] Information, and the quotations, pertaining to these grants come from the nine-page 'environment template' included by the Faculty in its submission to the REF 2014.

everything into teaching undergraduates who would surely seek careers in banks, multinationals and international finance. Is the wheel coming a full circle? Was this pay-back time from appreciative, enlightened and financially successful alumni? And could they make the piper play a very different tune? Money speaks. In the case of the Faculty at Cambridge, the benefactions had express intentions, of course carefully expressed, to shift the goal posts in the field of research.

In parallel is another huge donation, this one of $27 million, from the accomplished venture capitalist, Bill Janeway and his wife Weslie.[24] Bill is an alumnus of Pembroke College who, rather like Keynes, made his money through intelligent, carefully thought out financial investments.[25] And significantly, he had been supervised by Richard Kahn for his PhD in Cambridge. Again, the donation was to be shared between the Faculty and the donor's *alma mater*, Pembroke College. Janeway is himself an out-of-the-box, creative economist of heterodox orientation and is an associate fellow at the Faculty of Economics. As an active 'frontier' researcher, Bill Janeway's mission seems to

---

[24] A news release from the University of Cambridge announced a "major gift for Cambridge Economics Research": "Bill and Weslie Janeway have agreed to donate $27 million (£17.5 million) to the Faculty of Economics and to Pembroke College. The proposal, which will go for approval by the Regent House, the University's governing body, later this month, is to establish the Janeway Professorship of Financial Economics within the Faculty, with a linked Fellowship at the College, and to establish the Janeway Fund for Economics. The Fund will provide support in perpetuity to an Institute for fundamental research in economics. This Institute will provide funding for postdoctoral fellows, doctoral and research students, visitors and international conferences." Curiously, the write-up states: "Cambridge economists have made substantial contributions to the subject over the last two hundred years. Distinguished figures include Thomas Malthus, Alfred Marshall, John Maynard Keynes, Frank Ramsay [*sic*], Richard Stone, James Meade, Amartya Sen and James Mirrlees." The omission of all the major heterodox figures, Joan Robinson, Piero Sraffa, Maurice Dobb, Richard Kahn, Nicky Kaldor, makes one wonder from whose pen this blurb was scripted—Keynes is lucky to make the cut; perhaps the criteria later was winning the 'Nobel' prize. https://www.cantab.org/component/content/article/157-news/1613-major-gift-for-cambridge-economics-research

[25] Alex Izurieta, with knowledge at a close personal and professional level, points out that Bill Janeway is far from being the archetypical fast-bucks hedge-fund investor, "not the casino capitalist criticised by Keynes but the entrepreneur praised by him". Or in words ascribed to Paul Samuelson, "Investment should be dull ... it should be more like watching paint dry, or watching grass grow. If you want excitement, take $800 and go to Las Vegas." Ajit Singh, a great critic of the investment allocation role ascribed to stock markets, would have agreed with the emphasis on the long term, though without compromising the 'animal spirits' of the dynamic entrepreneur in the real economy. In his work, Ajit quoted Keynes: "the spectacle of modern investment markets has sometimes moved me towards the conclusion that to make the purchase of an investment permanent and indissoluble, like marriage, except by reason of death, or other great cause, might be a useful remedy for our contemporary evils" (Keynes, quoted in Singh, A. 1991: 44–45). For 'marriage', in the context of a progressive investor in the real economy, read 'one-night stand' for the casino hedge-fund investor in the financial pyramid. Janeway's description of himself that of a venture capital entrepreneur; Alex observes: "Bill has been working for a long, long time in venture capital projects around the world; he made his gains step by step through a long and persistent series of well-calibrated involvement in innovation firms worldwide. Bill is, what one could call, an unusually intelligent entrepreneur" (Personal communication, email dated 16 December 2021).

lie in making economics fit for socially meaningful policy purposes again by pushing the contours of new economic thinking. He clearly writes his own script and has provided his preferred musical score to the pipers at the Faculty.

What is this/his 'new economic thinking'? Bill Janeway (2015) has set down what he describes as its "four pillars". First, "decision-making under uncertainty" which includes "a variety of alternative approaches that acknowledge the ontologically inescapable limits on human knowledge, escaping from the caricature of the perfectly rational, omniscient economic agent ... this necessarily means challenging the simplistic pursuit of 'consistent' integration from rigorously unrealistic micro foundations to manifestly inaccurate macroeconomics", and "incorporating the influence of inherited institutions and the overlapping networks individuals inhabit"; relatedly, following Marshall and Pigouvian externalities and induced state interventions that "are themselves also embedded in structures of ideology and power ... as Karl Polanyi well understood, the overlapping but differing distributions of market and political power in symbiotic tension, generating occasions for conflict and opportunities for reciprocal rent seeking".

Second, integrating economics and finance: "Post-2008, the most obvious absurdity of the Dynamic Stochastic General Equilibrium (DSGE) models that dominated modern macroeconomics was their exclusion of a financial system ... macroeconomics abdicated from engaging with the world as it is, a world in which participants in the markets for goods and services also participate in the markets and institutions which enable intermediate savers and investors. That this retreat was accompanied by extreme 'financialization' of the economy is more than ironic, for financialization itself was enabled by the divorce of the discipline of finance from economics. Here the central challenge transcends the addition of financial frictions to DSGE models, an activity that smacks of adding layers of epicycles to a Ptolemaic model of the universe in order to keep the earth at the centre."

Third, "bringing distribution back in"—"the Lucasian Critique and the establishment of the Rational Expectations Hypothesis eliminated any role for government in stabilizing an economy destined for general equilibrium by the utility and profit-maximizing actions of its rational market participants whose expectations were informed by a shared model of the world that (happily and necessarily) was presumed to be correct. As for distribution, at the core of the neoclassical production function is the proposition that, in perfectly competitive markets for outputs and inputs, the factors of production receive their marginal products. More or less by stealth, this assertion became operational as both explanation and legitimization of the actual distribution of market rewards: the distribution of income is both definitionally 'fair' and, as the logical consequence of a consistent model, no longer a subject of study"; Piketty's evidence is "impossible to square with the neoclassical production function ... [and] the active critique of Piketty's own explanations may prove as valuable to new economic thinking as the data itself. Bringing distribution back in necessarily requires interaction with the other social sciences ... explicit retreat from the intellectual imperialism of methodological individualism and rational choice theory as universal solvents is a mark of new economic thinking."

And, finally the fourth pillar: "taking history seriously". "A generation ago, Cliometrics proposed to bring rigor to economic history by embedding historical data in the neoclassical production function, thereby imposing on history the radical counterfactuals that at all times resources are fully employed and optimally allocated. Far from honouring historical experience, it produced a travesty of it." Required are explorations of economic development over the past 250 years, involving the impact of technological innovation and its creative destruction. "New economic thinking means reading old economics books", Janeway quotes Mark Thoma with approval: "indeed he was right. Recognition that there is much to learn from past efforts to comprehend the dynamics of production and growth, employment and consumption, savings and investment, price discovery and price fixing—and the roles of the state with respect to all—is a marker not only of new economic thinking, but of the maturity of the discipline itself" (ibid.).

Bill Janeway's credo of new thinking is remarkable both in its challenge and rejections of the meaningless reifications imposed on the discipline by the orthodox mainstream over the decades leading to an intellectual blindness in seeing, comprehending, analysing and responding to the world, and also in its qualified revalidation of the accumulated learnings of the rich heterodox lineages that preceded it—albeit with the crucial insertion of the prime significance of the contemporary context of extreme financialisation, extreme inequality and existential global economic crises. Both on the side of the critiques and on the way forward, pulling in these strings brings back to the table some of the central concerns, and achievements, of his supervisor Richard Kahn, as well as Joan Robinson, Nicky Kaldor, Wynne Godley, and then articulates with some key strands of the work of the following generation in Cambridge.

Janeway's exposition of what 'new economic thinking' entails makes clear its distance from the standard orthodox approaches of general equilibrium, rational expectations models and so on. On the contrary, it demonstrates a deep affinity with the intellectual concerns and agendas of the Cambridge heterodox lineages, of course recast to be useful for contemporary times of global dislocations and crisis; the word 'equilibrium' would not find a place in this new lexicon. The implications are obvious: if the Faculty were to be leveraged into this mandate, it would be pointing in a direction very different from the one it had been made to march, in blinkers, over 25 years of the Hahn era, representing in many respects a wasted generation. In announcing the initiative, Willy Brown (2015) ends with his own rumination: "the intellectual challenge facing economics is as formidable as it is exciting. The Janeways' generosity will do much to help the Faculty address it." It is 'interesting' to see that Brown has come to this realisation in 2015, three decades after he condoned precisely the opposite project at the Faculty.

Another, very recent, gift comes from a Trinity alumnus Gavin Oldham, Chair and CEO of Share PLC, a private financial services company, supporting a Research Fellow (curiously) at King's College, and a PhD student at the Faculty for a period of four years for research on 'egalitarian capitalism'. The modesty of the budget notwithstanding, the gift carries the lofty ambitions of the donor. The announcement on the Faculty website[26] helpfully explains that Gavin Oldham has long been a proponent of egalitarian capitalism, which he defines as "people from all walks of life having the opportunity to experience a genuine sense of ownership and to feel in control of their own destiny. ... Political solutions to resolve inequality, particularly enforced redistribution of wealth through taxation or other means, have led to soaring public debt and social discord." Hence the eponymous "SHARE (Supporting Human Achievement through Research based on Egalitarian Principles) Egalitarian Capitalism Programme [which] will include four key areas of research: Intergenerational Wealth Transfer; Human capital, improving inequality and productivity through education and training; Disintermediation; Mass ownership". Professor Leonardo Felli, Chair of the Faculty, naturally expresses "absolute delight" and offers some do-no-harm anodyne words: "A more egalitarian system of capitalism, one that empowers and provides individuals from all walks of life with the opportunities to fulfil their potential, could offer an economic solution to addressing the increasingly serious problem of inequality". How might this be achieved? Further helpful words: "More research is certainly needed to understand how this would and could best function, and to give the subject the underpinning and credibility it needs to gain traction and move forwards". Absolutely. SHARE researchers will have a tall task: intergenerational wealth transfers seem to be blocked by the donor's thumbs-down on "enforced re-distribution through taxation" thereby ruling out inheritance taxes à la Meade (1964); human capital and education generally tend to increase inequality at the upper end of the income scale, if the American experience is anything to go by; 'disintermediation' requires some disambiguation; and a concern about 'mass ownership' might be that it could turn out to be, as it very nearly is now, a mass ownership of indebtedness. So, indeed much research to do. Meanwhile, Share PLC has been gobbled up by Interactive Investor, a larger fish in the choppy pool of private financial service; it is unknown whether the CEO of the new masters shares the SHARE philosophical perspective. These examples suggest though, that Cambridge economics notwithstanding its transformation into a mainstream enterprise, still attracts capitalist reformers of capitalism.

Two other notable interventions, with greater symbolic than material significance, take the form of open fellowships carrying names of two famous practitioners of heterodox economics covering nearly a century, Joan Robinson and Ajit Singh: the Joan Robinson Fellow in Heterodox Economics at Girton

---

[26] https://www.econ.cam.ac.uk/news/oldham-egalitarian-capitalism

College, presently held by Carolina Alves[27]; and the Ajit Singh—Cambridge-INET Doctoral Studentship at Queens' College; apart from these, there is an El-Erian Fellow in Macroeconomics, and a Janeway Fellow in Economics on the Faculty Staff.

Big money makes big waves, big news. But that should not diminish appreciation for other, more modest, endeavours of idealism and integrity seeking also to make a difference in their own fields. One such initiative worthy of special attention is the launching in 2005, prior to the shock of the financial crisis, of the Cambridge Trust for New Thinking by Terry Barker, who had worked as Richard Stone's deputy on the Cambridge Growth Project and then taken over on Stone's retirement, as director till 1987, when the unit was effectively closed down when ESRC funding was refused; Barker had gone on to significant work on modelling supporting global climate control initiatives, including the Nobel prize-winning IPCC. The website of the Trust provides a statement of its principles,[28] its objectives[29] and its activities which are focussed primarily on placing progressive ideas in the public domain.

These donor-driven shifts have been evident elsewhere as well, prominently through the initiatives of Leon Levy and George Soros, both occurring in times when research spaces of refuge were crucially needed at the height of mainstream orthodoxy; much valuable work was accomplished through these progressive initiatives, as for instance the work of Wynne Godley and his co-researchers at the Levy Institute. It is to be noted that some of the pathbreaking research on national and global imbalances, such that allowed Godley to sound the alarm of the likelihood of financial crises, was undertaken well before the crises broke; that little heed was paid to these warning points is another matter. It is ironic that it would need private philanthropists to fund work on

---

[27] https://www.econ.cam.ac.uk/people/postdoc/cca30 See, especially, her co-authored paper on heterodox economics as a positive project (Kvangraven & Alves, 2019).

[28] "Principles: (a) that economic behaviour is primarily social rather than individual; (b) that economic behaviour is influenced by aesthetic and ethical values as well as economic values; and (c) that the pursuit of self-interest in economic behaviour can impact adversely on both society and the environment. In particular, the Charity is to educate the public in developing practices and policies that recognise and redress the adverse effects that arise from lack of awareness of the principles stated above." http://www.neweconomicthinking.org/index.htm

[29] "Objectives: It is vital that two social problems be solved. The first is the obvious degradation of the planet and its atmosphere by over-consumption and over-production through the exploitation of resources in pursuit of monetary gain. The second problem is the toxic pollution of the global money supply, also obvious, caused by financial practices over the past twenty years, led by the investment banks of Wall Street and the City of London. The problems are related: both arise out of the pursuit of self-interest, sanctified by the crude economic utilitarianism that underlies equilibrium economics; both are non-linear catastrophic events, although on different time scales; and arguably both can be described, in different ways, as the greatest market failures in human history. The Trust has been founded to promote new thinking in economics that does not rely on equilibrium and instead recognises the inherent uncertainties in the understanding of behaviour and accepts that nearly all economic activity is social in nature, not individual; that human beings are social animals; and that successful economies are based on trust and integrity." http://www.neweconomicthinking.org/index.htm

radical economics. It cannot be gainsaid that such donors might not have other expectations or desires in relation to these benefactions, but then that applies to most donors; the crucial test is to examine what traction the donation has for making good change happen, and then for it to be sustained. Does the donor money push-start the research vehicle and send it on its 'new' pathway on its own power, or does it need to keep dangling the proverbial carrot in front perennially?

The larger part of the research budget comes from external donors, such as William Janeway, George Soros or Mohamed El-Erian, augmented by donations from other 'heterodox' sources, such as the Keynes Fund for Applied Economics. The agenda-changing impact of 'charitable' donations, for instance, of the Gates monies on such vital global bodies as the cash-strapped WHO, demonstrates how add-on, fungible money can shift the substantive orientation and practical priorities even of large organisations and agencies whose regular budgets are almost entirely absorbed in defraying salaries and establishment costs; the donor's funds then become the tail that wags the dog, or the dog is put on a leash held by the donor's hand. There is little that the Cambridge donors, Soros, El-Erian and Bill Janeway, would not know about leveraging. Of course, their financial and intellectual contributions have induced well deserved acts of public and professional acknowledgement: El-Erian had highly responsible University-level duties placed on him, and has also fully committed himself to a university life in taking on the position of President of Queens' College; Janeway's contributions are also well recognised and rewarded, not least with a CBE; Adrian, in the donors' camp even if not a financial donor, has an honorary degree from the University to add to his CBE. But the donors are surely not in the game for such honours; they are clearly drawn to their old university and to their discipline to attempt to reorient Cambridge economics in a more meaningful direction, to reverse some of the self-harm and collateral damage that three lost decades of orthodoxy might have done, to again make it fit for public purposes of policy, to restore some of the epistemological attributes that were jettisoned en route to the present where it had effectively side-lined itself from some of the burning strategic issues of the times, not least, multiple economic crises.

How strong is the Pied Piper effect? Are the donors leveraging a major reboot of the ideational template of Cambridge economics? Any such effort encounters a paradox. On the one side, fresh money can underwrite a wide range of 'greenfield' initiatives through the additions of optional extras that alter the balance of research. The funding of new research programmes, the Keynes Fund, the new units in the Judge Institute, new programmes for small research grants, fresh cohorts of PhD postdoctoral research projects and so on have the potential to collectively shift the coordinates of the overall research programme, and not just on the margins. This is amply evident from the central space occupied by these new donor-funded initiatives in the submission of the Faculty to the REF 2014.

However, on the other side, there are strong limits to the extent to which such changes in direction might enter the body or minds of Faculty staff, whose profile—the composition of human capital investment of the past—is an accretion of the previous decades of orthodox dominance and decisions on tenured appointments. Disciplinary mindsets are not as flexible and pliable as all resources are deemed to be in the orthodox theoretical paradigm. Hahn and Matthews had faced this 'brownfield' constraint in their campaigns against the heterodox groups and recognised that marginal changes would not have a macro impact, and that the only way of achieving their strategic goals was first, through the closure or expulsion of heterodox research units thereby changing the balance of political control, and then to follow up at the margin via hirings and firings through the instrumental use of the RAEs and the REFs. These instruments are not available to external donors, even if they were so minded. Further, the very fact of being donors also bars them, through the informal protocol of convention, and also formal procedures of governance, from directly entering certain decision-making spaces in the Faculty.

Thus, a somewhat schizophrenic outcome becomes quite likely where external research funds manage to discernibly shift the goal posts of funded research, but perhaps make little impact on the profile of the body of academic staff or its pattern of time use. Over time, an osmotic process can, if anything, dilute the force of funds to influence the totality. Is anything, such a tendency to walk rather awkwardly on two legs pulling in different directions, such a tendency already perceptible in the recent trends of teaching and research, where the 'old' persists in 'new' forms through cosmetic changes in dress and language? It is perhaps also pertinent to note that major shifts in paradigms usually involve powerful, charismatic personalities who have the accumulated intellectual capital and institutional authority to drive the agenda of change; the Faculty is devoid of any such force, and it would seem to be too tall an order to expect a bloc of like-minded senior imports—along the game-changing lines of the contemporaneous arrival of Gorman, Hahn, Johnson and Walters, at the LSE as the flag bearers of the American mathematical economics revolution in the 1960s.

There could be other issues as well, including especially the question of predictability and sustainability, as illustrated on a lesser scale by the changing fortunes and identity of Share Plc. More significantly, it has now been announced that the Cambridge-INET Institute will formally close down when its grant period expires in the summer of 2021. Explaining the development, Vasco Carvalho, Professor of Macroeconomics in the Faculty, notes that this Institute was set up in 2012 following the global financial crisis; "the time was ripe for some soul searching, and to determine whether and the profession had gone wrong". Of course, those with any kind of memory might feel that the time had been 'ripe' for a long time prior to 2012, though that in no way detracts intrinsically from the INET initiative, the three main objectives of which were "to produce world-leading research; to invest in the next generation of economists; and to encourage collaboration both within economics and across disciplines", through the creation of "four inter-disciplinary research groups: Networks, Crowds and Markets; Transmission Mechanisms and Economic Policy; Information, Uncertainty and Incentives; and Empirical Analysis of Financial Markets". Vasco Carvalho provides an assessment of the substantial impact of the Institute in reorienting aspects of the Faculty's activities: "These groups are very successful, with several leading the world in their field. Indeed, the INET Working Paper Series includes 211 papers with many published in top journals. Collectively these have helped redefine the research frontier in Economics." The postdoctoral research programme, which supported as many as 27 researchers, is especially singled out as a success: "young researchers are attracted by the freedom to pursue their own research interests while integrated in ambitious research groups, which is somewhat different to postdoctoral positions at other universities"; he feels that the programme has rejuvenated the Faculty. Fortunately, there will be lapsing of this valuable institutional capacity, because almost seamlessly, a new facility, the Weslie and William Janeway Institute for Economics is to be launched in October 2021 "which will invest in shaping young minds, transforming economic research and disseminating frontier work at Cambridge. Effectively, the Janeway Institute will take the place of Cambridge-INET", says Carvalho, "because the aims and objectives of the Janeway Institute will be similar, but the new Institute will benefit from being funded by an endowment[30] rather than a grant. A grant must deliver on what was promised at the beginning of the grant, which constrains research directions. By taking an endowment, it will allow us to be much more flexible and agile, reflecting both the evolving academic strengths of the Faculty and societal concerns ... tell new stories, change the narrative and tangibly impact the research frontier in Economics" by organically incorporating such new directions as "inequality, climate change, epidemics, gender, the digital economy, or the impact of automation and machine learning".[31] It remains a moot point what the locus and governance structure of such an institute might be within the framework of the Faculty—would it be akin to a semi-autonomous applied economics, policy-oriented, arm of the Faculty, as the DAE once used to be? In what ways would it exercise its professed corrective mandate? It should and can be expected that appropriate solutions will be available or evolve.

The irony will be lost on none that, rather like Frank Hahn was said by his friend Bob Solow to have dragged the erstwhile heterodox Cambridge economics kicking and screaming into mainstream economics, it is the intellectual progeny of those purged heterodox lineages that are committing very considerable personal fortunes to try to pull back the cleansed orthodox Faculty back

---

[30] "The Janeway Institute will be primarily funded by a grant from Weslie Janeway and William Janeway. ... The Janeway Institute will also be funded by the Keynes Fund and the Cambridge Endowment for Research in Finance (CERF)" (Heath, 2021).

[31] See: Heath, Rebecca (2021). Vasco Carvalho reflects on the success of Cambridge-INET https://www.inet.econ.cam.ac.uk/; and: https://www.econ.cam.ac.uk/economics-alumni/carvalho-inet-janeway-institute

into an economics of and for the real world. And virtually all attributes that are held desirable by them, as for instance conveyed by Bill Janeway in his enunciation of the meaning and purpose of 'new economic thinking' actually finds resonance in the characteristics of the Faculty and the DAE of the pre-orthodox period—of course, with due acknowledgement of the specificities and demands of the current economic and political conjunctures. What is sought is not any nostalgic retro re-creation of good old times. What is shared is the fundamental objective of making the discipline useful for societal policy purposes in an era of multiple global crises. The future course of Cambridge economics will reveal the balance of such inertial conservative constraints embedded in its body, and dynamic radical impulses injected into it by external funding. The fundamental generic issue lurking at a subterranean level concerns the conflation of the roles of the donor and the executive, regardless of how sympathetic the former might be in relation to the mandate of an institution such as the Faculty of a university.

14.10 The Great Banyan

The lineages of Cambridge heterodox traditions took root and shape over half a century, and were then pulled down in a decade; and the same time window witnessed the collapse of all the major oppositional projects that had intellectual roots in these heterodox branches: the welfare state, Keynesian macroeconomic management by the state; socialist development; and non-capitalist development paths in the Third World. The two trajectories were not unconnected; systemic forces that operated on the global and national stage dramatically altered the external environment for the battles for control within the Faculty of Economics in Cambridge. It is against this panoramic backdrop that the Cambridge purges have to be understood. Much of the untold story narrated has focussed on 'internal' explanations of the collapse, and indeed, these factors and forces were the agents through which the purges were enacted. However, the outcomes might have been rather different if the external political, ideological and material contexts had not turned from being benign to hostile to the Cambridge heterodox economics. Arguably, neither the internal, nor the external, set of factors might have been sufficient to force the change; it was the combination that gave to the Cambridge orthodox group the local power and external protection and support to stage its successful campaign of wresting control of the Faculty.

Endless counterfactuals are possible, starting for instance with one where Allyn Young would not have succumbed to the flu—Cambridge and LSE economics might well have evolved along a very different set of rails; or another where three senior professors had not, against all expectations, contributed to bringing Frank Hahn into the Faculty as professor; or yet another where the ailing Sir Alfred Broughton had actually been allowed to fulfil virtually his dying wish and travelled to Westminster to cast that single vote that would have kept Margaret Thatcher out of power, at least in 1979; and thus the list can be extended to suit any imagination.

Nevertheless, there is an unfortunate irony here. In the light of the global rightward shift, Cambridge economics should actually have gained significant ground for its relevance. And indeed, all this while, in parallel, the younger cohort of radical Cambridge economists had made steady and significant contributions to the analysis of the new phase of global capitalism, pointing out its agendas and dangers, and offering alternatives that went beyond academic critiques. But just as the general need for their creative alternative formulations became more acute, their own position within Cambridge was in a state of atrophy and decline due to this interplay of internal and external factors. Its fortress breached, Cambridge heterodox economics, instead of rising and flourishing, scattered, fragmented and withered. There were only peripheral marginalised job markets for young Post-Keynesians, neo-Ricardians, Sraffians, Marxists or Kaldorians,[32] including those who worked on applied economics within heterodox frameworks.

In the end, all said and done, and especially when reviewed retrospectively, the heterodox left had won most of their intellectual battles, but still wound up losing the war of territorial control over the discipline. "I think it is sensible, indeed necessary, to preserve what elsewhere I have called the Cambridge tradition" (Harcourt, 2017: 219). "The traditions ... are still carried on by a besieged minority, mostly centred around the *Cambridge Journal of Economics*. Some still have a foothold in the Faculty; others form a thriving colony in the Judge Institute of Management Studies or are scattered around in colleges, as college, not university, teachers.[33] More optimistically, in centres other than Cambridge, Keynes and the Cambridge tradition are to be found under the wide embrace and rubric of post-Keynesianism" (Harcourt & Kerr, 2003: 355–356). Ruefully, Geoff Harcourt records the scene the day after the battle was lost: "With the retirement and then death of many of the main *dramatis personae*" (ibid.) "the dominant group in the Faculty at present seems to wish the Faculty to be a clone of the leading United States departments, especially Harvard, MIT, Stanford and Yale, for example, but certainly not Chicago. In doing so it seems to have forgotten two important principles of good economics: comparative advantage and a role for differentiated products" (Harcourt, 2007: 219).[34]

---

[32] For a somewhat more optimistic take from outside of Cambridge, see Frederic Lee (2007).

[33] "There are still some colleagues in the Faculty at Cambridge working within the Cambridge tradition as I have defined it—Gabriel Palma, Bob Rowthorn, Ajit Singh, Frank Wilkinson, for example,—and on method, principally through Tony Lawson's influential contributions to critical realism. ... As I often tell Lawson the central core of truth in critical realism is to be found in Marx's method and Keynes's methodological critique of Tinbergen's early econometric work on investment" (Harcourt, 2007: 233).

[34] The Cambridge Realist Workshop (CRW) and the Cambridge Social Ontology Group (CSOG), both bearing Tony Lawson's hallmark, constitute not just one "differentiated product" but an entity in its own right engaging with all else, deepening and clarifying the epistemological

How is this tale to be read? Is it a story of defeat: Troy destroyed after the Trojan horse, bearing Frank Hahn and his foot soldiers, is pulled into the safe sanctuary of Cambridge heterodox economics by the unsuspecting and unlikely trio of Kaldor, Kahn and Reddaway? Or is it a case of checkmate in three moves by the international chess problematist, Robin Matthews? The reality of defeat is an undeniable and undoubtedly painful truth, but it is perhaps not the only one to take from this tale. A wider reflection is essential that looks not just at the day after the various battles, but also at the futures that subsequently rolled out. Nothing stays won, or lost, forever; and the various 'defeated' heterodox bands and brigades reassemble, reform and, phoenix like, rise again in their own 'peripheral' spaces, where defeats get transformed into fresh gains, and those marginalised refugee encampments become vibrant new hives of independent heterodox and radical intellectual activity. However reassuring and plausible such an interpretation of rebuilding victory from the dismantled bricks of defeat might be, there nevertheless remains the core inescapable truth of the proverbial paradise lost, even if in the form of a counterfactual imaginary, the loss of a world that might have been.

The diverse groups which were eased or pushed out from the Faculty, or matured and grew out of the original DAE home (such as CBR led by Hughes) settled in various new locations—some with marginal affinities (such as Land Economy) or others with strong synergies (such as the Judge Institute)—and can now be found on their feet and flourishing in their reincarnations. Sociology went and eventually built its own new home in an independent Department of Sociology. Economic historians found their individual ways to prominent success, as exemplified by Jane Humphries, CBE, Professor and Head of the Department of Economic History in Oxford. Applied economics, in the form of Alan Hughes and his group in the Centre for Business Research migrated with massive success to the Judge Business School when Alan was appointed to the competitive Margaret Thatcher Chair;[35] JBS also launched the Cambridge Endowment for Research on Finance; and John Eatwell, who had held a Faculty lectureship till then, became Professor of Financial Policy, and Director of the new, externally funded Centre for Financial Analysis and Policy at JBS was a Professor and Director; and Peter Nolan was appointed in sequence to two named chairs on China studies, raised huge funds to launch a high-profile programme for senior economic and finance executives, and is now regarded as one of the leading experts in his field; Gabriel Palma remained under-promoted and undervalued by the Faculty in contrast to the huge valuation placed on his work internationally; likewise, Ha-Joon Chang who is perhaps one of the most widely used authors in development economics with each of his many books

and methodological bases of "Cambridge" and wider heterodox traditions, extending the canvas into social theory and philosophy (Martins 2014, Pratten 2014).

[35] After his retirement as Director of the CBR and from the Margaret Thatcher Chair in 2013, Alan Hughes was elected to a Chair in Innovation at Imperial College Business School, and a Distinguished Professorship at Lancaster University Management School. He also served as a member of the UK Prime Minister's Council for Science and Technology from 2004 to 2014.

going into a score and more translations worldwide, is equally badly treated within the Faculty. This group, along with Ajit Singh (before and after his retirement) and other colleagues, including Shailaja Fennell, have been part of the impressive success of the Centre of Development Studies located outside the Faculty of Economics. The macroeconomics teams were effectively disbanded, but tracking the career paths of the researchers that were thereby expelled reveals an array of remarkable success stories in other universities and institutes; and as for their denigrated macroeconomic models, they live on: the CGP model was taken across from the DAE to Cambridge Econometrics, a private research company initiated within the DAE through the encouragement of the Treasury but then converted into an open private company; and the CEPG model was taken over and developed further by Francis Cripps and Terry Ward; both continue to use its versions and spinoffs for major engagements both with academic research as well as with high-profile clients drawn from international finance, including, for instance, the Bank of Tokyo; the downside, of course, is that the closure of the CEPG and the CGP teams has forced the privatisation of what were valuable public goods being used in national policy-oriented research. Individual staff who went their way almost all did brilliantly well; an inventorisation immediately gives the lie to the calumnious attempts at reputation assassination indulged by the Gang-of-Four orthodoxy and its camp followers. Quite legitimately, each of these emigrations and reinventions can and should be viewed as successes in their second lives.

All these glasses seem pretty much full to the brim, at least wearing one set of spectacles. But viewed through a different prism, light refracts differently and reveals the narrowness of the theoretical and methodological approach that captured authority and power in Cambridge. Several observations are pertinent. First, there was a very high cost of transition, and this was borne by the emigrants; second, those left behind as minorities suffered graver forms of internal exclusion and oppression; third, some changes also involved a mutation of a public good which addressed national policy issues, into a private enterprise which, by its very nature, could not; fourth, the vibrant and productive day-to-day cross-discipline and cross-team interactions, in the corridors and common rooms, that generated externalities and creativity, even through disagreements, were severely fragmented as life revolved around smaller more autarkic and specifically defined organisational units. And even as all these emigrants built new lives, economics in its old home, the Faculty, was converted increasingly into an intellectual pastime locked in the imaginary world of its own games, unable to interface meaningfully with the real world. The great banyan tree of Cambridge heterodox economics, root and branch, was hacked down, bit by bit, the ground dug up and replanted with a single genetically modified, monocrop species. Wearing these spectacles, the glass holding the heady elixir of what could have been, looks drained down to the dregs.

As post-Keynesian and other heterodox groups formed and reformed in new locations, they carried their approaches with them, and these often fertilised the further development of these traditions in these fresh sites, howsoever scattered, catalysing the emergence and strengthening of new intellectual and institutional networks through conferences, online interactions, and also new academic journals. However, that said, these networks were institutionally acephalous in character, in that they lacked a core institutional 'headquarters' or base camp, of the kind that the Faculty-DAE pairing in Cambridge had served for decades. Not to be overlooked also is the fact that within Cambridge economics, the ascent of orthodoxy meant that something like 40 to 50 cohorts of economics students were disciplined in the subject strictly in the orthodox mainstream template—despite protests from students about this. This cumulative damage in terms of intellectual orientation and capacity cannot be overlooked. In parallel, the Faculty and the DAE (while still existing) no longer provided opportunities for fresh young staff members to join and learn as teachers. Instead, the pattern of fresh appointments was unsurprisingly massively skewed towards the appointment of staff with mainstream orientation and research interests; since many of these staff became effectively permanent, they also set up a firewall against the re-entry, or reorientation in favour of selected heterodox lines. Any such initiatives have had to rely on external donor interventions. The implication is that the orthodox pattern of staffing is not putty that can be easily reshaped into heterodox forms; rather it has more the attributes of unreformable clay. Ergo, the fact that the purged or exiled heterodox lineages partially reassembled elsewhere and flourished in separate scattered locations cannot erase or discount the multiple forms of cumulative losses that were suffered as a result of the orthodox campaigns.

A parable might help. The violent and bleeding partitions of India made homeless, destitute refugees of millions, forced across hurriedly drawn borders; my family, no exception, came over with nothing more than a suitcase, while what was to become me travelled in my mother's womb. Punjab perhaps experienced more than its share of the upheavals and trauma that marked successive generations of migrants on either side, and the silence of the subconsciously repressed memories of that era have only recently been touched by historians, often children of parents who had lived through it all. At a collective level, there is a powerful discourse on the role of the historical roots, of the agency of the colonial regime, of conjunctural circumstances or of the machinations of ambitious political leaders on either side, in explaining the event, and given the way things have turned out, there is a body of opinion that interrogates and rejects the project of partition in the first place, even while pragmatically accepting that there is no turning back of history. Yet, the narratives of 'the way we were', of the peaceful and productive co-existence and interactions between different communities in the creative intellectual and cultural melting pot of old Punjab, subliminally point to the counterfactual of how an undivided India might have been and evolved had the toxin of the contentious and fatally divisive project of partition not been injected into the political imagination, never appeared on the horizon. As it happens, the Punjabi migrants eventually flourished in their new environs. The cross-product amalgam of being a Punjabi and a migrant defined an identity that was disproportionally endowed with dynamism, energy, resilience, ambition, stoicism and a willingness to sacrifice, never say die, and to work indefatigably; little surprise then that the displaced migrants reconstructed their lives, individually and collectively in groups, reinvented themselves as remarkably successful communities, recovering and ostensibly restoring Punjabi ethnic pride, with all its concomitants. Sikhs, with migration woven into their genetic code, epitomise such a narrative. But does the conventional success of the migrants erase the realities of their experience and their losses; and scaling up, does that current performance of the new countries invalidate the power of the latent counterfactual of an undivided subcontinent of say, the united states of India? That the refugees did well later does not validate their cleansing; that the emergent countries performed well does not legitimise the partition.

The stories of the successive episodes of intellectual purges and ideological cleansing of the diverse heterodox lineages in economics and related disciplines from the Faculty of Economics, relentlessly carried out by an orthodox camp in the grip of a revolutionary, à la Samuelson, disciplinary fundamentalism mirror this account. It was 1662 again, when by the Act of Uniformity, there was only the one god and the one gospel, and not swearing total allegiance attracted extreme exclusions and punishments, incidentally, also excluding non-conformists from receiving degrees from the Universities of Oxford and Cambridge. If Austin Robinson could have spoken from his place of rest, he might well have asked for the Faculty Building on Sidgwick Site to remove his name from its entrance; he had intended it to be a congenial interactive space for open intellectual exchange in the best Cambridge tradition, not a fortress of intellectual narrow-mindedness or a laboratory of lobotomisation. On the other hand, the far-sighted man that he was, might he have counselled patience, to keep calm and carry on, with a quiet confidence in another cycle of change, looking out for signs of successful re-rooting, of fresh green shoots?

Appendix 14.1: Letter of Protest by Graduate Students, 2001

Open Letter: Opening Up Economics - A Proposal by 27 PhD Students at Cambridge University

As students at Cambridge University, we wish to encourage a debate on contemporary economics. We set out below what we take to be characteristic of today's economics, what we feel needs to be debated and why:

> As defined by its teaching and research practices, we believe that economics is monopolised by a single approach to the explanation and analysis of economic phenomena. At the heart of this approach lies a commitment to formal modes of reasoning that must be employed for research to be considered valid. The evidence for this is not hard to come by. The contents of the discipline's major journals, of its faculties and its courses all point in this direction.

In our opinion, the general applicability of this formal approach to understanding economic phenomenon is disputable. This is the debate that needs to take place. When are these formal methods the best route to generating good explanations? What makes these methods useful and consequently, what are their limitations? What other methods could be used in economics? This debate needs to take place within economics and between economists, rather than on the fringe of the subject or outside of it all together.

In particular we propose the following:

1. That the foundations of the mainstream approach be openly debated. This requires that the bad criticisms be rejected just as firmly as the bad defences. Students, teachers and researchers need to know and acknowledge the strengths and weaknesses of the mainstream approach to economics.
2. That competing approaches to understanding economic phenomena be subjected to the same degree of critical debate. Where these approaches provide significant insights into economic life, they should be taught and their research encouraged within economics. At the moment this is not happening. Competing approaches have little role in economics as it stands simply because they do not conform to the mainstream's view of what constitutes economics. It should be clear that such a situation is self-enforcing.

This debate is important because in our view the status quo is harmful in at least four respects. Firstly, it is harmful to students who are taught the 'tools' of mainstream economics without learning their domain of applicability. The source and evolution of these ideas is ignored, as is the existence and status of competing theories. Secondly, it disadvantages a society that ought to be benefiting from what economists can tell us about the world. Economics is a social science with enormous potential for making a difference through its impact on policy debates. In its present form its effectiveness in this arena is limited by the uncritical application of mainstream methods. Thirdly, progress towards a deeper understanding of many important aspects of economic life is being held back. By restricting research done in economics to that based on one approach only, the development of competing research programs is seriously hampered or prevented altogether. Fourth and finally, in the current situation an economist who does not do economics in the prescribed way finds it very difficult to get recognition for her research.

The dominance of the mainstream approach creates a social convention in the profession that only economic knowledge production that fits the mainstream approach can be good research, and therefore other modes of economic knowledge are all too easily dismissed as simply being poor, or as not being economics. Many economists therefore face a choice between using what they consider inappropriate methods to answer economic questions, or to adopt what they consider the best methods for the question at hand knowing that their work is unlikely to receive a hearing from economists.

Let us conclude by emphasizing what we are certainly not proposing: we are not arguing against the mainstream approach per se, but against the fact that its dominance is taken for granted in the profession. We are not arguing against mainstream methods, but believe in a pluralism of methods and approaches justified by debate. Pluralism as a default implies that alternative economic work is not simply tolerated, but that the material and social conditions for its flourishing are met, to the same extent as is currently the case for mainstream economics. This is what we mean when we refer to an 'opening up' of economics.

Signed by 797, before signing was closed; released on 14 June 2001; for a list of names of the signatories, see: Cambridge Graduate Students (2001, June 14).

References

Atkinson, A. B., & Stern, N. (2017). Tony Atkinson on poverty, inequality, and public policy: The work and life of a great economist. *Annual Review of Economics, 9*, 1–20. https://doi.org/10.1146/annurev-economics-110216-100949

Backhouse, R. E. (1996). The changing character of British economics. In A. W. Coats (Ed.), *The post-1945 internationalization of economics*, Annual Supplement to volume 28, *History of political economy* (pp. 33–60). Duke University Press.

Besley, T., & Hennessy, P. (2009). The global financial crisis: Why didn't anybody notice? *British Academy Review, 14*, 8–10.

Besley, T., & Hennessy, P. (2010). *Financial and economic horizon scanning.* Letter sent to Her Majesty the Queen, February 8. https://www.thebritishacademy.ac.uk/sites/default/files/04besley-hennessy.pdf

Blinder, A. S. (1988). The fall and rise of Keynesian economics. *Economic Record, 64*(4, December), 278–294.

Blinder, A. S. (2000). How the economy came to resemble the model. *Business Economics, 35*(1), 16–25.

Blinder, A. S. (2014). *What did we learn from the financial crisis, the great recession, and the pathetic recovery?* Princeton University Griswold Center for Economic Policy Studies Working Paper No. 243. https://www.princeton.edu/ceps/workingpapers/243blinder.pdf

Bourguignon, F. (2012). Economics is not a science: Interview with Francois Bourguignon (Interview by C. Chavagneux). *L'Economie Politique, 55*, 7–13.

Brown, W. (2015). Distinguished alumnus: Bill Janeway. *Cambridge Economics: News from the Cambridge Faculty of Economics, 8*(Autumn), 3.

Brown, W., & Cockerill, T. (2015). Shaping the Faculty's future. *Cambridge Economics: News from the Cambridge Faculty of Economics, 8*(Autumn).

Cambridge Economics. (2012). *Cambridge Economics: News from the Cambridge Faculty of Economics, 5* (Autumn).

Cambridge Graduate Students. (2001, June 14). *Opening up economics: A proposal by Cambridge students.* Open letter. http://www.paecon.net/petitions/Camproposal.htm

Cockerill, T. (2012). The Marshall lectures. *Cambridge Economics: Cambridge Faculty of Economics Alumni Newsletter, 5*, 5–6. http://www.econ.cam.ac.uk/alumni/newsletters/Cambridge-Economics-Issue-5-2012.pdf

Cripps, F., & Izurieta, A. (2014). *The UN global policy model: Technical description.* Technical manual. https://unctad.org/en/PublicationsLibrary/tdr2014_GPM_TechnicalDescription.pdf

Cripps, F., Izurieta, A., & Singh, A. (2011). Global imbalances, under-consumption and over-borrowing: The state of the world economy and future policies. *Development and Change, 42*(1), 228–261.

Dasgupta, P. (2010). Interview with Partha Dasgupta 6th April 2010. In S. Harrison & A. Macfarlane, *Encounter with economics.* Interviews filmed by A. Macfarlane and edited by S. Harrison. University of Cambridge. http://sms.cam.ac.uk/collection/1092396

Dasgupta, P. (2013). Obituary: Frank Hahn. *Royal Economic Society Newsletter, 161*(April).

De Vroey, M. (2010). *Lucas on the Lucasian transformation of macroeconomics: An assessment.* Discussion Paper 2010-32. https://sites.uclouvain.be/econ/DP/IRES/2010032.pdf

Dow, S., Harcourt, G., Hodgson, G., et al. (2009, August 21). Her Majesty the Queen. *Revue du MAUSS permanente.* http://www.journaldumauss.net/./?Her-Majesty-the-Queen

Dunn, S. P. (2009). Cambridge economics, heterodoxy and ontology: An interview with Tony Lawson. *Review of Political Economy, 21*(3), 481–496.

Eatwell, J., & Milgate, M. (2011). *The fall and rise of Keynesian economics.* Oxford University Press.

Freeman, A. (2020). The second opinion: An ethical approach to learning and teaching economics. In S. Decker, W. Elsner, & S. Flechtner (Eds.), *Principles and pluralist approaches in teaching economics: Towards a transformative science* (pp. 13–30). Routledge.

Gillies, D. (2012). Economics and research assessment systems. *Economic Thought, 1*(1), 23–47. http://et.worldeconomicsassociation.org/files/ETGillies_1_1.pdf

Godley, W., & Zezza, G. (2006). *Debt and lending: A cri de coeur.* Policy Note 2006/4. The Levy Economics Institute of Bard College.

Harcourt, G. C. (2007). *What is the Cambridge approach to economics?* Republished in G. C. Harcourt, *On Skidelsky's Keynes and other essays: Selected essays of G. C. Harcourt* (pp. 219–240). Palgrave Macmillan, 2012.

Harcourt, G. C. (2010, October). Robin Matthews. *RES Newsletter,* No. 151. http://www.res.org.uk/SpringboardWebApp/userfiles/res/file/obituaries/matthews.pdf

Harcourt, G. C. (2017). Robert Charles Oliver (Robin) Matthews (1927–2010). In R. A. Cord (Ed.), *The Palgrave Companion to Cambridge economics* (pp. 955–978). Palgrave Macmillan.

Harcourt, G. C., & Kerr, P. (2003). Keynes and the Cambridge school. In W. J. Samuels, J. E. Biddle, & J. B. Davis (Eds.), *A companion to the history of economic thought* (pp. 343–359). Blackwell Publishing.

Heath, R. (2021). *Vasco Carvalho reflects on the success of Cambridge-INET.* https://www.inet.econ.cam.ac.uk/

Izurieta, A. (2017, August 11). *Economic models that reality can no longer afford.* Institute for New Economic Thinking. https://www.ineteconomics.org/perspectives/blog/economic-models-that-are-costing-us-all

Izurieta, A., & Singh, A. (2010). Does fast growth in India and China help or harm US workers? *Journal of Human Development and Capabilities, 11*(1), 115–140.

Janeway, W. (2015, April 14). *How to recognize new economic thinking.* Institute for New Economic Thinking. https://www.ineteconomics.org/perspectives/blog/how-to-recognize-new-economic-thinking

Kvangraven, I., & Alves, C. (2019). Heterodox economics as a positive project: Revisiting the debate. *ESRC Global Poverty & Inequality Dynamics Research Network Working Paper, 19,* 24p. https://gpid.univie.ac.at/wp-content/uploads/2019/07/GPID-WP-19.pdf

Lavoie, M. (2015, April). *Should heterodox economics be taught in economics departments, or is there any room for backwater economics?* Paper prepared for the session Teaching Economics, at the 2015 INET Annual Conference, Paris.

Lavoie, M. (2022). *Post-Keynesian economics: New foundations* (2nd ed.). Edward Elgar, forthcoming.

Lee, F. S. (2007, November 1–3). *Making history by making identity and institutions: The emergence of Post-Keynesian–heterodox economics in Britain, 1974–1996.* Paper presented at the EAPE Conference, Universidade Porto, Porto.

Lee, F. (2009). *A history of heterodox economics: Challenging the mainstream in the twentieth century.* Routledge.

Lucas, R. E. (1980, Winter). The death of Keynesian economics. *Issues and Ideas.*

Lucas, R. E. (2007, September 19). Mortgages and monetary policy. *Wall Street Journal.*

Lucas, R. E., Jr., & Sargent, T. (1994 [1978]). After Keynesian macroeconomics. In P. R. Miller (Ed.), *The rational expectations revolution: Readings from the front line* (pp. 5–30). The M.I.T. Press.

Meade, J. E. (1964). *Efficiency, equality and the ownership of property.* George Allen and Unwin.

Newbery, D. (1998). Foreword. In I. Begg & S. G. B. Henry (Eds.), *Applied economics and public policy* (pp. xix–xxii). Cambridge University Press.

Newbery, D. (2017). Frank Horace Hahn 1925–2013. *Biographical Memoirs of Fellows of the British Academy, XVI,* 485–525. https://www.britac.ac.uk/sites/default/files/23 Hahn 1837 9_11_17.pdf

Palley, T. (2006). *The fallacy of the revised Bretton Woods hypothesis: Why today's international financial system is unsustainable.* Public Policy Brief No. 85. The Levy Economics Institute of Bard College.

Palley, T. (2009, July 29). Letter to the Queen: Why no one predicted the crisis. *Economics for Open and Democratic Societies.* http://thomaspalley.com/?p=148

Piketty, T. (2014). *Capital in the twenty-first century* (A. Goldhammer, Trans.). Harvard University Press.

Robinson, J. (1977). What are the questions? *Journal of Economic Literature, 15*(4), 1318–1339.

Rothschild, E. (1996). The debate on economic and social security in the late eighteenth century: Lessons of a road not taken. *Development and Change, 27*(2), 331–351.

Samuelson, P. A. (1988). The passing of the guard in economics. *Eastern Economic Journal, 14*(4), 319–329.

Shute, J. (2017, October 12). Weatherman Michael Fish on missing the great storm of 1987: 'When I saw what happened I thought, "oh s***"'. *The Telegraph.* https://www.telegraph.co.uk/men/thinking-man/weatherman-michael-fish-missing-great-storm-1987-saw-happened/

Skrabec, Q. R., Jr. (2014). *The fall of an American Rome: De-industrialization of the American dream.* Algora Publishing.

Stern, N. (2016). *Building on success and learning from experience: An independent review of the Research Excellence Framework*. https://assets.publishing.service.gov.uk/government/uploads/system/uploads/attachment_data/file/541338/ind-16-9-ref-stern-review.pdf

Storm, S. (2009). Capitalism and climate change: Can the invisible hand adjust the natural thermostat? *Development and Change, 40*(6), 1011–1038.

Tarshis, L. (1989). Remembering Joan Robinson. In G. R. Feiwel (Ed.), *Joan Robinson and modern economic theory* (pp. 918–920). Palgrave Macmillan.

Tribe, K. (2002). *Economic careers: Economics and economists in Britain, 1930–1970*. Routledge Taylor & Francis.

Trinity College Cambridge. (2019). *Trinity colleagues pay tribute to Robert Neild, 1924–2018*. https://www.trin.cam.ac.uk/news/trinity-colleagues-pay-tribute-to-robert-neild-1924-2018/

Videler, T. (2011, November 26). 9 insights into leadership from Professor Dame Sandra Dawson. *Vitae*. https://www.vitae.ac.uk/doing-research/research-staff/the-best-of-the-research-staff-blog/9-insights-into-leadership-from-professor-dame-sandra-dawson

Wapshott, N. (2011). *Keynes Hayek: The clash that defined modern economics*. W.W. Norton & Company.

Ward, B. (1972). *What's wrong with economics?* Basic Books.

REFERENCES

Abdelrahman, M. (2019). A conversation with Ha-Joon Chang. *Development and Change, 50*(2), 573–591.

Acemoglu, D., & Robinson, J. (2012). *Why nations fail: The origins of power, prosperity and poverty.* Crown Business.

Ackerman, F. (1999). *Still dead after all these years: Interpreting the failure of general equilibrium theory.* Working Paper No. 00-01, Global Development and Environment Institute, Tufts University. https://sites.tufts.edu/gdae/files/2019/10/00-01Ackerman_StillDead.pdf

Ady, P. (1947). *Peter Ady's special section.* In: Fortes, Steel and Ady (1947).

Ady, P. (1954). Review of books: The measurement of colonial national incomes, 1948, and *Colonial Social Accounting, 1953. Africa, 24*(2), 173–174.

Ady, P. (1967). Teaching economic development in the U. K.: Some analytical aspects. In K. Martin & J. Knapp (Eds.), *The teaching of development economics. Its position in the present state of knowledge. The proceedings of the Manchester Conference on teaching economic development, April 1964.* Routledge.

Agarwal, B., Humphries, J., & Robeyns, I. (2004). *Capabilities, freedom, and equality: Amartya Sen's work from a gender perspective.* Oxford University Press.

Aidt, T. (2003). Economic analysis of corruption: A survey. *Economic Journal, 113*(491), F632–F652.

Aidt, T. S. (2016). Rent seeking and the economics of corruption. *Constitutional Political Economy, 27,* 142–157.

Aidt, T. S., & Albornoz, F. (2011). Political regimes and foreign intervention. *Journal of Development Economics, 94*(2), 192–201.

Aidt, T. S., & Dutta, J. (2017). Fiscal federalism and electoral accountability. *Journal of Public Economic Theory, 19*(1), 38–58.

Aidt, T. S., & Franck, R. (2019). What motivates an oligarchic elite to democratize? Evidence from the roll call vote on the Great Reform Act of 1832. *Journal of Economic History, 79*(3), 773–825.

Aidt, T. S., & Jensen, P. S. (2017). From open to secret ballot: Vote buying and modernization. *Comparative Political Studies, 50*(5), 555–593.

Aidt, T. S., & Leon, G. (2016). The democratic window of opportunity: Evidence from riots in sub-Saharan Africa. *Journal of Conflict Resolution, 60*(4), 694–717.

Aidt, T. S., & Rauh, C. (2018). The big five personality traits and partisanship in England. *Electoral Studies, 54*, 1–21.

Aidt, T. S., Albornoz, F., & Gassebner, M. (2017). The golden hello and political transitions. *Journal of Comparative Economics, 46*(1), 157–173.

Aidt, T. S., Castro, V., & Martins, R. (2018). Shades of red and blue: Government ideology and sustainable development. *Public Choice, 175*, 303–323.

Aidt, T. S., Chadha, J. S., & Sabourian, H. (2019). Breaking the Brexit impasse: Achieving a fair, legitimate and democratic outcome. *National Institute Economic Review*, February, F4–F11.

Aidt, T. S., Daunton, M., & Dutta, J. (2010). The retrenchment hypothesis and the extension of the franchise in England and Wales. *Economic Journal, 120*(547), 990–1020.

Aidt, T. S., Leon, G., & Satchell, M. (2021). The social dynamics of collective action: Evidence from the diffusion of the Swing riots. *The Journal of Politics* (ahead of print version).

Aidt, T. S., Lili, J., & Low, H. (2017). Are prices enough? The economics of material demand reduction. *Philosophical Transactions of the Royal Society A: Mathematical, Physical and Engineering Sciences, 375*(2095).

Aistleitner, M., Kapeller, J., & Steinerberger, S. (2018). The power of scientometrics and the development of economics. *Journal of Economic Issues, 52*(3), 816–834. https://doi.org/10.1080/00213624.2018.1498721

Albertson, K., & Stepney, P. (2020). 1979 and all that: A 40-year reassessment of Margaret Thatcher's legacy on her own terms. *Cambridge Journal of Economics, 44*(2), 319–342.

Alexander, J. A. (1995). Our ancestors in their successive generation. *Canadian Journal of Economics, 28*(1), 205–224.

Allan, L. (2008). *Thatcher's economists: Ideas and opposition in 1980s Britain*. Doctoral dissertation, Trinity College, Oxford.

Allsopp, C. J. (1973). Effects of the selective employment tax. Final report, Review by C. J. Allsopp. *Economic Journal, 83*(332), 1282–1284.

Annan, N. (1983, February 3). How should a gent behave? *New York Review of Books*. https://www.nybooks.com/articles/1983/02/03/how-should-a-gent-behave/?pagination=false

Appelbaum, B. (2019). *The economists' hour: False prophets, free markets, and the fracture of society*. Little, Brown and Company.

Apthorpe, R. (1971). The new generalism: Four phases in development studies in the first development decade. *Development and Change, 3*(1), 62–75.

Arena, R. (2006). *On the relation between economics and sociology: Marshall and Schumpeter*. https://www.lib.hit-u.ac.jp/service/tenji/amjas/Arena.pdf

Arestis, P., & Sawyer, M. C. (Eds.). (1992). *A biographical dictionary of dissenting economists*. Edward Elgar.

Arrow, K. J. (2010). Recollections on Cambridge economics. *Cambridge Economics: Cambridge Faculty of Economics Alumni Newsletter, 3*, 5. www.econ.cam.ac.uk/alumni/newsletters/Cambridge-Economics-Issue-3-2010.pdf

Arrow, K. J., Chenery, H. B., Minhas, B. S., & Solow, R. M. (1961). Capital–labour substitution and economic efficiency. *Review of Economics and Statistics, 43*(3), 225–250.

Aslanbeigui, N., & Oakes, G. (2002). The theory arsenal: The Cambridge circus and the origins of the Keynesian revolution. *Journal of the History of Economic Thought, 24*(1), 5–37.

Aspers, P. (2006). The economic sociology of Alfred Marshall: An overview. *American Journal of Economics and Sociology, 58*(4), 651–667.

Astorga, P., Berges, A., & Fitzgerald, V. (2005). The standard of living in Latin America during the twentieth century. *Economic History Review, 58*(4), 765–796.

Astorga, P., Bergés, A. R., & Fitzgerald, V. (2011). Productivity growth in Latin America over the long run. *Review of Income and Wealth, 57*(2), 203–244.

Atkinson, A. B., & Stern, N. (2017). Tony Atkinson on poverty, inequality, and public policy: The work and life of a great economist. *Annual Review of Economics, 9*, 1–20. https://doi.org/10.1146/annurev-economics-110216-100949

Audier, S. (2013). A German approach to liberalism? Ordoliberalism, sociological liberalism, and social market economy. *L'Economie Politique, 60*(4), 48–76. English translation at: https://www.cairn-int.info/article-E_LECO_060_0048%2D%2Da-german-approach-to-liberalism.htm

Austin, G. (2017, October 20). *Inaugural lecture. Three revolutions in economic history.* University of Cambridge. https://www.econsoc.hist.cam.ac.uk/podcasts.html

Austin, G., & Broadberry, S. (2014). Introduction: The renaissance of African economic history. *Economic History Review, 67*(4), 893–906.

Baccini, A. (2018). *Performance-based incentives, research evaluation systems and the trickle-down of bad science.* https://www.ineteconomics.org/uploads/papers/Baccini-Value-for-money-Berlin-final.pdf

Baccini, A., De Nicolao, G., & Petrovich, E. (2019). *How performance evaluation metrics corrupt researchers.* https://www.ineteconomics.org/perspectives/blog/how-performance-evaluation-metrics-corrupt-researchers

Bach, G. L. (1972). Symposium. Economics of the new left: Comment. *Quarterly Journal of Economics, 86*(4), 632–643.

Backhouse, R. E. (1996). The changing character of British economics. In A. W. Coats (Ed.), *The post-1945 internationalization of economics,* Annual Supplement to volume 28, History of political economy (pp. 33–60). Duke University Press.

Backhouse, R. E. (2000). Economics in mid-Atlantic: British economics, 1945–95. In A. W. Coats (Ed.), *The development of economics in Western Europe since 1945* (pp. 19–39). Routledge.

Backhouse, R. E., Caldwell, B., Goodwin, C., & Rutherford, M. (2008). A. W. (Bob) Coats 1924–2007. *History of Political Economy, 40*(3), 421–446.

Bagchi, A. K. (1976). Deindustrialization in India in the nineteenth century: Some theoretical implications. *Journal of Development Studies, 12*(2), 135–164.

Bagchi, A. K. (1982). *The political economy of underdevelopment.* Cambridge University Press.

Bagchi, A. K. (2004). *Keynes, Kaldor and development economics.* Occasional Paper No. 1. Institute of Development Studies.

Bagchi, A. K. (2010). Posner, Michael (1931–2006), economist. In *Oxford dictionary of national biography.* Oxford University Press. https://doi.org/10.1093/ref:odnb/97802

Bagchi, A. K. (2019, September 13). The practical economist. *Frontline.*

Baker, C. (2021). *National staff from overseas: Statistics.* Research Briefing, UK Parliament, House of Commons Library. https://commonslibrary.parliament.uk/research-briefings/cbp-7783/

Baranzini, M., & Marangoni, G.-D. (2015). *Richard Stone: An annotated bibliography.* Universita della Svizzera Italiana. https://core.ac.uk/download/pdf/43664097.pdf

Baranzini, M. L., & Mirante, A. (2018). *Luigi L. Pasinetti: An intellectual biography: Leading scholar and system builder of the Cambridge School of Economics.* Palgrave Macmillan.

Barker, T. (1996). *Space-time economics.* Cambridge Econometrics.

Barker, T. (1998). Large-scale energy-environment-economy modelling of the European economy. In I. Begg & S. G. B. Henry (Eds.), *Applied economics and public policy* (pp. 15–40). Cambridge University Press.

Barker, T. (2017). Richard Stone (1913–1991). In R. A. Cord (Ed.), *The Palgrave companion to Cambridge economics* (pp. 835–855). Palgrave Macmillan.

Barker, T., & Brailovsky, V. (Eds.). (1982). *Oil or industry? Energy, industrialisation and economic policy in Canada, México, the Netherlands, Norway and the United Kingdom.* Academic Press.

Barker, T., & Peterson, W. (Eds.). (1987). *The Cambridge multisectoral dynamic model of the British economy.* Cambridge University Press.

Barnard, A. (2011). John Arundel Barnes, 1918–2010. *Proceedings of the British Academy, 172,* 27–45.

Barnes, J. (1970). *Sociology in Cambridge: An inaugural lecture.* Cambridge University Press.

Barnes, J. A. (1971). *Three styles in the study of kinship.* University of California Press.

Barnes, J. (1983). *Interview of John Barnes by Jack Goody, Cambridge 19 December 1983.* Filmed and edited by Alan Macfarlane and Sarah Harrison. http://www.alanmacfarlane.com/DO/filmshow/barnes1_fast.htm

Barnes, J. A. (1986). Where lies the truth? *Australian Anthropological Society Newsletter, 64,* 4–9.

Barnes, J. A. (2007). *Humping my drum: A memoir.* https://www.amazon.com/Humping-my-drum-J-Barnes/dp/1409204006

Barnes, J. A. (2011). Sociology in Cambridge: An inaugural lecture. *Cambridge Journal of Anthropology, 29,* Special Issue in Memory of John Barnes, 45–60.

Barnett, W. A. (2004). An interview with Paul A. Samuelson, December 23, 2003. *Macroeconomic Dynamics, 8,* 519–542. Republished in Working Paper Series in Theoretical and Applied Economics, University of Kansas.

Barnett, V. (2008). Russian émigré economics in the USA. In J. Zweynert (Ed.), *Economics in Russia: Studies in intellectual history* (pp. 107–122). Ashgate Publishing.

Basili, M., & Zappia, C. (2005). An interview with Frank Hahn the occasion of his 80th birthday. *Storia del Pensiero Economico N. S., 2*(2), 13–18.

Bauer, P. T. (1957). *Economic analysis and policy in underdeveloped countries.* Cambridge University Press, for the Duke University Commonwealth Studies Center.

Bauer, P. T. (1981). *Equality, the third world and economic delusion.* Methuen University Paperbacks.

Bauer, P. T., & Yamey, B. S. (1957). *The economics of underdeveloped countries.* Cambridge University Press.

Baumol, W. J. (1990). Erik Lundberg, 1907–1987. *The Scandinavian Journal of Economics, 92*(1), 1–9.

BBC. (1997, June 11). http://www.bbc.co.uk/news/special/politics97/background/pastelec/ge87.shtml

BBC. (2011, June 27). *Margaret Thatcher Asprey handbag raises 'just' GBP 25,000.* https://www.bbc.com/news/uk-england-lincolnshire-13932845

BBC. (2017, January 26). Obituary: Tam Dalyell. *BBC News*. https://www.bbc.com/news/uk-politics-29367988

Beath, J. (2010). Comments recorded in the minutes of CHUDE Steering Committee Meeting of 26th March 2010, Item 5.2. Royal Economic Society Conference of Heads of Departments of Economics at the University of Surrey. https://www.google.com/url?sa=t&rct=j&q=&esrc=s&source=web&cd=13&ved=2ahUKEwjMrpeskPnjAhVH26QKHSNRAEQQFjAMegQIBxAC&url=https%3A%2F%2Fwww.jiscmail.ac.uk%2Fcgi-bin%2Fwebadmin%3FA3%3Dind1011%26L%3DCHUDE%26E%3Dbase64%26P%3D5048%26B%3D%2D%2D%253D_3fd5r5o4aeng%26T%3Dapplication%252Fpdf%3B%2520name%3D%2522chudeagendapapers061110.pdf%2522%26N%3Dchudeagendapapers061110.pdf%26attachment%3Dq&usg=AOvVaw0qi1hy_FArteCVhSF4cQHt

Beath, J. (2015). Obituary: Aubrey Silberston (1922–2015). *Royal Economic Society Newsletter, 171*, 17–18.

Beaud, M., & Dostaler, G. (1995). *Economic thought since Keynes: A history and dictionary of major economists*. Routledge.

Beckerman, W. (1968). *An introduction to national income analysis*. Weidenfeld & Nicolson.

Beckett, A. (2002). *Pinochet in Piccadilly: Britain and Chile's hidden history*. Faber & Faber.

Beckett, A. (2010). *When the lights went out: What really happened to Britain in the seventies*. Faber & Faber.

Beckett, A. (2015a, September 14). Toxteth, 1981: The summer Liverpool burned – By the rioter and economist on opposite sides. *The Guardian*. https://www.theguardian.com/cities/2015/sep/14/toxteth-riots-1981-summer-liverpool-burned-patrick-minford-jimi-jagne

Beckett, A. (2015b). *Promised you a miracle: Why 1980–82 made modern Britain*. Allen Lane.

Begg, I., & Henry, S. G. B. (Eds.). (1998). *Applied economics and public policy*. Cambridge University Press.

Begg, I., & Horrell, S. (2002). UK banking and other financial services and the euro. In A. El-Agraa (Ed.), *The Euro and Britain* (pp. 277–303). Prentice Hall.

Beloff, M. (1968, March). A plague of economists? *Encounter*, Letters, 91.

Benn, T. (2000). Interview. Commanding Heights, Public Broadcasting Service, Interviewed on 26 October 2000. https://www.pbs.org/wgbh/commandingheights/hi/people/pe_name.html

Berg, M. (1996). *A woman in history: Eileen Power, 1889–1940*. Cambridge University Press.

Bernal, M. (2012). *Geography of a Life*. IN Xlibris Corporation.

Berrill, K., Phelps Brown, E. H., & Williams, D. G. T. (1983, May). *The Berrill Report: Report of an investigation into certain matters arising from the Rothschild Report on the Social Science Research Council*. Social Sciences Research Council, RFK/14/6/1, Richard Kahn Papers, King's College Archives.

Berry, V., & Petty, C. (1992). *The Nyasaland survey papers 1938–1943, agriculture, food and health*. Academy Press.

Besley, T., & Hennessy, P. (2009). The global financial crisis: Why didn't anybody notice? *British Academy Review, 14*, 8–10.

Besley, T., & Hennessy, P. (2010). *Financial and economic horizon scanning*. Letter sent to Her Majesty the Queen, February 8. https://www.thebritishacademy.ac.uk/sites/default/files/04besley-hennessy.pdf

Bettio, F. (1984). *The sexual division of labour: The Italian case*. Unpublished Ph.D., University of Cambridge, UK.
Beveridge, W. (1929). Allyn Abbott Young. Address by Sir William Beveridge at memorial service, in the church of St Clement Danes, 11th March 1929. *Economica, 25*, 1–3.
Beveridge, W. B. (1944). *Full employment in a free society*. Allen and Unwin.
Bezemer, D. (2011). The credit crisis and recession as a paradigm test. *Journal of Economic Issues, 45*(1), 1–18.
Bhaduri, A. (1973). A study in agricultural backwardness under semi-feudalism. *Economic Journal, 83*(329), 120–137.
Bhaduri, A., & Steindl, J. (1983). The rise of monetarism as a social doctrine. *Thames Papers in Political Economy*, Autumn, 1–18.
Bhagwati, J. N., & Chakravarty, S. (1969). Contributions to Indian economic analysis: A survey. *American Economic Review, 59*(4, Part 2, supplement), 1–73.
Bhagwati, J. N., & Desai, P. (1970). *India: Planning for industrialization; industrialization and trade policies since 1951*. Oxford University Press, on behalf of OECD.
Bhagwati, J., & Srinivasan, T. N. (1975). *Foreign trade regimes and economic development: India*. National Bureau of Economic Research.
Bhagwati, J., & Srinivasan, T. N. (1993). *Report: India's economic reforms*. Associated Chambers of Commerce and Industry of India.
Birner, J. (2009). *F. A. Hayek's Monetary Nationalism after seven decades*. Paper Presented at the Storep Annual Conference, Florence. Universiti di Trento and University College, Maastricht.
Bispham, J. A. (1975). The new Cambridge and 'monetarist' criticisms of 'conventional' economic policy-making. *National Institute Economic Review, 74*, 39–55.
Blackburn, R. M., & Mann, M. (1979). *The working class in the labour market* (Cambridge studies in sociology) (Vol. 1). Palgrave Macmillan.
Blackburn, R. M., & Marsh, C. (1991). Education and social class: Revisiting the 1944 Education Act with fixed marginals. *British Journal of Sociology, 42*(4), 507–536.
Blackburn, R. M., & Stewart, A. (1977, September). Women, work and the class structure. *New Society*.
Blaug, M. (1975). Kuhn versus Lakatos, or paradigms versus research programmes in the history of economics. *History of Political Economy, 7*(4), 399–433.
Blaug, M. (1999). Brian Reddaway. In M. Blaug (Ed.), *Who's who in economics* (3rd ed.). Edward Elgar.
Blaug, M. (2001). No history of ideas, please, we're economists. *Journal of Economic Perspectives, 15*(1), 145–164.
Blaug, M., & Sturgis, P. (Eds.). (1983). *Who's who in economics*. MIT Press.
Blaug, M., & Towse, R. (1988). *The current state of the British economics profession*. Royal Economic Society.
Blecker, R. (2013). Long-run growth in open economies: Export-led cumulative causation or a balance-of-payments constraint? In G. C. Harcourt & P. Kriesler (Eds.), *The Oxford handbook of post-Keynesian economics* (Theory and origins (Paper 16)) (Vol. 1). Oxford University Press.
Blinder, A. S. (1988). The fall and rise of Keynesian economics. *Economic Record, 64*(4, December), 278–294.
Blinder, A. S. (2000). How the economy came to resemble the model. *Business Economics, 35*(1), 16–25.
Blinder, A. S. (2014). *What did we learn from the financial crisis, the great recession, and the pathetic recovery?* Princeton University Griswold Center for Economic Policy Studies Working Paper No. 243. https://www.princeton.edu/ceps/workingpapers/243blinder.pdf

Blinder, A. S., & Solow, R. M. (1978). What's 'new' and what's 'Keynesian' in the 'New Cambridge' Keynesianism? In K. Brunner & A. H. Meltzer (Eds.), *Carnegie-Rochester conference series on public policy* (Vol. 9, pp. 67–85). North-Holland.

Bliss, C. (2010). The Cambridge Post-Keynesians: An outsider's insider view. *History of Political Economy, 42*(4), 631–652.

Blitch, C. P. (1983). Allyn Young on increasing returns. *Journal of Post Keynesian Economics, 5*(3), 359–372.

Blitch, C. P. (1995). *Allyn Young: The peripatetic economist*. Macmillan Press.

Bloomberg News. (2013, October 21). *Lawrence Klein dies at 93; won Nobel Prize for his econometric models*. https://www.latimes.com/local/obituaries/la-me-lawrence-klein-20131022-story.html

Blundell, J. (1990). *Waging the war of ideas: Why there are no shortcuts*. Presentation given at the Heritage Foundation, Atlas Economic Research Foundation, January. https://web.archive.org/web/20050419113153/http://www.atlasusa.org/toolkit/waging_war.php

Blundell, J. (2004). *Introduction to the IEA condensed version of the Reader's Digest Road to serfdom*. Institute of Economic Affairs.

Blundell, J. (2010, October 15). *Obituary–Professor Sir Alan Walters*. Institute of Economic Affairs. https://iea.org.uk/blog/obituary-%E2%80%93-professor-sir-alan-walters

Bodkin, R. G., & Kanta, M. (1997). Klein, Lawrence Robert. In D. Glasner (Ed.), *Business cycles and depressions: An encyclopedia* (pp. 361–363). Garland Publishing Inc.

Boettke, P. J. (2006). Hayek and market socialism. In E. Feser (Ed.), *The Cambridge companion to Hayek* (pp. 51–66). Cambridge University Press.

Booth, P. (2006a, March 15). How 364 economists got it totally wrong. *The Telegraph*. https://www.telegraph.co.uk/comment/personal-view/3623669/How-364-economists-got-it-totally-wrong.html

Booth, P. (Ed.). (2006b). *Were 364 economists all wrong?* Institute of Economic Affairs.

Bortis, H. (2010). Political economy and economic science: The work of Phyllis Deane. *Journal of Economic Analysis, 1*(1), 49–77.

Bortis, H. (2017). Phyllis Deane (1918–2012). In R. Cord (Ed.), *The Palgrave companion to Cambridge economics* (pp. 871–892). Palgrave Macmillan.

Bortis, H. (2019). John Neville Keynes. In R. W. Dimand & H. Hagemann (Eds.), *The Elgar companion to John Maynard Keynes* (pp. 10–16). Edward Elgar.

Bourguignon, F. (2012). Economics is not a science: Interview with Francois Bourguignon (Interview by C. Chavagneux). *L'Economie Politique, 55*, 7–13.

Bowles, S., Kirman, A., & Sethi, R. (2017a). Retrospectives: Friedrich Hayek and the market algorithm. *Journal of Economic Perspectives, 31*(5), 215–230.

Bowles, S., Kirman, A., & Sethi, R. (2017b). *The market algorithm and the scope of government: Reflections on Hayek*. VOX CEPR Policy Portal, December 8. https://voxeu.org/article/reflections-hayek

Boynton, R. (1997). *The two Tonys: A profile of LSE's Anthony Giddens*. https://www.robertboynton.com/articleDisplay.php?article_id=41

Bradley, I. (1980, November 12). The Hayek cure: Bigger and better bankruptcies. *The Times*. Digitalised version available in the Margaret Thatcher Foundation Archives. Retrieved August 14, 2020, from https://www.margaretthatcher.org/document/114510

Brandolini, A., Jenkins, S. P., & Micklewright, J. (2018). Anthony Barnes Atkinson, 4 September 1944–1 January 2017. *Biographical Memoirs of Fellows of the British Academy, XVII*, 179–190.

Brantley, C. (2002). *Feeding families: African realities and British ideas of nutrition and development in early colonial Africa*. Heinemann.
Bray, F. S. (1949). *Social accounts and the business enterprise sector of the national economy*. Cambridge University Press.
Bray, F. S., & Stone, R. (1948). The presentation of the central government accounts. *Accounting Research, 1*(1).
Breit, W., & Hirsch, B. T. (2004). *Lives of Laureates: Eighteen Nobel economists*. MIT Press.
Brender, V. (2010). Economic transformations in Chile: The formation of the Chicago Boys. *The American Economist, 55*(1), 111–122.
Brito, K. (1982). Memorandum to Party Chairman Cecil Parkinson, dated 12/01/1982. Correspondence and memoranda concerning a project to increase public understanding of the workings of the economic system at Lord Rothschild's behest, and funded by him. Conservative Party Archive, Chairman's Office, Economic Policy, 1957–1982; CCO 20/9/7; catalogued at the Bodleian Library, University of Oxford by Emily Tarrant, 2003. http://www.bodley.ox.ac.uk/dept/scwmss/wmss/online/modern/cpa/cco/cco20.html
Broadbent, S. (2018, April 5). Christopher Taylor obituary. *The Guardian*. https://www.theguardian.com/business/2018/apr/05/christopher-taylor-obituary
Bronfenbrenner, M. (1971). The 'structure of revolutions' in economic thought. *History of Political Economy, 3*(1), 1–11.
Brown, W. (1998). Funders and research: The vulnerability of the subject. In K. Whitfield & G. Strauss (Eds.), *Researching the world of work: Strategies and methods in studying industrial relations* (pp. 267–285). ILR Press.
Brown, W. (2015). Distinguished alumnus: Bill Janeway. *Cambridge Economics: News from the Cambridge Faculty of Economics, 8*(Autumn), 3.
Brown, W., & Cockerill, T. (2015). Shaping the Faculty's future. *Cambridge Economics: News from the Cambridge Faculty of Economics, 8*(Autumn).
Bruland, K. (2004). Industrialisation and technological change. In R. Floud & P. Johnson (Eds.), *The Cambridge economic history of modern Britain* (Industrialisation, 1700–1860) (Vol. 1, pp. 117–146). Cambridge University Press.
Buchanan, J. M. (1954a). Social choice, democracy and free markets. *Journal of Political Economy, 62*(2), 114–123.
Buchanan, J. M. (1954b). Individual choice in voting and the market. *Journal of Political Economy, 62*(3), 334–343.
Buchanan, J. M. (1986). Prize Lecture. NobelPrize.org. Nobel Prize Outreach AB 2022. Sat. 11 Jun 2022. https://www.nobelprize.org/prizes/economic-sciences/1986/buchanan/lecture/
Buchanan, J. (2002). The sayer of truth: A personal tribute to Peter Bauer. *Public Choice, 112*(3–4), 233.
Buggeln, M., Daunton, M., & Nutzenadel, A. (2017). *The political economy of public finance: Taxation, state spending and debt since the 1970s*. Cambridge University Press.
Bulmer, M. (1981). Sociology and political science at Cambridge in the 1920s: An opportunity missed and an opportunity taken. *The Cambridge Review, CII*(22623, April 29), 156–159.
Bulmer, M. (1982). Support for sociology in the 1920s: The Laura Spelman Rockefeller memorial and the beginnings of modern, large-scale, sociological research in the university. *The American Sociologist, 17*, 185–192.

Bulmer, M. (1984). Philanthropic foundations and the development of the social sciences in the early twentieth century: A reply to Donald Fisher. *Sociology*, *18*(4), 572–579.

Bulmer, M. (Ed.). (1985a). *Essays on the history of British sociological research*. Cambridge University Press.

Bulmer, M. (1985b). The development of sociology and of empirical social research in Britain. In M. Bulmer (Ed.), *Essays on the history of British sociological research* (pp. 3–36). Cambridge University Press.

Bulmer, M. (Ed.). (1987). *Social science research and government: Comparative essays on Britain and the United States*. Cambridge University Press.

Burchardt, F., et al. (1944). *The economics of full employment*. Blackwell for the Oxford Institute of Economics and Statistics.

Burchell, B., & Marsh, C. (1992). The effect of questionnaire length on survey response. *Quality and Quantity*, *26*, 233–244.

Burchell, B., Horrell, S., & Rubery, J. (1989). Unequal jobs or unequal pay? *Industrial Relations Journal*, *20*(3), 176–191.

Burchell, B., Horrell, S., & Rubery, J. (1990). Gender and skills. *Work, Employment and Society*, *4*(2) Reprinted in *Gender and Economics*, J. Humphries (ed.), Edward Elgar, 1994.

Burchell, B., Deakin, S., Michie, J., & Rubery, J. (Eds.). (2002). *Systems of production: Markets organisation and performance*. Routledge.

Burgin, A. (2012). *The great persuasion: Reinventing free markets since the Depression*. Harvard University Press.

Buss, R. (2006, November 12). Talleyrand: Napoleon's master by David Lawday. *The Independent*. https://www.independent.co.uk/arts-entertainment/books/reviews/talleyrand-napoleons-master-by-david-lawday-424034.html

Butler, E. (2015). *Antony Fisher, Herald of Freedom*. Adam Smith Institute. https://www.adamsmith.org/blog/miscellaneous/antony-fisher-herald-of-freedom

Buzaglo, J. (2010, October 22). *The Nobel family dissociates itself from the economics prize*. Real-world Economics Review Blog. https://rwer.wordpress.com/2010/10/22/the-nobel-family-dissociates-itself-from-the-economics-prize/

Byres, T. J. (1984). Amiya Bagchi and the political economy of underdevelopment. *Social Scientist*, *12*(132), 64–75.

C. R. (2014, March 14). Keynes and Hayek: Prophets for today. *The Economist*. https://www.economist.com/free-exchange/2014/03/14/prophets-for-today

Cairncross, A. (1993). *The life of an economic adviser*. Palgrave Macmillan.

Cairncross, A. (1995). Economists in wartime. *Contemporary European History*, *4*(1), 19–36.

Cairncross, A. (1999). Economic advisers in the United Kingdom. *Contemporary British History*, *13*(2), 232–242.

Caldentey, E. P. (2019). *Roy Harrod*. Palgrave Macmillan.

Caldwell, B. (2006). Hayek and the Austrian tradition. In E. Feser (Ed.), *The Cambridge companion to Hayek* (pp. 1–12). Cambridge University Press.

Caldwell, B. (2010). Cambridge talk on Hayek. Presented at the INET Conference on *The Economic Crisis and the Crisis of Economics*, at King's College, Cambridge, April 8–11, 2010. https://www.ineteconomics.org/uploads/papers/INET-C@K-Paper-Dinner-1-Caldwell-upd.pdf

Caldwell, B. (2019). *The Road to Serfdom after 75 years*. CHOPE Working Paper No. 2019-13, Center for the History of Political Economy at Duke University, 60p.

Caldwell, B. (2020). Mont Pelerin 1947. Paper presented at the Conference commemorating the 40 Anniversary of the Mont Pelerin Society meeting of 1980 at Stanford University, Hoover Institution – Stanford University, January 15–17, 58p.

Caldwell, B., & Montes, L. (2015). Friedrich Hayek and his visits to Chile. *Review of Austrian Economics, 28*(3), 261–309. https://doi.org/10.1007/s11138-014-0290-8

Cambridge Economic Policy Review. (n.d.). Digital Archives maintained online by Cambridge Political Economy Society (CPES). http://cpes.org.uk/om/items/show/25

Cambridge Economics. (2012). *Cambridge Economics: News from the Cambridge Faculty of Economics, 5* (Autumn).

Cambridge Graduate Students. (2001, June 14). *Opening up economics: A proposal by Cambridge students*. Open letter. http://www.paecon.net/petitions/Camproposal.htm

Cambridge Journal of Economics Editors. (2006). Keynes's last time at the Political Economy Club: Editorial introduction. *Cambridge Journal of Economics, 30*(1), 1. https://doi.org/10.1093/cje/bei091

Cambridge Judge Business School. (2021). *Dame Sandra Dawson*. https://www.jbs.cam.ac.uk/faculty-research/fellows-associates/dame-sandra-dawson/#item3

Cambridge Political Economy Group. (1974). Britain's economic crisis. Spokesman pamphlet No. 44. Bertrand Russell Peace Foundation, for *The Spokesman*.

Cambridge University General Board. (2004, July 21). Report of the General Board on the Faculty of Economics and Politics and the Department of Applied Economics. *Cambridge Reporter*.

Cambridge University Reporter. (various years). University of Cambridge.

Cambridge University Sociology (2018). *Fifty years of sociology at the University of Cambridge*. https://www.50years.sociology.cam.ac.uk/panels

Carlton, A. (2016, August 10). How Tony Benn's deputy leadership campaign was defeated. *New Statesman*. https://www.newstatesman.com/politics/elections/2016/08/how-tony-benn-s-deputy-leadership-campaign-was-defeated

Cassidy, J. (2000, June 30). The Hayek century. *Hoover Digest, 3*. https://www.hoover.org/research/hayek-century

Caswill, C., & Shove, E. (2000). Introducing interactive social science. *Science and Public Policy, 27*(3), 154–157.

Catao, L. A. V., & Solomou, S. N. (2005). Effective exchange rates and the classical gold standard. *American Economic Review, 95*(4, September), 1259–1275.

Cato Journal. (1987). Essays in honour of Peter Bauer. *Cato Journal, 1* (Spring–Summer).

Cesarano, F., Freedman, C., Leeson, R., Robson, W., Rowe, N., Sandilands, R., & Young, R. (2010). Interview with David Laidler. In R. Leeson (Ed.), *David Laidler's contributions to economics* (pp. 1–40). Palgrave Macmillan.

Chakravarty, S. (1987). *Post-Keynesian theorists and the theory of economic development*. Working Paper No. 23. WIDER-UNU.

Chakravarty, S. (1989). Nicholas Kaldor on Indian economic problems. *Cambridge Journal of Economics, 13*(1), 237–244. Retrieved June 1, 2021, from http://www.jstor.org/stable/23598159

Chakravarty, S., & Singh, A. (1988, July). *The desirable forms of economic openness in the South*. Unpublished paper, First Draft, 53p.

Chambers, M. (2020). *London and the modernist bookshop*. Cambridge University Press.

Chandavarkar, A. (1989). *Keynes and India: A study in economics and biography.* Macmillan.
Chandavarkar, A. (1993). Keynes and the role of the state in developing countries. In D. Crabtree & A. P. Thirlwall (Eds.), *Keynes and the role of the state* (Keynes Seminars) (pp. 126–160). Palgrave Macmillan. https://doi.org/10.1007/978-1-349-22708-2_9
Chandra, R. (2004). Adam Smith, Allyn Young and the division of labour. *Journal of Economics Issues, XXXVIII*(3), 787–805.
Chang, H.-J. (2002). *Kicking away the ladder: Development strategy in historical perspective.* Anthem Press.
Chang, H.-J. (2007). *Bad Samaritans: The myth of free trade and the secret history of capitalism.* Random House.
Chang, H.-J. (2010). *23 things they don't tell you about capitalism.* Allen Lane.
Chang, H.-J. (2014). *Economics: The user's guide.* Bloomsbury.
Chang, H.-J., & Grabel, I. (2004). *Reclaiming development: An alternative economic policy manual.* Zed Books.
Chang, A. C., & Li, P. (2015). *Is economics research replicable? Sixty published papers from thirteen journals say 'usually not'.* Finance and Economics Discussion Series, 2015-083. Board of Governors of the Federal Reserve System.
Charlwood, A. M. (n.d.). *The anatomy of union membership decline in Great Britain, 1980–1998.* Doctoral dissertation, London School of Economics, London.
Chote, R. (1993, March 7). Lamont's 'seven wise men' fall out as professor goes on the attack. *The Independent.*
Clapham, J. (1940). Eileen Power, 1889–1940. *Economica, New Series, 7*(28), 351–359.
Clapham, J. (1944). *The Bank of England, Vol. I, 1694–1797; Vol. II, 1797–2014.* Cambridge University Press.
Clapham, J. (1949/1957). *A concise economic history of Britain from earlier times to 1750* (1st ed./3rd ed.). Cambridge University Press. [Prepared by John Saltmarsh after the death of John Clapham].
Clark, C. (1932). *The national income 1924–31.* Macmillan & Co.
Clark, C. (1937). *National income and outlay.* Macmillan & Co.
Clark, C. (1938). Determination of the multiplier from national income statistics. *Economic Journal, 48*(191), 435–448.
Clark, C. (1940). *The conditions of economic progress.* Macmillan & Co.
Clark, G. K. (1973). A hundred years of the teaching of history at Cambridge, 1873–1973. *Historical Journal, 16*(3), 535–553.
Clarke, P. (n.d.). *Obituary: Professor Sir Harry Hinsley, 1918–1998.* Obituaries, 1990s – St. John's College, pp. 100–106. https://www.joh.cam.ac.uk/sites/default/files/Eagle/Eagle%20Chapters/Obituaries/Obituaries_1990s.pdf
Clements, K. W. (2004). *Larry Sjaastad, the last Chicagoan.* http://www.library.uwa.edu.au/__data/assets/pdf_file/0009/99873/05_02_Clements.pdf
Coats, A. W. (1967). Alfred Marshall and the early development of the London School of Economics: Some unpublished letters. *Economica, 34*(136), 408–417.
Coats, A. W. (1969). Is there a 'structure of scientific revolutions' in economics? *Kyklos, 22*(2), 289–296.
Coats, A. W. (1971). The role of scholarly journals in the history of economics: An essay. *Journal of Economic Literature, 9*(1), 29–44.
Coats, A. W. (1982). The distinctive LSE ethos in the inter-war years. *Atlantic Economic Journal, 10*, 18–30.

Coats, A. W. (1993). *The sociology and professionalization of economics: British and American economic essays, volume II.* Routledge.

Coats, A. W. (Ed.). (1996). *The post-1945 internationalization of economics.* Annual Supplement to volume 28, History of Political Economy. Duke University Press.

Coats, A. W. (Ed.). (2000). *The development of economics in Western Europe since 1945.* Routledge.

Coats, A. W., & Coats, S. E. (1970). The social composition of the Royal Economic Society and the beginnings of the British economics 'profession', 1890–1915. *British Journal of Sociology, 21,* 75–85.

Cockerill, T. (2012). The Marshall lectures. *Cambridge Economics: Cambridge Faculty of Economics Alumni Newsletter, 5,* 5–6. http://www.econ.cam.ac.uk/alumni/newsletters/Cambridge-Economics-Issue-5-2012.pdf

Cockett, R. (1994). *Thinking the unthinkable: Think-tanks and the economic counter-revolution, 1931–1983.* Harper-Collins.

Colander, D. (Ed.). (1996). *Beyond microfoundations: Post-Walrasian macroeconomics.* Cambridge University Press.

Colander, D., & Landreth, H. (1996). *The coming of Keynesianism to America.* Edward Elgar.

Colander, D., & Landreth, H. (n.d.). *Political influence on the textbook Keynesian revolution: God, man, and Laurie (sic) Tarshis at Yale.* http://community.middlebury.edu/~colander/articles/Political%20Influence%20on%20the%20Textbook%20Keynesian%20Revolution.pdf

Colander, D., Föllmer, H., Haas, A., Goldberg, M., Juselius, K., Kirman, A., ... Sloth, B. (2009). The financial crisis and the systemic failure of academic economics. *Critical Review, 21*(2–3), 249.

Cole, W. A. (1967). *Economic history as a social science.* Inaugural lecture delivered at University College of Swansea on 14 October 1967, 1–23. https://collections.swansea.ac.uk/s/mitchell-welsh-arts-archive/item/2557#?c=&m=&s=&cv=

Cole, W. A. (2007). W. A. Cole interviewed by A. J. H. Latham. In J. S. Lyons, L. P. Cain, & S. H. Williamson (Eds.), *Reflections on the cliometric revolution: Conversations with economic historians* (pp. 146–154). Routledge. Interview on 17 April 1998 at University of Wales, Swansea, by A.J.H. Latham.

Coleman, D. C. (1956). Industrial growth and industrial revolutions. *Economica, 23*(89), 1–22.

Coleman, D. C. (1969a). *Courtaulds: An economic and social history: Volume 1 – Rope and silk.* Clarendon Press.

Coleman, D. C. (1969b). *Courtaulds: An economic and social history: Volume 2 – Rayon.* Clarendon Press.

Coleman, D. C. (1972). *What has happened to economic history? An inaugural lecture.* Cambridge University Press.

Coleman, D. C. (1980). *Courtaulds: An economic and social history: Volume 3 – Crisis and change.* Clarendon Press.

Coleman, D. C. (1983). Proto-industrialization: A concept too many. *The Economic History Review, 36*(3), 435–448.

Coleman, D. C. (1987). *History and the economic past. An account of the rise and decline of economic history in Britain.* Clarendon Press.

Coleman, D., & Rowthorn, B. (2004). The economic effects of immigration into the United Kingdom. *Population and Development Review, 30*(4), 579–624.

Collini, S. (2016, January 17). Obituary: Geoffrey Hawthorn. *The Guardian.*

Conference of Socialist Economists London Working Group. (1980). *The alternative economic strategy: A labour movement response to the economic crisis*. CSE Books.
Congdon, T. (1981, July 14). How 364 economists got it wrong .... Letter to the Editor. *The Times*.
Cooper, C., & FitzGerald, E. V. K. (Eds.). (1989). *Development studies revisited: Twenty-five years of the Journal of Development Studies*. Frank Cass.
Cord, R. (2013). *Reinterpreting the Keynesian revolution*. Routledge.
Cord, R. A. (Ed.). (2017). *The Palgrave companion to Cambridge economics*. Palgrave Macmillan.
Courvisanos, J., & Millmow, A. (2006). How Milton Friedman came to Australia: A case study of class-based political business cycles. *Journal of Australian Political Economy, 57*, 112–136.
Coutts, K. (2021). The legacy of Wynne Godley: Notes for a talk on the legacy of Wynne Godley, Wednesday 12 May 2020. *Journal of Post Keynesian Economics, 44*(1), 27–31.
Coutts, K., Tarling, R., Ward, T., & Wilkinson, F. (1981). The economic consequences of Mrs Thatcher. *Cambridge Journal of Economics, 5*(1), 81–93.
Crafts, N. F. R. (2007). Phyllis Deane, interviewed by Nicholas F. R. Crafts. In J. S. Lyons, L. P. Cain, & S. H. Williamson (Eds.), *Reflections on the cliometrics revolution: Conversations with economic historians* (pp. 132–145). Routledge.
Craig, C., Rubery, J., Tarling, R., & Wilkinson, F. (1982). *Labour market structure, industrial organisation and low pay*. Cambridge University Press.
Craver, E., & Leijonhufvud, A. (1987). Economics in America: The continental influence. *History of Political Economy, 19*(2), 173–182.
Craypo, C., & Wilkinson, F. (2011). The low road to competitive failure: Immigrant labour and emigrant jobs in the US. *The Handbook of Globalization* (2nd ed., pp. 356–380). Edward Elgar.
Creedy, J. (2008). *J. A. C. Brown (1922–1984): An appreciation*. Research Paper No. 1027, Department of Economics, University of Melbourne.
Cribb, J. (2013). *Income inequality in the UK*. https://www.ifs.org.uk/docs/ER_JC_2013.pdf
Cripps, F. (1973). *Growth in advanced capitalist economies, 1950–70*. Department of Applied Economics, Occasional Paper No. 40. Cambridge University Press.
Cripps, F. (2021). The legacy of Wynne Godley: Godley and the world today. *Journal of Post Keynesian Economics, 44*(1), 24–26.
Cripps, F., & Godley, W. (1976). A formal analysis of the Cambridge Economic Policy Group model. *Economica (New Series), 43*(172), 335–348.
Cripps, F., & Godley, W. (1978). Control of imports as a means to full employment and the expansion of world trade. *Cambridge Journal of Economics, 2*(3), 327–334.
Cripps, F., & Izurieta, A. (2014). *The UN global policy model: Technical description*. Technical manual. https://unctad.org/en/PublicationsLibrary/tdr2014_GPM_TechnicalDescription.pdf
Cripps, F., & Lavoie, M. (2017). Wynne Godley (1926–2010). In R. A. Cord (Ed.), *The Palgrave companion to Cambridge economics* (pp. 929–953). Palgrave Macmillan.
Cripps, T. F., & Tarling, R. (1973). *Growth in advanced capitalist economies, 1950–1970*. Cambridge University Press.
Cripps, F., Fetherston, M., & Godley, W. (1978). Simulations with the Cambridge Economic Policy Group model. In M. V. Posner (Ed.), *Demand management*. Heinemann.

Cripps, F., Gudgin, G., & Rhodes, J. (1979). Technical manual of the CEPG model of world trade. *Cambridge Economic Policy Review, 3*(June).

Cripps, F., Izurieta, A., & Singh, A. (2011). Global imbalances, under-consumption and over-borrowing: The state of the world economy and future policies. *Development and Change, 42*(1), 228–261.

Crotty, J. (2019). *Keynes against capitalism: His economic case for liberal socialism*. Routledge.

Cubitt, C. E. (2006). *A life of Friedrich August von Hayek*. Authors OnLine.

Cunningham, C. (1973). *A survey of economic forecasting*. Report submitted to the SSRC. SSRC.

Cunningham, C. (2006, March 17). Michael Posner: Applied economist and champion of the social sciences. *The Guardian*.

Daedalus. (1975). The oil crisis: In perspective. *Daedalus, 104*(4, Theme issue).

Dahrendorf, R. (1995). *A history of the London School of Economics and Political Science, 1895–1995*. Oxford University Press.

Dandekar, V. M. (1971). D. R. Gadgil. *Economic and Political Weekly, 6*(19), 938–942.

Dartington. (2019, October 15). *Michael Young*. Dartington Trust. https://www.dartington.org/michael-young/

Dasgupta, P. (1995). *An inquiry into wellbeing and destitution*. Clarendon Press.

Dasgupta, P. (2000). Economic progress and the idea of social capital. In P. Dasgupta & I. Serageldin (Eds.), *Social capital: A multifaceted perspective* (pp. 325–424). World Bank.

Dasgupta, P. (2002). *Social capital and economic performance: Analytics*. https://citeseerx.ist.psu.edu/viewdoc/download?doi=10.1.1.127.8067&rep=rep1&type=pdf. To appear in: Ostrom, Elinor, & Ahn, T. K. (Ed.). (2003). *Foundations of social capital*. Edward Elgar.

Dasgupta, P. (2010). Interview with Partha Dasgupta 6th April 2010. In S. Harrison & A. Macfarlane, *Encounter with economics*. Interviews filmed by A. Macfarlane and edited by S. Harrison. University of Cambridge. http://sms.cam.ac.uk/collection/1092396

Dasgupta, P. (2013). Obituary: Frank Hahn. *Royal Economic Society Newsletter, 161*(April).

Dasgupta, P., & Weale, M. (1992). On measuring the quality of life. *World Development, 20*(1), 119–131.

Daubenmier, J. (1990, February 25). Professors recall hard lessons of McCarthyism: Free speech: Some want the University of Michigan to apologize to three professors who were branded as potential subversives because of their former communist sympathies. *Los Angeles Times*. https://www.latimes.com/archives/la-xpm-1990-02-25-mn-1928-story.html

Daunton, M. (1995). *Progress and poverty: An economic and social history of Britain, 1700–1850*. Oxford University Press.

Daunton, M. J. (1996). How to pay for the War: State, society and taxation in Britain, 1917–24. *The English Historical Review, CXI*(443), 882–919.

Daunton, M. (2001). *Trusting Leviathan: The politics of taxation in Britain, 1799–1914*. Cambridge University Press.

Daunton, M. (2002). *Just taxes: The politics of taxation in Britain, 1914–1979*. Cambridge University Press.

Daunton, M. (2007). *Wealth and welfare: An economic and social history of Britain, 1851–1951*. Oxford University Press.

Daunton, M. (2008). Interview with Professor Martin Daunton interviewed by Danny Millum. *Making history: The discipline in perspective.* https://archives.history.ac.uk/makinghistory/resources/interviews/Daunton_Martin.html

Daunton, M. (2017a). Cambridge and economic history. In R. A. Cord (Ed.), *The Palgrave companion to Cambridge economics, Volume I* (pp. 157–186). Palgrave Macmillan.

Daunton, M. (2017b). John Harold Clapham (1873–1946). In R. A. Cord (Ed.), *The Palgrave companion to Cambridge economics, Volume I* (pp. 423–454). Palgrave Macmillan.

Davis, J. (2007). *Prime ministers and Whitehall 1960–74.* Hambledon Continuum.

Davis, J., & McWilliam, R. (Eds.). (2018). *Labour and the left in the 1980s.* Manchester University Press.

De Vries, J. (1994). The industrial revolution and the industrious revolution. *Journal of Economic History, 54*(2), 249–270.

De Vroey, M. (2010). *Lucas on the Lucasian transformation of macroeconomics: An assessment.* Discussion Paper 2010-32. https://sites.uclouvain.be/econ/DP/IRES/2010032.pdf

De Vroey, M., & Duarte, P. G. (2012). *In search of lost time: The neoclassical synthesis.* Working Paper No. 2012-07. Department of Economics, FEA-USP. http://www.repec.eae.fea.usp.br/documentos/PedroDuarteN07WP.pdf

De Vroey, M., & Malgrange, P. (2012). From the *Keynesian Revolution* to the Klein-Goldberger Model: Klein and the dynamization of Keynesian theory. *History of Economic Ideas, 20*(2), 113–135.

Deakin, S. F., & Ewing, K. D. (2021, April 13). *Frank Wilkinson 1934–2021.* Institute of Employment Rights. https://www.ier.org.uk/news/frank-wilkinson-1934-2021/

Deane, P. (1946). Measuring national income in Colonial Territories. In *Studies in Income and Wealth* (pp. 145–174). National Bureau on Economic Research.

Deane, P. (1947). National income: Problems in social accounting in Central Africa. *Human Problems in British Central Africa: The Rhodes-Livingstone Journal, 5,* 24–43.

Deane, P. (1948a). *The measurement of colonial national incomes: An experiment.* N.I.E.S.R. Occasional Papers XII. Cambridge University Press.

Deane, P. (1948b). *Village economic surveying in Central Africa.* Colonial Research Fellowships, Plans and Reports of Miss PM Deane, October 28, 1948, CO 927/17/5, UK National Archives.

Deane, P. (1949). Problems of surveying village economies. *Human Problems in British Central Africa: The Rhodes-Livingstone Journal, 8,* 42–49.

Deane, P. (1953). *Colonial social accounting.* N.I.E.S.R. Social Studies XI. Cambridge University Press.

Deane, P. (1965). *The first industrial revolution.* Cambridge University Press.

Deane, P. (1978). *The evolution of economic ideas.* Cambridge University Press.

Deane, P. (1988a). *The state and the economic system: Introduction to the history of political economy.* Oxford University Press.

Deane, P. (1988b). Review of: *The rise and fall of monetarism: The theory and politics of an economic experiment* by David Smith, and Why Reaganomics and Keynesian economics failed by James E. Sawyer. *International Affairs, 64*(3), 486–487.

Deane, P. (1991). Joan Robinson (1903–1983): A biographical memoir. In I. Rima (Ed.), *The Joan Robinson legacy* (pp. 15–19). M. E. Sharpe.

Deane, P. (2001). *The life and times of J. Neville Keynes: A beacon in the tempest.* Edward Elgar.

Deane, P. (2007). Phyllis Deane interviewed by Nicholas F. R. Crafts. In J. S. Lyons, L. P. Cain, & S. H. Williamson (Eds.), *Reflections on the cliometric revolution: Conversations with economic historians* (pp. 132–145). Routledge. Interview conducted in Spring, 1993.

Deane, P., & Cole, W. A. (1962). *British economic growth: 1688–1959*. Cambridge University Press.

Deaton, A. S. (1987). Stone, John Richard Nicholas. In J. Eatwell, M. Milgate, & P. Newman (Eds.), *The new Palgrave dictionary of economics* (Vol. IV, pp. 509–512). Macmillan.

Deaton, A. S. (1993). John Richard Nicholas Stone 1913–1991. *Proceedings of the British Academy, 82*, 475–492.

Deaton, A. (2008). Stone, John Richard Nicholas (1913–1991). In S. N. Durlauf & L. E. Blume (Eds.), *The new Palgrave dictionary of economics* (2nd ed.). Palgrave Macmillan. https://www.princeton.edu/~deaton/downloads/Deaton_STONE_JOHN_RICHARD.pdf

Deaton, A. (2011). My Cambridge in the 60s and 70s. *Cambridge Economics: Cambridge Faculty of Economics Alumni Newsletter, 4*, 3–4. www.econ.cam.ac.uk/alumni/newsletters/Cambridge-Economics-Issue-4-2011.pdf

Deaton, A. (2014). Puzzles and paradoxes: A life in applied economics. In M. Szenberg & L. Ramrattan (Eds.), *Eminent economists II: Their life and work philosophies* (pp. 84–101). Cambridge University Press. https://wws.princeton.edu/system/files/research/documents/deaton_puzzles_and_paradoxes.pdf

Deaton, A. (n.d.). *Puzzles and paradoxes: A life in applied economics*. https://wws.princeton.edu/system/files/research/documents/deaton_puzzles_and_paradoxes.pdf. Published subsequently as: Deaton, A. (2014). Puzzles and paradoxes: A life in applied economics. In M. Szenberg & L. Ramrattan (Eds.), *Eminent economists II: Their life and work philosophies* (pp. 84–101). Cambridge University Press.

Debreu, G. (1974). Excess demand functions. *Journal of Mathematical Economics, 1*(1), 15–21.

Decker, S., Elsner, W., & Flechtner, S. (Eds.). (2020). *Principles and pluralist approaches in teaching economics: Towards a transformative science*. Routledge.

Deng, A. (1994). Obituary: Paul Philip Howell, D.Phil, CMG, OBE. *The Cambridge Journal of Anthropology, 17*(1), 69–71.

Denham, A. (2005). *British think-tanks and the climate of opinion*. Routledge.

Denham, A., & Garnett, M. (2001). *Keith Joseph*. Routledge.

Denham, A., & Garnett, M. (1998). *British think-tanks and the climate of opinion*. UCL Press Ltd.

Dennis, N., Henriques, F., & Slaughter, C. (1956). *Coal is our life: An analysis of a Yorkshire mining community*. Eyre & Spottiswoode.

Dennison, T., & Ogilvie, S. (2007). Serfdom and social capital in Bohemia and Russia. *Economic History Review, 60*(3), 513–544.

Dennison, T., & Ogilvie, S. (2014). Does the European marriage pattern explain economic growth? *The Journal of Economic History, 74*(3), 651–693.

Dennison, T. K., & Ogilvie, S. (2016). Institutions, demography, and economic growth. *The Journal of Economic History, 76*(1), 205–217.

Department of Applied Economics. (n.d.). *The Cambridge Growth Project 1960–87: A catalogue of the collection*. Department of Applied Economics, University of Cambridge.

Department of Applied Economics. (various years). *DAE Annual Reports, 1946–48 to 1986–87*. Cambridge: Department of Applied Economics, Marshall Library Archives, digitalized.

Desai, P. (1963). The development of the Indian economy. An exercise in economic planning. *Oxford Economic Papers, 15*(3), 308–317.

Desai, M. (2005, July 20). I. G. Patel: Economic statesman and director of LSE. *The Independent*.

Desai, M. (2006). Hayek and Marx. In E. Feser (Ed.), *The Cambridge companion to Hayek* (pp. 67–81). Cambridge University Press.

Di Matteo, M. (Ed.). (1990). *Celebrating R. M. Goodwin's 75th Birthday Quaderni del Dipartimento di Economia Politica No. 100*. University of Siena.

Di Matteo, M., & Sordi, S. (2009). *Richard M. Goodwin: A pioneer in the field of economic dynamics between the two Cambridges*. DEPFID Working Paper No. 7/2009. Dipartimento di Politica Economica, Finanza e Sviluppo, University di Siena.

Diamond, A. M. (1989). The core journals of economics. *Current Contents, 21*(1), 4–11.

Dimand, R. W. (2008). How Keynes came to Canada: Mabel Timlin and Keynesian economics. In M. Forstater & L. R. Wray (Eds.), *Keynes for the twenty-first century* (pp. 57–79). Palgrave Macmillan. https://doi.org/10.1057/9780230611139_4

Dimand, R. W. (2019). Mabel Timlin. In R. Dimand & H. Hagemann (Eds.), *The Elgar Companion to John Maynard Keynes* (pp. 456–461). Edward Elgar.

Dirks, N. B. (2001). *Castes of mind: Colonialism and the making of modern India*. Princeton University Press.

Dobb, M. (1928). *Russian economic development since the revolution*. George Routledge & Sons.

Dobb, M. (1937). *Political economy and capitalism: Some essays in economic tradition*. Routledge.

Dobb, M. (1946). *Studies in the development of capitalism*. Routledge.

Dobb, M. (1948). *Soviet economic development since 1917*. Routledge.

Dobb, M. (1950). The transition from feudalism to capitalism: Reply to Paul Sweezy. *Science and Society, 14*(2), 157–167.

Dobb, M. (1951). *Some aspects of economic development*. Ranjit Printers and Publishers. (Reprinted in M. Dobb 1967).

Dobb, M. (1955). *On economic theory and socialism*. Routledge and International Publishers.

Dobb, M. (1960). *An essay on economic growth and planning*. Routledge and Kegan Paul.

Dobb, M. (1967). *Papers on capitalism, development and planning*. Routledge and Kegan Paul.

Dobb, M. (1969). *Welfare economics and the economics of socialism: Towards a commonsense critique*. Cambridge University Press.

Dobb, M. (1973). *Theories of value and distribution since Adam Smith: Ideology and economic theory*. Cambridge University Press.

Doherty, B. (1995, June). Best of both worlds: An interview with Milton Friedman. *Reason*. https://reason.com/1995/06/01/best-of-both-worlds/

Dow, S., Harcourt, G., Hodgson, G., et al. (2009, August 21). Her Majesty the Queen. *Revue du MAUSS permanente*. http://www.journaldumauss.net/./?Her-Majesty-the-Queen

Dow, J. C., with Hacche, G., & Taylor, C. (2013). *Inside the Bank of England: Memoirs of Christopher Dow, Chief Economist 1973–84*. Palgrave Macmillan.

Downes, D. (Ed.). (1992). *Unravelling criminal justice: Eleven British studies.* Macmillan.

Drewnowski, J. (1974). *On measuring and planning the quality of life.* Institute of Social Studies and Mouton.

Drury, I. (2015, December 4). Mass migration 'will wreck the dream of a high-wage Britain': Top economist says large numbers of unskilled workers is 'damaging' for job prospects. *The Daily Mail.* https://www.dailymail.co.uk/news/article-3345332/Mass-migration-wreck-dream-high-wage-Britain-economist-says-large-numbers-unskilled-workers-damaging-job-prospects.html

Dunn, S. P. (2009). Cambridge economics, heterodoxy and ontology: An interview with Tony Lawson. *Review of Political Economy, 21*(3), 481–496.

Durlauf, S., & Blume, L. (Eds.). (2008). *The new Palgrave dictionary of economics.* Palgrave Macmillan.

Earl, P. (2016). Pluralistic teaching: A student's memoir. In G. C. Harcourt, The legacy of Ajit Singh (11 September 1940–23 June 2015): Memories and tributes from former pupils, colleagues and friends. *The Economic and Labour Relations Review, 27*(3), 304–306.

Eatwell, J. (1977). Maurice Dobb. *Cambridge Journal of Economics, 1*(1), 1–3.

Eatwell, J. (1982). *Whatever happened to Britain: The economics of a decline.* Duckworth, BBC.

Eatwell, J. (1992). The development of labour policy, 1979–1992. In J. Michie (Ed.), *The economic legacy.* Academic Press.

Eatwell, J. (2008). Retirement of Professor Ajit Singh. *The Queens' College Record 2008,* 7–8.

Eatwell, J. (2016). Tribute to Ajit Singh. *Cambridge Journal of Economics, 40*(2), 365–372.

Eatwell, J. (2019). Singh, Ajit (1940–2015), economist. In *Oxford dictionary of national biography.* Oxford University Press. https://www.oxforddnb.com/search?q=ajit+singh&searchBtn=Search&isQuickSearch=true

Eatwell, J., & Milgate, M. (2011). *The fall and rise of Keynesian economics.* Oxford University Press.

Ebenstein, L. (2018). Hayek's divorce and move to Chicago. *Econ Journal Watch, 15*(3), 301–321. https://econjwatch.org/articles/hayeks-divorce-and-move-to-chicago

Economic Journal. (1898). After seven years. *Economic Journal, 8*(29), 1–2.

The Economist. (1986, September 6). The price of prediction. *The Economist.*

The Economist. (1995, June 3). Dustmen as economic gurus. *The Economist.*

Edgeworth, F. W. (1891). The British Economic Association. *Economic Journal, 1*(1), 1–14.

Edmunds, J. (1997). *The Left's views on Israel: From the establishment of the Jewish State to the Intifada.* PhD Thesis, London School of Economics and Politics. http://etheses.lse.ac.uk/2847/1/U615796.pdf

Edwards, K. J. R. (2009, February 5). *Ken Edwards, interviewed by Alan Macfarlane.* Film interview with leading thinkers, University of Cambridge. http://www.alan-macfarlane.com/DO/filmshow/edwardstx.htm

Edwards, J., & Ogilvie, S. (1996). Universal banks and German industrialization: A reappraisal. *Economic History Review, 49,* 427–446.

Edwards, J., & Ogilvie, S. (2012a). Contract enforcement, institutions, and social capital: The Maghribi Traders reappraised. *Economic History Review, 65*(2), 421–444.

Edwards, J., & Ogilvie, S. (2012b). What lessons for economic development can we draw from the champagne fairs? *Explorations in Economic History, 49*(2), 131–148.

Eldridge, J. (2011). Half-remembrance of things past: Critics and cuts of old. *Sociological Research Online, 16*(3), 20. http://www.socresonline.org.uk/16/3/20.html

Ellman, M. (1975). Did the agricultural surplus provide the resources for the increase in investment in the USSR during the first five year plan? *Economic Journal, 85*(340), 844–863.

Ellman, M. (2000). The 1947 famine and the entitlement approach to famines. *Cambridge Journal of Economics, 24*(5), 603–630.

Ellman, M., Rowthorn, B., Smith, R., & Wilkinson, F. (1974). *Britain's economic crisis*. Spokesman Books.

English Chess Forum. (n.d.). Modern chess openings, p. 118. https://www.ecforum.org.uk/viewtopic.php?t=10039

ESRC. (n.d.). *SSRC/ESRC: The first forty years*. ESRC. https://esrc.ukri.org/files/news-events-and-publications/publications/ssrc-and-esrc-the-first-forty-years/

Evaluation Associates. (1999). *Interdisciplinary research and the research assessment exercise: A report by Evaluation Associates Ltd*. Higher Education Funding Council for England.

Evans, R. (1997). Soothsaying or science? Falsification, uncertainty and social change in macroeconomic modelling. *Social Studies of Science, 27*(3), 395–438.

Evon, D. (2016). 'First they ignore you, then they laugh at you' quote isn't Gandhi's. https://www.snopes.com/fact-check/first-they-ignore-you/

Ewing, A. F. (1971). Review of *Welfare economics and the economics of socialism: Towards a common-sense critique*, Cambridge: Cambridge University Press. *Journal of Modern African Studies, 9*(2), 332–333.

Farnie, D. A., & Tweedale, G. (2009). *A bio-bibliography of economic and social history* (5th ed.) https://www.yumpu.com/en/document/read/9266699/a-bio-bibliography-of-economic-history-society

Feinstein, C. H. (1965). *Domestic capital formation in the United Kingdom*. Cambridge University Press.

Feinstein, C. H. (Ed.). (1967). *Socialism, capitalism and economic growth: Essays presented to Maurice Dobb*. Cambridge University Press.

Feinstein, C. H. (1972). *National income, expenditure and output of the United Kingdom, 1855–1965*. Cambridge University Press.

Feinstein, C. (1988). The rise and fall of the Williamson curve. *Journal of Economic History, 48*(3), 699–729.

Feinstein, C. H. (2007). Charles H. Feinstein interviewed by Mark Thomas. In J. S. Lyons, L. P. Cain, & S. H. Williamson (Eds.), *Reflections on the cliometric revolution: Conversations with economic historians* (pp. 286–300). Routledge. Interviewed by Mark Thomas on 2 August 2002 at All Souls, Oxford.

Feinstein, C., & Matthews, R. (1990). The growth of output and productivity in the UK: The 1980s as a phase of the post-war period. *National Institute Economic Review, 133*(1), 78–90.

Feinstein, C., & Reddaway, W. B. (1978). OPEC surpluses, the world recession and the U.K. economy. *Midland Bank Review*, Spring; reprinted in Matthews and Sargent (1983).

Feiwel, G. R. (1975). *The intellectual capital of Michal Kalecki: A study in economic theory and policy*. University of Tennessee Press.
Feiwel, G. R. (Ed.). (1989). *Joan Robinson and modern economic theory*. Palgrave Macmillan.
Feldstein, M. (2009, January). *The case for fiscal stimulus*. Reprinted by Project Syndicate. www.aei.org
Feser, E. (Ed.). (2006). *The Cambridge companion to Hayek*. Cambridge University Press.
Filip, B. (2018a). Hayek on limited democracy, dictatorships, and the 'free' market: An interview in Argentina, 1977. In R. Leeson (Ed.), *Hayek: A collaborative biography. Part XIII: 'Fascism' and liberalism in the (Austrian) classical tradition* (pp. 395–421). Palgrave Macmillan.
Filip, B. (2018b). Friedrich Hayek and his visits to Chile: Some Austrian misrepresentations. In R. Leeson (Ed.), *Hayek: A collaborative biography. Part XIII: 'Fascism' and liberalism in the (Austrian) classical tradition* (pp. 423–462). Palgrave Macmillan.
Fisher, D. (1980). American philanthropy and the social sciences in Britain, 1919–1939: The reproduction of a conservative ideology. *The Sociological Review, 28*, 297–315.
Fisher, D. (1983). The role of philanthropic foundations in the reproduction and production of hegemony: Rockefeller Foundations and the social sciences. *Sociology, 17*(2), 206–233.
Fisher, D. (1984). Philanthropic foundations and the social sciences: A response to Martin Bulmer. *Sociology, 18*(4), 580–587.
Fitzgerald, E. V. K. (1976). *The state and economic development: Peru since 1968*. Cambridge University Press.
Fitzgerald, E. V. K. (1978a). The fiscal crisis of the Latin American state. In J. F. J. Toye (Ed.), *Taxation and economic development: Twelve critical studies*. Frank Cass.
Fitzgerald, E. V. K. (1978b). *Public sector investment for developing countries*. Macmillan.
FitzGerald, E. V. K. (1991). Kurt Mandelbaum and the classical tradition in development theory. In K. Martin (Ed.), *Strategies of economic development*. Palgrave Macmillan. https://doi.org/10.1007/978-1-349-12625-5_1
Fitzsimons, C. (1984, November 10). University to investigate department. *Cambridge Evening News*.
Flather, P. (1982, May 21). Report condemns proposal as 'intellectual vandalism'. *Times Higher Education Supplement*.
Flather, P. (1987). 'Pulling through': Conspiracies, counterplots, and how the SSRC escaped the axe in 1982. In M. Bulmer (Ed.), *Social science research and government: Comparative essays on Britain and the United States* (pp. 353–372). Cambridge University Press.
Flather, P. (2019, January 9). *Paul Flather interviewed by Alan Macfarlane*. https://www.sms.cam.ac.uk/media/3058954
Fleming, G. (2014). A conversation with A. W. Bob Coats. In A. W. (Bob) Coats, *The historiography of economics: British and American economic essays*, compiled and edited by R. E. Backhouse and B. Caldwell (pp. 40–51). Routledge.
Fletcher, G. (2008). *Dennis Robertson*. Palgrave Macmillan.
Flinn, M. W., & Mathias, P. (1982). Obituary: Sir Michael Moissey Postan, 1899–1981. *Economic History Review, 35*(1), iv–vi.
Fluckiger, M. (2018). Teaching economics with economic history. In M. Blum & C. Colvin (Eds.), *An economist's guide to economic history* (pp. 55–59). Palgrave Macmillan.

Folbre, N. (1991). The unproductive housewife: Her evolution in nineteenth-century economic thought. *Signs, 16*(3), 463–484.
Fortes, M. (1947). *Meyer Fortes's special section.* In: Fortes, Steel and Ady (1947).
Fortes, M. (1953). *Social anthropology at Cambridge since 1900: Inaugural lecture.* Cambridge University Press.
Fortes, M. (1978). An anthropologist's apprenticeship. *Annual Review of Anthropology, 7,* 1–30.
Fortes, M., & Mayer, D. Y. (1966). Psychosis and social change among the Tallensi of Northern Ghana. *Cahiers d'Etudes Africaines, 6*(21), 5–40.
Fortes, M., Steel, R. W., & Ady, P. (1947). Ashanti survey, 1945–46: An experiment in social research. *The Geographical Journal, 110*(4/6), 149–177. https://doi.org/10.2307/1789946
Foundation for Economic Education. (2019, March 27). *Hayek Nobel Prize fetches $1.5 million at auction.* https://fee.org/articles/hayek-nobel-prize-fetches-15-million-at-auction/
Fourcade, M. (2009). *Economists and societies: Discipline and profession in the United States, Britain and France, 1890s to 1990s.* Princeton University Press.
Frank, A. G. (1976). Economic genocide in Chile: Open letter to Milton Friedman and Arnold Harberger. *Economic and Political Weekly, 11*(24), 880–888. https://www.jstor.org/stable/4364704?seq=1#page_scan_tab_contents
Frank, A. G. (1998). *ReOrient: Global economy in the Asian Age.* University of California Press.
Freeman, A. (2020). The second opinion: An ethical approach to learning and teaching economics. In S. Decker, W. Elsner, & S. Flechtner (Eds.), *Principles and pluralist approaches in teaching economics: Towards a transformative science* (pp. 13–30). Routledge.
Frey, B. S., & Pommerehne, W. W. (1988). The American domination among eminent economists. *Scientometrics, 14*(1–2), 97–110.
Friedman, M. (1976). *Milton Friedman: biographical.* https://www.nobelprize.org/prizes/economic-sciences/1976/friedman/biographical/
Frost, G. (2002). *Antony Fisher, champion of liberty.* https://www.iea.org.uk/sites/default/files/publications/files/upldbook443pdf.pdf
Fuelner, E. J. (2018, February 28). *The legacy of William F. Buckley Jr.* The Heritage Foundation. https://www.heritage.org/conservatism/commentary/the-legacy-william-f-buckley-jr
Fukuyama, F. (1989). The end of history? *The National Interest, 16,* 3–18.
Fuller, E. (2019). Was Keynes a socialist? *Cambridge Journal of Economics, 43*(6), 1653–1682.
Fuller, E. W. (2013a). Keynes and the ethics of socialism. *Quarterly Journal of Austrian Economics, 22*(2), 139–180.
Fuller, E. W. (2013b). The marginal efficiency of capital. *Quarterly Journal of Austrian Economics, 16*(4), 379–400.
Fuller, E. W. (2017). Keynes's politics and economics. *Procesos de Mercado: Revista Europea de Economia Politica, 14*(1), 41–88. http://www.procesosdemercado.com/wp-content/uploads/2017/07/41-88-170705-Visual-Procesos-de-Mercado-COMPLETO-n%C3%BAmero-27-Vol.-XIV-n.-1-3.pdf
Fuller, E. W. (2018). Keynes's fatal conceit. *Procesos de Mercado: Revista Europea de Economia Politica, 15*(2), 13–65. https://search.proquest.com/openview/a1a638fd68c12766b7878865efc4f8f3/1?pq-origsite=gscholar&cbl=686495

Fuller, E. W., & Whitten, R. C. (2017). Keynes and the first world war. *Libertarian Papers, 9*(1), 1–37.

Gadgil, D. R. (1924). *The industrial evolution of India in recent times.* Oxford University Press.

Gadgil, D. R. (1959). *Origins of the modern business class.* Institute of Pacific Relations.

Galbraith, J. K. (1967). *The new industrial state.* Princeton University Press.

Galbraith, J. K. (2012). Who are these economists anyway? In D. B. Papadimitriou & G. Zezza (Eds.), *Contributions to stock-flow modelling: Essays in honour of Wynne Godley* (Chapter 4). Palgrave Macmillan.

Galofre-Vila, G. (2019, May). The past's long shadow. A systematic review and network analysis of cliometrics or the new economic history. EDES Working Paper No: 154. University of Bocconi, 18p. http://ehes.org/EHES_154.pdf

Gamble, A. (2006). Hayek on knowledge, economy and society. In E. Feser (Ed.), *The Cambridge companion to Hayek* (pp. 111–131). Cambridge University Press.

GCHQ. (2021, April 19). *The bombing of Coventry in WWII*. Retrieved December 19, 2021, from https://www.gchq.gov.uk/information/the-bombing-of-coventry-in-wwii

Gerrard, B. (1991). Keynes's *General Theory*: Interpreting the interpretations. *Economic Journal, 101*(405), 276–287.

Giddens, A. (1971). *Capitalism and modern social theory.* Cambridge University Press.

Giddens, A. (1973). *The class structure of the advanced societies.* Hutchinson.

Giddens, A. (1976). *New rules of sociological method.* Hutchinson.

Giddens, A. (1979). *Central problems in social theory.* Macmillan.

Giddens, A. (1984). *The constitution of society.* Polity.

Giddens, A. (2011, October 22). Obituary: Professor Ilya Neustadt. *The Independent*. https://www.independent.co.uk/news/people/obituary-professor-ilya-neustadt-1473958.html

Giddens, A., & Mackenzie, G. (Eds.). (1982). *Social class and the division of labour: Essays in honour of Ilya Neustadt.* Cambridge University Press.

Gilbert, R. V., Hildebrand, G. H., Stuart, A. W., Sweezy, M. Y., Sweezy, P., Tarshis, L., & Wilson, J. D. (1938). *An economic program for American democracy by seven Harvard and Tufts economists.* Vanguard Press.

Gillies, D. (2012). Economics and research assessment systems. *Economic Thought, 1*(1), 23–47. http://et.worldeconomicsassociation.org/files/ETGillies_1_1.pdf

Giorgi, L., & Marsh, C. (1990). The protestant work ethic as a cultural phenomenon. *European Journal of Social Psychology, 20*(6), 499–517.

Giraud, Y. (2020). Addressing the audience: Paul Samuelson, radical economics, and textbook making, 1967–1973. *Journal of the History of Economic Thought, 42*(2), 177–198.

Girvan, N. (1975). Economic nationalism. *Daedalus, 104*(4), 145–158.

Glyn, A., Hughes, A., Lipietz, A., & Singh, A. (1988). *The rise and fall of the golden age.* UNU-WIDER Working Paper No. 43. UNU-WIDER.

Glyn, A., Hughes, A., Lipietz, A., & Singh, A. (1990). The rise and fall of the golden age. In S. A. Marglin & J. B. Schor (Eds.), *The golden age of capitalism: Reinterpreting the post-war experience* (pp. 39–125). Clarendon Press.

Godley, W. (1992). Maastricht and all that. *London Review of Books, 14*(19), 3–4.

Godley, W. (1998). Using figures to guide macroeconomic policy. In I. Begg & S. G. B. Henry (Eds.), *Applied economics and public policy* (pp. 258–263). Cambridge University Press.

Godley, W. (2001). Saving Masud Khan. *London Review of Books, 23*(4), 3–7.

Godley, W. (2004). *Towards a reconstruction of macroeconomics using a Stock Flow Consistent (SFC) model.* CFAP Working Paper No. 16. Judge Business School, University of Cambridge.

Godley, W. (2008, May 16). Interview with Wynne Godley. In S. Harrison & A. Macfarlane, *Encounter with economics.* Interviews filmed by A. Macfarlane and edited by S. Harrison. University of Cambridge. http://sms.cam.ac.uk/collection/1092396

Godley, W., & Cripps, F. (1973, January 8). GBP 1,000m payments deficit this year if economy grows at 5 per cent. *The Times.*

Godley, W., & Cripps, F. (1983). *Macroeconomics.* Oxford University Press.

Godley, W., & Lavoie, M. (2007). *Monetary economics: An integrated approach to credit, money, income, production and wealth.* Palgrave Macmillan.

Godley, W., & Zezza, G. (2006). *Debt and lending: A cri de coeur.* Policy Note 2006/4. The Levy Economics Institute of Bard College.

Goldschmidt-Clermont, L. (1990). Economic measurement of non-market household activities: Is it useful and feasible? *International Labour Review, 129*(3), 279–299. https://www.proquest.com/docview/224019616/fulltextPDF/D6BDE500E5134DACPQ/12?accountid=13598

Goldschmidt-Clermont, L. (1993). Monetary valuation of non-market productive time: Methodological considerations. *Review of Income and Wealth, 39*(4), 419–433.

Goldschmidt-Clermont, L., & Pagnossin-Aligisakis, E. (1995). *Measures of unrecorded economic activities in fourteen countries.* https://core.ac.uk/reader/6248730

Goldschmidt-Clermont, L., & Pagnossin-Aligisakis, E. (2005). Households' non-SNA production: Labour time, value of labour and of product, and contribution to extended private consumption. *Review of Income and Wealth, 45*(4), 519–529.

Goldthorpe, J. H., Lockwood, D., Bechhofer, F., & Platt, J. (1961–1962). *The Affluent Worker Collection.* University of Essex Special Collections, GB 301 Q045; twenty archival boxes, 6.60 metres. https://archiveshub.jisc.ac.uk/search/archives/3e385b64-60d5-3914-939d-8ae03d38c5ba

Goldthorpe, J., Lockwood, D., Bechhofer, F., & Platt, J. (1967). The affluent worker and the thesis of embourgeoisement: Some preliminary research findings. *Sociology, 1*(1), 11–31.

Goldthorpe, J., Lockwood, D., Bechhofer, F., & Platt, J. (1968a). *The affluent worker: Industrial attitudes and behaviour.* Cambridge University Press.

Goldthorpe, J., Lockwood, D., Bechhofer, F., & Platt, J. (1968b). *The affluent worker: Political attitudes and behaviour.* Cambridge University Press.

Goldthorpe, J., Lockwood, D., Bechhofer, F., & Platt, J. (1969). *The affluent worker in the class structure.* Cambridge University Press.

Gombrich, R. F. (2000, January 7). *British higher education policy in the last twenty years: The murder of a profession.* Lecture delivered at the Graduate Institute of Policy Studies, Tokyo. http://www.damtp.cam.ac.uk/user/mem/papers/LHCE/uk-higher-education.html

Goodhart, C. A. E. (2006). John Stanton Flemming, 1941–2003. *Proceedings of the British Academy, 138,* 71–95.

Goodwin, R. M. (1944). Review of *Keynesian economics* by Mabel Timlin. *Review of Economic Statistics, 26*(3), 162.

Goodwin, R. M. (1970). *Elementary economics from the higher standpoint.* Cambridge University Press.

Goodwin, R. M. (1989). Joan Robinson – Passionate seeker after truth. In G. R. Feiwel (Ed.), *Joan Robinson and modern economic theory* (pp. 916–917). Palgrave Macmillan.

Goodwin, R. M. (1991). Schumpeter, Keynes and the theory of evolution. *Journal of Evolutionary Economics, 1,* 29–47.

Goodwin, R. M. (1995). In memory of Sir Richard Stone. In ISTAT (Ed.), *Social statistics, national accounts and economic analysis. International conference in memory of Sir Richard Stone.* ISTAT.

Goodwin, D. (2001, December 19). The way we won: America's economic breakthrough during World War II. High growth needn't require a war. *The American Prospect.* https://prospect.org/health/way-won-america-s-economic-breakthrough-world-war-ii/

Goodwin, J., & Hughes, J. (2011). Ilya Neustadt, Norbert Elias, and the Leicester Department: Personal correspondence and the history of sociology in Britain. *British Journal of Sociology, 62*(4), 677–695.

Goody, J. (1991). *Jack Goody interviewed by Eric Hobsbawm.* Film interviews with leading thinkers, Alan Macfarlane archive, University of Cambridge. https://www.sms.cam.ac.uk/media/1117872

Gopal, S. (1979). *Jawaharlal Nehru: A biography, volume 2, 1947–1956.* Random House.

Gordon, R. J. (2009, September 14). Is modern macro or 1978-era macro more relevant to the understanding of the current economic crisis? *Economist's View.* https://economistsview.typepad.com/economistsview/2009/09/is-modern-macro-or-1978era-macro-more-relevant-to-the-understanding-of-the-current-economic-crisis.html

Gould, J. (1977). *The attack on higher education: Marxist and radical penetration. Report of a study group of the Institute for the Study of Conflict.* ISC.

de Graaff, J. V. (1957). *Theoretical welfare economics.* Cambridge University Press.

Green, A. (2014, October 24). A divisive peer for a divided time. *The Independent.* https://www.independent.co.uk/news/people/profiles/andrew-green-divisive-peer-divided-time-9817055.html

Grimley, M. (2019). You got an ology? The backlash against sociology in Britain, 1945–90. In L. Goldman (Ed.), *Welfare and social policy in Britain since 1870: Essays in honour of Jose Harris* (pp. 178–196). Oxford University Press.

Groenewegen, P. D. (1988). Alfred Marshall and the establishment of the Cambridge Economics Tripos. *History of Political Economy, 20*(4), 627–667.

Groenewegen, P. D. (2007). *Alfred Marshall: Economist 1842–1924.* Palgrave Macmillan.

Grove, J. (2013, April 8). Thatcher had 'immense impact' on higher education. *Times Higher Education.* https://www.timeshighereducation.com/news/thatcher-had-immense-impact-on-higher-education/2003059.article

Grove, J. (2017, June 11). Lord Giddens: Accidental academic who reached the top. *The Times Higher Education Supplement.* www.timeshighereducation.com/news/lord-giddens-accidental-academic-who-reached-top

Gudgin, G. (2021). The legacy of Wynne Godley: Notes from Graham Gudgin. *Journal of Post Keynesian Economics, 44*(1), 32–37.

Gudgin, G., Coutts, K., & Gibson, N. (2015). *The CBR macroeconomic model of the UK economy (UKMOD).* Working Paper No. 472. Centre for Business Research, University of Cambridge.

Guha, R. (2007). *India after Gandhi: The history of the world's largest democracy.* Harper Collins.

Guinan, J. (2015). Ownership and control: Bring back the Institute for Workers' Control. *Renewal: A Journal of Social Democracy, 23*(4), 11–36. https://www.academia.edu/20411866/Bring_back_the_Institute_for_Workers_Control

Gylfason, T. (2005). *Interview with Assar Lindbeck*. CESIFO Working Paper No. 1408.

Habakkuk, H. J. (1940a). English landownership, 1680–1740. *Economic History Review, 10*.

Habakkuk, H. J. (1940b). Free trade and commercial expansion, 1853–1870. In J. H. Rose, A. P. Newton, & E. Benians (Eds.), *Cambridge history of the British empire* (The new empire, 1783–1870) (Vol. 2, pp. 751–805). Cambridge.

Habakkuk, H. J. (1962). *American and British technology in the nineteenth century: The search for labour-saving inventions*. Cambridge University Press.

Habakkuk, H. J. (1994). *Marriage, debt, and the estates system: English landownership, 1650–1950*. Oxford University Press.

Haberler, G. (1961, October 15). *Mises's private seminar: Reminiscences by Gottfried Haberler*. Mises Institute; Reprinted from *The Mont Pelerin Quarterly, III*(3). https://mises.org/library/misess-private-seminar-reminiscences-gottfried-haberler

Haberler, G. (1986). Reflections on Hayek's business cycle theory. *The Cato Journal, 6*(2).

Hagemann, H. (2007). German-speaking economists in British exile, 1933–1945. *BNL Quarterly Review, 60*(242), 323–363.

Hagemann, H. (2011). European émigrés and the 'Americanization' of economics. *European Journal of the History of Economic Thought, 18*(5), 643–671.

Hagemann, H., & Krohn, C. D. (Eds.). (1999). *Biographical guide to the emigration of German-speaking economists after 1933*. K. G. Sauer.

Hahn, F. (1974). *Letter to Joan Robinson*. JVR/vii/182/1-2. In Joan Violet Robinson Papers held at King's College Archives, Cambridge.

Hahn, F. (1981a, April 28). The preposterous claims of monetarists. *The Times*.

Hahn, F. (1981b, July 29). Letter to the editor. *The Times*. (Response to Tim Congdon's letter in *The Times* of July 14.)

Hahn, F. H. (1984). *Equilibrium and macroeconomics*. Basil Blackwell.

Hahn, F. (1987). Information, dynamics and equilibrium. *Scottish Journal of Political Economy, 34*(4), 321–334.

Hahn, F. (Ed.). (1989a). *The economics of missing markets, information, and games*. Clarendon Press.

Hahn, F. (1989b). Robinson–Hahn love–hate relationship. In G. R. Feiwel (Ed.), *Joan Robinson and modern economic theory* (pp. 895–910). Palgrave Macmillan.

Hahn, F. H., & Matthews, R. C. O. (1964). Theory of economic growth: A survey. *Economic Journal, 74*(296), 779–902.

Hahn, F., & Neild, R. (1980, February 25). Monetarism: Why Mrs Thatcher should beware. *The Times*.

Hahn, F., & Neild, R. (1981, March 28). Letter signed by 364 economists. *The Times*.

Halcrow, M. (1989). *Keith Joseph: A single mind*. Macmillan.

Hallengren, A. (Ed.). (2004). *Nobel laureates in search of identity and integrity: Voices of different cultures*. World Scientific.

Halsey, A. H. (2004). *A history of sociology in Britain: Science, literature and society*. Oxford University Press.

Hammond, J. D. (1988, May 24). *An interview with Milton Friedman on methodology*. Hoover Institution, Stanford University. https://miltonfriedman.hoover.org/friedman_images/Collections/2016c21/Stanford_05_24_1988.pdf. Reprinted as

Hammond, J. D. (1992). An interview with Milton Friedman on methodology. In W. J. Samuels & J. Biddle (Eds.), *Research in the history of economic thought and methodology*. JAI Press.

Hamouda, O. F., & Price, B. B. (Eds.). (1998). *Keynesianism and the Keynesian revolution in America: A memorial volume in honour of Lorie Tarshis*. Edward Elgar.

Hamowy, R. (2008). *The encyclopedia of libertarianism*. Sage.

Hanappi, H. (2015). Schumpeter and Goodwin. *Journal of Evolutionary Economics, 25*(1). https://www.researchgate.net/publication/271732427_Schumpeter_and_Goodwin

Hanney, S. R. (1993). *Special advisers: Their place in British Government*. Doctoral dissertation, Department of Government, Brunel University, Uxbridge.

Harberger, A. (2000, March 10). Interview with Arnold "Al" Harberger. *Commanding Heights*. PBS. https://www.pbs.org/wgbh/commandingheights/shared/minitext/int_alharberger.html

Harcourt, G. C. (1964). Review of *An international comparison of factor costs and factor use*, by B. S. Minhas. *The Economic Journal, 74*(294), 443–445.

Harcourt, G. C. (1966). Biases in empirical estimates of the elasticities of substitution of CES production functions. *Review of Economic Studies, 33*(3), 227–233.

Harcourt, G. C. (1972). *Some Cambridge controversies in the theory of capital*. Cambridge University Press.

Harcourt, G. C. (1982). An early post Keynesian: Lorie Tarshis. *Journal of Post Keynesian Economics, 4*(4), 609–619.

Harcourt, G. C. (1985). A twentieth-century eclectic: Richard Goodwin. *Journal of Post-Keynesian Economics, 7*(3), 410–421.

Harcourt, G. C. (1987). Review of *economics in disarray* edited by Wiles, P. & Routh, G. *Economica, 54*(213), 113–114.

Harcourt, G. C. (1988). Nicholas Kaldor, 12 May 1908–30 September 1986. *Economica, 55*, 159–170.

Harcourt, G. C. (1993a, June 4). E. A. G. Robinson – Obituary. *The Independent*.

Harcourt, G. C. (1993b, October 9). Obituary: Professor Lorie Tarshis. *The Independent*.

Harcourt, G. C. (1995a). Lorie Tarshis, 1911–1993: In appreciation. *Economic Journal, 105*(432), 1244–1255.

Harcourt, G. C. (1995b). Interview with G. C. Harcourt. In J. E. King (Ed.), *Conversations with post Keynesians* (pp. 168–186). Palgrave Macmillan.

Harcourt, G. C. (1997). The Kaldor legacy: Reviewing Nicholas Kaldor, *Causes of growth and stagnation in the world economy* (Cambridge University Press, 1996). *Journal of International and Comparative Economics, 5*, 341–357.

Harcourt, G. C. (1998). Two views on development: Austin and Joan Robinson. *Cambridge Journal of Economics, 22*(3), 367–377.

Harcourt, G. C. (1999a). Horses for courses: The making of a post-Keynesian economist. In A. Heertje (Ed.), *The makers of modern economics* (Vol. IV, pp. 32–69). Edward Elgar.

Harcourt, G. C. (1999b, November 18). Obituary: John Wells. *The Independent*. https://www.independent.co.uk/arts-entertainment/obituary-john-wells-1126818.html

Harcourt, G. C. (2001). *Fifty years a Keynesian and other essays*. Palgrave Macmillan.

Harcourt, G. C. (2006). *The structure of post-Keynesian economics: The core contributions of the pioneers*. Cambridge University Press.

Harcourt, G. C. (2007a). *What is the Cambridge approach to economics?* Republished in G. C. Harcourt, *On Skidelsky's Keynes and other essays: Selected essays of G. C. Harcourt* (pp. 219–240). Palgrave Macmillan, 2012.

Harcourt, G. C. (2007b). Interview with Geoffrey Harcourt 15th May 2007. In S. Harrison & A. Macfarlane, *Encounter with economics*. Film interviews with leading thinkers, filmed by A. Macfarlane and edited by S. Harrison. University of Cambridge; Created 28 March 2011. http://sms.cam.ac.uk/collection/1092396

Harcourt, G. C. (2008). Preface. In P. Arestis & J. Eatwell (Eds.), *Essays in honour of Ajit Singh. Volume 2: Issues in economic development and globalization* (pp. xiii–xv). Palgrave Macmillan.

Harcourt, G. C. (2009). A revolution yet to be accomplished: Reviewing Luigi Pasinetti, *Keynes and the Cambridge Keynesians*. *History of Economic Ideas, 17*(1), 203–208.

Harcourt, G. C. (2010, October). Robin Matthews. *RES Newsletter*, No. 151. http://www.res.org.uk/SpringboardWebApp/userfiles/res/file/obituaries/matthews.pdf

Harcourt, G. C. (2011). The *General Theory* is not a book that you should read in bed! Interviewed by Eckhard Hein and Achim Truger, January 2010. *Intervention, 8*(1), 7–12.

Harcourt, G. C. (2012a, October). Phyllis Deane. *Royal Economic Society Newsletter, 159*.

Harcourt, G. C. (2012b). *The making of a post-Keynesian economist: Cambridge harvest. Selected essays of G. C. Harcourt*. Palgrave Macmillan.

Harcourt, G. C. (2012c). Interview with Geoffrey C. Harcourt. In S. Ederer et al. (Eds.), *Interventions: 17 interviews with unconventional economists (2004–2012)* (pp. 83–92). Metropolis Verlag GmbH.

Harcourt, G. C. (2012d). Keynes and his Cambridge pupils and colleagues. *Meiji Journal of Political Science and Economics, 1*, 12–25.

Harcourt, G. C. (2012e). *On Skidelsky's Keynes and other essays: Selected essays of G. C. Harcourt*. Palgrave Macmillan.

Harcourt, G. C. (2015). Fusing indissolubly the cycle and the trend: Richard Goodwin's profound insight. *Cambridge Journal of Economics, 39*(6), 1569–1578.

Harcourt, G. C. (2016a). Piero Sraffa: A tribute. In J. Halevi, G. C. Harcourt, P. Kriesler, & J. W. Neville (Eds.), *Post-Keynesian essays from down under* (Essays on ethics, social justice and economics – Theory and policy in an historical context) (Vol. III, pp. 258–261). Palgrave Macmillan.

Harcourt, G. C. (2016b). Frank Hahn, 1926–2013: A tribute. In J. Halevi, G. C. Harcourt, P. Kriesler, & J. W. Neville (Eds.), *Post-Keynesian essays from down under* (Essays on ethics, social justice and economics – Theory and policy in an historical context) (Vol. III, pp. 273–275). Palgrave Macmillan.

Harcourt, G. C. (2017). Robert Charles Oliver (Robin) Matthews (1927–2010). In R. A. Cord (Ed.), *The Palgrave Companion to Cambridge economics* (pp. 955–978). Palgrave Macmillan.

Harcourt, G. C., & Cohen, A. J. (1986). *International monetary problems and supply-side economics: Essays in honour of Lorie Tarshis*. Palgrave Macmillan.

Harcourt, G. C., & Cohen, A. J. (2012). Whatever happened to the Cambridge capital theory controversies? (Originally published 2003). In G. C. Harcourt (Ed.), *The making of a post-Keynesian economist: Cambridge harvest. Selected essays of G. C. Harcourt* (pp. 112–130). Palgrave Macmillan.

Harcourt, G. C., & Kerr, P. (2003). Keynes and the Cambridge school. In W. J. Samuels, J. E. Biddle, & J. B. Davis (Eds.), *A companion to the history of economic thought* (pp. 343–359). Blackwell Publishing.

Harcourt, G. C., & Kerr, P. (2009). *Joan Robinson*. Palgrave Macmillan.

Harcourt, G. C., & King, J. (1995). Talking about Joan Robinson: Geoff Harcourt in conversation with John King. In J. E. King (Ed.), *Conversations with post Keynesians* (pp. 168–186). Palgrave Macmillan. Also in: *Review of Social Economy, 53*(1), 31–64.

Harcourt, G. C., & Kitson, M. (1993). Fifty years of measurement: A Cambridge view. *Review of Income and Wealth, 39*(4), 435–447.

Harcourt, G. C., & Kriesler, P. (Eds.). (2013). *The Oxford handbook of post-Keynesian economics* (Theory and origins) (Vol. 1). Oxford University Press.

Harris, R. (2000, July 17). Interview. *Commanding Heights*. 28p. https://www.pbs.org/wgbh/commandingheights/hi/people/pe_name.html

Harrison, M. (2001). *My economic history: From revolutions to routines.* https://warwick.ac.uk/fac/soc/economics/staff/mharrison/comment/econhist.pdf

Harrod, R. F. (1951). *The life of John Maynard Keynes*. Harcourt, Brace and Company.

Hart, D. M. (2019). The Paris School of Liberal Political Economy. In: M. Moriarty and J. Jennings (Eds.), *The Cambridge History of French Thought*. Cambridge University Press, 301–312.

Harte, N. (1995, September 8). Obituary: Professor D. C. Coleman. *The Independent*. https://www.independent.co.uk/news/people/obituary-professor-d-c-coleman-1600207.html

Harte, N. (2002, November 14). Sir John Habakkuk. *The Guardian*. https://www.theguardian.com/news/2002/nov/14/guardianobituaries.highereducation

Harte, N. (2012, October 1). Professor Phyllis Deane: Leading and influential figure in the field of economic history. *The Independent*.

Hartwell, R. M. (1995). *A history of the Mont Pelerin Society*. Liberty Fund.

Harvey, A. (2012). Hashem Pesaran. *Cambridge Economics: News from the Cambridge Faculty of Economics, 5*(Autumn).

Hattersley, R. (2009, March 22). The party's over. *The Observer*.

Hawthorn, G. (1986, November 6). Sociology in Cambridge. *London Review of Books, 8*(19). https://www.lrb.co.uk/the-paper/v08/n19/geoffrey-hawthorn/sociology-in-cambridge

Hawthorn, G. (2009). *An interview of Professor Geoffrey Hawthorn about his life and work.* Filmed by Alan Macfarlane on 23rd April 2009 and edited by Sarah Harrison. https://www.sms.cam.ac.uk/media/1120434

Hawthorn, G. (2011). Across the fields: John Barnes in Cambridge. Special issue: In memory of John Barnes. *The Cambridge Journal of Anthropology, 29*, 35–44.

Hawthorn, G. (2014). *Thucydides on politics*. Cambridge University Press.

Hayek, F. A. (1944). *The road to serfdom*. Routledge.

von Hayek, F. (1967). *Studies in philosophy, politics and economics*. Routledge & Kegan Paul.

von Hayek, F. (1974). *The pretence of knowledge. Lecture to the memory of Alfred Nobel, December 11.* Sveriges Riksbank Prize in Economic Sciences in Memory of Alfred Nobel, 1974. https://www.nobelprize.org/prizes/economic-sciences/1974/hayek/lecture/

Hayek, F. A. (1980, March 5). Letter to *The Times*. *The Times*.

Hayter, T. (2007, March 16). Watching David Coleman. *The Guardian*. https://www.theguardian.com/commentisfree/2007/mar/16/watchingdavidcoleman1

Hazari, R. K. (1958, November 8). Inter-corporate investment: The Birla Group of companies. *Economic Weekly*.

Hazari, R. K. (1960, November 26, December 3, December 10). Ownership and control. *Economic Weekly*.

Hazari, R. K. (1961). *Big business in India: A study in ownership and control*. All India Trade Union Congress.

Hazari, R. K. (1966). *The structure of corporate private control*. Asia Publishing House.

Heath, R. (2021). *Vasco Carvalho reflects on the success of Cambridge-INET*. https://www.inet.econ.cam.ac.uk/

Heckman, J. J., & Moktan, S. (2020). *Publishing and promotion in economics: The tyranny of the Top Five*. https://voxeu.org/article/publishing-and-promotion-economics-tyranny-top-five. Published later as: *Journal of Economic Literature*, 58(2), June.

Heffernan, R. (1997). *Exploring political change: Thatcherism and the remaking of the Labour Party 1979–1997*. Ph.D. thesis, London School of Economics and Political Science, University of London. http://etheses.lse.ac.uk/2133/1/U613365.pdf

Heffernan, R., & Marqusee, M. (1992). *Defeat from the jaws of victory: Inside Kinnock's Labour Party*. Verso.

Hein, E. (2014). *Distribution and growth after Keynes: A post-Keynesian guide*. Edward Elgar.

Hendry, D. F. (2004). The *ET* interview: Professor David F. Hendry interviewed by Neil R. Ericsson. *Econometric Theory*, 20, 743–804. https://pdfs.semanticscholar.org/36d8/a192bbbab3703ea89febab1646e122bcee3b.pdf

Hendry, D. F., & Wallis, K. F. (Eds.). (1984). *Econometrics and quantitative economics*. Basil Blackwell.

Henley, P. (2011). John Barnes: An appreciation. *Cambridge Journal of Anthropology*, 29, 13–15.

Hennessy, P. (2015, August 5). A feeble minister blames the civil service for not delivering his policies: William Waldegrave interviewed by Peter Hennessy. *Civil Service World*. https://www.civilserviceworld.com/articles/interview/feeble-minister-blames-civil-service-not-delivering-his-policies-william

Hey, J. D., & Winch, D. (Eds.). (1990). *A century of economics: 100 years of the Royal Economic Society and the Economic Journal*. Blackwell.

Hiatt, L. (1986). An interview with John Barnes. *Australian Anthropological Society Newsletter*, 63, 4–15.

Hill, P. (1986). *Development economics on trial: The anthropological case for a prosecution*. Cambridge University Press.

Hill, R. (2001). *The Labour Party's economic strategy, 1979–1997: The long road back*. Palgrave.

Hill, R. (2021). *Letter of resignation to Keir Starmer*. https://www.jewishvoiceforlabour.org.uk/article/richard-hill-clp-chair-and-former-candidate-resigns-from-the-labour-party/

Hobsbawm, E. (1967). Maurice Dobb. In C. H. Feinstein (Ed.), *Socialism, capitalism and economic growth: Essays presented to Maurice Dobb* (pp. 1–12). Cambridge University Press.

Hobsbawm, E. (2002). *Interesting times: A twentieth-century life*. Knopf Doubleday Publishing Group.

Hobsbawm, E. (2012, September 21). Dorothy Wedderburn obituary. *The Guardian*.

Hobson, J. A. (1902). *Imperialism*. James Pott & Co.

Hodgson, G. M. (2004). Veblen and Darwinism. *International Review of Sociology*, 14(3), 343–361.

Hodgson, G. M., Gagliardi, F., & Gindis, D. (2018). From Cambridge Keynesian to institutional economist: The unnoticed contributions of Robert Neild. *Journal of Institutional Economics, 14*(4). https://doi.org/10.1017/S1744137417000534

Hollinger, D. A. (n.d.). *Academic culture at Michigan, 1938–1988: The apotheosis of pluralism*. https://www.rackham.umich.edu/downloads/Hollinger.pdf

Holroyd, M. (1995). *Lytton Strachey*. Vintage.

Horrell, S. (1996, September). Home demand and British industrialisation. *Journal of Economic History, 56*, 561–604.

Horrell, S. (1999). Economic history: Great Britain. In J. Peterson & M. Lewis (Eds.), *The Elgar Companion to feminist economics* (pp. 193–201). Edward Elgar.

Horrell, S. (2009). Interview of Jane Humphries for *The Cliometrics Society* newsletter, (24)2, 28–31.

Horrell, S. (n.d.). *Notes on construction of an input-output table for the UK economy in 1841*. Department of Applied Economics, University of Cambridge, mimeo.

Horrell, S., & Humphries, J. (1995a). Women's labour force participation and the transition to the male-breadwinner family, 1790–1865. *Economic History Review, 48*(1), 89–117.

Horrell, S., & Humphries, J. (1995b, October). The exploitation of little children: Child labor and the family economy in the Industrial Revolution. *Explorations in Economic History, 32*, 485–516.

Horrell, S., & Humphries, J. (1997). The origins and expansion of the male breadwinner family: The case of nineteenth-century Britain. *International Review of Social History, 42*, 25–64.

Horrell, S., & Humphries, J. (2019). Children's work and wages in Britain, 1280–1860. *Explorations in Economic History*.

Horrell, S., & Krishnan, P. (2007, November). Poverty and productivity in female-headed households in Zimbabwe. *Journal of Development Studies, 43*, 1351–1380.

Horrell, S., & Oxley, D. (1999). Crust or crumb?: Intrahousehold resource allocation and male breadwinning in late Victorian Britain. *Economic History Review, LII*, 494–522.

Horrell, S., & Oxley, D. (2016). Gender bias in nineteenth-century England: Evidence from factory children. *Economics and Human Biology, 22*, 47–64.

Horrell, S., & Rubery, J. (1989). The household distribution of income in the United Kingdom. *Trends and distribution of income: An overview*. European Federation for Economic Research, Commission of the European Community. ISBN: 92-825-9628-1.

Horrell, S., & Rubery, J. (1991). Gender and working time: An analysis of employers' working-time policies. *Cambridge Journal of Economics, 15*(4), 373–391.

Horrell, S., & Rubery, J. (1992/93). The 'new competition' and working time. *Human Resource Management Journal, 3*(2), 1–13.

Horrell, S., Hudson, J., & Mosley, P. (1992a). Aid, the public sector and the market in less developed countries: A return to the scene of the crime. *Journal of International Development, 4*(2), 139–150.

Horrell, S., Humphries, J., & Rubery, J. (1992b). Women's employment in textiles and clothing. In R. Lindley (Ed.), *Women's employment: Britain in the single European market* (pp. 81–100). HMSO.

Horrell, S., Humphries, J., & Rubery, J. (1992c). The SEM and employment in the banking sector. In R. Lindley (Ed.), *Women's employment: Britain in the single European market* (pp. 126–140). HMSO.

Horrell, S., Humphries, J., & Weale, M. (1994, August). An input-output table for 1841. *Economic History Review, XLVII*, 546–567.
Horrell, S., Humphries, J., & Voth, H.-J. (1998, May). Stature and relative deprivation: Fatherless children in early industrial Britain. *Continuity and Change, 13*, 73–115.
Horrell, S., Johnson, H., & Mosley, P. (2008). *Work, female empowerment and economic development*. Routledge.
Horrell, S., Meredith, D., & Oxley, D. (2009). Measuring misery: Body mass among Victorian London's poor. *Explorations in Economic History, 46*, 93–119.
Horrell, S., Humphries, J., & Sneath, K. (2015). Consumption conundrums unravelled. *Economic History Review, 68*, 830–857.
Horrell, S., Humphries, J., & Weisdorf, J. (2021). Family standards of living over the long run, England 1280–1850. *Past & Present, 250*(1), 87–134.
House of Lords. (1981, December 15). Debates on the Social Science Research Council. *Hansard*, Volume 426, Debate starting at 2:54 pm; Columns 87–89.
House of Lords. (1982, June 30). Debate on Social Science Research Council: Rothschild Report, 30 May 1982. *Hansard, 432*, 288–321.
Howson, S. (2011). *Lionel Robbins*. Cambridge University Press.
Hudson, H. R. (1957, December). A model of the trade cycle. *Economic Record, XXXIII* (66), 378–389.
Hughes, J., Hartwell, R. M., Supple, B., & Matthews, R. C. O. (1971). In D. McCloskey (Ed.), *Essays on mature economy: Britain after 1840. Papers and proceedings on the new economic history of Britain, 1840–1930* – The future of the new economic history in Britain, 401–433.
Humphries, J. (1976). Women, scapegoats and safety valves in the Great Depression. *Review of Radical Political Economics, 8*(1).
Humphries, J. (1977a). Class struggle and the persistence of the working class family. *Cambridge Journal of Economics, 1*(3).
Humphries, J. (1977b). The working class family, women's liberation and class struggle: The case of nineteenth century British history. *Review of Radical Political Economics, 9*(3).
Humphries, J. (1983). From the latent to the floating: The 'emancipation' of women in the 1970's and 1980's. *Capital and Class, 20*(1), 6–28.
Humphries, J. (1987). Inter-war house building, cheap money and building societies: The housing boom revisited. *Business History, XXIX*(3).
Humphries, J. (1988). Women's employment in restructuring America: The changing experience of women in three recessions. In J. Rubery (Ed.), *Women and recession* (pp. 20–47). Routledge.
Humphries, J. (2010). *Childhood and child labour in the British industrial revolution*. Cambridge University Press.
Humphries, J. (2012). Inspiration passes from generation to generation. In *Inspiring future generations of economists: The creation of the Phyllis Deane fund at Newnham to support teaching in economics*. http://www.newn.cam.ac.uk/sites/www.newnham.local/uploads/files/After-Newnham/Giving%20to%20Newnham/Economics%20Fund%20Leaflet%202.pdf
Humphries, J. (2018). Women and children. In M. Blum & C. Colvin (Eds.), *An economist's guide to economic history* (pp. 143–152). Palgrave Macmillan.
Humphries, J., & Rubery, J. (1984). The reconstitution of the supply side of the labour market: The relative autonomy of social reproduction. *Cambridge Journal of Economics, 8*(4), 331–346.

Humphries, J., & Weisdorf, J. (2019). Unreal wages? Real income and economic growth in England, 1260–1850. *Economic Journal, 129*(623), 2867–2887.

Hunold, A. (1958, September 8–15). *The story of the Mont Pelerin Society.* Paper for the 9th Meeting of the Mont Pelerin Society, Princeton, New Jersey.

Husbands, C. T. (1981). The anti-quantitative bias in postwar British sociology. In P. Abrams, R. Deem, J. Finch, & P. Rock (Eds.), *Practice and progress: British sociology 1950–1980.* Allen and Unwin.

Husbands, C. T. (2019). *Sound and fury: Sociology at the London School of Economics and Political Science, 1904–2015.* Palgrave Macmillan.

Hymer, S., & Roosevelt, F. (1972). Symposium. Economics of the New Left: Comment. *Quarterly Journal of Economics, 86*(4), 644–657.

Illarionov, A. (2008). Friedman and Russia. *Cato Journal, 28*(1), 1–10. https://object.cato.org/sites/cato.org/files/serials/files/cato-journal/2008/1/cj28n1-1.pdf

Indrani, D. E. (1990). *An inter-temporal study of Indian industrial economy with special reference to selected business houses.* PhD dissertation, University of Calcutta.

Inman, P. (2010, July 5). Martin Weale joins Bank of England's monetary policy committee. *The Guardian.* https://www.theguardian.com/business/2010/jul/05/martin-weale-bank-of-england-monetary-policy-committee

Innset, O. (2017). *Reinventing liberalism: Early neoliberalism in context, 1920–1947.* Thesis submitted for the degree of Doctor of History and Civilization of the European University Institute, Florence.

Ioannidis, J. P. A., Stanley, T. D., & Doucouliagos, H. (2017). The power of bias in economics research. *Economic Journal, 127*(605), F236–F265.

Irving, S. (2014). R. Leeson (Ed.), *Hayek: A collaborative biography. Part I: Influences, from Mises to Bartley. Oeconomia [Online], 4–3,* 451–458.

ITV News. (2014, March 14). Funeral for former Chesterfield MP Tony Benn. https://www.itv.com/news/calendar/update/2014-03-14/scargill-benn-was-an-outstanding-trade-unionist-and-friend/

Izurieta, A. (2017, August 11). *Economic models that reality can no longer afford.* Institute for New Economic Thinking. https://www.ineteconomics.org/perspectives/blog/economic-models-that-are-costing-us-all

Izurieta, A., & Singh, A. (2010). Does fast growth in India and China help or harm US workers? *Journal of Human Development and Capabilities, 11*(1), 115–140.

Jackson, B. (2010). At the origins of neo-liberalism: The free economy and the strong state, 1930–1947. *The Historical Journal, 53*(1), 129–151.

Jackson, D., Turner, H. A., & Wilkinson, F. (1972). *Do trade unions cause inflation?* Occasional Paper No. 36. Cambridge University Department of Applied Economics.

Janeway, W. (2015, April 14). *How to recognize new economic thinking.* Institute for New Economic Thinking. https://www.ineteconomics.org/perspectives/blog/how-to-recognize-new-economic-thinking

Jobling, R. (2005). Therapeutic research into psoriasis: Patients' perspectives, priorities and interests. In M. D. Rawlins & P. Littlejohns (Eds.), *Delivering quality in the NHS 2005* (pp. 53–56). Radcliffe Publishing.

Jobling, R., & Naldi, L. (2006). Assessing the impact of psoriasis and the relevance of qualitative research. *Journal of Investigative Dermatology, 126*(7), 1438–1440.

Jobling, R., et al. (2015). European S3-Guideline on the systemic treatment of psoriasis vulgaris. *Journal of the European Academy of Dermatology and Venereology, 29,* 2277–2794. http://publicatio.bibl.uszeged.hu/12736/1/3015633_Nast_et_

al_2015_Journal_of_the_European_Academy_of_Dermatology_and_Venereology_u.pdf
Johnson, H. G. (1968a). Canadian contributions to the discipline of economics since 1945. *Canadian Journal of Economics, 1*(1), 129–146.
Johnson, H. G. (1968b, May). A catarrh of economists? From Keynes to Postan. *Encounter*, 50–54.
Johnson, H. G. (1973). National styles in economic research: The United States, United Kingdom, Canada, and various European countries. *Daedalus, 102*(2), 65–74.
Johnson, H. G. (1977). Cambridge as an academic environment in the early 1930s: A reconstruction from the late 1940s. In D. Patinkin & J. C. Leith (Eds.), *Keynes, Cambridge and the general theory*. Palgrave Macmillan.
Johnson, H. G. (1978). The shadow of Keynes. In E. S. Johnson & H. G. Johnson (Eds.), *The shadow of Keynes: Understanding Keynes, Cambridge and Keynesian economics*. Basil Blackwell.
Johnson, N. (2020, July 17). Introducing: "An economic programme for American democracy". Re-posted by Yves Smith on *Naked Capitalism* from the original contribution on *Reviving Growth Keynesianism*. https://webcache.googleusercontent.com/search?q=cache:YUwMr12wFuwJ:https://www.nakedcapitalism.com/2020/07/introducing-an-economic-program-for-american-democracy.html+&cd=9&hl=en&ct=clnk&gl=nl&client=safari
Johnson, H. G. (n.d.). *Cambridge in the 1950s: Memoirs of an economist*. Men and Ideas, RFK/12/2/57/2-14, pp. 28–39. Richard Kahn Papers, King's College Archives, Cambridge.
Johnson, E. S., & Johnson, H. G. (1978). *The shadow of Keynes: Understanding Keynes, Cambridge and Keynesian economics*. Basil Blackwell.
Johnston, J., & Reeves, A. (2018). An investigation into the role played by research assessment in the socio-geographic fragmentation of undergraduate economics education in the UK. *Higher Education, 76*(4), 589–614.
Jones, G., Van Leeuwen, H. D., & Broadberry, S. (2012). The future of economic, business and social history. *Scandinavian Economic History Review, 60*(3), 225–253. https://www.tandfonline.com/doi/abs/10.1080/03585522.2012.727766
Joslin, D. (1963). *A century of banking in Latin America*. Oxford University Press.
Jump, P. (2013a, July 10). REF 'risks narrowing economics'. *Times Higher Education*. https://www.timeshighereducation.com/news/ref-risks-narrowing-economics/2005673.article
Jump, P. (2013b, October 17). Evolution of the REF. *Times Higher Education*. https://www.timeshighereducation.com/features/evolution-of-the-ref/2008100.article
Kahn, R. (1958). The pace of development. In A. Bonne (Ed.), *The challenge of development: Papers of a symposium held in Jerusalem* (pp. 153–191). Eliezer Kaplan School of Economics and Social Science, Hebrew University of Jerusalem.
Kahn, R. (1972). *Essays in the theory of growth*. Cambridge University Press.
Kahn, R. (1977). Malinvaud on Keynes. Reviewing: Edmond Malinvaud, *The theory of unemployment reconsidered*, Basil Blackwell, Oxford, 1977; Three lectures delivered for the Yrjo Jahnsson Foundation, Helsinki. *Cambridge Journal of Economics, 1*(4), 375–388.
Kahn, R., & Marcuzzo, M. C. (2020). Richard Kahn: A disciple of Keynes. *History of Economics Review*, 57p. https://doi.org/10.1080/10370196.2020.1767930
Kahn, R., & Posner, M. (1974). Cambridge economics and the balance of payments. *London and Cambridge Economic Bulletin, 85*, 19–32.

Kaldor, N. (1966). *Causes of the slow rate of economic growth of the United Kingdom*. Cambridge University Press.
Kaldor, N. (1967). *Strategic factors in economic development*. New York State School of Industrial and Labor Relations, Cornell University.
Kaldor, N. (1971). Conflicts in national economic objectives. *Economic Journal*, *81*(321), 1–16.
Kaldor, N. (1980, July). Evidence to the Treasury and Civil Service Committee. Reproduced in N. Kaldor, *The scourge of monetarism* (pp. 45–48). Oxford University Press, 1986.
Kaldor, N. (1982). *Letter to Lord Rothschild concerning the Enquiry into the SSRC*. NK/3/98/2-4; 22 February. King's College Archives, University of Cambridge.
Kaldor, N. (1996). *Causes of Growth and Stagnation in the World Economy. The Raffaele Mattioli Lectures delivered in 1984*. Cambridge: Cambridge University Press.
Kaldor, M. (2019, January 8). Robert Neild obituary. *The Guardian*.
Kaldor, N. (n.d.). *Nicholas Kaldor's notes on Allyn Young's LSE lectures 1927–1929*. https://www.emeraldinsight.com/doi/abs/10.1108/01443589010139958
Kaldor, N., & Kitson, M. (1986). *The impact of import restrictions in the interwar period*. Report to the ESRC. Department of Applied Economics, Cambridge.
Kalecki, M. (1943). Political aspects of full employment. *Political Quarterly*, *14*(4), 322–330.
Kalecki, M. (1944). Three ways to full employment. In F. A. Burchardt (Ed.), *The economics of full employment: Six studies in applied economics prepared at the Oxford University Institute of Statistics* (pp. 39–58). Basil Blackwell.
Kalecki, M. (1972). *Selected essays on the economic growth of the socialist and the mixed economy*. Edited by M. Nuti. Cambridge University Press.
Kaminsky, A. P. (1986). *The India Office, 1880–1910*. Contributions in comparative colonial studies 20. Greenwood Press.
Kanbur, R. (2015). *The end of laissez-faire, the end of history, and the structure of scientific revolutions*. Working Paper No. 2015-04. Charles H. Dyson School of Applied Economics and Management, Cornell University. http://publications.dyson.cornell.edu/research/researchpdf/wp/2015/Cornell-Dyson-wp1504.pdf
Karamessini, M., & Rubery, J. (Eds.). (2013). *Women and austerity: The economic crisis and the future for gender equality*. Routledge.
Kavanagh, D. (2006, August 29). Sir Alfred Sherman: Adviser who preached Thatcherism before the term was invented. *The Guardian*. https://www.theguardian.com/news/2006/aug/29/guardianobituaries.conservatives
Kaza, G. (1997, June 1). *The Mont Pelerin Society's 50th anniversary: The society helps keep alight the lamp of classical liberalism*. Foundation for Economic Education. https://fee.org/articles/the-mont-pelerin-societys-50th-anniversary/
Kearl, J. R., et al. (1979). A confusion of economists? *American Economic Review*, *69*(2), 28–37.
Keegan, W. (2010, May 20). Wynne Godley obituary: Economist with a flair for anticipating and responding to crises. *The Guardian*. https://www.theguardian.com/politics/2010/may/20/wynne-godley-obituary
Keegan, W. (2015, September 16). Barry Moore obituary: Economist who became a noted authority on the business of scientific innovation and the revival of ailing regions. *The Guardian*. https://www.theguardian.com/business/2015/sep/16/barry-moore

Kerr, P. (2007). Joan Robinson and socialist planning in the years of high theory. *Cambridge Journal of Economics, 31*(4), 489–505.
Keynes, J. M. (1913). *Indian currency and finance*. Macmillan and Co.
Keynes, J. M. (1921). *Treatise on probability*. Macmillan and Co.
Keynes, J. M. (1924). Alfred Marshall, 1842–1924. *The Economic Journal, 34*(135), 311–372.
Keynes, J. M. (1925). A short view of Russia. In J. M. Keynes (Ed.), *Essays in Persuasion*. The collected writings of John Maynard Keynes (Essays in Persuasion) (Vol. IX). Royal Economic Society, Palgrave Macmillan, 1972.
Keynes, J. M. (1926). The end of laissez-faire. Hogarth Press (pamphlet). In *The collected writings of John Maynard Keynes* (Essays in Persuasion) (Vol. IX). Royal Economic Society, Palgrave Macmillan, 1972.
Keynes, J. M. (1929). J. M. Keynes to Mrs Allyn A. Young, letter of condolence, 17 March 1929. Cited in C. P. Blitch, *Allyn Young: The peripatetic economist* (p. 208). Macmillan Press, 1995.
Keynes, J. M. (1936). *The general theory of employment, interest and money*. Macmillan.
Keynes, J. M. (1940). *How to pay for the war*. Macmillan and Co.
Khan, M. H. (1996). A typology of corrupt transactions in developing countries. *IDS Bulletin, 27*(2), 12–21.
King, J. E. (1995). *Conversations with post Keynesians*. Palgrave Macmillan.
King, D. (1998). The politics of social research: Institutionalizing public funding regimes in the United States and Britain. *British Journal of Political Science, 28*(3), 415–444.
King, R. (2003). *The university in the global age*. Macmillan International Higher Education.
King, J. E. (2009). *Nicholas Kaldor*. Palgrave Macmillan.
King, J. E., & Millmow, A. (2003). Death of a revolutionary textbook. *History of Political Economy, 35*(1), 105–134.
Kirk-Greene, A. (1999, May). The colonial service training courses: Professionalizing the colonial service. *Overseas Service Pensioners' Association (OSPA) Journal, 77*. https://www.britishempire.co.uk/ospa.htm
Kirman, A. (1989). The intrinsic limits of modern economic theory: The emperor has no clothes. *Economic Journal, 99*(395, Supplement Conference Papers), 126–139.
Kirman, A., & Koch, K. J. (1986). Market excess demand in exchange economies with identical preferences and collinear endowments. *Review of Economic Studies, 53*(3), 457–463.
Kitson, M. (1999). Recession and economic revival in Britain: The role of policy in the 1930s and 1980s. *Journal of Contemporary European History, 8*(1), 1–27.
Kitson, M. (2005). Economics for the future. *Cambridge Journal of Economics, 29*, 827–835.
Kitson, M. (2012). Britain's withdrawal from the gold standard: The end of an epoch. In R. Parker & R. Whaples (Eds.), *Handbook of major events in economic history*. Palgrave.
Kitson, M., & Michie, J. (1995). Trade and growth: An historical perspective. In J. Michie & J. Grieve Smith (Eds.), *Managing the global economy*. Oxford University Press.
Kitson, M., & Michie, J. (2014). The deindustrial revolution: The rise and fall of UK manufacturing, 1870–2010. In R. Floud & P. Johnson (Eds.), *The Cambridge economic history of modern Britain, Volume 2* (pp. 302–329). Cambridge University Press.

Kitson, M., & Solomou, S. (1989). The macroeconomics of protectionism: The case of Britain in the 1930s. *Cambridge Journal of Economics, 13*(1), 155–169. Retrieved June 1, 2021, from http://www.jstor.org/stable/23598154

Kitson, M., & Solomou, S. (1990). *Protectionism and economic revival.* Cambridge University Press.

Kitson, M., & Solomou, S. (1991). Trade policy and the regionalization of imports in interwar Britain. *Bulletin of Economic Research, 43*(2), 151–168.

Kitson, M., Solomou, S., & Weale, M. (1991). Effective protection and economic recovery in the United Kingdom during the 1930s. *Economic History Review, 44*(2), 328–338.

Klaus, V. (2018, March 27). *Notes for Peter Bauer's speech in Budapest.* https://www.klaus.cz/clanky/4254

Klausinger, H. (2011). Hayek and Kaldor: Close encounter at LSE. *History of Economic Ideas, 19*(3), 135–163.

Klein, L. R. (1944). *The Keynesian revolution.* Ph.D. thesis, Massachusetts Institute of Technology, Department of Economics. https://dspace.mit.edu/handle/1721.1/11300

Klein, L. R. (1947). *The Keynesian revolution.* Macmillan & Co.

Klein, L. (1951). The life of John Maynard Keynes. *Journal of Political Economy, 59,* 443–451.

Klein, L. R. (1961/1952). *The Keynesian revolution.* Macmillan & Co.

Klein, L. (1980). *Lawrence R. Klein: Biographical. The Sveriges Riksbank prize in economic sciences in memory of Alfred Nobel.* https://www.nobelprize.org/prizes/economic-sciences/1980/klein/biographical/

Klein, L. R. (1991). Econometric contributions of the Cowles Commission, 1944–47: A retrospective view. *BNL Quarterly Review, 177*(June), 107–117.

Klein, L. (2003). Some potential linkages for input-output analysis with flow of funds. *Economic Systems Research, 15*(3), 169–177.

Klein, L. (2005). *Lawrence R. Klein: Biographical: Addendum. The Sveriges Riksbank prize in economic sciences in memory of Alfred Nobel, 1980.* https://www.nobelprize.org/prizes/economic-sciences/1980/klein/biographical/

Klein, A., & Ogilvie, S. (2016). Occupational structure in the Czech lands under the Second Serfdom. *Economic History Review, 69*(2), 493–521.

Kneeland, H. (1929a). Women on farms average sixty-three hours work weekly in survey of seven hundred homes. In *US Department of Agriculture, Yearbook of Agriculture, 1928.* Government Printing Office.

Kneeland, H. (1929b). Is the modern housewife a lady of leisure? *Survey, 62.*

Kneeland, H. (1929c). Woman's economic contribution in the home. *Annals of the American Academy of Political and Social Science, 143,* 33–40.

Kogan, M., & Hanney, S. (2000). *Reforming higher education.* Jessica Kingsley Publishers.

Komine, A. (2018). William Henry Beveridge (1879–1963). In R. Cord (Ed.), *The Palgrave Companion to LSE economics* (pp. 239–262). Palgrave Macmillan.

Konzelmann, S., & Wilkinson, F. (2016). Cooperation in production, the organization of industry and productive systems: A critical survey of the 'district form of industrial organisation and development'. *CBR Working Paper No. 481.* Centre for Business Research.

Koopmans, T. (1947). Measurement without theory. *Review of Economics and Statistics, 29*(3), 161–172.

Kornai, J. (1990). *The road to a free economy: Shifting from a socialist system. The example of Hungary.* W.W. Norton & Company.

Kothari, U. (2005). From colonial administration to development studies: A postcolonial critique of the history of development studies. In U. Kothari (Ed.), *A radical history of development studies: Individuals, institutions and ideologies* (pp. 47–66). Zed Books.

Kregel, J. (1973). *The reconstruction of political economy: An introduction to post-Keynesian economics.* Macmillan.

Kregel, J. (2011). Evolution versus equilibrium. *Journal of Economic Issues, 45*(2), 269–275.

Kriedte, P., Medick, H., & Schlumbohm, J. (1981 [1979]). *Industrialization before industrialization* (B. Schempp, Trans.). Cambridge University Press.

Krishnaswami, A. (1942). Marshall's contribution to Indian economics. *Indian Journal of Economics, 22,* 875–897.

Krishnaswamy, K. S. (2002). V.K.R.V. Rao on some macroeconomic relationships. *Journal of Social and Economic Development, 4*(1), 81–87. http://webcache.googleusercontent.com/search?q=cache:MxfhZYX4cHUJ:http://www.isec.ac.in/JSED/JSED_V4_I1_81-87.pdf%2Bvkrv+rao+multiplier+agricultural&client=safari&rls=en&hl=en&ct=clnk

Krugman, P. (2011a, December 5). The conscience of a Liberal: Things that never happened in the history of macroeconomics. *The New York Times.*

Krugman, P. (2011b). The profession and the crisis. *Eastern Economic Journal, 37,* 307–312.

Kuczynski, M. (2006, March 9). Michael Posner: Versatile applied economist. *The Independent.*

Kuhn, T. S. (1970). *The structure of scientific revolutions* (2nd ed.). University of Chicago Press.

Kuiken, J. R. (2013). *Empires of energy: Britain, British petroleum, Shell and the remaking of the international oil industry, 1957–1979.* Doctoral dissertation, Department of History, Boston College. https://dlib.bc.edu/islandora/object/bc-ir:104079/datastream/PDF/view

Kuiken, J. R. (2014). Caught in transition: Britain's oil policy in the face of impending crisis, 1967–1973. *Historical Social Research / Historische Sozialforschung, 39*(4), 272–290.

Kumar, D. (1983a). Male utopias or nightmares? *Economic and Political Weekly, 18*(3).

Kumar, D. (1983b). Amniocentesis again. *Economic and Political Weekly, 18*(24).

Kumar, D. (1994, July 9). Left secularists and communalism. *Economic and Political Weekly, 29*(28), special article.

Kuper, A. (2016). Meyer Fortes: The person, the role, the theory. *Cambridge Journal of Anthropology, 34*(2), 127–139.

Kuznets, S. (1966). *Modern economic growth, rate, structure and spread.* Yale University Press.

Kvangraven, I., & Alves, C. (2019). *Heterodox economics as a positive project: Revisiting the debate.* ESRC Global Poverty & Inequality Dynamics Research Network Working Paper 19, 24p. https://gpid.univie.ac.at/wp-content/uploads/2019/07/GPID-WP-19.pdf

Laidler, D. (1976). Inflation in Britain: A monetarist perspective. *American Economic Review, 66*(4), 485–500.

Lal, D. (1983). *The poverty of 'development economics'.* Institute of Economic Affairs.

Lal, D. (2009, March 5). *The Mont Pelerin Society: A mandate renewed*. Presidential address, Mont Pelerin Society. http://www.econ.ucla.edu/lal/MPS%20 Presidential%20Address%203.5.09.pdf

Lane, M. (2013). The genesis and reception of *The Road to Serfdom*. In R. Leeson (Ed.), *Hayek: A collaborative biography. Part I: Influences, from Mises to Bartley*. Palgrave Macmillan.

Larmer, M. (Ed.). (2010a). *The Musakanya papers: The autobiographical writings of Valentine Musakanya*. Lembani Trust. https://books.google.nl/books?id=o4r6nO BcD9AC&pg=PA22&source=gbs_toc_r&cad=3#v=onepage&q&f=false

Larmer, M. (2010b). Chronicle of a coup foretold: Valentine Musakanya and the 1980 coup attempt in Zambia. *Journal of African History, 51*(3), 391–409.

Lavoie, M. (2007). *Introduction to post-Keynesian economics*. Palgrave Macmillan.

Lavoie, M. (2009). *Introduction to post-Keynesian economics*. Palgrave Macmillan.

Lavoie, M. (2010). *From macroeconomics to monetary economics: Some persistent themes in the theory work of Wynne Godley*. Department of Economics, University of Ottawa. http://www.levyinstitute.org/conferences/godley2011/Lavoie.pdf

Lavoie, M. (2015, April). *Should heterodox economics be taught in economics departments, or is there any room for backwater economics?* Paper prepared for the session Teaching Economics, at the 2015 INET Annual Conference, Paris.

Lavoie, M. (2021). The legacy of Wynne Godley: Wynne Godley's monetary circuit. *Journal of Post Keynesian Economics, 44*(1), 6–23.

Lavoie, M. (2022). *Post-Keynesian economics: New foundations* (2nd ed.). Edward Elgar.

Lavoie, M., & Zezza, G. (Eds.). (2012). *The stock-flow consistent approach: Selected writings of Wynne Godley*. Palgrave Macmillan.

Lawson, T. (2006). The nature of heterodox economics. *Cambridge Journal of Economics, 30*, 483–505.

Lawson, T. (2013). What is this 'school' called neoclassical economics? *Cambridge Journal of Economics, 37*(5), 947–983.

Lawson, T., Palma, J., & Sender, J. (1989). Kaldor's contribution to economics: An introduction. *Cambridge Journal of Economics, 13*(1), 1–8. Retrieved June 1, 2021, from http://www.jstor.org/stable/23598143

Layard, R. (1982). *More jobs, less inflation: The case for a counterinflation tax*. McIntyre.

Le Bas, C. (2019). Towards a deepening of knowledge in the economics of innovation: The intellectual legacy of Nick Von Tunzelmann. *Journal of Innovation Economics & Management, 3*(30), 235–238.

Leach, E. R. (1984). Glimpses of the unmentionable in the history of British social anthropology. *Annual Review of Anthropology, 13*, 1–23.

Lebaron, F. (2006). 'Nobel' economists as public intellectuals: The circulation of symbolic capital. *International Journal of Contemporary Sociology, 43*(1), 88–101.

Lee, F. S. (2007a, November 1–3). *Making history by making identity and institutions: The emergence of Post-Keynesian–heterodox economics in Britain, 1974–1996*. Paper presented at the EAPE Conference, Universidade Porto, Porto.

Lee, F. (2007b). The Research Assessment Exercise, the state and the dominance of mainstream economics in British universities. *Cambridge Journal of Economics, 31*(2), 309–325.

Lee, F. (2009). *A history of heterodox economics: Challenging the mainstream in the twentieth century*. Routledge.

Lee, F. S., & Cronin, B. (2010). Research quality rankings of heterodox economic journals in a contested discipline. *American Journal of Economics and Sociology, 69*(5), 1409–1452.
Lee, F., & Harley, S. (1998a). Peer review, the Research Assessment Exercise and the demise of non-mainstream economics. *Capital and Class, 22*(3), 23–51.
Lee, F., & Harley, S. (1998b). Economics divided: The limitations of peer-review in a paradigm bound social science. In D. Jary & M. Packer (Eds.), *The new higher education*. Staffordshire University Press.
Lee, F. S., Pham, X., & Gu, G. (2012a). *The UK Research Assessment Exercise and the narrowing of UK economics*. MPRA Paper No. 41842. https://mpra.ub.uni-muenchen.de/41842/1/MPRA_paper_41842.pdf
Lee, F. S., Pham, X., & Gu, G. (2012b, October 9). *The UK Research Assessment Exercise and the narrowing of UK economics – Appendices*. https://hetecon.net/documents/ResearchAssessment/UKRAE-Narrowing-Appendix.pdf
Lee, F. S., Pham, X., & Gu, G. (2013). The UK Research Assessment Exercise and the narrowing of UK economics. *Cambridge Journal of Economics, 37*(4), 693–717.
Leeson, R. (1995). *The distasteful hunt for 'guilty' economists*. Murdoch University.
Leeson, R. (1996). The rise and fall of the Phillips Curve in British policy-making circles. *History of Economics Review, 25*, 232–248.
Leeson, R. (1997). *The Chicago counter-revolution and the sociology of economic knowledge*. Murdoch University.
Leeson, R. (2000). *The eclipse of Keynesianism: The political economy of the Chicago counter-revolution*. Palgrave Macmillan.
Leeson, R. (Ed.). (2010a). *David Laidler's contributions to economics*. Palgrave Macmillan.
Leeson, R. (Ed.). (2010b). *The anti-Keynesian tradition*. Palgrave Macmillan.
Leeson, R. (Ed.). (2013). *Hayek: A collaborative biography. Part I: Influences, from Mises to Bartley*. Palgrave Macmillan.
Leeson, R. (Ed.). (2015). *Hayek: A collaborative biography. Part VI: Good dictators, sovereign producers and Hayek's 'ruthless consistency'*. Palgrave Macmillan.
Leeson, R. (Ed.). (2017). *Hayek: A collaborative biography. Part X: Eugenics, cultural evolution and the fatal conceit*. Palgrave Macmillan.
Leeson, R. (Ed.). (2018a). *Hayek: A collaborative biography. Part XIII: Fascism and liberalism in the (Austrian) classical tradition*. Palgrave Macmillan.
Leeson, R. (2018b). Introduction: 'How we developed a consistent doctrine and some international circles of communication'. In R. Leeson (Ed.), *Hayek: A collaborative biography. Part XIII: Fascism and liberalism in the (Austrian) classical tradition* (pp. 3–78). Palgrave Macmillan.
Lehmann, D. (2016). *Interview with David Lehmann*. 50th Anniversary Symposium, Centre of Latin American Studies, University of Cambridge. http://www.latin-american.cam.ac.uk/latest-news-and-events/50-years-media/memories-reflections-clas/interview-dr-david-lehmann
Leijonhufvud, A. (1973). Life among the econ. *Economic Inquiry, 11*(3), 327–337.
Leitch, D. (1994, October 23). Rothschild 'spied as the Fifth Man'. *The Independent*. https://www.independent.co.uk/news/uk/home-news/rothschild-spied-as-the-fifth-man-1444440.html
Letwin, O. (1994, May 26). Article in *The Times*.
Levine, Y. (2012, October 12). There is no Nobel Prize in economics. *Alternet*.

Levy, D. (1999, March 1). Interview with Arnold Harberger: An interview with the dean of the "Chicago Boys". *The Region*. Federal Reserve Bank of Minneapolis.
Levy, W. J. (1971). Oil power. *Foreign Affairs, 49,* 652–668.
Levy, W. J. (1982). *Oil strategy and politics, 1941–1981.* Westview Press.
Lewis, W. A. (1954). Economic development with unlimited supplies of labour. *The Manchester School, 22,* 139–191.
Lewis, W. A. (1955). *The theory of economic growth.* Allen and Unwin.
Lewis, L. S. (1988). *Cold war on campus: A study of politics of organizational control.* Transaction Books.
Lindahl, E. (Ed.). (1958). *Selected papers on economic theory.* George Allen and Unwin.
Lindbeck, A. (1970a). *Speech at the presentation of the prize for economic science in memory of Alfred Nobel to Paul A. Samuelson.*
Lindbeck, A. (1970b). Paul Anthony Samuelson's contribution to economics. *Swedish Journal of Economics, 72*(4), 342–354. https://www.nobelprize.org/prizes/economic-sciences/1970/ceremony-speech/
Lindbeck, A. (1971). *Political economy of the New Left: An outsider's view.* Harper and Row.
Lindbeck, A. (1972). Symposium. Economics of the New Left: Rejoinder. *Quarterly Journal of Economics, 86*(4), 665–683.
Lindbeck, A. (Ed.). (1992). *Economic sciences 1969–1980: Nobel lectures including presentation speeches and laureates' biographies.* The Sveriges Riksbank Prize in Economic Sciences in Memory of Alfred Nobel. World Scientific Publishing Co. and the Nobel Foundation.
Linehan, P. (1998, February 19). *Obituary: Professor Sir Harry Hinsley.* https://www.independent.co.uk/news/obituaries/obituary-professor-sir-harry-hinsley-1145675.html
Lippman, W. (1937). *An enquiry into the principles of the good society.* Little, Brown & Co.
Lipsey, R. (1963). *Positive economics.* Weidenfeld & Nicolson.
Livingstone, G. (2018). *Britain and the dictatorships of Argentina and Chile, 1973–82: Foreign policy, corporations and social movements.* Palgrave Macmillan.
Llewellyn, J. (1998). Empirical analysis as an underpinning to policy. In I. Begg & S. G. B. Henry (Eds.), *Applied economics and public policy* (pp. 247–257). Cambridge University Press.
Lloyd, I. (2006). Summary of an address by Lord Keynes to the Political Economy Club, Trinity College, Cambridge on the 2nd February 1946. *Cambridge Journal of Economics, 30*(1), 2–6. https://doi.org/10.1093/cje/bei096
Lockwood, D. (1958). *The blackcoated worker: A study in class consciousness.* Allen & Unwin.
Lucas, R. E. (1980, Winter). The death of Keynesian economics. *Issues and Ideas.*
Lucas, R. E. (2007, September 19). Mortgages and monetary policy. *Wall Street Journal.*
Lucas, R. E., Jr., & Sargent, T. (1994 [1978]). After Keynesian macroeconomics. In P. R. Miller (Ed.), *The rational expectations revolution: Readings from the front line* (pp. 5–30). The M.I.T. Press.
Luhnow, H. (n.d.). https://en.wikipedia.org/wiki/Harold_Luhnow
Lundberg, E. (1969). Speech at the presentation of the prize for economic science in memory of Alfred Nobel to Ragnar Frisch and Jan Tinbergen. In A. Lindbeck (Ed.), *Economic sciences 1969–1980: Nobel lectures including presentation speeches and laureates' biographies* (pp. 3–5). World Scientific Publishing Co. and the Nobel Foundation.

Lundberg, E. (1976). *Presentation speech for the award of the Sveriges Riksbank Prize in Economic Sciences in Memory of Alfred Nobel to Milton Friedman*. https://www.nobelprize.org/prizes/economic-sciences/1976/ceremony-speech/

Lyons, J. S., Cain, L. P., & Williamson, S. H. (Eds.). (2007). *Reflections on the cliometric revolution: Conversations with economic historians*. Routledge.

MacCarthy, F. (2019). *Walter Gropius: Visionary founder of the Bauhaus*. Faber and Faber.

Macekura, S. (2018, May 30). *Phyllis Deane and the limits of national accounting*. National Institute of Economic and Social Research, blog. https://www.niesr.ac.uk/blog/phyllis-deane-and-limits-national-accounting

Macfarlane, A. (2015). *Cambridge anthropology: Preliminary notes*. Berghahn Books.

Mackenzie, G. (1973). *The aristocracy of labour: The position of skilled craftsmen in the American class structure*. Cambridge University Press.

MacLean, N. (2017). *Democracy in chains: The deep history of the radical right's stealth plan for America*. New York: Viking, Penguin Random House.

Maddison, A. (1994, June). Confessions of a Chiffrephile. *Banca Nazionale del Lavoro Quarterly Review, 189*. http://www.ggdc.net/maddison/personal/autobiog1994.pdf

Mair, L. (1944). *Welfare in the British Colonies*. Royal Institute of International Affairs.

Maloney, J. (2008). Obituary: A. W. Bob Coats, 1924–2007. *European Journal of the History of Economic Thought, 15*(1), 129–133.

Maloney, J. (2012). The Treasury and the New Cambridge School in the 1970s. *Cambridge Journal of Economics, 36*(4), 997–1017. https://academic.oup.com/cje/article/36/4/997/1710182

Mandelbaum, K. (1944). An experiment in full employment: Controls in the German economy, 1933–1938. In F. A. Burchardt (Ed.), *The economics of full employment: Six studies in applied economics prepared at the Oxford University Institute of Statistics* (pp. 181–203). Basil Blackwell.

Mandelbaum, K. (1945). *The industrialization of backward areas*. Basil Blackwell.

Mankiw, N. G. (1992). The reincarnation of Keynesian economics. *European Economic Review, 36*, 559–565. Republished in B. Snowdon & H. R. Vane (Eds.), *A macroeconomics reader* (pp. 445–451). Routledge, 1997.

Mankiw, N. G. (1992/1997). The reincarnation of Keynesian economics. *European Economic Review, 36*, 559–565. Republished in Snowdon, B., & Vane, H. R. (Eds.). *A macroeconomics reader* (pp. 445–451). Routledge, 1997.

Manning, P. (1971). Review of *Studies in rural capitalism in West Africa* by Polly Hill. *African Historical Studies, 4*(1), 156–157.

Mantel, R. (1974). On the characterization of aggregate excess demand. *Journal of Economic Theory, 7*(3), 348–353.

Marcuzzo, M. C. (2003). Joan Robinson and the three Cambridge revolutions. *Review of Political Economy, 15*(4), 545–560.

Marcuzzo, M. C. (2008). Piero Sraffa at the University of Cambridge. In H. D. Kurz, L. Pasinetti, & N. Salvadori (Eds.), *Piero Sraffa: The man and the scholar. Exploring his unpublished papers* (pp. 51–77). Routledge.

Marcuzzo, M. C. (2012). *Fighting market failure: Collected essays in the Cambridge tradition of economics*. Routledge.

Marcuzzo, M. C. (2019). Whose Welfare State? Beveridge versus Keynes. In M. C. Marcuzzo (Ed.), *Essays in Keynesian Persuasion* (Chapter 9, pp. 199–217). Cambridge Scholars Publishing. Also in: Backhouse, R. E., & Nishizawa, T. (Eds.). (2010). *No wealth but life: Welfare economics and the welfare state in Britain, 1880–1945*. Cambridge University Press, 256p.

Marcuzzo, M. C., & Rosselli, A. (Eds.). (2005). *Economists in Cambridge: A study through their correspondence, 1907–1946*. Routledge.

Marcuzzo, M. C., & Rosselli, A. (2019). The Cambridge Keynesians: Kahn, J. Robinson and Kaldor: A perspective from the archives. In M. C. Marcuzzo (Ed.), *Essays in Keynesian persuasion* (Chapter 5, pp. 76–102). Cambridge Scholars Publishing.

Marcuzzo, M. C., & Sanfilippo, E. (2008). Dear John, Dear Ursula: Eighty-eight letters unearthed. In R. Scazzieri, A. Sen, & S. Zamagni (Eds.), *Markets, money and capital: Hicksian economics for the twenty first century* (pp. 72–91). Cambridge University Press.

Marcuzzo, M. C., Naldi, N., Sanfilippo, E., & Rosselli, A. (2008). Cambridge as a *place* in economics. *History of Political Economy, 40*(4), 569–593.

Margaret Thatcher Foundation. (n.d.). *Thatcher, Hayek & Friedman*. https://www.margaretthatcher.org/archive/Hayek.asp

Marriott, E. (2002, June 10). In bed with Chile's torturers. *Evening Standard*. https://www.standard.co.uk/showbiz/in-bed-with-chiles-torturers-6319873.html

Marris, R. (1964). *The economic theory of 'managerial' capitalism*. Macmillan.

Marris, R. (1971). Effects of the selective employment tax. First report, review by R. Marris. Her Majesty's Stationery Office. *Economic Journal, 81*(322), 393–395.

Marsh, C. (1979). Problems with surveys: Method or epistemology. *Sociology, 13*(2), 293–305. Reprinted as: Marsh, C. (1984). Problems with surveys: Method or epistemology? In M. Bulmer (Ed.), *Sociological research methods*. Palgrave. https://doi.org/10.1007/978-1-349-17619-9_5

Marsh, C. (1982). *The survey method: The contribution of surveys to sociological explanation*. Allen & Unwin.

Marsh, C. (1985). Back on the bandwagon: The effect of opinion polls on public opinion. *British Journal of Political Science, 15*(1), 51–74.

Marsh, C. (1988). *Exploring data: An introduction to data analysis for social scientists*. Polity Press.

Marsh, C., & Elliot, J. (2008). *Exploring data: An introduction to data analysis for social scientists* (2nd ed.). Polity Press.

Marsh, C., et al. (1991). The case for samples of anonymized records from the 1991 Census. *Journal of the Royal Statistical Society: Series A (Statistics in Society), 4*(2), 305–340.

Marshall, A. (1897, January). The old generation of economists and the new. *Quarterly Journal of Economics*, No. 11, 115–135.

Marshall, A. (1916 [1890]). *Principles of economics* (7th ed.). Macmillan.

Martin, K. (Ed.). (1991a). *Strategies of economic development: Readings in the political economy of industrialization*. Palgrave Macmillan.

Martin, K. (1991b). Modern development theory. In K. Martin (Ed.), *Strategies of economic development: Readings in the political economy of industrialization* (pp. 27–73). Palgrave Macmillan.

Martin, K., & Knapp, J. (Eds.). (1967). *The teaching of development economics. Its position in the present state of knowledge. The proceedings of the Manchester Conference on teaching economic development, April 1964*. Routledge.

Martins, N. O. (2014). *The Cambridge revival of political economy*. Routledge.

Marx, K., & Engels, F. (1967/1888). *The Communist manifesto*, with an Introduction by A.J.P. Taylor. Penguin.

Mata, T. (2012). Godley moves in mysterious ways: The craft of economic judgment in post-war Britain. In D. B. Papadimitriou & G. Zezza (Eds.), *Contributions to stock-flow modelling: Essays in honour of Wynne Godley* (pp. 12–35). Palgrave Macmillan.

Mathias, P. (2008). Clapham, John Harold. In *International encyclopedia of the social sciences*. Thomson Gale. https://www.encyclopedia.com/social-sciences/applied-and-social-sciences-magazines/clapham-john-harold

Mathias, P., & Thompson, F. M. L. (2002). Donald Cuthbert Coleman, 1920–1995. *Proceedings of the British Academy, 115*, 169–191.

Mathur, G. (1965). *Planning for steady growth*. Basic Blackwell.

Matthews, R. C. O. (1954a). The trade cycle in Britain, 1790–1850. *Oxford Economic Papers, 6*(1), 1–32.

Matthews, R. C. O. (1954b). *A study in trade cycle history: Economic fluctuations in Great Britain 1833–1842*. Cambridge University Press.

Matthews, R. C. O. (1968). Why has Britain had full employment since the war? *Economic Journal, 78*(311), 555–569.

Matthews, R. C. O. (1989). Joan Robinson and Cambridge – A theorist and her milieu: An interview. In G. R. Feiwel (Ed.), *Joan Robinson and modern economic theory* (pp. 911–915). Palgrave Macmillan.

Matthews, R. C. O. (2007). R. C. O. Matthews, interviewed by Nicholas von Tunzelmann and Mark Thomas. In J. S. Lyons, L. P. Cain, & S. H. Williamson (Eds.), *Reflections on the cliometric revolution: Conversations with economic historians* (pp. 155–170). Routledge. Interviewed on 25 August 2004 at the British Academy in London by Nick von Tunzelman and Mark Thomas.

Matthews, R. C. O., & Sargent, J. R. (Eds.). (1983). *Contemporary problems of economic policy: Essays from the CLARE Group*. Routledge.

Matthews, R. C. O., & Supple, B. (n.d.). *The ordeal of economic freedom: Marshall on economic history*. Typescript in E.A.G. Robinson Papers, Marshall Library Archives, University of Cambridge, EAGR 6/4/16, 23p. Also published as Matthews, R. C. O., & Supple, B. (1991). The ordeal of economic freedom: Marshall on economic history. *Quaderni di Storia dell'Economia Politica, 9*(2–3), 189–213.

Matthews, R. C. O., & Supple, B. (1991). The ordeal of economic freedom: Marshall on economic history. *Quaderni di Storia dell'Economia Politica, 9*(2–3), 189–213. Also available as a typescript in E.A.G. Robinson Papers, Marshall Library Archives, University of Cambridge, EAGR 6/4/16, 23p.

Matthews, R. C. O., Feinstein, C. F., & Odling-Smee, J. (1982). *British economic growth 1856–1973: The post-war period in historical perspective*. Oxford University Press.

Maxton, G., & Randers, J. (2016). *Reinventing prosperity: Managing economic growth to reduce unemployment, inequality and climate change. A report to the Club of Rome*. Greystone Books.

McCloskey, D. (2003). Milton. *Eastern Economic Journal, 29*(1), 143–146. http://www.deirdremccloskey.com/editorials/milton.php

McCloskey, D. N., & Ziliak, S. T. (1996). The standard error of regressions. *Journal of Economic Literature, 34*(1), 97–114.

McCormick, B. J. (1992). *Hayek and the Keynesian avalanche*. Harvester Wheatsheaf/University of Michigan.

McDonagh, E. C. (1989). Book review: *Cold war on campus: A study of politics of organizational control. Lionel S. Lewis. American Journal of Education, 97*(3), 315–318.

McDonnell, J. (2015). *Speech to Labour Party Annual Conference.* http://press.labour.org.uk/post/130055656854/speech-by-john-mcdonnell-to-labour-party-annual

McKendrick, N., & Outhwaite, R. B. (1986). Editorial preface. In N. McKendrick & R. B. Outhwaite (Eds.), *Business life and public policy: Essays in honour of D. C. Coleman* (pp. vii–xiii). Cambridge University Press.

McKittrick, D., & Dalyell, T. (2010, August 10). Robin Matthews: Leading economist and Master of Clare College, Cambridge. *The Independent.* https://www.independent.co.uk/news/obituaries/robin-matthews-leading-economist-and-master-of-clare-college-cambridge-2047930.html

McMahan, J. (2012). *Bernard Williams: A reminiscence.* http://jeffersonmcmahan.com/wp-content/uploads/2012/11/Williams-A-Reminiscence-FINAL.pdf

Meade, J. E. (1964). *Efficiency, equality and the ownership of property.* George Allen and Unwin.

Meade, J. E. (1977). *James E. Meade: Biographical.* https://www.nobelprize.org/prizes/economic-sciences/1977/meade/biographical/

Meade, J., & Stone, R. (1944). *National income and expenditure.* Oxford University Press.

Medema, S. G., & Waterman, A. M. C. (Eds.). (2015). *Paul Samuelson on the history of economic analysis: Selected essays.* Cambridge University Press.

Medhurst, J. (2014). *That option no longer exists: Britain 1974–76.* Zero Books.

Meek, R. (1978). Maurice Herbert Dobb, 1900–1976. *Proceedings of the British Academy, 63,* 332–344. https://www.thebritishacademy.ac.uk/publishing/memoirs/pba-63/dobb-maurice-herbert-1900-1976/

Meeks, G. (1974). Profit illusion. *Oxford Bulletin of Economics and Statistics, 36*(4), 267–285.

Meeks, G. (2017). Theories came and went, good data endured: Accounting at Cambridge. In R. A. Cord (Ed.), *The Palgrave Companion to Cambridge economics* (pp. 187–205).

Mendels, F. F. (1972). Proto-industrialization: The first phase of the industrialization process. *Journal of Economic History., 32*(1), 241–261.

de Ménil, G., & Gordon, R. J. (Eds.), (1985). Special issue. *European Economic Review, 28*(1–2).

Messac, L. M. (2016). *What is an economy? Women's work and feminist economics in the construction and critique of national income accounting.* Earlier version of paper presented at the New York Area African History Workshop. https://www.ineteconomics.org/uploads/papers/June-Messac_What-is-an-economy.pdf

Metcalf, D. (2019). *Tribute to Basil Yamey.* http://www.lse.ac.uk/economics/Assets/Documents/basil-yamey/david-metcalf-tribute-to-basil-yamey.pdf

Middleton, R. (2008, March 18–19). *'There is no alternative', or was there? Benchmarking the Thatcher years.* Paper for workshop, Department of Economics, University of Fukuoka. https://papers.ssrn.com/sol3/papers.cfm?abstract_id=2942693

Miliband, R. (1966). The Labour Government and beyond. *The Socialist Register, 1966,* 11–26. https://socialistregister.com/index.php/srv/article/view/5965

Miller, R. (2016). *The centre in the early years.* Presentation on the occasion of the 50th anniversary of the Centre of Latin American Studies, University of Cambridge. http://www.latin-american.cam.ac.uk/latest-news-and-events/50-years-media/memories-reflections-clas/early-years-dr-rory-miller

Millmow, A. (2003, October). Joan Robinson's disillusion with economics. *Review of Political Economy, 15*(4), 561–574.

Millmow, A. (2014, July). *The influence of Cambridge upon the professionalisation of postwar Australian economics.* Paper for the 27th HETSA conference, Auckland University, New Zealand. http://docs.business.auckland.ac.nz/Doc/16-Alex-Millmow.pdf

Minford, P. (1981, April 7). Letter in response to letter by 364 economists. *The Times.*

Minford, P. (1986). Rational expectations and monetary policy. President's lecture, Scottish Economic Society Conference. *Scottish Journal of Political Economy, 33*(4), 317–333.

Minford, P. (2013, April 9). We should treasure Margaret Thatcher for saving us from economic disaster. *WalesOnline.* https://www.walesonline.co.uk/news/wales-news/margaret-thatcher-saved-britain-economic-2569217

Mingers, J., & White, L. (2015). *Throwing out the baby with the bathwater: The undesirable effects of National Research Assessment Exercises on research.* https://arxiv.org/ftp/arxiv/papers/1502/1502.00658.pdf

Mirowski, P. (2013). *Never let a serious crisis go to waste: How neoliberalism survived the financial meltdown.* Verso Press.

Mirowski, P., & Plehwe, D. (2009). *The road from Mont Pelerin: The making of the neoliberal thought collective.* Harvard University Press.

Mirrlees, J. (2009). *Interview of Sir James Mirrlees, Nobel laureate in economics, covering aspects of his life and work.* Interview on 21 September 2009 filmed by Alan Macfarlane and edited by Sarah Harrison. https://www.sms.cam.ac.uk/media/1126590

Mirrlees, J. A. (1996). *James A. Mirrlees biographical.* https://www.nobelprize.org/prizes/economic-sciences/1996/mirrlees/facts/

Mishan, E. J. (1967). *The costs of economic growth.* Penguin Books.

Mitch, D. (2015). Morality versus money: Hayek's move to the University of Chicago. In R. Leeson (Ed.), *Hayek: A collaborative biography. Archival insights into the evolution of economics.* Palgrave Macmillan.

Mitchell, B. R. (1980). *European historical statistics 1750–1970.* Macmillan.

Mitchell, B. R. (1982). *International historical statistics: Africa and Asia.* Macmillan.

Mitchell, B. R. (1983). *International historical statistics: The Americas and Australasia.* Macmillan.

Mitchell, B. (2009). *Dr Brian Mitchell celebrated his eightieth birthday on 20 September 2009.* https://www.trin.cam.ac.uk/wp-content/uploads/mitchell_brian_80th_Birthday.pdf

Mitchell, B., & Deane, P. (1962). *Abstract of British historical statistics.* Cambridge University Press.

Mitchell, J., Solomou, S., & Weale, M. (2012). Monthly GDP estimates for inter-war Britain. *Explorations in Economic History, Elsevier, 49*(4), 543–556.

Mkandawire, T. (1987). Review: *The development of capitalism in Africa*, by John Sender and Sheila Smith. *Africa Development, 12*(2), 166–170. Published by CODESRIA.

Moggridge, D. (1973). *Collected writings of John Maynard Keynes, volume XIII.* Macmillan.

Moggridge, D. E. (2001). H. G. J. as a biographer's subject: Some autobiographical writings. *American Journal of Economics and Sociology, 60*(3), 651–666.

Moggridge, D. E. (2019). Harry Gordon Johnson. In R. Dimand & H. Hagemann (Eds.), *The Elgar companion to John Maynard Keynes* (pp. 506–509). Edward Elgar.

Monbiot, G. (2017, July 19). A despot in disguise: One man's mission to rip up democracy. *The Guardian*. https://www.theguardian.com/commentisfree/2017/jul/19/despot-disguise-democracy-james-mcgill-buchanan-totalitarian-capitalism

Mongiovi, G. (2001, October). The Cambridge tradition in economics: An interview with G. C. Harcourt. *Review of Political Economy, 13*(4), 503–521.

Mongiovi, G. (2020). Was Keynes a socialist. *Catalyst, 3*(4). https://catalyst-journal.com/vol3/no4/was-keynes-a-socialist

Mont Pelerin Society. (n.d.). Mont Pelerin Society. *Wikipedia*. https://en.wikipedia.org/wiki/Mont_Pelerin_Society

Monthly Review Editors. (2016). Notes by the editors. *Monthly Review, 68*(7).

Moore, C. (2013). *Margaret Thatcher: The authorized biography. Volume one: Not for turning*. Penguin Books.

Moreno, F. (2008). Silent revolution: An early export from Pinochet's Chile. *Globalization, Competitiveness & Governability, 2*(2), 90–99. https://www.google.com/url?sa=t&rct=j&q=&esrc=s&source=web&cd=10&ved=2ahUKEwjypdCnq7TkAhUPPVAKHeplCk0QFjAJegQIARAC&url=https%3A%2F%2Fgcg.universia.net%2Farticle%2Fdownload%2F339%2F465&usg=AOvVaw24IyK-3m_XXS2rNJVtqaZ6

Moreno-Brid, J. C., & Ros, J. (2007). *Mexico's economic development in historical perspective*. Oxford University Press.

Morgan, M. (2011). Seeking parts, looking for wholes. In L. Daston & E. Lunbeck (Eds.), *Histories of scientific observation*. Chicago University Press.

Morrish, L. (2019, May 23). *The university has become an anxiety machine*. Guest blog contribution, Higher Education Policy Institute. https://www.hepi.ac.uk/2019/05/23/the-university-has-become-an-anxiety-machine/

Moser, P., Voena, A., & Waldinger, F. (2014). German Jewish emigres and US invention. *American Economic Review, 104*(10), 3222–3255.

Moss, R. (1975). *The collapse of democracy*. Maurice Temple Smith Ltd.

Moss, L. S. (2005). Richard A. Musgrave and Ludwig von Mises: Two cases of émigré economists in America. *Journal of the History of Economic Thought, 27*(4), 443–450.

Musakanya, V. (2010). *The Musakanya Papers: The autobiographical writings of Valentine Musakanya*. Edited by M. Larmer. Lembani Trust. https://books.google.nl/books?id=o4r6nOBcD9AC&pg=PA22&source=gbs_toc_r&cad=3#v=onepage&q&f=false

Naoroji, D. (1901). *Poverty and un-British rule in India*. S. Sonnenschein & Co.

Naylor, R. T. (1981). Johnson on Cambridge and Keynes. *Canadian Journal of Political and Social Theory/Revue Canadienne de Theorie Politique et Sociale, 5*(1–2), 216–229.

Necker, S. (2014). Scientific misbehaviour in economics. *Research Policy, 43*(10), 1747–1759.

Neild, R. (1986, October 2). Kaldor of Kings. *The Guardian*.

Neild, R. (2012a). The '1981 statement by 364 economists' revisited. *Royal Economic Society Newsletter, 159*, 11–14.

Neild, R. (2012b). *What next? A memoir*. Privately published.

Neild, R. (2013a). *Economics in disgrace: The need for a reformation*. GIDS Discussion Paper No. 01-13. Graduate Institute of Development Studies.

Neild, R. (2013b, December 10). Interview with Robert Neild by F. Gagliardi, D. Gindis and G. M. Hodgson. Cited in Hodgson, Gagliardi and Gindis (2018).

Neild, R. (2017a). The future of economics: The case for an evolutionary approach. *Economic and Labour Relations Review, 28*(1), 1–9.
Neild, R. (2017b, February 7). Interview with G. M. Hodgson. Cited in Hodgson, G. M., Gagliardi, F., & Gindis, D. (2018). From Cambridge Keynesian to institutional economist: The unnoticed contributions of Robert Neild. *Journal of Institutional Economics, 14*(4), 767–786.
Neild, R. (2018). The first serious optimist: A. C. Pigou and the birth of welfare economics. Review. *Contributions to Political Economy, 37*(1), 138–140.
Network. (1985a). Glittering prizes. *Newsletter of the British Sociological Association, 32*, 1. https://www.britsoc.co.uk/files/NETWORK%20NO32%20MAY1985.pdf
Network. (1985b). New ventures in social science publishing. *Newsletter of the British Sociological Association, 32*, 2. https://www.britsoc.co.uk/files/NETWORK%20NO32%20MAY1985.pdf
New Scientist. (1975, March 20). Towards a self-sufficient Britain? *65*(941).
Newbery, D. (1998). Foreword. In I. Begg & S. G. B. Henry (Eds.), *Applied economics and public policy* (pp. xix–xxii). Cambridge University Press.
Newbery, D. (2017). Frank Horace Hahn 1925–2013. *Biographical Memoirs of Fellows of the British Academy, XVI*, 485–525. https://www.britac.ac.uk/sites/default/files/23 Hahn 1837 9_11_17.pdf
Nickell, S. (2006). The budget in 1981 was over the top. In P. Booth (Ed.), *Were 364 economists all wrong?* (pp. 54–61). Institute of Economic Affairs.
Nickell, S. (n.d.). *Basil Yamey.* http://www.lse.ac.uk/economics/Assets/Documents/basil-yamey/steve-nickell-tribute-to-basil-yamey.pdf
Nicol, A. (2001). *The social sciences arrive: The Social Science Research Council is established.* Economic and Social Research Council.
Nicolas, S. (1982). Total factor productivity growth and the revision of post-1870 British economic history. *Economic History Review (New Series), 35*(1), 83–98.
Nikiforos, M., & Zezza, G. (2017). Stock-flow consistent macroeconomic models: A survey. *Journal of Economic Surveys, 31*(5), 1204–1239.
Nilsson, M. (2011). The editor and the CIA. Herbert Tingsten and the Congress for Cultural Freedom: A symbiotic relationship. *European Review of History/Revue Europeeanne d'histoire, 18*(2), 147–174.
Nolan, P. (1976). Collectivization in China: Some comparisons with the USSR. *Journal of Peasant Studies, 3*(2), 192–220.
Nolan, P. (1988). *The political economy of collective farms: An analysis of China's post-Mao rural reforms.* Routledge.
Nolan, P., & Paine, S. (1986a). Towards an appraisal of the impact of rural reform in China, 1978–85. *Cambridge Journal of Economics, 10*(1), 83–99.
Nolan, P., & Paine, S. (1986b). *Rethinking socialist economics: A new agenda for Britain.* St. Martin's Press.
Nurkse, R. (1953). *Problems of capital formation in underdeveloped countries.* Basil Blackwell.
Nuti, D. M. (1971). 'Vulgar Economy' in the theory of income distribution. *Science and Society, 35*(1), 27–33.
O'Connor, J. J., & Robertson, E. F. (2014). *David Gawen Champernowne.* http://mathshistory.st-andrews.ac.uk/Biographies/Champernowne.html
O'Donnell, R. (1999). Keynes's socialism: Conception, strategy and espousal. In P. Kriesler & C. Sardoni (Eds.), *Keynes, post-Keynesianism and political economy: Essays in honour of Geoff Harcourt* (Vol. 3, pp. 149–175). Routledge.

O'Hear, A. (2006). Hayek and Popper: The road to serfdom and the open society. In E. Feser (Ed.), *The Cambridge companion to Hayek* (pp. 132–147). Cambridge University Press.

OAC (Online Archive of California). (2015). *Register of the Vervon Orval Watts papers*. https://oac.cdlib.org/findaid/ark:/13030/kt7c60394c/entire_text/

Offer, A. (2008). *Charles Feinstein (1932–2004), and British Historical National Accounts*. Discussion papers in Economic and Social History No. 70. University of Oxford.

Offer, A., & Soderberg, G. (2016). *The Nobel factor: The prize in economics, social democracy, and the market turn*. Princeton University Press.

Ogilvie, S. (1993). Proto-industrialization in Europe. *Continuity and Change, 8*(2), 159–179.

Ogilvie, S. (1997). *State Corporatism and Proto-Industry: The Wurttemberg Black Forest 1580–1797*. Cambridge University Press.

Ogilvie, S. (2008). Protoindustrialization. In S. Durlauf & L. Blume (Eds.), *The new Palgrave dictionary of economics. 6* (pp. 711–714). Palgrave Macmillan.

Ogilvie, S. (2015). *Medieval Champagne fairs: Lessons for development*. https://voxeu.org/article/medieval-champagne-fairs-lessons-development

Ogilvie, S. (2019). *The European guilds: An economic analysis*. Princeton University Press.

Ogilvie, S., & Edwards, J. (1998). Women and the 'Second Serfdom': Evidence from Bohemia, 1381–1722. *CESifo Working Papers*, 0177.

Ogilvie, S., & Edwards, J. (2000). Women and the "Second Serfdom": Evidence from early modern Bohemia. *Journal of Economic History, 60*(4), 961–994.

Okon, H. (2018). The Austrian revival. In R. Leeson (Ed.), *Hayek: A collaborative biography. Part XIII: Fascism and liberalism in the (Austrian) classical tradition* (pp. 213–244). Palgrave Macmillan.

Pace, I. (2018, April 3). The RAE and REF: Resources and critiques. *Desiring Progress*. https://ianpace.wordpress.com/2018/04/03/the-rae-and-ref-resources-and-critiques/

Paine, S. (1971a). Lessons for LDCs from Japan's experience with labour commitment and subcontracting in the manufacturing sector. *Bulletin of the Oxford Institute of Economics and Statistics, 33*(2), 115–133.

Paine, S. (1971b). Wage differentials in the Japanese manufacturing sector. *Oxford Economic Papers, 23*(2), 212–238.

Paine, S. (1972). Turkey's first five-year development plan (FFYDP) 1963–67: A different assessment. *Economic Journal, 82*(326), 693–699.

Paine, S. (1973). Review of *Economic theory and the underdeveloped countries* by Hla Myint. *Modern Asian Studies, 7*(2), 311–313.

Paine, S. (1974). *Exporting workers: The Turkish case*. Occasional Paper 41, Department of Applied Economics, Cambridge University Press.

Paine, S. (1976a). Balanced development: Maoist conception and Chinese practice. *World Development, 4*(4), 277–304.

Paine, S. (1976b). Development with growth: A quarter century of socialist transformation in China. *Economic and Political Weekly, 11*(31/33), 1349–1382.

Paine, S. (1977). Agricultural development in less developed countries (particularly South Asia): An introduction to Bhaduri. *Cambridge Journal of Economics, 1*(4), 335–339.

Paine, S. (1978). Some reflections on the presence of 'rural' or of 'urban bias' in China's development policies, 1949–1976. *World Development, 6*(5), 693–707.

Paine, S. (1981). Spatial aspect of Chinese development: Issues, outcomes and policies, 1949–1979. *Journal of Development Studies, 17*(2), 133–195.

Paine, S., & Singh, A. (1973). The Shanghai diesel engine factory. *The Cambridge Review, 94*.

Palley, T. (2006). *The fallacy of the revised Bretton Woods hypothesis: Why today's international financial system is unsustainable*. Public Policy Brief No. 85. The Levy Economics Institute of Bard College.

Palley, T. (2009, July 29). Letter to the Queen: Why no one predicted the crisis. *Economics for Open and Democratic Societies*. http://thomaspalley.com/?p=148

Palma, J. G. (2009). The revenge of the market on the rentiers. Why neo-liberal reports of the end of history turned out to be premature. *Cambridge Journal of Economics, 33*(4), 829–869. https://doi.org/10.1093/cje/bep037

Palma, J. G. (2015). *Why corporations in developing countries are likely to be even more susceptible to the vicissitudes of international finance than their counterparts in the developed world: A tribute to Ajit Singh*. CWPE Working Paper No. 1539. Cambridge University.

Palma, J. G., & Marcel, M. (1989). Kaldor on the 'discreet charm' of the Chilean bourgeoisie. *Cambridge Journal of Economics, 13*(1), 245–272.

Pande, R., & Roy, H. (2021). "*If you compete with us, we shan't marry you*" – *The (Mary Paley and) Alfred Marshall lecture*. Working Paper 29481. National Bureau of Economic Research, 33p.

Papadimitriou, D. B., & Zezza, G. (Eds.). (2012). *Contributions to stock-flow modelling: Essays in honour of Wynne Godley*. Palgrave Macmillan.

Papadimitriou, D. B. & Zezza, G. (ed.) (2021). The legacy of Wynne Godley. Special issue, *Journal of Post Keynesian Economics, 44*(1).

Parkin, M., & Nobay, A. R. (Eds.). (1975). *Contemporary issues in economics: Proceedings of the conference of the Association of University Teachers of Economics, Warwick, 1973*. Manchester University Press.

Parsons, W. (1983). Keynes and the politics of ideas. *History of Political Thought, 4*(2), 367–392.

Pasinetti, L. L. (1991). Richard Ferdinand Kahn, 1905–1989. *Proceedings of the British Academy, 76*, 423–443.

Pasinetti, L. L. (1996). Richard Murphey Goodwin (1913–1996): A pupil's tribute to a great teacher. *Cambridge Journal of Economics, 20*(6), 645–649.

Pasinetti, L. L. (2005). The Cambridge School of Keynesian economics. *Cambridge Journal of Economics, 29*(6), 837–848.

Pasinetti, L. L. (2007). *Keynes and the Cambridge Keynesians. A 'revolution in economics' to be accomplished*. Cambridge University Press.

Patel, I. G. (1989). Images of Joan. In G. R. Feiwel (Ed.), *Joan Robinson and modern economic theory* (pp. 863–865). Palgrave Macmillan.

Patinkin, D., & Leith, J. C. (Eds.). (1977). *Keynes, Cambridge and the general theory*. Macmillan.

Patnaik, P. (2015a). Ajit Singh (1940–2015): A formidable economist. *Economic & Political Weekly, 50*(30), 32–34.

Patnaik, P. (2015b). Goodwin on the optimal growth path for a developing economy. *Cambridge Journal of Economics, 39*(6), 1579–1586.

Peel, M. (2013, October 16). Shirley Williams the dazzling flirt could have been Britain's first woman PM. *Mail Online*. https://www.dailymail.co.uk/femail/article-2463621/Shirley-Williams-dazzling-flirt-Britains-woman-PM.html

Penrose, E. (1975). The development of crisis. *Daedalus, 104*(4), 39–57.
Pepper, G. (1998). Early monetarism in the UK. In G. Pepper (Ed.), *Inside Thatcher's monetarist revolution* (pp. 3–5). Palgrave Macmillan.
Pernecky, M., & Wojick, P. (2019). The problematic nature and consequences of the effort to force Keynes into the conceptual cul-de-sac of Walrasian economics. *Cambridge Journal of Economics, 43*(3), 769–783. https://doi.org/10.1093/cje/bey039
Pernecky, M., & Wojick, P. (2020). A response to 'Keynes, Kuhn and the sociology of knowledge: A comment on Pernecky and Wojick'. *Cambridge Journal of Economics, 44*(6), 1425–1428. https://doi.org/10.1093/cje/beaa017
Thomas, R. (2020). Keynes, Kuhn and the sociology of knowledge: A comment on Pernecky and Wojick. *Cambridge Journal of Economics, 44*(6), 1415–1424. https://doi.org/10.1093/cje/beaa016
Pesaran, M. H. (1987). *The limits to rational expectations*. Basil Blackwell.
Pesaran, M. H. (1991). The ET interview: Professor Sir Richard Stone. *Econometric Theory, 7*(1), 85–123.
Pesaran, M. H. (2014, June 6). *Reflections on my time with Ron*. Speech at Conference Dinner, Conference in Honour of Professor Ron Smith, Birkbeck College.
Pesaran, M. H., & Harcourt, G. C. (2000). Life and work of John Richard Nicholas Stone 1913–1991. *The Economic Journal, 110*, F146–F165.
Peterson, W. (n.d.). *James Meade (1907–1995)*. Christ's College Cambridge Alumni. https://alumni.christs.cam.ac.uk/james-meade
Philpot, R. (2017). *Margaret Thatcher: The honorary Jew. How Britain's Jews helped shape the Iron Lady and her beliefs*. Biteback Publishing.
Pigou, A. C. (1920). *The economics of welfare*. Macmillan.
Piketty, T. (2014). *Capital in the twenty-first century* (A. Goldhammer, Trans.). Harvard University Press.
Platt, J. (2003). *The British sociological association: A sociological history*. Routledge.
Plehwe, D., Walpen, B., & Neunhoffer, G. (Eds.). (2006). *Neoliberal hegemony: A global critique*. Routledge.
POLIS. (n.d.). *Home page of the Department of Politics and International Development*. University of Cambridge. https://www.polis.cam.ac.uk/about-us
Pomeranz, K. (2001). *The great divergence: China, Europe and the making of the modern world economy*. Princeton University Press.
Portes, R. (2008, July). The annual report of the Secretary-General. *Royal Economic Society Newsletter*, No. 142.
Posner, M. (Ed.). (1978). *Demand management*. Heinemann.
Posner, M. V. (1981a). *The organisation and finance of the modelling effort in the UK* (Unpublished). Paper for The Bank of England Panel of Economic Advisors.
Posner, M. (1981b). *Macro-economic research in the United Kingdom: The report of a Social Science Research Council Sub-committee, chaired by Michael Posner*. SSRC.
Posner, M. V. (2002). Social sciences under attack in the UK (1981–1983). *La revue pour l'histoire du CNRS, 7*. https://doi.org/10.4000/histoire-cnrs.547
Postan, M. M. (1939). *The historical method in social science: An inaugural lecture*. Cambridge University Press.
Postan, M. M. (1946). Obituary notice: Sir John Clapham. *Economic History Review, 16*(1), 56–59.
Postan, M. M. (1968a). A plague of economists? On some current myths, errors, and fallacies. *Encounter, 30*(1), 42–47.

Postan, M. M. (1968b). The uses and abuses of economics. *Encounter, 31*(3), 85–90.

Prandy, K., Stewart, A., & Blackburn, R. M. (1982). *White collar work* (Cambridge studies in sociology) (Vol. 3). Palgrave Macmillan.

Prandy, K., Stewart, A., & Blackburn, R. M. (1983). *White collar unionism* (Cambridge studies in sociology) (Vol. 4). Palgrave Macmillan.

Pratten, S. (ed.) (2014). *Social ontology and modern economics*. London: Routledge.

Prest, A. R., & Coppock, D. J. (Eds.). (1966). *The UK economy: A manual of applied economics*. Weidenfeld and Nicholson.

Prest, A. R., & Stewart, I. G. (1953). *The national income of Nigeria, 1950–51*. Colonial research studies No. 11. HMSO for the Colonial Office.

Preston, P. (2017, May 9). Lord Thomas of Swynnerton: Obituary. *The Guardian*. https://www.theguardian.com/books/2017/may/09/lord-thomas-of-swynnerton-obituary

Puttaswamaiah, K. (1995). *Nobel economists: Lives and contributions* (3 Vols.). Indus Publishing Company.

Pyatt, G. (1990). Accounting for time use. *Review of Income and Wealth, 36*(1), 33–52.

Pyatt, G. (2005). *Sir Richard Stone: An appreciation*. https://www.copsmodels.com/webhelp/viewhar/index.html?hc_stone2.htm

Pyatt, G., & Ward, M. (1999). An appreciation of Eden's contribution to the study of poverty. In G. Pyatt & M. Ward (Eds.), *Identifying the poor: Papers on measuring poverty to celebrate the bicentenary of the publication in 1797 of 'The State of the Poor' by Sir Frederick Morton Eden* (pp. 17–34). IOS Press.

Queens' College. (2016). Largest gift in modern times. *The Bridge, 4*, 16. https://www.queens.cam.ac.uk/sites/www.queens.cam.ac.uk/files/publicationFiles/final_mu20301_queens_bridge_-_march_2016_-_low_res_2.pdf

Quinn, J., & Hall, J. (2009, October 21). Goldman Sachs vice-chairman says: 'Learn to tolerate inequality'. *The Telegraph*. https://www.telegraph.co.uk/finance/recession/6392127/Goldman-Sachs-vice-chairman-says-Learn-to-tolerate-inequality.html

Radice, H. (1971). The conference of socialist economics. *Bulletin of the Conference of Socialist Economics, I*(1), 1–5.

Radice, L. (1984). *Beatrice and Sidney Webb: Fabian socialists*. Macmillan.

Ragupathy, V., Zambelli, S., & Velupillai, K. V. (2013). A non-linear model of the trade cycle: Mathematical reflections on Hugh Hudson's classic. *Australian Economic Papers, 52*(2), 115–125.

Rai, L. L. (1917). *England's debt to India: A historical narrative of Britain's fiscal policy in India*. B. W. Huebsch.

Raj, K. N. (1960). *Some economic aspects of the Bhakra Nangal project: A preliminary analysis of selected investment criteria*. Asia Publishing House.

Rao, V. K. R. V. (1937). *The national income of British India, 1931–32*. PhD Dissertation, Faculty of Economics and Politics, University of Cambridge, UK.

Rao, V. K. R. V. (1952, February). Investment, income and the multiplier in an underdeveloped economy. *The Indian Economic Review*.

Ravelli, G., & Bull, A. C. (2018). The Pinochet regime and the trans-nationalization of Italian neo-fascism. In R. Leeson (Ed.), *Hayek: A collaborative biography. Part XIII: Fascism and liberalism in the (Austrian) classical tradition* (pp. 361–393). Palgrave Macmillan.

Razavi, S. (2011). Nancy Folbre: Interviewed by Shahra Razavi. *Development and Change, 42*(1), 315–329.

Reason Online. (n.d.). Interview of F. A. Hayek. http://www.reasonmag.com/hayekint.html
Reddaway, W. B. (1939). *The economics of a declining population*. George Allen and Unwin.
Reddaway, B. (1962). *The development of the Indian economy*. George Allen and Unwin.
Reddaway, W. B. (1963). The development of the Indian economy: The objects of the exercise restated. *Oxford Economic Papers, 15*(3), 318–332.
Reddaway, W. B. (1995). Recollections of a lucky economist. *BNL Quarterly Review, 192*, 3–16.
Reddaway, W. B. and Associates. (1970). *Effects of the selective employment tax. First report*. Her Majesty's Stationery Office.
Reddaway, W. B. and Associates. (1973). *Effects of the selective employment tax. Final report*. University of Cambridge Department of Applied Economics. Cambridge University Press.
Reed, J. (1919). *Ten days that shook the world*. Boni and Liveright, Inc.
Reid, M. (2019, January 9). Peter Swinnerton-Dyer: Obituary. *The Guardian*. https://www.theguardian.com/science/2019/jan/09/sir-peter-swinnerton-dyer-obituary
Renfro, C. (2004). Econometric software: The first fifty years in perspective. *Journal of Economic and Social Measurement, 29*(1–3).
Repapis, C. (2014). J. M. Keynes, F. A. Hayek and the common reader. *Economic Thought, 3*(2), 1–20.
Repapis, C. (2019). Cambridge economics: A place, a people, an academic community and its Palgrave Companion. Book review. *Journal of Economic Methodology, 26*(2), 171–175.
Reyes, E. (2014, October 20). Interview: David Howarth. *The Law Society Gazette*. https://www.lawgazette.co.uk/people/interview-david-howarth/5044394.article
Ristuccia, C. A., & Solomou, S. (2014). Can general purpose technology theory explain economic growth? Electrical power as a case study. *European Review of Economic History, 18*(3), 227–247.
Robbins, L. (1932). *An essay on the nature and significance of economic science*. Macmillan.
Robbins, L. (1963). *The Robbins Report. Higher education: Report of the Committee appointed by the Prime Minister under the Chairmanship of Lord Robbins 1961–1963*. Her Majesty's Stationery Office.
Robinson, E. A. G. (1948). Foreword. In P. Deane (Ed.), *The measurement of colonial incomes: An experiment*. Cambridge University Press.
Robinson, E. A. G. (1978). Comment on Brian Corry's presentation at the Third Keynes Seminar, "Keynes and Laissez Faire", held at the University of Kent, Canterbury in 1976. In Thirlwall, A. P. (Ed.). (1978). *Keynes and Laissez Faire: The Third Keynes Seminar held at the University of Kent, Canterbury 1976*. Palgrave Macmillan.
Robinson, E. A. G. (1989). Colin Clark. In *E. A. G. Robinson Papers* held at the Marshall Library Archives, University of Cambridge, 5/7/15/1.
Robinson, J. (1933). *The economics of imperfect competition*. Macmillan.
Robinson, J. (1945). The economics of full employment. Review of *Six studies in applied economics*, prepared at the Oxford Institute of Statistics, 1944. *Economic Journal, 55*.
Robinson, J. (1949, October). The theory of planning. Review of *Soviet development since 1917* by Maurice Dobb. *Soviet Studies*.

Robinson, J. (1956). *The accumulation of capital.* Macmillan.
Robinson, J. (1961). *Exercises in economic analysis.* Macmillan.
Robinson, J. (1964). Factor prices not equalized. *Quarterly Journal of Economics, 78*(2), 202–207.
Robinson, J. (1966). *The new mercantilism: An inaugural lecture.* Cambridge University Press.
Robinson, J. (1972). The second crisis of economic theory. *American Economic Review, 62*(1–2), 1–10. Richard T. Ely Lecture delivered in New Orleans in 1971.
Robinson, J. (1974, Autumn). History versus equilibrium. *Thames Papers in Political Economy,* 11p. https://docs.gre.ac.uk/__data/assets/pdf_file/0025/122578/TP_PPE_74_3_compressed.pdf
Robinson, J. (1976). *The state of play.* RFK/12/2/81/81-82. 2p. Typed note by Joan Robinson held in the Richard F. Kahn Papers, King's College Archives, University of Cambridge.
Robinson, J. (1977). What are the questions? *Journal of Economic Literature, 15*(4), 1318–1339.
Robinson, J. (1978). *Contributions to modern economics.* Academic Press.
Robinson, J. (1979a). *Aspects of development and underdevelopment.* Cambridge University Press.
Robinson, J. (1979b). The disintegration of economics. In *Collected economic papers* (Vol. V, pp. 289–297). Basil Blackwell.
Robinson, J. (1981, April 14 and 16). *The arms race. The Tanner lectures on human values delivered at the University of Utah.* https://tannerlectures.utah.edu/_documents/a-to-z/r/robinson82.pdf
Robinson, P. (2009, February 20). Paul Samuelson vs. Milton Friedman (a debate). *Forbes.* http://www.freerepublic.com/focus/news/2190904/posts
Robinson, J., & Eatwell, J. (1973). *An introduction to modern economics.* McGraw Hill.
Rocha, B., & Solomos Solomou, S. (2015). The effects of systemic banking crises in the inter-war period. *Journal of International Money and Finance, 54,* 35–49.
Roehner, B. M. (2007). *Driving forces in physical, biological and socio-economic phenomena: A network science investigation of social bonds and interactions.* Cambridge University Press.
Rose, D. (1996). For David Lockwood. *British Journal of Sociology, 47*(3), 385–396.
Rose, D. (2014, June 29). David Lockwood obituary. *The Guardian.* https://www.theguardian.com/education/2014/jun/29/david-lockwood
Rosenheim, A. (1994, April 9). Obituary: Paul Howell. *The Independent.*
Rosenthal, T. (2006, February 5). How Malcolm Bradbury killed sociology. *The Independent.*
Ross, R. (2013). The politics of household budget research in colonial Central Africa. *Zambia Social Science Journal, 4*(1), Article 4. http://scholarship.law.cornell.edu/zssj/vol4/iss1/4
Roth, A. (2002, May 6). Obituary: Lord Bauer – Thatcher's rightwing economist opposed to third world aid. *The Guardian.*
Rothbard, M. N. (1973, August 17). *Floyd Arthur 'Baldy' Harper, RIP.* Mises Daily Articles, Mises Institute. https://mises.org/library/floyd-arthur-baldy-harper-rip
Rothbard, M. N. (n.d.). *Ludwig von Mises: Scholar, creator, hero.* https://www.rothbard.it/books/mises-scholar-creator-hero.pdf
Rothbard, M. N., & Gordon, D. (2010). *Strictly confidential: The private Volker fund – Memos of Murray N. Rothbard,* edited by D. Gordon. Ludwig von Mises Institute.

Rothschild, N. M. V. (1982). *An enquiry into the Social Science Research Council*. Her Majesty's Stationery Office.

Rothschild, E. (1996). The debate on economic and social security in the late eighteenth century: Lessons of a road not taken. *Development and Change, 27*(2), 331–351.

Rowthorn, R. E. (1974). Neo-classicism, neo-Ricardianism and Marxism. *New Left Review, 86*, 63–87.

Rowthorn, R. (2008). Interview with Bob Rowthorn 13th June 2008. In I. S. Harrison & A. Macfarlane (Eds.), *Encounter with economics*. Interviews filmed by A. Macfarlane and edited by S. Harrison. University of Cambridge. http://sms.cam.ac.uk/collection/1092396

Rowthorn, R. E., & Wells, J. R. (1987). *De-industrialisation and foreign trade*. Cambridge University Press.

Roy, A. (1999). *The greater common good*. India Book Distributor Ltd.

Roy, S. (2013, January 30). Frank Hahn has passed away. *Marginal Revolution*, blog. https://marginalrevolution.com/marginalrevolution/2013/01/frank-hahn-has-passed-away.html

Rubery, J. (Ed.). (1988). *Women and recession*. Routledge and Kegan Paul.

Rubery, J., & Karamessini, M. (Eds.). (2014). *Women and austerity: The economic crisis and the future of gender equality*. Routledge.

Rubery, J., Burchell, B., Deakin, S., & Konzelmann, S. J. (2022). A tribute to Frank Wilkinson. *Cambridge Journal of Economics, 46*(3), 429–445.

Rudra, A. (1996). *Prasanta Chandra Mahalanobis: A biography*. Indian Statistical Institute; Oxford University Press.

Runciman, W. G. (1989). *A treatise on social theory: Volume II, Substantive social theory*. Cambridge University Press.

Runciman, W. G. (2014, June 3). *Garry Runciman interviewed by Alan Macfarlane*. Film interviews with leading thinkers. Alan Macfarlane archive, University of Cambridge. https://www.sms.cam.ac.uk/media/1729998

Saari, D. G. (1992). The aggregated excess demand function and other aggregation procedures. *Economic Theory, 2*(3), 359–388.

Saari, D. G. (1996). The ease of generating chaotic behavior in economics. *Chaos, Solitons & Fractals, 7*(12), 2267–2278.

Saith, A. (2008). Joan Robinson and Indian planning: An awkward relationship. *Development and Change, 39*(6), 1115–1134.

Saith, A. (2011). Inequality, imbalance, instability: Reflections on a structural crisis. *Development and Change, 42*(1), 70–86.

Saith, A. (2018). Ajit Singh (1940–2015), the radical Cambridge economist: Anti-imperialist advocate of third world industrialization. *Development and Change, 49*(2), 561–628.

Saith, A. (2019). *Ajit Singh of Cambridge and Chandigarh: An intellectual biography of the radical Sikh economist*. Palgrave Macmillan.

Samuelson, P. A. (1947). *Foundations of economic analysis*. Harvard University Press.

Samuelson, P. A. (1948). *Economics*. McGraw-Hill.

Samuelson, P. A. (1955). *Economics* (3rd ed.). McGraw Hill.

Samuelson, P. A. (1958). Review: *Theoretical welfare economics*, by J. de V. Graaff. *Economic Journal, 68*(271), 539–541.

Samuelson, P. (1971). Introduction. In A. Lindbeck (Ed.), *Political economy of the New Left: An outsider's view*. Harper and Row.

Samuelson, P. A. (1987). Out of the closet: A program for the Whig history of economic science. *History of Economics Society Bulletin, 9*(1), 51–60. Reprinted in Medema, S. G., & Waterman, A. M. C. (Eds.). (2015). *Paul Samuelson on the history of economic analysis: Selected essays* (pp. 25–36). Cambridge University Press.
Samuelson, P. A. (1988). The passing of the guard in economics. *Eastern Economic Journal, 14*(4), 319–329.
Samuelson, P. A. (1989, September 19). *Letter from Paul A. Samuelson to Austin Robinson*. EAGR Archives, Marshall Library, Cambridge; #389.
Samuelson, P. A. (1994). Richard Kahn: His welfare economics and lifetime achievement. *Cambridge Journal of Economics, 18*(1), 55–72.
Samuelson, P. A. (1997). Credo of a lucky textbook author. *Journal of Economic Perspectives, 11*(2), 153–160.
Samuelson, P. A. (1998). Requiem for the classic Tarshis textbook that first brought Keynes to introductory economics. In O. Hamouda & B. B. Price (Eds.), *Keynesianism and the Keynesian revolution in America: A memorial volume in honour of Lorie Tarshis*. Edward Elgar.
Samuelson, P. A. (2004). William A. Barnett: An interview with Paul A. Samuelson, December 23, 2003. *Macroeconomic Dynamics, 8*, 519–542. Republished in Working Paper Series in Theoretical and Applied Economics, University of Kansas.
Samuelson, P. A. (2009). A few remembrances of Friedrich von Hayek. *Journal of Economic Behavior and Organization, 69*(1), 1–4.
Sanchez-Ancochea, D. (2017). Conflict, inequalities and development: Celebrating the work of Valpy FitzGerald. Special Issue in Honour of Professor Valpy FitzGerald. *Oxford Development Studies, 45*(2), 113–115.
Sandilands, R. (1997). Review of Charles P. Blitch, *Allyn Young: The peripatetic economist*. *Economic Journal, 107*(443), 37–39.
Sandilands, R. (1999). New evidence on Allyn Young's style and influence as a teacher. *Journal of Economic Studies, 26*(6), 453–479.
Sarvary, M. (2012). *Gurus and oracles: The marketing of information*. MIT Press.
Savage, M. (2016). The fall and rise of class analysis in British sociology, 1950–2016. *Tempo Social, 28*(2), 57–72. http://eprints.lse.ac.uk/68676/1/Savage_The_fall_and_rise_of_class_analysis_published_LSERO.pdf
Sayer, D. (2015). *Rank hypocrisies: The insult of the REF*. Sage Swifts.
Scanlon, H. (1968). *The way forward for workers' control*. Pamphlet Series No. 1. Institute for Workers' Control.
Schiffman, D. (2013). *Richard Kahn and Israeli economic policy, 1957 and 1962*. Ariel University. https://ssrn.com/abstract=2373517
Schlefer, J. (2012). *The assumptions economists make*. Harvard University Press.
Schlefer, J. (2013, September 10). Embracing Wynne Godley, an economist who modeled the crisis. *The New York Times*.
Schlesinger Jr., A. M. (1949/2014). *The vital center: The politics of freedom*. Houghton Mifflin Co.
Schrecker, E. W. (1986). *No Ivory Tower: McCarthyism and the universities*. Johns Hopkins University Press.
Schumpeter, J. A. (1954). *History of economic analysis*. Oxford University Press.
Schur, T. (Ed.). (2014). *From the Cam to the Zambezi: Colonial service and the path to new Zambia*. I. B. Taurus.
Scott, A., Skea, J., Robinson, J., & Shove, E. (1999). *Designing 'interactive' environmental research for wider social relevance*. ESRC Global Environmental Change Programme, Special Briefing no 4, May.

Scranton, P. (2013, July 9). Why John Maynard Keynes supported the New Deal. *Bloomberg Opinion*. https://webcache.googleusercontent.com/search?q=cache:ITa deOyjZKsJ:https://www.bloomberg.com/opinion/articles/2013-07-08/why-john-maynard-keynes-supported-the-new-deal+&cd=21&hl=en&ct=clnk&gl=nl&client=safari

Seers, D. (1963a). The limitations of the special case. *Bulletin of the Oxford Institute of Economics and Statistics, 25*(2), 77–98.

Seers, D. (1963b). Big companies and small countries: A practical proposal. *Kyklos, 16*(4), 599–608.

Seers, D. (1969). The meaning of development. *IDS Communications Series, 44*.

Seers, D. (1972). What are we trying to measure? *Journal of Development Studies, 8*(3), 21–36.

Seers, D. (1979). The birth, life and death of development economics: Revisiting a Manchester conference. *Development and Change, 10*(4), 707–719.

Sefton, J., & Weale, M. (1995). *Reconciliation of national income and expenditure: Balanced estimates of national income for the United Kingdom, 1920–1990*. Cambridge University Press.

Seldon, A. (1977, May 9). The liberal teacher who turned his back on old age to lead world thought. *The Times*. https://www.margaretthatcher.org/document/114629

Sen, A. (1982, March 4). Just deserts. Review of *Equality, the third world, and economic delusion*, Harvard University Press. *The New York Review of Books*.

Sen, A. (1990). Maurice Herbert Dobb. In J. Eatwell, M. Milgate, & P. Newman (Eds.), *Marxian economics. The new Palgrave* (pp. 141–147). Palgrave Macmillan.

Sen, A. (1998). *Amartya Sen – Biographical*. https://www.nobelprize.org/prizes/economic-sciences/1998/sen/biographical/

Sen, A. (2020). Marx after Kornai. *Public Choice*. https://doi.org/10.1007/s11127-020-00838-x

Sen, A. (2021). *Home in the world: A memoir*. Allen Lane and Penguin Random House.

Sen, A., Deaton, A., & Besley, T. (2020). Economics with a moral compass? Welfare economics: Past, present, and future. *Annual Review of Economics, 12*, 1–21. https://www.annualreviews.org/doi/10.1146/annurev-economics-020520-020136

Sen, R. K. (2002). On Professor P. R. Brahmananda and his writings. In R. K. Sen & C. Biswajit (Eds.), *Indian economy agenda for the 21st century: Essays in honour of Professor P. R. Brahmananda* (pp. 1–45). Deep and Deep Publications.

Sender, J., & Smith, S. (1986). *The development of capitalism in Africa*. Methuen.

Serra, G. (2018). Pleas for fieldwork: Polly Hill on observation and induction, 1966–1982. In F. Fiorito, S. Scheall, & C. E. Suprinyak (Eds.), *Research in the history of economic thought and methodology. Including a symposium on Mary Morgan: Curiosity, imagination, and surprise* (pp. 93–108). Emerald Publishing.

Seton, F. (1962). Review: *An essay on economic growth and planning* by M.H. Dobb. *Economic Journal, 72*(286), 376–379.

Shammas, V. L. (2017). Burying Mont Pelerin: Milton Friedman and neoliberal vanguardism. *Constellations*. https://doi.org/10.1111/1467-8675.12322

Shaxson, N. (2011). *Treasure islands: Tax havens and the men who stole the world*. Penguin Random House.

Shearmur, J. (2015). The other path to Mont Pelerin. In R. Leeson (Ed.), *Hayek: A collaborative biography. Archival insights into the evolution of economics*. Palgrave Macmillan.

Shenk, T. (2013). *Maurice Dobb: Political economist*. Palgrave Macmillan.

Shipman, A. (2019). *Wynne Godley: A biography*. Palgrave Macmillan.
Shove, G. F. (1942). The place of Marshall's principles in the development of economic theory. *Economic Journal*, 52(208), 294–329.
Shute, J. (2017, October 12). Weatherman Michael Fish on missing the great storm of 1987: 'When I saw what happened I thought, "oh s***"'. *The Telegraph*. https://www.telegraph.co.uk/men/thinking-man/weatherman-michael-fish-missing-great-storm-1987-saw-happened/
Silberston, Z. A. (1939–1940). *Notes made by Zangwill Aubrey Silberston on early modern English economic history, 1939–1940*. University of Leeds Archives, Special Collections, 2 volumes. GB 206 MS 556. https://archiveshub.jisc.ac.uk/data/gb206-ms556
Silberston, A. (1972–1992). *1972–92: Correspondence as secretary-general of Royal Economic Society*. Held by London University, London School of Economics Library, Archives and Special Collections. Reference: "RES". "NRA 30256 Royal Economic Soc".
Silberston, A. (2011a, January). Robin Matthews. *Royal Economic Society Newsletter*, 152. http://www.res.org.uk/SpringboardWebApp/userfiles/res/file/obituaries/matthews.pdf
Silberston, A. (2011b). Ken Arrow, James Meade and the secret seminar. *Cambridge Economics: Cambridge Faculty of Economics Alumni Newsletter*, 4, 4. www.econ.cam.ac.uk/alumni/newsletters/Cambridge-Economics-Issue-4-2011.pdf
Singer, H. (1979). A generation later: Kurt Mandelbaum's *The Industrialisation of Backward Areas* revisited. *Development and Change*, 10(4), 577–584.
Singh, A. (1971). *Take-overs: Their relevance to the stock market and the theory of the firm*. Cambridge University Press.
Singh, M. (1972). Jagdish N. Bhagwati and Padma Desai, India: Planning for industrialization; Industrialization and trade policies since 1951, published on behalf of OECD, Oxford University Press, 1970, pp. xx+537; Book Review, *Indian Economic and Social History Review*, 9(4), 413–417.
Singh, A. (1973). Political economy of socialist development in China since 1949. *Economic & Political Weekly*, 8(47), 2097–2111.
Singh, A. (1975a). Takeovers, economic natural selection and the theory of the firm: Evidence from the post-war UK experience. *Economic Journal*, 85(339), 497–515.
Singh, A. (1975b). *An essay on the political economy of Chinese development. Thames Papers in Political Economy*. Thames Polytechnic.
Singh, A. (1977). UK industry and the world economy: A case of de-industrialisation? *Cambridge Journal of Economics*, 1, 113–136.
Singh, A. (1982). *The structural disequilibrium of the Tanzanian economy*. Cambridge University, Department of Applied Economics (unpublished).
Singh, A. (1983). *Industrialisation, employment and basic needs in a fast-growing agrarian state: A study of the Indian Punjab*. Basic Needs and Development Programme Working Paper WEP 2-32/WP4. International Labour Organisation.
Singh, A. (1986). Tanzania and the IMF: The analytics of alternative adjustment programmes. In B. Van Arkadie (Ed.), *External finance and policy adjustment in Africa*, Special Issue. *Development and Change*, 17(3), 425–454.
Singh, A. (1990a). The institution of a stock market in a socialist economy: Notes on the Chinese economic reform programme. In D. Fureng & P. Nolan (Eds.), *The Chinese economy and its future: Achievements and problems of post-Mao reforms* (pp. 162–178). Polity Press.

Singh, A. (1990b). Global rules and a new golden age: Southern competition, labour standards and industrial development in the North and the South. In US Dept of Labor (Ed.), *Labor standards, development and the global economy*. US Department of Labor.

Singh, A. (1991). *The stock market and economic development: Should developing countries encourage stock markets?* Faculty of Economics, University of Cambridge. http://mpra.ub.uni-muenchen.de/54927/

Singh, A. (1993). The stock market and economic development: Should developing countries encourage stock markets? *UNCTAD Review, 4*(1), 1–74.

Singh, A. (1994). *The state and industrialisation in India: Successes and failure and the lessons for the future*. University of Cambridge. https://mpra.ub.uni-muenchen.de/54986/1/MPRA_paper_54986.pdf

Singh, A. (1995). 'Close' vs. 'strategic' integration with the world economy and the 'market-friendly approach to development' vs. an 'industrial policy': A critique of the World Development Report 1991 and an alternative policy perspective. MPRA Paper No 53562. http://mpra.ub.uni-muenchen.de/53562/

Singh, A. (1996a). The world economy under the market supremacy model and third world industrialisation. *Indian Economic Journal, 44*(1), 1–16.

Singh, A. (1996b). The plan, the market and evolutionary economic reform in China. In A. Abdullah & A. R. Khan (Eds.), *State, market and development: Essays in honour of Rehman Sobhan* (pp. 193–230). Dhaka University Press.

Singh, A. (1996c). The stock market, the financing of corporate growth and Indian industrial development. *Journal of International Finance, 4*(2), 1–17.

Singh, A. (1999). Should Africa promote stock market capitalism? *Journal of International Development, 11*(3), 343–367.

Singh, A. (2003). Competition, corporate governance and selection in emerging markets. *Economic Journal, 113*, F443–F464.

Singh, A. (2007a). Does integration of India and China with the world economy harm the US workers? A commentary on the Freeman thesis. *Indian Journal of Labour Economics, 50*(3), 457–466.

Singh, A. (2007b). *Globalisation, industrial revolutions in India and China and labour markets in advanced countries: Implications for advanced and developing economies and for national and international policies*. Working Paper No. 81. Policy Integration Department, International Labour Organisation.

Singh, A. (2007c). Capital account liberalisation, free long-term capital flows, financial crises and economic development. In A. Shaikh (Ed.), *Globalization and the myths of free trade* (pp. 259–287). Routledge.

Singh, A. (2008). *Better to be rough and relevant than to be precise and irrelevant: Reddaway's legacy to economics*. Working Paper No. 379. Cambridge University Centre for Business Research. www.cbr.cam.ac.uk/fileadmin/user_upload/centre-for-business-research/downloads/working-papers/wp379.pdf

Singh, A. (2009). Better to be rough and relevant than to be precise and irrelevant: Reddaway's legacy to economics. *Cambridge Journal of Economics, 33*(3), 363–379.

Singh, D. (2014). *Strictly personal: Manmohan and Gursharan*. Harper Collins.

Singh, A., & Weisse, B. (1998). Emerging stock markets, portfolio capital flows and long-term economic growth: Micro and macroeconomic perspectives. *World Development, 26*(4), 607–622.

Singh, A., & Weisse, B. (1999). The Asian model: A crisis foretold? *International Social Science Journal, 51*(160), 203–215.

Singh, A., & Whittington, G. (1968). *Growth, profitability and valuation: A study of United Kingdom quoted companies*. Cambridge University Press.

Singh, A., & Zammit, A. (2000). *The global labour standards controversy: Critical issues for developing countries*. South Centre.

Singh, A., & Zammit, J. A. (2004). *Labour standards and the 'race to the bottom': Re-thinking globalization and workers' rights from developmental and solidaristic perspectives*. CBR Working Paper 279. Cambridge Centre for Business Research.

Singh, A., Singh, A., & Weisse, B. (2000). *Information technology, venture capital and the stock market*. Discussion Paper in Accounting and Finance, No. AF47. Cambridge University Department of Applied Economics.

Skidelsky, R. (1992). *John Maynard Keynes: The economist as saviour, 1920–1937*. Macmillan.

Skidelsky, R. (2006). Hayek versus Keynes: The road to reconciliation. In E. Feser (Ed.), *The Cambridge companion to Hayek* (pp. 82–110). Cambridge University Press.

Skidelsky, R. (2007). What is essential about Keynes today? *Annals of the Fondazione Luigi Einaudi, LI*, 5–16.

Skidelsky, R. (2009, September 17). Keynes: The return of the master. *The New York Times*.

Skidelsky, R. (2020, January 15–17). *Keynes v Hayek: The Four Buts*. Paper presented at the Conference commemorating the 40 Anniversary of the Mont Pelerin Society meeting of 1980 at Stanford University, Hoover Institution – Stanford University, pp. 160–167.

Skinner, C., Marsh, C., Openshaw, S., & Wyner, C. (1994). Disclosure control for census microdata. *Journal of Official Statistics, 10*(1), 31–51.

Sklair, L. (1981). Sociologies and Marxisms: The odd couples. In P. Abrams, R. Deem, J. Finch, & P. Rock (Eds.), *Practice and progress: British sociology 1950–1980* (pp. 163–167). Allen and Unwin.

Skousen, M. (1997). The perseverance of Paul Samuelson's *economics*. *Journal of Economic Perspectives, 11*(2), 137–152.

Skrabec, Q. R., Jr. (2014). *The fall of an American Rome: De-industrialization of the American dream*. Algora Publishing.

Slade-Caffarel, Y. (2019). The nature of heterodox economics revisited. *Cambridge Journal of Economics, 43*(3), 527–539. https://doi.org/10.1093/cje/bey043

Slobodian, Q. (2018). *Globalists: The end of empire and the birth of neoliberalism*. Harvard University Press.

Smith, R. P. (1976). Demand management and the 'New School'. *Journal of Applied Economics, 8*(3), 193–205.

Smith, D. (1987). *The rise and fall of monetarism: The theory and politics of an economic experiment*. Penguin.

Smith, C. S. (1991). Networks of influence: The social sciences in the United Kingdom since the war. In P. Wagner et al. (Eds.), *Social sciences and modern states: National experiences and theoretical crossroads* (pp. 131–147). Cambridge University Press.

Smith, R. P. (1998). The development of econometric methods at the DAE. In I. Begg & S. G. B. Henry (Eds.), *Applied economics and public policy* (pp. 88–103). Cambridge University Press.

Smith, S. (2008). 'Hard as the metal of my gun': John Cornford's Spain. *Journal of English Studies, 5*, 357–373.

Smith, Y. (2013, January 10). Philip Pilkington: The origins of neoliberalism part II – The Americanisation of Hayek's delusion. Blog post, *Naked Capitalism.* https://www.nakedcapitalism.com/2013/01/philip-pilkington-the-origins-of-neoliberalism-part-ii-the-americanisation-of-hayeks-delusion.html

Smith, G. (2016). *The New Cambridge School: Contribution and legacy.* http://www.cpes.org.uk/dev/wp-content/uploads/2016/07/Graeme_Smith.pdf

Smith, R. P. (2014). Richard Stone. Published later as Smith, R. P. (2019). In R. Dimand & H. Hagemann (Ed.), *The Elgar Companion to John Maynard Keynes* (pp. 419–423). Edward Elgar.

Smith, R. P. (2019). Richard Stone. In R. Dimand & H. Hagemann (Eds.), *The Elgar companion to John Maynard Keynes* (pp. 419–423). Edward Elgar.

Smith, A. K. (2020, January 19). *Women at Cambridge: Eileen Power.* https://akennedysmith.com/tag/eileen-power/

Snooks, G. D. (1993). *Economics without time: A science blind to the forces of historical change.* Macmillan.

Snowdon, B., & Vane, H. (1995). New-Keynesian economics today: The empire strikes back. *American Economist, 39,* 48–55. Reproduced in Snowdon, B., & Vane, H. (Eds.). (1997), *A macroeconomics reader* (pp. 452–477). Routledge.

Snowdon, B., & Vane, H. (1997). *A macroeconomics reader.* Routledge.

Sociology, University of Cambridge. (2018). 50 years of sociology at the University of Cambridge. *Panel discussion: Sociology at Cambridge: Past, present and future* (Patrick Baert, John Thompson, Anthony Giddens, Jacqueline Scott, Ali Meghji). Video recording at: https://www.50years.sociology.cam.ac.uk/events/sociology-cambridge-past-present-and-future

Soderberg, J. (2018). A response to Steve Fuller: The differences between social democracy and neoliberalism. *Blog.* https://blogs.lse.ac.uk/europpblog/2018/08/21/a-response-to-steve-fuller-the-differences-between-social-democracy-and-neoliberalism/

Soderberg, G., Offer, A., & Bjork, S. (2013). Hayek in citations and the Nobel Memorial Prize. In R. Leeson (Ed.), *Hayek: A collaborative biography. Archival insights into the evolution of economic series* (pp. 61–70). Palgrave Macmillan.

Solomou, S. (1986a). Non-balanced growth and Kondratieff waves in the world economy, 1850–1913. *Journal of Economic History, 46*(1), 165–169.

Solomou, S. (1986b). Innovation cluster and Kondratieff long waves in economic growth. *Cambridge Journal of Economics, 10*(2), 101–112.

Solomou, S. (1990). *Phases of economic growth, 1850–1973.* Cambridge University Press.

Solomou, S. (1996). *Themes in macroeconomic history.* Cambridge University Press.

Solomou, S., & Weale, M. (1996). UK national income, 1920–1938: The implications of balanced estimates. *Economic History Review, 49*(1), 101–115.

Solomou, S., & Weale, M. (1997). Personal sector wealth in the United Kingdom, 1920–56. *Review of Income and Wealth, 43*(3), 297–318.

Solomou, S., & Weale, M. (2010). Unemployment and real wages in the great depression. *National Institute Economic Review, 214*(1), 51–61.

Solow, R. M. (2012, November 16). Hayek, Friedman, and the illusions of conservative economics. *The New Republic.*

Solow, R. M. (2017). Frank Hahn (1925–2013). In R. A. Cord (Ed.), *The Palgrave Companion to Cambridge economics* (pp. 915–927). Palgrave Macmillan.

Solow, R. M. (2019). Interview. *Infinite History* (Video). https://infinitehistory.mit.edu/video/robert-m-solow

Sonnenschein, H. (1972). Market excess demand functions. *Econometrica, 40,* 549–563.
de Sousa, F. (2020, October 7). Keynes: The object of Hayek's passion? *Cambridge Journal of Economics, 45*(1), 1–18. https://doi.org/10.1093/cje/beaa043
Spafford, D. (1977). In memoriam: Mabel Timlin. *Canadian Journal of Economics, 10*(2), 279–281.
Sraffa, P. (1925). Sulle relazioni fra costo e quantita produtta. [On the relation between cost and quantity produced. J. Eatwell & A. Roncaglia, Trans.]. In L. L. Pasinetti (Ed.), (1998) *Italian economic papers, Vol. III* (pp. 323–363). Il Mulino; Oxford University Press.
Sraffa, P. (1926). The laws of returns under competitive conditions. *Economic Journal, 36*(144), 535–550.
Sraffa, P. (1932, March). Dr. Hayek on money and capital. *Economic Journal, 42*(165), 42–53.
Sraffa, P. (1960). *Production of commodities by means of commodities: Prelude to a critique of economic theory*. Cambridge University Press.
SSRC. (1981). *A review of macroeconomic research in the UK. The report of a Social Science Research Council Sub-committee*. SSRC.
Standing, G. (2011). *The precariat: The new dangerous class*. Bloomsbury Publishing.
Stanford University. (1993). *Author of first US college textbook on Keynesian economics dies*. News Release, Stanford University News Service, 10/11/93. https://news.stanford.edu/pr/93/931011Arc3112.html
Stern, N. (2016). *Building on success and learning from experience: An independent review of the Research Excellence Framework*. https://assets.publishing.service.gov.uk/government/uploads/system/uploads/attachment_data/file/541338/ind-16-9-ref-stern-review.pdf
Stewart, M. (1967). *Keynes and after*. Penguin Books.
Stewart, M. (1968a, May). A plague of politicians. *Encounter,* 54–56.
Stewart, M. (1968b). A plague of economists? *Encounter,* Letters, 94–95.
Stewart, M. (1978). *Politics and economic policy in the UK since 1964: The Jekyll and Hyde years*. Pergamon Press.
Stewart, H. (2002, September 16). View from the terraces. *The Guardian*.
Stewart, A., & Blackburn, R. M. (1975). The stability of structural inequality. *The Sociological Review, 23*(3), 481–508.
Stewart, A., Prandy, K., & Blackburn, R. (1973). Measuring the class structure. *Nature, 245,* 415–417. https://doi.org/10.1038/245415a0
Stewart, A., Prandy, K., & Blackburn, R. M. (1980). *Social stratification and occupations* (Cambridge studies in sociology) (Vol. 2). Palgrave Macmillan.
Stigler, G. (1982). *Nobel prize biographical*. https://www.nobelprize.org/prizes/economic-sciences/1982/stigler/biographical/
Stigler, G. J. (1985). *Memoirs of an unregulated economist*. University of Chicago Press.
Stigler, S. M. (2005). Aaron Director remembered. *Journal of Law and Economics, 48*(2), 307–311. https://www.jstor.org/stable/10.1086/498417?seq=1#page_scan_tab_contents
Stiglitz, J. E. (2002). *Biographical*. https://www.nobelprize.org/prizes/economic-sciences/2001/stiglitz/biographical/
Stockhammer, E., Dammerer, Q., & Kapur, S. (2017, October). *The research excellence framework 2014, journal ratings and the marginalization of heterodox economics*. Working Paper No. PKWP1715, Post Keynesian Economics Society (PKES). Version 1.05.

Stockwell, S. (2018). *The British end of the British empire.* Cambridge University Press.
Stokes, E. T. (1959). *The English utilitarians in India.* Clarendon Press.
Stone, J. R. N. (1975). *Towards a system of social and demographic statistics.* Studies in Methods, Series F, No. 2. United Nations Statistical Office.
Stone, J. R. N. (1980). Political economy, economics and beyond. Royal Economic Society, presidential address. *Economic Journal, 90,* 719–736.
Stone, J. R. N. (1984). Richard Stone: Biographical. *The Nobel Prize.* https://www.nobelprize.org/prizes/economics/1984/stone/auto-biography/
Stone, R. (1985). James Alan Calvert Brown: An appreciation. *Oxford Bulletin of Economics and Statistics, 47*(3), 191–197.
Stone, J. R. N. (1997). Some British empiricists in the social sciences, 1650–1900. In A. M. Cardani & G. Stone (Eds.), *Raffaele Mattioli lectures 1986.* Cambridge University Press.
Stonier, A. W., & Hague, D. C. (1953). *A textbook of economic theory.* Longmans, Green & Co.
Storm, S. (2009). Capitalism and climate change: Can the invisible hand adjust the natural thermostat? *Development and Change, 40*(6), 1011–1038.
Storm, S., & Naastepad, C. W. M. (2011). *Macroeconomics beyond the NAIRU.* Harvard University Press.
Stray, C. (2019). An Irishman abroad. In C. Stray, C. Pelling, & S. Harrison (Eds.), *Rediscovering E. R. Dodds: Scholarship, education, poetry and the paranormal* (pp. 10–35). Oxford University Press.
Streeten, P. P. (1986/1989). Aerial roots. *Banca Nazionale del Lavoro Quarterly Review, 39*(157): 135–159. (Reprinted: [1989]. In J. A. Kregel (Ed.), *Recollections of eminent economists,* Vol. 2. Macmillan, pp. 73–98).
Streeten, P. (1989). Joan Robinson: Utter fearlessness. In G. R. Feiwel (Ed.), *Joan Robinson and modern economic theory* (pp. 861–862). Palgrave Macmillan.
Supple, B. (1964). *Commercial crisis and change in England, 1600–1642.* Cambridge University Press.
Supple, B. (1970). *The royal exchange assurance: A history of British insurance, 1720–1970.* Cambridge University Press.
Supple, B. (1987). *The history of the British coal industry. Volume 4: 1914–1946, The political economy of decline.* Clarendon Press.
Supple, B. (2011). *An interview of the economic historian and former Master of St. Catharine's College, Cambridge, Professor Barry Supple, talking about his life and work.* Filmed by Alan Macfarlane on 3rd July 2010 and edited by Sarah Harrison. https://www.sms.cam.ac.uk/media/1130704
Sweezy, P. (1950). The transition from feudalism to capitalism. *Science and Society, 14*(2), 134–157.
Sweezy, P. (1972). Symposium. Economics of the New Left: Comment. *Quarterly Journal of Economics, 86*(4), 658–664.
Swinnerton-Dyer, P. (2008, May 12). Interview with Sir Peter Swinnerton-Dyer. In S. Harrison & A. Macfarlane (Eds.), *Encounter with economics.* Interviews filmed by A. Macfarlane and edited by S. Harrison. University of Cambridge. https://www.sms.cam.ac.uk/media/1131073
Szenberg, M., & Ramrattan, L. B. (2017). *Collaborative research in economics: The wisdom of working together.* Palgrave Macmillan.

Tanenhaus, S. (2017). The architect of the radical right: How the Nobel Prize-winning economist James M. Buchanan shaped today's antigovernment politics. *The Atlantic*, July–August.

Targetti, F. (1992). *Nicholas Kaldor: The economics and politics of capitalism as a dynamic system*. Clarendon Press.

Targetti, F. (2005). Nicholas Kaldor: Key contributions to development economics. *Development and Change*, 36(6), 1185–1200.

Tarling, R., & Wilkinson, F. (1977). The social contract: Post-war incomes policies and their inflationary impact. *Cambridge Journal of Economics*, 1(4), 395–414.

Tarshis, L. (1947). *The elements of economics*. Houghton Mifflin.

Tarshis, L. (1989). Remembering Joan Robinson. In G. R. Feiwel (Ed.), *Joan Robinson and modern economic theory* (pp. 918–920). Palgrave Macmillan.

Tarshis, L., et al. (1938). *An economic program for American democracy by seven Harvard and Tufts economists*. Vanguard Press. See Gilbert, R. V. (1938).

Taylor, L. (1984). Review: Social choice theory and the world in which we live. Review of *Choice, Welfare and Measurement* by Amartya Sen. *Cambridge Journal of Economics*, 8(2), 189–196.

Taylor, L. (2004). *Reconstructing macroeconomics: Structuralist proposals and critiques of the mainstream*. Harvard University Press.

Teacher, D. (2018a). 'Neutral academic data' and the international right. In R. Leeson (Ed.), *Hayek: A collaborative biography. Part XIII: Fascism and liberalism in the (Austrian) classical tradition* (pp. 245–320). Palgrave Macmillan.

Teacher, D. (2018b). Private club and secret service Armageddon. In R. Leeson (Ed.), *Hayek: A collaborative biography. Part XIII: Fascism and liberalism in the (Austrian) classical tradition* (pp. 321–360). Palgrave Macmillan.

Temin, P. (2013, June 5). *The rise and fall of economic history at MIT*. Working Paper 13-11. Department of Economics, M.I.T.

Tew, B., & Henderson, R. F. (Eds.). (1959). *Studies in company finance: A symposium on the economic analysis and interpretation of British company accounts*. Cambridge University Press.

Thatcher, M. (1993). *The Downing Street years*. Harper-Collins.

Thatcher, M. (1999, October 6). Pinochet was this country's staunch, true friend. Full text of Margaret Thatcher's speech to the Blackpool fringe. *The Guardian*.

The Telegraph. (2010a, May 21). Professor Wynne Godley. *The Telegraph*. https://www.telegraph.co.uk/news/obituaries/finance-obituaries/7750835/Professor-Wynne-Godley.html

The Telegraph. (2010b, July 13). Professor Robin Matthews. *The Telegraph*. https://www.telegraph.co.uk/news/obituaries/finance-obituaries/7888512/Professor-Robin-Matthews.html

The Telegraph. (2015, March 2). Sir Douglas Hague, economist – Obituary. https://www.telegraph.co.uk/news/obituaries/11444810/Sir-Douglas-Hague-economist-obituary.html

The Times. (2006, March 20). Michael Posner: Cambridge economics lecturer turned government adviser who later worked to safeguard social science research in the UK. *The Times*.

The Times. (2015, July 14). Obituary: Ajit Singh. *The Times*.

Thirlwall, A. P. (Ed.). (1978). *Keynes and laissez-faire: The third Keynes seminar held at the University of Kent at Canterbury, 1976*. Macmillan.

Thirlwall, A. (1987a). *Nicholas Kaldor*. New York University Press.

Thirlwall, A. (1987b). Nicholas Kaldor 1908–1986. *Proceedings of the British Academy, LXXIII*, 517–566.

Thirlwall, A. P. (1989). Kaldor as a policy adviser. *Cambridge Journal of Economics, 13*(1), 121–139.

Thomas, P. (1982). Review: Social sciences and government policy-making. *Government and Opposition, 17*(4), 501–504.

Thomas, M. (2007). Charles Feinstein interviewed by Mark Thomas. In J. S. Lyons, L. P. Cain, & S. H. Williamson (Eds.), *Reflections on the cliometrics revolution: Conversations with economic historians* (pp. 286–300). Routledge.

Thomas, R. (2020). Keynes, Kuhn and the sociology of knowledge: A comment on Pernecky and Wojick. *Cambridge Journal of Economics*, beaa016. https://doi.org/10.1093/cje/beaa016

Thompson, J. B. (1991). Mass communication and modern culture: Contribution to a critical theory of ideology. *Sociology, 22*(3), 359–383.

Thompson, J. B. (1993). The theory of the public sphere: A review article. *Theory, Culture and Society, 10*(3), 173–189.

Thompson, F. M. L. (2004). Hrothgar John Habakkuk, 1915–2002. *Proceedings of The British Academy, 124*, 91–114. https://www.thebritishacademy.ac.uk/documents/1779/124p091.pdf

Thompson, J. B. (2005). The new visibility. *Theory, Culture and Society, 6*, 31–51.

Thompson, J. B. (2011). Shifting boundaries of public and private life. *Theory, Culture and Society, 28*(4), 49–70.

Times Higher Education Supplement. (1982, May 28). Lord Rothschild's truce. *Times Higher Education Supplement*.

Timlin, M. F. (1942). *Keynesian economics*. University Press.

Tobin, J.. (n.d.). Lost star. *Heritage Project*. University of Michigan. https://heritage.umich.edu/stories/lost-star/

Toporowski, J. (2010). Obituary: Wynne Godley. *Royal Economic Society Newsletter, 150*, 15–16. http://www.res.org.uk/SpringboardWebApp/userfiles/res/file/newsletters/July_2010.pdf

Toye, J. F. J. (1983). The disparaging of development economics. *Journal of Development Studies, 20*(1), 87–107.

Toye, J. (1989). Nicholas Kaldor and tax reform in developing countries. *Cambridge Journal of Economics, 13*(2), 183–200.

Toye, J. (1993). *Dissent of development: Reflection on the counter-revolution in development economics* (2nd ed.). Blackwell.

Toye, J. (2006). Keynes and development economics: A sixty-year perspective. *Journal of International Development, 18*(7), 983–995.

Toye, J. (2017). Valpy FitzGerald: Radical macroeconomist of development. *Oxford Development Studies, 45*(2), 116–124.

Travis, A. (2011, December 30). Thatcher government toyed with evacuating Liverpool after 1981 riots. *The Guardian*.

Tremlett, G. (2020, September 3). Operation Condor: The cold war conspiracy that terrorised South America. *The Guardian*.

Tribe, K. (Ed.). (1997). *Economic careers: Economics and economists in Britain 1930–1970*. Routledge.

Tribe, K. (2001). German émigré economists and the internationalisation of economics. Book Review of Harald Hagemann and Claus-Dieter Krohn (eds.), 1999, *Biographical guide to the emigration of German-speaking economists after 1933*, Munich: K. G. Sauer. *Economic Journal, 111*, F740–F746.

Tribe, K. (1992). The *Economic Journal* and British economics, 1891–1940. *History of the Human Sciences*, 5(4), 33–58.
Tribe, K. (2002). *Economic careers: Economics and economists in Britain, 1930–1970.* Routledge Taylor & Francis.
Trinity College Cambridge. (2019). *Trinity colleagues pay tribute to Robert Neild, 1924–2018.* https://www.trin.cam.ac.uk/news/trinity-colleagues-pay-tribute-to-robert-neild-1924-2018/
Tsuru, S. (1993). *Japan's capitalism: Creative defeat and beyond.* Cambridge University Press.
Turner, M. S. (1989). *Joan Robinson and the Americans.* M.E. Sharpe.
Tylecote, A. (1988). Review of *Phases of economic growth: 1850–1973: Kondratieff Waves and Kuznets Swings*, by Solomos Solomou. *Economic Journal*, 98(392), 855–857.
Ulph, A. M., & Reynolds, I. K. (1979). An activities model of consumer behaviour with special reference to outdoor recreation. *Scottish Journal of Political Economy*, 26(1), 33–60.
UNSO. (1975). *Towards a system of social and demographic statistics.* United Nations. ST/ESA/STAT/SER.F/18.
Valdes, J. G. (1995). *Pinochet's economists: The Chicago School in Chile.* Cambridge University Press.
Varottil, U. (2015). *Corporate law in colonial India: Rise and demise of the managing agency system.* NUS Working Paper No. 2015/016. Department of Law, National University of Singapore. http://law.nus.edu.sg/wps/pdfs/016_2015_Umakanth Varottil.pdf
Veblen, T. (1898). Why is economics not an evolutionary science? *Quarterly Journal of Economics*, 12(3), 373–397.
Veblen, T. (1904). *The theory of business enterprise.* Charles Scribners.
Velupillai, V. (1996, August 9). Obituary: Professor Richard Goodwin. *The Independent*.
Velupillai, K. V. (2015a). Richard Goodwin: The Indian connection. *Economic and Political Weekly*, 50(15), 80–84.
Velupillai, K. V. (2015b). Perspectives on the contributions of Richard Goodwin. *Cambridge Journal of Economics*, 39(6). Special Issue: *Perspectives on the contributions of Richard Goodwin*, 1485–1496.
Venkatachalam, R., Velupillai, K. V., & Zambelli, S. (2012). *A non-linear model of the trade cycle: Mathematical reflections on Hugh Hudson's classic.* https://econpapers.repec.org/paper/trnutwpas/1215.htm. Also in: *Australian Economic Papers*, 52(2), 115–125.
Vernengo, M. (2013, September 14). Hydraulic Krugman on Wynne Godley. *Naked Keynesianism: Hemlock for Economics Students.* http://nakedkeynesianism.blogspot.com/2013/09/hydraulic-krugman-on-wynne-godley.html
Vernon, R. (1975). An interpretation. *Daedalus*, 104(4), 1–14.
Vervaecke, P. (2011). Review of William C. Lubenow, *The Cambridge Apostles, 1820–1914: Liberalism, imagination and friendship in British intellectual and professional life*, Cambridge University Press, 1998. *Cercles, Revue Pluridisciplinaire du Monde Anglophone.* http://www.cercles.com/review/r47/Lubenow.html
Videler, T. (2011, November 26). 9 insights into leadership from Professor Dame Sandra Dawson. *Vitae.* https://www.vitae.ac.uk/doing-research/research-staff/the-best-of-the-research-staff-blog/9-insights-into-leadership-from-professor-dame-sandra-dawson

Volcker, P. (2000). *Interview. Commanding heights, public broadcasting service.* Interviewed on 26 September, 2000. https://www.pbs.org/wgbh/commanding-heights/hi/people/pe_name.html

Von Neumann, J., & Morgenstern, O. (1944). *Theory of games and economic behaviour.* Princeton University Press.

Von Tunzelmann, G. N. (1978). *Steam power and British industrialization to 1860.* Clarendon Press.

Von Tunzelmann, G. N. (1982). Structural change and leading sectors in British manufacturing 1907–68. In Kindleberger & di Telia (Eds.), *Economics in the long view* (Vol. Ill). Macmillan.

Von Tunzelmann, G. N. (1995). *Technology and industrial progress: The foundations of economic growth.* Edward Elgar.

Von Tunzelmann, G. N., & Thomas, M. (2007). R. C. O. Matthews interviewed by Nicholas von Tunzelmann and Mark Thomas. In J. S. Lyons, L. P. Cain, & S. H. Williamson (Eds.), *Reflections on the cliometrics revolution: Conversations with economic historians* (pp. 155–170). Routledge.

Voorhees, E. D. (1929). Emotional adjustment of women in the modern world and the choice of satisfactions. *Annals of the American Academy of Political and Social Science, 143,* 368–373. http://www.jstor.org/stable/1017216

Wagner, P., Hirschon Weiss, C., Wittrock, B., & Wollman, H. (Eds.). (1991). *Social sciences and modern states: National experiences and theoretical crossroads.* Cambridge University Press.

Waldegrave, W. (2013). *William Waldegrave interviewed by Alan Macfarlane.* Film interviews with leading thinkers. University of Cambridge. https://www.sms.cam.ac.uk/media/1901304

Walker, D. (2016). *Exaggerated claims? The ESRC, 50 years on.* Sage Publications.

Walters, A. (1981). *Alan Walter's diary 1981.* Transcribed from the original at Churchill Archive Centre (WTRS 3/1/1). https://www.margaretthatcher.org/document/137536

Wapshott, N. (2011). *Keynes Hayek: The clash that defined modern economics.* W.W. Norton & Company.

Ward, B. (1972). *What's wrong with economics?* Basic Books.

Ward, T. (1982). Mrs. Thatcher's economic strategy in practice. *Cambridge Journal of Economics, 4*(4), 516–530.

Waring, M. (1999). *Counting for nothing: What men value and what women are worth* (2nd ed.). University of Toronto Press, Scholarly Publishing Division.

Warren, B. (1980). *Imperialism: Pioneer of capitalism.* Verso Press.

Warsh, D. (2016, December 4). Presentiments of Nobel future. *Economic Principals – A Weekly Column about Economics and Politics.* http://www.economicprincipals.com/issues/2016.12.04/1950.html

Waterman, A. M. C. (2003). Joan Robinson as a teacher. *Review of Political Economy, 15*(4), 589–596.

Weale, M. (1985). Testing linear hypotheses on national account data. *Review of Economics and Statistics, 67*(4), 685–689.

Weale, M. (1993). Fifty years of national income accounting. *Economic Notes, 22*(2), 178–199.

Webb, S. (1926). The end of laissez-faire. *Economic Journal, 36*(143), 434–441.

Weintraub, E. R. (1985). Joan Robinson's critique of equilibrium: An appraisal. *The American Economic Review*, 75(2), 146–149. http://www.jstor.org/stable/1805586

Weintraub, E. R. (2017). McCarthyism and the mathematization of economics. *Journal of the History of Economic Thought*, 39(4), 571–597.

Whitaker, J. K. (Ed.). (1996a). *The correspondence of Alfred Marshall, economist* (Climbing, 1681–1890) (Vol. 1). Royal Economic Society Publication. Cambridge University Press.

Whitaker, J. K. (Ed.). (1996b). *The correspondence of Alfred Marshall, economist* (At the summit, 1891–1902) (Vol. 2). Royal Economic Society Publication. Cambridge University Press.

Whitaker, J. K. (Ed.). (1996c). *The correspondence of Alfred Marshall, economist* (Towards the close, 1903–1924) (Vol. 3). Royal Economic Society Publication. Cambridge University Press.

White, L. H. (2015). Susan Howson, *Lionel Robbins*. Book review. *Oeconomia*, 5-3, 419–422. https://journals.openedition.org/oeconomia/2104#quotation

Whitehead, P. (1985). *The writing on the wall: Britain in the 1970s*. Michael Joseph.

Whitfield, S. J. (1987). Review of Ellen W. Schrecker, *No ivory tower: McCarthyism and the universities*. *Reviews in American History*, 15(3), 480–485.

Whittington, G. (2016). Wit and empirical rigour in pursuing debate. In G. C. Harcourt, The legacy of Ajit Singh (11 September 1940–23 June 2015): Memories and tributes from former pupils, colleagues and friends. *The Economic and Labour Relations Review*, 27(3), 302–303.

Wickham-Jones, M. (1992). Monetarism and its critics: The university economists' letter of protest of 1981. *Political Quarterly*, 63(2), 171–185.

Wicksell, K. (1904). Ends and means in economics. Inaugural lecture delivered at the University of Lund on 16 September 1904. Reprinted in E. Lindahl (Ed.), *Selected papers on economic theory* (pp. 51–66). George Allen and Unwin, 1958.

Wiles, P. (1968, July). Stalin on sterling. *Encounter*, Notes and Topics, 56–59.

Wilkins, M. (1975). The oil companies in perspective. *Daedalus*, 104(4), 159–178.

Wilkinson, F. (Ed.). (1981). *Dynamics of labour market segmentation*. Academic Press.

Wilkinson, F. (1983). Productive systems. *Cambridge Journal of Economics*, 7(3–4), 413–429.

Wilkinson, F. (2003). Productive systems and the structuring role of Economic and social theories. In B. Burchell, S. Deakin, J. Michie, & J. Rubery (Eds.), *Systems of production: Markets, organisations and performance* (pp. 10–39). Routledge.

Wilkinson, C. (2017). The East India College debate and the fashioning of imperial officials, 1806–1858. *The Historical Journal*, 60(4), 943–969.

Wilson, T. (1943). Review of Mabel F. Timlin, *Keynesian Economics*, Toronto: University Press, 1942. *Economic Journal*, 53(210/211), 224–226. https://doi.org/10.2307/2226324

Wilson, B. (2017, January 26). Tam Dalyell obituary. *The Guardian*. https://www.theguardian.com/politics/2017/jan/26/tam-dalyell-obituary

Woolbert, R. G. (1939, October). A defense of new deal economics, a review of: *An economic program for American democracy* by Seven Harvard and Tufts Economists. *Foreign Affairs*.

Wright, D. M. (1948, March). Review: The Keynesian revolution by Lawrence R. Klein. *American Economic Review*, 38(1), 145–152.

Yamey, B. S. (1987). Peter Bauer: Economist and scholar. *Cato Journal, 7*(1), 21–27. https://www.cato.org/sites/cato.org/files/serials/files/cato-journal/1987/5/cj7n1-2.pdf

Yergin, D., & Stanislaw, J. (1988). *The commanding heights*. Simon and Schuster.

Yokoyama, K. (2006). The effect of the research assessment exercise on organizational culture in English universities: Collegiality versus managerialism. *Tertiary Education and Management, 12*, 311–322.

Youkee, M. (1999, October 4). Thatcher sent Pinochet finest scotch during former dictator's UK house arrest. *The Guardian*.

Young, A. A. (1928). Increasing returns and economic progress. *Economic Journal, 38*(152), 527–542.

Young, M. Y. (2011). John Arundel Barnes (1918–2010). *Cambridge Journal of Anthropology, 29*, 4–12.

Name Index[1]

A

Abdel-Fadil, M., 312, 695, 824
Abdelrahman, M., 60
Abel-Smith, B., 154n82, 733n42, 1048
Abizaid, General J., 263
Abramovitz, M., 139n64
Abrams, P., 693, 698, 705, 710, 719
Abramsky, C., 883
Abulafia, A., 883
Acemoglu, D., 930
Adams, A. A., 865n14
Adler, S., 250
Ady, P., 938, 939, 939n102, 943–947, 943n104, 949
Agarwal, B., 952
Agnew, S., 1024
Ahmed, I., 344n60, 820
Aidt, T., 900, 902, 924–925, 924n87, 928
Albertson, K., 477n25
Albornoz, F., 924n86
Allais, M., 219, 222n23, 239
Allende, S., 245, 248, 254, 257–260, 375, 461n14
Allsopp, C. J., 889
Amjad, R., 344n60, 820, 823, 825n71
Anderlini, L., 134, 364
Anderson, D., 729n37

Annan, Lord (Noel), 234n38, 538, 543, 699, 699n1, 700, 730, 732
Antoni, C., 222n23
Anyadike-Danes, M., 320
Appelbaum, B., 193, 200, 275
Archer, D., 335, 335n51
Arestis, P., 327, 360–361, 970, 981, 985–987, 1037
Armstrong, W., 454n7
Aron, R., 213
Arrow, K., 77, 106, 252, 272n62, 328, 350, 351, 353, 358
Artis, M. J., 147, 166, 568n8, 586, 971, 980, 985–987
Arulampalam, W., 981
Arumugam, H., xviii
Asbrink, P., 236, 237
Ashton, T. S., 969
Asimakopoulos, T., 341, 343n59
Aslanbegui, 28, 29, 29n17
Aspers, P., 702, 702n10
Asquith, H. H., 502n41
Atkinson, A. B., 83, 147, 160–162, 165, 626, 980, 981, 985–987
Atkinson, F., 459n13
Attlee, C., 86n13, 727
Auden, W. H., 133n57, 335n51

[1] Note: Page numbers followed by 'n' refer to notes.

Audier, S., 56
Austin, G., 846n1, 931, 933

B

Backhouse, R., 166, 305n18, 970–972, 972n5, 989, 1009, 1010, 1032n8
Bagchi, A., xvii, xix, 314n30, 474n23, 511n49, 770, 771n3, 774, 775, 819, 820, 821n66, 868
Bain, A. D., 980
Baker, C., 121, 821n67
Ball, C., 974
Ball, R. J., 980
Balls, E., 981
Balogh, Lord (Thomas, "Tommy"), 132, 457, 459, 805
Banks, J. A., 694, 695
Baran, P., 190, 238, 375, 777
Baranzini, M. L., 96n23, 128, 128n52, 317n35, 340n56, 342, 372
Bardhan, P., 820
Bardon, A., 258
Barker, J., 947
Barker, K., 981
Barker, T., xvii, xix, 7n3, 10, 70n1, 103n31, 111, 111n35, 164, 362, 363, 399, 400, 420, 427, 427n11, 435n24, 443n2, 507, 523, 558, 558n21, 566, 566n4, 567, 568n8, 569–574, 569n9, 570n10, 571n12, 576–581, 579n22, 581n24, 584, 584n26, 585n27, 586, 588–590, 613, 613n12, 625, 630, 658, 662, 662n55, 667n61, 673, 678, 823, 827, 828, 932n93, 936, 937n97, 1037, 1057n20, 1064
Barnard, A., 707, 941
Barnes, J. A., 81, 114, 338, 699–701, 699n2, 701n6, 705–708, 706n16, 710, 710n19, 714–716, 714n25, 715n26, 725, 733n42, 734, 736–738, 737n47, 743, 753, 941–943, 952
Barnes, M., xviii
Barnett, V., 188n3
Barnett, W. A., 185, 205n11, 390n105
Barth, H., 222n23
Barton, A., 341

Basili, M., 54
Bauer, P. T., 91, 108, 232, 266, 267, 542n7, 775, 775n8, 775–776n9, 797, 805, 822n69, 826, 867n16, 870n22, 966
Baumol, W. J., 239
Bayly, C., 821n67, 867n16
Bean, C., 154, 165, 977, 981
Beath, J., 74, 584n26, 976, 977, 979n9, 981, 985–987
Beaud, M., 47, 48, 724
Bechhofer, F., 682, 684n78, 693, 698, 708
Becker, G., 57n33, 205n11, 231, 239, 250, 264
Beckerman, W., 459n13, 882n33, 981
Beckett, A., 258, 472, 473
Bedi, B. S., 98
Begg, I., 320, 435n24, 619, 651n48, 675, 911
Beinart, W., 932n91
Beloff, M., 266, 267, 533, 534, 540, 543–545, 546n12, 556, 732, 884n37, 889–891
Beloff, Lord, 526
Benn, A. W. "Tony," xiii, 30n18, 71, 72, 116, 118, 193, 308, 446n4, 449n5, 456, 457, 458n11, 465, 471, 472, 472n20, 479, 480n30, 482–484, 812n41
Bennathan, E., 980
Bennett, D., 791n21, 795n26
Bentham, J., 27, 28
Bentzel, R., 239
Berg, E., 797
Berg, M., 849, 851, 882
Bergstrom, V., 247
Berlin, I., 200, 730
Bernal, M., 77
Berrill, K. E., 91, 92, 300, 300n5, 347, 351, 442, 444, 445, 458, 459n13, 509, 540n5, 544–546, 546n12, 630, 630n30, 664, 746, 802–804, 980
Berry, V., 942n103, 947
Berry, WTC, 947
Bertrand, M., 167
Bescoby, J., 693
Besicovitch, A. S., 818n59

Besley, T., 146, 148, 155, 167, 988, 1029–1031
Bettelheim, C., 813
Bevan, A., 191, 459
Beveridge, W. B., xii, 111, 182, 185, 185n2, 191, 213, 243, 345, 448, 783, 969, 970
Beveridge, W. H., 111, 165, 182, 185, 185n2, 191, 213, 243, 345, 448, 783, 969, 970
Bezemer, D., 988
Bhaduri, A., v, 813, 820, 822n68, 823, 827
Bhagwati, J., 60, 186, 201, 816, 816n57, 820, 885
Bharadwaj, K., 820, 824
Binmore, K., 363, 981
Birch, B., 973n6
Birnbaum, I., 696
Birner, J., 30, 199
Black, F., 1025
Black, J., 166, 980
Black, R. D. C., 980
Blackaby, F., 980
Blackburn, R. M. "Bob," xvii, 651, 651n48, 682, 683n77, 693–698, 709, 712, 733n42, 736, 736–737n46, 738n50, 739, 744, 747, 749n59, 750–752
Blair, T., 122–124, 232n34, 483, 638n37, 665, 1059n22
Blaug, M., 27, 186, 970
Blinder, A., 34–39, 39n24, 58n34, 723, 1023–1027, 1053–1054
Bliss, C., 58n24, 134, 136, 154, 154n82, 343n58, 361, 821n68
Bliss, C. J., 58n34, 134, 136, 154, 154n82, 167, 343n58, 361, 821n68, 971, 981
Bloch, M., 733, 876
Blundell, J., 165, 198, 203, 204, 211, 229, 230, 230n31, 230n32, 244, 258, 259, 264, 981
Blundell, R., 154, 977, 981
Bode, K., 216n20
Boehm, K. H., 693, 698
Bohm-Bawerk, E. von, 214, 214n19, 315n32
Bolton, J. R., 211n15

Bonn, J.M., 185, 189
Bonnier, 240
Booth, A., 981, 985–987
Booth, C., 676, 907n53
Booth, P., 467–470, 468n17, 468n18
Borges, J. L., 78
Borooah, V. K., xvii, xx, 7n3, 70n1, 98, 98n26, 98n27, 355–357, 355n68, 358n72, 589, 651, 823, 827
Borpujari, J. G., 821n66
Bortis, H., xvii, xx, 343n59, 869–870n20, 870n21, 872
Bose, S., 820
Bottomore, T. B., 733n42
Bourdieu, P., 703n12, 711, 992
Bourguignon, F., 1052–1053
Bowles, S., 272n62, 1011
Bownas, P., xviii
Bradbury, M., 729, 729n38, 730
Brading, D., 889n39, 894
Bradley, I., 273, 274
Bradley, J., xvii, 306, 307, 312, 316, 321
Brand, R. H., 165
Brandenburger, A., 51, 134
Brandt, K., 212n17, 222n23
Bray, M., 643n39, 746, 936n94
Bray, S., 932n94, 936n94
Brentano, L. J., 702, 702n7
Brito, K., 535n4
Brittan, S., 232, 430, 504, 542n7
Britten, Benjamin, xv
Britton, A. J. C., 147, 444, 980
Broadbent, S., 587
Broadberry, S., 931–933
Bromwich, M., 138n63
Bronfenbrenner, M., 27
Broughton, A., xii, 465, 466, 1068
Brown, A. J., 165, 980
Brown, J. A. C. "Alan," 9, 70n1, 71–73, 103n31, 154, 419, 421, 423, 425, 564, 566, 569, 613n12, 614, 716, 719, 936, 977
Brown, L., 211n15
Brown, Miss, 455n8
Brown, W., 82, 86, 86n12, 114, 165, 366n80, 433, 533, 542, 544, 545, 615, 632, 632n32, 651, 653, 653n51, 654, 668n62, 687, 745, 756, 1022, 1036, 1062

Brown, W. A., 82–84, 147, 365n79
Bruland, K., 880
Bryce, B., 376, 403
Buchanan, J., 201, 231, 233, 239, 249, 250, 256, 257, 261n53, 276, 284n70, 776n9
Buckley Jr., W. F., 373, 375
Budd, A., 980
Buffet, H., 211
Buggeln, M., 900
Buiter, W., 83, 166, 981
Bull, A. C., 257n52
Bulmer, M., 701, 703–704n12, 704, 705, 710n22, 717n30, 718
Bundy, C., 932n91
Buiter, W., 83, 166, 981
Burbidge, J., 343n59
Burchell, B., xvii, xx, 651, 651n48, 683–687, 687n88, 697, 698, 705n14, 735n45, 738n51, 742, 742n56, 756, 911n61, 912
Burdett, K., 981
Burgin, A., 27n14, 219, 220, 224n26, 227
Burn, G., 220
Burns, A. F., 211n15, 379
Burns, T., 586, 980
Bush, G. W., 211n15
Bush, George H. W., 263, 264
Buss, R., 152n80
Butler, C., 981
Butler, E., 234, 234n40
Butler, H., 220
Butler, R. A. "Rab," 717n30, 818n59
Butterfield, J., 576n18, 600, 605, 656
Buzaglo, J., 236
Byatt, I. C. R., 971, 980, 985
Byres, T. J., 774

C

Caesar, J., xi, 285
Caine, S., 165
Cairncross, A., 71n2, 146, 147, 165, 336, 336n54, 337, 364, 365, 458, 617, 801, 805, 871n24
Cairncross, F., 980
Caldentey, E. P., 338

Caldwell, B., 202n9, 203, 204, 210, 212n17, 220, 221n21, 222n23, 224n26, 228, 256, 257n51, 280, 281
Callaghan, J., xii, xiii, 140n67, 195, 195n6, 450, 463–466, 472n20, 482, 483, 605, 812n41
Cameron, D., 125
Cannan, E., 165, 181, 182
Canning, D., 134, 364
Cardoso, F. H., 894
Carlin, W. J., 147, 148
Carlisle, M., 487, 522, 525, 534
Carlson, S., 238n43
Carr, E.H., 143, 455n8
Carr Saunders, A. M., 165
Carrington, Lord, 262, 794n24
Carruth, A., 981
Carter, C. F., 166, 299n4
Carter, J., 391, 476
Carvalho, V., 1066, 1067
Casey, W. J. "Bill," 233
Cassel, G., 237, 247, 336
Cassell, F., 455n8
Cassidy, J., 242, 243
Casson, M. C., 980
Castro, F., 375, 783
Castro, V., 924n86
Cexbres, B. de J., 222n23
Chadha, J. S., 924n86
Chakravarty, S., 316, 511n49, 770, 772, 773, 816n57, 886, 887
Chambers, M., 335, 335n51
Chambers, R., 42n26, 952
Champernowne, D. G., 7, 70n1, 71, 73, 73n4, 81, 82, 85, 86, 108, 132n56, 166, 297, 301, 310n23, 339n55, 351, 358, 360, 416, 417, 425, 432, 826
Chandavarkar, A., 770
Chang, A. C., 999
Chang, H-J., xvii, 60, 61, 506n46, 779n11, 781, 797, 823, 825n71, 828–832, 835, 1007, 1023, 1044, 1070
Chapman, A., 863n11, 865n14
Chatterjee, M., 820
Chatterjee, R., 820
Chatterji, M., 344n60

Chayanov, A. V., 921
Chenery, H., 771n4
Cheney, D., 211n15
Cherwell, Viscount, 73n4
Chesher, A., 165, 981, 982
Cheung, S., 167
Chiang Kai-shek, 782
Chick, V., 981, 985
Chowdhury, N., 344n60, 820
Christodoulakis, N., 651
Churchill, W., 73n4, 130, 131, 133, 135, 160, 191, 193, 307, 328, 343, 357, 360–362, 361n75, 364, 367, 630n30, 710n21, 737n47, 812n41, 863n10, 979, 1055n18
Ciccone, A., 167
Clack, G., 693, 694
Clapham, J., 203, 220, 221, 221n21, 277, 303, 727, 847–852, 876, 877, 879, 881, 892, 905n53, 907n53, 931
Clark, C., 230, 417, 418, 418n2, 421, 436n26, 805, 807, 819, 819n62, 861, 863, 877, 884, 887
Clark, G. Kitson, 846, 847, 849, 869n18
Clarke, P., 113, 114
Clay, 109
Clegg, N., 125
Clements, K. W., 253, 254
Coase, R., 186, 205n11, 211n15, 231, 239, 241, 250
Coats, A. W. "Bob," 27, 300–304, 301n7, 302n9, 302n10, 302n12, 303n13, 304n17, 968n1, 971n3
Coats, S. E., 301n7, 968n1
Cochrane, D., 421, 564
Cockerill, T., 1036, 1054
Cockett, R., 231
Cohen, A., 107
Cohen, R., 87, 95n22, 351
Colander, D., 52, 372–376, 393
Cole, D. E., 693–694, 717, 865n14
Cole, W. A. "Max," 421, 717, 863, 863n10, 863n11, 864n12, 865, 870, 903, 908
Coleman, D., 114, 115, 120, 121, 606n6, 895–899, 896n45, 907n53
Collard, D. A., 166
Collini, S., 756n63

Colson, E., 942, 943
Congdon, T., 468n18, 525
Cornford, J., 335n50, 655, 876
Cornuelle, H., 208, 211
Cornuelle, R., 208
Corry, B., 969n2
Cortney, P., 373
Cosh, A., xvii, 121, 358, 627, 669n63, 827, 937n97, 1042, 1059
Coutts, K. J., xvii, xxii, 7n3, 70n1, 151, 312, 317, 320, 321, 344, 360, 361, 428, 429, 475, 476, 492, 496, 498, 499, 525, 651, 651n48, 695, 827, 913n70
Cowen, M. P., 695
Cowling, K. G., 980
Coxeter, H. S. M., 405
Coyle, D., 981
Craig, J. C., 685, 693–697
Crane, E., 211n16
Crane, J., 203
Craver, E., 189, 214
Craypo, C., 684, 684n82
Creedy, J., 72, 73
Cripps, F., xii, xvii, xxi, xxii, 7n3, 9, 13, 14n7, 70n1, 103n31, 113, 117, 118, 118n42, 122, 146, 305n18, 306–308, 312, 313, 314n30, 320, 321, 359, 399–402, 419, 425, 440, 442, 443, 446n4, 448, 449n5, 453, 454n7, 457, 458n11, 460, 472n20, 479n28, 483, 484, 490, 491, 495, 496, 497n38, 498, 498n39, 499, 502n41, 503, 503n42, 504, 507–509, 599, 600n2, 647n44, 651, 658, 661–664, 673, 811, 812n42, 822, 827, 828, 865n15, 867, 1000, 1010, 1037, 1042n11, 1071
Cripps, M., 167
Cripps, S., 449n5, 472n20, 481, 811, 812n41
Crompton, R., 693
Crook, C., 981, 985
Crossman, R., 76n6, 458
Crotty, J., 281
Croxford, P. M., 882n36
Crozier, B., 260, 261, 729n37
Cuadro, S. de la, 260

Cubitt, C. E., 185n2
Cunningham, C., 464, 520, 533, 534, 537, 540, 565, 847–849
Cunningham, W., 847–849, 848n2
Cupitt, D., 655n52
Currie, D., 981
Curry, E., 269

D

Dahrendorf, R., 181, 183, 184, 534, 699n2, 708, 733n42
Dalton, H., 851
Daly, H., 167
Dalyell, T., 78, 145n75, 146, 333, 333n46
Daniel, P., 695, 696
Daniel, S. S., 980
Dara Singh (wrestler), 322n40
Darwin, C., 119, 335n50
Dasgupta, A. K., 346, 352
Dasgupta, P., xii, xix, 11, 14, 51, 52, 54, 82–84, 86, 101, 114, 129, 132–134, 134n59, 152n81, 154, 154n82, 160–162, 164, 342, 346, 350, 355, 358, 363, 432, 435, 448, 496, 611, 612, 616, 625, 643n39, 659n54, 668n62, 674n68, 734, 746, 827–829, 915, 918, 919–920n77, 952, 967, 968, 971, 973n6, 976, 977, 979–981, 995, 1022, 1032, 1036, 1046, 1054–1056, 1058
Dasgupta, S., 821
Daunton, M., 846, 849, 850, 852, 877, 881–883, 891, 892, 899–902, 919n76, 920, 924n87, 925, 926, 933, 1002
Davenant, C., 421, 862n9
Davenport, J., 222n23, 222n24
David Easley, D. or Kelsey, 363, 364
David, P. A., 974, 981
Davies, G., 123, 980
Davies, T., xviii
Davis, E., 981
Davis, J., 459
De Vroey, M., 34n21, 58n34, 378, 1024, 1024n3
Deakin, B. M., 694–696

Dean, K., xviii, 386n101
Deane, P. M., 7, 40, 70n1, 73, 82, 114, 136, 154, 165, 298, 301, 310n23, 421, 422, 432, 450, 565n1, 578n21, 793, 793n23, 802, 804, 806, 822–824, 826, 860, 862–866, 863n11, 864n12, 869–875, 899n46, 902–906, 908–911, 910n60, 927, 933, 938–953, 980, 1043, 1043n12
Deaton, A., 7n3, 70n1, 72, 136, 138n61, 154, 154n83, 159, 168n85, 241, 355, 356, 420–423, 423n10, 440, 564, 567, 575, 575n15, 575–576n17, 584, 584n25, 643, 824, 827, 862n9, 873n24
Debreu, G., 51
Dell, E., 446n4
Den Haan, W., 167
Deng, A., 789
Deng, Xiaoping, 774
Denham, A., 230, 492, 532, 534
Dennison, S. R., 87, 213, 223, 276
Dennison, T., 921, 922
Derkson, J. B. D., 819n63
Desai, A., 820
Desai, M. J., 33n20, 280, 820n64, 834, 971, 980, 984–987
Desai, P., 60, 813n50, 815–817, 815n54, 816n57
Devereux, J., 683, 698, 910n58
Devlin, Lord, 297, 492, 701n6, 706n16
Dewas, Raja of, 811n38
Di Matteo, M., 315n32, 372n85, 372n86, 372n87
Diamond, J., 446n4
Diamond, P., 353, 1049, 1054
Dickens, C., 907n53
Dickinson, Goldsworthy Lowes, 335, 335n52
Dilnot, A., 981
Dimand, R. W., 404
Director, A., 202, 203, 205, 205n11, 212n17, 219, 220, 222n23
Dirks, N. B., 821n67
Disney, R., 981
Dixon, H., 167, 981
Dixon, K., 694, 695

Dobb, M. C., xix, 5, 7, 70n1, 87, 87n15, 91, 92, 96, 112, 115, 116, 117n41, 136, 141, 142, 142n71, 144, 306, 309, 310n24, 313, 314, 318, 331, 335, 337, 348, 370, 716, 769, 772, 774, 812n45, 818, 826, 852–860, 863n10, 864n11, 864n13, 865, 874n27, 881n32, 883, 886, 903, 904, 909, 931, 1060n24
Doherty, B., 197, 206, 206n12, 275
Dolton, P. J., 166
Domar, E., 186, 337, 542n7
Donald, D., 694–696
Dostaler, G., 47, 48, 724
Doucoudliagos, H., 999
Douglas, C.H., 381n98
Dow, C., 457, 458, 459n13
Dow, J. C. R., 456, 457, 980
Dow, S., 981, 1029, 1029n7
Downes, D., 700, 700n3
Downie, J., 814n53
Drewnowski, J., 721, 951
Dreze, J., 723, 1049
Dribbin, J. D., 980
Driffil, J., 981
Duarte, P. G., 34n21, 58n34
Duesenberry, J., 246
Dunlop, J. T., 340
Dunn, J., 756n63
Durbin, E. F. M., 851
Durbin, J., 421, 564
Durkheim, E., 701
Durrell, L., ix, 599
Dutta, J., 167, 900, 924n86, 925

E
Earhart, P., 203
Eastman, M., 204
Eatwell, J. L., xxii, 7n3, 70n1, 104, 117, 117n41, 121–124, 124n44, 136, 305–307, 305n18, 309, 309n22, 310n24, 312–314, 314n30, 315n31, 316, 316n33, 320, 321, 360, 394–398, 401, 483, 499, 506n46, 642, 823, 826, 858, 858n6, 859, 1041, 1042, 1058, 1059, 1070
Ebenstein, L., 206
Eden, F. M., 676n70
Edgeworth, F. Y., 166, 297–299, 305
Edmunds, J., 446n4
Edwards, J. S. S., 643n39, 746
Edwards, K. J. R., 114, 576n18, 600, 602, 602n4, 604–606, 608, 608n9, 610–613, 615, 617, 618, 621, 621n18, 623, 626, 627, 629, 633, 636–638, 642–648, 645n43, 648n45, 652n49, 654–657, 655n52, 659, 660, 745–747, 748n58, 752
Einstein, A., 1025
Eisenhower, D. D., 200, 201, 398, 818n59
Eldridge, J., 729, 729n38, 730
El-Erian, M., 1059, 1064, 1065
Ellis, H. S., 216n20
Ellman, M. J., xvii, xxi, 7n3, 70n1, 117, 117n41, 118, 305n18, 311n26, 312, 314n30, 321, 480, 575, 643, 859n7
Engels, F., 41, 121, 850, 863n10, 907n53
English, M., 431
Epstein, J., xv, 493, 493n36
Erlander, T., 235
Eucken, W., 213n18
Evans, B., 364
Evans, R., 52, 134
Evans-Pritchard, E. E., 784, 789, 941
Evon, D., 30n18
Ewing, A. F., 769
Eyck, E., 222n23

F
Faber, M. L. O., 824
Fanon, F., 785
Farmer, B., 796
Farnie, D. A., 895
Farrell, M. J., 70n1, 91, 328, 350
Fawcett, H., 79, 80, 847

Feinstein, C. H., 70n1, 115, 116, 117n41, 125, 126, 132n56, 133n57, 136, 139–147, 139n64, 140n65, 140n66, 140n69, 141n70, 142n71, 144n73, 166, 170n86, 234n38, 310n23, 341, 364, 365n79, 366, 366n81, 421, 422, 432, 447, 464, 552n15, 553n16, 568n8, 586, 627–630, 629n27, 695, 697, 822n68, 860, 863, 863–864n11, 864n12, 865, 866, 868, 887, 891, 899, 899n46, 906, 909–910n56, 910, 910n60, 911, 918, 919, 919n74, 927, 976n8, 980, 981, 983, 985–987, 989, 1043
Feiwel, G., 106, 378n96
Feldman, G., 5
Feldstein, M., 211n15, 226n29, 571n11, 586, 626
Felli, L., 52, 164, 167, 1063
Fells, A. H. M., 694
Fennell, S., 779n12, 1071
Feser, E., 281
Fetherston, M., 7n3, 320, 442, 509, 651, 827
Feulner, E. J. Jr., 211, 233, 263, 264
Fforde, A., 822n68
Fieldhouse, D. K., 821n67
Filip, B., 256, 257, 257n51
Finley, M., 714
Firth, R., 727n35, 733n42
Fischer, S., 186, 771n4
Fish, M., 1027, 1028
Fisher, A., 192, 229–234, 234n40, 257, 266, 267, 542n7
Fisher, D., 703n12
Fisher, J., 897
Fisher, Malcolm, 350
Fisher, Mark, 229
FitzGerald, E. V. K. "Valpy," xvii, 793, 793n23, 796, 797, 805, 822, 826n71, 827, 893
Fitzmaurice, H. G., 947
Flather, P., 532, 536–538, 540, 541, 541n6, 544, 545, 731
Flemming, J. S., 137, 146, 147, 155, 159–163, 166, 170n86, 280, 299n4, 365, 366, 489n33, 568n8, 571n11, 586, 587n28, 626, 669, 971, 980, 984–987

Fletcher, C. H., 882n36
Fletcher, G., 75, 333, 346
Flinn, M. W., 851, 875n31, 882, 883, 892
Florence, P. S., 335, 335n49, 336
Floud, J., 733n42
Fluckiger, M., 933
Folbre, N., 905, 950n106
Foot, M., 243, 265, 483
Ford, G., 211n15
Fores, M., 693, 695
Forster, E. M., 811n38, 818n59
Fortes, M., 87n14, 706, 707, 784, 938n98, 941, 943–946
Fosh, P., 695
Foxwell, H. S., 75n5, 165, 330
Franck, R., 924n86
Franco, General F., 50, 52, 782
Frank, A. G., 934
Fraser, C., 683, 697, 698
Frearson, K., 341
Freeman, A., 1031
Freeman, R., 372, 981
Freire, P., 42n26, 952
Friedman, A., 133n58, 192
Friedman, M., 8, 33, 36, 40, 77, 112, 187, 193, 195n6, 196–201, 205, 205n11, 206, 210, 211n15, 219, 222, 223, 223n25, 225, 225n28, 226, 228, 228n30, 231, 232, 234n38, 235, 238, 239, 242, 245–251, 254, 256–259, 256n50, 263–265, 267–270, 272–278, 274n66, 276n68, 280, 283, 284n70, 296, 337, 354, 355, 369, 375, 379, 403, 452, 460, 469n19, 470, 473, 542n7, 771n4, 775n9, 1023
Friedman, R., 267
Frisch, R., 240–241, 251, 377, 421n9, 576n17, 812n44, 812n46, 813, 813n51
Frohlich, W., 216n20
Frost, M., xvii
Frost, S., xviii
Fullbrook, E., 367, 1033
Fuller, E., 281–283, 282n69
Furth, H. von, 216n20

G

Gadgil, D. R., 807, 819, 819n61, 868
Gailord, A. Hart, 216n20
Gaitskell, H., 216n20, 851
Galbraith, James, 498, 501
Galbraith, John K., 235, 376, 394, 492, 581n24
Gale, D., 51, 134, 364
Gallagher, J., 821n67, 867n16
Galeotti, A., 167
Galofre-Vila, G., 913
Gama (wrestler), 322n40
Gandhi, M. K. "Mahatma," 30n18
Garcia, A., 461n14
Garegnani, P., 7, 70n1, 309, 309n22, 341
Garnett, M., 230, 492, 532, 534
Garman, K., xv
Garnsey, E., 683n75, 683n76, 696
Garonna, P., 343n59
Gassebner, M., 924n86
Gatsios, C., 364
Geanakoplos, J., 363
Geeta and Babita (wrestlers), 322n40
Gellner, E., 716, 738
George, K. D., 980, 984–987
Georgescu-Roegen, N., 186
Geroski, P., 981
Gerschenkron, A., 142n71, 186, 190, 777, 868
Ghose, A. K., 344n60, 820, 823
Ghosh, J., 820, 825n71
Giap, General, 97
Gibson, N., 499
Giddens, A., 82, 114, 469, 694, 695, 711, 711n23, 715
Gideonse, H. D., 222n23
Giersch, H., 244n46
Gilbert, R. V., 373, 373n89, 393
Gillies, D., 968, 1029
Gingrich, N., 211n15
Ginsburg, D., 446n4
Giraud, Y., 373, 374
Girvan, N., 461, 462
Gladstone, W., 502n41
Gluckman, M., 941–943
Glyn, A., 102, 195n6, 269n61, 430, 464, 465, 867n15, 936
Glynn, Alan, 465

Godley, C., 498n29
Godley, J. A., 502n41, 812
Godley, J. R., 502n41
Godley, W., xii, xv, xxii, 7, 9, 10, 17, 20, 70, 70n1, 71, 82, 86, 86n13, 87, 103–104, 111, 115, 122, 129, 152n80, 164, 307, 309, 310n23, 320, 321, 321n39, 359, 370n84, 392, 401, 402, 419, 419n7, 419n8, 426–432, 427n11, 429n14, 429n15, 430n17, 431n19, 440, 442–444, 453, 454n7, 456–458, 456n10, 458n11, 459n13, 460, 474, 479n28, 490–494, 493n36, 497–507, 498n39, 502n41, 504n44, 506n46, 508n48, 509, 518, 519, 521–531, 574, 585, 587, 589, 598–604, 602n4, 609, 617, 619–622, 622n21, 624–627, 625n23, 632, 633, 634n33, 635, 643–650, 645n43, 647n44, 650n47, 652, 653, 655–663, 668n62, 671, 673, 677, 678n72, 680, 682, 684, 687n87, 749n59, 811, 812, 826, 827, 860, 867, 892, 915, 1022, 1030, 1032, 1037, 1038, 1041, 1042n11, 1055, 1058, 1062, 1064
Goldschmidt-Clermont, L., 950, 951
Goldthorpe, J. H., 682, 684n78, 693, 698, 704n13, 705, 708–710, 708n17, 709n18, 711n23, 712, 713n24, 714, 719, 736n46, 742, 744, 745, 750, 751
Goldwater, B., 200, 256, 263, 375
Goodhart, C. A. E., 147, 155, 365, 365n79, 980, 985–987
Goodrich, P., 203, 211
Goodwin, D., 194
Goodwin, R. M. "Dick," xii, 5, 7, 70, 70n1, 91n20, 96, 108, 112, 115, 117n41, 136, 146, 194, 309, 309n22, 310n23, 314–316, 315n31, 315n32, 317n35, 342, 349, 351, 370–372, 372n85, 391, 391n107, 396, 404, 404n118, 405, 425, 432, 742n57, 812, 812n46, 813n51, 816n58, 818, 823, 886

Goody, J., 705, 715n26, 716, 716n28, 733n42, 753, 776, 799
Gopal, S., 818n59
Gordon, R. J., 58n34, 206, 206n12, 207, 587n28
Gorky, M., 863n10
Gorman, W. M. "Terence," xii, 47, 108, 132, 134, 138, 138n63, 154, 160–163, 168n85, 184, 197n8, 571n11, 586, 966, 971, 979, 1010, 1046, 1066
Goschen, G. J., 165
Gottardi, P., 364
Goudie, A., 651
Gould, J., 728, 729
Gowers, E., 548
Goyal, S., 52, 164
Graaff, J. de V., 769
Graham, F. D., 222n23
Gramsci, A., v, 703n12, 782
Grantchester, Lord, 220, 230
Green, M., 694, 695
Greenaway, D., 166, 981, 985–987
Gregory, M. B., 35, 980
Griffith, R., 167
Griffiths, B., 138n63, 266
Griffiths, E., 260
Grimley, M., 700, 700n3, 730
Grimshaw, D., 685
Groenewegen, P. D., 335n49
Grossman, H., 214n19
Grossman, S., 363
Grove, J., 725, 974
Gudgin, G., 320, 428, 429, 499, 651
Guevara, C., 783
Guha, Ramachandra, 812n44
Guha, Ranajit, 821n67
Guillebaud, C. W., 87
Gupta, S., xviii
Gwalior, Maharaja of, 801, 811
Gylfason, T., 237–240, 245

H

Habakkuk, J. H., 875–879, 882, 899, 919n74
Haberler, G., 185, 186, 213, 214, 216, 218, 223, 226n29
Habermas, J., 740
Hadjimatheou, C., 427n11, 557, 558n21, 566n4, 567–574, 576, 577, 579, 579n22, 614
Hagemann, H., 76n6, 186–190, 188n3
Hague, D. C., 169, 170n86, 205n11, 232, 266, 268, 544, 557–560, 583, 586, 627, 980
Hahn, A., 132
Hahn, D., 131, 222n23, 276, 362
Hahn, F. H., v, xii, xix, xxi, 13, 14, 17, 19, 33, 44n27, 46–56, 54n30, 62, 70n1, 75, 76, 81, 85, 86, 96, 96n24, 101, 102, 104, 108, 127, 127n50, 129–132, 133n58, 134, 138, 138n63, 146, 150, 154n82, 155, 160–165, 168, 184, 222n23, 234n38, 276, 277, 279, 328, 342, 343, 347, 350–352, 354–356, 358, 359, 361, 364, 366, 367, 369, 395, 399, 401, 403, 424, 429, 433–435, 444, 445, 448, 466–468, 489, 493, 499, 519, 523–525, 573, 593, 608, 608n9, 611, 617, 621, 630, 638, 643n39, 655, 661, 662n55, 666, 667, 668n62, 669, 706, 725, 746, 822n68, 898, 899, 901n46, 902, 928, 967, 970–976, 980, 985, 995, 1005, 1009–1011, 1020n1, 1021, 1021n2, 1022, 1036, 1045–1047, 1055, 1056, 1067, 1068, 1070
Hahn, M., 132
Hailsham, Lord, 727
Haldane, R. B., 165
Hall, R. L., 165
Halsey, A. H., 544, 544n10, 546, 692, 699, 699n2, 700, 704, 705, 708, 728, 729, 731, 732, 733n42
Hammond, J. D., 197, 369
Hammond, P. J., 980
Hamouda, O. F., 377
Hamowy, R., 221, 283
Hanappi, H., 315n32
Handy, L. J., 682, 693–695
Hanney, S., 974
Haq, M. ul, 820
Harberger, A., 200, 201, 253–255, 256n50, 460, 461, 461n14, 1049
Harcourt, G. C., xii, xvii, xviii, xxi, xxii, 7, 10, 13, 13n6, 20, 23n11, 70n1,

77, 92, 92n21, 95–97, 95n22,
  96n24, 103, 107, 112, 112n36,
  116, 121, 127, 130, 131, 132n56,
  135, 136, 146, 149, 154, 167, 297,
  298n2, 304n17, 309, 314n30,
  315n32, 318, 334, 339, 341, 345,
  347, 348, 370n84, 372, 376, 396,
  417, 419–423, 429n15, 435n24,
  467, 618, 638n37, 661, 779n12,
  811n40, 812n46, 820n64, 826,
  860, 862n9, 870n20, 892, 916,
  934, 937–938n97, 973n6, 981,
  1001n17, 1029, 1045,
  1069, 1069n33
Harcourt, W., xvii
Hardayal, L., 779
Harding, J., 230
Harley, B., 149
Harper, F. A. "Baldy," 207, 208, 210,
  211, 220, 222n23, 230, 232
Harper, J., 341
Harper, P., 211
Harris, C. J., 83
Harris, Ralph, 198, 203, 222, 223, 225,
  228–233, 264, 265, 267, 533,
  543, 728
Harris, Robin, 260
Harrison, W., 465
Harrod, R. F., 165, 251, 282, 302,
  332n44, 337, 338, 916, 969
Hart, D. M., 212
Hart, J., 794n24
Hart, M. K., 374
Hart, O., 134, 136, 363
Hart, P. E., 980
Hart, R. A., 971
Harte, N., 870, 872, 875–878, 895, 898
Hartwell, R., 220, 224n26
Harvey, A., 164, 663n56
Hattersley, R., xii, 122, 464, 465
Hawthorn, G., 700, 700n4, 714, 714n25,
  716, 734n44, 737, 743, 744, 753,
  754, 754n62, 756n63, 799, 867
Hawtrey, R. G., 165, 336, 405n120
Hay, D. A., 147, 365n79
Hayek, F. A., xii, 8, 19, 24, 30–33, 40,
  61n36, 76, 77, 91, 92, 109, 110,
  112, 183, 184, 185n2, 191, 192,
  196–199, 201–208, 210, 212–232,
  213n18, 222n23, 230n31, 234n38,
  238–247, 245n47, 250, 251, 253,
  256, 257, 257n51, 263–267, 269,
  270, 272–274, 272–273n62,
  274n66, 276–278, 280–285,
  282n69, 284n70, 296, 346, 375,
  380, 390n105, 403, 405n120, 433,
  460, 470, 542n7, 775, 775n9, 783,
  850, 851, 890, 978, 1023, 1045
Hayek, Helene, 206
Hayek, Hella, 206
Hayek, L., 229
Hazari, R. K., 170, 171n88
Hazlitt, H., 222n23, 224n27
Heal, G., 134, 136, 154n82, 159, 342,
  343n58, 971
Healey, D., xiii, 458, 483, 492
Heath, E., 145, 145n75, 268, 401, 431,
  463, 492, 630n30, 794n24, 935
Heffer, E., 446n4
Hegel, G. W. F., 30, 31
Held, D., 739, 739n53
Heller, W. Jr., 134
Helliwell, J., 570, 571, 571n11, 580,
  581n24, 586, 587n28
Henderson, D., 146, 147, 365
Henderson, H., 6, 165
Henderson, Lord, 776n9
Henderson, R. F., 87, 92, 109, 117, 350,
  937–938n97
Hendry, D. F., xii, 134, 138n63, 146,
  154, 160–162, 165, 166, 170n86,
  365, 489n33, 490, 659n54, 971,
  977, 980, 981, 985–987
Hennessey, P., 535, 535n3, 1029–1031
Henry, S. G. B., 435n24, 675
Herklotts, G., 947
Heseltine, M., 473, 474
Hey, J., 300n5
Hey, J. D., 166, 971n3, 980
Hibberd, J., 455n8
Hicks, J., 58, 109, 110, 118, 133n57,
  139, 165, 231, 241, 250, 346,
  405n120, 772, 775n9
Higgins, B., 404
Higgs, H., 166
Hildebrand Jr., G. H., 373n89
Hilferding, R., 214n19
Hill, P., xxi, 806, 822, 822n69,
  867n16, 873
Hilton, J., 80

Hines, A. G., 980
Hinsley, H., 113, 114, 798, 799
Hirschman, A., 186, 190, 343, 777, 806, 806n33
Hobsbawm, E., 87n14, 119, 242, 313, 331, 656, 657, 664, 665, 665n58, 715n26, 818n59, 849, 852, 858–860, 858n5, 892, 899, 931
Hobson, J. A., 806
Hobson, O., 230
Hodgson, G., 91–93, 305n19, 333, 1029
Hoff, T. J. B., 222n23
Hogg, S., 980, 981
Hoiles, R. C., 207, 211
Holmwood, J., 696
Holroyd, M., 283, 890
Hoover, H., 206, 229, 247, 256n50, 263, 281
Hopkin, Bryan, 453, 876
Hopkins, A. G., 821n67
Hopper, E. I., 693
Horrell, S., 683, 685, 685n84, 687n88, 698, 865, 866, 880, 902–914, 907n54, 920, 928, 952, 1043
Hoskyns, J., 266, 267, 473, 473n22
Hossain, Mahabub, 344n60
Hossain, Mahboob, 820, 825n71
Hossain, Monowor, 820
Howarth, D., 125, 125n47
Howarth, T. E. B., 335n53
Howe, G., 278, 355, 450, 473, 526, 534, 536
Howell, P. P., 800
Howson, S., 109, 183, 185, 310n23, 360, 969
Hsu, Y. H., 339n55
Hudson, H., 341, 405
Hudson, J., 912
Hughes, A., xvii, xxi, 84, 127, 136, 164, 312, 419n8, 467, 496, 601, 609, 622, 627, 632, 633, 652–654, 659, 661, 664, 664n57, 669n63, 670–674, 673n66, 674n69, 681, 682, 684, 687, 826, 829, 881, 902, 937n97, 983, 990, 1038, 1040–1042, 1058, 1070, 1070n35
Hughes, G. A., 356, 359
Hughes, M., 695

Huhne, C., 981
Hume, D., 36
Humphries, J., xvii, xxii, 136, 143, 316, 614, 618, 637, 638, 679, 685, 687n88, 698, 865, 866, 869, 869n20, 874n27, 880, 899n46, 902–914, 917–920, 931, 950n106, 952, 981, 1023, 1043, 1070
Hunold, A., 219, 222n23, 224n26, 227
Hunt, E. H., 375
Hurwicz, L., 186
Husbands, C. T., 728
Hutchins, R. M., 206
Hutchinson, B. E., 203, 1046
Hutton, G., 230
Hutton, J. P., 166, 980
Hutton, M. A., 696
Hymer, S., 823n70, 824, 826

I
Ibbs, R., 266, 473
Illarionov, A., 247
Illsley, R., 733n42
Imam Bux (wrestler), 322n40
Indrani, D. E., 171n88
Ingham, G., 694, 695, 709n18, 741, 742
Innset, O., 223–225, 224n26, 224n27, 225n28
Ioannidis, J. P. A., 999
Ironmonger, D., 341
Irving, S., 244n46
Iversen, C., 222n23
Izurieta, A., xvii, xxii, 429, 429n14, 496, 497n38, 499, 501, 504, 506n46, 822, 1041, 1041–1042n11, 1058, 1060n25

J
Jackman, R., 979
Jackson, D. A. S., 309, 682, 694, 695
James, R. R., 794n24
Janeway, Weslie, 1041, 1058, 1060n24
Janeway, William, 929, 1059, 1065, 1067, 1067n30
Jayawardena, L., 820
Jenner, P., 693

Jensen, P. S., 924n86
Jerven, M., 933
Jewkes, J., 222n23, 223, 890
Jobling, R. G., 683, 696–698, 741, 741n54, 745, 911n61
Joginder Singh, Tiger (wrestler), 322n40
Johnson, C., 980, 985
Johnson, D. Gale, 776n9
Johnson, E., 89n18
Johnson, G., 979
Johnson, H. G., 87–91, 87n15, 88n17, 89n18, 111, 132, 134, 184, 187, 301, 302n10, 331, 332, 332n44, 336, 347, 351, 352, 404, 405, 405n119, 444, 445, 469, 542n7, 704, 884n37, 889, 891, 966, 1010
Johnson, J., xviii, 1003n19
Johnson, P., 232, 232n34
Johnston, J., 995n14
Jolley, A. N. E., 695
Jolly, A. R., 794n24, 824
Jones, A., 694, 695
Jones, E., 876
Jones, G., 313, 876
Jones-Lee, M., 980
Joseph, K., 3, 231–233, 234n38, 264, 267, 268, 270, 278, 473, 487, 492, 493, 518, 519, 521–545, 540n5, 541n6, 542n8, 542n9, 548–550, 554, 556, 560, 566n3, 727, 728, 731, 731n41, 973n7, 1013
Joshi, H., 981
Joslin, D., 846n1, 892–895, 897, 899, 931, 933, 934
Jowett, B., 779
Judd, F., 794n24
Judge, G., 166
Julius, D., xi, 981
Jump, P., 27, 974, 975, 1003n19

K

Kahn, R. F., xii, 7, 11, 13, 23n11, 30, 34–36, 58, 70n1, 71, 76, 79–81, 85–87, 87n14, 87n15, 89–91, 93, 96, 99, 103, 110, 112, 112n36, 112n37, 112n38, 115–118, 126, 127, 131, 140, 146, 192, 228, 271, 306, 306n20, 309–312, 309n22, 310n23, 310n24, 311n26, 314, 314n29, 315, 316n34, 317, 328, 330–334, 334n47, 337, 338, 341, 343, 345–353, 345n63, 356–362, 357n71, 359n73, 361n75, 366n81, 370, 376, 397, 398n112, 402, 403, 405n120, 416, 418n2, 422, 425, 432, 443–445, 446n4, 447, 449–455, 449n5, 455n8, 458–460, 464, 509, 511n49, 519, 622–623n21, 630n30, 664, 705n15, 771, 771n4, 772, 806, 818, 826, 929, 1000, 1021, 1055, 1055n18, 1060, 1060n24, 1062, 1070
Kaldor, M., 73, 74
Kaldor, N., xi, xii, xix, xxii, 5, 7, 11, 17, 23n11, 25, 46, 47, 50, 70, 70n1, 71, 81, 85, 86n13, 87–92, 92n21, 96, 97, 103, 103n30, 103n31, 104, 108, 110, 112, 112n36, 112n38, 115–118, 122, 126n49, 127, 128, 130–132, 146, 154, 165, 184, 197n8, 250–252, 282n69, 297n1, 306, 309, 310n24, 311, 314–318, 315n31, 347, 348, 350, 351, 356, 357n71, 359, 362, 370, 370n84, 402, 403, 405n120, 425, 426, 432, 440–445, 446n4, 449n5, 453–459, 458n11, 459n13, 466, 474, 492, 499, 503n43, 504, 508n48, 509, 510, 511n49, 522, 528, 549, 773, 777, 805, 813, 813n48, 814, 814n53, 818, 820n65, 823, 831, 851, 858n5, 867, 867n15, 868, 882n32, 883, 884, 886–888, 890, 892, 895, 898, 913n71, 917, 977, 980, 1021, 1028, 1046, 1054, 1055, 1055n18, 1060n24, 1062, 1070
Kalecki, M., v, 13, 25, 96n24, 97, 251, 282n69, 305n19, 307, 309, 312, 315, 315n31, 318, 339n55, 340, 376, 378n96, 380–382, 381n97, 382n99, 385, 393, 401, 405n120, 463, 770–772, 771n4, 813, 819, 826, 868
Kaletsky, A., 981
Kaminsky, A. P., 502n41

NAME INDEX

Kanbur, R., 27, 37
Kannan, K. P., 833
Kantorowicz, L., 185
Kapur, S., xvii
Karadzic, R., 233, 268
Karshenas, M., 825n71
Kaser, K., 980
Kaser, M. C., 980
Kast, M., 260
Kaufmann, F., 214, 216n20
Kaunda, K., 786
Kavanagh, D., 233, 267
Kay, J. A., 147, 166, 299n4, 365n79
Kay, P., 980
Kaza, G., 219, 222n24
Keegan, W., 493, 496
Kehoe, T. J., 134, 643n39, 746
Kelly, R., 981
Kelsey, D. or Easley, 364
Kennedy, C. M., 980
Kennedy, J. F., 234
Kerr, P., 1069
Kettlewell, R., 947
Keynes, J. M., xi, xii, xxii, xxv, 4, 70, 166, 182, 299, 416, 622n21, 704n12, 766, 849, 969, 1023
Keynes, J. N., 94, 702, 870n20, 873n25
Khan, A. R., 820
Khan, M., 797, 797n28, 827, 925
King Kong (wrestler), 322n40
King, G., 421, 862n9, 870–872
King, J., 116, 117, 394n110, 395, 397, 398n113, 458, 459, 938n97
King, M., 125, 136, 138n61, 146, 147, 149, 151, 154, 155, 159, 237, 365, 468, 564, 567, 584, 584n25, 827, 981
King, M. A., 980
Kinnock, N., xiii, 121–124, 124n44, 483
Kipling, R., 723
Kirk-Greene, A., 788, 939n101
Kirkaldy, H., 80, 81
Kirman, A., 50
Kirzner, M., 217
Kissinger, H., xxiii
Kitson, M., 319, 360–361, 419, 651n48, 679, 902, 914–918, 934, 1042
Klein, L., viii, 377–394, 377n95, 378n96, 381n98, 382n99, 385n100, 386n101, 390n105, 391n108, 403–405, 405n120, 503, 504, 504n44
Klein, N., 30n18
Klein, R., 216n20
Klemperer, P., 981
Knapp, J., 190, 803, 805, 942n102
Kneeland, H., 949n105
Knight, F. H., 51, 204, 205n11, 208, 379, 405n120
Koch, C., 211, 211n16
Kogan, M., 974
Komine, A., 969, 970, 971n4
Konzelmann, S., 684, 686n86
Koopmans, T., 186, 188n3, 379
Kothari, U., 788
Kregel, J., 49, 370n84
Kreps, D., 363
Krishnan, P., 912
Krishnaswami, A., 811n37
Krishnaswamy, K. S., 819n63
Kristol, I., 211n15
Krohn, C-D., 186, 187
Krugman, P., 245, 246, 264, 272, 392, 503
Kuczynski, M., 7n3, 70n1, 532, 534, 540, 544
Kuhn, T. S., 27, 35
Kuiken, J., 464n15
Kumar, A., 820
Kumar, D., 57n33, 110
Kumar, M., 651
Kurosawa, A., ix, 599
Kuznets, S., 139n63, 186, 187, 188n3, 200, 241, 251, 392, 771n4, 772, 812n43, 813, 819n63, 868, 886, 909n56, 914

L

Laclau, E., 894
Laidler, D., 30n19, 199, 244, 244n46, 278, 469, 469n19, 490, 586
Lakatos, I., 44
Lal, D., 226, 226n29, 259, 775, 775–776n9
Lall, S., 880
Lamont, N., 500

Landesmann, M., xvii, 7n3, 14n8, 316, 589, 651, 651n48, 827
Landreth, H., 372–376, 393
Lane, M., 284
Lane, R. W., 373, 374
Lange, O., 91, 92, 142, 404n118, 405n120, 768, 813
Larmer, M., 784–786, 784n16, 785n17
Lavington, F., 6
Lavoie, M., xvii, xxii, 58n34, 60n35, 126n49, 370n84, 497–499, 504, 504n44, 647n44, 1009n20, 1032, 1033, 1037
Law, William L., 211
Lawrence, P., 818n59
Lawson, T., xvii, 7n3, 11, 12, 14, 14n8, 56, 58, 60n35, 70n1, 111, 318, 357n71, 582, 584n26, 589, 641, 642, 745, 1001, 1023, 1028, 1069n33
Layard, R., 138n63, 451, 647, 971
Le Bas, C., 880
Le Pen, Jean-Marie, 233, 268
Lea, R., 981
Leach, E., 714n25, 716, 733n42
Lebaron, F., 235, 244
Lee, F., 60n35, 117n41, 305, 305n19, 308n21, 310n24, 440, 968, 970, 983–985, 988n11, 1004, 1006, 1007, 1051, 1069n32
Lee-Potter, L., 730
Leeson, R., 185n2, 221, 226, 243, 244, 244n46, 257n52, 390n105
Lehmann, D., 696, 797, 888n38, 893, 894
Leijonhufvud, A., 2n1, 48, 53, 79n9, 189, 251, 828
Leitch, D., 535n3
Leith, J. C., 331
Lenin, V. I., 185–191, 204, 206, 207
Leon, G., 924n86
Leontief, W., 185–187, 188n3, 349, 572
Lerner, A., 346, 347, 376, 405n120, 771n4
Letwin, O., 234, 234n38, 531, 541, 542, 542n7
Letwin, S. R., 232, 234n38, 542, 542n7
Letwin, W., 234n38, 541
Levy, D., 254, 255, 461, 461n14

Levy, G., 167, 254, 255, 461
Levy, L., 1064
Lewis, G., 256n50
Lewis, J., 200, 576n18, 605, 615n14, 620, 649n46, 653, 656
Lewis, W. A., 190, 241, 251, 871, 871n24, 873, 933, 952
Lewney, R., 651
Li, P., 999
Liesner, H. H., 455n8, 980, 985
Liggio, L. P., 211
Lili, J., 924n86
Lindahl, E., 44, 372n88
Lindbeck, A., 236–244, 247, 249, 250, 252, 722, 723
Linehan, P., 113
Lipietz, A., 102, 195n6, 269n61, 430, 464, 867n15
Lippmann, W., 183, 212, 213, 218
Lipton, M., 150, 794n24, 822n69
Little, A., 700n4
Little, G., 156
Livingstone, G., 259–262
Llewellyn, J., 7n3, 70n1, 399, 424, 827
Llosa, M. V., 249, 267
Lloyd, I., vi, 332n44
Loasry, B. J., 980
Lockwood, B., 364
Lockwood, D., 681, 682, 684n78, 693, 698, 699, 699n2, 704n13, 705, 708–710, 709n18, 711n23, 712, 712–713n24, 714, 719, 736, 737, 746
Lomax, J. R., 981
Lovatt, D., 651, 697, 752
Low, H., 924n86
Lowe, G., 697
Lowes-Dickinson, G., 335
Lucas, R. Jr, 33–35, 34n21, 38, 42, 52, 197n8, 249, 252, 1023, 1024, 1024n3, 1027–1029, 1029n6
Luce, R., 260
Luhnow, H., 191, 192, 202–211, 203n10, 217, 220, 232
Lundberg, E., 236, 238–241, 238n43, 243, 244n46, 246, 249, 252
Lydall, H. F., 980
Lyon, A., 794n24

M

Macaulay, T. B., 779, 810
MacBean, A. I., 980
MacCarthy, F., 335n49
Macdonald, R., 109
MacDougall, D., 165, 459, 459n13, 551
Macekura, S., 872–874
Macfarlane, A., 11, 118, 152n80, 348, 392, 602n4, 654, 674n68, 714, 715, 715n26
Macgregor, D. H., 166, 299n4, 303
Machiavelli, N., 114, 636, 655–657, 660
Machin, S., 167
Machina, M., 134, 363
Machlup, F., 203, 213, 215–217, 216n20, 219, 222n23, 243, 302n10, 405n120
MacLean, N., 261n53
MacLennan, B., 305n19
MacMahon, K., 459n13
MacNeice, L., 335n49
Macpherson, G., 695
MacPherson, W. J. "Iain," 860, 867n16
Macrae, D. G., 733n42
Maddison, A., 110, 111, 333
Mahalanobis, P. C., 771, 772, 806, 812, 812n44, 812n46, 813n51, 814, 814n52, 816n58, 819n63, 862
Mahmud, W., 823
Mair, L., 948
Makowski, L., 363, 364
Malcomson, J., 981, 985–987
Malinvaud, E., 314n29, 317, 622n21, 626, 1010
Maloney, J., 442, 443n1, 458n11, 460, 498
Malraux, A., 297
Malthus, T., 31, 59, 94, 779, 779n12, 810, 926, 1060n24
Mandelbaum (Martin), K., 190, 381, 777
Mani, S., xviii
Mankiw, G., xxii, 35, 36, 36n22, 40–42, 58n34
Mann, J. M., 693–697
Mannheim, H., 185
Manning, P., 792n22, 873
Mao, Tse Tung, 152, 398, 771, 774, 783, 806

Marcel, M., 813n48
Marcuzzo, M. C., xvii, xxiii, 8, 13, 109, 110, 316n34, 330, 331, 334, 337–340, 339n55, 345–348, 446n4, 447, 449n5, 450, 451, 455, 705n15, 771, 818n59, 1000
Markowitz, H., 1025
Marquez, G. G., 248, 249
Marriott, E., 258
Marris, R., 70n1, 91, 341, 342, 347, 424, 672, 681, 705, 826, 882n36, 888, 889, 937n97
Marschak, J., 186, 188n3, 189, 204, 380, 405n120
Marsh, C., 683, 686, 687, 697, 698, 741, 741–742n56, 911n61
Marshall, A., 4, 6, 28n15, 35, 56n32, 70, 75n5, 79, 80, 89, 93, 94, 109, 110, 128, 135, 136, 181, 182, 183n1, 319, 329, 330, 335n49, 335n52, 369, 395, 398n112, 421, 429n15, 598, 679, 686n86, 701–703, 702n7, 702n10, 703n11, 767, 779, 811, 811n37, 818n59, 826, 847–849, 848n2, 860, 899, 903n51, 905, 934, 1060n24, 1061
Marshall, M. P., 335, 905
Marshall, T. H., 704, 704n13, 706, 709, 709n18, 711, 711n23, 718, 727n35, 742
Marsland, D., 729n37
Martin (Mandelbaum), K., 190, 803, 805, 941n102
Martins, N. O., 59, 368, 1070n34
Martins, R., 736
Marwah, H., 933
Marx, K., 11, 31, 41, 55, 56n32, 115, 121, 144, 190, 201, 282n69, 285, 305n19, 312, 315, 315n31, 315n32, 316n33, 318, 329, 331, 724, 851, 860, 863n10, 868, 882, 932, 1069n33
Maskin, E., 51, 134, 363
Mata, T., 443, 443n3, 456n10, 460, 492, 493, 498
Mathias, P., 221, 851, 875n31, 882, 883, 892, 895–898, 895n42, 919n74
Mathur, G., 770, 820, 820n64

NAME INDEX 1163

Matthews, R. C. O., xii, xix, 7, 11, 14, 17, 19, 70n1, 79, 82, 83, 86, 91–94, 96, 102, 106–108, 115, 116, 125, 126, 129, 133n57, 139, 139n64, 140, 142n71, 143, 145–147, 145n75, 145n76, 149–154, 160–163, 165, 184, 242n44, 280, 299n4, 333n46, 342, 347–349, 351, 362–367, 363n77, 365n79, 366n80, 419n8, 421, 429, 432, 433, 435, 444, 446, 458, 467, 467n16, 489, 489n33, 493, 499, 507n47, 519, 533, 552n15, 560, 568, 568n7, 568n8, 573, 592, 593, 602, 606, 606n6, 607n7, 609, 610, 617, 621–623, 621n18, 625–627, 629n27, 630–633, 636, 648, 653, 653n51, 654, 660, 661, 664–666, 668n62, 669, 703, 722, 727, 734, 746–748, 820n64, 821–822n68, 829, 848, 849, 857, 863, 864n11, 865, 865n15, 868, 879, 887, 899, 901n46, 902, 910n60, 916–918, 966, 967, 973n6, 976, 976n8, 977, 979, 980, 983, 984, 1006, 1021, 1021n2, 1022, 1036, 1045–1046, 1046n15, 1066, 1070
Mattioli, R., 103, 103n30, 871
Mattis, General J., 263
Maxton, G., 263
Mayer, C. P., 147, 981
Mayer, H., 215
Mayer, M., 981
Mayes, D. G., 166
Mayhew, H., 907n53
Maywald, K., 140n66, 863n11, 865n14
McCarthy, J., 189n5, 191, 192, 201, 341, 371–377, 386–388, 391
McCloskey, D., 256, 256n50, 900, 998
McCombie, J., 1037
McCormick, B. J., 971
McCrone, G., 980
McGuire, P., xviii
McKittrick, D., 145n75, 146
McLeod, N., 211
McMahan, J., 538
Meade, J. E., 10, 61, 70n1, 71, 73n4, 77, 79, 81, 85, 89, 154n82, 165, 191, 231, 241, 250, 276, 304n17, 310n23, 337, 345, 345n63, 346, 350–352, 356, 358, 381n98, 405n120, 425, 451, 620, 621, 628n25, 826, 860, 871, 915, 1048, 1050, 1051, 1060n24, 1063
Meade, M., 345, 345n63
Meadows, S., 693
Medio, A., 343n59
Meek, R., 858, 859
Meeks, G., 575, 615, 615n14, 619, 643, 643n40, 932n93, 934–937, 937n97, 1042
Meghir, C., 167
Mehrotra, S., 820, 825n71
Meltzer, A., 253, 254
Menger, C., 214n19, 216n20
Menger, K., 216n20
Menon, V. Krishna, 818n59
Meredith, D., 913n67
Messac, L. M., 872, 938n98, 942n103, 943n104, 947–951
Metcalf, D., 138n63, 147
Meza, D. de, 167, 981
Michael, Saint, xv, 490n35
Miles, D. K., 148
Milgate, M., 315n31, 316n33, 499, 1041n10
Mill, James S., 812
Miller-Bernal, L., 696, 697
Miller, E., 881
Miller, L. B. "Red," 203–205, 211, 220, 222n23, 224n27
Miller, M. H., 146, 147, 365, 365n79, 626, 971, 981
Miller, R., 886n38, 889n39, 893, 894
Miller, T., 730
Millmow, A., 54, 87n15, 99, 394n110, 395, 397, 398n113
Mills, C. Wright, 201
Minford, A. P. I., 980
Minford, A. P. L., 267, 278, 440, 468, 469, 472, 473, 475, 484, 485, 524, 525, 530, 541n6, 547, 548, 585
Mingers, J., 992, 993, 995, 996
Minhas, B. S., 250
Minsky, H., 40, 1053
Mirante, A., 96n23, 128, 128n52, 317n35, 340n56, 342, 372
Mirowski, P., 19, 224n26

Mirrlees, J. A., 14n8, 79, 83, 84, 134, 136, 138, 154, 155, 159–162, 165, 241, 342, 343n58, 352, 564, 826, 827n72, 971, 972, 976n8, 977, 980, 981, 984–987, 989, 1049
Mises, L. von, 19, 185, 186, 202, 202n9, 207, 208, 210, 213–218, 213n18, 214n19, 216n20, 222, 222n23, 223, 225n28, 257, 268, 282, 283, 375, 405n120
Mishra, S., 344n60, 820, 823
Mitchell, B. R., 421, 693, 860, 863n11, 864, 864n12, 865, 868n17, 869, 870, 911, 917
Mitchell, C., 941
Mkandawire, T., 927n90, 932n90
Modigliani, F., 246, 390n105
Moggridge, D., 282, 332n44, 345n63, 352n66
Monbiot, G., 261n53
Mongiovi, G., 282, 283
Monteith, P., xviii
Montes, L., 256, 257n51
Moore, B., 312, 320, 496, 600, 651, 696, 697, 827
Moore, C., 232, 232n34, 259, 542n7
Moore, J. H., 165, 981, 982
Moreno, F., 257n51, 258
Morgan, M., 981
Morgenstern, O., 186, 188n3, 213, 216n20, 890
Morishima, M., 966
Morley, F., 212n17, 222n23, 224n27
Morrish, L., 996
Morrison, H., 727
Mortimer, Mr., 455n8
Moser, Lord, 727
Moser, P., 188n4
Mosley, P., 912
Moss, R., 260
Mountbatten, Earl of, 818n59
Muellbauer, M., 981
Mujahid, G., 344n60, 820
Mundell, R., 253, 254
Muqtada, M., 344n60, 820
Murmis, M., 696, 697
Musakanya, V., 784–787, 784n16, 785n17
Muscatelli, A., 981
Musgrave, R., 186, 189, 390n105

Myatt, D., 167
Myint, H., 822n68
Myrdal, G., 235, 236, 242–246, 244n46, 248, 251, 777, 888
Myrdal, S., 244

N

Namm, Colonel, 373
Naoroji, D., 42n26
Nash, E., 230
Nasser, G. A., 824n70
Naylor, R., 89, 89n18, 90
Neary, J. P., 165, 166, 977, 980–982, 985, 988
Necker, S., 999
Needham, J., 818n59, 821, 867n16
Nef, J., 205n11
Nehru, J. L., xxiv, 60, 61n36, 192, 806, 813n51, 818n59, 819n63
Neild, R. R., xii, 7, 47, 55, 55n31, 70n1, 71, 73, 81, 82, 85, 86, 92, 93, 99, 114, 116, 117, 126, 129, 131, 146, 164, 276, 279, 310n23, 311–313, 311n27, 332, 333n45, 346, 354, 355, 359, 402, 431n18, 432, 441–445, 443n3, 448, 456, 460, 466–468, 499, 509, 523, 524, 625, 632, 701n6, 706n16, 724, 725, 725n33, 826, 1054–1056, 1055n18
Neruda, P., 249
Newbery, D. G., 10, 33n20, 44n27, 47, 52, 54n30, 76n7, 83, 84, 87, 93, 99, 129–134, 137, 137n60, 138n62, 154, 154n82, 155, 159–162, 164, 166, 170n86, 184, 274, 279, 300, 342, 343n58, 350, 355, 356, 358–364, 419, 419n8, 420, 429n15, 435, 435n24, 466, 502, 506, 590, 606, 610, 611, 613, 617, 622, 622n19, 627, 631, 637, 643n39, 660, 660n54, 661, 667, 668, 669n63, 670, 672–678, 673n66, 674n69, 678n71, 678n72, 680n73, 695, 746, 747, 823, 826, 827, 829, 862, 916, 967, 971, 978–980, 983, 985, 991, 1006, 1007, 1032, 1043, 1047–1048, 1055, 1055n18, 1058
Newby, H., 727, 728

Newton, A., 34, 316
Nicholson, J. L., 155, 986, 987
Nicholson, J. Shield, 304
Nicholson, L., 459n13, 983, 985
Nicholson, R. J., 157
Nickell, S. J., 134, 136, 154, 159–163, 165, 170n86, 468, 469, 568, 586, 623, 626, 647, 659n54, 977, 980, 981, 985
Nicol, A. D. I., 114, 600–602, 602n3, 604, 605, 609, 727n35, 792n22, 796
Nightingale, F., 676, 862
Nikiforos, M., 321
Nilsson, M., 243n45
Nobay, A. R., 971, 980
Nobel, A., 236, 237, 241, 377, 567n6
Nobel, M., 237
Nobel, P., 236, 237
Noel-Baker, P., 74
Nolan, P. H., xvii, 84, 618, 697, 779n12, 781, 821, 822, 822n68, 825n71, 828, 830–832, 835, 1023, 1040, 1042, 1044, 1070
North, D., 231
Nott, J., 431
Nove, A., 142, 307
Nozick, R., 206n12
Nurkse, R., 213, 216n20, 772, 777
Nuti, M., v, xviii, 7n3, 70n1, 117n41, 136, 144, 306–308, 311, 312, 314n30, 318, 401, 771, 814, 826
Nutzenadel, A., 900

O

Oakes, G., 28, 29, 29n17, 110, 345n63
O'Brien, D. P., 980
O'Brien, R., 981
O'Connor, J. J., 73n4
Odling-Smee, J., 552n15, 864n11, 980
O'Donnell, G., 894, 981
O'Donnell, J. S., 882n36
O'Donnell, R., 281, 284
Offer, A., 133n57, 139–145, 140n65, 140n69, 141n70, 235, 236, 238n43, 239, 240, 244, 247, 272n62, 276n68, 552n15, 864n11, 865, 866, 909–910n56, 919n74, 929

Ogilvie, S., 679, 882, 901, 902, 909, 914, 918–924, 924n85, 928, 1043
Ohlin, B., 109, 218, 236, 238n43, 239, 240, 243, 249, 336, 405n120
Okon, H., 245n47
Oppenheimer, P., 146, 147, 365
Orcutt, G., 421, 564
O'Rourke, K., 909n56, 914, 919n74
Orwell, G., 191, 388
Osborn, D., 981
Ostrom, E., 231, 250, 251
Ostroy, J., 134
Oswald, A., 166, 981
Owen, D., 446n4, 452
Oxford, K., 474
Oxley, D., 909, 913, 913n67, 914, 931, 952

P

Page, J., 888n38
Page, S., 981
Pain, W. H., xviii
Paine, S., 117n41, 312, 314n30, 467, 793, 821, 821–822n68, 824
Paish, F., 469
Palazzi, M., 372n85
Palley, T., 1030
Palma, J. G., xvii, xxiii, 318, 506n46, 781, 796, 796–797n27, 797n28, 798, 799, 813n48, 822, 823, 825n71, 828, 831, 831n74, 831n75, 835, 893, 1023, 1044, 1059, 1069n33, 1070
Palme, O., 247
Palmer, R., 932n91
Pant, P., 815
Papadimitriou, D. B., 321, 498
Papanek, G., 200
Papola, T. S., 695
Parboni, R., 343n59
Pardoe, J., 430, 430n17, 431, 431n18
Pareto. V., 35, 237, 769
Parkin, M., 971
Parkinson, C., 262, 355
Parkinson, J. A., 980
Parry, J. H., 893
Parson, T., 699, 704, 705, 707, 740

Pasinetti, L. L., xii, xviii, 5, 7, 7n4, 21, 23, 23n11, 34, 35, 59, 70n1, 88, 91n20, 96, 96n23, 103, 112, 112n37, 112n38, 117n41, 118, 118n42, 121, 127, 128, 128n51, 135, 136, 140, 309, 309n22, 310n23, 312, 314–318, 315n31, 317n35, 341, 342, 345, 347, 348, 351, 352, 358, 370n84, 372n87, 376, 432, 445, 446n4, 447, 448, 453, 496, 499, 509, 826, 1000
Patel, I. G., 349, 350, 820, 820n64, 834, 980
Patinkin, D., 35, 58, 331, 405n120, 446n4
Patnaik, P., xvii, xxiv, 117n41, 315n32, 356n69, 812n46, 813n51, 820, 868
Peacock, A., 233
Pechman, J., 626
Penrose, E., 461, 980
Perkins, J. O. N., 823n70
Perle, R., 211n15
Pernecky, M., 27n13
Peron, I., 461n14
Peron, J., 782
Perris, 792n22
Person, J., 792n22
Pesaran, H., xii, 7n3, 70n1, 83, 84, 136, 137, 316, 420, 423, 490, 503, 564, 614, 661, 663, 663n56, 664, 667, 668, 673, 823, 827, 832n75, 862n9, 915
Peston, M. H., 467, 980
Peterson, A. W. A. "Bill," 312, 643n39
Peterson, W., 351, 427n11, 478, 558n21, 575, 582, 584n26, 590, 643, 643n39, 651, 827, 916, 936n93, 937n97
Petty, C., 942n103, 947
Petty, W., 329, 421, 676, 862, 862n9
Pew, J. H., 211
Phelps, E., 231, 250
Phillips, D., 974
Philpot, R., 446n4
Pierse, R., 590
Pigou, A. C., 4, 6, 8, 70, 75, 75n5, 79, 80, 89, 109, 128, 165, 221, 280, 300, 303, 304n17, 318, 331, 335, 369, 395, 416, 457, 622n20,
722n32, 767–769, 805, 826, 901n50, 903n50, 905, 952, 1000
Piketty, T., 1033, 1061
Pinchbeck, I., 907n53
Pinera, J., 260
Pinochet, General, 119, 192, 225, 245, 247, 248, 253–262, 255n49, 256n50, 261n53, 274n66, 375, 453, 470, 829, 894
Pischke, S., 167
Pissarides, C., 138n63, 981
Plant, A., 230
Platt, B. S., 942n103, 947, 948
Platt, C., 889n39, 894
Platt, J., 682, 684n78, 693, 708, 728
Plehwe, D., 19, 224n26
Ploeg, R. van der, 7n3, 651
Podolski, T. M., 985–987
Polanyi, K., 1061
Polanyi, M., 213n18, 222n23, 932
Polemarchakis, H., 363
Pomeranz, K., 933
Popper, K., 212n17, 222n23, 265–267, 533, 540, 543, 1013
Porter, R. S. "Bob," 791, 792, 792n22, 800
Portes, R., 154, 979n9, 980, 981, 985, 1010, 1011
Posner, M., xiii, 88, 116, 130n54, 140, 140n67, 145, 146, 164, 169, 170n86, 351, 359, 364, 366, 366n81, 399–402, 427n11, 434, 439, 441, 443–446, 449n5, 454, 455n8, 459n13, 460, 464, 464n15, 484–493, 509, 517–560, 565, 569, 583, 590, 598, 602, 613, 625, 627–630, 628n25, 647, 664, 826, 938n97, 974n7
Posner, M. V., xiii, 88, 116, 126, 130n54, 140, 140n67, 145–147, 164, 169, 170n86, 351, 359, 364, 365n79, 366, 366n81, 399–402, 427n11, 434, 441, 443–446, 443n3, 449n5, 454, 455, 455n8, 459n13, 460, 464, 464n15, 466, 484–493, 499, 506n45, 509, 518–560, 565, 569, 579, 583, 590, 598, 602, 613, 625, 627–630, 628n25, 647, 664, 826, 937n97, 974n7, 980

Postan, "Munia" M.M., xxi, 310n23, 849–852, 875n31, 876, 877, 879, 881–892, 896, 899, 901, 905n53, 909, 914, 920, 926
Poster, M., 740
Potter, J.G., 823n70
Powell, E., 267, 465, 492
Power, E. E. Le Poer, 851, 852, 907n53
Prais, S. J., 980
Prandy, K., 651, 651n48, 683n77, 693–698, 736n46, 738n50, 739n52, 750, 752
Pratten, 59, 367, 368, 1070n34
Prebisch, R., 60, 253, 462, 777, 806
Prest, A. R., 87, 87n15, 99, 146, 147, 365, 863n11, 865, 865n14, 870n22
Prest, W., 87
Price, B. B., 377
Priemel, K., 225
Princip, G., xiii
Propper, C., 981
Pryce, V., 981
Pryme, G., 79, 80
Purdy, D., 305n19
Puttaswamaiah, K., 235
Pyatt, F. G., 421, 567, 676, 676n70, 693, 698, 719, 721n31, 814, 827, 873–874n26

Q
Quinton, A., 243

R
Radford, R. A., 74
Rahim, S., 344n60, 820
Rahman, A., 344n60, 820
Raico, R., 283
Raj, K. N., 804
Rajania, B., 167
Ramsey, F., 49, 52, 152n80, 331, 616n15, 722n32
Rand, A., 283
Randers, J., 263
Ranis, G., 300, 300n6, 805
Rao, S. K., 117n41, 820, 821n66
Rao, V. K. R. V., 418, 770, 807, 819, 819n62, 819n63, 868

Rappard, W. E., 213, 222n23, 225, 225n28
Rauh, C., 924n86
Ravelli, G., 257n52
Ravn, M., 167
Razavi, S., 906
Reach, G., 211
Read, L. E., 5, 206n12, 207, 208, 210, 211, 220, 222n23, 224n27, 232
Read, M., 947, 951
Reagan, R., xix, xxiii, 77, 195, 200, 225, 232–234, 247, 256, 259, 262–265, 269, 270, 280, 285, 375, 375n94, 433, 471, 472, 476, 477, 632, 797
Reddaway, W. B., vi, vii, xii, xix, 7, 9, 10, 17, 70, 70n1, 71, 73, 79, 81, 82, 85, 86, 86n13, 91, 96, 115, 116, 125, 126, 127n50, 129–131, 130n54, 139, 140, 140n66, 146, 147, 150, 164, 166, 297–299, 299n4, 301, 302, 302n12, 306, 310n23, 316, 316n34, 317, 321, 351, 354, 364, 365n79, 366, 366n81, 398n112, 403, 405n120, 419, 419n7, 422–426, 428–430, 429n15, 432, 432n21, 436, 464, 479, 502, 506, 575, 575n16, 599, 608, 621, 632, 634n33, 643, 647, 648, 677, 681, 682, 717, 718, 720–722, 746, 749n59, 804, 804n32, 813, 813n50, 815–818, 815n54, 815n55, 815n56, 816n57, 816n58, 820n65, 822n68, 823n70, 824, 827, 860, 861, 864n11, 867, 882n36, 886, 888, 889, 915, 933, 935, 980, 998, 1021, 1022, 1048, 1055, 1070
Reed, J., 833
Rees, P., 260
Reeves, A., 995n14
Reid, G. A., 605, 606, 620, 626, 680, 681
Reinhart, C., 1053
Renault, Mr., 223
Rendle, G., 695
Revell, J. R. S., 980
Reyes, E., 125, 125n47
Rhodes, J., 320, 496, 604, 642, 643, 651, 651n48, 696, 697

Ricardo, D., 5, 11, 31, 94, 144, 341, 847
Rice, C., 263
Richards, A., 784, 784n16
Richards, M., 714
Richardson, G., 232n34, 310n24
Richardson, M., 266
Richardson, R., 138n63
Ridley, N., 259
Riley, Mr., 455n8
Ristuccia, C. A., 914
Robbins, L., xi, xii, 89, 109–111, 130, 132, 165, 183–185, 185n2, 213, 221–223, 226n29, 230, 245n47, 265, 333, 346, 469, 543, 700, 775n9, 805, 851, 969, 970, 1045, 1046
Roberts, D. J., 693, 694
Roberts, G., 693–695
Robertson, D. H., 6, 73, 75, 79–81, 87–89, 91, 94, 118, 128, 146, 165, 223, 276, 328, 331, 333n46, 334, 337, 346, 348, 405n120, 969
Robertson, S., 797
Robeyn, I., 952
Robinson, E. A. G. (Austin), xix, 6, 7, 7n4, 10, 13, 70n1, 71, 75, 78, 79, 89, 96, 109, 110, 146, 162, 163, 192, 198, 226n29, 299–304, 302n9, 302n12, 304n17, 331, 336, 339, 339n55, 344–346, 348, 352, 353, 416, 417, 418n2, 418n4, 423, 425, 428, 436n26, 448, 565n1, 704n12, 704n13, 715n27, 725, 775, 801, 802, 805, 807, 811, 814, 814n53, 818, 820, 858n5, 861, 870n22, 871, 873, 873n24, 873n25, 933, 940–942, 949, 952, 969, 969n2, 971n3, 972, 976n8, 977, 1000, 1014, 1073
Robinson, F., 821n67
Robinson, J., vii, viin1, xii, xix, xxii, 5, 7–9, 11, 13, 15n9, 20, 25, 36, 43–49, 54, 56n32, 58n34, 62, 70, 74, 78, 81, 87–91, 88n17, 93, 96, 97, 101–103, 106, 107, 110, 111, 115, 116, 117n41, 118, 127, 131, 136, 137n60, 138n62, 144n73, 145n74, 146, 154n83, 183, 192, 196n7, 242n44, 250–252, 282n69, 296, 309, 310n24, 311, 313, 314, 317n35, 318, 333n46, 337, 339n55, 342, 345–347, 350, 351, 353, 356–358, 370, 376, 394–396, 398, 398n113, 399, 405n120, 417, 425, 432, 445, 448, 459, 476, 509, 552n15, 639, 686n86, 698, 720, 722, 722n32, 767, 770, 771, 774, 800, 811n40, 812, 812n46, 814–815n53, 818, 820n64, 821, 822n69, 858n5, 873n25, 876, 882n32, 886, 893n41, 928, 941, 1000, 1001, 1020, 1021, 1043n12, 1054, 1055n18, 1060n24, 1062, 1063
Robinson, P., 272
Robinson, R., 821n67, 867n16
Rocha, B., 915
Rodgers, "Bill," 446n4
Roehner, B. M., 212
Rogoff, K., 1053
Roosevelt, F., 183, 379, 390
Ropke, W., 109, 213n18, 218, 222n23, 224, 405n120
Roseberry, Lord, 502n41
Rosenheim, A., 788
Rosenstein-Rodan, P. N., 186, 215, 405n120, 777
Rosenthal, T., 730
Ross, R., 938n98, 940–942
Rosselli, A., 109, 338, 446n4
Rostas, L., 87, 333
Rostow, W. W., 777, 868
Roth, A., 776n9
Rothbard, M., 206–210, 206n12, 211n16, 214–217, 216n20, 232, 283
Rothschild, E., 280, 754n62, 922
Rothschild, Lord, 521–531
Rothschild, V., 533, 535, 539, 541n6, 547, 550, 551, 551n14, 557, 559, 731, 732
Rougier, L., 212, 213, 213n18, 217
Rowbotham, S., 97
Rowlatt P., 981
Rowntree, S., 42n26, 182, 683, 907n53
Rowthorn, B., xi, 7n3, 70n1, 94, 96, 96n24, 112n36, 117–121, 117n41,

127, 136, 137n60, 143, 146,
305–308, 305n18, 311, 311n26,
312, 314n30, 315, 316, 320, 321,
343, 357, 360, 435, 436, 467, 480,
608n9, 631, 633, 638n37, 643,
645–648, 648n45, 661, 701n6,
746, 747, 824, 826, 892, 1000,
1007, 1032, 1032n8, 1069n33
Rowthorn, R. E., xi, 83, 84, 117, 164, 746, 892
Roy, S., 274–276
Rubery, J., xvii, xxiv, 429, 480n29, 496, 614, 618, 650, 650–651n48, 651, 654, 683–687, 684n82, 686n86, 687n88, 696–698, 741n56, 750, 827, 902, 909, 910n59, 911n65, 912, 912n66, 913
Rudra, A., 771, 812n44
Ruel, M., 714
Runciman, W. G., 55, 699, 699n1, 700, 704, 705, 707, 708, 714, 715n26, 724, 733n42, 757
Russell, B., 388n104, 818n59
Rybczynski, T., 976
Ryunosuke Akutagawa, ix

S

Sabourian, H., 51, 134, 164
Saith, A., v, xix–xxv, 344n60, 403n116, 428, 630n30, 634n33, 685n82, 701n6, 706n16, 770, 770n2, 771, 773n6, 774n7, 812n44, 813n47, 820, 823, 825n71, 833n77, 882n35
Saith, S., xviii
Salter, A., 218
Salvanes, K., 167
Samarasinghe, S. "Sam," 344n60, 820
Samuelson, P. A., 5, 8, 9, 19, 24, 25, 30, 32, 33, 42, 43, 58, 87n14, 103–104, 106, 112, 121, 144, 144n73, 181, 185–187, 191, 192, 194, 196–198, 197n8, 202, 205, 205n11, 223, 227–229, 238, 241–242, 242n44, 245, 251, 252, 263, 272, 272n62, 275, 277, 296, 299, 310, 310n23, 315n32, 328, 344, 349, 349n64, 350, 358, 369–379, 375n92, 377n95,
393–398, 401, 403, 405n120, 421n9, 722, 769, 968, 1000, 1010, 1020, 1027, 1050, 1060n25, 1073
Sanderson, N., 446n4
Sanfilippo, E., 109, 110, 331, 345–347
Sangster, R., xviii
Sargan, D., xii, 132, 155, 966, 971, 1010
Sargent, D. R. "Dick," 52, 146, 365, 365n79, 569
Sargent, J. R., 971, 1024
Sarvary, M., 555n17
Satchell, M., 924n86
Savage, L., 49
Sawyer, M., 62, 92
Sayer, D., 975, 1012
Scargill, A., 449n5
Schams, E., 216n20
Schefold, B., 309, 309n22
Schiff, E., 216n20
Schiffman, D., 446n4, 771n4
Schlefer, J., 275, 493
Schlesinger, K., 216n20
Scholes, M., 1025
Schor, J., 251
Schultz, T., 192, 200, 205n11, 249, 253, 822n69, 1047
Schumpeter, J., 87n14, 185–187, 189, 190, 214n19, 227–229, 315, 315n32, 376, 777, 868, 1000
Schutz, A., 213, 216n20, 217
Schwartz, G., 230
Schwarz, A. J., 246, 469n19
Scitovsky, T., 186
Scott, A., 167
Scott, J., 695, 847, 1003n18
Scott, M. F-G., 147, 365n79, 599n1, 980
Scott, W. R., 165
Scranton, P., 183
Seabright, P., 134, 147, 364
Seal, A., 821n67, 867n16
Seavers, S., 167
Sedgwick, P., 455n8
Seers, D., 30, 777, 805, 806, 806n33, 824, 942n102, 951
Sefton of Garston, Lord, 543, 547, 548, 733, 733n43
Sefton, J. A., 915

1170   NAME INDEX

Seldon, A., 223n25, 229–231, 266, 267, 728
Sen, Abhijit, 344n60
Sen, Amartya, xi, 91, 92, 115, 138n63, 154, 241, 251, 280, 284, 284n70, 313, 318, 341, 341n57, 347, 351, 496, 550, 551, 769, 776n9, 812n45, 820, 820n64, 859, 860n8, 950n105, 952, 966, 1011, 1060n24
Sen, A. K., 980
Sen, R. K., 815n53
Sen, S., xvii
Sender, J., 781, 796, 796n27, 797, 822, 825n71, 828, 835, 926–927n90, 1023, 1044
Serra, G., 873
Sethi, R., 272n62
Seton, F., 774, 821n68
Shackleton, J. R., 980, 985
Shanin, T., 733n42
Sharpe, M. E., 1025
Shaw, E., 123, 375
Shaw, G. B., 181
Shaxson, N., 219, 220
Shepherd, J. R., 455n8
Sherman, A., 232, 233, 266–268
Shipman, A., 321, 428, 499
Shove, G., 6, 331, 417, 826, 1000, 1003n18
Shultz, G., 263
Shute, J., 1028
Sibert, A., 981
Sickle, J. V. Van, 213, 216n20
Sidgwick, H., 94, 328, 330, 701, 706, 718, 848
Silberston, A., 74, 91, 131, 146, 147, 150, 164, 341, 347, 350, 351, 356n69, 364–366, 972, 976, 976n8, 979, 979n9, 1010, 1055n18
Silberston, Z. A., 147, 365n79
Simon, A., 74
Simons, H., 221, 379, 850
Sinclair, P., 981
Singer, H., 189, 190, 819, 819n62
Singh, A., v, vi, ix, xii, xviii, xxii, 7n3, 14, 62, 76, 83, 84, 94, 96, 101, 105, 106, 117, 117n41, 118n42, 121, 122, 127, 127n50, 130, 136, 137n60, 146, 170, 298, 305–308,

305n18, 312, 316, 318, 320, 321, 327, 328, 333, 334n47, 343, 353–362, 361n75, 399, 424, 425, 428, 432n21, 443, 445, 467, 496, 497n38, 506n46, 575, 607n7, 608n9, 621, 622, 627, 630n30, 631–634, 634n33, 636, 638n37, 645–647, 661, 663, 669n63, 672, 673, 681, 685n82, 701n6, 718, 738n49, 740, 746, 747, 770, 770n2, 773, 779, 781, 798, 804n32, 810, 812n46, 813n50, 815, 819–823, 821–822n68, 825n71, 826, 828, 831, 831n74, 835, 886, 935, 937n97, 998, 1000, 1007, 1021n2, 1023, 1028n5, 1032, 1040–1042, 1042n11, 1046n15, 1058, 1059, 1060n25, 1063, 1064, 1069n33, 1071
Singh, D., 90n19
Singh, M., 90, 820, 820n64
Singh, Maharaja Ranjit, 97
Sjaastad, L., 253, 254, 256n50
Skidelsky, R., 41n25, 58n34, 226n29, 228n30, 232, 245n47, 281–284, 418n2, 542n7, 551n14
Skinner, A. S., 980
Sklair, L., 728n36
Skouras, A., 980
Skouras, T., 970
Skousen, M., 395
Skrabec Jr. Q. R., 1023
Slater, L., 694, 695
Sloan, P., 335, 335n50
Sloane, P., 335n50, 586, 984–987
Slobodian, Q., 214, 217, 218
Smedley, O., 230
Smith, A., 119, 122, 231, 232, 234n40, 250, 259, 260, 318, 334n47, 584n26, 870, 897, 1024, 1026, 1027
Smith, A. K., 852
Smith, C.S., 970
Smith, Clifford, 894
Smith, Cyril, 537, 540, 970
Smith, D., 450
Smith, G. (Graeme), 460, 498, 499
Smith, M. A. M., 166

NAME INDEX 1171

Smith, R. "Ron," xvii, xxv, 7n3, 70n1, 91n20, 105, 108n33, 116n40, 117n41, 118, 136, 164, 311n26, 313, 314n30, 321, 334n47, 353n67, 361, 361n75, 419n6, 420, 422, 456n9, 479, 480
Smith, S., 335n50, 797, 822, 827, 927n90
Smith, V., 231, 776n9
Smuts, J., 818n59
Sneath, K., 908n54
Snell, A., 590, 651
Snowdon, B., 27n12
Sobhan, R., 820
Soderberg, G., 235, 236, 238n43, 239, 240, 244, 247, 272n62, 276n68
Solomons, D., 74
Solomou, S., 857, 902, 914–918, 928, 932n92, 934
Solow, R. M., 19, 24, 42–43, 58n34, 77, 112, 143, 144, 154n82, 155, 168n85, 187, 227–229, 250, 252, 275, 277, 310, 328, 355, 552n15, 864n11, 1024, 1054
Sordi, S., 315n32, 372n85, 372n86, 372n87
Soros, G., 500, 1059n22, 1064, 1065
Sousa, F. de, 282n69
Spafford, D., 404, 404n117
Spaventa, L., 309n22
Spencer, H., 702
Sraffa, P., xi, 5, 7, 8, 11, 70, 75, 87, 90–92, 96, 108, 110–112, 115, 116, 118, 121, 142, 151, 182, 183, 228, 309, 310n24, 314, 315, 315n31, 316n33, 318, 328, 339–345, 339n55, 344n62, 348, 349, 351, 353, 370, 396, 417, 432, 669n63, 767, 769, 773, 774, 782, 818n59, 826, 1060n24
Srinivasan, T. N., 816, 885
Srivastava, R., 820, 825n71
Stahl, I., 238n43
Stalin, J., 204, 882, 885
Stamler, 453, 455n8
Stamp, J., 109
Stanislaw, J., 263, 264
Stanley, T. D., 999
Stanworth, P. H., 694, 695
Starr, R., 134

Starrett, D., 134
Steedman, I., 305n19, 309n22, 314n30
Steel, D., 452
Steel, R., 943
Stepney, P., 477n25
Stern, N. H., 137, 154, 155, 165, 575n16, 723, 827, 896n43, 977, 981, 982, 985, 1003n19, 1045, 1048, 1048n16, 1049, 1051
Steuer, M., 985–987
Steward, F., 980, 985
Stewart, A., 651, 693–696, 698, 739n52
Stewart, F., 463
Stewart, H., 500
Stewart, I. G., 871n22
Stewart, M., 890, 891
Stewart, S., 738n50
Stigler, G. J., 205, 210, 224n26, 231
Stigler, S., 203, 205, 206
Stiglitz, J., 51, 134, 342, 827, 1011, 1047, 1048
Stockhammer, E., 968, 984, 997–999
Stockwell, S., 784, 784n15, 785, 787, 788
Stokes, E. T., 779, 782, 821n67, 867n16
Stone, F., 870–871
Stone, J. R. N., 165, 422, 727n35, 980
Stone, R., 5, 7, 9, 10, 70, 70n1, 71, 79, 80, 87, 91, 91n20, 103n31, 115, 129, 130n54, 164, 191, 353–356, 377, 420, 421, 429n15, 432, 502, 507, 554, 557, 563, 564, 566, 567, 568n8, 569, 570, 575, 578n21, 585n27, 597, 613, 614, 623, 625, 632, 634n33, 634n34, 636, 637, 658, 667n61, 676, 686n87, 716, 718–721, 721n31, 772, 811, 814n52, 818, 819n63, 822, 860–863, 863n11, 870–873, 874n26, 886, 933, 936, 937, 948, 949, 952, 976, 1037, 1050, 1060n24
Stonier, A., 213, 216n20, 268
Storm, S., xvii, xxv, 50, 52, 54, 285, 581, 581n24, 1038
Stout, D. K., 664, 980
Strachey, L., 890
Strathern, M., 716
Stray, C., 335n49
Streeten, P., 76n6, 190, 777

1172 NAME INDEX

Stuart, A. W., 373n89
Sturgis, P., 186
Suenson-Taylor, A., 220, 230
Sukarno, 461n14
Sultanpuri, M., 367n83
Supple, B., 93, 94, 114, 420, 433, 539, 601, 602, 605, 606, 606n6, 606–607n7, 626, 633, 668n62, 703, 848, 849, 898–899, 899n46, 901n46, 973n6
Supple, B. E., 680
Suriya Aratchi, S. M. P., 821n66
Surrey, M. J. C., 259, 590, 980, 1007
Sutton, J., 154, 165, 977, 981
Svennilson, I., 236, 239
Sweeney, "Rifleman," 535n3
Sweezy, M. Y., 373n89
Sweezy, P., 238, 242, 373n89, 382
Swinnerton-Dyer, P., 973–977, 1012
Szenberg, M., 132

T

Tagore, R., 367, 367n82, 368
Talleyrand-Perigord, C.-M. de, 152n80
Tarling, R., 7n3, 70n1, 312, 314n30, 320, 475, 496, 614, 651, 683–685, 683n76, 685n84, 687, 687n88, 696–698, 750, 827, 911n65
Tarshis, L., 13, 191, 192, 296, 331, 331n43, 339, 340, 371–378, 373n89, 375n92, 382, 393, 403, 814, 814n53, 1020n1
Taylor, A. J. P., 193
Taylor, C., 586, 587
Taylor, J. John, 655n52
Taylor, L., 107, 499
Taylor, M., 981
Teacher, D., 257n52
Tedder, Lord, 818n59
Temin, P., 878, 929, 931
Templeton, K., 208
Templeton, K. S. Jr., 211
Tew, Brian, 146, 339, 339n55, 365, 938n97
Tew, J. H. B., 147, 339, 339n55, 365n79
Thatcher, D., 266
Thatcher, M., xii, xix, xxi, xxiii, 3, 33, 77, 78, 84, 93, 113, 114, 122, 123, 126, 145, 145n76, 169, 170n86,
195, 196, 225, 231–234, 232n34, 234n38, 257–262, 264–270, 273, 274, 274n66, 278–280, 285, 354, 355, 365, 403, 431, 433, 440, 441, 443, 450, 452, 453, 460, 461, 464–467, 469–477, 472n20, 473n22, 474n23, 482–484, 493, 501, 518, 519, 521–530, 532, 533, 535, 539, 542, 542n7, 544, 548, 549, 555, 557, 557n19, 558, 560, 578, 585, 586, 605, 627, 632, 674, 729, 731, 732, 740, 775, 775n9, 788, 796–798, 834, 890, 897n45, 973n6, 974, 975, 992, 994, 1007, 1013, 1038, 1040, 1058, 1069
Theil, H., 186
Thirlwall, A. P., 116, 444, 851, 858n5, 882n35, 892, 980, 985
Thoma, M., 1062
Thomas, D., 335n51
Thomas, H., 266–268
Thomas, J., 364, 779
Thomas, M., 140n69, 142n71, 144n73, 929
Thompson, E. P., 899
Thompson, F. M. L., 874n28, 876–879, 895–898, 895n42
Thompson, J., 739, 739n53, 741, 741n55
Timlin, M., 403–405, 405n119, 405n120
Tinbergen, J., 240–241, 251, 393, 417, 421n9, 422, 722, 813, 815n55, 861, 1069n33
Tingsten, H., 222n23, 243, 243n45
Tintner, G., 216, 216n20
Tocqueville, A. de, 201
Todd, Mr., 455n8
Tomlinson, B. R., 821n67, 867n16
Townsend, P., 42n26, 154n82, 733n42, 1048
Towse, R., 970
Toye, John, xvii, xviii, 770, 775n8, 779n12, 793n23, 796, 798, 806, 806n33, 813n48, 823, 825–826n71, 827
Toynbee, A., 779, 850
Trapido, S., 932n91
Travis, A., 473, 474
Trevoux, F., 222n23

Tribe, K., 47, 187, 459n13, 819n60, 819n62, 1046
Trollope, A., 133n57, 234n38
Trotsky, L., 204, 782
Tullock, G., 257
Tunzelmann, N. von, 7n3, 879–881, 902, 917
Turing, A., 73
Turner, H. A. F. "Bert," 81, 86, 86n13, 114, 309, 682, 682n74, 687, 693–696
Turner, M., 243, 250
Turvey, R., 459n13
Tweedale, G., 895
Tylecote, A., 914

U
Ulph, A. M., 971, 981, 985
Ulph, D., 981
Uswatte-Aratchi, G., 821n66
Utting, J. E. G., 693, 717, 863n11, 865n14

V
Vaizey, J. E., 333
Vakil, C. N., 814n53, 815n53
Valdes, J. G., 253
Van Arkadie, B., xvii, 822, 889n39, 893n39, 894
Van den Berg, G., 167
Vane, H. R., 27n12
Varottil, U., 171n88
Veblen, T., 702
Velupillai, K. V., 315n32, 344n60, 405, 493, 812n46, 820
Venables, A. J., 981
Venkatachalam, R., 405
Ventura, J., 167
Verdoorn, P. J., 117
Vermeulen, F., 167
Vernon, R., 461, 463
Vervaecke, P., 351
Vickers, J. S., 147, 154, 159, 165, 365n79, 977, 981
Videla, R., 257
Viner, J., 109, 182, 205n11, 379
Vines, D., 575, 584n26, 643, 651, 980
Vinson, N., 266

Vivo, G. de, 315n31, 316n33
Voegelin, E., 216n20
Voena, A., 188n4
Volcker, P., 269, 269n61, 270, 470, 471, 476
Volker, W., 191, 202, 203, 209, 211, 270, 470
Volpato, R., 696, 697
von Euler, U., 237
Von Strigl, R., 216n20
Voorhees, E. D., 949n105, 950n105
Voth, H-J., 167, 908n54
Vyasulu, V., 73n3

W
Wadhwani, S., 148, 365n79
Waldegrave, W., 535, 535n3, 536, 973–974n7
Waldinger, F., 188n4
Walker, D., 535–538, 542n7, 543, 546, 732
Wallenberg, 240
Wallis, K. F., 488, 579, 981
Walras, L., 35, 50, 59, 237, 273n62, 722n32
Walters, A. A., 47, 132, 134, 138n63, 169, 184, 232, 233, 257–260, 266, 278, 279, 354, 445, 467–470, 472, 473, 474n23, 776n9, 979, 1010, 1046, 1066
Walters, P. "Paddie," 258
Wapshott, N., 1023
Ward, A., 869n17
Ward, B., 1021, 1021n2
Ward, M., 676n70, 823n70
Ward, T., xviii, xxvi, 116, 118, 320, 431n19, 431n20, 475, 476, 492, 494, 495, 495n36, 497n38, 505n45, 508, 651, 1071
Ward, T. S., 888n36
Waring, M., 949–951
Warren, B., 926n90, 927n90
Warsh, D., 276n68
Washbrook, D., 821n67
Wass, D., 444, 509
Waterman, A. M. C., 337
Watson, G., 421, 564
Watts, V. O., 207, 210, 220, 222n23
Wazir, R., xviii

Weale, M. R., 7n3, 125, 125n45, 147, 584n26, 589, 651, 902, 911, 914–918, 934
Weaver, H., 203
Webb, B., 181
Webb, D., 695
Webb, S., xii
Webb, U., 346
Weber, M., 214, 701, 702
Wedderburn, D. E. C., 664, 665n58, 682n74, 693–695, 717, 717n30, 718
Wedgewood, C. V., 222n23
Weidenfeld, G., 446n4
Weintraub, E. Roy, 43–46, 189n5, 1029
Weisdorf, J., 910
Wells, H. G., 218
Wells, J. W., 638, 746
Whitaker, J. K., 183n1, 848, 848n2
White, D. G., 697
White, L., 992, 993, 995, 996
Whitehead, C., 138n63
Whitelaw, W., 474, 474n23
Whitelock, J., xviii
Whitten, R., 282, 283
Whittington, G., 7n3, 70n1, 77, 83, 84, 98, 129n53, 575, 627, 643, 672, 681, 827, 937n97
Wickens, M., 167
Wickramasekhara, P., 344n60, 820
Wicksell, K., 26, 27, 27n12, 44, 237, 342
Wilder, L. I., 373
Wilkinson, C., 779
Wilkinson, F., vii, viin1, xvii, xviii, 7n3, 70n1, 118, 305, 305n18, 307, 308, 311n26, 312, 313, 314n30, 318, 320, 321, 475, 480, 480n29, 492, 496, 614, 683, 684n82, 685–687, 686n86, 687n88, 694–698, 745, 750, 827, 912, 1042, 1069n33
Wilkinson, S. F., 694, 695
Williams, A., 459n13
Williams, B., 538, 539
Williams, S., 116, 140n67, 466, 974n7
Williamson, J. G., 908n56, 909n56
Williamson, J. H., 166, 299n4
Williamson, O., 231, 250
Wilson, B., 78

Wilson, H., 445, 458, 459, 463, 481, 482, 492, 888
Wilson, J. D., 373n89
Wilson, T., 405, 535, 812n41
Winch, D., 131, 166, 300n5, 302, 302n10, 302n12, 303, 971n3
Winters, A., 312, 575, 584n26, 984, 985
Winters, L. A., 166, 981, 985–987
Witcomb, R., 584n26
Wojick, P., 27n13
Wold, H., 239
Wolf, M., 981, 985
Wolfowitz, P., 211n15, 390n105, 783
Wood, A., 136, 310n23, 509, 826, 981
Woodward, V., 312, 584n26
Wootton, B., 6
Worlock, D., 474
Worms, R., 702
Worrall, T., 651
Worswick, G. D. N., 165, 980
Wren-Lewis, S., 981
Wrigley, E. A., 846n1, 899, 909
Wynne, G. C., 502n41

Y
Yale, D. E. C., 247, 374, 379, 605, 606, 620, 659, 680, 681, 750, 1008, 1069
Yamey, B. S., 138n63, 775, 776n9
Yergin, D., 263, 264
Yokoyama, K., 993n12
Young, A. A., xi–xii, 5, 112, 182, 183, 183n1, 197n8, 221, 773, 851, 888, 1068
Young, D., 266, 267
Young, H., 940
Young, M. Y., 114, 699, 699n2, 705, 706, 710, 710n21, 712, 713, 726, 733, 733n42, 737n47

Z
Zambelli, S., 405
Zammit, A., xvii
Zappia, C., 54
Zezza, G., 321, 498, 499, 1030
Ziliak, S. T., 998
Zinkin, M., 980
Zoll, 373

Subject Index[1]

A

Act of Uniformity, England, Charles II, 1662, 1013, 1073
Adam Smith Institute, 232, 234n40, 259
Adam Smith Prize, 334n47, 820n64, 1024
Admiral Belgrano, 453, 797
Alliance Manchester Business School, 687, 912
Alphametrics Co. Ltd., Bangkok, Francis Cripps, 495, 495n37, 576
Alternative Economic Strategy 'leftist' pamphlet by Cambridge dons, 118, 311n26, 479
American Economic Association, 186, 227, 275, 315n32, 394
Anglo-Israeli Bank (AIB), 446n4
Anti-Vietnam War movement/protests, 77, 97, 492
Apostles, Cambridge, 7, 108, 331, 351, 455, 656
Applica, Brussels, Terence Ward, 495, 495n37
Argentina, 254, 255, 255n49, 257, 257n52, 259, 262, 461n14, 782, 815n55, 893, 894
Association of Polytechnic Teachers of Economics (APTE), 970, 985
Association of the Teachers of Economics/association of the teachers of economics (ATE), 968, 969, 969n2, 971n4
Association of University Teachers (AUT), 650, 651, 654
Association of University Teachers of Economics (AUTE), 33n20, 48, 50, 133, 168, 724, 969–972, 969n2, 971n4, 976–979
Asterix and Obelix, 285
Atlas Network, 233, 234, 257
Auctions
 of Hayek's Medal, 229, 230, 234n38
 of Mrs Thatcher's handbag, 269
Austin Robinson Building, Faculty of Economics & DAE, 352, 587, 658, 725, 755
Australia, 42, 77, 108, 314n30, 417, 418, 685, 737, 801, 802, 877, 913
Australian National University (ANU), 707, 710n19
Austrian Economics Newsletter, 245n47

---

[1] Note: Page numbers followed by 'n' refer to notes.

© The Author(s), under exclusive license to Springer Nature Switzerland AG 2022
A. Saith, *Cambridge Economics in the Post-Keynesian Era*, Palgrave Studies in the History of Economic Thought,
https://doi.org/10.1007/978-3-030-93019-6

B

Banca d'Italia, 219
Bangladesh, 344, 772, 792, 814, 815n55, 822n68, 823
Bank Leumi, Israel, 446n4
Bank of England
   Monetary Policy Committee/ monetary policy committee (MPC), 125, 125n48, 126, 149, 469, 589, 915
   Panel of Academic Consultants, R.C.O. Matthews, 145, 467n16, 573, 606
Bank of London and South America, 892
Banks, and bank finance, 219
BBC weather forecast, Michael Fish, 1987, 1027
Berkeley, University of California, 76, 77, 97, 131, 354, 424, 607n7, 878, 1008, 1021n2
Beveridge Report, 191, 381, 384
Big Bang approach to deflation (Friedman, Hayek, Thatcher), 270, 274n66
Birkbeck College, London, 108n33, 420, 468, 485, 710n21, 1007
Birmingham Group, 335n49
Bletchley Park, code-breaking, intelligence, 72, 798
Bloomsbury set, group, 283, 335n49, 335n52
Bretton Woods Institutions, IMF, World Bank, 42n26, 52, 56, 77, 159, 191, 254, 258, 421, 462, 465, 492, 506, 589, 610, 650, 725, 773, 783, 797, 800, 810, 815n55, 821, 827, 829, 831, 923n85, 995n13, 1030, 1052
British Academy, Fellow of (FBAs), 149, 154, 155, 875, 922, 1043
British Council, 789n20
British Petroleum (BP), 260, 584n26, 1059n22
'Buda' and 'Pest', Kaldor and Balogh, 457
Business and Management Studies, Cambridge, 990, 991, 1034, 1036, 1036n9

C

Cambridge Circus, 110, 344–345, 347, 405n120, 883
Cambridge Econometrics (CE), DAE, 554, 565, 577–579, 588, 590–592, 686n87, 1037, 1071
Cambridge Economic Policy Group (CEPG), 2, 3, 9, 10, 16, 70, 86, 103n31, 104, 111, 115, 116, 118, 122, 129, 140, 151, 152, 168, 170n86, 296, 297, 307, 308n21, 309, 319–322, 366, 401, 402, 419, 420, 426, 427, 433, 434, 435n24, 440–511, 518–560, 564, 566, 573n13, 574, 585, 590–593, 598, 607, 613, 616, 617, 623–625, 627–630, 632, 634n34, 643, 647, 648, 653, 658, 661, 662, 671–673, 678, 681, 682, 684, 686n87, 719, 734, 740, 811, 827, 867, 902, 913n71, 924n88, 967, 991, 1000, 1007, 1010, 1014, 1021, 1037–1038, 1071
Cambridge Endowment for Research in Finance (CERF), 497, 506n46, 507, 1040–1042, 1041n11, 1058, 1059, 1067n30
Cambridge Growth Project (CGP), 2, 3, 9, 10, 16, 103n31, 111, 111n35, 140, 151, 152, 168, 362–363, 366, 402, 419–423, 425, 427, 427n11, 434, 435n24, 478, 484–486, 489, 489n33, 489n34, 500, 502, 506, 507, 548–550, 553, 554, 557–559, 558n21, 564–593, 573n13, 576–577n19, 598, 607, 613, 613n12, 614, 616, 617, 623–625, 628–630, 629n27, 634n34, 637, 643, 648, 653, 658, 661, 662, 662n55, 667n61, 671–673, 677, 678, 681, 686, 686–687n87, 716, 719, 827, 867, 902, 914–916, 924n88, 936, 967, 991, 1001, 1014, 1022, 1037–1038, 1064, 1071
Cambridge Indian Majlis, 811n36
Cambridge in India, 810–818
Cambridge Journal of Economics, viin1, 14, 27n13, 117, 282n69, 296, 297,

305, 305n19, 308, 313, 315n32, 318, 321, 332n44, 433, 445, 475, 479n28, 496, 740, 901n48, 906, 1069
Cambridge Political Economy Society (CPES), 305, 305n19, 311n26, 315n31, 318, 319, 320n38, 679
Cambridge Political Economy Society Trust, 357n70
Cambridge Realist Workshop (CRW), 58, 367, 1069n34
Cambridge Social Ontology Group (CSOG), 58, 368, 1069n34
Cambridge Union, 811n36
CAMPOP, Cambridge, 909, 931
Canada, 76n6, 108, 126n49, 388, 403, 704n12, 801, 802, 918, 1010
Catholic University, Santiago, Chile, 253, 258
Cato Institute, 206n12, 211, 211n16, 775n9
Centennial Chair, London School of Economics, 918n73, 919
Center for Policy Studies, Chile, 254
Central Intelligence Agency (CIA), U.S. Government, 77, 202, 233, 249, 255n49, 259, 375
Central Policy Review Staff (CPRS), Prime Minister's Office, UK, 535, 535n3, 536, 630n30
Centre for Business Research (CBR), 435n24, 496, 499, 627n24, 673, 674, 682, 684, 916, 935, 938, 990, 991, 1036n9, 1038, 1040, 1041, 1058, 1070, 1070n35
Centre for Development Studies, Cambridge, 756, 798, 808, 809, 831, 934, 1040
Centre for Latin American Studies, Cambridge, 822, 894
Centre for Policy Studies (CPS), UK, 231–233, 258–260, 264
Centres for South Asia Studies, Cambridge, 766
CES-'SMAC' production function, 250
Chandigarh, 779, 810, 820n64
Chequers, 97, 280

Chicago Boys, Friedman, Harberger, 192, 247, 249, 253–255, 258–261, 460, 470, 829
Chicago economics, 192, 197, 255, 272, 369, 460
Chichele Professor of Economic History, Oxford, 727n35, 917n72
Chile
 Alan Walters and Chile, 258, 259, 470
 CIA involvement, 77
 Hayek's visits, 256, 257, 257n51
 Mrs Thatcher and General Pinochet, 257–262
China
 Ajit Singh and Suzy Paine Research Trip 1973, 819, 820
 Cultural Revolution, 101, 398, 402
Churchill College Economics Seminar (the 'Hahn Seminar'), 360, 361n75
City University Business School (CUBS), 468, 560, 565n1, 582, 585
Civil rights movement, 97
Clapham Report 1946, 704
CLARE Group at Clare College, 125, 126, 140, 140n66, 143, 146–149, 146n78, 280, 296, 364–367, 446, 458, 464, 489n33, 519, 560, 568n8, 593, 627, 915, 976
Cliometrics, 144, 846, 878, 896, 900, 910n56, 916, 925, 928–931, 933, 1062
CND, 308, 433
Colleges, Cambridge
 Churchill, 133, 274, 357, 362, 364, 660n54, 699n2, 737n47, 1048
 Clare, 86, 115, 129, 139, 141, 142, 145, 146, 149, 150, 356n69, 364–366, 459, 606, 627, 737n46, 822n68, 865, 915, 973n6, 1021
 Darwin, 756
 Downing, 600, 605
 Girton, 664, 1064
 Jesus, 779n12, 878
 King's, 19, 32, 73, 88n16, 103n31, 112n37, 128n52, 191, 221n21, 271, 276, 280, 284, 335n52, 346, 352n66, 356n69, 359n73, 361, 480n29, 704n13, 709n18, 738, 783, 811n38, 848n2, 1063
 New Hall, 910n59

Colleges, Cambridge (*cont.*)
  Pembroke, 484, 877, 1060, 1060n24
  Peterhouse, 234n38, 864n11
  Queens, 98, 121, 122, 307, 328, 333, 334n47, 343, 352, 353, 355–362, 361n75, 445, 634, 638n37, 756, 889n39, 893n39, 1059, 1064, 1065
  St. Catherine's, 318, 358, 360–361, 605, 607n7, 656, 785, 973n6
  St. John's, 87, 114, 329, 605, 708, 798
  Sidney Sussex, 801, 1040, 1041
  Trinity, vi, 91, 92, 116, 121, 122, 128, 229, 271–285, 328, 329, 333, 335n50, 342, 699n1, 705, 818n59, 847, 848n2, 859, 868n17, 869, 911, 918, 1039, 1054, 1055, 1063
Colleges, elsewhere
  All Souls, Oxford, 139, 535, 699n1, 908–909n56, 913, 919
  Balliol, Oxford, 502n41, 779, 782, 787, 969, 969n2
  Birkbeck College, London, 108n33, 136, 420, 468, 485, 710n21, 1007
  Nuffield, Oxford, 154, 163, 306, 606n6, 709n18, 744, 750
  Ruskin College, Oxford, 480n29
  St. Stephen's College, Delhi, 811n38
  Wadham, Oxford, 147, 156, 161
Colloque Lippmann, Paris, 1938, 212, 213
Comite Internationale d'etude pour le Renouveau du Liberalisme (CIERL), 212
Communist Party
  of Great Britain (CPGB), 335n50, 335n51
  of United States of America, 388n103
Conference of Heads of University Departments of Economics (CHUDE), 168, 971, 972, 976–979, 979n9, 983, 984, 984n10, 988
Conference of Socialist Economists, 117, 117n41, 480n30

Congress for Cultural Freedom (CCF, Svenska kommittén för kulturens frihet, SKfKF), 243n45
Conservative Party Research Department, 260, 269, 535n4
Corporate finance, 202, 424, 718
Cowles Commission, viii, 188, 188n3, 377, 379–380, 387, 392, 423n10
Credit Suisse, 219
Cricket, vi, 98, 785, 792
Cripps Mission to India, 1942, 811
Cumulative causation, 49, 773, 888, 898, 917

D
DAE
  50th Anniversary, 321, 399, 424, 435n24, 440, 502, 506n46, 675
  Centre for Business Studies, 687
  Closure in 2004, 17, 415, 420, 588, 673, 727, 1021
  DAE Review by the General Board of the Faculties, 1984-87, 598
  DAE Review Committees, membership, 140, 445, 607n7
  development research, 827
  directorships, 9, 79, 86, 86n13, 115, 422–424, 434, 435n24, 508, 634n33, 641, 647, 660, 663, 668, 736n46, 912, 967, 991, 1014, 1022, 1039
  economic history, 4, 93, 424, 434, 681, 687, 718, 758, 861–863, 863n10, 865n14, 868n16, 872, 902, 934–938, 1042, 1043
  formation, 171, 416, 435, 440, 622, 632, 718, 751
  housing of, 10
  national accounts and statistics, 861–869
  Sociology group, 434, 682
  Staff leaving DAE 1984-1987, 642, 643
De-industrialisation/de-industrialization, 13, 297, 310, 359, 399, 401, 443, 455, 461, 479n28, 638n37, 714, 773, 819, 824, 868, 888, 1000
Delhi School of Economics, 418, 747, 812n45

SUBJECT INDEX 1179

Department for International Development (DfID), UK, 778
Department of Politics and International Studies (POLIS), University of Cambridge, 756, 756n63, 766, 778, 835, 1040
Department of Sociology, University of Cambridge, 692
Department of Sociology, University of Leicester, 709n18
Devaluation, 402, 442, 479n28, 500, 773, 824, 888, 916, 917, 1003
Development and Change, 496
Development Diploma, Cambridge, 740, 825n71
Development economics, 2, 3, 17, 60, 117n41, 511n49, 752, 758, 771, 775n8, 776, 783, 792, 793, 800–808, 819, 823, 825n71, 826–827n72, 828, 829, 831, 832, 834, 836, 875, 893, 909, 933, 939n102, 953, 1022, 1040, 1044, 1049, 1070
Development studies, 17, 56, 105, 127, 190, 422, 725, 752, 755, 758, 767–800, 807, 808, 810, 825, 825n71, 828–832, 831n74, 834–839, 835n78, 875, 894, 933–935, 953, 1005, 1034, 1040, 1043, 1044, 1071
Development Studies Institute (DESTIN), London School of Economics, 825n71, 834, 835
Devlin Enquiry
  Ajit Singh's Submission to Enquiry, 701n6
  meeting with Lord Devlin, 706n16
  report of enquiry, 706n16
"Devonshire" Courses on Development, 775
Donors and Donations
  by Bill and Weslie Janeway to Pembroke College and Faculty of Economics, 1058
  Donor re-boot of Cambridge Economics?, 1057–1068
  by Mohamed El-Erian to Queens' College and Faculty of Economics, 1059

E
Early retirements of Professors, Faculty of Economics, 114
East India College, Malthus, 779, 810
Ecole Normale Superieure, Paris, 1033
Econometric Society, 576n17, 676
Economic and Social Research Council (ESRC), 16, 111, 139, 140, 145n76, 168–170, 170n86, 279, 363, 363n77, 420, 434, 435n24, 484, 492, 496, 500, 507, 520, 531, 532, 537, 541n6, 544, 544n10, 554, 554n17, 557, 557n19, 558, 560, 564–572, 566n3, 566n4, 571n11, 571n12, 574, 574n14, 575, 577–579, 578n21, 580n23, 581n24, 582, 583, 585, 586, 588, 589, 592, 607, 613, 614, 617, 623–625, 627–630, 627n24, 634n34, 637, 649, 651, 652, 661, 672, 683, 686, 686n87, 687, 698, 719, 726, 727, 731, 732, 734, 742, 745, 917, 935, 936, 937n95, 994, 1003n18, 1022, 1051, 1059n22, 1064
Economic Affairs Committee, 140, 566n4, 567, 571n12
Economic history
  cliometrics and quantitative economic history, 925
  at Faculty of Economics and DAE, Cambridge, 113
  at Faculty of History, Cambridge, 606n6, 925, 926, 931, 1002
  significance of, 822, 896
Economic Journal, 2, 5, 16, 47, 73, 125, 143, 183, 198, 296–298, 300, 300n5, 301, 302n9, 304n17, 305, 305n18, 306, 309, 312, 313, 336, 340, 341, 341n57, 403, 418n2, 454, 631, 767, 782, 823, 870, 875, 910, 914, 968, 983, 984, 988, 999, 1021
Economic Problems of the British Empire, Course by Austin Robinson, Cambridge, 807
An Economic Programme for American Democracy, 373, 382, 386
Econ Tribe, A. Leonhufvud, 79n9

Education Reform Act, 1988,
    1007, 1012
Ellen McArthur Lectures, Faculty of
    History, Cambridge, 907n55
Ely, Richard T. Lecture 1971, 138n62,
    394, 401
Émigré economists
    'Americanization' of economics, 186
    Beveridge and LSE, 185
    and development economics, 187, 190
    flows into USA and UK, 76, 185–191,
        257, 371
    mathematisation of economics, 188n3,
        192, 371
English Sociological Association, 702

F
Faculty of Archaeology and
    Anthropology, University of
    Cambridge, 692, 738
Faculty of Economics and Politics,
    University of Cambridge, 21, 100,
    127, 608, 639, 681, 692, 705,
    705n15, 717, 720, 733n42, 738,
    758, 767, 789n20, 790, 791n21,
    793, 794, 800, 807, 808, 810,
    834–836, 846, 852, 879, 891,
    893n39, 898, 915n72, 1023, 1032,
    1034, 1047
Faculty of Economics, University of
    Cambridge, 3, 4, 11, 12, 16, 17, 62,
    73, 87, 100, 102, 113, 114, 128,
    151, 169, 181, 285, 328, 376, 391,
    416, 433, 444, 588, 598, 599,
    602–605, 615, 617, 640, 642,
    649n46, 653, 655, 673, 679,
    704n13, 706, 709n18, 720, 735,
    736, 746–748, 748n58, 752, 755,
    757, 778, 782, 797, 797n27, 799,
    802, 807, 808, 825, 826, 828, 829,
    834, 835, 846–953, 966, 968, 993,
    1021n2, 1032, 1034, 1038–1040,
    1042, 1056, 1059, 1060, 1060n24,
    1068, 1071, 1073
Faculty of Human, Social and Political
    Sciences, 687, 756
Faculty of Social and Political Sciences,
    University of Cambridge,
    737n48, 755

Falklands/Malvinas, 78
Federal Reserve U.S.A., 262
Festschrift, 5, 141, 142, 742, 860
Firm, theories of, 899, 1049
Fiscal redistribution, 500
Foreign aid, 775n9, 797, 885
Foundation for Economic Education
    (FEE), USA, 191, 199, 202n9, 203,
    204, 206–211, 206n12, 220,
    222n23, 230
France, 76, 364, 428, 532, 559n22, 699,
    913, 914, 924n86, 973n6,
    997n15, 1033
Free Speech Movement, 97
Friedman Prize, 775n9
Friedman's Chicago Boys, 192

G
Gang of Four, China, 674
Garden House Hotel, Cambridge;
    protest, 973n6
Gender issues, 1047
General Board of the Faculties,
    University of Cambridge, 113, 114,
    151, 427, 434, 598, 607, 633, 654,
    655, 670, 734, 736
Geneva school of neoliberals, 218
Germany, 23, 109, 186, 188,
    188n4, 194, 213n18, 227,
    255n49, 262, 265, 381, 425,
    559n22, 699, 782, 822n68,
    901, 914, 918, 921,
    922n84, 1033
Gleichschaltung, 639, 640
    Kaldor on, 639
Globalisation and labour outcomes/
    standards, 581n24
Godley Family, 502n41
Gokhale Institute of Economics and
    Politics, Pune, 819n61
The "Golden Age," 30, 195, 269n61,
    425, 430–433, 711, 867n15
Graduate Students Letter of Protest By
    Faculty of Economics, 1031–1032,
    1073–1075
Greece, 54, 1046
Greek Colonels Protest week,
    Cambridge, 433
Gwalior, E.A.G., 811

H

Harcourt Butler Committee, India, 1927, 811n39
Harvard, 56n32, 121, 181, 185, 197, 227, 241, 256n50, 272, 277, 279, 307, 315n32, 369, 372, 373, 376, 390n105, 404, 445, 607n7, 734–735n44, 754, 878, 908n56, 922, 1069
HEFCE, 993, 994
Heritage Foundation, 211, 233, 263, 264, 375n94
Her Majesty's Treasury (HMT), 485, 487, 488, 566, 578
Heterodox economics
  definitions, 8
  identity, 56, 59, 61
High Court, Madras, 811
History vs. Equilibrium, Joan Robinson vs. Frank Hahn, 46–56
Honours awarded in tenure of Margaret Thatcher as Prime Minister, 266–268
Hoover Institution, Stanford, 229, 247, 256n50, 263, 281, 729n37
House of Commons Expenditure Committee, 431
House of Lords
  Debate on Report of Rothschild Enquiry on SSRC, 547, 555, 556n18
  debate on SSRC, 555, 700
House Un-American Activities Committee (HUAC), 387–389, 388n104, 393

I

Import controls
  bogey of wartime rationing, 477
  New Scientist symposium at Café Royal, London, 477
  policy debates, 481
Increasing returns and economic growth, 888
India
  Cambridge in India, 810–818
  Delhi School of Economics, 418, 772, 812n45
  India in Cambridge, 818–821
  Input-Output Table, 812n46, 816
  Mahalanobis's 'brain irrigation' scheme, 813, 816n58
  partition of, 1072
  planning, 771, 803, 813n51
  Planning Commission, 813n51
  Robinsons in Gwalior, 1920s, 800, 811
  steel industry, 885
  Third Five Year Plan, 816
Indian Civil Service, 779, 782
Industrial economics, 434, 627, 669n63, 681, 719, 861, 902, 914, 934, 937n97, 1038, 1041
Industrial Relations Research Unit (IRRU), University of Warwick, and Rothschild Enquiry, 542n8, 544, 545, 548, 559, 732
Inequality, 42n26, 45, 51, 61, 235, 275, 304n17, 340, 358, 638, 710, 711, 713, 719, 739, 809, 828, 831, 833, 833n77, 903n51, 908n56, 912, 913, 928, 995, 1002, 1004, 1027, 1044, 1056, 1062, 1063, 1067
Institute for New Economic Thinking (INET), 929, 1057, 1059, 1059n22, 1066
Institute for the Study of Conflict, 260
Institute for Workers' Control (IWC), 124n44, 311n26, 480, 480n30, 481
Institute of Economic Affairs (IEA), 192, 229–232, 230n31, 234, 249, 257–260, 278–280, 468, 542n7, 728, 729n37, 775
  Social Affairs Unit, 728, 729n37
Institute of Humane Studies, 245n47
Institute of Social Studies, The Hague, 190, 796, 826n71, 827, 873n26, 1042n11
Institut International de Sociologie, 702
International Center for Economic Policy Studies (ICEPS), 233
International Cooperation Administration (ICA), precursor of U.S. Agency for International Development, of U.S. State Department, 253

International Monetary Fund (IMF)
  in Mexico, 773, 823
  in Tanzania, 773, 822
International Monetary Fund (IMF),
  World Bank, Bretton Woods
  Institutions (BWI), 42n26, 52,
  56, 77, 159, 191, 254, 258, 462,
  465, 492, 506, 589, 610, 650,
  725, 773, 783, 797, 800, 810,
  815n55, 821, 827, 829, 831,
  923n85, 995n13, 1030,
  1042n11, 1052
International Panel on Climate Change
  (IPCC), 1057n20
International Student Initiative for
  Pluralism in Economics
  (ISIPE), 1033
Iran, 256n50, 463, 813n48, 823

J

Janeway Institute, Cambridge,
  1067, 1067n30
Japan, 191, 425, 859, 868n16, 880,
  886, 914
Journals
  Cambridge Journal of Economics, 14,
    27n13, 117, 295, 305, 305–319,
    305n19, 306n20, 308, 313,
    314n29, 315n32, 317n35, 321,
    332n44, 369, 433, 445, 475,
    479n28, 496, 622n21, 679, 684,
    740, 858, 903n48, 906,
    1067, viin1
  Contributions to Political Economy,
    315n31, 316n33
  Economic Journal, 2, 5, 16, 47,
    73, 125, 143, 183, 198,
    295–298, 300, 300n5, 301,
    302n9, 305n18, 306, 309,
    312, 313, 336, 340, 341,
    341n57, 403, 418n2, 454,
    631, 767, 782, 823, 870,
    875, 910, 914, 968, 983,
    984, 988, 999, 1019
  Economica, 74, 301
  Economic Policy Review of the
    Cambridge Economic Policy
    Group, Cambridge, 295, 319–322

Judge Business School (JBS), University
  of Cambridge, 496, 497, 587, 627,
  673, 674, 682, 683n75, 684, 766,
  828, 831, 879–880, 916, 938, 989,
  990, 1036n9, 1038–1042,
  1058, 1070

K

Kaldorian Industrialisation, 443
Kaldor, Selective Employment Tax
  (SET), 887–889
Kaldor's Laws, 117
Keynes Fund, Cambridge, 1057, 1058,
  1065, 1067n30
King's College/Lord Kahn Economics
  Seminar, 356n69
Klein-Goldberger model, 503
Kondratieff, Kondratiev cycles, long
  wave, 914
Korea, 16n9, 823

L

Labour Studies Group/labour studies
  group (LSG), DAE, 86n13, 496,
  612, 614, 615, 682, 902, 912
Lady Mitchell Hall, Economics Staff-
  Student Meeting, 701n6
Lahore, 825n71
Lahore School of Economics, 825n71
Land Economy, Department of,
  University of Cambridge, 496, 588,
  778, 789n20, 790, 799, 807, 808,
  829, 834, 1037, 1038
Land, reforms, redistribution,
  holdings, 824
Latin American Studies, "Parry
  Centres," 893
Le Cercle, 729n37
Lehmann Brothers, 1028
Letter of Protest by Cambridge Graduate
  Students in economics, 62,
  1033, 1056n19
Letter of Protest by Economics Students
  in Paris, 1032–1033
Letter of 364 economists against
  Thatcher Government policies,
  'Hahn-Neild' letter, 353, 1007

Levy Institute, 429, 501, 1030, 1064
LINK model, Lawrence Klein, 3929
Liverpool street protests, Toxteth, 472–474, 525
Liverpool University, Liverpool macroeconomic model, Patrick Minford, 585
London and Cambridge Economic Bulletin, 430n17
London Business School (LBS), 485, 565n1, 577n20, 582, 586, 979n9
London Economics, 302n9, 565n2
London School of Economics
  Academic atmosphere, comparison with Cambridge, 11–14, 183–185
  "Uncles" and "Nephews," 138n63, 181, 342
LSE vs. Cambridge, 229–234

M

Maastricht treaty, Wynne Godley on, 500
Machiavelli, 114, 636, 655–657
Malvinas, Falklands, 78
Managerial capitalism, 592, 937n97
Manchester Conference on the Teaching of Development Economics, 803–805
Manchester School of Management, 912
Mankiw's Pendulum, 40–42
Mao Tse Tung, 77, 398
McCarthyism, 192, 194, 371, 374, 378, 378n96, 386–391, 394, 1008
McGill University, 388
Mergers and takeovers, 934
Mexico, 375, 813n48, 823, 826, 827, 885
MIT, 24, 56n32, 181, 197–200, 227, 241, 246, 271, 272, 274, 277, 279, 369, 372, 373, 375n92, 379, 387, 404, 922, 930, 1069
Monetary Policy Committee (MPC) of the Bank of England (BOE), 125, 126, 149, 469, 589, 915
Mont Pelerin Society (MPS)
  anniversaries, 219, 226, 229, 243, 269, 281
  Bank of England, 220, 221, 230
  Conference at Stanford University, 216n20, 229, 281
  financing, 219
  formation, 32, 208, 217
  Foundation for Economic Education (FEE), 199
  inaugural meeting, Mont Pelerin, Switzerland, 202, 204, 205
  influence of, 61n36, 247
  linkage with Chicago economists, 191
  linkage with "nobel" Economics prize winners, 261n53
  presidents of, 212, 226, 249, 264
  The "Stockholm connection," 235–240
Movements
  anti-apartheid, 864n11
  anti-Vietnam War, 77, 97
  civil rights, 97
  CND, 308, 433
  Free Speech, 97
  Quit India, 812n41

N

National Association for Freedom (NAFF), 260
National income accounting
  Ghana, 813n48
  India, 418, 804, 819, 819n62, 868
  UK, 428
National Institute of Economic and Social Research (NIESR), 125, 126, 149, 231, 300, 417, 468, 485, 549, 551, 554, 555, 565n1, 577, 577n20, 582, 583, 585, 586, 589, 635, 663, 673, 869n19, 902, 915, 917, 934, 937n97
National Union of Miners (NUM), 449n5
Nehru, Jawaharlal, Campaign for Chancellorship of Cambridge University, 818n59
Neoliberalism, 19, 22–26, 195, 218, 251, 252, 280, 452, 481, 507, 519, 591, 593, 809

New Cambridge, equation, model, paradigm, controversies, 58n34, 97, 145n75, 317, 321, 359, 441–444, 449n5, 453–456, 477, 484, 498–499, 509–511, 755
   Exchange of letters, 443–444, 454–455, 509–510
New Scientist Symposium, 477, 478n26
New Deal democrats, 379
"New economic thinking", four pillars, William Janeway, 929
"Nobel" prizes
   awarded to members/presidents of Mont Pelerin Society, 249–250
   links between memberships of selection committees and of Mont Pelerin, 238, 243, 245, 251
   Nobel Family, objections from, 237
   Nobel Prize Committee for economics, 239
   not awarded to Joan Robinson, 250–251
   Selection Committees, members, 243, 244, 448
North Sea oil, 443, 461, 463, 476, 481

O
O.D.A., 791n21
O.D.A. and Development Courses in Cambridge, 836, 838, 867
OPEC oil-prices, 31, 77, 195, 195n6, 307, 430, 492, 797, 831, 832
Open University, Michael Young, 710n21
Operation Condor, U.S.A. in Latin America, 255, 255n49
Oxford
   Economic Journal moves to, 305
Oxford Economic Forecasting, 565n2

P
Pakistan, 200, 256n50, 772, 792, 814n53, 820, 823
Panjab University, Chandigarh, 820n64
   Economics, 820n64
Paris Peace Accord, Conference 1919, 282, 283

Parkinson's Disease, 831
Parry Parliamentary Committee on Latin American Studies, 893
Pluralist teaching in economics, PEPS-Economie, 1033
Political arithmeticians, 421
Political parties
   British Communist Party, 99, 308, 863n10
   Conservative Party, U.K., 119, 234n38, 258, 264, 535, 535n4, 728, 729n39, 731n41, 1039
   Labour Party, U.K., xiii, 116, 122, 123, 124n44, 146, 195n6, 216n20, 234n38, 308, 311n26, 335n52, 431, 445, 446n4, 450, 451, 453, 459, 464, 479–481, 480n30, 638n37, 710n21, 712; Bennite wing, Bennism, 477–484, 494; Labour Friends of Israel, 446n4; Liberal-SDP Alliance, Lib-Dems, 125, 452, 915; Tribune Group, 472n20, 483
   Social Democratic Party U.K., 140, 140n69, 238, 366n81, 446, 448, 450–452; SDP Friends of Israel, 446n4
Poverty, 42n26, 45, 53, 182, 329, 333, 382, 500, 547, 638, 731n41, 733, 809, 827, 885, 912, 921, 923, 952
Prebisch-Singer thesis, 462
Presidential
   Medal of Freedom, U.S. A., 263
Programme for Britain 1973, 480n30, 481
Protection, xiii, 191, 389, 432, 441, 455, 456, 463, 479n28, 492, 502n41, 505, 543, 586, 632, 651, 795, 801, 812, 916, 917, 1068
Pugwash Conference, 388n104
Punjab, 97, 823, 1072, 1073
   migration at Partition, parable of, 1072, 1073

Q
QS World University Rankings, 1034
Quaker Seminar, Frank Hahn, 51, 52, 136, 363, 364, 366, 620, 622n19
Queens' College

Ajit Singh Fellowship, 121
Director of Studies in
   Economics, 893n39
Political Economy Seminar, 328, 343,
   356–360, 445, 1028n5
President, John Eatwell, 121, 122
President, Mohamed El Erian,
   1064, 1065
Queen's Question about Financial
   Crisis, 988

R
Racism, 283, 713, 786
Radcliffe Report, 337, 469
Raffaele Mattioli Lectures
   Nicholas Kaldor, 103, 370n84
   Richard Kahn, 103
   Richard Stone, 676, 862, 870
Reader's Digest, 204, 229, 264
'Reddaway-type' economics/'Reddaway
   method,' vii, 96, 424, 429n15, 935
Reform Club, London
   Munia Postan on Kaldor, 884
   Wilfred Beckerman on Kaldor and
      Balogh, 459n13, 882n33
Research Assessment Exercise (RAE), 2,
   4, 12, 17, 149, 152, 153, 168, 170,
   279, 734, 758, 830, 918n73, 927,
   966–1014, 1022, 1023, 1029,
   1033–1036, 1051, 1066
   Economics Panels, 140, 154n82, 971,
      979, 983, 984, 986, 987,
      1006, 1051
Research Excellence Framework (REFs),
   17, 153, 168, 830, 968, 975, 987,
   987n11, 990, 992, 995, 995n14,
   997, 998, 1000n16, 1001–1005,
   1007, 1010, 1023, 1033–1036,
   1039, 1051, 1059n23, 1065, 1066
   Stern Review, 1003
Riots
   Brixton, 472–474, 474n23
   Cambridge, 472–474
   Liverpool/Toxteth, 472–474
The Road to Serfdom, Friedrich Hayek, 8,
   19, 32, 76, 191, 198, 203–205,
   211, 219, 222, 227–229, 228n30,
   231, 240, 245, 246, 264, 280, 281,
   284, 375, 380, 978

Robbins Report on Higher Education
   1963, 700, 730, 970
Root and branch, 482, 891, 1071
Rothschild Enquiry on SSRC, 3, 445,
   503n43, 518, 519, 534, 544,
   546n13, 548, 549, 727, 740
Royal Economic Society (RES), 139,
   146, 149, 153–155, 159, 163,
   168, 279, 297, 297n1, 300,
   301n7, 312, 366, 437, 567, 606,
   870, 875, 903, 968–972, 968n1,
   971n3, 975–989, 976n8, 979n9,
   1005, 1006, 1009–1011, 1014,
   1022, 1051
Royal Swedish Academy of Sciences,
   236, 239
Russia, 143, 187, 192, 371, 386, 392,
   429n15, 877n32, 879n32,
   882, 921

S
St Michael slaying the devil, Sir
   Jacob Epstein, Wynne
   Godley, 493n36
Sanskrit, 779, 810, 992, 994
Schooling, 907, 908n55, 918
Science Policy Research Unit (SPRU),
   Sussex, 879
Scottish Economic Society, 983, 984
Selective Employment Tax (S.E.T),
   Kaldor, 887–890
Seminars elsewhere
   Eugen von Bohm-Bawerk Seminar,
      Vienna, 214n19, 315n32
   Lionel Robbins Seminar, London
      School of Economics, 346
   Ludwig von Mises Privatseminar,
      Vienna, 214n19, 217
   Tuesday Club, 346
Seminars in Cambridge
   Cambridge Circus, 110, 344–345,
      347, 405n120, 883
   Cambridge Economic Club, 329–330
   Cambridge Growth Project Seminar at
      DAE, 362–363
   Cambridge-LSE joint
      seminar, 345–347
   Churchill College Economics, Hahn,
      133, 343, 362

Seminars in Cambridge (*cont.*)
  CLARE GROUP, Matthews &
    Cairncross, 125–126, 125n46,
    140, 140n66, 143, 146, 146n77,
    149, 280, 295, 296, 364–367,
    464, 489, 489n33, 517, 560,
    568n8, 593, 627, 976
  King's College Economics, 'Secret'
    Seminar, Lord Kahn, 110, 306,
    328, 330, 334n47, 337–338,
    347–353, 356–359, 1055
  Marshall Society, 330, 334–338
  Political Economy Club, Keynes, 146,
    328, 330–334, 336, 343,
    810, 969
  Political Economy Seminar; Queens'
    College, Ajit Singh, 343, 1028n5;
    St. Catherine's College, Arestis &
    Kitson, 360–361
  'Quaker' Risk Seminar, Hahn,
    363–364, 367
  Research Students Seminar, Piero
    Sraffa, 309, 339–344
  Richard Stone Common
    Room, 353–356
  South Asian research scholars
    seminar, 822n68
Shanghai, 947, 948
Share Plc, 1063, 1066
SNA and invisibility of women's work
  and contribution, Phyllis
  Deane, 947–953
SNA application in African colonial
  economies, Phyllis Deane, Peter
  Ady, 938–939, 943–949
SNA system, Richard Stone, 862
Social Affairs Unit, Institute of Economic
  Affairs, 729n37
Social and Political Science Committee
  (SPS), 611, 619, 640, 669, 673,
  674, 678, 681, 683, 687, 699n2,
  705, 710n22, 714, 715, 715n26,
  720, 734, 734n44, 736–738,
  737n46, 737n48, 741n56,
  742–752, 748n58, 755–757,
  756n63, 766, 790, 791, 797, 799,
  838, 894
Social ontology, 59, 367–368

Social Science Research Council, Lord
  Rothschild Enquiry, Keith
  Joseph, 727
Social Science Research Council,
  Macroeconomic Modelling Bureau,
  554n17, 565, 579
Social Science Research Council (SSRC),
  xiii, 3, 9, 16, 111, 116, 140n67,
  145, 145n76, 149, 151, 154n82,
  168–170, 170n86, 209, 234n38,
  279, 319–321, 363, 363n77,
  365–367, 420, 427, 427n11, 433,
  441, 445, 460, 464, 466, 474,
  484–494, 496, 497, 500, 503n43,
  504, 505, 507–509, 518–560,
  541n6, 564–566, 566n3, 568, 569,
  571n11, 574, 578, 579, 583, 585,
  586, 588, 590, 592, 598, 602, 607,
  613, 617, 623, 625–630, 629n27,
  634n34, 635n35, 637, 643, 647,
  649, 672, 686n87, 699n2, 700,
  700n5, 710n21, 725–734, 740,
  741n56, 778, 795, 973n6, 974n7,
  1003n18, 1022, 1051
Social Science Research Council (SSRC)
  Consortium, 320
Sociology, vi, viii, 2, 4, 10, 17, 56, 119,
  137n60, 214, 216, 242n44, 302,
  424, 536, 537, 541n6, 546, 548,
  549, 551, 559, 560, 605, 614,
  638n37, 640, 668, 678, 680–682,
  683n77, 687, 687n87, 692–758,
  791, 793, 794, 827, 829, 867, 893,
  908, 924n88, 935, 937, 941, 969,
  1005, 1030, 1043, 1047, 1053,
  1057, 1070
South Asian research scholars in
  Cambridge
  mentored by Ajit Singh, 822n68
  Research Scholars' Seminar, 1041n11
  Supervised by Suzy Paine,
    821n68, 822n68
Spanish Civil War, 119, 233, 297,
  335n50, 335n51, 388, 876
  Battle of Teruel, 296–297, 403
Sports
  cricket in Cambridge, vi, 98, 785, 792
  South Asian XI, 792

SPS Committee, Faculty of Economics, 640, 705, 746, 748, 893
Sri Lanka, 262, 813n48, 814, 820, 822n68, 827
SSRC's Ad hoc Committee on Macroeconomic Models in U.K., 489, 491, 509
Stafford Cripps Mission (1942), India, 811
State, role of, 27, 58, 71, 182, 194, 277, 380, 453, 483, 638, 770, 822, 828, 929, 1049, 1062
Stock-flow-consistent modelling (SCF), Wynne Godley, 499
Stock markets, 511n49, 630n30, 770, 1060n25
Student protests
  anti-Vietnam War protests, 433
  Free Speech movement, California, 97
  Garden House Riot (Cambridge 'Greek Colonels' protest), 121, 973n6
  Students Sit-in at Faculty of Economics over Tripos Reform, 99, 121, 319, 433, 618, 701, 701n6, 706n16, 973n6
Supporting Human Achievement through Research based on Egalitarian Principles (SHARE) Egalitarian, 1063
  Capitalism Programme, 1063
Sverige Riksbank Prize in Economic Science in memory of Alfred Nobel ("Nobel" economics prize), 237
Swedish Academy of Letters, 249
Swinnerton-Dyer, P., 973–977, 1012

T
Takeovers and mergers, 934
The Talmud, 54, 1046
Tanzania, 822
Tea-room, Faculty of Economics, Cambridge (Richard Stone Common Room), 328
Technological capability, construction of, 880
Textbooks

Alfred Marshall, 4, 6, 28n15, 79, 110, 135, 329, 686n86, 701, 767, 779, 811n37, 849, 903n51, 934
Alfred Stonier & Douglas Hague, 268
Joan Robison et al on *Applied Economics*, 399–403
Joan Robinson & John Eatwell, *An Introduction to Modern Economics*, 121, 310n24, 394, 394n110
Lawrence Klein, *The Keynesian Revolution*, 377–394, 377n95, 504n44
Lorie Tarshis, *The Elements of Economics*, 191, 331n43, 372, 374
Mabel Timlin, *Keynesian Economics*, 403–405
Paul Samuelson, *Economics*, 32, 33, 191, 369, 370, 372, 373, 373n90, 377n95, 394–397, 401
Richard Lipsey *Positive Economics*, 398
Trade unions, 71, 126, 195, 201, 233, 240, 247, 259, 260, 270, 273, 307–309, 401, 448, 463, 471, 473n22, 474n23, 480n29, 481–483, 533, 544, 552n15, 556, 650, 683, 685, 713, 739, 949n105, 969n2, 970
Treasury Cafeteria, Reform Club, 459n13, 882n33
Treaty of Versailles, 282
Tripos, Economics Cambridge curriculum and examination reforms, 701n6
  Marshall and establishment of, 94, 181
  Students Sit-in, 121, 297
Trojan Horse, 17, 70, 129–132, 271, 403, 1021, 1070
Trollope, Anthony, novels, 133n57
Tropical African Services (TAS), 782
Turkey, 809, 813n48, 822n68

U
Under-consumption, and Rosa Luxemburg, 496
UNESCO, 704n13, 709
Union of Radical Political Economics (URPE), 117n41, 238

University College London (UCL), 153, 155, 163, 213, 216n20, 345, 468, 709n18, 900, 1007
University of Birmingham, 47, 108, 131, 132, 136, 139, 141, 143, 153, 163, 328, 335n49, 342, 362, 467, 831, 1046
University of Bristol, 584n26
University of California, Berkeley, 76, 77, 97, 131, 216n20, 354, 424, 607, 878, 1008, 1021n2
   Described by Henry Kissinger as 'University of Saigon,' 607
University of Glasgow, 584n26, 1013
University of Illinois, Urbana, 302n9
University of Manchester, 687, 742n56, 1006
University of Massachusetts, Amherst, 905, 950n106
University of Michigan (UMich), 377, 378n96, 386–391, 386n101, 387n102, 390n105
University of Notre Dame du Lac, Indiana, 684, 684n82
University of Toronto, 388, 404, 405
University of Ulster, 98n27, 589

University of Wales, Bangor, 584n26
University of Warwick, 137, 138, 146, 153, 531, 540n5, 542n8, 544, 545, 548, 556, 565, 579, 615, 721n31, 727, 732, 970, 1007
University of Zurich, 219

V

Verdoorn's Law, 117, 898
Vice Chancellor, Cambridge University, 973n6
Vietnam, 23, 76, 77, 99, 101, 121, 137n60, 248, 270, 297, 310, 355, 398, 425, 471, 492, 607n7, 797, 822n68, 833
Volker Fund, 191, 192, 199, 200, 202–204, 202n9, 206, 206n12, 208–211, 208n13, 220

W

Washington, 203, 418
"What if?" counterfactuals, xi, 183
World Bank, IMF, Bretton Woods Institutions (BWI), 191